BUSINESS

Ricky W. Griffin

Ronald J. Ebert

Frederick A. Starke

FOURTH CUSTOM EDITION FOR DAWSON COLLEGE

Taken from:

Business, Sixth Canadian Edition
by Ricky W. Griffin, Ronald J. Ebert, and Frederick A. Starke

DAWSON COLLEGE

Custom Publishing

New York   Boston   San Francisco
London   Toronto   Sydney   Tokyo   Singapore   Madrid
Mexico City   Munich   Paris   Cape Town   Hong Kong   Montreal

Cover Art: Courtesy of PhotoDisc, DigitalVision/Getty Images

Taken from:

Business, Sixth Canadian Edition
by Ricky W. Griffin, Ronald J. Ebert and Frederick A. Starke
Copyright © 2008, 2005, 2002, 1999, 1996, 1993 by Pearson Education Canada
Published by Prentice Hall
Toronto, Ontario
Canada

Printed in Canada

10 9 8 7 6 5 4 3 2 1

2008160442

BK

Pearson
Custom Publishing
is a division of

www.pearsonhighered.com

ISBN 10: 0-555-02454-7
ISBN 13: 978-0-555-02454-6

OVERVIEW

CONTENTS

PART FOUR
Managing Marketing   468

APPENDICES

Welcome to the sixth Canadian edition of *Business*! In this edition, we continue to emphasize our principle of *"Doing the Basics Best."* Cutting-edge firsts, up-to-date issues that shape today's business world, and creative pedagogy help students build a solid foundation of business knowledge. This new, sixth edition continues with the strengths that made the first five editions so successful—comprehensiveness, accuracy, currency, and readability.

Changes in the Sixth Canadian Edition

Business incorporates the rapid changes taking place as well as many of the changes suggested by instructors and students involved in Introductory Business. The key changes are:

- The chapter on business ethics and social responsibility (Chapter 3, Conducting Business Ethically and Responsibly) now occupies an earlier spot in the text so that students will have an increased consciousness of the importance of this area as they read subsequent chapters in the text.

- Chapter 4 (Understanding Entrepreneurship, Small Business, and New Venture Creation) has been significantly revised to include a larger focus on how new businesses are started.

- More than 95% of the opening cases, boxed inserts, and end-of-chapter cases are either new or updated.

- Many new examples of business practice have been included in each of the chapters. For example, new material on income trusts and hedge funds has been added to Chapter 19. Some of these examples are brief and some are more detailed, but they all increase students' understanding of important business issues.

- Each chapter contains two new boxed inserts. The first of these, "Entrepreneurship and New Ventures," provides real-life examples of Canadian entrepreneurs who saw an opportunity to provide a new product or service in the marketplace and the activities they carried out in order to be successful. The second series, entitled "Business Accountability," focuses student attention on business behaviour that is of significant public concern. Each insert describes an accountability issue that is currently confronting a real Canadian or international company and the steps that are being taken to make business managers more accountable for their actions.

- New CBC *Venture* video cases are included at the end of each major section of the text.

- A new feature called "Planning for Your Career" has been introduced at the end of each major section of the text. This feature contains career-planning activities that help students tie the content of each major section of the text to their career-planning efforts. For example, the focus of this feature at the end of the marketing section of the text is on how students can present themselves as business professionals to prospective employers.

- Another new feature, "Managing Your Personal Finances," is contained in Appendix B at the end of the text. This feature has been overwhelmingly requested by students and instructors and presents a down-to-earth, hands-on approach that will help students manage their personal finances. The practical information found in this feature includes a work-sheet for determining net worth, insightful examples demonstrating the time value of money, a method for determining how much to invest now in order to build a future nest egg of a certain size, suggestions on how to manage credit card debt, guidelines for purchasing a house, and a personalized worksheet for setting financial goals. The information contained in this feature will be immensely useful to students.

- The business law material is found in Appendix A and the material on insurance from the fifth edition has been moved to the CD-ROM that comes with the text.

- Yet another new feature is the inclusion of five supplementary cases in Appendix C at the end of the text. These cases are more detailed than those found at the end of each chapter, and allow students to consider more extensive information as they do their analysis and make recommendations about how to resolve the issue presented in the case.

- The "Crafting Your Business Plan" exercises (which were found at the end of each chapter in the fifth edition) are now included on a CD-ROM that comes with the text. This exercise gives students the opportunity to apply text material to the task of developing a business plan, using the Business Plan Pro software. The new version of this software allows users to create plans with greater ease and speed.

Major Themes

Five major themes are evident throughout this new edition. It is important that students understand these themes since their careers in business will be significantly affected by them.

- **The theme of change.** The dramatic changes that have been occurring during the past decade continue apace. The development of new business processes, new products, and new services all make the study of change in business exciting and necessary. In nearly every aspect of business today there are totally new ways of doing things. These new ways are replacing traditional business practices, usually with surprising speed and often with better competitive results. Given these developments, we as authors felt that our goal had to be to communicate the theme of change by describing how real-world business firms cope with organizational change and conflict. Thus, we have tried to capture the flavour and convey the excitement of the "new economy" in all of its rapidly evolving practices.

- **The growth of international business.** The globalization of the economy is one of the dominant challenges of the twenty-first century. To keep students aware of this challenge, we've included many examples and cases that describe the experiences of Canadian companies in the global marketplace. We also describe how global companies have impacted the domestic Canadian market. In addition to these examples throughout the text, we devote an entire chapter to international business (Chapter 5, Understanding International Business).

- **The role of ethics and social responsibility.** Business ethics and social responsibility are generating a sharply increased level of discussion and debate as a result of the highly publicized criminal trials of top managers at companies like Enron, WorldCom, and others. We devote an entire chapter to the discussion of ethical and social responsibility issues (Chapter 3, Conducting Business Ethically and Responsibly) because these issues are so important to modern business. Ethical issues are also raised in nearly every chapter of the text.

■ **The significance of small business.** Since many students will not work for major corporations, we have provided coverage of both large and small companies throughout the text. In various chapters, the implications of various ideas for small business are discussed. As well, a major section in Chapter 4 (Understanding Entrepreneurship, Small Business, and New Venture Creation) is devoted to small business and new business start-ups.

■ **The importance of information and communication technology.** In our information-based society, the people and organizations that learn how to obtain and use information will be the ones that succeed. The explosive growth and change in these systems is recognized as we devote an entire chapter to the management of information (Chapter 13, Managing Information Systems and Communication Technology).

■ **The quality imperative.** Quality and productivity became the key to competitive success for many companies in the global marketplace during the 1990s. These topics continue to dominate the thinking of managers in the twenty-first century, and we devote a full chapter to their coverage (Chapter 12, Increasing Productivity and Quality).

Major Features of the Text

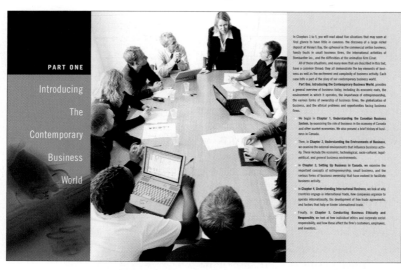

The text contains the following features to stimulate student interest in, and understanding of, the material that is presented about business.

Part Opener

At the beginning of each of the five parts of the book is a brief outline introducing the material that will be discussed in that part. These outlines give students a glimpse of the "big picture" as they start reading about a new area of the business world.

Chapter Materials

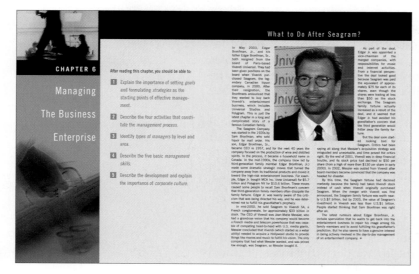

Each chapter contains several features that are designed to increase student interest in, and understanding of, the material being presented. These features are as follows:

Chapter learning objectives. A list of numbered learning objectives is presented at the beginning of each chapter. These objectives—which guide students in determining what is important in each chapter—are also referenced in the margins opposite the relevant content in the chapter.

Chapter opening case. Each chapter begins with a description of a situation that is faced by a real Canadian or international company. The subject matter of the opening case is relevant to the material presented in the chapter, and therefore helps students bridge the gap between theory and practice.

Boxed inserts. Each chapter contains two boxed inserts: "Business Accountability" and "Entrepreneurship and New Ventures." As noted above, the *Business Accountability* boxes raise student consciousness about business responsibility to its constituents. The *Entrepreneurship and New Ventures* boxes tell interesting stories of how Canadian entrepreneurs identified a need for a new product or service, and how they set up a company to effectively satisfy that need.

End-of-Chapter Materials

Several important pedagogical features are found at the end of each chapter. These are designed to help students better understand the contents of the chapter.

Summary of learning objectives. The material in each chapter is concisely summarized, using the learning objectives as the organizing scheme. This helps students understand the main points that were presented in the chapter.

Key terms. In each chapter, the key terms that students should know are highlighted in the text, defined in the margin, and listed alphabetically at the end of the chapter (with page references).

Questions and exercises. There are two types of questions here: *analysis questions* (which require students to think beyond simple factual recall and apply the concepts they have read about), and *application exercises* (which require students to visit local businesses or to interview managers and gather additional information that will help them understand how business firms operate).

Building your business skills. This feature involves in-depth exercises that allow students to examine some specific aspect of business in detail. The exercise may ask students to work individually or in a group to gather data about an interesting business issue, and then develop a written report or a class presentation based on the information that was gathered. Each exercise begins with a list of goals, a description of the situation, a step-by-step methodology for proceeding, and follow-up questions to help students focus their responses to the challenge.

Exercising your ethics. In this feature, students are presented with a description of a situation that leads to an ethical dilemma, and are then asked several questions that focus on how to approach and resolve the ethical challenge.

Concluding cases. Each chapter concludes with two case studies that focus on real Canadian or international companies. These cases are designed to help students apply the chapter material to a real company that is currently in the news. At the end of each case, several questions guide students in their analysis.

End-of-Part Material

CBC video cases. At the end of each of the five major parts of the text, two CBC video cases are presented. The instructor can show the *Venture* episode in class and then either conduct a class discussion using the questions at the end of the written case as a guide, or ask students to complete a written assignment which requires answering the questions at the end of the case. This approach to teaching adds a major new dynamic to classes because students will be able to relate text material to actual Canadian business situations. The cases are also available on the Companion Website for *Business*, Sixth Canadian Edition.

Planning for your career. This new feature helps students relate their career-planning activities to the chapters in each major section of the text. This very practical feature requires students to think about some very specific things they will need to do to be effective in career planning.

Supplementary Materials

MyBusinessLab is an online grading, assessment, and study tool for faculty and students. It engages students and helps them focus on what they need to study. It can help students get a better grade because they are learning in an interactive and focused environment.

MyBusinessLab delivers all classroom resources for instructors and students in one place. All resources are organized by Learning Objective so that lectures and studying can be customized more conveniently than ever before. Resources include:

■ **Diagnostic tests** for student review. This quizzing can be monitored by professors. Results reveal which learning objectives students are struggling with so professors can customize their review and assessment.

■ **Personalized Study Plan** based on each student's results in the diagnostic test offers students remediation (by learning objective) to help them focus on the concepts they find most challenging.

- **Links** to the Griffin/Ebert/Starke *Business*, Sixth Canadian Edition, **eText**.

- **Business News Cases.** Business concepts come to life for your students. Online Canadian news articles are linked to three mini cases with questions for your students to answer. These will be updated twice a year to ensure relevance and currency. The Business News cases will be linked to specific chapters within *Business,* Sixth Canadian Edition. Solutions will be made available to faculty.

- Ability to mark homework, quizzes, and tests automatically and have them automatically populate in your grade book.

- **Glossary Flashcards.** Quick and fun study of business terms.

- **Additional quizzing** for review. Pretest and Post Test.

For Instructors

Instructor's Resource Centre. Instructor resources are password protected and available for download via **www.pearsoned.ca**. For your convenience, these resources are also available on the Instructor's Resource CD-ROM.

MyTest (www.pearsonmytest.com). MyTest from Pearson Canada is a powerful assessment generation program that helps instructors easily create and print quizzes, tests, and exams, as well as homework or practice handouts. Questions and tests can all be authored online, allowing instructors ultimate flexibility and the ability to efficiently manage assessments at any time, from anywhere.

Pearson TestGen (ISBN-13: 978-0-13-179202-9). *Pearson TestGen* is a special computerized test item file that enables instructors to view and edit the existing questions, add questions, generate tests, and print the tests in a variety of formats. Powerful search and sort functions make it easy to locate questions and arrange them in any order desired. TestGen also enables instructors to administer tests on a local area network, have the tests graded electronically, and have the results prepared in electronic or printed reports. The Pearson TestGen is compatible with IBM or Macintosh systems.

Instructor's Resource Manual   (ISBN-13: 978-0-13-179199-2). The *Instructor's Resource Manual* contains chapter outlines, teaching tips, and suggestions on how to use the text effectively. It includes material for classroom use, such as careers in business and additional cases. The manual also provides answers to the end-of-chapter questions and cases (including Building Your Business Skills, Exercising Your Ethics, and the CBC Video Cases).

PowerPoint® Presentations   (ISBN-13: 978-0-13-1791200-5). *PowerPoint Presentations*, which are also available for downloading from the Companion Website, offer an average of about 40 PowerPoint slides per chapter, outlining the key points in the text. The slides include lecture notes that provide page references to the text, summaries, and suggestions for student activities or related questions from the text.

CBC Video Library   (VHS: ISBN-13: 978-0-13-244002-8. DVD: ISBN-13: 978-0-13-244001-1). The CBC Video Library for *Business*, Sixth Canadian Edition, includes 10 segments from the CBC program *Venture* that accompany the video cases found at the end of each part in the text. These cases focus on Canadian companies and discuss business issues from a Canadian point of view. The cases are also available on the Companion Website, and answers are discussed in the Instructor's Resource Manual. (Please contact your Pearson Education Canada sales representative for details.)

Videos. Twenty custom videos help students see how real-life businesses and the people who run them apply fundamental business principles on a daily basis. Ask your Pearson Education Canada sales representative for details!

Pearson Custom Publishing (www.prenhall.com/custombusiness). Pearson Custom Publishing can provide you and your students with texts, cases, and articles to enhance your course. Choose material from Darden, Ivey, Harvard Business School Publishing, NACRA, and Thunderbird to create your own custom casebook. Contact your Pearson Education Canada sales representative for details.

Online Learning Solutions. Pearson Education Canada supports instructors interested in using online course management systems. We provide text-related content in WebCT, Blackboard, and Course Compass. To find out more about creating an online course using Pearson content in one of these platforms, contact your Pearson Education Canada sales representative.

New! Instructor's ASSET. Pearson Education Canada is proud to introduce Instructor's ASSET, the Academic Support and Service for Educational Technologies. ASSET is the first integrated Canadian service program committed to meeting the customization, training, and support needs for your course. Ask your Pearson Education Canada sales representative for details!

Your Pearson Education Canada Sales Representative. Your Pearson sales rep is always available to ensure you have everything you need to teach a winning course. Armed with experience, training, and product knowledge, your Pearson rep will support your assessment and adoption of any of the products, services, and technology outlined here to ensure our offerings are tailored to suit your individual needs and the needs of your students. Whether it's getting instructions on TestGen software or specific content files for your new online course, your Pearson sales representative is there to help. (Also available for your students. Ask your Pearson sales rep for details!)

For Students

Student CD-ROM. Designed to complement the content of the text, the Companion CD-ROM features loads of useful information to help and encourage students: the CBC videos and their cases, a glossary organized by chapter, Crafting your Business Plan exercises, and additional material on insurance.

Crafting Your Business Plan. Chapter-ending exercises apply text material to the task of developing a business plan using Business Plan Pro software. The new version of this software allows users to create plans with greater ease and speed. The education version of the best-selling Business Plan Pro software can be packaged with the text for an extra charge in a value pack.

Business PlanPro Software. Business PlanPro (BPP) provides students with a step-by-step approach to creating a comprehensive business plan. The software is designed to stimulate student thinking about the many tasks and decisions that go into planning and running a business. Preformatted report templates, charts, and tables handle the mechanics so that students can focus on the thinking. Planners can also publish to a protected internet site, where readers can access all or part of posted plans. Available for a small extra charge in a value-package. Ask your Pearson sales representative for details!

Companion Website. The Companion Website provides an audio glossary to help students with pronunciation of terms and "flashcards" to help students review key terms and concepts. The PowerPoint® Presentations are available for downloading by both students and instructors. The Instructor's Resource Manual is also available for downloading in a protected area for instructors. Visit the site at **www.pearsoned.ca/griffin**.

Acknowledgments

We owe special thanks to Catharine Haggert, for her excellent copy editing; Claudia Forgas, for her careful proofreading; Cheryl Jackson, Production Editor, for her efficient management of this project; and Natalie Barrington for her fine photo research. Thanks are also due to Steve O'Hearn, Publisher; Gary Bennett, Editor-in-Chief; Karen Elliott, Acquisitions Editor; Michelle Harrington and Pamela Voves, Developmental Editors; Eileen Lasswell, Marketing Manager, Business and Economics; and all the members of the Pearson Education Canada sales team.

We appreciate the insights and suggestions of the following individuals who provided feedback on the fifth edition or reviewed the manuscript for the new edition:

Sofy Carayannopoulos, Wilfrid Laurier University
Alex Faseruk, Memorial University of Newfoundland
Suzanne Iskander, Humber College Institute of Technology
   & Advanced Learning
Bob Sproule, University of Waterloo
Patricia Stoll, Seneca College of Applied Arts and Technology
William Thurber, Brock University
Heather Johnston, Brandon University
Cindy Stewart, University of British Columbia
Lesley J. Moffitt, Assiniboine Community College
Dwight Heinrichs, University of Regina

Frederick A. Starke
2007

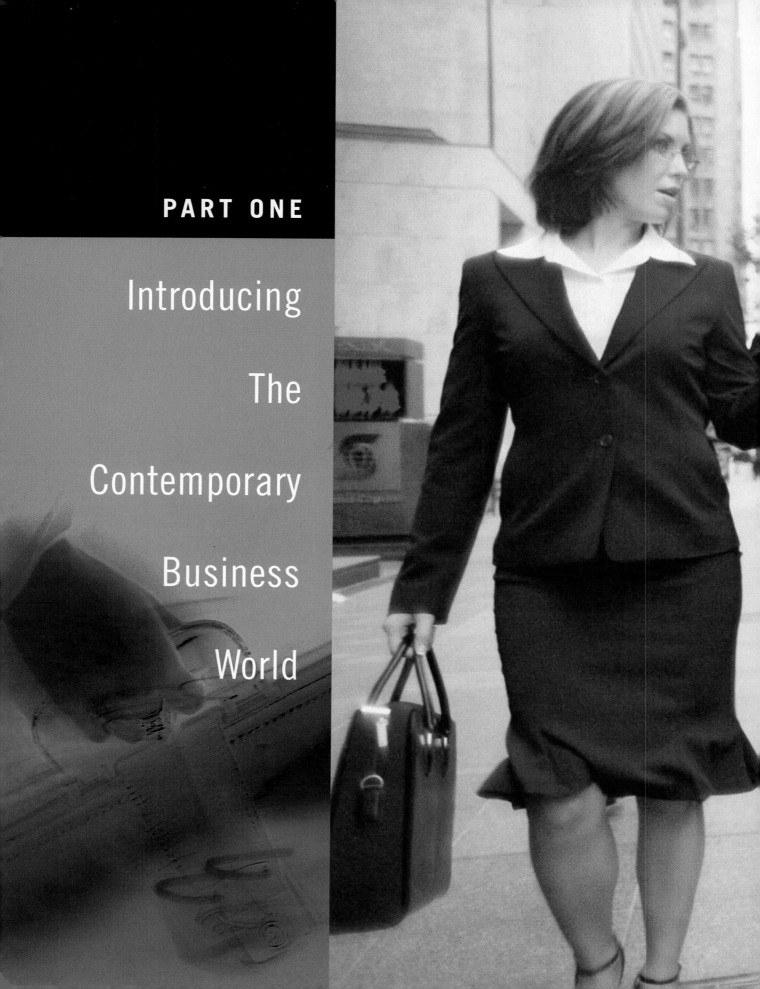

PART ONE

Introducing

The

Contemporary

Business

World

In the Opening Cases in Chapters 1 to 5, you will read about five situations that may seem to have little in common at first glance: Canadian megaprojects that focus on the extraction of oil and nickel, the importance of productivity for our standard of living, the unethical behaviour of some business managers, entrepreneurs starting new businesses, and the exporting of Canadian goods and services to other countries. All of these situations, and many more that are described in this text, have a common thread—they all demonstrate the key elements of business as well as the excitement and complexity of business activity. Each case tells a part of the story of our contemporary business world.

Part One, Introducing the Contemporary Business World, provides a general overview of business today, including its economic roots, the environment in which it operates, the importance of entrepreneurship, the various forms of ownership of business firms, the globalization of business, and the ethical problems and opportunities facing business firms.

- We begin in **Chapter 1, Understanding the Canadian Business System**, by examining the role of business in the economy of Canada and other market economies. We also present a brief history of business in Canada.

- Then, in **Chapter 2, Understanding the Environments of Business**, we examine the external environments that influence business activity. These include the economic, technological, socio-cultural, legal-political, and general business environments.

- Next, in **Chapter 3, Conducting Business Ethically and Responsibly**, we look at individual ethics and corporate social responsibility, and how these affect the firm's customers, employees, and investors.

- In **Chapter 4, Understanding Entrepreneurship, Small Business, and New Venture Creation**, we examine the important concepts of entrepreneurship, small business, and the various forms of business ownership that have evolved to facilitate business activity.

- Finally, in **Chapter 5, Understanding International Business**, we look at why countries engage in international trade, how companies organize to operate internationally, the development of free trade agreements, and factors that help or hinder international trade.

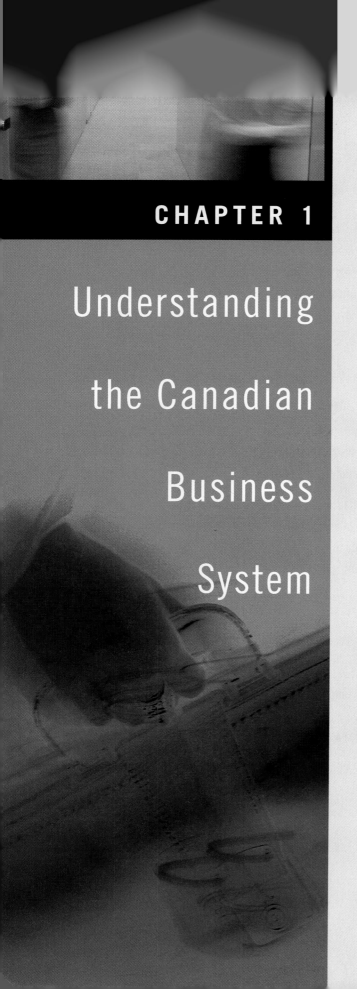

CHAPTER 1

Understanding the Canadian Business System

After reading this chapter, you should be able to:

1 Define the nature of Canadian *business* and identify its main goals.

2 Describe different types of global *economic systems* according to the means by which they control the *factors of production* through *input* and *output markets*.

3 Show how *demand* and *supply* affect resource distribution in Canada.

4 Identify the elements of *private enterprise* and explain the various *degrees of competition* in the Canadian economic system.

5 Trace the *history of business* in Canada.

In the world of business, Canada is famous for its rich supply of natural resources such as oil, gas, gold, nickel, and copper. Extracting and selling these resources has long been an important activity for Canadian business firms. Two major projects currently underway in Canada's north—the Alberta Tar Sands and Voisey's Bay—illustrate the rewards and risks associated with such business activity. Both of these cases show that the process can be long and complex, particularly for megaprojects.

alone required 21 million construction hours, 3 million engineering hours, and 150 000 cubic metres of concrete. At its peak, the Syncrude upgrader project employed 6000 workers. By 2010, nearly 30 000 tradespeople will be needed in the area, and this number does not include those who will actually be needed to work in the mines. Approximately 80 000 people will find work in this area by 2014, and another 240 000 jobs will appear elsewhere as a result of the mining activity in the tar sands.

The plans being made by Canadian Natural Resources Ltd. are typical. It will spend $25 billion on tar sands development by 2017. This is in addition to the $11 billion the company has already spent. Although the company only started operations in 1989, it has now become the #2 oil and gas producer in Canada. If events unfold as planned, the company will be producing approximately one million barrels of oil a day.

THE ALBERTA TAR SANDS

People have known about the sticky bitumen of northern Alberta for many years. Attempts were made to drill conventional oil wells there nearly 100 years ago, but they were unsuccessful. In 1967 the Great Canadian Oil Sands Project began the modern era in tar sands development. But ups and downs in oil prices in the 1970s and 1980s led many businesspeople to believe the tar sands were not economically viable. More recently, with the strong surge in oil prices and talk of future oil shortages, the rate of development of the tar sands has increased dramatically.

It is estimated that there are 2.5 *trillion* barrels of oil trapped in the tar sands around Fort McMurray, Alberta. That far exceeds the reserves of even Saudi Arabia. Over the last 30 years, various companies have spent about $34 billion dollars to develop this area. Over the next 10 years another $87 billion is likely to be spent. By then, production will reach about two million barrels of oil each day. This is comparable to the major oil producers in the Middle East. All of this activity is making the rest of the world sit up and take notice of Canada's potential.

Several companies are important players in the development of the tar sands, including Suncor Energy Inc., Canadian Natural Resources Ltd., Petro-Canada, and Syncrude Canada Ltd. The megaprojects currently underway at these companies have generated a huge demand for both people and raw materials. One project at Suncor

VOISEY'S BAY

After years of delay, the nickel mining project at Voisey's Bay in Labrador is finally going ahead. The story began in 1993, when two diamond prospectors stumbled upon one of the world's richest nickel finds in the rolling hills of northeast Labrador. In 1996, Inco bought controlling interest in the site for $4.3 billion so it could maintain its dominance in world nickel markets. But in 1997, Inco announced that it would have to delay development of the site because of a time-consuming and expensive environmental review process. To complicate matters, the government of Newfoundland was demanding that Inco build a smelter in the province, and the Innu Nation was asking for a 3 percent smelter royalty.

Over the next eight years, many further delays took place as Inco tried to negotiate a deal that was acceptable to the government of Newfoundland. After many false starts, an agreement was finally reached in 2002. The agreement included the provision that the mine would become operational in 2006 and that a smelter would be built in Argentia in 2011. In 2004 alone, Inco poured nearly $250 million dollars into the project.

The project is not without risk to Inco because it plans to use an unproven technology at Argentia that relies on chemicals instead of heat to produce nickel from concentrate. To explore this new process, Inco has built a test facility in a 1:10 000 scale model. By 2008, Inco must tell the province whether it will use the new technology or the conventional one. Whatever decision is made on the processing technology, once the mine is operational, each year it will produce 110 million pounds of nickel concentrate, 70 million pounds of copper concentrate, and will add about $300 million to Inco's cash flow. In 2005, the project at Voisey's Bay provided employment for about 1000 people, but that will drop to about 400 once regular operations begin. The Argentia smelter will also employ about 400 people. About one-third of the workers at Voisey's Bay are Aboriginal.

Industry observers agree that Inco paid too much for Voisey's Bay and that it took far too long to develop the site. But with nickel prices at 16-year highs and customers demand for the product at high levels as well, Inco is poised to reap considerable rewards from the project. ◆

THE CONCEPT OF BUSINESS AND PROFIT

business An organization that seeks to earn profits by providing goods and services.

profit What remains (if anything) after a business's expenses are subtracted from its sales revenues.

The stories of Inco's involvement with the nickel discovery at Voisey's Bay and the development of the Alberta tar sands are classic Canadian business stories. But what do you think of when you hear the word *business*? Does it conjure up images of large and successful corporations like Inco and Wal-Mart? Or do you think of less successful companies like Jetsgo or Enron? Perhaps you think of smaller companies like your local supermarket or favourite restaurant. Actually, each of these firms is a **business**—an organization that produces or sells goods or services in an effort to make a profit. **Profit** is what remains after a business's expenses have been subtracted from its revenues. Profits reward the owners of businesses for taking the risks involved in investing their time and money. These amounts can be very

"Your Honor, my client pleads guilty to an overzealous but well-intentioned pursuit of the profit motive."

large if the business is managed well. Among the most profitable companies in 2005 were the Royal Bank of Canada ($3.3 billion), Manulife Financial ($3.2 billion), and Imperial Oil Ltd. ($2.6 billion).[1]

In Canada's economic system, businesses exist to earn profits for owners who are free to set them up. But consumers also have freedom of choice. In choosing how to pursue profits, businesses must take into account what consumers want or need. No matter how efficient a business is, it won't survive if there is no demand for its goods or services. Neither a snow-blower shop in Victoria nor a beach-umbrella store in Rankin Inlet is likely to do very well.

But if enterprising business people can identify either unmet consumer needs or better ways of satisfying consumer needs, they can be successful. In other words, someone who can spot a promising opportunity and then develop a good plan for capitalizing on it can succeed. The opportunity always involves goods or services that consumers want or need—especially if no one else is supplying them or if existing businesses are doing so inefficiently or incompletely.

Businesses produce most of the goods and services we consume and employ the majority of working people. They create most new innovations and provide opportunities for other businesses, which serve as their suppliers. A healthy business climate also contributes directly to our quality of life and standard of living. New forms of technology, service businesses, and international opportunities promise to keep production, consumption, and employment growing indefinitely. Business profits enhance the personal incomes of millions of owners and stockholders, and business taxes help to support governments at all levels. Many businesses support charities and provide community leadership.

In this chapter, we begin your introduction to Canadian business by looking at its role in our economy and society. Because a variety of economic systems are found around the world, we will first consider how the dominant ones operate. Once you have some understanding of different systems, you can better appreciate the workings of our own system. As you will see, the effect of economic forces on Canadian businesses and the effect of Canadian businesses on our economy produce dynamic and sometimes volatile results. We conclude the chapter by briefly tracing the history of Canadian business.

> **1** Define the nature of Canadian *business* and identify its main goals.

ECONOMIC SYSTEMS AROUND THE WORLD

A Canadian business is different in many ways from one in China. And both are different from businesses in Japan, France, or Peru. A major determinant of how organizations operate is the kind of economic system that characterizes the country in which they do business. An **economic system** allocates a nation's resources among its citizens. Economic systems differ in terms of who owns and controls these resources, known as the "factors of production" (see Figure 1.1).

> **2** Describe different types of global *economic systems* according to the means by which they control the *factors of production* through *input* and *output markets*.

economic system The way in which a nation allocates its resources among its citizens.

Factors of Production

The key difference between economic systems is the way in which they manage the **factors of production**—the basic resources that a country's businesses use to produce goods and services. Traditionally, economists have focused on four factors of production: *labour, capital, entrepreneurs,* and *natural resources. Information resources* are now often included as well.[2]

factors of production The resources used to produce goods and services: labour, capital, entrepreneurs, and natural resources.

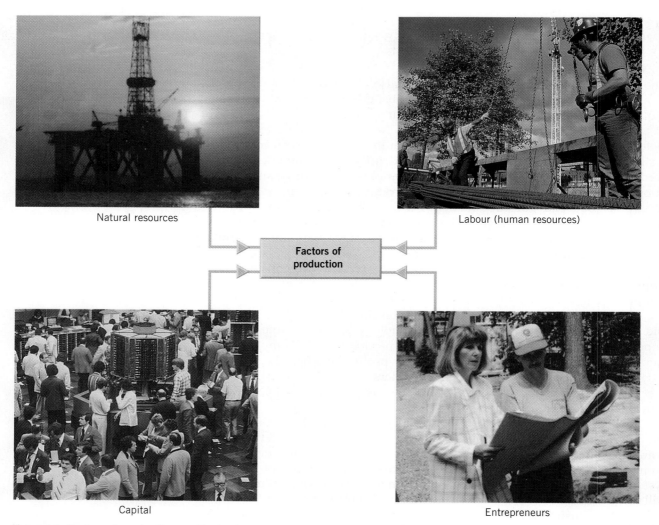

Natural resources

Labour (human resources)

Factors of production

Capital

Entrepreneurs

Figure 1.1 Factors of production are the basic resources a business uses to create goods and services. The four basic factors are natural resources, labour, capital, and entrepreneurs.

Labour

labour The mental and physical training and talents of people; sometimes called human resources.

The people who work for a company represent the first factor of production, **labour**. Sometimes called *human resources*, labour is the mental and physical capabilities of people. Carrying out the business of such a huge company as Imperial Oil, for example, requires a labour force with a wide variety of skills ranging from managers to geologists to truck drivers. Employees who are well trained and knowledgeable can be a real competitive advantage for a company.

Capital = $

capital The funds needed to operate an enterprise.

Obtaining and using labour and other resources requires **capital**—the financial resources needed to operate an enterprise. You need capital to start a new business and then to keep it running and growing. Inco needs millions of dollars in cash (and millions more in equipment and other assets) to run its operations. A major source of capital for small businesses is personal investment by owners. Investments can come from individual entrepreneurs, from partners who start businesses together, or from investors who buy stock. Revenue from the sale of products is a key and ongoing source of capital once a business has opened its doors.[3]

Entrepreneurs ↑ thâu khoáng

The people who accept the opportunities and risks involved in creating and operating businesses are entrepreneurs. Jimmy Pattison and Izzy Asper (who died in 2003) are well-known Canadian **entrepreneurs**. AOL was started by James Kimsey, who had the technical skills to understand how the internet works, the conceptual skills to see its huge future potential, and the risk-taking acumen to bet his own career and capital on the idea of AOL.

entrepreneur An individual who organizes and manages labour, capital, and natural resources to produce goods and services to earn a profit, but who also runs the risk of failure.

Natural Resources

Land, water, mineral deposits, and trees are examples of **natural resources**. Newer perspectives, however, tend to broaden the idea of "natural resources" to include all physical resources. For example, Imperial Oil makes use of a wide variety of natural resources. It obviously has vast quantities of crude oil to process each year. But Imperial Oil also needs the land where the oil is located, as well as land for its refineries and pipelines.

natural resources Items used in the production of goods and services in their natural state, including land, water, mineral deposits, and trees.

Information Resources

While the production of tangible goods once dominated most economic systems, today **information resources** play a major role. Businesses themselves rely heavily on market forecasts, the specialized expertise and knowledge of people, and various forms of economic data for much of their work. Much of what they do results in either the creation of new information or the repackaging of existing information for new users and different audiences. America Online, for example, does not produce tangible products. Instead, it provides numerous online services for its millions of subscribers in exchange for monthly access fees. AOL is in the information business.

information resources Information such as market forecasts, economic data, and specialized knowledge of employees that is useful to a business and that helps it achieve its goals.

Types of Economic Systems

Different types of economic systems manage the factors of production in different ways. In some systems, ownership is private; in others, the government owns the factors of production. Economic systems also differ in the way that decisions are made about production and allocation. A **command economy**, for example, relies on a centralized government to control all or most factors of production and to make all or most production and allocation decisions. In **market economies**, individuals—producers and consumers—control production and allocation decisions through supply and demand. We will describe each of these economic types and then discuss the reality of the *mixed market economy*.

command economy An economic system in which government controls all or most factors of production and makes all or most production decisions.

market economy An economic system in which individuals control all or most factors of production and make all or most production decisions.

Command Economies

The two most basic forms of command economies are communism and socialism. As originally proposed by the nineteenth-century German economist Karl Marx, **communism** is a system in which the government owns and operates all sources of production. Marx envisioned a society in which individuals would ultimately contribute according to their abilities and receive economic benefits according to their needs. He also expected government ownership of production factors to be only temporary. Once society had matured, government would "wither away" and the workers would gain direct ownership. But as the Business Accountability box demonstrates, things have not worked out the way Marx predicted, and most countries have now abandoned communism in favour of a more market-based economy.

communism A type of command economy in which the government owns and operates all industries.

In a less extensive command economic system called **socialism**, the government owns and operates only selected major industries. Smaller businesses such as clothing stores and restaurants may be privately owned.

socialism A kind of command economy in which the government owns and operates the main industries, while individuals own and operate less crucial industries.

BUSINESS ACCOUNTABILITY

Whatever Happened to Communism?

In 2005, GlobeScan conducted a poll of over 20 000 people in 20 different countries and asked them whether they agreed with the following statement: "The free market economy is the best system." Where do you think the highest support for capitalism was found? Not in the United States or Canada or Germany or Italy or Japan, but in *China*, where 74 percent of people polled agreed with the statement. This is a surprising finding, given the Chinese government's strong support of the communist economic ideology. Other countries with high agreement scores were the United States (71 percent), India (70 percent), and South Korea (66 percent). Countries with surprisingly low scores were Argentina (42 percent), Brazil (57 percent), and Mexico (61 percent). These low scores are likely the result of rushing free market reforms amid much corruption in Latin American countries.

It is surprising how rapidly free market systems have become popular. Until the 1980s, the former Soviet Union, most Eastern European countries, China, North Korea, Vietnam, Albania, and Cuba all embraced communist economic systems. During the early 1990s, however, one country after another renounced communism as both an economic and a political system. Today, Cuba, North Korea, Vietnam, and the People's Republic of China are among the few nations that claim to have a communist system. But while these countries may claim to be communist, the reality is quite different. They have all been swept up in the worldwide movement toward free market systems (some more than others).

Cuba's movement toward free markets has been underway for about a decade. Even though free-market activities are technically illegal, they have been increasing since the mid-1990s. Now, special shops that once were reserved for diplomats sell goods to Cubans from all walks of life. These stores are surrounded by paid bicycle-parking lots, car washes, and stalls selling homegrown produce and homemade handicrafts. This "street-corner commerce" reflects a rapid growth in private enterprise as a solution to problems that Cuba's centralized economy was never able to solve.

Dramatic and highly publicized changes are taking place in China, which has suddenly burst upon the world scene as an awakening economic giant. It seems hard to believe now, but before 1979 people who sold watches on street corners in China were sentenced to years of hard labour. In 1999, China's constitution was amended to elevate private enterprise to a place alongside the state sector in China's official economic ideology. Since that time, the private sector has become incredibly productive, and China is the world's fastest growing economy. For example, it is estimated that China produces 60 percent of all the toys in the world. China's reputation for being a low-cost producer of goods is legendary. It is also a vast and rapidly growing market for many of the products that Canadian firms produce—chemicals, ores, cereals, and wood products. Over the longer term, it will be difficult for the Chinese government to maintain a communist economic and political ideology while the people of China eagerly embrace the free market system.

In terms of movement away from the communist ideology, perhaps the most striking changes are those occurring in North Korea. Until very recently, North Korea was an extreme example of the communist economic system, and the country was so isolated from world commerce that it was known as the "Hermit Kingdom." Now, large numbers of "sidewalk entrepreneurs" sell items like food and drinks in public places in North Korea, where just a few years ago they would have been imprisoned for "profiteering." In the Yanggakdo Hotel, visitors can play slot machines or roulette at the Casino Pyongyang.

As recently as the late 1990s, the official government position was that merchants were a class of people who should be eradicated because they bought products at low prices and sold them to consumers at high prices (and, it was argued, they used deceit and fraud in the process). Now, the communist party newspaper quotes North Korean dictator Kim Jong Il as saying that he favours profits under socialist economic management. These changes in the government's position have attracted the attention of foreign companies who are becoming more interested in investing in North Korea. In 2005, for example, the London-based Anglo-Sino Capital Partners formed the Chosun Development & Investment Fund and planned to raise $50 million for investment in North Korea. North Korea still has a long way to go toward a free market system, but the movement has started. These changes in so many different countries reflect consumer beliefs that market-based economies are more responsive and accountable to consumer needs.

Although workers in socialist countries are usually allowed to choose their occupations or professions, a large proportion generally works for the government. Many government-operated enterprises are inefficient, since management positions are frequently filled based on political considerations rather than on ability. Extensive public welfare systems have also resulted in very high taxes. Because of these factors, socialism is generally declining in popularity.[4]

Market Economies

A **market** is a mechanism for exchange between the buyers and sellers of a particular good or service. To understand how a *market economy* works, consider what happens when a customer goes to a fruit stand to buy apples. Let's say that while one vendor is selling apples for $1 per kilogram, another is charging $1.50. Both vendors are free to charge what they want, and customers are free to buy what they choose. If both vendors' apples are of the same quality, the customer will buy the cheaper ones. But if the $1.50 apples are fresher, the customer may buy them instead. In short, both buyers and sellers enjoy freedom of choice.

The internet is a technologically sophisticated market that brings buyers and sellers together through ecommerce. When people talk about ecommerce, they usually think of business-to-consumer (B2C) transactions such as buying books over the internet for personal use. But business-to-business (B2B) transactions are also very important.

B2B involves businesses joining together to create ecommerce companies that make them more efficient when they purchase the goods and services they need. B2B transactions actually far exceed B2C transactions in dollar value. Worldwide, B2B transactions exceed $200 billion.

Thirty of the world's large commercial airlines, including Air Canada, have joined forces to purchase fuel, equipment, aircraft parts, and maintenance through an ecommerce site called Aeroxchange Ltd. In total, the airlines purchase about U.S.$50 billion on the site. Air Canada expects to save $11 million–$14 million on the items it buys through the exchange. The exchange also lowers transaction, processing, and inventory costs for the airlines.

Input and Output Markets. Figure 1.2 provides a useful and more complete model for better understanding how the factors of production work in a pure market economy. According to this view, businesses and households interact in two different market relationships.[5] In the **input market**, firms buy resources from households, which are thus resource suppliers. In the **output market**, firms supply goods and services in response to demand on the part of households. (We will provide a more detailed discussion of supply and demand later in this chapter.)

As you can see in Figure 1.2, the activities of these two markets create a circular flow. Ford Motor Co., for example, relies on various kinds of inputs. It buys labour directly from households, which may also supply capital from accumulated savings in the form of stock purchases. Consumer buying patterns provide information that helps Ford decide which models to produce and which to discontinue. In turn, Ford uses these inputs in various ways and becomes a supplier to households when it designs and produces various kinds of automobiles, trucks, and sports utility vehicles and offers them for sale to consumers.

Capitalism. Individuals, meanwhile, are free to work for Ford or an alternative employer and to invest in Ford stock or alternative forms of saving or consumption. Similarly, Ford can create whatever vehicles it chooses and

market A mechanism for exchange between the buyers and sellers of a particular good or service.

input market Firms buy resources that they need in the production of goods and services.

output market Firms supply goods and services in response to demand on the part of consumers.

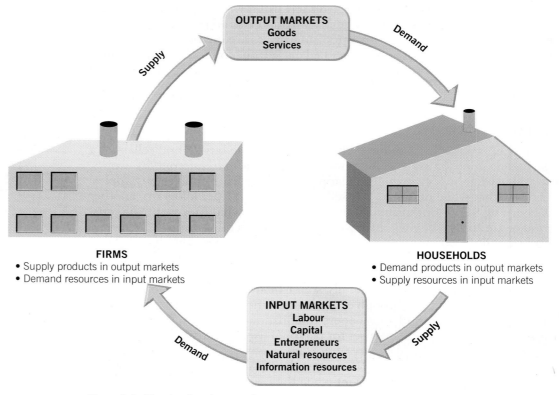

Figure 1.2 Circular flow in a market economy.

price them at whatever value it chooses. But consumers are then free to buy their next car from Ford or Toyota or BMW. This process contrasts markedly with that of a command economy, in which individuals may be told where they can and cannot work, companies are told what they can and cannot manufacture, and consumers may have little or no choice as to what they purchase or how much they pay for items. The political basis of market processes is called **capitalism**, which sanctions the private ownership of the factors of production and encourages entrepreneurship by offering

capitalism An economic system in which markets decide what, when, and for whom to produce.

According to the model of circular flow in a market economy, shoppers at a Wal-Mart de Mexico play the same role in the output market as consumers everywhere. They demand goods supplied by a retail firm. Likewise, you can think of the employees who work for companies from which Wal-Mart buys its products as households that supply the input market with labour, time, and skills.

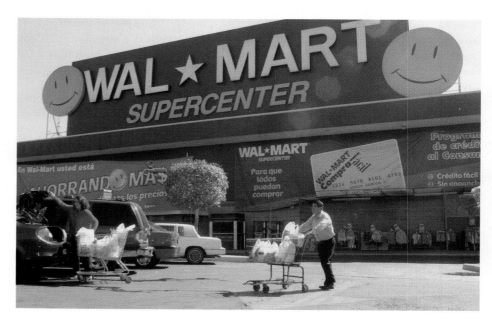

profits as an incentive. The economic basis of market processes is the operation of demand and supply, which we discuss later in the chapter.

Mixed Market Economies

In their pure forms, command and market economies are often viewed as two extremes or opposites. In reality, however, most countries rely on some form of **mixed market economy**—a system featuring characteristics of both command and market economies. For example, most countries of the former Eastern bloc have now adopted market mechanisms through a process called **privatization**—the process of converting government enterprises into privately owned companies. In recent years this practice has also begun to spread to many other countries as well. For example, the postal system in most countries is government-owned and -managed, regardless of whether the country has a command or market economy. The Netherlands, however, recently began the process of privatizing its TNT Post Group N.V., already among the world's most efficient post office operations. Similarly, Canada has recently privatized its air traffic control system. In each case, the new enterprise reduced its payroll, boosted efficiency and productivity, and quickly became profitable.[6]

Another trend is **deregulation**—the reduction in the number of laws affecting business activity and in the powers of government enforcement agencies. In most cases, deregulation frees companies to do what they want without government intervention, thereby simplifying the task of management. Deregulation is evident in many industries, including airlines, pipelines, banking, trucking, and communication.

mixed market economy An economic system with elements of both a command economy and a market economy; in practice, typical of most nations' economies.

privatization The process of converting government enterprises into privately owned companies.

tư hữu hóa

deregulation A reduction in the number of laws affecting business activity.

sự điều chỉnh?

INTERACTIONS BETWEEN BUSINESS AND GOVERNMENT

In Canada's mixed economic system, there are many important interactions between business and government. We first look at how government influences business, and then examine the way that business influences government.

How Government Influences Business

Government plays several different roles in the Canadian economy, and each of these roles influences business activity in some way. The roles government plays follow.

Government as Customer

Government buys thousands of different products and services from business firms, including office supplies, office buildings, computers, battleships, helicopters, highways, water treatment plants, and management and engineering consulting services. The government is also the largest purchaser of advertising in Canada. Many businesses depend on government purchasing, if not for their survival, at least for a certain level of prosperity. Government expenditures on goods and services amount to billions of dollars each year.

Government as Competitor

Government also competes with business through Crown corporations, which are accountable to a minister of parliament for their conduct.

Crown corporations exist at both the provincial and federal level, and account for a significant and wide variety of economic activity in Canada (see Table 1.1).

Government as Regulator

Federal and provincial governments in Canada regulate many aspects of business activity. Government regulates business through many administrative boards, tribunals, or commissions. At the federal level, examples include the **Canadian Radio-television and Telecommunications Commission (CRTC)**, which issues and renews broadcast licences, the **Canadian Transport Commission (CTC)**, which makes decisions about route and rate applications for commercial air and railway companies, and the **Canadian Wheat Board**, which regulates the prices of wheat. Provincial boards and commissions also regulate business through their decisions. Sometimes business people feel that government is unfair in the way it performs its role as regulator. Concluding Case 1-2 gives an example of one such situation.

There are several important reasons for regulating business activity. These include protecting competition, protecting consumers, achieving social goals, and protecting the environment.

Protecting Competition. One of the reasons that government regulates business is to ensure that healthy competition exists among business firms, because competition is crucial to a market economy. Without restrictions, a large company with vast resources could drive smaller firms out of the market. Competition policy tries to eliminate restrictive trade practices and thereby stimulate maximum production, distribution, and employment.

The guidelines for Canada's competition policy are contained in The Competition Act, which prohibits a variety of practices (see Table 1.2). Section 38, for example, prohibits something called *resale price maintenance*. In 2005, Labatt Brewing Co. pleaded guilty to resale price maintenance and was fined $250 000 after its sales representatives gave money to store operators who agreed to not lower prices on some brands of beer. This activity meant that customers had to pay higher prices for beer. A Labatt competitor, Sleeman Breweries, was also fined for resale price maintenance in 2002.[7]

Protecting Consumers. The federal government has initiated many programs that protect consumers. Consumer and Corporate Affairs Canada administers many of these. Important legislation includes the **Hazardous Products Act** (which requires poisonous, flammable, explosive, or corrosive products to be

Canadian Radio-television and Telecommunications Commission (CRTC) A federal regulatory agency that issues and renews broadcast licences.

Canadian Transport Commission (CTC) A federal regulatory agency that makes decisions about route and rate applications for commercial air and railway companies.

Canadian Wheat Board A federal regulatory agency that regulates the prices of wheat.

Hazardous Products Act Regulates banned products and products that can be sold but must be labelled hazardous.

Table 1.1	The Top 10 Crown Corporations in Canada, 2005
Company	**Annual Revenues (in billions of $)**
1. Hydro-Quebec	$ 10.8
2. Canada Post Corp.	6.6
3. Ontario Lottery and Gaming Corp.	5.8
4. Ontario Power Generation Inc.	5.7
5. Canada Mortgage and Housing Corp.	5.2
6. Caisse de dépôt et placement du Québec	4.7
7. Canadian Wheat Board	3.7
8. Insurance Corp. of British Columbia	3.7
9. British Columbia Hydro and Power Authority	3.7
10. Liquor Control Board of Ontario	3.5

Table 1.2	The Competition Act
Section 32	Prohibits conspiracies and combinations formed for the purpose of unduly lessening competition in the production, transportation, or storage of goods. Persons convicted may be imprisoned for up to five years or fined up to $1 million or both.
Section 33	Prohibits mergers and monopolies that substantially lessen competition. Individuals who assist in the formation of such a monopoly or merger may be imprisoned for up to two years.
Section 34	Prohibits illegal trade practices. A company may not, for example, cut prices in one region of Canada while selling at a higher price everywhere else if this substantially lessens competition. A company may not sell at "unreasonably low prices" if this substantially lessens competition. (This section does not prohibit credit unions from returning surpluses to their members.)
Section 35	Prohibits giving allowances and rebates to buyers to cover their advertising expenses, unless these allowances are made available proportionally to other purchasers who are in competition with the buyer given the rebate.
Section 36	Prohibits misleading advertising including (1) false statements about the performance of a product, (2) misleading guarantees, (3) pyramid selling, (4) charging the higher price when two prices are marked on an item, and (5) referral selling.
Section 37	Prohibits bait-and-switch selling. No person can advertise a product at a bargain price if there is no supply of the product available to the consumer. (This tactic baits prospects into the store, where salespeople switch them to higher-priced goods.) This section also controls the use of contests to sell goods, and prohibits the sale of goods at a price higher than the advertised one.
Section 38	Prohibits resale price maintenance. No person who produces or supplies a product can attempt to influence upward, or discourage reduction of, the price of the good in question. It is also illegal for the producer to refuse to supply a product to a reseller simply because the producer believes the reseller will cut the price.

appropriately labelled), the **Tobacco Act** (which prohibits cigarette advertising on billboards and in stores), the **Weights and Measures Act** (which sets standards of accuracy for weighing and measuring devices), the **Textile Labelling Act** (which regulates the labelling, sale, importation, and advertising of consumer textile articles), and the **Food and Drug Act** (which prohibits the sale of food that contains any poisonous or harmful substances). Consumers are also protected by municipal bylaws such as the "no-smoking" bylaws that are so controversial in some Canadian cities.

Achieving Social Goals. Social goals promote the well-being of our society. Social goals include universal access to health care, safe workplaces, employment insurance, and decent pensions. All of these goals require the interaction of business firms and government.

Protecting the Environment. Key government legislation designed to protect the environment includes the **Canada Water Act** (which controls water quality in fresh and marine waters), the **Fisheries Act** (which controls the discharge of any harmful substance into water), and the **Environmental Contaminants Act** (which establishes regulations for airborne substances that are a danger to human health or the environment).

Government as Taxation Agent

Taxes are imposed and collected by federal, provincial, and local governments. **Revenue taxes** (e.g., income taxes) are levied by governments primarily to provide revenue to fund various services and programs. **Progressive revenue taxes** are levied at a higher rate on higher-income taxpayers and at a lower rate on lower-income taxpayers. **Regressive revenue taxes** (e.g., sales tax) are levied at the same rate regardless of a person's income. They cause poorer people to pay a higher percentage of their

Tobacco Act Prohibits cigarette advertising on billboards and in retail stores, and assigns financial penalties to violators.

Weights and Measures Act Sets standards of accuracy for weighing and measuring devices.

Textile Labelling Act Regulates the labelling, sale, importation, and advertising of consumer textile articles.

Food and Drug Act Prohibits the sale of food unfit for human consumption and regulates food advertising.

Canada Water Act Controls water quality in fresh and marine waters of Canada.

Fisheries Act Regulates the discharge of harmful substances into water.

Environmental Contaminants Act Establishes regulations for airborne substances that are a danger to human health or to the environment.

revenue taxes Taxes whose main purpose is to fund government services and programs.

progressive revenue taxes Taxes levied at a higher rate on higher-income taxpayers and at a lower rate on lower-income taxpayers.

regressive revenue taxes Taxes that cause poorer people to pay a higher percentage of income than richer people pay.

restrictive taxes Taxes levied to control certain activities that legislators believe should be controlled.

income for these taxes than rich people pay. **Restrictive taxes** (e.g., taxes on alcohol, tobacco, and gasoline) are levied partially for the revenue they provide, but also because legislative bodies believe that the products in question should be controlled.

Government as Provider of Incentives

Federal, provincial, and municipal governments offer incentive programs that help stimulate economic development. In Quebec, for example, Hyundai Motors received $6.4 million to build a production facility and an additional $682 000 to train workers. Both Toyota and Hyundai have received millions of dollars in incentives from government in the form of training incentives, interest-free loans, and the suspension of customs duties.[8]

Governments also offer incentives through the many services they provide to business firms through government organizations. These include the Export Development Corporation (which assists Canadian exporters by offering export insurance against nonpayment by foreign buyers and long-term loans to foreign buyers of Canadian products), Energy, Mines and Resources Canada (which provides geological maps of Canada's potential mineral-producing areas), and Statistics Canada (which provides data and analysis on almost every aspect of Canadian society).

There are many other government incentive programs, including municipal tax rebates for companies that locate in certain areas, design assistance programs, and remission of tariffs on certain advanced technology production equipment. Government incentive programs may or may not have the desired effect of stimulating the economy. They may also cause difficulties with our trading partners.

Government as Provider of Essential Services

The federal, provincial, and municipal governments facilitate business activity through the wide variety of services they supply. The federal government provides highways, the postal service, the minting of money, the armed forces, and statistical data on which to base business decisions. It also tries to maintain stability through fiscal and monetary policy. Provincial and municipal governments provide streets, sewage and sanitation systems, police and fire departments, utilities, hospitals, and education. All of these activities create the kind of stability that encourages business activity.

How Business Influences Government

lobbyist A person hired by a company or an industry to represent its interests to government officials.

While government activity influences what businesses do, businesses also influence the government through lobbyists, trade associations, and advertising (see Figure 1.3). A **lobbyist** is a person hired by a company or industry to represent its interests to government officials. The Association of Consulting Engineers of Canada, for example, regularly lobbies the federal and provincial governments to make use of the skills possessed by private sector consulting engineers on projects like city water systems. Some business lobbyists have training in the particular industry, public relations experience, or a legal background. A few have served as legislators or government regulators.

The Lobbyists Registration Act came into effect in 1989. Lobbyists must register with the Registrar of Lobbyists so that it is clear which individuals are being paid for their lobbying activity. For many lobbying efforts, there are opposing points of view. The Canadian Cancer Society and the Tobacco Institute present very different points of view on cigarette smoking and cigarette advertising.

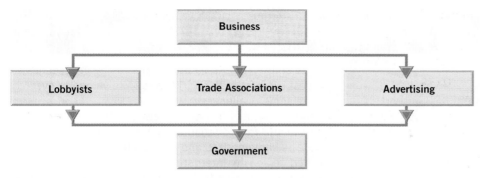

Figure 1.3 Business influences the government in a variety of ways.

Employees and owners of small businesses that cannot afford lobbyists often join **trade associations**, which may act as an industry lobby to influence legislation. They also conduct training programs relevant to the particular industry, and they arrange trade shows at which members display their products or services to potential customers. Most publish newsletters featuring articles on new products, new companies, changes in ownership, and changes in laws affecting the industry.

Corporations can influence legislation indirectly by influencing voters. A company can, for example, launch an advertising campaign designed to get people to write their MPs, MPPs, or MLAs demanding passage—or rejection—of a particular bill that is before parliament or the provincial legislature.

trade association An organization dedicated to promoting the interests and assisting the members of a particular industry.

THE CANADIAN MARKET ECONOMY

Understanding the complex nature of the Canadian economic system is essential to understanding Canadian businesses. In the next few pages, we will examine the workings of our market economy in more detail. Specifically, we look at demand and supply in a market economy, private enterprise, and degrees of competition.

Show how *demand* and *supply* affect resource distribution in Canada.

3

Demand and Supply in a Market Economy

In economic terms, a market is not a specific place, like a supermarket, but an exchange process between buyers and sellers. A market economy consists of many different markets. We have already described input and output markets, but we need to remember that the inputs used by business and the products created by business have their own markets. In each of these markets, businesses decide what inputs to buy, what to make and in what quantities, and what prices to charge. Likewise, customers decide what to buy and how much they want to pay. Literally billions of such exchanges take place every day between businesses and individuals; between businesses; and among individuals, businesses, and governments. Moreover, exchanges conducted in one area often affect exchanges elsewhere.

The Laws of Demand and Supply

On all economic levels, decisions about what to buy and what to sell are determined primarily by the forces of demand and supply.[9] **Demand** is the willingness and ability of buyers to purchase a product (a good) or a service.

demand The willingness and ability of buyers to purchase a product or service.

ENTREPRENEURSHIP AND NEW VENTURES

Pulse of a Nation

At 33 years of age, Murad Al-Katib has put Canada—and its lentils—on the international map. As president and CEO of Saskcan Pulse Trading of Regina, Al-Katib has, in three years, taken his company from a home-based venture to an award-winning agribusiness that processes and exports pulse—lentils, chick peas, and peas—to more than 60 countries.

Observing the growth in the export of lentils to Turkey, Al-Katib saw the opportunity for value-added processing. "I didn't want to see the lentil story end up like the mustard story," he said, where Saskatchewan supplies the raw material for almost all of the many prepared mustards made in France. "I identified potential partners there [in Turkey], including one of the world's largest buyers of red lentils [Arbel] and convinced them that we should do the processing in Saskatchewan. That's how Saskcan was born." The company has attracted millions of dollars in investment, largely due to Arbel's proprietary technology for splitting and oiling the red lentils and their expertise in setting up and operating the processing plant. Indeed, the facility has added about 40 percent to the market value of the crops.

Several factors have contributed to the boom in lentil crops over the past several years: international demand; a desire to produce a commodity that is less volatile in price than wheat; the drive to avoid a price-fixing, central marketing agency such as the Saskatchewan Wheat Board; and the need to rotate traditional crops with ones that restore nitrogen levels to the soil, which lentil plants do.

Product quality is important at Saskcan. "At first, we were a bit of a mystery to clients who wondered if, in Canada, we could produce a red split lentil that lived up to Turkish and Indian quality standards," Al-Katib recalls. "But the quality of our first shipment of red split lentils was likely among the best in the world. From then on, our business just continued to grow." As Al-Katib explains, "January 2003 was our first load of red split lentils. To go from that to being the second-largest exporter in the world...yeah, we've had to overcome some challenges."

Transportation is one of those challenges, particularly in the face of soaring fuel costs. All the lentils must be containerized and shipped by rail from a land-locked region to international ports. "We are so far from world markets that transit time can take several weeks. Our competitors can deliver faster, so we have to be very competitive with our pricing," explains Al-Katib. The transportation costs alone make up about 20 percent of the market cost of Canadian lentils, as compared to about seven percent for rival Turkish lentils. "We've designed an automated system that makes us very efficient at processing, and that has been a big help," he says.

Another challenge is dealing with customers from 33 different countries, with many distinct cultures and languages. For example, in the Middle East, bright, shiny red lentils are considered the most valuable, while in Europe, a dull finish is more popular. That means some of Saskcan's product is highly polished with oil, while other batches are untouched.

From a relatively minor specialty crop five years ago, Canada's lentil production has grown to more than 900 000 tonnes annually, of which 98 percent is produced in Saskatchewan. "This has become a $1-billion industry in Canada," says Al-Katib, and Saskcan has grown along with it. The company is the largest processor and exporter of red lentils in the western hemisphere, and the second-largest exporter of red lentils in the world. For Saskcan's business model to continue working, however, the venture must constantly race to remain the world's lowest-cost producer of lentils.

Despite unpredictable growing conditions and the strong Canadian dollar, Al-Katib is optimistic that given the continuing shift from green to red lentils, crops which command a premium price on international markets, ongoing investment in the development of new seeds and refined varieties will foster Saskcan's growth.

---

supply The willingness and ability of producers to offer a good or service for sale.

law of demand The principle that buyers will purchase (demand) more of a product as price drops.

law of supply The principle that producers will offer (supply) more of a product as price rises.

Supply is the willingness and ability of producers to offer a good or service for sale. Generally speaking, demand and supply follow basic "laws":

- The **law of demand**: Buyers will purchase (demand) more of a product as its price drops and less of a product as its price increases.

- The **law of supply**: Producers will offer (supply) more of a product for sale as its price rises and less as its price drops.

The Demand and Supply Schedule

To appreciate these laws in action, consider the market for pizza in your town. If everyone in town is willing to pay $25 for a pizza (a high price), the town's only pizzeria will produce a large supply. If everyone is willing to pay only $5 (a low price), however, the restaurant will make fewer pizzas. Through careful analysis, we can determine how many pizzas will be sold at different prices. These results, called a **demand and supply schedule**, are obtained from marketing research and other systematic studies of the market. Properly applied, they help managers better understand the relationships among different levels of demand and supply at different price levels.

demand and supply schedule Assessment of the relationships between different levels of demand and supply at different price levels.

Demand and Supply Curves

The demand and supply schedule, for example, can be used to construct demand and supply curves for pizza in your town. A **demand curve** shows how many products—in this case, pizzas—will be demanded (bought) at different prices. A **supply curve** shows how many pizzas will be supplied (cooked) at different prices.

Figure 1.4 shows hypothetical demand and supply curves for pizzas. As you can see, demand increases as price decreases; supply increases as price increases. When the demand and supply curves are plotted on the same graph, the point at which they intersect is the **market price** or **equilibrium price**—the price at which the quantity of goods demanded and the quantity of goods supplied are equal. Note in Figure 1.4 that the equilibrium price for pizzas in our example is $10. At this point, the quantity of pizzas demanded and the quantity of pizzas supplied are the same: 1000 pizzas per week.

demand curve Graph showing how many units of a product will be demanded (bought) at different prices.

supply curve Graph showing how many units of a product will be supplied (offered for sale) at different prices.

market price (or equilibrium price) Profit-maximizing price at which the quantity of goods demanded and the quantity of goods supplied are equal.

Surpluses and Shortages

But what if the restaurant chooses to make some other number of pizzas? For example, what would happen if the owner tried to increase profits by making more pizzas to sell? Or what if the owner wanted to reduce overhead, cut back on store hours, and reduce the number of pizzas offered for sale? In either case, the result would be an inefficient use of resources—and perhaps lower profits. For example, if the restaurant supplies 1200 pizzas and tries to sell them for $10 each, 200 pizzas will not be purchased. The demand schedule clearly shows that only 1000 pizzas will be demanded at this price. The pizza maker will have a **surplus**—a situation in which the quantity supplied exceeds the quantity demanded. The restaurant will thus lose the money it spent making those extra 200 pizzas.

surplus Situation in which quantity supplied exceeds quantity demanded.

Conversely, if the pizzeria supplies only 800 pizzas, a **shortage** will result: the quantity demanded will be greater than the quantity supplied. The pizzeria will "lose" the extra money that it could have made by producing 200 more pizzas. Even though consumers may pay more for pizzas because of the shortage, the restaurant will still earn lower profits than it would have if it had made 1000 pizzas. In addition, it will risk angering customers who cannot buy pizzas. To optimize profits, therefore, all businesses must constantly seek the right combination of the price charged and the quantity supplied. This "right combination" is found at the equilibrium point.

shortage Situation in which quantity demanded exceeds quantity supplied.

When there are shortages of commodities, the price of the commodity rises and there may be an increase in criminal behaviour. For example, as the price of stainless steel and aluminum rose during the last few years, thieves began stealing items such as beer kegs, railway baggage carts, railroad tracks, light poles, and guard rails along highways. These items were then sold to scrap yards for cash.[10]

Ginseng—a plant known for its healing properties—demonstrates the ideas about shortages and surpluses. In 1982, less than 25 metric tonnes of ginseng were grown in Canada, and growers received about $187 per kilogram for it. There was essentially a shortage of ginseng. Many new growers therefore got into the market because they saw a chance to make money supplying ginseng. With more growers, production increased rapidly, and by 1999, 2200 metric tonnes were being produced. But by then, growers were getting only about $33 per kilogram. By 2001, there was a surplus of ginseng.[11]

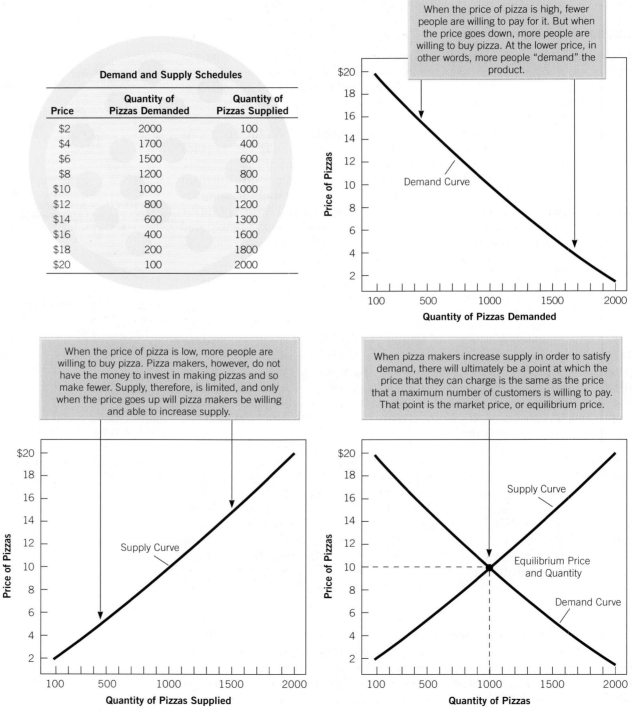

Figure 1.4 Demand and supply.

Applied Materials specializes in the high-tech equipment used to make flat panel TV screens. You can buy a 40-inch TV with a plasma-display screen for $4000. That's down about 45 percent in just two years because flat screen TVs have caught on and demand has grown dramatically. The latest thing is the liquid crystal display (LCD) panel, but because it's still new, a 40-inch LCD TV costs more than twice as much as a flat screen TV.

Private Enterprise and Competition in a Market Economy

Market economies rely on a **private enterprise** system—one that allows individuals to pursue their own interests with minimal government restriction. In turn, private enterprise requires the presence of four elements: private property rights, freedom of choice, profits, and competition.

- *Private property rights*. Ownership of the resources used to create wealth is in the hands of individuals.[12]

- *Freedom of choice*. You can sell your labour to any employer you choose. You can also choose which products to buy, and producers can usually choose whom to hire and what to produce.

- *Profits*. The lure of profits (and freedom) leads some people to abandon the security of working for someone else and to assume the risks of entrepreneurship. Anticipated profits also influence individuals' choices of which goods or services to produce.

- *Competition*. If profits motivate individuals to start businesses, **competition** motivates them to operate those businesses efficiently. Competition occurs when two or more businesses vie for the same resources or customers. To gain an advantage over competitors, a business must produce its goods or services efficiently and be able to sell at a reasonable profit. To achieve these goals, it must convince customers that its products are either better or less expensive than those of its competitors. Competition, therefore, forces all businesses to make products better or cheaper. A company that produces inferior, expensive products is likely to fail. We discuss competition more fully in the next section.

Degrees of Competition

Even in a free enterprise system, not all industries are equally competitive. Economists have identified four degrees of competition in a private enterprise system: *perfect competition, monopolistic competition, oligopoly,* and *monopoly*. Table 1.3 summarizes the features of these four degrees of competition.

private enterprise An economic system characterized by private property rights, freedom of choice, profits, and competition.

Identify the elements of *private enterprise* and explain the various *degrees of competition* in the Canadian economic system.

4

competition The vying among businesses in a particular market or industry to best satisfy consumer demands and earn profits.

Table 1.3	Degrees of Competition			
Characteristic	**Perfect Competition**	**Monopolistic Competition**	**Oligopoly**	**Monopoly**
Example	Local farmer	Stationery store	Steel industry	Public utility
Number of competitors	Many	Many, but fewer than in perfect competition	Few	None
Ease of entry into industry	Relatively easy	Fairly easy	Difficult	Regulated by government
Similarity of goods or services offered by competing firms	Identical	Similar	Can be similar or different	No directly competing goods or services
Level of control over price by individual firms	None	Some	Some	Considerable

perfect competition A market or industry characterized by a very large number of small firms producing an identical product so that none of the firms has any ability to influence price.

Perfect Competition. For **perfect competition** to exist, two conditions must prevail: (1) all firms in an industry must be small and (2) the number of firms in the industry must be large. Under these conditions, no single firm is powerful enough to influence the price of its product. Prices are therefore determined by such market forces as supply and demand. In addition, these two conditions also reflect four principles:

1. The products of each firm are so similar that buyers view them as identical to those of other firms.

2. Both buyers and sellers know the prices that others are paying and receiving in the marketplace.

3. Because each firm is small, it is easy for firms to enter or leave the market.

4. Going prices are set exclusively by supply and demand and accepted by both sellers and buyers.

Canadian agriculture is a good example of perfect competition. The wheat produced on one farm is the same as that from another. Both producers and buyers are aware of prevailing market prices. It is relatively easy to start producing wheat and relatively easy to stop when it's no longer profitable.

monopolistic competition A market or industry characterized by a large number of firms supplying products that are similar but distinctive enough from one another to give firms some ability to influence price.

Monopolistic Competition. Fewer sellers are involved in **monopolistic competition** than in perfect competition, but because there are still many buyers, sellers try to make products at least *seem* to differ from those of competitors. Differentiating strategies include brand names (Tide and Cheer), design or styling (Polo and Tommy Hilfiger jeans), and advertising (Coke and Pepsi). For example, in an effort to attract health-conscious consumers, the Kraft Foods division of Philip Morris promotes such differentiated products as low-fat Cool Whip, low-calorie Jell-O, and sugar-free Kool-Aid.

Monopolistically competitive businesses may be large or small, but they can still enter or leave the market easily. For example, many small clothing stores compete successfully with large apparel retailers such as Liz Claiborne and Limited Brands. bebe Stores is a good case in point. The small clothing chain controls its own manufacturing facilities and can respond just as quickly as firms like Gap Inc. to changes in fashion tastes.[13] Many single-store clothing businesses in college towns compete by developing their own T-shirt and cap designs with copyrighted slogans and logos.

Product differentiation also gives sellers some control over prices. For instance, even though Sears shirts may have similar styling and other features, Ralph Lauren Polo shirts can be priced with little regard for lower Sears prices. But there are limits. Although Polo might be able to sell shirts for, say, $20 more than a comparable Sears shirt, it could not sell as many shirts if they were priced at $200 more.

Oligopoly. When an industry has only a handful of sellers, an **oligopoly** exists. As a general rule, these sellers are quite large. It is difficult for new competitors to enter the industry because large capital investment is needed. Thus oligopolistic industries like the automobile, airline, and steel industries tend to stay that way.[14] For example, only two companies make large commercial aircraft: Boeing (a U.S. company) and Airbus (a European consortium). Furthermore, as the trend toward globalization continues, most experts believe that, as one forecaster puts it, "global oligopolies are as inevitable as the sunrise."[15]

Oligopolists have more control over their strategies than monopolistically competitive firms, but the actions of one firm can significantly affect the sales of every other firm in the industry. For example, when one firm cuts prices or offers incentives to increase sales, the others usually protect sales by doing the same. Likewise, when one firm raises prices, others generally follow suit. Therefore, the prices of comparable products are usually similar. When an airline announces new fare discounts, others adopt the same strategy almost immediately. Just as quickly, when discounts end for one airline, they usually end for everyone else.

Monopoly. When an industry or market has only one producer, a **monopoly** exists. Being the only supplier gives a firm complete control over the price of its product. Its only constraint is how much consumer demand will fall as its price rises. Until 1992, the long-distance telephone business was a monopoly in Canada, and cable TV, which has had a local monopoly for years, will lose it when telephone companies and satellite broadcasters are allowed into the cable business.[16]

In Canada, laws such as the Competition Act forbid many monopolies, and the prices charged by so-called "natural monopolies" are closely watched by provincial utilities boards. **Natural monopolies** are found in industries in which one company can most efficiently supply all the product or service that is needed. For example, the argument is typically made that a single provincial electric company can supply all the power (product) needed in an area. The argument is made that duplicate facilities—such as two nuclear power plants, two sets of power lines, and so forth—would be wasteful. The assumption that certain activities qualify as natural monopolies is increasingly being challenged, however. For example, the Royal Mail Group's 350-year monopoly of the British postal service ended in 2006 and rival companies are now allowed to compete with Royal Mail.[17]

oligopoly A market or industry characterized by a small number of very large firms that have the power to influence the price of their product and/or resources.

monopoly A market or industry with only one producer, who can set the price of its product and/or resources.

natural monopoly A market or industry in which having only one producer is most efficient because it can meet all of consumers' demand for the product.

A BRIEF HISTORY OF BUSINESS IN CANADA

A look at the history of business in Canada shows a steady development from sole proprietorships to the complex corporate structures of today. In this section, we will trace the broad outlines of the development of business

Consumers often buy products under conditions of monopolistic competition. For example, there are few differences between various brands of toothpaste, cold tablets, detergents, canned goods, and soft drinks.

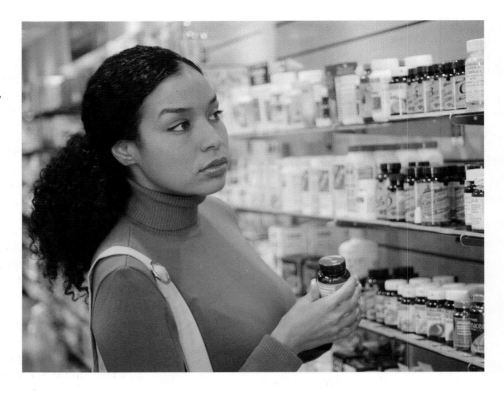

5   Trace the *history of business* in Canada.

in Canada. Table 1.4 highlights some of the specific events in Canadian business history.[18]

The Early Years

Business activity and profit from commercial fishing were the motivation for the first European involvement in Canada. In the late 1400s, ships financed by English entrepreneurs came to the coast of Newfoundland to fish for profit. By the late 1500s, the Newfoundland coast was being visited by hundreds of fishing vessels each year.

Beginning in the 1500s, French and British adventurers began trading with the native peoples. Items such as cooking utensils and knives were exchanged for beaver and other furs. One trading syndicate made over 1000 percent profit on beaver skins sold to a Paris furrier. Trading was aggressive and, over time, the price of furs rose as more and more Europeans bid for them. Originally the fur trade was restricted to eastern Canada, but by the late 1600s, coureurs de bois were travelling far to the west in search of new sources of furs.

European settlers who arrived in Canada in the sixteenth and seventeenth centuries initially had to farm or starve. Gradually, however, they began to produce more than they needed for their own survival. The governments of the countries from which the settlers came (notably England and France) were strong supporters of the mercantilist philosophy. Under mercantilism, colonists were expected to export raw materials like beaver pelts and lumber at low prices to the mother country. These raw materials were then used to produce finished goods such as fur coats, which were sold at high prices to settlers in Canada. Attempts to develop industry in Canada were thwarted by England and France, who enjoyed large profits from mercantilism. As a result, Canadian manufacturing was slow to develop.

Table 1.4	Some Important Dates in Canadian Business History

1490	English fishermen active off the coast of Newfoundland	1897–99	Klondike gold rush
1534	Account of first trading with native peoples written by Jacques Cartier	1917–22	Creation of Canadian National Railways
1670	Hudson's Bay Company founded	1926	U.S. replaces Great Britain as Canada's largest trading partner
1730–40	Hat-making industry arises in Quebec and is stifled by French home officials	1927	Armand Bombardier sells first "auto-neige" (forerunner of the snowmobile)
1779	North West Company forms	1929	Great stock market crash
1785	Molson brewery opens	1929–33	Great Depression
1805	First Canadian paper mill built at St. Andrew's, Quebec	1930	Canadian Airways Limited formed
		1932	Canadian Radio Broadcasting Corporation formed (it became the CBC in 1936)
1809	First steamboat (the *Accommodation*) put into service on the St. Lawrence River by John Molson	1935	Bank of Canada begins operations
1817	Bank of Montreal chartered	1937	Canadian Breweries Limited is formed
1821	Hudson's Bay Company and North West Company merge	1947–51	Early computer built at the University of Toronto
		1947	Leduc Number 1 oil well drilled in Alberta
1830–50	Era of canal building	1949	A.V. Roe (Avro) makes Canada's first commercial jetliner
1850–60	First era of railroad building	1965	Auto Pact signed with the U.S.
1855	John Redpath opens first Canadian sugar refinery in Montreal	1969	Canada becomes world's largest potash producer
1857–58	First oil well in Canada drilled near Sarnia, Ontario	1989	Free trade agreement with U.S. comes into effect
1861	Toronto Stock Exchange opens	1993	North American Free Trade Agreement comes into effect
1869	Eaton's opens for business in Toronto		
1880–90	First western land boom	1995–99	Rapid increase in stock prices
1885	Last spike driven to complete the Canadian Pacific Railroad	2000	Prices of most stocks decline sharply
		2003–04	Canadian internet pharmacies begin selling prescription drugs to U.S. citizens
1896	First large pulp and paper mill in Canada opened at Sault Ste. Marie, Ontario	2006	Softwood lumber dispute with U.S. settled

The Factory System and the Industrial Revolution

British manufacturing took a great leap forward around 1750 with the coming of the **Industrial Revolution**. A new level of production was made possible by advances in technology and by the development of the **factory system**. Instead of hundreds of workers turning out items one at a time in their cottages, the factory system brought together in one place all of the materials and workers required to produce items in large quantities, along with newly created machines capable of **mass production**.

Mass production offered savings in several areas. It avoided unnecessary duplication of equipment. It allowed firms to purchase raw materials at better prices by buying large lots. And most important, it encouraged **specialization** of labour. No longer did production require highly skilled craftspeople who could do all the different tasks required to make an item. A series of semiskilled workers, each trained to perform only one task and supported by specialized machines and tools, greatly increased output.

In spite of British laws against the export of technology and against manufacturing in North America, Canadian manufacturing existed almost from the beginning of European settlement. Modest manufacturing operations were evident in sawmills, breweries, gristmills for grinding grain, tanneries, woollen mills, shoemakers' shops, and tailors' shops. These operations were so successful that by 1800, exports of manufactured goods were more important than exports of fur.

Industrial Revolution A major change in goods production that began in England in the mid-eighteenth century and was characterized by a shift to the factory system, mass production, and specialization of labour.

factory system A process in which all the machinery, materials, and workers required to produce a good in large quantities are brought together in one place.

mass production The manufacture of products of uniform quality in large quantities.

specialization The breaking down of complex operations into simple tasks that are easily learned and performed.

With the advent of steam power in the early 1800s, manufacturing activity began to increase rapidly. By 1850, more than 30 factories—employing more than 2000 people—lined the Lachine Canal in Montreal alone. Exports of timber to England in 1850 were 70 times greater than what they had been in 1800. The demand for reliable transportation was the impetus for canal building in the mid-1800s and then the railroad-building boom in the mid- and late-1800s.

The Entrepreneurial Era

One of the most significant features of the last half of the nineteenth century was the emergence of entrepreneurs willing to take risks in the hope of earning huge profits. Adam Smith in his book *The Wealth of Nations* argued that the government should not interfere in the economy, but should let businesses function without regulation or restriction. The Canadian government often adopted this laissez-faire attitude. As a result, some individuals became immensely wealthy through their aggressive business dealings. Some railway, bank, and insurance executives made over $25 000 per year in the late 1800s, and their purchasing power was immense. Entrepreneurs such as Joseph Flavelle, Henry Pellatt, and John MacDonald lived in ostentatious mansions or castles.

The size and economic power of some firms meant that other businesses had difficulty competing against them. At the same time, some business executives decided that it was more profitable to collude than to compete. They decided among themselves to fix prices and divide up markets. Hurt by these actions, Canadian consumers called for more regulation of business. In 1889, the first anti-combines legislation was passed in Canada, and legislation regulating business has increased ever since.

The Production Era

The concepts of specialization and mass production that originated in the Industrial Revolution were more fully refined as Canada entered the twentieth century. The Scientific Management Movement focused management's attention on production. Increased efficiency via the "one best way" to accomplish tasks became the major management goal.

production era The period during the early twentieth century when businesses focused almost exclusively on improving productivity and manufacturing methods.

Henry Ford's introduction of the moving assembly line in the United States in 1913 ushered in the **production era**. During the production era, less attention was paid to selling and marketing than to technical efficiency when producing goods. By using fixed workstations, increasing task specialization, and moving the work to the worker, the assembly line increased productivity and lowered prices, making all kinds of products affordable for the average person. It also increased the available labour pool because many people could be trained to carry out assembly line tasks. Formerly, the labour pool was limited because relatively few people had the high skill levels of craftspeople.

During the production era, large businesses began selling stock—making shareholders the owners—and relying on professional managers. The growth of corporations and improved production output resulting from assembly lines came at the expense of worker freedom. The dominance of big firms made it harder for individuals to go into business for themselves. Company towns run by the railroads, mining corporations, and forest products firms gave individuals little freedom of choice over whom to work for and what to buy. To restore some balance within the overall system, both government and labour had to develop and grow. Thus, this period saw the rise of labour unions and collective bargaining. We will look at this development in more detail in Chapter 9. The Great Depression of the 1930s and the Second World War caused the federal government to intervene in the economic system on a previously unimaginable scale.

Today, business, government, and labour are frequently referred to by economists and politicians as the three *countervailing powers* in our society. All are big. All are strong. Yet, none totally dominates the others.

The Sales and Marketing Eras

By the 1930s, business's focus on production had resulted in spectacular increases in the amount of goods and services for sale. As a result, buyers had more choices and producers faced greater competition in selling their wares. Thus began the so-called **sales era**. According to the ideas of this time, a business's profits and success depended on hiring the right salespeople, advertising heavily, and making sure products were readily available. Business firms were essentially production- and sales-oriented, and they produced what they thought customers wanted, or simply what the company was good at producing. This approach is still used by firms that find themselves with surplus goods that they want to sell (e.g., used-car dealerships).

sales era The period during the 1930s and 1940s when businesses focussed on sales forces, advertising, and keeping products readily available.

Following the Second World War, pent-up demand for consumer goods kept the economy rolling. While brief recessions did occur periodically, the 1950s and 1960s were prosperous times. Production increased, technology advanced, and the standard of living rose. During the **marketing era**, business adopted a new philosophy of how to do business—use market research to determine what customers want, and then make it for them. Firms like Procter & Gamble and Molson were very effective during the marketing era, and continue to be profitable today. Each offers an array of products within a particular field (toothpaste or beer, for example) and gives customers a chance to pick what best suits their needs.

marketing era The period during the 1950s and 1960s when businesses began to identify and meet consumer wants to make a profit.

The Finance Era

In the 1980s, emphasis shifted to finance. In the **finance era** there was a sharp increase in mergers and in the buying and selling of business enterprises. Some people now call it the "decade of greed." As we will see in the next chapter, during the finance era there were many hostile takeovers and a great deal of financial manipulation of corporate assets by so-called corporate raiders. Critics charged that these raiders were simply enriching themselves and weren't creating anything of tangible value by their activity. They also charged that raiders were distracting business managers from their main goals of running the business. The raiders responded that they were making organizations more efficient by streamlining, merging, and reorganizing them.

finance era The period during the 1980s when there were many mergers and much buying and selling of business enterprises.

The Global Era

The last few years have seen the continuation of technological advances in production, computer technology, information systems, and communication capabilities. They have also seen the emergence of a truly global economy. Canadians drive cars made in Japan, wear sweaters made in Italy, drink beer brewed in Mexico, and listen to stereos made in Taiwan. But we're not alone in this. People around the world buy products and services from foreign companies.

While it is true that many Canadian businesses have been hurt by foreign imports, numerous others have profited by exploring new foreign markets themselves. And domestic competition has forced many businesses to

China opened its economy to foreign investors in the 1980s and joined the World Trade Organization in 2001. Now the Chinese buy as many cars as the Germans and more photographic film than the Japanese. They also buy more cellphones than anyone anywhere, and the opening of the Chinese market has created a windfall for makers of wireless handsets, including Motorola (U.S.), Siemens (Germany), Samsung (South Korea), and Nokia (Finland).

work harder than ever to cut costs, increase efficiency, and improve product and service quality. We will explore a variety of important trends, opportunities, and challenges of the global era throughout this book.

Most of these software developers are among the 65 000 engineers that the Indian State of Andhra Pradesh graduates every year—up from 7500 just 10 years ago. Microsoft operates an R&D centre in the capital city of Hyderabad, where Oracle, Computer Associates, and IBM also have facilities. The city is prospering as a hub not only for software programming, but for telephone call centres and pharmaceuticals as well.

The Internet Era

The turn of the century has been accompanied by what many experts are calling the internet era of business. Internet usage in North America grew from about 100 users per 1000 people in 1995 to over 750 users per 1000 people in 2005. The growth rate in Western Europe and the Asia-Pacific region, however, is expected to be even faster. The growth of the internet affects business in at least three different ways:

1. The internet will give a dramatic boost to trade in all sectors of the economy, especially services. If the internet makes it easier for all trade to grow, this is particularly true for trade in services on an international scale.

2. The internet will level the playing field, at least to some extent, between larger and smaller enterprises, regardless of what products or services they sell. In the past, a substantial investment was typically needed to enter some industries and to enter foreign markets. Now, however, a small business based in central Alberta, southern Italy, eastern Malaysia, or northern Brazil can set up a website and compete quite effectively with much larger businesses located around the world.

3. The internet holds considerable potential as an effective and efficient networking mechanism among businesses. Business-to-business (B2B) networks can link firms with all of their suppliers, business customers, and strategic partners in ways that make it faster and easier for them to do business together.

Summary of Learning Objectives

1. **Define the nature of Canadian *business* and identify its main goals.** *Businesses* are organizations that produce or sell goods or services to make a profit. *Profits* are the difference between a business' revenues and expenses. The prospect of earning profits encourages individuals and organizations to open and expand businesses. The benefits of business activities also extend to wages paid to workers and to taxes that support government functions.

2. **Describe different types of global *economic systems* according to the means by which they control the *factors of production* through *input* and *output markets*.** An *economic system* is a nation's system for allocating its resources among its citizens. Economic systems differ in terms of who owns or controls the basic *factors of production*: labour, capital, entrepreneurs, natural resources, and, more recently, information resources. In *command economies*, the government controls all or most of these factors. In *market economies*, which are based on the principles of capitalism, individuals and businesses control the factors of production and exchange them through *input and output markets*. Most countries today have *mixed market economies* that are dominated by one of these systems but include elements of the other. The process of *privatization* is an important means by which many of the world's planned economies are moving toward mixed market systems.

3. **Show how *demand* and *supply* affect resource distribution in Canada.** The Canadian economy is strongly influenced by markets, demand, and supply. *Demand* is the willingness and ability of buyers to purchase a good or service. *Supply* is the willingness and ability of producers to offer goods or services for sale. Demand and supply work together to set a *market* or *equilibrium price*—the price at which the quantity of goods demanded and the quantity of goods supplied are equal.

4. **Identify the elements of *private enterprise* and explain the various *degrees of competition* in the Canadian economic system.** The Canadian economy is founded on the principles of *private enterprise: private property rights*, *freedom of choice*, *profits*, and *competition*. Degrees of competition vary because not all industries are equally competitive. Under conditions of *perfect competition*, numerous small firms compete in a market governed entirely by demand and supply. An *oligopoly* involves a handful of sellers only. A *monopoly* involves only one seller.

5. **Trace the *history of business* in Canada.** Modern business structures reflect a pattern of development over centuries. Throughout much of the colonial period, sole proprietors supplied raw materials to English manufacturers. The rise of the factory system during the Industrial Revolution brought with it mass production and specialization of labour. During the entrepreneurial era in the nineteenth century, large corporations—and monopolies—emerged. During the production era of the early twentieth century, companies grew by emphasizing output and production. During the sales and marketing eras of the 1950s and 1960s, business began focussing on sales staff, advertising, and the need to produce what consumers wanted. In the 1980s there was increased buying and selling of businesses, and in the 1990s a significant global economy emerged. Many Canadian companies have profited from exporting their goods to foreign markets. The most recent development is the use of the internet to boost business. To some extent, the internet should level the playing field between large and small companies.

KEY TERMS

business,   6
Canada Water Act,   15
Canadian Radio-television and
   Telecommunications Commission
   (CRTC),   14
Canadian Transport Commission
   (CTC),   14
Canadian Wheat Board,   14
capital,   8
capitalism,   12
command economy,   9
communism,   9
competition,   21
demand,   17
demand and supply schedule,   19
demand curve,   19
deregulation,   13
economic system,   7
entrepreneur,   9
Environmental Contaminants Act,
   15
factors of production,   7
factory system,   25

finance era,   27
Fisheries Act,   15
Food and Drug Act,   15
Hazardous Products Act,   14
Industrial Revolution,   25
information resources,   9
input market,   11
labour (or human resources),   8
law of demand,   18
law of supply,   18
lobbyist,   16
market,   11
market economy,   9
market price (or equilibrium price),
   19
marketing era,   27
mass production,   25
mixed market economy,   13
monopolistic competition,   22
monopoly,   23
natural monopoly,   23
natural resources,   9
oligopoly,   23

output market,   11
perfect competition,   22
private enterprise,   21
privatization,   13
production era,   26
profit,   6
progressive revenue taxes,   15
regressive revenue taxes,   15
restrictive taxes,   16
revenue taxes,   15
sales era,   27
shortage,   19
socialism,   9
specialization,   25
supply,   18
supply curve,   19
surplus,   19
Textile Labelling Act,   15
Tobacco Act,   15
trade association,   17
Weights and Measures Act,   15

QUESTIONS FOR ANALYSIS

1. Is one factor of production more important than the others? If so, which one? Why?

2. On various occasions, government provides financial incentives to business firms. For example, the Canadian government provided expert assistance to Bombardier Inc. with its Technology Transfer Program. Is this consistent with a basically free market system? Explain how this might distort the system.

3. In recent years, many countries have moved from planned economies to market economies. Why do you think this has occurred? Can you envision a situation that would cause a resurgence of planned economies?

4. Find an example where a surplus of a product led to decreased prices. Then find an example where a shortage led to increased prices. What eventually

happened in each case? Why? Is what happened consistent with what economics predicts? Why?

5. Familiarize yourself with a product or service that is sold under conditions of perfect competition. Explain why it is an example of perfect competition and identify the factors that make it so. Then do the same for a product in each of the other three competitive situations described in the chapter.

6. Analyze how the factors of production work together for a product or service of your choice.

7. Government plays a variety of roles in the Canadian mixed economy. Consider each of the roles discussed in the text and state the criteria you would use to decide whether government involvement in each role is excessive, insufficient, or about right.

APPLICATION EXERCISES

1. Choose a locally owned business. Interview the owner to find out how the business uses the factors of production and have the owner describe the means of acquiring them.

2. Visit a local shopping mall or shopping area. List each store that you see and determine what degree of competition it faces in its immediate environment. For example, if there is only one store in the

mall that sells shoes, that store represents a monopoly. Note those businesses with direct competitors (two jewellery stores) and show how they compete with one another.

3. Go to the library or log onto the internet and research 10 different industries. Classify each according to degree of competition.

BUILDING YOUR BUSINESS SKILLS

Analyzing the Price of Doing Ebusiness

Goal

To encourage students to understand how the competitive environment affects a product's price.

The Situation

Assume that you own a local business that provides internet access to individuals and businesses (this kind of business is called an ISP, or internet service provider). Yours is one of four such businesses in the local market. Each of the four companies charges the same price: $20 per month for unlimited dial-up service. Your business also provides users with email service; two of your competitors also offer email service. One of these same two competitors, plus the third, also provides the individual user with a free, basic personal webpage. One competitor just dropped its price to $14 per month, and the other two have announced their intentions to follow suit. Your break-even price is $10 per customer; that is, you must charge $10 for your service package to cover your costs (but not earn any profit). You are concerned about getting into a price war that may destroy your business.

Method

Divide into groups of four or five people. Each group is to develop a general strategy for handling competitors' price changes. In your discussion, take the following factors into account:

■ how the demand for your product is affected by price changes

■ the number of competitors selling the same or a similar product

■ the methods—other than price—you can use to attract new customers and/or retain current customers

Analysis

Develop specific pricing strategies based on each of the following situations:

■ Within a month after dropping the price to $14, one of your competitors raises its price back to $18.

■ Two of your competitors drop their prices further—to $12 per month. As a result, your business falls off by 25 percent.

■ One of your competitors that has provided customers with a free webpage has indicated that it will start charging an extra $4 per month for this optional service.

■ Two of your competitors have announced that they will charge individual users $12 per month, but will charge businesses a higher price (not yet announced).

■ All four providers (including you) are charging $11 per month. One goes out of business, and you know that another is in poor financial health.

Follow-Up Questions

1. Discuss the role that various inducements other than price might play in affecting demand and supply in the market for internet service.

2. Is it always in a company's best interest to feature the lowest prices?

3. Eventually, what form of competition is likely to characterize the market for internet service?

EXERCISING YOUR ETHICS

Prescribing a Dose of Competitive Medicine

The Purpose of the Assignment

Demand and supply are key elements of the Canadian economic system. So, too, is competition. This exercise will challenge you to better understand the ethical dimensions of a system that relies on demand, supply, and competition.

The Situation

You are a business person in a small town, where you run one of two local pharmacies. The population and economic base are fairly stable. Each pharmacy controls about 50 percent of the market. Each is reasonably profitable, generating solid if unspectacular revenues.

The Dilemma

The owner of the other pharmacy has just approached you. He has indicated an interest either in buying your pharmacy or in selling his to you. He argues that neither of you can substantially increase your profits and complains that if one pharmacy raises its prices, customers will simply go to the other one. He tells you outright that if you sell to him, he plans to raise prices by 10 percent. He believes that the local market will have to accept the increase for two reasons: (1) The town is too small to attract national competitors, and (2) local customers aren't likely to go elsewhere to shop because the nearest town with a pharmacy is 60 kilometres away.

Questions for Discussion

1. What are the roles of supply, demand, and competition in this scenario?
2. What are the underlying ethical issues?
3. What would you do if you were actually faced with this situation?

CONCLUDING CASE 1-1

Supply and Demand: Some Practical Lessons

The prices of many different commodities are influenced by the supply of, and demand for, these commodities. Variations in demand and supply have implications for both businesses and for consumers, as the following stories about oil, palladium, and coffee demonstrate.

Oil

The sign in front of one gas station summed it up nicely: The prices listed for the three grades of gasoline were "An arm," "A leg," and "Your firstborn." While the sign no doubt led to a few smiles from motorists, its sentiments were far from a laughing matter. Indeed, in early 2006, retail gasoline prices in Canada and the United States were very high, exceeding $2.30 per gallon in the U.S. and $0.95 per litre in Canada.

Gasoline prices have fluctuated many times in the past. For example, an Arab embargo on petroleum in 1971 led to a major price jump. But the higher prices spurred new exploration, and as new oil fields came online and supplies increased, prices eventually dropped again. Subsequent supply disruptions due to political problems in Venezuela, Nigeria, and Iraq have also caused short-term price jumps, after which the price again dropped.

But people who are knowledgeable about oil say that from now on the price of oil is likely to go in only one direction—up. Why? Because the supply of easily recoverable oil is limited, and demand continues to increase because of the surging global economy, particularly in China and India. What's worse, the global supply of oil will soon peak and then slowly begin to decline. While no one can pinpoint exactly when the decline will start, virtually all the experts agree that it will happen well before 2050. Canada's prominence in energy production will increase as the output from the tar sands steadily increases during this same period of time (see the Opening Case).

What happens then? Although there will be gradual reductions in supply, oil and gas will remain available for at least another century—but at prices that will make those of today seem like a bargain. Firms that can produce alternative sources of energy will spring up, and those who find viable answers will prosper.

▶▶▶

Palladium

Most people have never heard of palladium, a greyish metal produced primarily in Russia and South Africa. In the 1990s, when automakers adopted tighter pollution emission standards, they switched from platinum to palladium because palladium does a better job of cleaning auto emissions, and because at that time palladium was much cheaper than platinum. The automobile manufacturers knew that switching to palladium would cause demand to exceed world production, which was then about 5 million ounces per year. They also knew that this increased demand would cause the price of palladium to rise, but they were not prepared for the price rise that actually occurred when Russian exports of palladium suddenly ceased in 1997. The official explanation was a bureaucratic problem, and when supplies resumed, the price dropped again to about $200 per ounce.

In 1998, the same thing happened, but this time the price went up to over $400 per ounce. When supplies resumed, the price dropped back to only $300 per ounce. Now the auto manufacturers were becoming very concerned, and they began trying to figure out how to use less palladium and still meet the tighter pollution standards. By 2000, when the price of palladium had risen to over $1000 per ounce, automakers took the unprecedented step of stipulating the maximum amount of palladium that would be allowed in engineers' car designs.

In 2002, Ford Motor Company took a $1 billion write-off on the value of the palladium it had stockpiled for use in its automobile catalytic converters. Ford originally stockpiled this raw material because it thought it would need increasing amounts of palladium, and because it was concerned that palladium was going to be high-priced and hard to get. At the same time, however, Ford's engineers were succeeding in figuring out ways to reduce the amount of palladium they needed. So, Ford's purchasing agents were buying lots of palladium at high prices (fearing the price would go even higher) while Ford's engineers were figuring out ways to reduce the company's need for the metal.

By 2001, the price of palladium had again dropped to about $400 dollars per ounce. This happened because demand dropped (other automakers had also discovered ways to get by with less palladium) and supplies increased (because the extremely high prices of palladium in 1999–2000 had caused more producers to get into the business of supplying the market).

Coffee

This is another commodity whose price soared in 2005. Between October 2004 and February 2005, for example, the price of high quality Arabica coffee beans (the type used by specialty coffee stores like Starbucks) increased by 79 percent. High demand from consumers, coupled with falling supplies caused the price increase. The increased cost of this popular commodity is quickly passed on to consumers.

Like oil, coffee is a commodity that has experienced many ups and downs over the years. The current high-price situation is a dramatic change from 2001, when coffee prices hit a 30-year low because of an oversupply of coffee beans. The low prices in 2001 were, in turn, caused by the high coffee prices in 1994 and 1995, which motivated farmers to plant a lot of acres of coffee beans in an attempt to cash in on the high prices. Since it takes 3–4 years for a coffee tree to mature, a lot of coffee beans started hitting the market in 1998 and 1999, and that increased the supply and drove prices down. But by 2001 the low prices had discouraged growers from planting more coffee trees, and that caused production to fall, leading to the current drop in supply. This up-and-down cycle is hard to break.

Questions for Discussion

1. What are the basic factors of production in the petroleum industry?

2. Describe the concepts of input and output markets as they apply to the petroleum industry.

3. Explain how the concepts of demand and supply combine to determine market prices for diverse commodities like palladium, oil, and coffee.

4. Does the global energy situation increase or decrease your confidence in a capitalistic system based on private enterprise?

5. Did automakers respond to increases in the price of palladium in the way predicted by economic theory? Explain.

6. Not everyone agrees that there is an impending oil crisis. Develop arguments that we are not likely to run out of oil any time soon.

Business, Government, and Liquor

The liquor business is no stranger to controversy. In addition to the moral and health issues with regard to the use of alcohol, there are also complex issues of who should control the sale of liquor, and how closely regulated the industry should be.

For many years, all provincial governments held a monopoly on the sale of liquor. But with the worldwide move to privatization that began in the 1990s, various provinces began looking at the possibility of privatizing liquor sales. In 2005, a government-appointed panel in Ontario called for the privatization of the Liquor Control Board of Ontario (LCBO). But the Ontario finance minister rejected the idea, apparently because the Crown Corporation is popular with consumers, and because liquor suppliers like dealing with just one big buyer instead of many smaller ones. The LCBO's unionized employees were also very vocal in their opposition to privatization.

Critics of the LCBO say that it should be privatized because it is inefficient and it doesn't make any profit. Supporters, on the other hand, argue that it *is* profitable. Which claim is more reasonable? Consider these numbers: In its 2003–2004 financial statement, the LCBO reported a gross margin on sales of 47.6 percent (most food retailers, by comparison achieve 2–3 percent). The LCBO achieved this high return by counting the provincial liquor tax it collected as profit. Critics point out that if this tax is subtracted from the LCBO's net income, there is no profit at all. The critics say this tax revenue *should* be subtracted, since private sector firms are not be able to claim government taxes they collect as profit.

The Ontario dispute is just one example of the long-running debate about privatization. In Alberta, for example, the province announced in 1993 that it was getting out of the liquor business and that it would allow private sector operators to begin selling liquor. It was doing so because it said it would save $65 million annually in salaries and operating costs. Within a year, 500 privately owned liquor stores had opened up. In 2003, a policy research group at the University of Alberta issued a report that analyzed the province of Alberta's 10-year experience with privatized liquor stores. The report reached the following conclusions:

- Liquor prices had increased by about one-third since 1993 (12 percent more than inflation for the period).
- The province had lost $511 million in revenue since liquor stores were privatized.
- The number of liquor stores had more than tripled since privatization.

The report concluded that the benefits of privatization were modest at best.

Also in 2003, the B.C. branch of the Consumers Association of Canada (CAC) compared liquor prices in British Columbia (where the government had a monopoly on liquor sales) with prices in Alberta. It found that B.C. prices were competitive with, or lower, than prices in Alberta. The study also concluded that if British Columbia privatized its liquor sales consumers would pay 10–20 percent more. The B.C. government had, in fact, been looking at the possibility of closing 224 government liquor stores and replacing them with privately owned stores. But the provincial government put the plan on hold so they could do more analysis of the situation. Not surprisingly, the Government and Service Employees Union expressed concerns about what privatization would do to its members' jobs.

Another interesting comparison involves Quebec and Ontario, both of which have provincial monopolies in the sale of liquor. Prices of most liquor products are higher in Quebec than they are in Ontario. Even when a Société des alcools du Québec (SAQ) store in Quebec has a sale, prices may be higher than non-sale items in Ontario. For example, during one period in 2006, a bottle of Australian Wyndham Estate Cabernet Merlot that was on sale at SAQ cost $17, while the regular price in Ontario was just $14.60. Critics of the Quebec government's liquor monopoly argue that SAQ's new "Customer First" slogan is a joke. The government's position was not helped when newspapers reported that several European wine distributors claimed that SAQ had urged them to raise their prices rather than pass on savings to Quebec consumers as a result of the rising value of the Canadian dollar relative to the euro. All of this negative publicity has given supporters of privatization some hope that the government will get out of the liquor business.

The dispute about privatization is not the only issue that has arisen in the liquor industry. There is also debate about which roles the government should play. In the recent past, government has acted as both a regulator and competitor of private sector liquor companies. In the late 1990s, for example, Magnotta Winery Corp. was denied shelf space for its products by the LCBO. Magnotta therefore started selling its wine at its own on-site store at the vineyard. The company wanted to charge $3.95 for a 750-mL bottle, which was lower than the LCBO's price of $5.15. But the LCBO ruled that Magnotta couldn't sell its products for less than the cheapest wine carried in an LCBO store. Magnotta was also involved in several other well-publicized disputes with the LCBO. Finally, in 2000, the

▶▶▶

province of Ontario stripped its government-owned liquor stores of their regulatory status to make competition fairer.

The same sort of dispute was evident in Manitoba, where 6 privately owned wine stores sold over half the wine in Winnipeg, while 22 Manitoba Liquor Control Commission (MLCC) stores sold the rest. A Probe Research poll showed that 90 percent of Winnipeggers didn't want the province to phase out private wine stores. More than half of those polled said that private wine stores forced the MLCC stores to improve their service by providing competition. The private wine sellers in Manitoba also argued that the MLCC was in a conflict of interest because it had the power to regulate its competitors. They filed a lawsuit against the MLCC in 2000, claiming that the MLCC had engaged in various unfair business practices in an attempt to steal customers from the private wine stores. In 2006, it was disclosed that the MLCC had paid $8 million to the wine stores in an out-of-court settlement.

Questions for Discussion

1. What are the different roles that government plays in the Canadian mixed economic system? What are the appropriate roles that the government should play in the liquor business?

2. What roles does government play in, say, retail trade and manufacturing? Should the government's role in the liquor business be different from its role in retail trade or manufacturing?

3. Should the sale of liquor be a government monopoly, or should other provinces do what Alberta did? Defend your answer.

4. Critics argue that government-run monopolies like liquor stores should make a profit. Is this a reasonable claim? Explain.

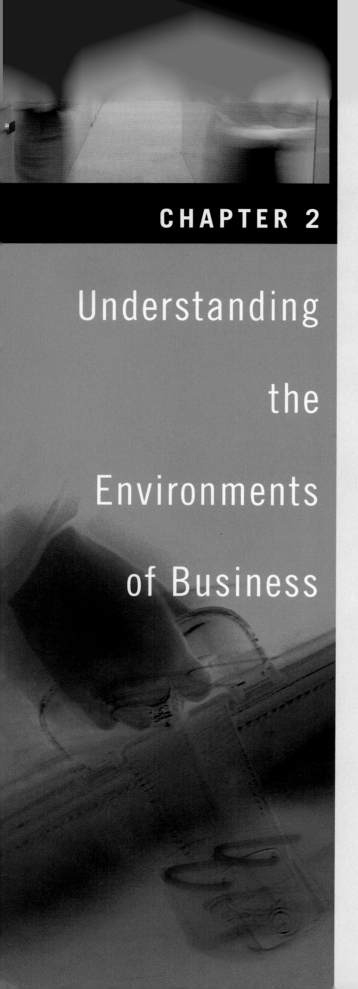

CHAPTER 2

Understanding the Environments of Business

After reading this chapter, you should be able to:

1 Explain the concepts of *organizational boundaries* and *multiple organizational environments*.

2 Explain the importance of the *economic environment* to business and identify the factors used to evaluate the performance of an economic system.

3 Describe the *technological environment* and its role in business.

4 Describe the *political-legal environment* and its role in business.

5 Describe the *socio-cultural environment* and its role in business.

6 Identify emerging challenges and opportunities in the *business environment*.

7 Understand recent trends in the *redrawing of corporate boundaries*.

Compared with the United States, Canada's standard of living has been slipping for the last two decades. In 1980, Canada's standard of living was 90 percent of the U.S. level. By 2002, it had slipped to 87 percent, and by 2004 to 84 percent. It is projected to drop to 77 percent by 2010. If our standard of living continues to drop, Canadians will experience a decline in the quality of health care, social programs, and overall quality of life. We also risk losing our finest brains, talent, and companies if we fail to hold our own against the United States.

What is causing the standard of living to drop in Canada relative to the United States (and to other countries)? One major factor is Canada's relatively slow *productivity growth rate*. Data developed by the Paris-based Organisation for Economic Co-operation and Development (OECD) show that Canada's labour productivity (that is, GDP per hour worked) did not increase at all in 2004. Most other industrialized countries achieved increases of 1.5–2.5 percent. The same kinds of concerns are expressed in the Conference Board of Canada's annual "Performance and Potential Report" which rates the world's 24 richest economies on various factors, including productivity. In the 2005 Report, Canada ranked only 12th in productivity (down from 3rd place in 2003 and 6th place in 2004). The Conference Board attributed this downward trend to poor productivity growth.

As the number of working-age people decreases over the next several decades, our standard of living will decline further unless the remaining people in the workforce can produce more per person—in other words, productivity must increase. If we are going to compete with the surging economies of India and China in the global market, we must become more productive. If we don't, we will lose export possibilities and the jobs that go with them. That will also contribute to a decline in the Canadian standard of living.

Why is Canadian productivity growing so slowly? Various organizations, including the Ottawa-based Centre for the Study of Living Standards, have identified several different causes:

- Productivity in the information and communications technology sector has dropped off sharply since 2000; prior to that time it was increasing rapidly.

- The prices of commodities like oil and gas have increased dramatically in the last few years, and this has motivated companies to exploit marginal reserves where productivity is low.
- R&D intensity (the ratio of R&D spending to gross GDP) has dropped.
- Exports, as a percent of GDP, dropped from 45.6 percent in 2000 to 38.2 percent in 2004.
- The scale of manufacturing firms in Canada is smaller than in the United States, and small plants are less productive than large ones.
- Worker stress is reducing productivity (66 percent of Canadian CEOs who were polled in 2005 by Ipsos-Reid said that employee stress was the biggest drain on productivity); other factors reducing productivity were poor management practices and lack of effective training programs.
- The decline of the Canadian dollar between 1995 and 2001 meant that manufacturers had little incentive to increase productivity (because they could sell their goods easily in the United States).
- Canadian business firms conduct less research and development (R&D) than companies in many other countries. For example, Canadian R&D as a percentage of GNP was less than half that of Sweden. In a survey of 24 countries, Canada ranked 11th in R&D spending.

What is the solution to the productivity problem? Clearly, we must boost our productivity growth rate if we are to raise our standard of living. The following actions have been suggested:

- Put more money into post-secondary education.
- Develop more partnerships between business and academic institutions.
- Invest in upgrading workforce skills, and increase the availability of vocational, technical, and apprenticeship programs for students who don't attend university.
- Create greater incentives to rejoin the workforce for those on welfare.
- Levy training costs on businesses like some European countries do.
- Stop subsidizing uncompetitive industries like shipbuilding.

- Cut personal and corporate income tax rates.
- Allow more aggressive write-off schedules for capital investments by businesses.

What do Canadians think about the issue of productivity and the standard of living? Surveys that have been conducted during the last few years reveal the following answers to several important questions:

- *"How do you think the average personal income for a Canadian worker compares with that for a U.S. worker?"* (half of the respondents said it was lower, one-fifth said it was higher, and one-fifth said it was the same).
- *"How do you think Canada compares with the United States in terms of quality of life?"* (70 percent said it was higher and 18 percent said it was the same).

- *"How do you think Canada compares with the United States in terms of standard of living?"* (37 percent said it is higher in Canada, 34 percent thought it was the same, and 28 percent said it was lower).
- *"How do you think Canada's level of productivity compares with that of the United States?"* (50 percent felt it was worse, 25 percent felt it was the same, and 20 percent felt it was better).

When asked if they agreed or disagreed with the statement "Increasing productivity is essential to improving our standard of living," 82 percent agreed. When asked if they agreed or disagreed with the statement "If we don't improve our productivity, our quality of life will suffer," 70 percent agreed. ◆

ORGANIZATIONAL BOUNDARIES AND ENVIRONMENTS

external environment Everything outside an organization's boundaries that might affect it.

All businesses, regardless of their size, location, or mission, operate within a larger external environment. This **external environment**—which consists of everything outside an organization's boundaries that might affect it—plays a major role in determining the success or failure of any organization. Managers must therefore have an accurate understanding of the environment facing their company, and then strive to operate and compete within it. While no single firm can control the environment, managers should not simply react to changes; they should also be proactive and at least try to influence their environment.

To better explain the environment of business, we begin by discussing *organizational boundaries*, and then we introduce the concept of *multiple organizational environments*.

Organizational Boundaries

organizational boundary That which separates the organization from its environment.

1 Explain the concepts of *organizational boundaries* and *multiple organizational environments*.

An **organizational boundary** separates the organization from its environment. Boundaries were once relatively easy to identify, but they are becoming increasingly complicated and hard to pin down. Consider the simple case of a small neighbourhood grocery that includes a retail customer area, a storage room, and an owner/manager's office. In many ways, the store's boundary coincides with its physical structure. When you walk through the door, you're crossing the boundary into the business, and when you go back onto the sidewalk, you cross the boundary back into the environment.

But even this simple example isn't as simple as it seems. During the course of the business day, distributors of soft drinks, beer, snack foods, ice, and bread products may enter the store, inventory the products that they distribute, and automatically refill coolers and shelves just as if they were employees. Although these distributors are normally considered part of the environment rather than the organization, during the time that they're inside the store, they are essentially part of the business. Assuming that they're store employees, customers may ask them questions as they restock shelves. The bread distributor may even offer someone a fresh loaf instead of the one that he or she has taken from the shelf.

Now consider the case of a large domestic business (such as GM Canada) that is owned by an even larger international corporation (U.S.-based General Motors). The domestic business has a complex network of relationships with other businesses. GM Canada, for example, deals with companies that supply tires, glass, steel, and engines. But GM Canada also functions within the boundaries of its international parent, which has its own network of business relationships, some overlapping and some distinct from GM Canada's network.

We can also examine similar complexities from the customer's perspective. McDonald's, for example, has a contract with Coca-Cola, stipulating that it will sell only Coke soft-drink products. McDonald's also has partnerships with Wal-Mart and Disney that allow it to open stores inside those firms' facilities. So when you buy a Coca-Cola soft drink from a McDonald's restaurant located inside a Wal-Mart store or Disney theme park, you are essentially affecting, and being affected by, multiple businesses. As you can see, the boundaries of any specific business are becoming increasingly difficult to define and more complicated to manage.

Multiple Organizational Environments

Although we tend to speak of "the external environment" as if it were a single entity, organizations actually have multiple environments. Some of them are relatively general. Prevailing economic conditions, for instance, will affect the performance of almost every business. But other dimensions are much more precise. Our neighbourhood grocery will be influenced not only by an increase in unemployment in the area, but also by the pricing and other marketing policies of its nearest competitor.

Figure 2.1 shows the major dimensions and elements of the external environment as it affects most businesses. As you can see, these include economic conditions, technology, political-legal considerations, social issues, the global environment, issues of ethical and social responsibility, the business environment itself, and numerous other emerging challenges and opportunities. Because this book provides detailed coverage of global and ethical issues in Chapters 3 and 5, respectively, we will introduce them here only as they relate directly to the other areas in this chapter.

THE ECONOMIC ENVIRONMENT

The **economic environment** refers to the conditions of the economic system in which an organization operates.[1] For example, McDonald's Canadian operations are (as of this writing) functioning in an economic environment characterized by moderate growth, moderate unemployment, and low inflation. Moderate unemployment means that most people can afford to eat out, but it also means that McDonald's must pay higher wages to attract employees. Low inflation means that McDonald's pays relatively constant prices for its supplies, but it also means that McDonald's can't really increase the prices it charges consumers.

economic environment Conditions of the economic system in which an organization operates.

Explain the importance of the *economic environment* to business and identify the factors used to evaluate the performance of an economic system.

2

Given the importance of the economic environment, we will closely examine the three key goals of the Canadian economic system: *economic growth*, *economic stability*, and *full employment*. We begin by focussing on the tools we use to measure economic growth, including *aggregate output*, *standard of living*, *gross domestic product*, and *productivity*. We then discuss the main threats to economic stability—namely, *inflation* and *unemployment*. We conclude this section by discussing government attempts to manage the Canadian economy in the interest of meeting national economic goals.

Figure 2.1 Dimensions of the external environment.

Economic Growth

At one time, about half the population of Canada was involved in producing food. Today, less than 2.5 percent of the population works in agriculture. Agricultural efficiency has improved because we devised better ways of producing products and invented better technology for getting the job done. We can therefore say that agricultural production has grown because we have been able to increase total output in the agricultural sector.

The Business Cycle

business cycle Pattern of short-term ups and downs (expansions and contractions) in an economy.

recession Period during which aggregate output, as measured by real GDP, declines.

depression Particularly severe and long-lasting recession.

We can apply the same concepts to a nation's economic system, but the computations are much more complex. A fundamental question, then, is how we know whether or not an economic system is growing. Experts call the pattern of short-term ups and downs in an economy the **business cycle**. It has four recognizable phases: peak, recession, trough, and recovery (see Figure 2.2). A **recession** is a period during which aggregate output declines. If a recession lasts for a prolonged period, it is called a **depression**. Periods

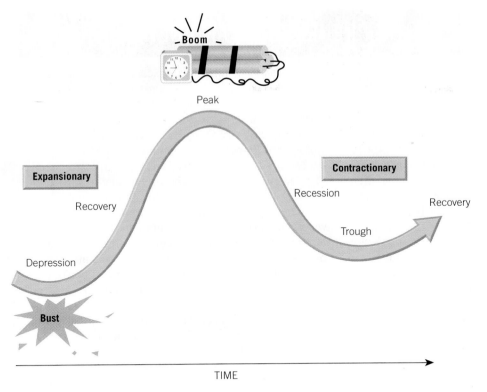

Figure 2.2 The business cycle.

of expansion and contraction can vary from several months to several years. During the latter half of the 1990s, the Canadian economy was continuously expanding, leading some people to believe that the business cycle was a thing of the past. This belief was particularly evident among people who invested in high-tech stocks. They learned a hard lesson when tech stocks crashed in 2000.

Aggregate Output and the Standard of Living

The main measure of growth in the business cycle is **aggregate output**: the total quantity of goods and services produced by an economic system during a given period.[2] To put it simply, an increase in aggregate output is growth (or economic growth).[3] When output grows more quickly than the population, two things usually follow: Output per capita—the quantity of goods and services per person—goes up and the system provides relatively more of the goods and services that people want.[4] And when these two things occur, people living in an economic system benefit from a higher **standard of living**, which refers to the total quantity and quality of goods and services that they can purchase with the currency used in their economic system.

Among other things, then, growth makes possible higher standards of living. Thus, to know how much your standard of living is improving, you need to know how much your nation's economic system is growing.

Gross Domestic Product

The term **gross domestic product (GDP)** refers to the total value of all goods and services produced within a given period by a national economy through domestic factors of production. If GDP is going up, the nation is experiencing economic growth. Canada's GDP in 2005 was $1.3 trillion.[5]

aggregate output Total quantity of goods and services produced by an economic system during a given period.

standard of living Total quantity and quality of goods and services that a country's citizens can purchase with the currency used in their economic system.

gross domestic product (GDP) Total value of all goods and services produced within a given period by a national economy through domestic factors of production.

ENTREPRENEURSHIP AND NEW VENTURES

Want a MacBrioche with That MacEspresso?

McDonald's has become an international icon of the fast-food industry. With 30 000 restaurants in 121 countries, the Golden Arches have become as recognizable to foreign consumers as the shape of a Coca-Cola bottle. Yet in recent years, McDonald's seems to have lost its competitive edge both at home and abroad. In the United States, for example, the company's menu is seen as unhealthy, its stores are outdated, and its customer service skills seem to be slipping. McDonald's no longer leads in technology, with rivals inventing new processing and cooking technologies. The firm's traditional markets, children and young men, are spending less on food while markets McDonald's doesn't target, notably women and older consumers, spend more. Profits have dropped and Starbucks has replaced McDonald's as the food industry success story.

To grow, McDonald's has had to expand aggressively into foreign markets, especially in Europe and Asia. However, consumers in many of those countries do not always like McDonald's "Americanized" look and products. So the burger maker has had to cater to local tastes. That means serving brioche and espresso in France, salmon sandwiches in Scandinavia, and beer in Germany. A Premiere line features more expensive and upscale offerings, such as chicken served on focaccia bread with salsa.

McDonald's is also customizing the look of its stores. In France, the "Mountain" has ski-chalet décor—hardwood floors, televisions, and armchairs. The "Music" features 1950s-style booths with their own CD players. Managers hope that the customers attracted to the more upscale restaurants may also be willing to pay more for premium food. Charlie Bell, McDonald's European president, claims, "Our future business will be selling more than burgers and fries."

So far the new appearance and menu are paying off. U.S. sales continue their downward trend, but French sales increased after the makeover. Ken Clement, a franchisee and former McDonald's vice president, claims the changes are not necessary in the United States. "People are not coming to swoon over the décor," he says. "They are coming in and getting out of here. They don't give a rip what is inside." However, if the French market continues to improve, the innovations may make it to the States, where the risk and the return could be great. The change could alienate McDonald's traditional customers, or it could revitalize the firm and spark a renaissance for the entire fast-food industry.

---

gross national product (GNP)
Total value of all goods and services produced by a national economy within a given period regardless of where the factors of production are located.

Sometimes, economists also use the term **gross national product (GNP)**, which refers to the total value of all goods and services produced by a national economy within a given period regardless of where the factors of production are located. Thus, the profits earned by a Canadian company abroad are included in GNP, but not in GDP. Conversely, profits earned by foreign firms in Canada are included in GDP. Consider the example of a Canadian-owned manufacturing plant in Brazil. The profits earned by the factory are included in Canadian GNP—but not in GDP—because its output is not produced domestically (that is, in Canada). Conversely, those profits are included in Brazil's GDP—but not GNP—because they are produced domestically (that is, in Brazil). Calculations like these quickly become complex because of different factors of production. The labour, for example, will be mostly Brazilian but the capital mostly Canadian. Thus, wages paid to Brazilian workers are part of Brazil's GNP even though profits are not.

GDP and GNP are useful measures of economic growth because they allow us to track an economy's performance over time. An organization called Redefining Progress has proposed a more realistic measure to assess economic activity—the Genuine Progress Indicator (GPI). GPI treats activities that harm the environment or our quality of life as costs and gives them negative values. For example, the Exxon Valdez oil spill in 1986 increased GDP because the activities required to clean up the mess were included in traditional measurements of economic growth. But the oil spill was not a good thing. The new GPI measure shows that while GDP has been increasing for many years, GPI has been falling since the 1970s.[6]

Real Growth Rates. GDP and GNP usually differ slightly, but GDP is the preferred method of calculating national income and output. The *real growth rate of GDP*—the growth rate of GDP *adjusted for inflation and changes in the value of the country's currency*—is what counts. Remember that *growth depends on output increasing at a faster rate than population*. If the growth rate of GDP exceeds the rate of population growth, then our standard of living should be improving.

GDP per Capita. *GDP per capita* means GDP per person. We get this figure by dividing total GDP by the total population of a country. As a measure of economic well-being of the average person, GDP per capita is a better measure than GDP. The United States has the highest GDP per capita of any country ($33 123), followed by Ireland ($30 910), Switzerland ($28 684), and Canada ($28 344).[7]

Real GDP. "Real GDP" means that GDP has been adjusted. To understand why adjustments are necessary, assume that pizza is the only product in an economy. Assume that in 2005, a pizza cost $10, and in 2006 it cost $11. In both years, exactly 1000 pizzas were produced. In 2005, the GDP was $10 000 ($10 × 1000); in 2006, the GDP was $11 000 ($11 × 1000). Has the economy grown? No. Since 1000 pizzas were produced in both years, aggregate output remained the same. The point is that we should not be misled into believing that an economy is doing better than it is. If it is not adjusted, GDP for 2006 is **nominal GDP**, that is, GDP measured in current dollars or with all components valued at current prices.[8]

nominal GDP GDP measured in current dollars or with all components valued at current prices.

Purchasing Power Parity. In our example, current prices would be 2006 prices. On the other hand, we calculate **real GDP** when we calculate GDP to account for *changes in currency values and price changes*. When we make this adjustment, we account for both GDP and **purchasing power parity**— the principle that exchange rates are set so that the prices of similar products in different countries are about the same. Purchasing power parity gives us a much better idea of *what people can actually buy with the financial resources allocated to them by their respective economic systems*. In other words, it gives us a better sense of standards of living around the world.

real GDP GDP calculated to account for changes in currency values and price changes.

purchasing power parity Principle that exchange rates are set so that the prices of similar products in different countries are about the same.

Productivity

A major factor in the growth of an economic system is **productivity**, which is a measure of economic growth that compares how much a system produces with the resources needed to produce it. Let's say, for instance, that it takes 1 Canadian worker and 1 Canadian dollar to make 10 soccer balls in an 8-hour workday. Let's also say that it takes 1.2 Saudi workers and the equivalent of $1.2 (in riyals, the currency of Saudi Arabia) to make 10 soccer balls in the same 8-hour workday. We can say, then, that the Canadian soccer-ball industry is more *productive* than the Saudi soccer-ball industry. The two factors of production in this extremely simple case are labour and capital.

productivity Measure of economic growth that compares how much a system produces with the resources needed to produce it.

Now let's look at productivity from a different perspective. If more products are being produced with fewer factors of production, what happens to the prices of these products? They go down. As a consumer, therefore, you would need less of your currency to purchase the same quantity

Extremely high productivity levels can be attained using automated equipment such as that in this soft drink bottling operation. Productivity is high because relatively few workers are able to produce large quantities of the product.

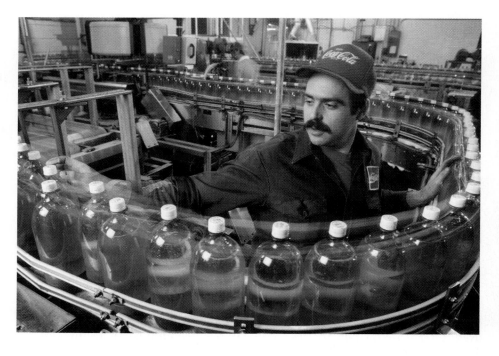

of these products. In short, your standard of living—at least with regard to these products—has improved. If your entire economic system increases its productivity, then your overall standard of living improves. In fact, *standard of living improves only through increases in productivity*.[9] Real growth in GDP reflects growth in productivity. We examine productivity in more detail in Chapter 12.

There are several factors that can help or hinder the growth of an economic system, but we'll focus on just two of them: *balance of trade* and the *national debt*.

balance of trade The total of a country's exports (sales to other countries) minus its imports (purchases from other countries).

Balance of Trade.   The **balance of trade** is the economic value of all the products that a country *exports* minus the economic value of its *imported* products. The principle here is quite simple:

- A *positive* balance of trade results when a country exports (sells to other countries) more than it imports (buys from other countries). A positive balance of trade helps economic growth.

- A *negative* balance of trade results when a country imports more than it exports. A negative balance of trade inhibits economic growth.

A negative balance of trade is commonly called a *trade deficit*. Canada usually has a positive balance of trade. It is therefore a *creditor nation* rather than a *debtor nation*. In 2005, for example, Canada received $66.6 billion more for exports than it spent on imports.[10] By contrast, the United States usually has a negative balance of trade. In 2005, for example, it spent $725 billion more on imports than it received for exports.[11] It is therefore a debtor nation rather than a creditor nation. A trade deficit negatively affects economic growth because the money that flows out of a country can't be used to invest in productive enterprises, either at home or overseas.

national debt The total amount of money that the government owes its creditors.

National Debt.   A country's **national debt** is the amount of money that the government owes its creditors. Like a business, the government takes in revenues (primarily in the form of taxes) and has expenses (military spending, social programs, and so forth). For many years, the government of Canada incurred annual **budget deficits**; that is, the government spent more money each year than it took in. These accumulated annual deficits have created a huge national debt—the amount of money that Canada owes its creditors.

Until the mid-1990s annual budget deficits and the total national debt were increasing at an alarming rate. From Confederation (1867) to 1981, the *total* accumulated debt was only $85.7 billion, but in the period 1981–94, *annual deficits* were in the $20- to $40-billion range. Since 1994, however, things have changed dramatically. Annual deficits declined rapidly between 1994 and 1996, and in 1997 the first budget surplus in many years occurred. Now, Canada is the only highly industrialized country in the world that continues to have a budget surplus. In 2005, government revenues were $234.9 billion and expenditures were $219.8 billion.[12]

How does the national debt affect economic growth? While taxes are the most obvious way the government raises money, it also sells *bonds*—securities through which it promises to pay buyers certain amounts of money by specified future dates. The government sells bonds to individuals, households, banks, insurance companies, industrial corporations, non-profit organizations, and government agencies, both at home and overseas.[13] These bonds are attractive investments because they are extremely safe: The Canadian government is not going to *default* on them (that is, fail to make payments when due). Even so, they must also offer a decent return on the buyer's investment, and they do this by paying interest at a competitive rate. By selling bonds, therefore, the Canadian government competes with every other potential borrower—individuals, households, businesses, and other organizations—for the available supply of loanable money. The more money the government borrows, the less money is available for the private borrowing and investment that increases productivity.

Economic Stability

We have now learned a great deal about a market economy and the way it allocates resources among its citizens. We know that households, for example, receive capital in return for labour. We know that when households enter consumer markets to purchase goods and services, their decisions (and those of the firms trying to sell them goods and services) are influenced by the laws of demand and supply. We know that the laws of demand and supply result in equilibrium prices when the quantity of goods demanded and the quantity of goods supplied are equal. We know that households enjoy higher standards of living when there is balanced growth in the quantity of goods demanded and the quantity of goods supplied. We know that we can measure growth and productivity in terms of gross domestic product and standard of living in terms of the purchasing power parity of a system's currency: Living standards are stable when purchasing power parity remains stable.[14]

We may thus conclude that a chief goal of an economic system is **stability**: a condition in which the amount of money available in an economic system and the quantity of goods and services produced in it are growing at about the same rate. Now we can focus on certain factors that threaten stability—namely, *inflation*, *deflation*, and *unemployment*.

Inflation

Inflation occurs when there are widespread price increases throughout an economic system. How does it threaten stability? Inflation occurs when the amount of money injected into an economy outstrips the increase in actual output. When this happens, people will have more money to spend, but there will still be the same quantity of products available for them to buy.

budget deficit The result of the government spending more in one year than it takes in during that year.

stability Condition in an economic system in which the amount of money available and the quantity of goods and services produced are growing at about the same rate.

inflation Occurrence of widespread price increases throughout an economic system.

As they compete with one another to buy available products, prices go up. Before long, high prices will erase the increase in the amount of money injected into the economy. Purchasing power, therefore, declines.

Obviously, then, inflation can also hurt you as a consumer because your primary concern when deciding whether to purchase a product is often price. In other words, you will probably decide to make a purchase if the value of the product justifies the price that you'll have to pay. Now look at Table 2.1, which reduces a hypothetical purchase decision to three bare essentials:

1. Your household income over a three-year period

2. The price of a hamburger over a three-year period

3. The rates of increase for both over a three-year period

In which year did the cost of a hamburger go up? At first glance, you might say in both YR2 and YR3 (to $4 in YR2 and to $7.50 in YR3). In YR2, your income kept pace: Although a hamburger cost twice as much, you had twice as much money to spend. In effect, the price to you was actually the same. In YR3, however, your income increased by 250 percent while the price of a hamburger increased by 275 percent. In YR3, therefore, you got hit by inflation (how hard, of course, depends on your fondness for hamburgers). This ratio—the comparison of your increased income to the increased price of a hamburger—is all that counts if you want to consider inflation when you're making a buying decision. Inflation, therefore, can be harmful to you as a consumer because *inflation decreases the purchasing power of your money.*

Measuring Inflation: The CPI. Remember that inflation means widespread price increases throughout an economic system. It stands to reason, therefore, that we can measure inflation by measuring price increases. To do this, we can turn to such price indexes as the **consumer price index (CPI)**, which measures changes in the cost of a "basket" of 600 different goods and services that a typical family might buy. What is included in the basket has changed dramatically over the years as new products and services have become available and old ones fall out of favour. For example, the first CPI in 1913 included items like coal, spirit vinegar, and fruit, while in 2005 the index included DVD home theatre systems, MP3 portable players, and plasma televisions.[15] These changes in the CPI reflect changes that have occurred in the pattern of consumer purchases. For example, in 1961, about 53 percent of consumer spending went to necessities like food, housing, and clothing. By 2000, only 40 percent of consumer spending went to necessities.[16] Figure 2.3 shows how inflation has varied over the last 20 years in Canada.

consumer price index (CPI)
Measure of the prices of typical products purchased by consumers living in urban areas.

Table 2.1	When Did the Cost of a Hamburger Go Up?			
YR1 Income	YR2 Income	YR2 % Increase Over YR1 Base	YR3 Income	YR3 % Increase Over YR1 Base
$5000	$10 000	100	$17 500	250
YR1 Hamburger Price	YR2 Hamburger Price	YR2 % Increase Over YR1 Base	YR3 Hamburger Price	YR3 % Increase Over YR1 Base
$2	$4	100	$7.50	275

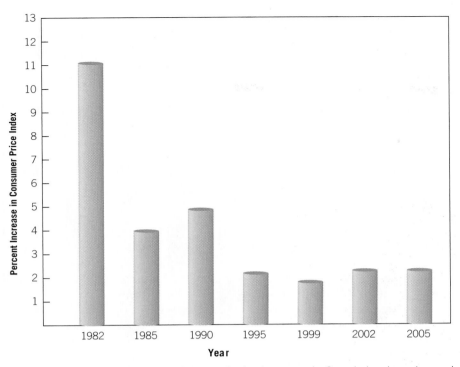

Figure 2.3 During the past decade, the rate of price increases in Canada has been low and quite stable.

Deflation

When **deflation** (generally falling prices) occurs, the Bank of Canada reduces interest rates in an attempt to increase consumer demand. Prices may fall because industrial productivity is increasing and cost savings can be passed on to consumers (this is good), or because consumers have high levels of debt and are therefore unwilling to buy very much (this is bad).

deflation A period of generally falling prices.

Unemployment

Unemployment is the level of joblessness among people actively seeking work. There are various types of unemployment: *frictional unemployment* (people are out of work temporarily while looking for a new job); *seasonal*

unemployment Level of joblessness among people actively seeking work in an economic system.

During the depression of the 1930s, unemployment was very high, with nearly one-quarter of the population unable to find work. Lines of unemployed workers outside soup kitchens were an unfortunate reality during those difficult economic times.

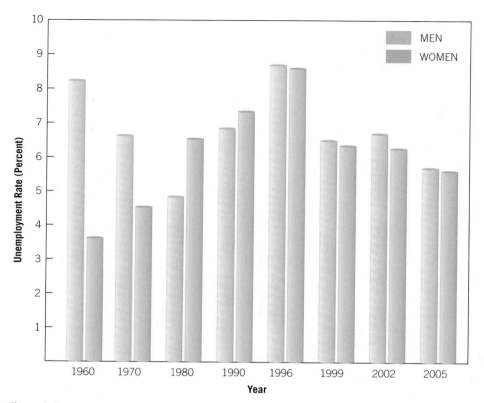

Figure 2.4 Historical unemployment rate.
During the period 1970–96, there was a steady upward trend in unemployment rates, but the rate began to decline in the late 1990s.

unemployment (people are out of work because of the seasonal nature of their jobs); *cyclical unemployment* (people are out of work because of a downturn in the business cycle); and *structural unemployment* (people are unemployed because they lack the skills needed to perform available jobs). Unemployment rates have varied greatly over the years, as Figure 2.4 shows, with the rates for men generally being higher than the rates for women.

When unemployment is low, there is a shortage of labour available for businesses. As these businesses compete with one another for the available supply of labour, they raise the wages that they are willing to pay. Then, because higher labour costs eat into profit margins, businesses raise the prices of their products. Thus, although consumers have more money to inject into the economy, this increase is soon erased by higher prices. Purchasing power declines.

If wage rates get too high, businesses will respond by hiring fewer workers and unemployment will go up. But if that happens, demand may decline because unemployed workers don't purchase as much. Because of reduced sales, companies may further cut back on hiring and unemployment will go even higher. What if the government tries to correct this situation by injecting more money into the economic system—say, by cutting taxes or spending more money? Prices in general may go up because of increased consumer demand, but then inflation sets in, and purchasing power declines.[17]

Managing the Canadian Economy

fiscal policies Policies by means of which governments collect and spend revenues.

The government acts to manage the Canadian economic system through two sets of policies: fiscal and monetary. It manages the collection and spending of its revenues through **fiscal policies**. Tax increases can function as fiscal policies, not only to increase revenues but to manage the economy as well. When there is evidence that the growth rate of the economy is decreasing, tax cuts will normally stimulate renewed economic growth. When the government of Canada cuts taxes that people have to pay, government action is being taken to bring stability to the economic system.

Monetary policies focus on controlling the size of the nation's money supply. Working primarily through the Bank of Canada (the nation's central bank), the government can influence the ability and willingness of banks throughout the country to lend money. It can also influence the supply of money by prompting interest rates to go up or down. The power of the Bank of Canada to make changes in the supply of money is the centrepiece of the Canadian government's monetary policy. The principle is fairly simple:

- Higher interest rates make money more expensive to borrow and thereby reduce spending by both those who produce goods and services and by those who buy those goods and services. When the Bank of Canada restricts the money supply, we say that it is practising a *tight monetary policy*.

- Lower interest rates make money less expensive to borrow and thereby increase spending by both those who produce goods and services and by the consumers who buy those goods and services. When the Bank of Canada loosens the money supply—and thus stimulates the economy—we say that it is practising an *easy monetary policy*.

In both Canada and the United States, the interest rate was cut several times in late 2001 to help the economy recover from the terrorist attacks in the United States on September 11. But in Canada, we experienced a recovery during 2002, so the Bank of Canada had actually been raising interest rates to head off the possibility of inflation. By mid-2003, however, the Bank of Canada decided to hold interest rates steady to protect the economic recovery. But by 2006, interest rates were again on the rise, and the economy was very strong.

In short, the Bank of Canada can influence the aggregate market for products by influencing the supply of money. Taken together, fiscal policy and monetary policy make up **stabilization policy**: government economic policy whose goal is to smooth out fluctuations in output and unemployment and to stabilize prices.

monetary policies Policies by means of which the government controls the size of the nation's money supply.

stabilization policy Government policy, embracing both fiscal and monetary policies, whose goal is to smooth out fluctuations in output and unemployment and to stabilize prices.

THE TECHNOLOGICAL ENVIRONMENT

Technology has a variety of meanings, but as applied to the environment of business, it generally includes all the ways firms create value for their constituents. Technology includes human knowledge, work methods, physical equipment, electronics and telecommunications, and various processing systems that are used to perform business activities. Although technology is applied within the organization, the forms and availability of that technology come from the general environment.

technology All the ways firms create value for their constituents.

Describe the *technological environment* and its role in business.

3

Research and Development (R&D)

Technological improvements and innovation in general are important contributors to the economic development of a country. The innovation process includes **research and development (R&D)**, which provides new ideas for products, services, and processes. (See Chapter 16 for a discussion of the importance of R&D in the marketing of products.) There are two types of

research and development (R&D) Those activities that are necessary to provide new products, services, and processes.

basic (or pure) R&D Improving knowledge in an area without a primary focus on whether any discoveries that might occur are immediately marketable.

applied R&D Focussing specifically on how a technological innovation can be put to use in the making of a product or service that can be sold in the marketplace.

R&D. **Basic (or pure) R&D** involves improving knowledge in an area without a primary focus on whether any discoveries that might occur are immediately marketable. For example, chemists in a laboratory might examine how certain chemical compounds behave. The knowledge gained from this activity might or might not result in a marketable product. **Applied R&D**, on the other hand, means focussing specifically on how a technological innovation can be put to use in the making of a product or service that can be sold in the marketplace.

R&D spending in Canada in 2005 totalled about $13.8 billion.[18] The Canadian private sector accounts for about 54 percent of R&D, the government 9 percent, and universities 35 percent.[19] In the private sector, a large proportion of R&D is carried out by just a few large firms, and just 0.8 percent of firms accounted for 56 percent of the R&D performed.[20] A large proportion of R&D personnel in Canada are concentrated in industries like computer system design, information, communications equipment, and scientific research.[21] Quebec and Ontario accounted for 84 percent of all R&D activities in Canada.[22]

As a proportion of GDP, Canada's level of R&D lags behind that of other countries (see Figure 2.5). This lag exists partly because many Canadian businesses are subsidiaries of large U.S. companies that carry out their R&D in the United States. When we take into account that the GDP of countries like Japan, the United States, and Germany is much larger than the GDP of Canada, it means that R&D spending in Canada (in terms of absolute dollars) is a tiny fraction of what is spent in other countries.

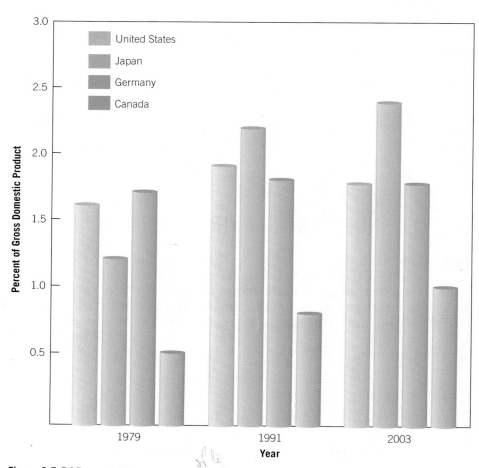

Figure 2.5 R&D expenditures as a proportion of GDP.

Product and Service Technologies

Product and service technologies are the technologies employed for creating products—both physical goods and services—for customers. Although many people associate technology with manufacturing, it is also a significant force in the service sector. Just as an automobile is built as it follows a predetermined pathway along an assembly line, a hamburger at McDonald's is cooked, assembled, and wrapped and bagged as it moves along a predefined path. The rapid advancement of the internet into all areas of business is also a reflection of the technological environment. Indeed, new technologies continue to revolutionize nearly every aspect of business, ranging from the ways that customers and companies interact to where, when, and how employees perform their work.

Companies must constantly be on the lookout for technological breakthroughs that might make their products or services obsolete and thereby threaten their survival. Many of these breakthroughs do not come from direct competitors or even from the industry the company is part of. Microsoft, for example, originally didn't pay much attention to internet technology because it was busy competing with companies like WordPerfect in the word processing and operating software market. When Netscape entered the market with a browser program that threatened to make operating systems unnecessary, Microsoft had to spend a lot of time and money developing its own Internet Explorer browser.[23]

Companies must decide how much emphasis they are going to place on R&D as a competitive tool. **R&D intensity** refers to R&D spending as a percentage of the company's sales revenue. Research has shown that companies with a high R&D intensity are better able to gain market share in global markets.[24] If a company has a strategy to be the technological leader in its industry, it will likely have a high R&D intensity. Alternatively, if its strategy is to be a technology follower, it will likely have a much lower R&D intensity. Being a technological leader is riskier, but can yield very large profits if technological innovations are developed and marketed effectively. Being a technological follower is less risky, but presents fewer opportunities for large profits because very few technological innovations will be evident.

Technology is the basis of competition for some firms, especially when the company's goal is to be the technology leader in their industry. A company, for example, might focus its efforts on being the low-cost producer or always having the most technologically advanced products on the market. But because of the rapid pace of new developments, keeping a leadership position based on technology is increasingly difficult. Another challenge is meeting constant demands to decrease *cycle time*—the time that it takes a firm to accomplish some recurring activity or function from beginning to end. **Technology transfer** refers to the process of getting a new technology out of the lab and into the marketplace where it can generate profits for the company. Efficient technology transfer means an increased likelihood of business success.

Businesses are more competitive if they can systematically decrease cycle times. Many companies, therefore, now focus on decreasing cycle times in areas ranging from developing products to making deliveries and collecting credit payments. Twenty years ago, it took an automaker about five years from the decision to launch a new product until it was available in dealer showrooms. Now most companies can complete the cycle in less than two years. The speedier process allows them to respond more quickly to changing economic conditions, consumer preferences, and new competitive products while recouping their product-development costs more quickly.

R&D intensity R&D spending as a percentage of a company's sales revenue.

technology transfer The process of getting a new technology out of the lab and into the marketplace.

Some firms compete directly on how quickly they can get things done for consumers. In the early days of personal computers, for instance, getting a made-to-order system took six to eight weeks. Today, firms like Dell can usually ship exactly what the customer wants in a matter of days.

Intel exemplifies the challenge and the risks of adopting a strategic dependence on technological leadership. In 1964, before co-founding Intel with Bob Noyce in 1968, Gordon Moore made a prediction about transistors on integrated circuits (the processing components of microcomputers) that eventually became known as Moore's Law: He said that the amount of information stored on a given amount of silicon would double every two years. In effect, this rate would entail a twofold increase in processing power every 24 months—a seemingly impossible pace. Intel, however, has adopted Moore's Law as a performance requirement for each new generation of processor since 1970, up through the Itanium 2.

Intel spent $7.5 billion in 2001 for research and development, and is aggressively searching for ways to cram twice as many transistors into a space that already holds millions. Such a task will require a revolution in technology that, as yet, Intel hasn't found. Without a technological breakthrough, Moore's Law—and Intel's technological leadership position—may not be sustainable. The financial stakes, of course, are high. If Intel can't meet industry-wide goals, it faces threats from new competitors, such as Advanced Micro Devices (AMD), whose microprocessor market share recently grew from 13 percent to 18 percent in just one year.

Process Technologies

Process technologies are used to improve a firm's performance of its internal operations (such as accounting, managing information flows, creating activity reports, and so forth). They also help create better relationships with external constituents, such as suppliers and customers. One recent process technology innovation that is worthy of special mention is **enterprise resource planning (ERP)**, a large-scale information system for organizing and managing a firm's processes across product lines, departments, and geographic locations. Company-wide processes—such as materials management, production planning, order management, and financial reporting—can all be managed by ERP. Figure 2.6 shows some of the areas

enterprise resource planning (ERP) Large-scale information system for organizing and managing a firm's processes across product lines, departments, and geographic locations.

On the surface, low-fat corn and salmon that grow twice as fast would seem to be a good way of improving the food supply. But not everybody is happy about such developments in the modern technological environment. Environmentalists are afraid that genetically modified crops (which they call "Frankenfoods") will sneak into natural populations, outbreed wild species, and threaten biodiversity. Or else they'll cross-pollinate and engineer species that are downright dangerous for human consumption.

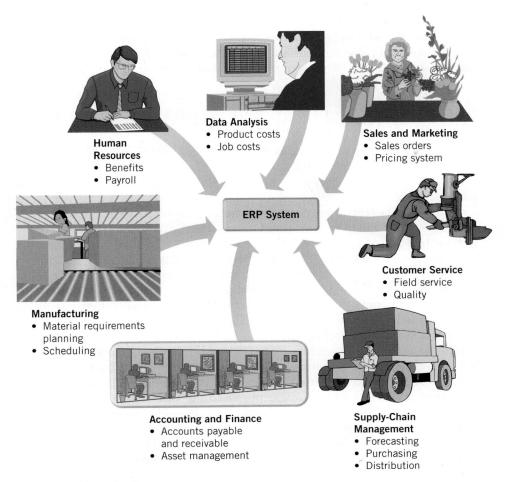

Human Resources
- Benefits
- Payroll

Data Analysis
- Product costs
- Job costs

Sales and Marketing
- Sales orders
- Pricing system

Manufacturing
- Material requirements planning
- Scheduling

ERP System

Customer Service
- Field service
- Quality

Accounting and Finance
- Accounts payable and receivable
- Asset management

Supply-Chain Management
- Forecasting
- Purchasing
- Distribution

Figure 2.6 ERP applications.

in which ERP can be applied, including some of the common processes performed in each area.[25]

In developing the ERP system, the firm starts by identifying the processes that need critical attention, such as supplier relationships, materials flows, or customer order fulfillment. The resulting system would thus integrate the sales process with production planning and then both of these operations into the financial accounting system. Let's say that a customer in Rome orders a product to be manufactured in Ireland. The ERP-integrated seller can schedule the order shipment via air cargo to Rome, where it can be picked up by a truck at the airport and delivered to the customer's warehouse by a specified date. All of these activities are synchronized in one massive database.

The ERP also stores updated real-time information on activities, reports recent and upcoming transactions, and posts electronic notices that certain action is required if certain schedules are to be met. It coordinates internal operations with activities by outside suppliers and notifies customers of current order status and upcoming deliveries and billings. It can integrate financial flows among the firm, its suppliers, customers, and banks and generate up-to-the-minute financial reports at a moment's notice (reduced from the traditional one-month time span).

One Canadian company that uses ERP is Crestline Coach Ltd., a relatively small company in Saskatoon that builds customized emergency vehicles and replacement parts. When problems developed with Crestline's old software—for example, customers had to wait days for parts—management decided to buy an ERP system called Business One from SAP Canada Inc. This was a scaled-down, less expensive version of the ERP systems that are usually sold to large companies. With the new ERP system, if Crestline receives an order for a replacement part it can usually ship it the same day.[26]

THE POLITICAL-LEGAL ENVIRONMENT

political-legal environment
Conditions reflecting the relationship between business and government, usually in the form of government regulation.

4 Describe the *political-legal environment* and its role in business.

The **political-legal environment** reflects the relationship between business and government, usually in the form of government regulation of business. It is important for several reasons. First, the legal system defines in part what an organization can and can't do. Although Canada is a free market economy, it still has major regulation of business activity, as we saw in Chapter 1.

Pro- or anti-business sentiment can further influence business activity. During periods of pro-business sentiment, firms find it easier to compete and have fewer concerns about antitrust issues. On the other hand, during a period of anti-business sentiment, firms may find their competitive activities more restricted. There may, for example, be fewer opportunities for mergers and acquisitions because of antitrust concerns. When the Royal Bank wanted to merge with the Bank of Montreal, the Canadian government blocked the merger on the grounds that it would reduce competition and harm consumers. Nestlé has considered buying Hershey for some time, but the Swiss-owned company worries that the acquisition would be blocked because the two firms, if combined, would dominate the U.S. confectionery market at a level unacceptable to the U.S. government.

Political stability is also an important consideration, especially for international firms. No business wants to set up shop in another country unless trade relationships with that country are relatively well defined and stable. Thus, Canadian firms are more likely to do business with England, Mexico, and the United States than with Haiti and Afghanistan. Similar issues also pertain to assessments of local and provincial governments. A new mayor or provincial leader can affect many organizations, especially small firms that do business in a single location and are thus susceptible to zoning restrictions, property and school taxes, and the like.

Relations between sovereign governments can also affect business activity. When Canada refused to send troops to support the U.S.-led invasion of Iraq, relations between the United States and Canada were very cool for a time. A survey revealed that nearly half the Americans polled said they would consider switching away from Canadian goods in favour of goods from other countries because of Canada's lack of support of the war. This would obviously have a negative effect on Canadian exports if U.S. consumers acted on these opinions.[27]

THE SOCIO-CULTURAL ENVIRONMENT

socio-cultural environment
Conditions including the customs, values, attitudes, and demographic characteristics of the society in which an organization functions.

5 Describe the *socio-cultural environment* and its role in business.

The **socio-cultural environment** includes the customs, values, attitudes, and demographic characteristics of the society in which an organization functions. Socio-cultural processes determine the goods and services as well as the standards of business conduct that a society is likely to value and accept.

Customer Preferences and Tastes

Customer preferences and tastes vary both across and within national boundaries. In some countries, consumers are willing and able to pay premium prices for designer clothes with labels such as Armani or Calvin

Klein. But the same clothes have virtually no market in other countries. Product usage also varies between nations. In China, bicycles are primarily seen as a mode of transportation, but in Canada, they are marketed primarily for recreational purposes.

Similarly, consumer preferences can also vary widely within the same country. Customs and product preferences in Quebec, for example, differ from those in other parts of Canada. In the United States, pre-packaged chili is more popular in the southwest states than in the northeast. McDonald's is just one company that is affected by socio-cultural factors. In response to concerns about nutrition and health, McDonald's has added salads to its menus and experimented with other low-fat foods. It was the first fast-food chain to provide customers with information about the ingredients in its products, and it attracted media attention when it announced that it would reduce the fat content in its popular french fries.

Consumer preferences and tastes also change over time. Preferences for colour, style, and so forth change from season to season. In some years, brightly coloured clothes sell best, while in other years people want more subdued colours. Some of these changes are driven by consumers, and some are driven by companies trying to convince consumers to adopt new styles. Soft drinks usually sell better during the hot summer months than in the cold winter months. Drinking whiskey, vodka, and gin and smoking cigarettes are less common today than they were just a few years ago. These and many other related issues regarding businesses and their customers are explored more fully in Part 4 of this book, which deals with the marketing of products and services.

Finally, socio-cultural factors influence the way workers in a society feel about their jobs and organizations. In some cultures, work carries meaningful social significance, with certain employers and job titles being highly desired by workers. But in other cultures, because work is simply a means to an end, people are concerned only with pay and job security. McDonald's has occasionally struggled with its operations in the Middle East because many people there are not interested in working in food-service operations.

Ethical Compliance and Responsible Business Behaviour

An especially critical element of the socio-cultural environment is the practice of ethical conduct and social responsibility. We cover these areas in detail in Chapter 3, but a preview of them is justified here. The central issue revolves around the fact that rapid changes in business relationships, organizational structures, and financial flows pose difficulties in keeping accurate track of a company's financial position. The public—current and potential investors—often gets blurred pictures of a firm's competitive health. The stakeholders of business firms—employees, stockholders, consumers, unions, creditors, and government—are entitled to a fair accounting so they can make enlightened personal and business decisions. Keeping up with today's increasingly fast-paced business activities is putting a strain on the accounting profession's traditional methods for auditing, financial reporting, and time-honoured standards for professional ethics.

The Enron scandal in the United States, for example, involved fast-moving financial transactions among layers of subsidiary firms, which were designed to conceal Enron's shaky financial condition. Enron's accounting reports failed completely to reflect the firm's disastrous financial and managerial condition. In a blatant display of social irresponsibility and unethical behaviour, Enron's public reports concealed many of its partnerships (and obligations) with other companies, thus hiding its true operating condition. This activity netted prison terms for several Enron executives.

Arthur Andersen LLP, the accounting firm that audited Enron's finances, did not catch its client's distorted reports. Perhaps Andersen's desire for future high-revenue consulting services with Enron motivated the auditors to turn a blind eye to questionable practices that eventually showed up during audits of Enron's finances. Andersen's unethical and illegal practices—including obstruction of justice for shredding and doctoring documents related to Enron audits—destroyed the public's trust and Arthur Andersen as a company.

These activities were not limited to U.S. companies. In a report released on July 28, 2003, court-appointed examiner Neal Batson charged that the Canadian Imperial Bank of Commerce, one of Enron's lenders, knew that Enron was concealing billions of dollars in debts. The report further charged that CIBC helped Enron executives manipulate their financial statements. In 2004, CIBC agreed to pay $480 million to settle allegations that it facilitated accounting fraud at Enron. The CEO of CIBC admitted that the company had "stumbled" in the area of trust and reputation.[28]

Appropriate standards of business conduct vary across cultures. In Canada, accepting bribes in return for political favours is unethical. In other countries, however, payments to local politicians are expected in return for favourable responses to such common business transactions as zoning and operating permits. The shape of the market, the ethics of political influence, and the attitudes of its workforce are only a few of the many ways in which culture can affect an organization. We examine these issues in more detail in Chapter 6.

THE BUSINESS ENVIRONMENT

6 Identify emerging challenges and opportunities in the *business environment*.

Business today is faster paced, more complex, and more demanding than ever before. The 2005 KPMG/Ipsos-Reid poll of CEOs found that the three most serious issues facing Canadian businesses are (1) taxation, (2) the value of the Canadian dollar, and (3) the need for an educated/skilled workforce.[29] These three issues are all important elements of the business environment.

The business environment is complex. As businesses aggressively try to differentiate themselves, there has been a trend toward higher quality products, planned obsolescence, and product life cycles measured in weeks or months rather than years. This, in turn, has created customer expectations for instant gratification. Ultimately consumers and business customers want high-quality goods and services—often customized—with lower prices and immediate delivery. Sales offices, service providers, and production facilities are shifting geographically as new markets and resources emerge in other countries. Employees want flexible working hours and opportunities to work at home. Stockholder expectations also add pressure for productivity increases, growth in market share, and larger profits. At the same time, however, a more vocal public demands more honesty, fair competition, and respect for the environment.

The Industry Environment

Each business firm operates in a specific industry, and each industry has different characteristics. The intensity of the competition in an industry has a big influence on how a company operates. To be effective, managers must understand the company's competitive situation, and then develop a competitive strategy to exploit opportunities in the industry.

One of the best known examples of an effective competitive strategy is Wal-Mart's satellite-based distribution system (discussed in Chapter 17). WestJet has a unique management system that helps it minimize aircraft turnaround time and thus keep its costs lower than its competitors. Managers try hard to find a competitive strategy for their firm, because doing so will slow down or stop new competitors from entering the industry.

One of the most popular tools to analyze competitive situations in an industry is Michael Porter's five forces model.[30] The model (see Figure 2.7) helps managers analyze five important sources of competitive pressure, and then decide what their competitive strategy should be. We briefly discuss each of the elements of the model in the following paragraphs.

Rivalry Among Existing Competitors

The amount of rivalry between companies varies across industries. Rivalry can be seen in activities like intense price competition, elaborate advertising campaigns, and an increased emphasis on customer service. For many years, the rivalry among Chartered Accountants, Certified General Accountants, and Certified Management Accountants in Canada was low-key, but it has recently become much more intense. These firms are responding by trying to attain more market power, cutting costs, making pricing deals with clients, and trying to find ways to differentiate themselves from their competitors.

Threat of Potential Entrants

When new competitors enter an industry, they may cause big changes. For example, when Microsoft introduced Encarta, it caused the sale of hard-copy encyclopedias by companies like Encyclopaedia Britannica to drop sharply. If it is easy for new competitors to enter a market, competition will likely be intense and the industry will not be very attractive. Some industries (for example, automobile manufacturing) are very capital-intensive and are therefore difficult to enter, but others (for example, home cleaning or lawn care services) are relatively easy to enter.

Suppliers

The amount of bargaining power suppliers have in relation to buyers helps determine how competitive an industry is. When there are only a few

Figure 2.7 Michael Porter's five forces model.

suppliers in an industry, they tend to have great bargaining power. The power of suppliers is influenced by the number of substitute products that are available (i.e., products that perform the same or similar functions). When there are few substitute products, suppliers obviously have more power.

Buyers

When there are only a few buyers and many suppliers, the buyers have a great deal of bargaining power. Retail powerhouse Wal-Mart, for example, is often cited as a buyer that puts tremendous pressure on its suppliers to reduce their prices. Wal-Mart can do this because it buys so much from these suppliers.

Substitutes

If there are many substitute products available, the industry is more competitive. For example, various synthetic fibres can be used as substitutes for cotton.

Managers use Porter's ideas to help them decide the level of competitive intensity in an industry. A good example is the emergence of the internet in the sale of airline tickets. By making it easier for consumers to compare prices, the internet has increased the competitive intensity of the airline industry (and many other industries, for that matter). In the airline industry, the internet increased the bargaining power of ticket buyers.

Emerging Challenges and Opportunities in the Business Environment

The most successful firms are dealing with challenges and opportunities in today's business environment by focussing on their **core competencies**—the skills and resources with which they compete best and create the most value for owners. They outsource non-core business processes, paying suppliers and distributors to perform them and thereby increasing their reliance on suppliers. These new business models call for unprecedented coordination—not only among internal activities, but also among customers, suppliers, and strategic partners—and they often involve globally dispersed processes and supply chains.

In this section, we'll discuss some of the most publicized steps that companies have taken to respond to challenges and opportunities in the business environment. These developments include *outsourcing*, *viral marketing*, and *business process management*.

core competency Skills and resources with which an organization competes best and creates the most value for owners.

Outsourcing

outsourcing Strategy of paying suppliers and distributors to perform certain business processes or to provide needed materials or services.

Outsourcing is the strategy of paying suppliers and distributors to perform certain business processes or to provide needed materials or services. For example, the cafeteria in a museum may be important to employees and customers, but running it is not the museum's main line of business and expertise. The museum's primary focus is on exhibits that will interest the general public, not on food-service operations. That's why museums usually outsource cafeteria operations to food-service management companies whose main line of business is to run cafeterias. The result is more attention to museum exhibits and better food service for customers. Firms today outsource numerous activities, including payroll, employee training, and research and development. As the Business Accountability box illustrates, concerns about outsourcing have increased as it has become more and more widely used.

Outsourcing: Good or Bad?

Outsourcing is an increasingly popular strategy because it helps firms focus on their core activities and avoid getting sidetracked by secondary activities. The Bank of Montreal (BMO), for example, outsourced its human resource processing services to Exult Inc. Over 100 people who used to work for BMO now work for Exult. They manage payroll and benefits administration, employee records, HR call centre services, and other functions that used to be performed in-house at BMO. The new arrangement will mean a 20 percent reduction in HR costs for BMO. It will also free up BMO managers to concentrate on more "value-added" work.

The Bank of Montreal outsourcing decision involved moving jobs from one company to another within Canada. But a lot of outsourcing involves moving jobs from Canada to a foreign country, and that is why there is so much concern about it. In the short run, it is obvious that Canadian jobs will be lost when outsourcing takes place. But in the longer run, it is possible that outsourcing may be beneficial. How can that be? The reasoning goes something like this: Canadian companies will continue to outsource more manufacturing work to take advantage of low-cost foreign suppliers. This will allow the Canadian companies to reduce their costs and be more effective in highly competitive global markets. This, in turn, will raise Canadian productivity and improve the standard of living in Canada.

The chief economist for the Export Development Corporation (EDC) says that the main reason for the large increases in U.S. productivity between 1998 and 2002 was outsourcing, so Canada may get the same benefit if it outsources increasing amounts of work. On the negative side, it will obviously reduce the number of jobs in Canada, at least in the short run. That, in turn, may reduce demand and cause economic growth to decline. Our balance of trade might also be negatively affected.

In an increasingly global economy, competitive pressures are intense, and these can cause sweeping change in certain industries. In the automobile business, for example, companies like Ford and GM have to compete with highly efficient Japanese companies like Toyota and Honda. Ford and GM must therefore cut costs wherever possible. But they have rather restrictive labour contracts with the United Auto Workers union that prevent them from easily cutting costs in terms of their own employees, so they have hit upon a new strategy: Put pressure on the companies that supply them with auto parts.

The case of Superior Industries International, a California-based company that makes aluminum wheels for Ford and GM, is instructive. Superior got blunt messages from both Ford and General Motors to match the price that Chinese wheel suppliers were charging or they would buy from a company that could match the price. Since 85 percent of Superior's business was with Ford and GM, it had little alternative but to start outsourcing some work to Chinese factories to lower their costs. To do this, Superior got involved in a joint venture with a Chinese company near Shanghai to build aluminum wheels. The operation will start small and increase as years go by. This means that there is no guarantee that North American jobs at Superior will continue in the long run.

Wages in China average about 90 cents per hour compared to $22 per hour in North America. Even after taking into account the large distance between China and North American markets, the cost of Chinese-made radios, cables, brakes, and wheels is still 20 to 40 percent lower than products made in North America. This is causing jobs in the North American auto parts industry to disappear at a rapid rate. What is interesting is that this trend has just started. Since Ford and GM currently buy less than 5 percent of their parts from China, there is room for dramatically increased amounts of outsourcing. The implication for jobs is not positive.

In addition to the loss of *workers'* jobs, there can also be a downside for the *business* as well. At Superior, for example, profit margins have taken a hit as the company has lowered prices to keeps its business with Ford and GM. In earlier years, Superior usually achieved profit margins of 12 percent, but now that has been reduced to 5.5 percent.

There are other problems with outsourcing. A Dun & Bradstreet study found that one-quarter of all outsourcing relationships fail within two years, and one-half within five. In addition, many executives feel that suppliers too often don't understand what they are supposed to do, that they charge too much, and that they provide poor service. Moreover, when disruptions occur in the supply chain, the costs to both parties can be high. For one thing, replacing failed outsourced operations can be very expensive, especially if the firm wants to go back to performing the outsourced activity itself. Another risk in outsourcing is the loss of control over both operations and information.

▶▶▶

▶▶▶

In spite of these problems, outsourcing is here to stay because of the increasingly global nature of business, and because competitive pressures to reduce costs are so great. But the "look" of outsourcing may change. Consider the "reverse outsourcing" that occurred when India's Bharti Tele-Ventures Ltd. signed a $400 million outsourcing deal with three European companies—Ericsson (Sweden), Nokia (Finland), and Siemens (Germany). Hundreds of technicians who used to maintain Bharti's wireless network are now employed by these European companies (but the employees work in India, not in Europe). Bharti also outsourced most of its information technology services to IBM. To get the contract, IBM had to beat out several Indian companies that were competing for the contract. As a result of these outsourcing deals, Bharti now has just a few of its own employees. It is using outsourcing to reduce its costs so that it will be the lowest-cost provider of cellphone minutes in India.

Viral Marketing

viral marketing Strategy of using the internet and word-of-mouth marketing to spread product information.

Combining technology with marketing methods usually results in new ways to attract customers. **Viral marketing**, which uses word of mouth that spreads information like a virus from customer to customer, relies on the vast reaches of the internet to replace face-to-face communications. Messages about new cars, sports events, and numerous other goods and services travel on the internet among potential customers who pass the information on to others. Using various formats—games, contests, chat rooms, and bulletin boards—marketers encourage potential customers to try out products and tell other people about them.[31]

The Organic Trade Association (OTA), which promotes organic foods, created a successful viral marketing program when it partnered with Free Range Graphics, and produced a 5-minute online spoof of the latest Star Wars movie. The film—which is called *Store Wars: The Organic Rebellion*—has characters such as Cuke Skywalker and Darth Tater, and has been passed around the internet by consumers who favour organic foods.[32]

Viral marketing leads to faster consumer awareness and wider reach than traditional media messages, and at a lower cost. The OTA's short film, for example, was seen by 10 million people in its first four months. Viral marketing works because people increasingly rely on the internet for information that they used to get from other media such as newspapers, and because the customer becomes a participant in the process of spreading the word by forwarding information to other internet users.

Business Process Management

Every company performs numerous processes that provide the goods or services, whether for customers or for other departments within the firm. Human resource departments perform interviewing and hiring processes; payroll departments perform the employee-payment process; the purchasing department performs the process of ordering materials; accounting performs the financial reporting process; marketing performs the process of taking orders from customers. A **process**, in short, is any activity that adds value to some input, transforming it into an output for a customer (whether external or internal).[33]

process Any activity that adds value to some input, transforming it into an output for a customer (whether external or internal).

business process management An approach by which firms move away from department-oriented organization and toward process-oriented team structures that cut across old departmental boundaries.

In today's business environment, many firms are moving away from the department-oriented organization (one that is organized around departments grouped according to processes or functions). Firms are moving toward process-oriented team structures that cut across old departmental boundaries. This approach is called **business process management**. Often, companies begin by asking, "What must we do well to stay in business and win new orders?" Next, they identify the major processes that must be performed well to satisfy these general goals. Then they organize resources and skills around those essential processes. By organizing according to processes rather than functional departments, they gain a number of benefits. Decision making is faster and more customer-oriented, materials and operations are coordinated, and products get to customers more rapidly.[34]

REDRAWING CORPORATE BOUNDARIES

Successful companies are responding to challenges in the environment by redrawing traditional organizational boundaries, and by joining together with other companies to develop new goods and services. Some of these relationships are permanent, but others are temporary alliances formed on short notice so that, working together, partners can produce and deliver products with shorter lead times than either firm could manage alone.

> Understand recent trends in the *redrawing of corporate boundaries.*
>
> **7**

Several trends in redrawing corporate boundaries have become evident in recent years. They include *acquisitions and mergers, divestitures and spinoffs, employee-owned corporations, strategic alliances,* and *subsidiary/parent corporations.*

Acquisitions and Mergers

In an **acquisition**, one firm simply buys another firm. For example, America Online bought Time Warner and Air Canada bought Canadian Airlines International. The transaction is similar to buying a car that then becomes your property. In contrast, a **merger** is a consolidation of two firms, and the arrangement is more collaborative. For example, Canadian National Railways merged with the Illinois Central Railroad, Rogers Communication merged with Groupe Videotron Ltd., and Toronto-Dominion Bank merged with Canada Trust. When the companies are in the same industry, as when Agricore and United Grain Growers merged to form Agricore United, it is called a **horizontal merger**. When one of the companies in the merger is a supplier or customer to the other, it is called a **vertical merger**. Finally, when the companies are in unrelated businesses, it is called a **conglomerate merger**.

A merger or acquisition can take place in one of several different ways. In a **friendly takeover**, the acquired company welcomes the acquisition, perhaps because it needs cash or sees other benefits in joining the acquiring firm. But in a **hostile takeover**, the acquiring company buys enough of the other company's stock to take control even though the other company is opposed to the takeover.

A **poison pill** is a defence that management adopts to make a firm less attractive to an actual or potential hostile suitor in a takeover attempt. The objective is to make the "pill" so distasteful that a potential acquirer will not want to swallow it. BCE Inc., for example, adopted a poison pill that allowed its shareholders to buy BCE stock at a 50 percent discount if another company announced its intention to acquire 20 percent or more of BCE's shares.[35]

acquisition One firm buys another firm and absorbs it into its operations.

merger The union of two companies to form a single new business.

horizontal merger A merger of two firms that have previously been direct competitors in the same industry.

vertical merger A merger of two firms that have previously had a buyer-seller relationship.

conglomerate merger A merger of two firms in completely unrelated businesses.

friendly takeover An acquisition in which the management of the acquired company welcomes the firm's buyout by another company.

hostile takeover An acquisition in which the management of the acquired company fights the firm's buyout by another company.

poison pill A defence that management adopts to make a firm less attractive to an actual or potential hostile suitor in a takeover attempt.

Divestitures and Spinoffs

A **divestiture** occurs when a company decides to sell part of its existing business operations to another corporation. For example, Unilever—the maker of Close-Up toothpaste, Dove soap, Vaseline lotion, and Q-tips—at

divestiture Occurs when a company sells part of its existing business operations to another company.

one time owned several specialty chemical businesses that made ingredients for its consumer products. The company decided that it had to focus more on the consumer products themselves, so it sold the chemical businesses to ICI, a European chemical company.

In other cases, a company might set up one or more corporate units as new, independent businesses because a business unit might be more valuable as a separate company. This is known as a **spinoff**. For example, PepsiCo spun off Pizza Hut, KFC, and Taco Bell into a new, separate corporation called Tricon Global Restaurants (now called Yum! Brands Inc.). Canadian Pacific spun off Canadian Pacific Railways, CP Ships, PanCanadian Petroleum, and Fording Coal.

spinoff Strategy of setting up one or more corporate units as new, independent corporations.

Employee-Owned Corporations

Corporations are sometimes owned by the employees who work for them. While the individuals who founded them own many smaller corporations, there is a growing trend today for employees to buy significant stakes of larger corporations. The current pattern is for this ownership to take the form of **employee stock ownership plans**, or **ESOPs**.

A corporation might decide to set up an ESOP to stimulate employee motivation or to fight a hostile takeover attempt. Here's how it works: The company first secures a loan, which it then uses to buy shares of its stock on the open market. Some of the future profits made by the corporation are used to pay off the loan. The stock, meanwhile, is controlled by a bank or other trustee. Employees gradually gain ownership of the stock, usually on the basis of seniority. But even though they might not have physical possession of the stock for a while, they control its voting rights immediately.

A survey of 471 Canadian and U.S. companies conducted by Western Compensation & Benefits Consultants of Vancouver found that three-quarters of the companies that have adopted ESOPs have experienced improvement in both sales and profits. Canadian companies such as Celestica and St. Laurent Paperboard Inc. have found that ESOPs give employees an increased sense of belonging in the company.[36]

employee stock ownership plan (ESOP) An arrangement whereby a corporation buys its own stock with loaned funds and holds it in trust for its employees. Employees "earn" the stock based on some condition such as seniority. Employees control the stock's voting rights immediately, even though they may not take physical possession of the stock until specified conditions are met.

Strategic Alliances

A **strategic alliance**, or joint venture, involves two or more enterprises co-operating in the research, development, manufacture, or marketing of a product. For example, GM and Suzuki formed a strategic alliance at the Ingersoll, Ontario, plant where Trackers and Grand Vitaras are made. Northern Empire, Stornoway, and Hunter Exploration Group formed a three-way joint venture to explore for diamonds on Melville Island in the Arctic Ocean.[37] Inco Ltd. and LionOre Mining International formed a joint venture to do research on processing technologies for the recovery of base metals from sulphide ores.[38]

Companies form strategic alliances for two main reasons: (1) to help spread the risk of a project, and (2) to get something of value (like technological expertise) from their strategic partner.

strategic alliance An enterprise in which two or more persons or companies temporarily join forces to undertake a particular project.

Subsidiary and Parent Corporations

Sometimes corporations own other corporations. A **subsidiary corporation** is one that is owned by another corporation. The corporation that owns the subsidiary is called the **parent corporation**. For example, Unilever is the parent corporation of Lever Brothers, Lipton, and Chesebrough Ponds.

subsidiary corporation One that is owned by another corporation.
parent corporation A corporation that owns a subsidiary.

Summary of Learning Objectives

1. **Explain the concepts of *organizational boundaries* and *multiple organizational environments.*** All businesses operate within a larger *external environment*. An *organizational boundary* is that which separates the organization from its environment. Boundaries were once relatively easy to identify; they are becoming harder to pin down. Organizations have multiple environments. Some environments are relatively general, such as prevailing economic conditions. Others are much more precise, such as the pricing policies of competitors. A full picture of a company's organizational environments would include the following elements: economic conditions, technology, political-legal considerations, social issues, the global environment, issues of ethical and social responsibility, the business environment itself, and numerous other emerging challenges and opportunities.

2. **Explain the importance of the *economic environment* to business and identify the factors used to evaluate the performance of an economic system.** The *economic environment* is the economic system in which business firms operate. The health of this environment affects business firms. The three key goals of the Canadian system are economic growth, economic stability, and full employment. *Economic growth* is influenced by the pattern of short-term ups and downs in an economy known as the *business cycle*. The main measure of *growth* in this cycle is *aggregate output*. An increase in aggregate output is growth. *Gross domestic product (GDP)* is the total value of all goods and services produced within a given period by a national economy through domestic factors of production. If GDP is going up, so is aggregate output; if aggregate output is going up, we have economic growth.

    Economic stability means that the amount of money available in an economic system and the quantity of goods and services produced in it are growing at about the same rate. There are three threats to stability: inflation, deflation, and unemployment.

    Unemployment is the level of joblessness among people actively seeking work. If people in different sectors lose their jobs at the same time, overall income and spending drop and businesses cut spending further—including spending on labour—and unemployment goes up further. This kind of unemployment is called *cyclical unemployment*. Meanwhile, producers also start producing less because they can't sell as much. Aggregate output then decreases and we have a *recession*. A prolonged and deep recession is a *depression*.

    The government manages the economy through *fiscal policies* and *monetary policies*. Through the Bank of Canada, the Canadian government can influence the ability and willingness of banks to lend money. It can also influence the supply of money by prompting interest rates to go up or down.

3. **Describe the *technological environment* and its role in business.** *Technology* refers to all the ways by which firms create value for their constituents, including human knowledge, work methods, physical equipment, electronics and telecommunications, and various processing systems. There are two general categories of business-related technologies: *product and service technologies* and *business process technologies*. Product and service technologies create products—both physical goods and services—for customers. Business process technologies are used to improve a firm's performance of internal operations (such as accounting) and to help to create better relationships with external constituents, such as suppliers and customers. *Enterprise resource planning (ERP)* is a large-scale information system for organizing and managing a firm's processes across product lines, departments, and geographic locations.

4. **Describe the *political-legal environment* and its role in business.** The *political-legal environment* reflects the relationship between business and government, usually in the form of government regulation. The legal system defines in part what an organization can and can't do. Various government agencies regulate important areas such as advertising practices, safety and health considerations, and acceptable standards of business conduct. Pro- or anti-business sentiment in government can further influence business activity. During periods of pro-business sentiment, firms find it easier to compete and have fewer concerns about antitrust issues. During periods of anti-business sentiment, firms may find their competitive activities more restricted.

5. **Describe the *socio-cultural environment* and its role in business.** The *socio-cultural environment* includes the customs, values, and demographic characteristics of the society in which an organization functions. Socio-cultural processes determine the goods and services as well as the standards of business conduct that a society values and accepts. Appropriate standards of conduct also vary across cultures. The shape of the market, the ethics of political influence, and the attitudes of its workforce are only a few of the many ways in which culture can affect an organization.

6. **Identify emerging challenges and opportunities in the** *business environment.* Successful companies are responding to challenges in new ways. They are focussing on their core competencies. The innovative ways in which companies respond to emerging challenges and opportunities include *outsourcing, viral marketing,* and *business process management.* Outsourcing is the strategy of paying suppliers and distributors to perform certain business processes or to provide needed materials or services. Viral marketing relies on the internet to replace face-to-face communications. Many firms are moving away from the department-oriented organization and toward process-oriented team structures that cut across old departmental boundaries—an approach called business process management.

7. **Understand recent trends in the** *redrawing of corporate boundaries.* An *acquisition* occurs when one firm buys another outright. A *merger* occurs when two firms combine to create a new company. A *divestiture* occurs when a corporation sells a part of its existing business operations or sets it up as a new and independent corporation. When a firm sells part of itself to raise capital, the strategy is known as a *spinoff.* The *employee stock ownership plan* (ESOP) allows employees to own a significant share of the corporation through trusts established on their behalf. In a *strategic alliance*, two or more organizations collaborate on a project for mutual gain.

KEY TERMS

acquisition,   61
aggregate output,   41
applied R&D,   50
balance of trade,   44
basic (pure) R&D,   50
budget deficit,   45
business cycle,   40
business process management,   60
conglomerate merger,   61
consumer price index (CPI),   46
core competency,   58
deflation,   47
depression,   40
divestiture,   61
economic environment,   39
employee stock ownership program (ESOP),   62
enterprise resource planning (ERP),   52

external environment,   38
fiscal policies,   48
friendly takeover,   61
gross domestic product (GDP),   41
gross national product (GNP),   42
horizontal merger,   61
hostile takeover,   61
inflation,   45
merger,   61
monetary policies,   49
national debt,   44
nominal GDP,   43
organizational boundary,   38
outsourcing,   58
parent corporation,   62
poison pill,   61
political-legal environment,   54
process,   60

productivity,   43
purchasing power parity,   43
R&D intensity,   51
real GDP,   43
recession,   40
research and development (R&D),   49
socio-cultural environment,   54
spinoff,   62
stability,   45
stabilization policy,   49
standard of living,   41
strategic alliance,   62
subsidiary corporation,   62
technology,   49
technology transfer,   51
unemployment,   47
vertical merger,   61
viral marketing,   60

QUESTIONS FOR ANALYSIS

1. It has been argued that inflation is both good and bad. How can this be? Explain. Are government efforts to control inflation well-advised? Explain.

2. What are the benefits and risks of outsourcing? What, if anything, should be done about the problem of Canadian companies outsourcing jobs to foreign countries? Defend your answer.

3. Why is it important for managers to understand the environment in which their businesses operate?

4. Explain how current economic indicators such as inflation and unemployment affect you personally. Explain how they will affect you as a manager.

5. Using a product or service of your choice, explain how the various environments of business impact the sales possibilities of the product or service.

6. What is the current climate regarding the regulation of business? How might it affect you if you were a manager today?

7. At first glance, it might seem as though the goals of economic growth and stability are inconsistent with one another. How can you reconcile this apparent inconsistency?

APPLICATION EXERCISES

1. Select two businesses with which you are familiar. Identify the major elements of their external environments that are most likely to affect them in important and meaningful ways.

2. Using the internet, identify the major suppliers of software for enterprise resource planning. Try to locate information about their primary customers.

3. Interview two business owners or managers. Ask them to describe for you the following things: (a) what business functions, if any, they outsource; (b) whether or not they are focussing more attention on business process management now than in the past; and (c) how the events of September 11, 2001, have affected their work.

BUILDING YOUR BUSINESS SKILLS

The Letdown from Environmental Upheaval

Goal

To encourage students to understand how local events can affect other businesses in a number of ways.

The Situation

The collapse of Enron affected literally hundreds of other businesses. While attention has been directed primarily at the demise of Arthur Andersen, many other businesses suffered as well. For example, Enron's headquarters was located in a large office building on the edge of Houston's downtown business district. Because of both Enron's rapid growth and the prosperity of its employees, numerous other service providers had set up shop nearby—a shoeshine stand, a coffee shop, a bank branch, a dry cleaner, and two restaurants. When Enron collapsed, the demand for services provided by these small businesses dropped sharply.

Larger businesses were also caught up in the ripple effect. Enron, for example, had bought the rights to name the new home of baseball's Houston Astros Enron Field. The Astros were forced to remove all Enron signage and seek a new sponsor. Continental Airlines dominates the air traffic market out of Houston, and Enron was one of Continental's largest corporate clients. Combined with the events of September 11, 2001, and major staff reductions at Compaq Computer, another big Continental client, the end of business travel by Enron managers cost the airline considerable revenue.

Assignment

Divide up into groups of four or five students. Each group should begin by doing the following:

Step 1

Identify five kinds of small businesses likely to have been affected by Enron's collapse. You can include some of those identified above, but identify at least two others.

Step 2

Identify five kinds of large businesses likely to have been affected by Enron's collapse. Again, you can use some of those identified above, but identify at least two others.

Step 3

As a group, develop answers to each of the following:
1. For each company that you identify, both small and large, describe the specific effects of the Enron collapse on its business.
2. Describe the most logical organizational response of each company to these effects.
3. What kinds of plans, if any, should each organization develop in the event of similar future events?
4. Identify businesses that might have benefited economically from the collapse of Enron.

Alternative Assignment

Select a different high-profile environmental upheaval, such as the U.S. duties that were placed on Canadian softwood lumber being shipped to the United States, and substitute it for Enron. Then proceed with Steps 1–3 above.

Follow-Up Questions

1. What does this exercise demonstrate about the pitfalls of relying too heavily on one business?
2. Could any of these businesses have been better prepared for the Enron collapse?
3. Managers must be on the alert for environmental changes that might negatively affect their business. Is it possible for a manager to spend too much time trying to anticipate future events? Why or why not?

Assessing the Ethics of Trade-Offs

The Purpose of the Assignment

Managers must often make choices among options that are presented by environmental circumstances. This exercise will help you better appreciate the nature and complexity of the kinds of trade-offs that often result.

The Situation

You are owner and manager of a medium-sized non-unionized manufacturing company located in a town of about 15 000 people. The nearest major city is about 200 kilometres away. With about 500 workers, you are one of the five largest employers in town. A regional recession has caused two of the other largest employers to close down (one went out of business and the other relocated to another area). A new foreign competitor has set up shop in the area, but local unemployment has still risen sharply. All in all, the regional economic climate and the new competitor are hurting your business. Your sales have dropped 20 percent this year, and you forecast another drop next year before things begin to turn around.

The Dilemma

You face two unpleasant choices.

Choice 1: You can tell your employees that you need them to take cuts in pay and benefits. You know that because of the local unemployment rate, you can easily replace anyone who refuses. Unfortunately, you may need your employees to take another cut next year

if your forecasts hold true. At the same time, you do have reason to believe that when the economy rebounds (in about two years, according to your forecasts), you can begin restoring pay cuts. Here are the advantages of this choice: You can probably (1) preserve all 500 jobs, (2) maintain your own income, (3) restore pay cuts in the future, and (4) keep the business open indefinitely. And the disadvantages: Pay cuts will (1) pose economic hardships for your employees and (2) create hard feelings and undercut morale.

Choice 2: You can maintain the status quo as far as your employees are concerned, but in that case, you'll be facing two problems: (1) You'll have to cut your own salary. While you can certainly afford to live on less income, doing so would be a blow to your personal finances. (2) If economic conditions get worse and/or last longer than forecast, you may have to close down altogether. The firm has a cash surplus, but because you'll have to dip into these funds to maintain stable wages, they'll soon run out. The advantages of this option: You can (1) avoid economic hardship for your workers and (2) maintain good employee relations. The downside: You will reduce your own standard of living and may eventually cost everyone his or her job.

Questions for Discussion

1. What are the basic ethical issues in this situation?
2. Can you identify any other options?
3. Of the two options posed in the situation as presented, which would you choose? Why?

Corporate Reputations: Mixed Evidence

During the last few years, there has been a great deal of negative publicity about business activity. Because of illegal and unethical behaviour, sky-high executive salaries, or simply poor performance, business has lost a lot of respect lately. But there is another side to the story, and it doesn't get enough attention. That story concerns the large number of corporations that perform well and do good things for the constituents in their external environment. And they do it without a lot of fanfare.

Who are these companies? Each year since 1994, KPMG/Ipsos-Reid has published a list of the most respected corporations in Canada. In 2005, 250 leading Canadian CEOs were asked to assess Canadian corporations on eight performance categories such as long-term investment value, innovation and product/service development, financial performance, corporate social responsibility, corporate governance, human resource management, and customer service. The winner for 2005 was the Royal Bank of Canada (RBC) by a wide margin (RBC also came in first in the 2004 survey). The next four companies (in order) were Research In Motion, EnCana Corp., WestJet Airlines, and the Bank of Nova Scotia.

Some critics say that banks have an undue advantage in surveys like these because they are so rich that they are able to be very involved in philanthropy. Both CEOs and the general public are likely to be impressed by large charitable donations that banks make, and such activity gives banks a lot of free publicity. On the other hand, Canadian consumers are often not very impressed with banks, arguing that they charge too much for services and do not pay high enough interest on money deposited with them.

Respect and reputation are things that can quickly change. For example, in 1999, Nortel Networks ranked first in the survey, but with its recent troubles it ranked only 40th in the 2005 survey. And Bombardier, which ranked first in 2001, dropped to 28th place in 2005. Negative publicity about a company can obviously cause it to drop in the rankings. Canadian Imperial Bank of Commerce dropped from 10th place in 2004 to 18th place in 2005 after it received negative publicity about its role in the Enron debacle.

Surveys about corporate reputations are also conducted in the United States. The Reputation Quotient study is a joint effort of Harris Interactive Inc., a Rochester, New York-based research firm, and the Reputation Institute of New York. A 2005 survey asked nearly 20 000 people to name two companies with the best reputation and two companies with the worst reputation. Respondents evaluated the companies on factors such as emotional appeal, financial performance, social responsibility, and workplace environment. In total, 60 companies were named by those who were surveyed.

The company with the best reputation was Johnson & Johnson, a manufacturer of baby products and pharmaceuticals. The next four companies (in order) were Coca-Cola, Google, United Parcel Service, and 3M. Johnson & Johnson has had considerable success staying at the top of the Reputation Quotient (it has been ranked first every year since 1999). Apparently, consumers have warm feelings about the company because of its baby products.

The worst company was Enron (ranked 60th). Other poorly ranked companies were MCI (formerly WorldCom), Adelphia Communications, and Halliburton. All of these companies have received significant negative publicity in recent years for various misdeeds. The actions of a relatively small number of companies have influenced how people in the United States view business. In the 2005 survey, 71 percent of respondents rated the reputation of American business as either "not good" or "terrible."

It's not just individual companies that can run into difficulty. During the last few years, the reputations of entire industries have declined. For example, consumer impressions of the pharmaceutical and oil industries are negative because of a widely held belief that these industries are overcharging consumers for the products they sell. The tobacco industry has also had problems because consumers think that information about the negative effects of smoking and nicotine was withheld from the public.

When we consider negative information about business firms, we must remember that only a very small proportion of them are actually engaging in illegal or unethical behaviour. A review of the Canadian and U.S. reputation lists—and the criteria that are used to generate them—provides some reassuring testimony on the vitality and values of many businesses. It also shows the manner in which they conduct their operations, and gives us some insights into how companies must perform to gain the kind of stellar reputation necessary to get on the list.

These criteria all have one underlying theme: They reflect in one way or another the extent to which an organization and its managers effectively meet or exceed the needs and expectations of their external constituents. For example, hiring and developing the brightest and most motivated people from the labour market results in high levels of employee talent. Likewise, respecting the needs of shareholders and other investors affects several criteria, including financial soundness, use of corporate assets, and long-term investment value. Says one expert, "We admire companies that cater to their constituents."

Questions for Discussion

1. What is your opinion of the value of the rankings like these? How might the different ways the Canadian and U.S. surveys are conducted influence the results?

2. Do you think the criteria that are used are appropriate? Can you suggest others?

3. Is the ranking something that investors should rely on in buying stock?

4. If you were a top manager and wanted your firm to move up in the rankings, how would you proceed?

Maybe Malthus Was Wrong

Most people have heard of Thomas Malthus, who became famous by proposing that all species have a tendency to reproduce to the point where their food supply runs out. The application of this idea to human population was simple: The world's population would tend to increase until the food supply was no longer sufficient to support everyone. Starvation would then result. But is this correct? Recent population trends are very startling, and call into question the predictions of Malthus.

The fertility rate—the average number of lifetime births per woman—declined in many industrialized European countries in the mid-twentieth century, and has stayed low ever since. In fact, it has stayed below the "replacement rate"—the rate needed to ensure that the population maintains itself. That rate is 2.1 births per woman. Some of the implications of Europe's declining fertility rate are profound. In Russia, for example, the current population of 150 million people will drop to 105 million by 2050 if current trends continue.

While the fertility rate is low in industrialized Europe, in developing countries it has always been high. And, until recently, it was assumed that it would always be high. This would lead, it was feared, to eventual overpopulation of the world and Malthusian famine on a large scale. But something unexpected is happening. Fertility rates in most developing countries, including India, Mexico, and Iran, are declining.

In 2000, the United Nations population division predicted that the fertility rate in developing countries in 2050 would be 2.1 children per woman. But in 2002, it revised its prediction downward to 1.85 children per woman. If this latest prediction turns out to be accurate, the world's population should stabilize at about 9 billion people by 2050. This is a significant change from predictions that were made in 1992, when it was thought that world population would reach 12 billion people by 2050. There are several interesting implications of a stabilizing world population:

- In the future, a smaller proportion of the population in most countries will be children, and a larger proportion will be very old people.

- More and more women will be involved in the worldwide workforce because they are having fewer children, and they are having them later in life.
- The population of Japan will start declining in 2006, so businesses there will have to find ways to increase productivity to cope with the decline in the working population.
- Mexico's fertility rate has dropped precipitously in the last 25 years (from 7.0 to 2.1), and that means that for the first time in its history Mexico has the opportunity to develop a significant middle class of consumers; but this development may also make it difficult for Mexico to compete with other emerging markets for foreign investment.
- Countries where the fertility rate has dropped sharply will benefit from a so-called demographic bonus: Labour costs decline because a greater proportion of the population works when there are fewer children; Thailand and China are just two countries that have benefited this way, and India will soon start benefiting.

Some countries are so concerned about the decline in fertility rates that they have begun offering incentives to convince women to have more babies. In Australia, for example, couples that have a baby can put off a house loan payment for three months. In Singapore, parents are paid a bonus in cash if they have one more child. But these initiatives have had virtually no effect. It seems that the combination of high literacy rates, increasing prosperity, and improvements in women's rights are an irresistible force in reducing fertility rates.

Questions for Discussion

1. Consider each of the issues discussed in the chapter with regard to the economic environment. What will be the impact of declining fertility rates on each of these issues? Be specific.

2. What will be the impact of declining fertility rates on the technological, political-legal, and socio-cultural environments? Be specific.

3. If the fertility rate continues to decline worldwide, what are the implications for individual business firms? Be specific.

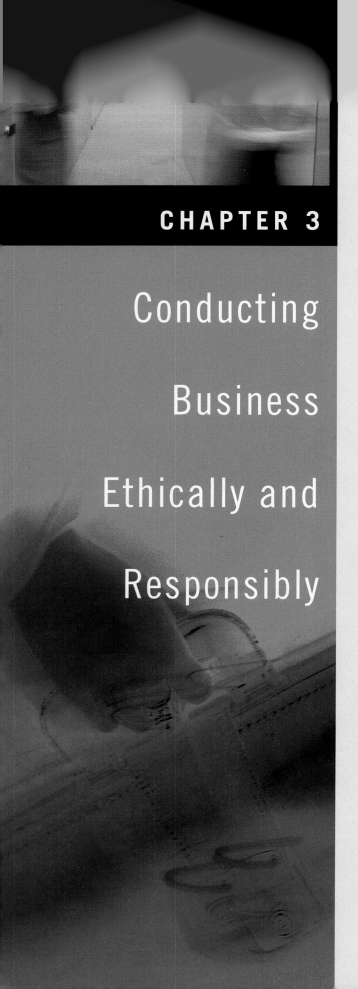

CHAPTER 3

Conducting Business Ethically and Responsibly

After reading this chapter, you should be able to:

1 Explain how individuals develop their personal *codes of ethics* and why ethics are important in the workplace.

2 Distinguish *social responsibility* from *ethics*, identify *organizational stakeholders*, and characterize social consciousness today.

3 Show how the concept of social responsibility applies both to environmental issues and to a firm's relationships with customers, employees, and investors.

4 Identify four general *approaches to social responsibility* and describe the four steps a firm must take to implement a *social responsibility program*.

5 Explain how issues of social responsibility and ethics affect small businesses.

During the last few years, many business executives have been hit with charges that they made undisclosed loans to shareholders, obstructed justice, engaged in insider trading and tipping, manipulated financial statements, and misled clients and investors. Some of these executives—for example, Garth Drabinsky and Myron Gottlieb (Livent Inc.), Bernie Ebbers (WorldCom), Ken Lay (Enron), Conrad Black (Hollinger International), and Jean Brault (Groupaction Marketing)—received a lot of publicity. Three Canadian banks that were involved in the Enron debacle also received bad press.

Garth Drabinsky and Myron Gottlieb. Livent Inc., a live theatre company with theatres in Toronto, Vancouver, Chicago,

and New York, was founded by Drabinsky and Gottlieb. In 1998, questions were raised about Livent's finances by new owners who had bought into the company. Shortly thereafter, Drabinsky and Gottlieb were fired. They were eventually charged with defrauding investors and creditors of about $500 million. Progress in the case has been very slow, and the trial is not expected to start until 2007. Drabinsky and Gottlieb have consistently denied any wrongdoing. In a related development, the Institute of Chartered Accountants of Ontario (ICAO) charged four partners of Deloitte & Touche LLP with breaching the Institute's rules of professional conduct regarding Livent. Deloitte also denies any wrongdoing.

Bernie Ebbers. Canadian-born Bernie Ebbers had risen from Alberta milkman and nightclub bouncer to become CEO of WorldCom, one of the largest companies in the United States. It was alleged that Ebbers conspired with subordinates to "cook the books" when a business downturn occurred. These actions wiped out $100 billion of the company's market value, cost 17 000 people their jobs, and lost some investors their life savings. Scott Sullivan, one of Ebbers' subordinates, pled guilty and testified that Ebbers had ordered him to cook the books to hit earnings targets. In March 2005, Ebbers was found guilty on nine charges of securities fraud and filing false documents. He was sentenced to 25 years in prison for his role in the collapse of WorldCom Inc.

Ken Lay. The former CEO of Enron was well-known as a "hands-off" manager, and he claimed that he was unaware of the financial manipulations that had been carried out by some of his subordinates, notably Andrew Fastow, the chief financial officer. These manipulations included moving debt "off the balance sheet" to make it look like Enron was in better financial shape than it was. The jury didn't buy Lay's story that he was the victim of his subordinates' misbehaviour, and in 2006 he was convicted of a variety of charges, including conspiracy and securities fraud. His sentencing hearing was scheduled for September 11, 2006, but he died of a heart attack in July 2006.

Conrad Black. In 2005, David Radler, Conrad Black's longtime business partner, pled guilty to his part in a $32 million fraud at Hollinger International where Black was CEO. Radler was given 29 months in jail and a $250 000 fine. He also agreed to cooperate with a criminal investigation of Conrad Black. Radler's guilty plea was not good news for Conrad Black, who was still awaiting trial on charges that he and three associates illegally diverted $84 million out of investors' pockets and into their own. Black denies any wrongdoing and notes that all his actions were approved by the board of directors of Hollinger. Prosecutors charge that Black used fraud to obtain board and audit committee approval to make payments to himself, and that he made false statements and omitted facts about the payment to shareholders and regulators. Black's trial had not started as of July 2006.

Jean Brault. In 2002, rumours began circulating that the federal Liberal government had paid millions of dollars to the advertising firm Groupaction Marketing to help raise Canada's profile in Quebec after the 1995 sovereignty referendum. The trouble was, no work was ever done. An inquiry resulted in many criminal charges being laid, including six charges of fraud against Jean Brault, who ran Groupaction Marketing. He eventually pled guilty to five of the charges and admitted to paying salaries to Liberal party workers who never did any work. He was sentenced to 30 months in prison.

Canadian Banks. The Royal Bank of Canada (RBC), the Toronto-Dominion (TD) bank, and the Canadian Imperial Bank of Commerce (CIBC) were among many defendants in a $25 billion class action suit filed against financial institutions by individuals who lost money when Enron went under in 2001. In 2005, RBC paid $25 million to settle its liability, and the interim CEO at Enron agreed that RBC played only a minor role in Enron's collapse. Also in 2005, CIBC agreed to pay $2.4 *billion* to get out of the Enron class action lawsuit. That is the biggest payout of any of the financial institutions that were sued (U.S.-based JP Morgan Chase & Co. paid $2.2 billion and Citigroup paid $2 billion). CIBC denied any wrongdoing and said the payment was designed to reduce the uncertainty of future litigation over Enron.

As we consider these cases, we might conclude that the ethical level of business executives has declined in recent years. That's a possibility, but a more likely explanation is that the stock market "bubble" of the late 1990s magnified some already existing human weaknesses, including greed and a tendency to "skate on the edge." Human greed probably hasn't increased in the last few years, but the opportunities to satisfy it have. Another reason is the failure of checks and balances that were supposed to prevent this kind of behaviour. Professionals such as accountants, lawyers, audit committees, government regulators, the press, and securities analysts are supposed to make sure that executives do not do things that are detrimental to shareholders, but critics feel that they often fail to do their job. A third reason is stock options (see Concluding Case 19-2), which may give executives an incentive to behave badly.

The best explanation of unethical executive behaviour is probably a combination of these three reasons. But what does the future hold? Were the excesses of the executives listed above caused by just a "few bad apples," or is the system broken? The view that there are just a "few bad apples" is supported by some statistics. For example, in the United States (where much of the high-profile bad behaviour has occurred), the Securities and Exchange Commission (SEC) investigated 570 companies in 2001. That sounds like a lot, but it's only slightly higher than the number investigated in 1994. Another statistic: only about one company in 100 restates its earnings. This suggests that the system needs only a minor fix-up.

The counter view is that there really has been a decline in the general level of ethical behaviour, and that the headline cases are just symptomatic of a very big problem. If we accept this view, it follows that the current legislation is inadequate to deal with the problem, and the only solution is to develop tough new legislation that will control the tendency of executives to behave in an unethical and illegal fashion. ◆

ETHICS IN THE WORKPLACE

ethics Individual standards or moral values regarding what is right and wrong or good and bad.

ethical behaviour Behaviour that conforms to individual beliefs and social norms about what is right and good.

unethical behaviour Behaviour that individual beliefs and social norms define as wrong and bad.

business ethics Ethical or unethical behaviours by a manager or employee of an organization.

Ethics are beliefs about what is right and wrong or good and bad. An individual's personal values and morals and the social context in which they occur determine whether a particular behaviour is perceived as ethical or unethical. **Ethical behaviour** is behaviour that conforms to individual beliefs and social norms about what is right and good. **Unethical behaviour** is behaviour that individual beliefs and social norms define as wrong and bad. **Business ethics** is a term often used to refer to ethical or unethical behaviour by a manager or employee of an organization.

Individual Ethics

1 Explain how individuals develop their personal *codes of ethics* and why ethics are important in the workplace.

Because ethics are based on both individual beliefs and social concepts, they vary from person to person, from situation to situation, and from culture to culture. Social standards are broad enough to support differences in beliefs. Without violating general standards, therefore, people may develop personal codes of ethics reflecting a wide range of attitudes and beliefs.

Thus ethical and unethical behaviour is determined partly by the individual and partly by culture. For instance, virtually everyone would agree that if you see someone drop a $20 bill in a store, it would be ethical to return it to the owner. But there'll be less agreement if you find $20 and don't know who dropped it. Should you turn it in to the lost-and-found department? Or, since the rightful owner isn't likely to claim it, can you just keep it?

Societies generally adopt formal laws that reflect prevailing ethical standards or social norms. For example, because most people regard theft as unethical, we have laws against such behaviour and ways of punishing those who steal. We try to make unambiguous laws, but interpreting and applying them can still lead to ethical ambiguities. Real-world situations can often be interpreted in different ways, and it isn't always easy to apply statutory standards to real-life behaviour. Samuel Waksal, former CEO of ImClone, was convicted of insider trading for tipping off certain investors, including Martha Stewart and members of his own family, about the impending fall of ImClone stock. Stewart said that she simply ordered her broker to sell the stock if it slipped below $60. But in 2004, she was convicted of lying to investigators and served several months in prison. Meanwhile, Waksal's daughter, who also sold her ImClone stock after getting information from her father, has so far been treated as an "innocent tippee"—someone who got inside information but didn't think that's what it was at the time.[1]

The epidemic of scandals ranging from Enron and Arthur Andersen to Tyco and WorldCom only serves to show how willing people can be to take advantage of potentially ambiguous situations. The Business Accountability box describes another situation where there are conflicting views about what is ethical.

Individual Values and Codes

How should we deal with business behaviour that we regard as unethical—especially when it's legally ambiguous? No doubt we have to start with the individuals in a business—its managers, employees, agents, and other legal representatives. Each of these people's personal code of ethics is determined by a combination of factors. We start to form ethical standards as children in response to our perceptions of the behaviour of parents and other adults. Soon, we enter school, where peers influence us, and as we grow into adulthood, experience shapes our lives and contributes to our ethical beliefs and our behaviour. We also develop values and morals that contribute to ethical standards. If you put financial gain at the top of your priority list, you may develop a code of ethics that supports the pursuit of material comfort. If you set family and friends as a priority, you'll no doubt adopt different standards.

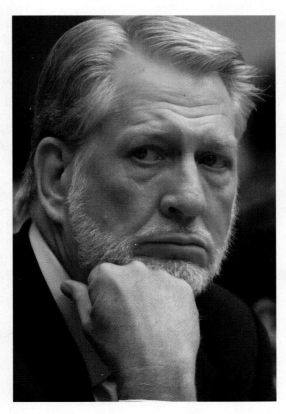

When telecommunications giant WorldCom (now MCI) collapsed amid a record-setting $1 billion bankruptcy in 2003, just about everybody who had anything to do with corporate accounting was arrested. Chief Financial Officer Scott Sullivan pleaded guilty to criminal charges and agreed to testify against his former boss, Canadian-born Bernard Ebbers (pictured here). In 2006, Ebbers was sentenced to 25 years in prison for his role in the collapse.

Because ethics are both personally and culturally defined, differences of opinion can arise as to what is ethical or unethical. For example, many people who would never think of taking a candy bar from a grocery store routinely take home pens and pads of paper from their offices. Other people who view

BUSINESS ACCOUNTABILITY

Crossing the Ethical Line?

In 2005, the CIBC World Markets sued six former employees after they left the company and started a new rival firm, Genuity Capital Markets (a total of 18 people left CIBC for Genuity). While asking for $10 million in damages, CIBC charged that the six people (a) planned their new company while they were still on CIBC's payroll, (b) took confidential information with them when they left CIBC, and (c) attempted to steal both top performers and clients from CIBC for the new company. All of this occurred, it is alleged, while the six executives were being handsomely paid by CIBC.

The defendants in the lawsuit are David Kassie (formerly CEO of CIBC World Markets), Daniel Daviau (formerly an investment banker at CIBC who specialized in the technology and media sectors), Phil Evershed (former head of mergers and acquisitions at CIBC), Earl Rotman (CIBC World Markets vice-chairman), John Esteireiro (head trader at CIBC), and David Morrsion (a top salesman). Evershed, Rotman, and Daviau each received more than $3 million in salary and severance pay from the bank just before they left for Genuity. One of the conditions of their leaving was that they would not try to hire any CIBC employees for 21 months.

In the document it filed with a Toronto court, CIBC provided detailed information from hundreds of pages of emails allegedly showing how the six former employees had frequently discussed the formation of Genuity while they were still employed at CIBC. It was also alleged that these emails listed the names of CIBC employees who were to be recruited for the new company. One other serious allegation has been made by CIBC: that an IT specialist downloaded confidential client information before she left CIBC (the IT specialist claims that she was simply copying disks for her successor, that she didn't give the information to Genuity, and that Genuity is willing to open its computers to support her story).

The founders of Genuity argue that they have done nothing unethical or illegal. One of the key points in their defence is that they didn't break any rules by hiring employees of CIBC to work at Genuity, because these employees had already decided to leave CIBC. Genuity simply provided them with a new place to work.

Some observers think this lawsuit is not so much about Genuity as it is about duty, integrity, honour, and trust. In other words, it's about business ethics. As the leader in the industry, CIBC is not really very concerned about a small new competitor like Genuity being started, but it is concerned about the "slippery" way that it was formed. CIBC also wants to send a message to its remaining employees that CIBC's corporate culture is all about honesty and fair dealing, and that its culture is so important that CIBC will pursue employees (or former employees) who don't act appropriately. The CIBC also wants to hold the six former employees to a certain ethical standard because they were paid very well for the work they did.

Others who have analyzed this interesting situation question the quality of the leadership that was evident at CIBC in the year or so before the employee exodus. They ask, for example, what the board of directors at CIBC was doing when rumours about the start of Genuity were swirling around Bay Street. They also ask what effect the hiring of Kassie's replacement at CIBC had on employees who did not leave (the defendants claim that once Kassie's replacement was announced, that Genuity received many applications from CIBC employees).

It is not clear that this dispute will ever actually be heard in court because both sides have much to lose. CIBC has the financial resources to support an expensive court battle, but if it loses it will not be able to make its point about the importance of ethical behaviour. Genuity, on the other hand, is a new company that needs to establish a reputation of integrity, and a nasty court fight isn't going to do much to help the company achieve that goal.

In the past, lawsuits like this one usually did not result in a full trial, but were settled with a small award (for example, the loser made a contribution to charity). When a full trial does happen, the usual ruling is that individuals have the right to work where they want, but that taking data or enticing a group to leave are not acceptable. Since CIBC alleged that the latter two things occurred, a full trial would be very interesting.

themselves as law-abiding citizens have no qualms about using radar detectors to avoid speeding tickets. In each of the situations, people will choose different sides of the issue and argue that their actions are ethical.

Managerial Ethics

Managerial ethics are the standards of behaviour that guide individual managers in their work.[2] Although your ethics can affect your work in any number of ways, it's helpful to classify them in terms of three broad categories.

managerial ethics Standards of behaviour that guide individual managers in their work.

Behaviour Toward Employees

This category covers such matters as hiring and firing, wages and working conditions, and privacy and respect. Ethical and legal guidelines suggest that hiring and firing decisions should be based solely on ability to perform a job. A manager who discriminates against any ethnic minority in hiring exhibits both unethical and illegal behaviour. But what about the manager who hires a friend or relative when someone else might be more qualified? Such decisions may not be illegal; but they may be objectionable on ethical grounds.

Wages and working conditions, though regulated by law, are also areas for controversy. Consider a manager who pays a worker less than he deserves because the manager knows that the employee can't afford to quit or risk his job by complaining. While some people will see the behaviour as unethical, others will see it as smart business. Cases such as these are hard enough to judge, but consider the behaviour of Enron management toward company employees. It encouraged employees to invest retirement funds in company stock and then, when financial problems began to surface, refused to permit them to sell the stock (even though top officials of the company were allowed to sell their stock). Ultimately, the firm's demise cost thousands of jobs.

Behaviour Toward the Organization

Ethical issues also arise from employee behaviour toward employers, especially in such areas as conflict of interest, confidentiality, and honesty. A conflict of interest occurs when an activity may benefit the individual to the detriment of his or her employer. Most companies have policies that forbid buyers from accepting gifts from suppliers. Businesses in highly competitive industries—software and fashion apparel, for example—have safeguards against designers selling company secrets to competitors. Relatively common problems in the general area of honesty include such behaviour as stealing supplies, padding expense accounts, and using a business phone to make personal long-distance calls. Most employees are honest, but most organizations are nevertheless vigilant. Again, Enron is a good example of employees' unethical behaviour toward an organization. Top managers not only misused corporate assets, but they often committed the company to risky ventures to further personal interests.

Behaviour Toward Other Economic Agents

Ethics also come into play in the relationship between the firm and its so-called primary agents of interest—mainly customers, competitors, stockholders, suppliers, dealers, and unions. In dealing with such agents, there is room for ethical ambiguity in just about every activity—advertising, financial disclosure, ordering and purchasing, bargaining and negotiation, and other business relationships.

For example, businesses in the pharmaceuticals industry are under criticism because of the rising prices of drugs. They argue that high prices cover the costs of research and development programs to develop new drugs. The solution to such problems seems obvious: Find the right balance between reasonable pricing and *price gouging* (which means responding to increased demand with overly steep price increases). But like so many questions involving ethics, there are significant differences of opinion about the proper balance.[3]

Another area of concern is competitive espionage. In 2004, Air Canada sued WestJet for $220 million, claiming that a WestJet executive had electronically snooped on Air Canada's confidential reservation database, which contained important competitive information that would be beneficial to WestJet. WestJet then filed a $30 million counter-suit, claiming that Air Canada had filed its suit in an attempt to destroy WestJet's reputation. It also claimed that Air Canada had "set up" WestJet by allowing one of WestJet's executives to get into the supposedly confidential Air Canada database. WestJet also charged that Air Canada had hired a firm to steal the garbage of a WestJet executive in the hopes of finding important financial information about WestJet.[4] In 2005, a judge denied WestJet's claim. In mid-2006, the Air Canada claim was still in process.

The difficulty of dealing with these problems is compounded by the fact that business practices vary globally. In many countries, bribes are a normal part of doing business. However, in Canada and the United States, bribes are seen as unethical and illegal. For example, in 2006 the Gemological Institute of America (GIA) fired several employees after they had accepted bribes from diamond dealers. In return for the bribes, the GIA employees rated the dealers' diamonds higher than they should have been, and this allowed the dealers to sell them for a much higher price. The GIA also banned two groups of dealers from having their diamonds rated by the GIA.[5]

Assessing Ethical Behaviour

By definition, what distinguishes ethical behaviour from unethical behaviour is often subjective and subject to differences of opinion.[6] So, how does one go about deciding whether a particular action or decision is ethical? A three-step model can be used for applying ethical judgments to situations that may arise during the course of business activities:

1. Gather the relevant factual information.

2. Determine the most appropriate moral values.

3. Make an ethical judgment based on the rightness or wrongness of the proposed activity or policy.

Unfortunately, the process does not always work as smoothly as the three steps suggest. What if the facts are not clear-cut? What if there are no agreed-upon moral values? Nevertheless, a judgment and a decision must be made. Experts point out that, otherwise, trust is impossible; and trust, they add, is indispensable to any business transaction.

To more fully assess the ethics of a particular behaviour, we need a more refined process. Let's consider a common dilemma faced by managers involving their expense accounts. Companies routinely provide managers with accounts to cover work-related expenses when they are travelling on company business and/or entertaining clients for business purposes. Common examples of such expenses include hotel bills, meals, rental cars or taxis, and so forth. Employees, of course, are expected to claim only those expenses that are accurate and work-related. For example, if a manager takes a client to dinner while travelling on business and spends $100, submitting a receipt for that dinner to be reimbursed for $100 is clearly accurate and appropriate. Suppose, however, that the manager then has a

$100 dinner the next night in that same city with a good friend for purely social purposes. Submitting that receipt for full reimbursement would be unethical. A few managers, however, will rationalize that it is acceptable to submit a receipt for dinner with a friend. They will argue, perhaps, that they are underpaid and are simply increasing the income due to them.

Other principles that come into play in a case like this include various ethical norms. Consider four such norms and the issues that they entail:

Utility: Does a particular act optimize what is best for those who are affected by it?
Rights: Does it respect the rights of the individuals involved?
Justice: Is it consistent with what we regard to be fair?
Caring: Is it consistent with people's responsibilities to each other?

Figure 3.1 incorporates the consideration of these ethical norms.

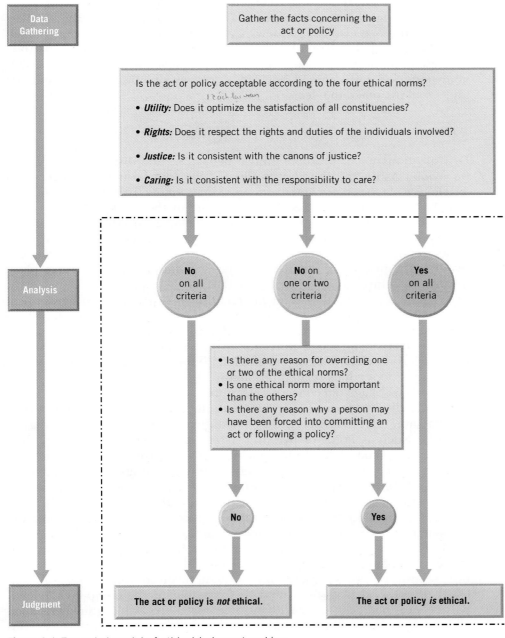

Figure 3.1 Expanded model of ethical judgment making.

Now, let's return to the case of the inflated expense account. While the utility norm would acknowledge that the manager benefits from padding an expense account, others, such as co-workers and owners, do not. Likewise, most experts would agree that it does not respect the rights of others. Moreover, it is clearly unfair and compromises the manager's responsibilities to others. This particular act, then, appears to be clearly unethical.

Figure 3.1, however, also provides mechanisms for considering unique circumstances—those that apply only in certain limited situations. Suppose, for example, that the manager loses the receipt for the legitimate dinner but retains the receipt for the social dinner. Some people will argue that it is acceptable to submit the illegitimate receipt because the manager is only doing so to be reimbursed for what he or she is entitled to. Others, however, will continue to argue that submitting the other receipt is wrong under any circumstances. We won't pretend to arbitrate the case. For our purposes, we will simply make the following point: Changes in the situation can make issues more or less clear-cut.

When judging how ethical a certain behaviour is, one of the simplest "tests" to use is the so-called "newspaper test." This means asking yourself this question: If you were to make a decision on an ethical issue and then read about it on the front page of tomorrow's paper, how would you feel? If you would feel embarrassed, you are very likely violating ethical standards and shouldn't make the decision.

Company Practices and Business Ethics

Organizations try to promote ethical behaviour and discourage unethical behaviour. As unethical and even illegal behaviour by both managers and employees plagues more and more companies, many firms have taken additional steps to encourage ethical behaviour in the workplace. Many, for example, establish codes of conduct and develop clear ethical positions on how the firm and its employees will conduct its business. An increasingly controversial area regarding business ethics and company practices involves the privacy of email and other communications that take place inside an organization.

Technological developments are creating all sorts of brand-new ethical problems—cloning, satellite reconnaissance, and bioengineered foods, to name just a few. For every innovation that promises convenience or safety, there seems to be a related ethical issue. The internet and email, for example, are certainly convenient and efficient, but they present business people with a variety of ethics-related problems.

In one set of age-old concerns, electronic communications merely substitute for traditional forms of communication, such as mail or the telephone. By the same token, however, they make it possible to run all the classic swindles, such as Ponzi or pyramid schemes, with greater efficiency than ever before. Federal law-enforcement personnel routinely surf the web looking for illegal or unethical practices, often finding hundreds of questionable sites in a typical sting. Employers are also using email to test employee loyalty, as in the case of the manager who sent false emails to his workers, pretending to be a recruiter from a competing firm. Any employees who responded were skipped for promotion.

Perhaps the single most effective step a company can take is to demonstrate top management support of high ethical standards. A classic illustration of the power of ethical commitment involved Johnson & Johnson (J&J). In 1982, it was discovered that capsules of the company's Tylenol pain reliever had been laced with cyanide. Managers at J&J quickly recalled all Tylenol bottles still on retailers' shelves and then went public with candid information throughout the crisis. J&J's ethical choices proved to be a crucial factor in its campaign to rescue its product. Both the firm and the brand bounced back much more quickly than anyone thought possible. More recently, when some Belgian schoolchildren became ill after drinking Coke, the company quickly determined what the problem was and Coke's CEO made a public apology. The furor died down almost immediately.[7]

In addition to demonstrating an attitude of honesty and openness, firms can take specific and concrete steps to formalize their commitment to ethical business practices. Two of the most common approaches to formalizing commitment are adopting written codes and instituting ethics programs.

Adopting Written Codes

Many companies have adopted written codes of ethics that formally acknowledge their intent to do business in an ethical manner. Most codes of ethics are designed to perform one or more of the following functions:

- They may increase public confidence in a firm or its industry.
- They may help stem the tide of government regulation—that is, aid in self-regulation.
- They may improve internal operations by providing consistent standards of both ethical and legal conduct.
- They can help managers respond to problems that arise as a result of unethical or illegal behaviour.

Figure 3.2 shows the code of ethics adopted by Mountain Equipment Co-op.

Figure 3.3 illustrates the central role that corporate ethics and values should play in corporate policy. Although strategies and practices can change frequently and objectives can change occasionally, an organization's core principles and values should remain steadfast.

Our Purpose To support people in achieving the benefit of wilderness-oriented recreation.	Our **purpose** is what we resolve to do.
Our Vision Mountain Equipment Co-op is an innovative, thriving co-operative that inspires excellence in products and services, passion for wilderness experiences, leadership for a just world, and action for a healthy planet.	Our **vision** is our picture of the future and outlines where we want to go.
Our Mission Mountain Equipment Co-op provides quality products and services for self-propelled wilderness-oriented recreation, such as hiking and mountaineering, at the lowest reasonable price in an informative, respectful manner. We are a member-owned co-operative striving for social and environmental leadership.	Our **mission** tells us what business we are in, who we serve, and how. It represents the fundamental reason for MEC's existence.
Our Values We conduct ourselves ethically and with integrity. We show respect for others in our words and actions. We act in the spirit of community and co-operation. We respect and protect our natural environment. We strive for personal growth, continual learning, and adventure.	Our **values** influence our conduct both collectively as an organization, and individually as employees, directors and members of our community. We strive to have our actions reflect these values, demonstrate personal accountability, and be publicly defensible.

Figure 3.2 Mountain Equipment Co-op's statements of purpose, vision, mission, and values make up their code of ethics.

Figure 3.3 Core principles and organizational values.

Two-thirds of Canada's largest corporations have codes of ethics (90 percent of large U.S. firms do). More and more regulatory and professional associations in Canada are recommending that corporations adopt codes of ethics. The Canada Deposit Insurance Corp., for example, requires that all deposit-taking institutions have a code of conduct that is periodically reviewed and ratified by the board of directors. The Canadian Competition Bureau, the Canadian Institute of Chartered Accountants, and the Ontario Human Rights Commission are all pushing for the adoption of codes of ethics by corporations.[8] Many Canadian and U.S. firms are adding a position called "Ethics Director" or "Ethics Officer."

Instituting Ethics Programs

Many examples suggest that ethical responses can be learned through experience. For instance, in the Tylenol case, company employees didn't wait for instructions or a company directive for dealing with the problem. They knew that they should get to retailers' shelves and pull the product as quickly as possible. They reported simply "knowing" that this was what the company should do.

But can business ethics be taught, either in the workplace or in schools? Not surprisingly, business schools have become important players in the debate about ethics education. Even though business schools must address the issue of ethics in the workplace, the practical reality is that companies must take the chief responsibility for educating employees. In fact, more and more firms are doing so. Imperial Oil, for example, conducts workshops for employees that emphasize ethical concerns. The purpose of these workshops is to help employees put Imperial Oil's ethics statement into practice.

SOCIAL RESPONSIBILITY

social responsibility A business's collective code of ethical behaviour toward the environment, its customers, its employees, and its investors.

organizational stakeholders Groups, individuals, and organizations that are directly affected by the practices of an organization and that therefore have a stake in its performance.

2 Distinguish *social responsibility* from *ethics*, identify *organizational stakeholders*, and characterize social consciousness today.

Ethics affect individual behaviour in the workplace. **Social responsibility**, however, refers to the way in which a business tries to balance its commitments to certain groups and individuals in its social environment. **Organizational stakeholders** are those groups, individuals, and organizations that are directly affected by the practices of an organization and that therefore have a stake in its performance.[9]

But which of these stakeholders should be given the most attention? One view, often called *managerial capitalism*, is that a company's only social responsibility is to make as much money as possible for its shareholders, as long as it doesn't break any laws. An opposing view is that companies must be responsible to various stakeholders, including *customers, employees, investors, suppliers*, and the *local communities* in which they do business. Some of these stakeholders may be particularly important to the organization and so it will have to pay particular attention to their needs and expectations.

The Stakeholder Model of Responsibility

Most companies that strive to be responsible to their stakeholders concentrate on the five groups shown in Figure 3.4. They may then select other stakeholders that are particularly relevant or important to the organization and try to address their needs and expectations as well.

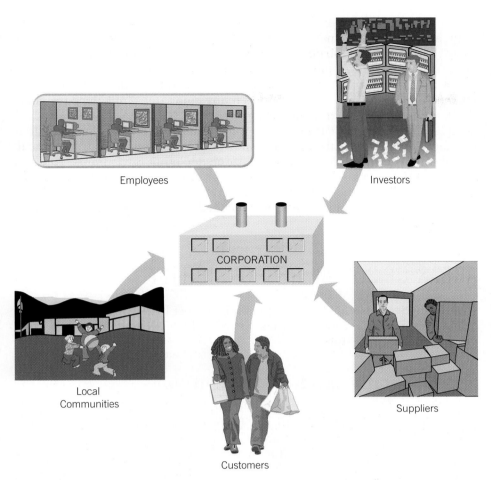

Figure 3.4 Major corporate stakeholders.

Contemporary Social Consciousness

Canadian society and Canadian business have changed dramatically in the last two centuries. Not surprisingly, so have views about social responsibility. The late nineteenth century was characterized by the entrepreneurial spirit and the laissez-faire philosophy. During this era of labour strife and predatory business practices, both individual citizens and the government became concerned about unbridled business activity. This concern was translated into laws regulating basic business practices.

During the Great Depression of the 1930s, many people blamed the failure of businesses and banks and the widespread loss of jobs on a general climate of business greed and lack of restraint. Out of the economic turmoil emerged new laws that described an increased expectation that business should protect and enhance the general welfare of society.

During the social unrest of the 1960s and 1970s, business was often characterized as a negative social force. Eventually, increased activism prompted increased government regulation in a variety of areas. Health warnings, for example, were placed on cigarettes, and stricter environmental protection laws were enacted.

Social consciousness and views toward social responsibility continue to evolve in the twenty-first century. Today's attitudes seem to be moving toward an enlightened view stressing the need for a greater social role for business. An increased awareness of the global economy and heightened campaigning on the part of environmentalists and other activists have combined to make many businesses more sensitive to their social responsibilities.

For example, retailers such as Sears have policies against selling hand-guns and other weapons, and toy retailer Toys "R" Us refuses to sell toy guns that look too realistic. Firms in numerous other industries have also integrated socially conscious thinking into their production plans and marketing efforts. The production of environmentally safe products, for example, has become a potential boom area, as many companies introduce products designed to be "environmentally friendly."

Electrolux, a Swedish appliance maker, has developed a line of water-efficient washing machines, a solar-powered lawnmower, and, for Brazil, the first refrigerators that are free of ozone-depleting refrigerants. Herman Miller, a Michigan-based office-furniture business, uses recycled materials and focuses on products that are simple in design, durable, and recyclable. Ford has set up an independent brand called Th!nk to develop and market fuel cells.[10]

AREAS OF SOCIAL RESPONSIBILITY

3 Show how the concept of social responsibility applies both to environmental issues and to a firm's relationships with customers, employees, and investors.

In defining its sense of social responsibility, most firms must confront four areas of concern: responsibilities toward the environment, customers, employees, and investors.

Responsibility Toward the Environment

pollution The injection of harmful substances into the environment.

One critical area of social responsibility involves how the business relates to its physical environment. In the following sections, we focus on the nature of the problems in these areas and on some of the current efforts to address them.[11] Controlling **pollution**—the injection of harmful substances into the environment—is a significant challenge for contemporary business. Although noise pollution is attracting increased concern, air pollution, water pollution, and land pollution are the subjects of most anti-pollution efforts by business and governments.[12]

The Kyoto Summit in 1997 was an attempt by various governments to reach agreement on ways to reduce the threat of pollution. Australia is the world's largest greenhouse gas emitter per capita, contributing 7.3 percent of the world's total. The United States (at 6.5 percent) and Canada (at

Why would a Western environmental group team up with a domestic logging company to help local villagers log a forest in a remote area of Indonesia? For one thing, the villagers are very poor. For another, the Nature Conservancy believes that it can enforce sustainable practices if the logger, Sumalindo Lestari Jaya, co-operates. The group also thinks that it can trust Sumalindo because it's already been successful in applying pressure to Western retailers like Home Depot and IKEA, who buy wood and paper from the Indonesian supplier.

ENTREPRENEURSHIP AND NEW VENTURES

Actions Speak Louder Than Words

When it comes to corporate social responsibility (CSR), one notable Canadian trailblazer is Mountain Equipment Co-op (MEC). MEC was formed in 1971 by four students from the University of British Columbia whose vision was to "inspire excellence in products and services, passion for wilderness experiences, leadership for a just world, and action for a healthy planet." The company's actions speak louder than words.

MEC's commitment to the environment is demonstrated in many aspects of its business, including the name of its CSR program: Social and Environmental Responsibility. The program's mandate ensures that environmental and social issues are weighed equally.

As a co-operative, MEC does not issue investment shares. Only MEC members—the customers—are permitted to own shares in the company, which are valued at five dollars apiece. Because MEC does not issue investment shares, maximizing shareholder wealth is not its exclusive focus. While MEC members may not see a direct financial return on their shares, in effect, they pass the returns on to the communities and groups that benefit from MEC's altruistic activities.

Some of MEC's revenue each year is allocated to sustainable community development projects, typically through donations for charitable or educational purposes. The MEC Endowment Fund for the Environment—MEC's own registered charity—was created in 1993. Each year, 0.4 percent of the previous year's sales are injected into MEC's Environment Fund. At first glace, this may not seem like a substantial amount, but that 0.4 percent translates into an average of $750 000 per year in contributions to environmental conservation and wilderness protection projects, research, and education. The endowment fund, which accepts tax deductible donations, is currently valued at $1.2 million and has historically been used to support land acquisition projects.

But to truly practise social and environmental responsibility, MEC recognizes that it must do more than provide money to environmental organizations.

Product manufacturers must adhere to a strict set of guidelines established to ensure that the products sold in MEC stores are manufactured in safe and healthy workplaces where human and civil rights are respected.

The co-op is even more scrupulous about MEC-brand products (58 percent of which are manufactured in Canada), which comprise approximately 60 percent of sales. In addition to its own Supply Team Evaluation Process, MEC uses third-party, independent audits to ensure that the suppliers of MEC-brand products avoid child and forced labour and that workers are treated with respect and dignity and are not subjected to harassment, discrimination, or abuse. Workers must be allowed to join unions and bargain collectively, and they must be paid fairly and directly. Safe and healthy work environments must comply with local health and safety laws and regulations. Suppliers of MEC-brand products are also required to implement and maintain systems to minimize negative impacts of manufacturing and packaging on the environment and to ensure that waste is disposed of in an environmentally responsible manner.

For the past five years, MEC has been greening its buildings by making design, materials, and construction decisions based on environmental considerations. To be considered green by MEC's standards, a building must be built and sustained by resources available within its immediate area. And it should enhance (or at least not detract from) its natural environment. MEC building designers scrutinize every building element and make choices based on a number of criteria, including embodied energy and pollution content, energy efficiency, and recycling potential. Some of the more tangible innovations found in MEC's green buildings include the use of geothermal energy heat pumps in Montreal, a demonstration straw-bale wall in Ottawa, and composting toilets in Winnipeg.

When construction on MEC's Winnipeg store was completed in 2002, it became the second retail building in Canada to meet the national C2000 Green Building Standard—second only to MEC's Ottawa location.

6.4 percent) are close behind. Canada is the only one of the three leading emitters that has signed the Protocol. Transalta is the Canadian company with the biggest emission problem, but it has a plan to reduce its greenhouse gas emissions by 15 percent.[13] In 2006, the Conservative government said Canada would not be able to meet the targets for reducing pollution, and that it would continue with the Protocol only if the targets were renegotiated.[14]

Air Pollution

Air pollution results when a combination of factors converge to lower air quality. Large amounts of chemicals, such as the carbon monoxide emitted by automobiles, contribute to air pollution. Smoke and other chemicals emitted by manufacturing plants also help to create air pollution.

Legislation has gone a long way toward controlling air pollution. Under new laws, many companies have had to install special devices to limit the pollutants they expel into the atmosphere. Such clean-up efforts are not without costs, however. The bill to private companies for air pollution control devices runs into billions of dollars.

Figure 3.5 tells a troubling story. The chart shows atmospheric carbon dioxide (CO_2) levels for the period between 1750 and 2000, and it offers three possible scenarios for future levels under different sets of conditions. The three projections—lowest, middle, highest—were developed by the Intergovernmental Panel on Climate Change, which calculated likely changes in the atmosphere during this century if no efforts were made to

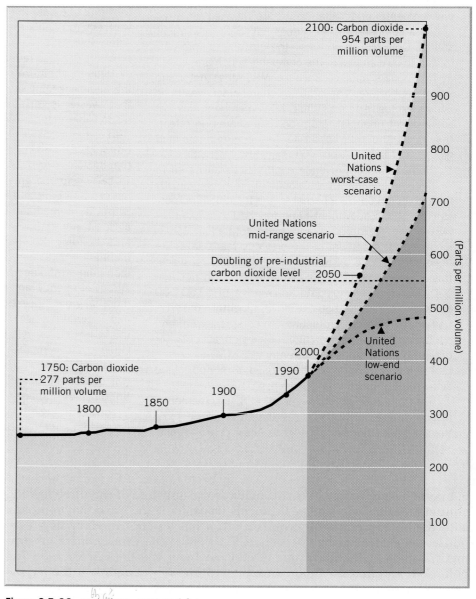

Figure 3.5 CO_2 emissions, past and future.

reduce so-called greenhouse emissions—waste gases that trap heat in the atmosphere. The criteria for estimating changes are population, economic growth, energy supplies, and technologies: The less pressure exerted by these conditions, the less the increase in CO_2 levels. Energy supplies are measured in exajoules—roughly the annual energy consumption of a large metropolitan area like New York or London.

Under the lowest, or best-case, scenario, by 2100 the population would only grow to 6.4 billion people, economic growth would be no more than 1.2 to 2.0 percent a year, and energy supplies would require only 8000 exajoules of conventional oil. However, under the highest, or worst-case, scenario, the population would increase to 11.3 billion people, annual economic growth would be between 3.0 and 3.5 percent, and energy supplies would require as much as 18 400 exajoules of conventional oil.

The resulting changes in climate would be relatively mild, and we would not experience dramatic changes in the weather. We would, however, increase the likelihood of having troublesome weather around the globe: droughts, hurricanes, and so forth. The charges levelled against greenhouse emissions are disputed, but as one researcher puts it, "The only way to prove them for sure is hang around 10, 20, or 30 more years, when the evidence would be overwhelming. But in the meantime, we're conducting a global experiment. And we're all in the test tube."[15]

Water Pollution

For years, businesses and municipalities dumped their waste into rivers, streams, and lakes with little regard for the effects. Thanks to new legislation and increased awareness on the part of businesses, water quality is improving in many areas. Millar Western Pulp Ltd. built Canada's first zero-discharge pulp mill at Meadow Lake, Saskatchewan. There is no discharge pipe to the river, no dioxin-forming chlorine, and next to no residue. Dow Chemical built a plant at Fort Saskatchewan that will not dump any pollutants into the nearby river.[16]

Land Pollution

Two key issues are associated with land pollution. The first issue is how to restore the quality of land damaged and abused in the past. In 1998, 5 million cubic litres of toxic waste escaped from a holding pond at a zinc mine in Spain that was operated by the Canadian firm Boliden Ltd. Thousands of hectares of agricultural land were contaminated.[17] A second issue is how to prevent such problems in the future. Changes in foresting practices, limits on types of mining, and new forms of solid waste disposal are all attempts to address this issue, although such changes are often opposed.

Concern for the environment has influenced the actions of many Canadian firms as they do business abroad. In many cases, there is opposition to a project by the local people because they fear that some sort of pollution will result. For example, Calgary-based TVI Pacific Inc.'s planned open-pit mine and cyanide processing plant in the Philippines led to violent clashes between the company and the Subanon people. Critics of Inco Ltd.'s Goro mine in New Caledonia claimed that it would damage the second-largest barrier reef system in the world. And a group of villagers in Thailand objected to a potash mine that was proposed by Asia Pacific Potash Corp., arguing that the project would increase salt levels in the soil and damage their ability to grow rice.[18]

Toxic Waste Disposal. Toxic wastes are dangerous chemical and/or radioactive by-products of various manufacturing processes. Because toxic waste cannot usually be processed into harmless material or destroyed, it must be stored somewhere. The problem is—where? Few people want a toxic waste storage facility in their town. Toxic waste disposal and clean-up have become increasingly important areas of debate and concern in recent years.

Many business firms are now acting to reduce various forms of pollution. Under the Canadian and Ontario environmental protection acts, liability for a business firm can run as high as $2 million per day. To protect themselves, companies must prove that they showed diligence in avoiding an environmental disaster such as an oil or gasoline spill.[19] The Environmental Choice program, sponsored by the federal government, licenses products that meet environmental standards set by the Canadian Standards Association. Firms whose products meet these standards can put the logo— three doves intertwined to form a maple leaf—on their products.[20]

Recycling. The conversion of waste materials into useful products—recycling—is a relatively new industry that has developed as part of increased consciousness about land pollution. Certain products, such as aluminum beverage cans and glass, can be very efficiently recycled. Others, such as plastics, are more troublesome. Many local communities actively support various recycling programs, including curbside pickup of aluminum, plastics, glass, and pulp paper.

biomass The plant and animal waste that is used to produce energy.

The plant and animal waste used to produce energy is referred to as **biomass**. Waste materials like sawdust, manure, and sludge are increasingly being turned into useful products. Ensyn Corp., for example, converts sawdust into liquid fuel by blasting wood waste with a sand-like substance that is heated. What's left is bio-oil.[21]

Responsibility Toward Customers

Social responsibility toward customers generally falls into one of two categories: providing quality products and pricing those products fairly. As with the environment, firms differ in their level of concern about responsibility to customers. Yet unlike environmental problems, customer problems do not require expensive technological solutions. Most such problems can be avoided if companies obey the laws regarding consumer rights, avoid illegal pricing practices, and behave ethically when advertising their products.

Rights of Consumers

consumerism A social movement that seeks to protect and expand the rights of consumers in their dealings with businesses.

Much of the current interest in business responsibility toward customers can be traced to the rise of consumerism. **Consumerism** is a form of social activism dedicated to protecting the rights of consumers in their dealings with businesses.

Consumers have the following rights:

1. The right to safe products. For example, when you buy a new paint sprayer, it must be safe to use for spraying paint. It must come with instructions on how to use it, and it must have been properly tested by its manufacturer. Dow Corning Corp. halted production of silicone breast implants after questions were raised about the product's safety. When the British government announced a possible link between "mad cow disease" and Creutzfeld-Jakob disease, McDonald's and Burger King suspended the sale of all British beef products. More recently, Canadian beef was banned from the United States when one case of mad cow disease was found in Alberta.

2. The right to be informed about all relevant aspects of a product. Food products must list their ingredients. Clothing must be labelled with information about its proper care. And banks must tell you exactly how

much interest you are paying on a loan. Cereal companies have come under fire recently for some of the claims they have made about the oat bran content of their cereals, as well as its likely effects.

3. **The right to be heard.** Many companies today have complaints offices. Retailers like Kmart offer a money-back guarantee if consumers aren't satisfied. Procter & Gamble puts a toll-free number on many of its products that consumers can call if they have questions or complaints. When companies refuse to respond to consumer complaints, consumer protection agencies such as the Better Business Bureau and consumer interest groups such as the Airline Passengers Association may intervene.

4. **The right to choose what they buy.** Central to this right is free and open competition among companies. In times past, "gentlemen's agreements" were often used to avoid competition or to divide up a market so that firms did not have to truly compete against each other. Such practices are illegal today and any attempts by business to block competition can result in fines or other penalties.

5. **The right to be educated about purchases.** All prescription drugs now come with detailed information regarding dosage, possible side effects, and potential interactions with other medications.

6. **The right to courteous service.** This right is hard to legislate, but as consumers become increasingly knowledgeable, they're more willing to complain about bad service. Consumer hotlines can also be used to voice service-related issues.

The problems with the diet pill called Pondimin illustrate what can happen to a firm that violates one or more of these consumer rights. Throughout the early 1990s, American Home Products aggressively marketed the drug, which contained fenfluramine. Doctors wrote millions of prescriptions for Pondimin and other medications containing fenfluramine. In 1997, however, a link was discovered between the pills and heart-valve disease. A class-action lawsuit followed, and the firm eventually agreed to pay $3.75 billion to individuals who had used the drug.[22]

Unfair Pricing

Interfering with competition can also mean illegal pricing practices. **Collusion** among companies—getting together to "fix" prices—is against the law. Polar Plastic Ltd. of Montreal pled guilty to conspiring to fix prices of disposable cups, glasses, and cutlery in the U.S. market. Although secret meetings and phone conversations took place between executives of competing companies as they tried to fix prices, the conspiracy was not successful.[23]

collusion An illegal agreement among companies in an industry to "fix" prices for their products.

The U.S. Justice Department is investigating 150 cases of pricing fraud by some of the world's biggest drug companies. The main allegation is that drug companies inflate prices of the drugs they sell to government-paid programs. In 2003 and 2004, several drug companies paid the following penalties: Pfizer ($430 million), Schering-Plough ($345 million), Bayer ($257 million), and GlaxoSmithKline ($88 million). The new charges may mean that up to $1 billion in fines will eventually be levied.[24]

Under some circumstances, firms can also come under attack for price gouging—responding to increased demand with overly steep (and often unwarranted) price increases. For example, when DaimlerChrysler launched its PT Cruiser in 2000, demand for the vehicles was so strong that some dealers sold them only to customers willing to pay thousands of dollars over sticker prices. Some Ford dealers adopted a similar practice when the new Thunderbird was launched in 2002. As we saw in Chapter 1, this illustrates what can happen when there is a shortage of a product.

Of all roadway accidents, 25 percent are distraction-related, and the biggest distractions for motorists are handheld gadgets like cellphones, pagers, and the like. In fulfilling their responsibility to consumers, some companies are conducting tests which yield important data about roadway accidents. Ford Motor Co., for example, has a Virtual Test Track Experiment simulator that determines how often drivers get distracted. Under normal circumstances, an adult driver will miss about 3 percent of the simulated "events" (like an ice patch or a deer on the road) that Ford contrives for a virtual road trip. If they're on the cellphone, they'll miss about 14 percent. Teenagers miss a scary 54 percent of the events.

Ethics in Advertising

In recent years increased attention has been given to ethics in advertising and product information. Because of controversies surrounding the potential misinterpretation of words and phrases such as "light," "reduced calorie," "diet," and "low fat," food producers are now required to use a standardized format for listing ingredients on product packages. There are several key ethical issues in advertising, including truth-in-advertising claims, the advertising of counterfeit brands, the use of stealth advertising, and advertising that is morally objectionable.

Truth in Advertising. Concerns about truth in advertising are becoming more noticeable on the international scene. In July 2005, for example, Chinese government officials investigated Procter & Gamble's claim that its Pantene shampoo made hair "10 times stronger." A few months earlier, P&G paid a $24 000 fine after one consumer complained that SK-II Skin Cream was not the "miracle water" it claimed to be and that it did not make her skin "look 12 years younger in 28 days."[25]

Advertising of Counterfeit Brands. Another issue concerns the advertising and sale of counterfeit brand names. Canadians tourists who visit New York often go to booths on Canal Street, which is famous for the "bargains" that can be had on supposedly name brand items like Cartier, Panerai, Vacheron, Montblanc, and Louis Vuitton. Many of the items being sold are counterfeit, although it can be very hard to tell the difference between these "knockoffs" and the genuine article. A fake Cartier Roadster watch, for example, can be bought on Canal Street for U.S.$45, while a real one costs about U.S.$3400. Naturally, legitimate manufacturers of these high-end products are trying to stamp out this counterfeit trade in their products.[26]

China is the source of many counterfeit products. For example, knockoffs of Suzuki motorcycles hit the market just a few weeks after the genuine product became available. These knockoffs were sold to customers as the real thing, but they had not been subjected to rigorous quality control like real Suzuki motorcycles are. Robert Kwauk, a Beijing lawyer, says that the idea of producing knockoffs is tolerated much more in the Chinese culture than it is in Western culture.[27] North Korea has become one of the leading counterfeiters of name brand cigarettes like Marlboro.[28]

stealth (undercover) advertising Involves companies paying individuals to extol the virtues of their products, without disclosing that they are paid to do so.

Stealth (Undercover) Advertising. **Stealth (or undercover) advertising—**which is a variation of viral marketing that we discussed in Chapter 2—involves companies paying individuals to extol the virtues of their products to other individuals. The ethics of this are questionable when the paid individuals do not reveal that they are being paid by a company, so the recipient of the advertising is not aware that it is advertising. For example, one advertising agency hired models to pose as "tourists." These models asked real tourists to take their picture with a new Sony Ericsson camera cellphone. The models then talked up the advantages of the new product to the unsuspecting real tourists. Commercial Alert, a U.S.-based consumer protection group, wants a government investigation of these undercover marketing tactics.[29]

Morally Objectionable Advertising. A final ethical issue concerns advertising that consumers consider to be morally objectionable. Benetton, for example, aired a series of commercials featuring inmates on death row. The ads, dubbed "We, on Death Row," prompted such an emotional outcry that Sears dropped the Benetton USA clothing line.[30] Other ads receiving criticism include Victoria's Secret models in skimpy underwear, and campaigns by tobacco and alcohol companies that allegedly target young people.

Responsibility Toward Employees

Organizations also need to employ fair and equitable practices with their employees. Later, in Chapter 8, we describe the human resource management activities essential to a smoothly functioning business. These same activities—recruiting, hiring, training, promoting, and compensating—are also the basis for social responsibility toward employees. A company that provides its employees with equal opportunities for rewards and advancement without regard to race, sex, or other irrelevant factors is meeting its social responsibilities. Firms that ignore their responsibility to employees leave themselves open to lawsuits. They also miss the chance to hire better and more highly motivated employees.

Legal and Social Commitments

Some progressive companies go well beyond these legal requirements, hiring and training the so-called hard-core unemployed (people with little education and training and a history of unemployment) and those who have disabilities. The Bank of Montreal, for example, sponsors a community college skills upgrading course for individuals with hearing impairments. The Royal Bank provides managers with discrimination awareness training. Rogers Cablesystems Ltd. provides individuals with mobility restrictions with telephone and customer-service job opportunities.[31] Bell Canada employs more than 1000 people with disabilities (2 percent of its permanent workforce). But, in Canada, over 50 percent of those with physical disabilities are still unemployed.[32]

In addition to their responsibility to employees as resources of the company, firms have a social responsibility to their employees as people. Firms that accept this responsibility ensure that the workplace is safe, both physically and emotionally. They would no more tolerate an abusive manager or one who sexually harasses employees than they would a gas leak.

Business firms also have a responsibility to respect the privacy of their employees. While nearly everyone agrees that companies have the right to exercise some level of control over their employees, there is great controversy about exactly how much is acceptable in areas such as drug testing and computer monitoring. When Canadian National Railways instituted drug testing for train, brake, and yard

The safety of workers is an important consideration for all organizations. The required use of hardhats, for example, is designed to protect workers from head injuries.

employees, 12 percent failed. Trucking companies have found that nearly one-third of truckers who have been involved in an accident are on drugs.[33]

Employees are often unaware that they are being monitored by managers who are using new computer technology. Computer software firms even sell programs called "Spy" and "Peek" to facilitate monitoring. This type of monitoring increases employee stress levels because they don't know exactly when the boss is watching them. A lawsuit was brought against Nortel Networks by employees who charged that the firm installed telephone bugs and hidden microphones in one of its plants.[34]

Whistle-Blowers. Respecting employees as people also means respecting their behaviour as ethically responsible individuals. Suppose, for instance, an employee discovers that a business has been engaging in practices that are illegal, unethical, or socially irresponsible. Ideally, this employee should be able to report the problem to higher-level management, confident that managers will stop the questionable practices. Enron's Sherron Watkins reported concerns about the company's accounting practices well before the company's problems were made public, warning top management that Enron would "implode in a wave of accounting scandals." CEO Kenneth Lay commissioned a legal review of the firm's finances but told his investigators not to "second-guess" decisions by Enron's auditor, accounting firm Arthur Andersen.[35]

Too often, people who try to act ethically on the job find themselves in trouble with their employers. If no one in the organization will take action, the employee might elect to drop the matter. Occasionally, however, the individual will inform a regulatory agency or perhaps the media. At this point, he or she becomes a **whistle-blower**—an employee who discovers and tries to put an end to a company's unethical, illegal, or socially irresponsible actions by publicizing them.[36] The 1999 Al Pacino–Russell Crowe movie *The Insider* told the true story of a tobacco-industry whistle-blower named Jeffrey Wigand.

Unfortunately, whistle-blowers are often demoted—and even fired— when they take their accusations public. Jeffrey Wigand was fired. "I went from making $300 000 a year," he reports, "plus stock options, plus, plus, plus—to making $30 000. Yes, there is a price I've paid."[37] Even if they retain their jobs, they may still be treated as outsiders and suffer resentment or hostility from co-workers. Many co-workers see whistle-blowers as people who simply can't be trusted. One recent study suggests that about half of all whistle-blowers eventually get fired, and about half of those who get fired subsequently lose their homes and/or families.[38] New federal legislation to protect whistle-blowers was introduced in Canada in 2003.

When Phillip Adams worked in the computer industry, he discovered a flaw in the chip-making process that, under certain circumstances, could lead to data being randomly deleted or altered. He reported the flaw to manufacturers, but several years later, he found that one company, Toshiba, had ignored the problem and continued to make flawed chips for 12 years. He went on to report the problem and became actively involved in a class-action lawsuit based heavily on his research. Toshiba eventually agreed to a U.S.$2.1 billion settlement. Adams's share was kept confidential, but he did receive a substantial reward for his efforts.[39] Unfortunately, the prospect of large cash rewards has also generated a spate of false or questionable accusations.

whistle-blower An individual who calls attention to an unethical, illegal, and/or socially irresponsible practice on the part of a business or other organization.

Responsibility Toward Investors

It may sound odd to say that a firm can be irresponsible toward investors, since they are the owners of the company. But if managers abuse their firm's financial resources, the ultimate losers are the owners, since they do not receive the earnings, dividends, or capital appreciation due them.

Improper Financial Management

Occasionally, organizations are guilty of financial mismanagement. In other cases, executives have been "guilty" of paying themselves outlandish salaries, spending huge amounts of company money for their own personal comfort, and similar practices. Creditors can do nothing. Even shareholders have few viable options. Trying to force a management changeover is not only difficult, it can drive down the price of the stock, a penalty shareholders are usually unwilling to assign themselves.

Cheque Kiting

Cheque kiting involves writing a cheque from one account, depositing it in a second account, and then immediately spending money from the second account while the money from the first account is still in transit. A cheque from the second account can also be used to replenish the money in the first account, and the process starts all over again. This practice obviously benefits the person doing the cheque kiting, but is irresponsible because it involves using other peoples' money without paying for it.

cheque kiting The illegal practice of writing cheques against money that has not yet arrived at the bank on which the cheque has been written, relying on that money arriving before the cheque clears.

Insider Trading

Another area of illegal and socially irresponsible behaviour by firms toward investors is the practice of insider trading. **Insider trading** occurs when someone uses confidential information to gain from the purchase or sale of stocks. The most famous recent example is, of course, Martha Stewart, who served jail time. More detail about insider trading is provided in the Opening Case for Chapter 19.

insider trading The use of confidential information to gain from the purchase or sale of stock.

Misrepresentation of Finances

Certain behaviours regarding financial representation are also illegal. In maintaining and reporting its financial status, every corporation must conform

"*From a purely business viewpoint, taking what doesn't belong to you is usually the cheapest way to go.*"

to generally accepted accounting principles (GAAP)—see Chapter 14. Sometimes, however, unethical managers project profits far in excess of what they actually expect to earn; others go so far as to hide losses and/or expenses to boost paper profits. When the truth comes out, however, the damage is often substantial.

Various issues involving the misrepresentation of finances were central in the Enron case. One review, for example, called Enron's accounting practices "creative and aggressive." It seems that CFO Andrew Fastow had set up a complex network of partnerships that were often used to hide losses. Enron, for instance, could report all the earnings from a partnership as its own while transferring all or most of the costs and losses to the partnership. Inflated profits would then support increased stock prices.[40]

IMPLEMENTING SOCIAL RESPONSIBILITY PROGRAMS

Thus far, we have discussed social responsibility as if a consensus exists on how firms should behave in most situations. In fact, dramatic differences of opinion exist as to the appropriateness of social responsibility as a business goal. As you might expect, some people oppose any business activity that cuts into profits to investors. Others argue that responsibility must take precedence over profits.

Even people who share a common attitude toward social responsibility by businesses may have different reasons for their beliefs. Some opponents of such activity fear that if businesses become too active in social concerns, they will gain too much control over how those concerns are addressed. They point to the influence many businesses have been able to exert on the government agencies that are supposed to regulate their industries. Other critics of business-sponsored social programs argue that companies lack the expertise needed. They believe that technical experts, not businesses, should decide how best to clean up a polluted river, for example.

Supporters of social responsibility believe that corporations are citizens just like individuals and therefore need to help improve our lives. Others point to the vast resources controlled by businesses and note that since businesses often create many of the problems social programs are designed to alleviate, they should use their resources to help. Still others argue that social responsibility is wise because it pays off for the firm.

The late Max Clarkson, formerly a top-level business executive and director of the Centre for Corporate Social Performance and Ethics at the University of Toronto, said that business firms that had a strong consciousness about ethics and social responsibility outperform firms that do not. After designing and applying a social responsibility rating system for companies, he found that companies that had the highest marks on questions of ethics and social responsibility also had the highest financial performance.[41]

Approaches to Social Responsibility

4 Identify four general *approaches to social responsibility* and describe the four steps a firm must take to implement a *social responsibility program.*

Given these differences of opinion, it is little wonder that corporations have adopted a variety of approaches to social responsibility. As Figure 3.6 illustrates, the four stances an organization can take concerning its obligations to society fall along a continuum ranging from the lowest to the highest degree of socially responsible practices.

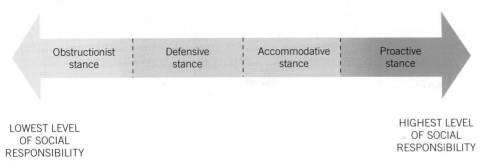

Figure 3.6 Spectrum of approaches to corporate social responsibility.

Obstructionist Stance

The few organizations that take what might be called an **obstructionist stance** to social responsibility usually do as little as possible to solve social or environmental problems. When they cross the ethical or legal line that separates acceptable from unacceptable practices, their typical response is to deny or cover up their actions. Firms that adopt this position have little regard for ethical conduct and will generally go to great lengths to hide wrongdoing.

obstructionist stance A company does as little as possible to solve social or environmental problems.

Defensive Stance

One step removed from the obstructionist stance is the **defensive stance**, whereby the organization will do everything that is required of it legally but nothing more. This approach is most consistent with arguments against corporate social responsibility. Managers who take a defensive stance insist that their job is to generate profits. Such a firm, for example, would install pollution-control equipment dictated by law, but would not install higher-quality equipment even though it might further limit pollution.

Tobacco companies generally take this position in their marketing efforts. In Canada and the United States, they are legally required to include warnings to smokers on their products and to limit advertising to prescribed media. Domestically, they follow these rules to the letter of the law but use more aggressive marketing methods in countries that have no such rules. In many Asian and African countries, for example, cigarettes are heavily promoted, contain higher levels of tar and nicotine than those sold in Canada and the United States, and carry few or no health warning labels. Firms that take this position are unlikely to cover up wrongdoing, will generally admit to mistakes, and will take appropriate corrective actions.

defensive stance An organization does only what is legally required and nothing more.

Accommodative Stance

A firm that adopts an **accommodative stance** meets its legal and ethical requirements, but will also go further in certain cases. Such firms voluntarily agree to participate in social programs, but solicitors must convince them that these programs are worthy of their support. Many organizations respond to requests for donations to community hockey teams, Girl Guides, youth soccer programs, and so forth. The point, however, is that someone has to knock on the door and ask; accommodative organizations do not necessarily or proactively seek avenues for contributing.

accommodative stance A company meets all of its legal and ethical requirements, and in some cases even goes beyond what is required.

Proactive Stance

The highest degree of social responsibility a firm can exhibit is the **proactive stance**. Firms that adopt this approach take to heart the arguments in

proactive stance An organization actively seeks opportunities to be socially responsible.

favour of social responsibility. They view themselves as citizens in a society and proactively seek opportunities to contribute. The most common—and direct—way to implement this stance is by setting up a foundation through which to provide direct financial support for various social programs.

These stances are not sharply distinct; they merely label stages along a continuum of social responsibility. Organizations do not always fit neatly into one category or another. The Ronald McDonald House program has been widely applauded, for example, but McDonald's has also come under fire for allegedly misleading consumers about the nutritional value of its food products. Likewise, while UPS has sincere motives for helping Olympic athletes, the company will also benefit by featuring their photos on its envelopes and otherwise promoting its own benevolence.

Corporate Charitable Donations. Donating money to different "causes" is one way that business firms try to show that they are socially responsible. Many groups that used to receive government funding (but no longer do because of government spending cuts) are increasingly seeking corporate support for their activities. More and more corporations are being asked to donate money to educational institutions, welfare agencies, service clubs, arts and culture groups, and athletic organizations.

A Decima Research survey found that 80 percent of Canadians think that businesses should give some of their profits to social causes.[42] An Environics survey of people in 23 different countries found that two-thirds of them thought that business was not doing enough if it simply abided by the law and provided employment. Instead, these people think that companies should also contribute to the broader goals of society.[43] A third survey, conducted by the Centre for Philanthropy, found that Canadian corporations contributed less than 2 percent of all charitable revenue. Canadians think that this number is closer to 20 percent, and that it should be 30 percent.[44]

Corporations that gave substantial amounts of money to charity in 2005 were the RBC Financial Group ($40 million), BMO Financial Group ($29.5 million), and TELUS Corp. ($11 million). Corporations typically give less than half of 1 percent of their pre-tax profits to charity, but many have demonstrated a willingness to give money and products when disasters strike.

When seven people died in Walkerton, Ontario, as a result of drinking contaminated water, companies such as Petro-Canada, Shoppers Drug Mart, Sobeys, and Zellers contributed products such as bleach and bottled water. And when thousands of people died in the Asian tsunamis of 2004, companies from around the world rushed aid to the stricken areas. They donated drugs, mobile telephones, machinery, medical equipment, water, and free travel for relief workers.[45] Companies generally receive favourable publicity when they make contributions like these, but they can be accused of being opportunistic if they attempt to publicize their donations.[46]

Most large business firms in Canada have clear procedures for dealing with requests from charities and community organizations. The company first determines how much money it will give each year, usually stated as a percentage of profit. It then decides which specific organizations will receive the money and the amount each will receive. The board of directors makes these decisions after it receives a recommendation from a committee that has been set up to consider charitable requests. Companies are increasingly taking a community-based approach to giving; they try to determine how they can achieve value for the community (and the company) with their donations.

Managing Social Responsibility Programs

Making a company truly socially responsible in the full sense of the proactive stance takes an organized and managed program. In particular, managers must take four steps to foster social responsibility, as shown in Figure 3.7.

1. Social responsibility must start at the top and be considered as a factor in strategic planning. Without the support of top management, no program can succeed. Thus, top management must embrace a strong stand on social responsibility and develop a policy statement outlining that commitment.

2. A committee of top managers must develop a plan detailing the level of management support. Some companies set aside percentages of profits for social programs. Levi Strauss, for example, earmarks 2.4 percent of pre-tax earnings for worthy projects. Managers must also set specific priorities. For instance, should the firm train the hard-core unemployed or support the arts?

3. One executive must be put in charge of the firm's agenda. Whether the role is created as a separate job or added to an existing one, the selected individual must monitor the program and ensure that its implementation is consistent with the firm's policy statement and strategic plan.

4. The organization must conduct occasional social audits. **Social audits** are systematic analyses of its success in using funds earmarked for its social responsibility goals.[47] Consider the case of a company whose strategic plan calls for spending $100 000 to train 200 hard-core unemployed people and to place 180 of them in jobs. If at the end of a year, the firm has spent $98 000, trained 210 people, and filled 175 jobs, a social audit will confirm the program's success. But if the program has cost $150 000, trained only 90 people, and placed only 10 of them, the audit will reveal the program's failure. Such failure should prompt a rethinking of the program's implementation and its priorities.

social audit A systematic analysis of how a firm is using funds earmarked for social-responsibility goals and how effective these expenditures have been.

In addition to social audits, Canadian businesses are increasingly publishing sustainability reports. These reports go beyond simply financial

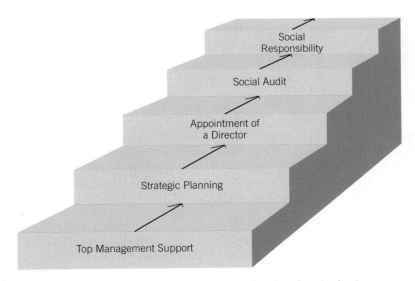

Figure 3.7 Establishing a social responsibility program involves four basic steps.

Ronald McDonald House helps the families of children who are in hospital care. It is supported by McDonald's and is an excellent example of socially responsible behaviour by a business corporation.

triple bottom line reporting
Measuring the social, environmental, and economic performance of a company.

reporting and explain how the company is performing on issues such as the environment, employee relations, workplace diversity, and business ethics. A study by Ottawa-based Stratos Inc. found that 70 percent of Canada's largest public companies now report at least some sustainability performance information.[48] Social audits and sustainability reports together constitute **triple bottom line reporting**—measuring the social, environmental, and economic performance of a company.[49]

Social Responsibility and the Small Business

5 Explain how issues of social responsibility and ethics affect small businesses.

Although many of the examples in this chapter illustrate responses to social responsibility and ethical issues by big business, small businesses face many of the same questions. As the owner of a garden supply store, how would you respond to a building inspector's suggestion that a cash payment would expedite your application for a building permit? As the manager of a nightclub, would you call the police, refuse service, or sell liquor to a customer whose ID card looks forged? Or as the owner of a small laboratory, would you actually call the board of health to make sure that it has licensed the company you want to contract with to dispose of the lab's medical waste? Is the small manufacturing firm justified in overcharging a customer by 5 percent whose purchasing agent is lax? Who will really be harmed if a small firm pads its income statement to help get a much-needed bank loan?

Can a small business afford a social agenda? Should it sponsor hockey teams, make donations to the United Way, and buy light bulbs from the Lion's Club? Is joining the Chamber of Commerce and supporting the Better Business Bureau too much or just good business? Clearly, ethics and social responsibility are decisions faced by all managers in all organizations, regardless of rank or size. One key to business success is to decide in advance how to respond to these issues.

Summary of Learning Objectives

1. **Explain how individuals develop their personal *codes of ethics* and why ethics are important in the workplace.** Individual codes of ethics are derived from social standards of right and wrong. Ethical behaviour is behaviour that conforms to generally accepted social norms concerning beneficial and harmful actions. Because ethics affect the behaviour of individuals on behalf of the companies that employ them, many firms are adopting formal statements of ethics. Unethical behaviour can result in loss of business, fines, and even imprisonment.

2. **Distinguish *social responsibility* from *ethics*, identify *organizational stakeholders*, and characterize social consciousness today.** Social responsibility refers to the way a firm attempts to balance its commitments to organizational stakeholders. One way to understand social responsibility is to view it in terms of stakeholders— those groups, individuals, and organizations that are directly affected by the practices of an organization and that therefore have a stake in its performance. Until the second half of the nineteenth century, businesses often paid little attention to stakeholders. Since then, however, both public pressure and government regulation, especially as a result of the Great Depression of the 1930s and the social activism of the 1960s and 1970s, have forced businesses to consider public welfare, at least to some degree. A trend toward increased social consciousness, including a heightened sense of environmental activism, has recently emerged.

3. **Show how the concept of social responsibility applies both to environmental issues and to a firm's relationships with customers, employees, and investors.** Social responsibility toward the environment requires firms to minimize pollution of air, water, and land. Social responsibility toward customers requires firms to provide products of acceptable quality, to price products fairly, and to respect consumers' rights. Social responsibility toward employees requires firms to respect workers both as resources and as people who are more productive when their needs are met. Social responsibility toward investors requires firms to manage their resources and to represent their financial status honestly.

4. **Identify four general *approaches to social responsibility* and describe the four steps a firm must take to implement a *social responsibility program*.** An obstructionist stance on social responsibility is taken by a firm that does as little as possible to address social or environmental problems and that may deny or attempt to cover up problems that may occur. The defensive stance emphasizes compliance with legal minimum requirements. Companies adopting the accommodative stance go beyond minimum activities, if asked. The proactive stance commits a company to actively seek to contribute to social projects. Implementing a social responsibility program entails four steps: (1) drafting a policy statement with the support of top management, (2) developing a detailed plan, (3) appointing a director to implement the plan, and (4) conducting social audits to monitor results.

5. **Explain how issues of social responsibility and ethics affect small businesses.** Managers and employees of small businesses face many of the same ethical questions as their counterparts at larger firms. Small businesses face the same issues of social responsibility and the same need to decide on an approach to social responsibility. The differences are primarily differences of scale.

KEY TERMS

accommodative stance,   93
biomass,   86
business ethics,   72
cheque kiting,   91
collusion,   87
consumerism,   86
defensive stance,   93
ethical behaviour,   72

ethics,   72
insider trading,   91
managerial ethics,   75
obstructionist stance,   93
organizational stakeholders,   80
pollution,   82
proactive stance,   93
social audit,   95

social responsibility,   80
stealth (undercover) advertising,   88
triple bottom line reporting,   96
unethical behaviour,   72
whistle-blower,   90

QUESTIONS FOR ANALYSIS

1. Write a one-paragraph description of an ethical dilemma which you, or someone you know, faced recently. What was the outcome in the situation? Was it consistent with what you thought should have occurred? Why or why not? Analyze the situation using the ideas presented in the chapter. Make particular reference to the ethical norms of utility, rights, justice, and caring in terms of how they impacted the situation. What would each of these suggest about the correct decision? Does this analysis lead you to a different conclusion about the best outcome? Explain.

2. Develop an example of the way in which your personal code of ethics might clash with the operations of a specific company. How might you try to resolve these differences?

3. What kind of wrongdoing would most likely prompt you to be a whistle-blower? What kind of wrongdoing would be least likely? Why?

4. In your opinion, which area of social responsibility is most important? Why? Are there areas other than those noted in the chapter that you consider important?

5. Identify some specific ethical or social responsibility issues that might be faced by small business managers and employees in each of the following areas: environment, customers, employees, and investors.

6. Choose a product or service and explain the social responsibility concerns that are likely to be evident in terms of the environment, customers, employees, and investors.

7. Analyze the forces that are at work from both the company's perspective and the whistle-blower's perspective. Given these forces, what characteristics would a law to protect whistle-blowers have to have to be effective?

8. Pick a product or service that demonstrates the defensive approach to social responsibility. What has been the impact of that stance on the company that is using it? Now pick a product or service for each of the other stances (obstructionist, accommodative, and proactive) and do the same analysis. Why did these companies adopt the particular stance they did?

APPLICATION EXERCISES

1. Develop a list of the major stakeholders of your college or university. As a class, discuss the ways in which you think the school prioritizes these stakeholders. Do you agree or disagree with this prioritization?

2. Using newspapers, magazines, and other business references, identify and describe at least three companies that take a defensive stance to social responsibility, three that take an accommodative stance, and three that take a proactive stance.

BUILDING YOUR BUSINESS SKILLS

To Lie Or Not to Lie: That Is the Question

Goal

To encourage students to apply general concepts of business ethics to specific situations.

Background

Workplace lying, it seems, has become business as usual. According to one survey, one-quarter of working adults said that they had been asked to do something illegal or unethical on the job. Four in 10 did what they were told. Another survey of more than 2000 secretaries showed that many employees face ethical dilemmas in their day-to-day work.

Assignment

Step 1

Working with four other students, discuss ways in which you would respond to the following ethical dilemmas. When there is a difference of opinion among group members, try to determine the specific factors that influence different responses.

■ Would you lie about your supervisor's whereabouts to someone on the phone?

■ Would you lie about who was responsible for a business decision that cost your company thousands of dollars to protect your own or your supervisor's job?

▶ ▶ ▶

▶▶▶

- Would you inflate sales and revenue data on official company accounting statements to increase stock value?

- Would you say that you witnessed a signature when you did not if you were acting in the role of a notary?

- Would you keep silent if you knew that the official minutes of a corporate meeting had been changed?

- Would you destroy or remove information that could hurt your company if it fell into the wrong hands?

Step 2

Research the commitment to business ethics at Johnson & Johnson (www.jnj.com/our_company/our_credo/index. htm) and Texas Instruments (www.ti.com/corp/docs/ company/citizen/ethics/index.shtml) by visiting their respective websites. As a group, discuss ways in which these statements are likely to affect the specific behaviours mentioned in Step 1.

Step 3

Working with group members, draft a corporate code of ethics that would discourage the specific behaviours mentioned in Step 1. Limit your code to a single type-written page, but make it sufficiently broad to cover different ethical dilemmas.

Follow-Up Questions

1. What personal, social, and cultural factors do you think contribute to lying in the workplace?

2. Do you agree or disagree with the following statement? "The term *business ethics* is an oxymoron." Support your answer with examples from your own work experience or that of a family member.

3. If you were your company's director of human resources, how would you make your code of ethics a "living document"?

4. If you were faced with any of the ethical dilemmas described in Step 1, how would you handle them? How far would you go to maintain your personal ethical standards?

EXERCISING YOUR ETHICS

Taking a Stance

The Situation

A perpetual debate revolves around the roles and activities of business owners in contributing to the greater social good. Promoting the so-called proactive stance, some people argue that businesses should be socially responsible by seeking opportunities to benefit the society in which they are permitted to conduct their affairs. Others maintain a defensive stance, saying that because businesses exist to make profits for owners, they have no further obligation to society.

The Dilemma

Pair up with one of your classmates. Using a coin toss, each of you should be assigned to one side of this debate. You and your partner should then enter into a dialogue to formulate the three most convincing arguments possible to support each side. Then select the single strongest argument in support of each position. Each team of two partners should then present to the class its strongest arguments for and against social responsibility on the part of business.

Questions for Discussion

1. Which side of the debate is easier to defend? Why?

2. What is your personal opinion about the appropriate stance that a business should take regarding social responsibility?

3. To what extent is the concept of social responsibility relevant to non-business organizations such as universities, government units, health-care organizations, and so forth?

High Seas Dumping

Cruising has become a very popular vacation. More than eight million passengers take an ocean voyage each year, cruising many areas of the world's oceans in search of pristine beaches and clear tropical waters. The Caribbean Sea, the Mediterranean Sea, and the coast of Alaska are among the most popular destinations, while the coasts of Europe and Asia are also growing in popularity. The tourists and the giant ships that carry them are usually welcome for the revenues that they bring, but these ships also bring something much less desirable—pollution.

A modern cruise ship carries an average of 2000 passengers and 1000 crew members. That many people generate a lot of waste. On a typical day, a ship will produce seven tons of solid garbage, which is incinerated and then dumped (15 gallons of highly toxic chemical waste; 30 000 gallons of sewage; 7000 gallons of bilge water containing oil; and 225 000 gallons of "grey" water from sinks and laundries). Cruise ships also pick up ballast water whenever and wherever it's needed and then discharge it later, releasing animals and pollution from other parts of the world. Multiply this problem by more than 167 ships worldwide, cruising 50 weeks per year, and the scope of the environmental damage is staggering.

Environmental groups see the top pollution-related problem as death of marine life, including extinction. Foreign animals bring parasites and diseases, and in some cases, replace native species entirely. Bacteria that are harmless to human beings can kill corals that provide food and habitat for many species. Oil and toxic chemicals are deadly to wildlife even in minute quantities. Turtles swallow plastic bags, thinking they are jellyfish, and starve, while seals and birds drown after becoming entangled in the plastic rings that hold beverage cans.

Other problems include the habitat destruction or disease that affects certain industries. For example, cholera, picked up in ships' ballast water off the coast of Peru, caused a devastating loss to fish and shrimp harvesters in the Gulf of Mexico in the 1990s when infected catches had to be destroyed. Heavy metal poisoning of fish is rising, and concern is on the rise that the poisons are moving up the food chain from microscopic animals, to fish, and ultimately to humans. Phosphorus found in detergents causes an overgrowth of algae, which then consume all the available oxygen in the water, making it incapable of supporting any flora or fauna.

Lack of regulation is the biggest obstacle to solving the problem. By international law, countries may regulate oceans for three miles off their shores. International treaties provide some additional regulation up to 25 miles offshore. Beyond the 25-mile point, however, ships are allowed free rein. Also, each country's laws and enforcement policies vary considerably, and even when laws are strict, enforcement may be limited. One would think that cruise lines would be cognizant of the importance of clean and safe seas for their own economic well-being. Sadly, however, this is often not the case.

Intentional illegal dumping may be growing in scope. Over the last decade, for instance, as enforcement has tightened, 10 cruise lines have collectively paid $48.5 million in fines related to illegal dumping. In the largest settlement to date, Royal Caribbean paid $27 million for making illegal alterations to facilities, falsifying records, lying to the U.S. Coast Guard, and deliberately destroying evidence. The fine may seem high, but it covers 30 different charges and 10 years' of violations and seems small compared to the firm's billions of profits over the past few years. Royal Caribbean's fine was less than what the firm would have paid to dispose of the waste properly over a one-year period. In addition, a lawsuit is pending regarding the firing of a whistle-blower, the firm's former vice president for safety and environment. "This [case] is like the Enron of the seas," says attorney William Amlong, who represents the whistle-blower.

Critics are speaking out against the cruise lines' profiteering from an environment that they are destroying, but they note that the companies won't stop as long as the profits continue. Technology exists to make the waste safe, but industry experts estimate that dumping can save a firm millions of dollars annually. From that perspective, Royal Caribbean and Norwegian are making understandable decisions.

Questions for Discussion

1. What are the major legal issues in this case? What are the major ethical issues?

2. Aside from personal greed, what factors might lead a cruise line to illegally dump waste into the ocean?

3. Which approach to social responsibility do cruise lines appear to be taking?

4. Distinguish between ethical issues and social responsibility issues as they apply to this problem.

CONCLUDING CASE 3-2

Ethical Lapses at Volkswagen

In 2005, a middle manager named Klaus-Joachim Gebauer was fired from Volkswagen (VW) for allegedly embezzling money from the company. A few weeks later, he began making serious allegations about unethical behaviour at VW. Specifically, he claimed that VW had sent several German labour leaders to Brazil so they could tour VW's production facilities in Sao Paulo and meet with local Brazilian union officials. Gebauer (who went along on the trip) alleged that after the business part of the trip was over, the group checked into the Othon Palace and then explored the "nightlife" of Rio. This included visits to prostitutes. Gebauer paid for everything and then submitted phony receipts so that VW would reimburse him for all the expenses the group incurred on the trip. He says he was told by his boss to do this in order to gain worker representatives' support for VW management.

Gebauer claims that this was just one of many trips that VW paid for during the period 1996–2004. Visits were also made to Argentina, India, Portugal, France, Poland, and the Czech Republic. For each of these trips, Gebauer drew up a legitimate-looking business agenda, which he says was a complete fake. German state prosecutors are now looking into the allegations, particularly the ones that VW illegally used company funds to pay for labour leaders to go on pleasure junkets.

There has long been a "cozy" relationship between management and labour in German companies, partly as a result of German laws. For example, approximately half the positions on supervisory boards of German companies are occupied by workers' representatives. In addition, German law requires that companies pay for legitimate business expenses of its labour representatives. Many observers have concluded that the close relationship between labour and management explains Germany's economic success during the past 30 years because Germany was able to avoid much of the labour strife that occurred in so many other countries. But now, critics are pointing to the problems that such a close relationship can cause.

When Gebauer initially made his charges, VW dismissed his claims and pointed out that he had been fired for embezzlement and for seeking kickbacks from possible VW business partners. But as time passed, Gebauer's allegations began to look more credible. By early 2006, prosecutors had identified nine individuals (including some labour representatives) who may have been involved. The prosecutors also said they had uncovered evidence of criminal wrongdoing.

VW now appears to be accepting that something was not right, because it asked KPMG to investigate the abuse of travelling expenses by some employees. The CEO of VW, Bernd Pischetsrieder, said that the auditors found that $740 000 had been paid to an acquaintance of VW's labour leader Klaus Volkert for "services" that were not approved. VW also acknowledged that the necessary control system to catch improper expenses was not in place.

This unpleasant situation is not the only one that VW has been involved in during the last decade. In the 1990s, the company also received bad publicity when its chief purchasing agent, Jose Ignacio Lopez de Arriortua, was charged by the U.S. Justice Department with stealing secret General Motors documents and turning them over to VW (Lopez had previously been the chief purchasing agent for General Motors and had access to GM's plans). GM also filed a civil suit against VW claiming that Lopez stole GM's plans for new cars, parts lists, price lists, and plans for a secret manufacturing plant. It claimed that VW used this information to lower its costs and to gain market share at GM's expense.

VW originally denied the allegations, but then the district attorney of Darmstadt, Germany, discovered confidential GM documents at the home of another former GM executive who had, like Lopez, defected to VW. At stake was the public's perception of VW's ethics—an intangible factor that could affect the company's sales. When a German polling organization asked 1000 Germans what they thought of the Lopez affair, 65 percent believed that there was "something to" the allegations, while only 7 percent felt they were unfounded.

VW eventually agreed to give GM $100 million in cash, and to purchase $1 billion in parts from GM. Lopez also resigned from VW and GM dropped its civil suit.

Questions for Discussion

1. What factors at VW encouraged the behaviour that Mr. Gebauer described?

2. What steps should VW take to ensure that such behaviour is not allowed to occur again?

3. How concerned should a company like VW be with the public's reaction to questionable behaviour by its managers? Defend your answer.

4. Consider the Lopez situation. Does an employee have an ethical responsibility to maintain the confidentiality of information gained on the job with one company when taking a job with a competing company? Explain your reasoning.

CHAPTER 4*

Understanding Entrepreneurship, Small Business, and New Venture Creation

After reading this chapter, you should be able to:

1 Explain the meaning of and inter-relationship among the terms *small business*, *new venture creation*, and *entrepreneurship*.

2 Describe the role of small and new businesses in the Canadian economy.

3 Explain the *entrepreneurial process* and describe its three key elements.

4 Describe three alternative strategies for becoming a business owner—*starting*, *buying an existing business*, and *buying a franchise*.

5 Describe four forms of *legal organization* for a business and discuss the advantages and disadvantages of each.

6 Identify four key reasons for success in small businesses and four key reasons for failure.

*This chapter was written by Dr. Monica Diochon, St. Francis Xavier University.

The year was 1994. Sandra Wilson, a young wife and mother, was downsized out of her airline job. She welcomed the chance to spend more time with her 18-month-old son Robert, and became inspired by his tiny feet. Lovingly she handcrafted a pair of brightly coloured, soft-soled leather shoes for young Robert. Indeed, the shoes seemed to improve his balance as the soft soles allowed him to "feel" the floor while he toddled about.

Wilson began to wonder: If these soft-soled shoes worked so well for Robert, perhaps other mothers would find them a good product for their children's developing feet. Wilson saw this as an opportunity to start her own business. Naming the footwear after her son, "Robeez" was born. After hand-stitching 20 pairs of her footwear, she attended the 1994 Vancouver Gift Show trade exhibition. The response? Overwhelming. The orders flooded in and she signed up 15 retailers ready to sell her product.

Wilson threw herself into production. Her home's basement became Robeez Footwear's early headquarters, and she quickly immersed herself into learning all there was to know about leather, cutting, sewing, design, sales, and distribution. It was the beginning of an incredible growth story.

To keep up with the booming sales, Wilson hired her first sales representative in March 1995 and by May 1997, Robeez was online. The company moved out of Wilson's basement in May 1999 and into its first commercial space. Since then, the company has relocated and expanded into larger premises to accommodate its rapidly expanding operations. In August 2001, sales topped $1.2 million and doubled by the following year. Today, sales of this Burnaby, British Columbia, business exceed the $25 million mark and continue to grow rapidly.

In June 2006, for the fourth year in a row, Robeez achieved a top-20 spot on the prestigious *Profit* 100 ranking of Canada's fastest-growing companies. Not bad for a business that started out in Wilson's basement with three employees. Wilson says Robeez' relaxed supportive culture is vital to its growth. Robeez weaves fun and training into the routine, which breaks the monotony of many of the sewing jobs. Wilson's belief in her company's culture explains why Robeez' European headquarters was started by a Welsh couple with a passion for Robeez' values. Today, the European office leads plans for cross-Atlantic distribution, with over two dozen full-time employees and regional sales representatives. "People ask, 'What the heck are you doing in Wales?'" says Wilson. "Well, that's where the right people are. We felt it was really important to get the people first, then do the business."

Today, Robeez is recognized as the world's leading manufacturer of soft-soled leather footwear for newborns to four-year-olds. The company has 450 employees and sells more than 90 designs of shoes and booties in over 6500 stores in countries throughout North America, Europe, Australia, and parts of Asia. Recommended by experts and the first choice of parents, the hallmark of the meticulously crafted footwear is the skid-resistant soles that promote the healthy development of little feet by encouraging feet to flex and toes to grip. In September 2006, Robeez joined The Stride Rite Corporation's family of well-known footwear brands including Keds, Sperry Top-Sider, Tommy Hilfiger Footwear, Stride Rite, and Saucony. Wilson remains with the company as a consultant, and her ongoing participation will ensure the continuation of the unique Robeez design and brand vision. ◆

THE LINKS AMONG SMALL BUSINESS, NEW VENTURE CREATION, AND ENTREPRENEURSHIP

Every day, approximately 380 businesses are started in Canada.[1] New firms create the most jobs,[2] are noted for their entrepreneurship, and are typically small. But does this mean that most small businesses are entrepreneurial? Not necessarily.

The terms *small business, new venture,* and *entrepreneurship* are closely linked terms, but each idea is distinct. In the following paragraphs we will explain these terms to help you understand these topics and how they are interrelated.

Small Business

1   Explain the meaning of and inter-relationship among the terms *small business, new venture creation,* and *entrepreneurship.*

Defining a "small" business can be a bit tricky. Various measures might be used, including the number of people the business employs, the company's sales revenue, the size of the investment required, or the type of ownership structure the business has. Some of the difficulties in defining a small business can be understood by considering the way the Canadian government collects and reports information on small businesses.

Industry Canada is the main federal government agency responsible for small business. In reporting Canadian small business statistics, the government relies on two distinct sources of information, both provided by Statistics Canada: the Business Register (which tracks businesses), and the Labour Force Survey (which tracks individuals). To be included in the register, a business must have at least one paid employee, annual sales revenues of $30 000 or more, or be incorporated (we describe incorporation later in the chapter). A goods-producing business in the register is considered small if it has fewer than 100 employees, while a service-producing business is considered small if it has fewer than 50 employees.

The Labour Force Survey uses information from *individuals* to make estimates of employment and unemployment levels. Individuals are classified as self-employed if they are working owners of a business that is either incorporated or unincorporated, if they work for themselves but do not have a business (some musicians, for example, would fall into this category), or if they work without pay in a family business.[3]

In its publication *Key Small Business Statistics* (www.strategis.gc.ca/epic/internet/insbrp-rppe.nsf/en/rd00760e.html), Industry Canada reports that there are 2.2 million "business establishments" in Canada and about 2.5 million people who are "self-employed."[4] There is no way of identifying how much overlap there is in these two categories, but we do know that an unincorporated business operated by a self-employed person (with no employees) would *not* be counted among the 2.2 million *businesses* in the register. This is an important point because the majority of businesses in Canada have no employees (just the owner), nor are they incorporated.

These facts need to be kept in mind when considering statistics or research that excludes these firms. When either of these indicators is used to find businesses to study, the number of new firms will be underestimated. A study by the Panel Study of Entrepreneurial Dynamics (PSED), conducted by members of the Entrepreneurship Research Consortium (ERC), tracked a sample of Canadian **nascent entrepreneurs**—people who were trying to start a business—over four years. Only 15 percent of those who reported establishing an operating business had incorporated their firm.[5]

nascent entrepreneurs People who are trying to start a business from scratch.

For our purposes, we define a **small business** as an owner-managed business with less than 100 employees. We do so because it enables us to make better use of existing information, and because you are now aware of how definitions can affect our understanding of small businesses.

small business An owner-managed business with less than 100 employees.

The New Venture/Firm

Various criteria can also be used to determine when a new firm comes into existence. Three of the most common are when it was formed, whether it was incorporated,[6] and if it sold goods and/or services. A business is considered to be new if it has become operational within the previous 12 months, if it adopts any of the main organizational forms (proprietorship, partnership, corporation, or co-operative), and if it sells goods or services. Thus, we define a **new venture** (or **new firm**) as a recently formed commercial organization that provides goods and/or services for sale.

new venture/firm A recently formed commercial organization that provides goods and/or services for sale.

Entrepreneurship

Entrepreneurship is the process of identifying an opportunity in the marketplace and accessing the resources needed to capitalize on that opportunity.[7] **Entrepreneurs** are people who recognize and seize opportunities. For example, Ken Woods and John Gagliardi are two entrepreneurs who recognized an opportunity in the marketplace for higher quality beer and formed the Ontario-based Black Oak Brewing Company. They've already developed several award-winning beers such as Black Oak Nut Brown Ale, Pale Ale, and Premium Lager. A website for Toronto beer lovers called The Bar Towel rates these beers very positively.[8]

entrepreneurship The process of identifying an opportunity in the marketplace and accessing the resources needed to capitalize on it.

entrepreneurs People who recognize and seize opportunities.

Small businesses are usually independently owned and influenced by unpredictable market forces. As a result, they often provide an environment to use personal attributes—such as creativity—that have come to be associated with entrepreneurs.[9] But do not assume that only small business owners exhibit entrepreneurial characteristics. Many successful managers in large organizations in both the public and private sectors also exhibit similar characteristics.[10] Entrepreneurship therefore occurs in a wide range of contexts:[11] not just in small or new firms, but also in old firms, in large firms, in firms that grow slowly, in firms that grow rapidly, in non-profit organizations, and in the public sector.

People who exhibit entrepreneurial characteristics and create something new within an existing large firm or organization are called **intrapreneurs**. One large firm renowned for encouraging intrapreneurship is Procter & Gamble. It has earned this reputation by having divisions that focus on creating new products for specific markets.[12] The Swiffer product line is one example. Once the basic Swiffer mop was launched successfully, a whole range of products was added such as the Swiffer WetJet and Swiffer Dusters. A key difference between intrapreneurs and entrepreneurs is that intrapreneurs typically don't have to concern themselves with getting the resources needed to bring the new product to market since their employer provides the resources.

intrapraneurs People who create something new within an existing large firm or organization.

Starting a business from scratch involves dealing with a great deal of uncertainty, ambiguity, and unpredictability. For example, who knows how many customers the business will attract or where the needed financial resources will come from? This means that every new venture founder needs to exercise some of the personal attributes that entrepreneurs are noted for. Therefore, when we explore the entrepreneurial process later in the chapter, we will do so within a new venture context. Before doing so, we will outline the role of small and new businesses in the Canadian economy.

A common type of small business in Canada is the convenience store. It attracts customers from its immediate area through its long hours of operation and the product lines it carries.

THE ROLE OF SMALL AND NEW BUSINESSES IN THE CANADIAN ECONOMY

2   Describe the role of small and new businesses in the Canadian economy.

As we will see in this section, small and new businesses play a key role in the Canadian economy. However, recognition of this role is relatively recent. Prior to the 1980s, large businesses were the focus of attention in terms of economic impact within industrialized nations.

Small Businesses

It may surprise you to learn that close to 98 percent of all businesses in Canada are small (having less than 100 employees). As Figure 4.1 shows, this percentage holds true at the provincial level as well. In terms of distribution, you can see that approximately 58 percent of all business establishments in Canada—whether small or large—are located in Ontario and Quebec. Virtually all the rest are divided up between the western provinces (36 percent) and the Atlantic provinces (6 percent). The Northwest Territories, the Yukon, and Nunavut only represent 0.3 percent of Canada's businesses.

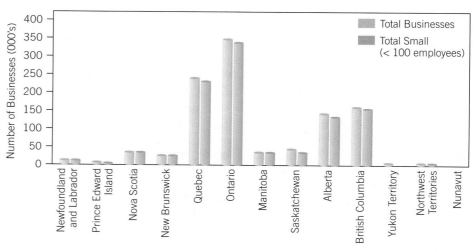

Figure 4.1 Employer businesses by firm size (number of employees) in provinces and territories, June 2005.

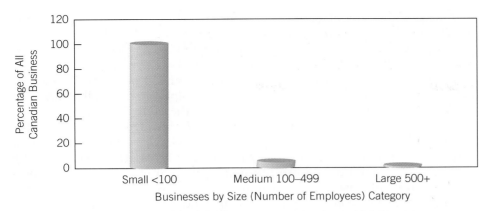

Figure 4.2a Small, medium, and large businesses as a percentage of total businesses.

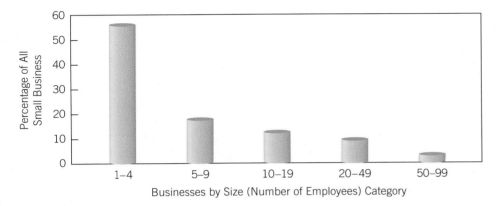

Figure 4.2b Small business size categories as a percentage of all small businesses.

How does the Canadian allocation of small (fewer than 100 employees), medium (100–499 employees), and large businesses (500+ employees) compare to that of the United States? Virtually identical! In Canada, as Figure 4.2a illustrates, 97.6 percent of the 1 048 286 employer businesses (or approximately half of the 2.2 million business establishments[13]) are small, 2.1 percent are medium-sized, and 0.3 percent are large. In the United States, slightly more than 97 percent are small, 2 percent are medium-sized, and 0.3 percent are large. As Figure 4.2b shows, when we further subdivide the Canadian "small" size category, we can see that the majority of small businesses (57 percent) have fewer than five employees.

While the previous figures profile the number of businesses in Canada by size, we now look at how many people work in small- versus medium- and large-sized businesses. According to Statistics Canada, there were 10 317 481 **private sector** employees in 2005. The term private sector generally refers to the part of the economy that is made up of companies and organizations that are not owned or controlled by the government.

Figure 4.3a shows that close to 49 percent of these employees (5.0 million) worked for small businesses; 16 percent (over 1.6 million) worked for medium-sized enterprises (those with 100 to 499 employees); and 35 percent (3.7 million) for large businesses.[14] These proportions have changed little over the last decade. When the small firm category is further subdivided (fewer than 4 employees, 5 to 19, 20 to 49, and 50 to 99), we see from Figure 4.3b that businesses with between 5 and 19 employees account for the highest percentage of employment.

private sector The part of the economy that is made up of companies and organizations that are not owned or controlled by the government.

The distribution of employment by size of firm varies considerably across industries. According to Industry Canada, small businesses account for over two-thirds of employment in four industries:[15] non-institutional health care (90 percent), the construction industry (77 percent), other services (73 percent), and accommodation and food (69 percent). In another five industries at least half of the workforce is employed by small businesses.

We conclude this section by considering the contribution small businesses make to the economy in terms of *gross domestic product (GDP)*. GDP refers to the market value of all final goods and services produced within a country in a given period of time. While GDP figures are not available by firm size, Industry Canada uses an approximation in estimating the percentage of small business's contribution to Canada's GDP. Over the past decade, the annual contribution has been valued at 25 percent[16]—less than the sector's contribution to employment but significant nonetheless.

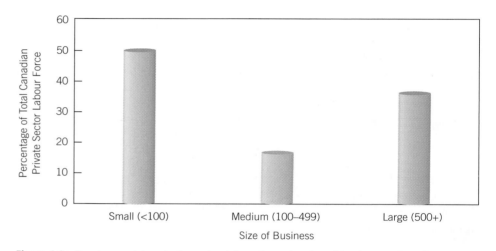

Figure 4.3a Employment in private sector labour force by size of business enterprise.

Note: SEPH data exclude self-employed workers who are not on a payroll and employees in the following industries: agriculture, fishing and trapping, private household services, religious organizations, and military personnel of defence services. The data breaking down employment by size of firm also exclude unclassified industries.

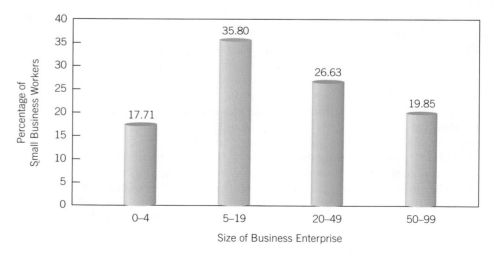

Figure 4.3b Small business employment of private sector labour force by size category.

Note: SEPH data exclude self-employed workers who are not on a payroll and employees in the following industries: agriculture, fishing and trapping, private household services, religious organizations, and military personnel of defence services. The data breaking down employment by size of firm also exclude unclassified industries.

New Ventures

New firms are not only the main source of job creation, they are also responsible for the vast majority of new products and services.[17] According to Statistics Canada, the number of firms in Canada grew 12 percent between 1991 and 2003. Alberta led in growth with 38 percent; British Columbia and Ontario followed with 20 percent and 14 percent, respectively.[18]

Most of the growth in firms occurred in the services-producing sector, with the number of firms in high-knowledge industries such as high-technology and biotechnology nearly doubling (from 32 000 to 62 000 firms). In the goods-producing sector, the number of firms in high-knowledge industries also grew at a much faster pace than in other industries.

Between 1991 and 2003, the number of businesses grew by an average of 9300 each year, with 8800 of these being small- and medium-sized enterprises (SMEs). In terms of who has been responsible for the growth in new firms, it may surprise you to learn that women are playing a far more prominent role than ever before. Kyla Eaglesham, the owner of Madeleines Cherry Pie and Ice Cream Parlour, is typical. After doing a lot of research on the ice cream and dessert industry, she left her job as a flight attendant and opened a dessert café in Toronto's trendy Annex neighbourhood. The store attracts customers who want "a little bit of cottage country in the heart of Toronto."[19]

There are now more than 800 000 women entrepreneurs in Canada, and the number has been increasing by more than 3 percent each year in recent years.[20] Female entrepreneurs are honoured each year at the Canadian Woman Entrepreneur Awards. In 2005, four women were honoured for the businesses they founded. They were Andrea Feunekes (New Brunswick-based Remsoft Inc.), Sherri Stevens (Ontario-based Stevens Resource Group), Sharon McNamara (Nova Scotia-based KilnArt), and Lynda Powless (Ontario-based Turtle Island News).[21]

Research conducted by Industry Canada shows that over the past two decades the number of female entrepreneurs has grown by 208 percent compared with just a 38 percent increase for men.[22] Between 1991 and 2001, self-employment among women increased by 43 percent, as compared with an increase of 21 percent among men. In 2000, majority women-owned SMEs had annual revenues of $72 billion, which is about 8 percent of all revenues from Canada's SMEs; in 2001, majority female-owned businesses employed 974 000 full or contract employees.

Many young entrepreneurs are also involved in creating new ventures in Canada. Consider the following examples:

- Geraldine McManus, who started Ab-Original Wear, buys artwork from Aboriginal artists and then reproduces it on T-shirts, crew-neck shirts, and sweatshirts. The clothing products feature Aboriginal artwork on the front and an inspirational message from a chief or elder on the back. The store also sells crafts made by local Aboriginal artists and miniature log cabins that McManus makes herself from recycled wood.[23]

- The Ben Barry Agency is an Ottawa-based modelling businesses that promotes models who are considered unorthodox—various sizes and ages, different racial backgrounds, and those who have physical disabilities. The models have appeared in government advertising campaigns, and on fashion runways in shopping malls. Barry works with company management to define their clientele and then chooses models who will best reflect the store's typical shoppers.[24]

- Tell Us About Us (TUAU) is a Winnipeg-based company specializing in market research and customer satisfaction programs. Owners Tyler Gompf and Scott Griffith recently signed a seven-figure deal to provide mystery shopper service to Dunkin Donuts, Baskin-Robbins, and Togo's in the United States and Canada. The mystery shoppers will note any problems at a retail site and TUAU will then measure how quickly the problems are fixed.[25]

In considering the government statistics on new ventures, we must be mindful that they exclude businesses without employees. Conceivably, a business counted as "new" could have been operating for several years before being statistically counted as a new business. How can this happen? Recall, from our earlier discussion, that an unincorporated business operated by a self-employed person (with no employees) would *not* be included in Statistics Canada's Business Register. If such a business operated for several years prior to hiring employees it would only be classified as a new business when the employees were acquired.

We began the discussion of small and new businesses in the Canadian economy by stating that 98 percent of all businesses are small. While individually, one large business easily outperforms the contribution of a countless number of small businesses, collectively, SMEs outperform large businesses in many areas, particularly in terms of their contribution to employment. New businesses, too, lead the way when it comes to innovation and new technology.

THE ENTREPRENEURIAL PROCESS

3 Explain the *entrepreneurial process* and describe its three key elements.

The entrepreneurial process is like a journey (see Figure 4.4). To get to the destination (the start-up of a new venture), the entrepreneur must identify a business opportunity and access the resources needed to capitalize on it. Along the way, social, economic, political, and technological factors in the broader environment will have an influence, but we will focus our attention on understanding the three key process elements—the entrepreneur, the opportunity, and resources—and how they interact. As these key elements interact, they may be mismatched or well-matched. If elements are mismatched (a "misfit"), the journey may be abandoned before the destination is reached. For example, if an entrepreneur identifies an opportunity for a new health service but does not have the relevant background and skills to deliver the service, the business may never get off the ground. Conversely, if the process elements are well-matched (a "fit"), the new business venture will likely become operational. After start-up, the venture's next phase of development will result in one of the following outcomes: growth, stability (staying the same), decline, or demise (ceasing to exist).

The Entrepreneur

Since the entrepreneur is at the heart of the entrepreneurial process, researchers have paid considerable attention to identifying the personal characteristics of entrepreneurs. The profiles provided in Table 4.1 illustrate how wide-ranging these characteristics are.[26] Some are behavioural (for example, high energy level), others are personality traits (for example, independence), and still others are skills (for example, problem solving).

While the idea that people are "born" entrepreneurs is still quite popular, nothing could be further from the truth.[27] In fact, entrepreneurial characteristics have been found to be widely distributed in the population.[28] We also know that personal characteristics often have less impact on a person's actions than the situation a person is in.[29] What is really important is not who the person *is* but what the person *does*.[30] The two main things that entrepreneurs need to do are to identify an opportunity and access resources.

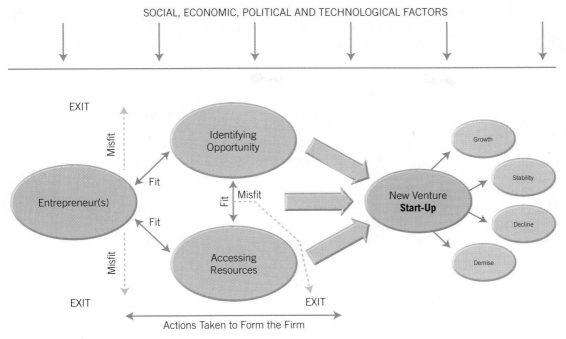

SOCIAL, ECONOMIC, POLITICAL AND TECHNOLOGICAL FACTORS

Figure 4.4 The entrepreneurial process in a new venture context.

Identifying Opportunities

Identifying opportunities involves generating ideas for new (or improved) products, processes, or services, screening those ideas so that the one that presents the best opportunity can be developed, and then developing the opportunity.

Table 4.1	Entrepreneurial Characteristics	
Kuratko and Hodgetts (2007)	**Hornday (1982)**	**Timmons and Spinelli (2007)**
Commitment, Determination, and Perseverance	Self-Confidence	Commitment and Determination
Drive to Achieve	Perseverence, Determination	Leadership
Opportunity Orientation	Drive to Achieve	Opportunity Obsession
Initiative and Responsibility	Energy, Diligence	Tolerance of Risk, Ambiguity, and Uncertainty
Persistent Problem Solving	Resourcefulness	Creativity, Self-Reliance, and Adaptability
Seeking Feedback	Calculated Risk Taking	Motivation to Excel
Internal Locus of Control	Need to Achieve	Courage
Tolerance for Ambiguity	Creativity	Creativity and Innovativeness
Calculated Risk Taking	Initiative	Energy, Health, and Emotional Stability
Integrity and Reliability	Flexibility	Values
Tolerance for Failure	Positive Response to Challenges	Capacity to Inspire
High Energy Level	Independence	Intelligence
Creativity and Innovativeness	Perceptiveness	
Vision	Dynamism, Leadership	
Self-Confidence and Optimism	Positive Attitude	
Independence	Ability to Get Along with People	
Team Building	Responsiveness to Suggestions and Criticism	
	Profit Orientation	
	Perceptiveness	

ENTREPRENEURSHIP AND NEW VENTURES

A Web-Hosting Vision

Vision, they say, is the ability to look at something and see what isn't there. Franc Nemanic's vision was 20/20 back in 1999, when he started eyeing online business opportunities. He noticed that while Canada's big phone companies and cable operators were rushing to offer web access, they weren't doing much to help small businesses build websites to cash in on the internet boom.

Franc's brother John, then the CEO of popular download site Tucows, warned that web hosting is a technically demanding business. But Franc saw that as a plus. If he could sell web-hosting services wholesale rather than retail, he figured, complexity would work in his favour, motivating telcos and internet service providers to private-label his services rather than develop their own web-hosting infrastructure.

Nemanic quit his job, wrote a business plan, and launched Mississauga, Ontario–based Hostopia.com Inc. Fortunately, he had another asset besides vision: big brother John and his business partners at Tucows, brothers Bill and Colin Campbell, had just sold that firm and were happy to be lead investors in Hostopia's U.S.$2.6-million financing. That first year, Hostopia attracted U.S.$109 202 in revenue. And despite the internet bust—which Nemanic, the firm's 37-year-old president, remembers as "nuclear winter"—sales grew to U.S.$14.3 million, a five-year sales growth of 13 000 percent that led to a top spot on the 2005 *Profit* 100.

How did Hostopia survive the meltdown and grow? Nemanic's tactics could fill a textbook on coping with hard times. "You either fight or die," he says. "I never spent a moment not trying to find customers." In September 2000, Nemanic called a staff meeting and explained that Hostopia had to sign up 100 new websites a day by the end of 2001, a fourfold increase that required more and bigger telco clients. "A sense of urgency motivates the whole organization," says Nemanic. "We told them where we were and what we had to accomplish to survive. It made them realize we were all going to sink or swim as a team."

Nemanic kept his team paddling by providing a daily report on Hostopia's progress toward its target. "It was a continuous process of communication." He says even non-sales staff adopted the mission, with administrators and programmers focussing their efforts on helping sales. "As long as you have a customer-centric attitude and you're focussed on helping other people achieve their goals," says Nemanic, "everyone will achieve their goal."

Hopes were rising and so were the numbers when Hostopia signed up TELUS Corp. in 2001, a big deal that ensured Hostopia's survival. Better yet, in August 2001, TELUS Ventures, the phone giant's venture-capital arm, invested U.S.$5 million in the company. Suddenly, Hostopia was cash-flow positive with a marquee customer.

In the summer of 2002, Nemanic moved to Ft. Lauderdale, Florida, to oversee U.S. sales. Today, he says Hostopia owns 40 percent of the U.S. and Canadian market for private-label, small-biz website hosting. But there's still room for growth, because its biggest rivals are telcos that run these services in-house, and they might be persuaded to outsource that business to specialists. Hostopia certainly has an appealing sales pitch: "We cut their operating expenses by 30 to 40 percent," says Nemanic, "and we wipe out their capital expenditures."

Hostopia's three major investors remain active players. Chairman John Nemanic keeps tabs on Hostopia's software development office in Ukraine. Bill Campbell is CEO and CTO, while Colin Campbell is COO. With Franc, they focus on maintaining the company's technological edge, introducing product updates quarterly. Plus, Hostopia is eyeing a public offering in early 2006, Franc says, "provided we build appropriate momentum." That shouldn't be a problem: After growing 60 percent last year, Franc says, Hostopia will probably expand 35 percent more this year, "but we're pushing for a higher number." That's persistence of vision.

Idea Generation

Typically, generating ideas involves abandoning traditional assumptions about how things work and how they ought to be, and seeing what others do not. If the prospective new (or improved) product, process, or service can be profitably produced and is attractive relative to other potential venture ideas, it might present an opportunity.

Where do ideas come from? Most new ventures do not emerge from a deliberate search for viable business ideas. Rather the majority originate from events relating to work or everyday life.[31] In fact, work experience is the most common source of ideas, accounting for 45 to 85 percent of those generated. As an employee, the prospective entrepreneur is familiar with the product or service, and the customers, suppliers, and competitors. He or she is aware of marketplace needs, can relate those needs to personal capabilities, and can determine whether he or she is capable of producing products or services that can fill the void. The next most frequent sources of venture ideas are a personal interest/hobby (16 percent) and a chance happening (11 percent).[32] A chance happening refers to a situation where a venture idea comes about unexpectedly. For example, while on vacation in another country you might try a new snack food that you feel would be in demand if introduced to the Canadian market.

Screening

Entrepreneurs often generate many ideas, and screening them is a key part of the entrepreneurial process. The faster you can weed out the "dead-end" venture ideas, the more time and effort you can devote to the ones that remain. The more of the following characteristics that an idea has, the greater the opportunity it presents.

The Idea Creates or Adds Value for the Customer. A product or service that creates or adds value for the customer is one that solves a significant problem, or meets a significant need in new or different ways. Consider Sally Fox's idea for eliminating the dyeing process in textile operations.[33] By cross-breeding long-fibre white cotton and short-fibre coloured cotton she developed FoxFibre®, an environmentally friendly new cotton fibre that is naturally grown in several colours and is long enough to be spun commercially.

The Idea Provides a Competitive Advantage that Can Be Sustained. A competitive advantage exists when potential customers see the product or service as better than that of competitors. Sustaining a competitive advantage involves maintaining it in the face of competitors' actions or changes in the industry. All other things being equal, the longer markets are in a state of flux, the greater the likelihood of being able to sustain a competitive advantage. The absence of a competitive advantage or developing a competitive advantage that is not sustainable constitute two fatal flaws of many new ventures.[34]

To continue Sally Fox's story, shortly after she sold her first crop she was running a $10 million business with well-known companies like Levi's, L.L. Bean, Land's End, and Esprit as customers. But Fox's journey turned out to be bumpy. She had to relocate twice in response to pressure from powerful cotton growers who were afraid that her coloured varieties would contaminate their own crops. Also, once spinning mills began moving to Southeast Asia and South America, Fox's cotton lost the financial advantage it had over traditional cotton. (In their new locations, spinning mills no longer had to treat and dispose of the toxic waste from the cotton-dyeing process—a cost saving of about $2 per pound.) Because the overseas mills were unwilling or unable to process the relatively small quantities of cotton her farmers produced, she lost her big customers. Fox now concentrates on smaller mills and smaller customers, and she is rebuilding her business and her network of growers.

The Idea Is Marketable and Financially Viable. While it is important to determine whether there are enough customers who are willing to buy the product or service, it is also important to determine whether sales will lead to profits.[35] Estimating the market demand requires an initial understanding of who the customers are, what their needs are, and how the product or service will satisfy their needs better than competitors' products will. It also requires a thorough understanding of the key competitors who can provide similar products, services, or benefits to the target customer. For example, 10 years ago few people thought that manufacturers of cellphones would be competitors of camera manufacturers in providing real-time photos through digital imaging. Customers define the competition in terms of who can best satisfy their needs.

After learning about the competition and customers, the entrepreneur must prepare a sales forecast. A **sales forecast** is an estimate of how much of a product or service will be purchased by the prospective customers for a specific period of time—typically one year. Total sales revenue is estimated by multiplying the units expected to be sold by the selling price. The sales forecast forms the foundation for determining the financial viability of the venture and the resources needed to start it.

sales forecast An estimate of how much of a product or service will be purchased by prospective customers over a specific period.

Determining financial viability involves preparing financial forecasts, which are two- to three-year projections of a venture's future financial position and performance. They typically consist of an estimate of *start-up costs, a cash budget, an income statement,* and *a balance sheet* (see Chapter 14 for more detail about these financial documents). A cash budget forecasts the cash receipts and cash disbursements of the business; the income statement shows the profit or loss; and the balance sheet shows the assets (what the business owns), the liabilities (what is owed), and the owners' equity (owners' investment, including any profits that the business retains). These projections serve as the basis for decisions regarding whether to proceed with the venture, and if so, the amount and type of financing to be used in financing the new business.

The Idea Has Low Exit Costs. The final consideration is the venture's exit costs. Exit costs are low if a venture can be shut down without a significant loss of time, money, or reputation.[36] If a venture is not expected to make a profit for a number of years, its exit costs are high, since the project cannot be reasonably abandoned in the short term. On the other hand, if the venture is expected to make a profit quickly, its exit costs will be lower, making the idea more attractive.

Developing the Opportunity

As the "dead-end" venture ideas are weeded out, a clear notion of the business concept and an entry strategy for pursuing it needs to be developed. As the process proceeds, the business concept often changes from what was originally envisioned. Some new ventures develop entirely new markets, products, and sources of competitive advantage once the needs of the marketplace and the economies of the business are better understood. So, while a vision of what is to be achieved is important, it is equally important to be responsive to new information and to be on the lookout for opportunities that were not originally anticipated. For example, if customers are not placing orders, as was the case with Sally Fox, it is important to find out why and make the appropriate adjustments.

New ventures use one or more of three main entry strategies: They introduce a totally new product or service; they introduce a product or service that will compete directly with existing competitive offerings but add a new twist (such as offering the option of customizing the standard product); or they franchise.[37] A **franchise** is an arrangement in which a buyer (franchisee) purchases the right to sell the product or service of the seller (franchiser). We discuss franchising in more detail later in the chapter.

franchise An arrangement in which a buyer (franchisee) purchases the right to sell the product or service of the seller (franchiser).

When capital requirements are high, such as when a manufacturing operation is being proposed, there is a need for considerable research and planning. Similarly, if product development or operations are fairly complex, research and analysis will be needed to ensure that the costs associated with effectively coordinating tasks will be minimized. In these circumstances, or when the aim is to attract potential investors, then a comprehensive written business plan will be required. A **business plan** is a document that describes the entrepreneur's proposed business venture; explains why it is an opportunity; and outlines its marketing plan, its operational and financial details, and its managers' skills and abilities.[38] The contents of a business plan are shown in Table 4.2.

business plan A document that describes the entrepreneur's proposed business venture; explains why it is an opportunity; and outlines its marketing plan, its operational and financial details, and its managers' skills and abilities.

If market conditions are changing rapidly, the benefits gained from extensive research and planning diminish quickly. By the time the entrepreneur is ready to start, new competitors may have entered the market, prices may have changed, a location may no longer be available, and so on. Similarly, if the product is highly innovative, market research is of less value since the development of entirely new products involves *creating* needs and wants rather than simply responding to existing needs. Consequently, measuring the capacity of the product or service to fill existing customer needs or wants is less critical.

Table 4.2	A Business Plan

A well-written business plan is formally structured, easy to read, and avoids confusion. By organizing the information into sections, it makes dealing with the information more manageable. The amount of detail and the order of presentation may vary from one venture to another and according to whom the plan is being prepared for (an investor will require more detail than if the plan is being prepared for internal use by the entrepreneur). An outline for a standard business plan is provided below. While formats vary, with some better suited to the type of venture being proposed than others, most contain the following elements.

I. **Cover Page**: Name of venture and owners, date prepared, contact person, his/her address, telephone and fax numbers, email address, and the name of the organization the plan is being presented to. The easier it is for the reader to contact the entrepreneur, the more likely the contact will occur.

II. **Executive Summary**: A one- to three-page overview of the total business plan. Written after the other sections are completed, it highlights their significant points, and aims to create enough excitement to motivate the reader to continue.

III. **Table of Contents**: This element lists major sections with page numbers for both the body and the appendices of the plan.

IV. **Company Description**: Explains the type of company and tells whether it is a manufacturing, retail, service, or other type of business. It also describes the proposed form of organization: sole proprietorship, partnership, corporation, or co-operative. A typical organization of this section is as follows: name and location; company objectives; nature and primary product or service of the business; current status (start-up, buyout, or expansion) and history if applicable; and legal form of organization.

V. **Product or Service Description**: Describes the product or service and indicates what is unique about it. This section explains the value that is added for customers—why people will buy the product or service; features of the product or service providing a competitive advantage; legal protection (patents, copyrights, trademarks, if relevant); and dangers of technical or style obsolescence.

VI. **Marketing**: This section has two key parts, the market analysis and the marketing plan. The market analysis convinces the reader that the entrepreneur understands the market for the product or service and can deal effectively with the competition to achieve sales projections. The marketing plan explains the strategy for achieving sales projections.

VII. **Operating Plan**: Explains the type of manufacturing or operating system to be used. Describes the facilities, labour, raw materials, and processing requirements.

VIII. **Management**: Identifies the key players—the management team, active investors, and directors—and cites the experience and competence they possess. This section includes a description of the management team, outside investors and directors and their qualifications, outside resource people, and plans for recruiting and training employees.

IX. **Financial Plan**: Specifies financial needs and contemplated sources of financing. Presents projected financial statements, including a cash budget, a balance sheet, and an income statement.

X. **Supporting Details/Appendix**: Provides supplementary materials to the plan such as résumés and other important supporting data.

Contrary to what many people might think, planning does not have to be completed before action is taken. For example, if an electrical contracting business is being proposed in an area where there is a shortage of tradespeople, it would be important to seek out qualified employees prior to conducting other analyses that are needed to complete the business plan. Such early action also helps to build relationships that can be drawn on later. Obviously, some ventures do not lend themselves to early action, particularly those which are capital intensive. Since most entrepreneurs have limited resources, it is important to concentrate on the issues that can be dealt with, *and* that will help determine whether to proceed and how to proceed.[39]

Accessing Resources

bootstrapping Doing more with less.

Typically, entrepreneurs acquire the various resources needed to make the venture a reality by **bootstrapping**, which means "doing more with less." Usually the term refers to financing techniques whereby entrepreneurs make do with as few resources as possible and use other peoples' resources wherever they can. However, bootstrapping can also refer to the acquisition of other types of resources such as people, space, equipment, or materials that are loaned or provided free by customers or suppliers.

Financial Resources

There are two main types of financing—*debt* and *equity* (see Chapter 20 for a detailed discussion of debt and equity). Briefly, *debt financing* refers to money that is borrowed. The borrower is obliged to repay the full amount of the loan in addition to interest charges on the debt. *Equity financing* refers to money that the entrepreneur (or others) invests in a business in return for an ownership interest. Equity investors, as owners, are keenly interested in how any profit will be distributed. Choosing between debt and equity involves trade-offs with regard to potential profitability, financial risk, and control. On the one hand, borrowing money increases the potential for higher rates of return to the entrepreneur when the business is performing well. On the other hand, equity makes it possible to reduce risk by giving up some control.

collateral Assets that a borrower uses to secure a loan or other credit, and that are subject to seizure by the lender if the loan isn't repaid according to the specified repayment terms.

Since a business is at its riskiest point during the start-up phase, equity is usually more appropriate and accessible than debt. However, most new venture founders prefer debt because they are reluctant to give up any control to outsiders. To obtain debt financing the entrepreneur must have an adequate equity investment in the business—typically 20 percent of the business's value—and collateral (or security). **Collateral** refers to items (assets) owned by the business (such as a building and equipment) or by the individual (such as a house or car) that the borrower uses to secure a loan or other credit. These items can be seized by the lender if the loan isn't repaid according to the specified terms. To lenders, equity investment demonstrates the commitment of the entrepreneur, as individuals tend to be more committed to a venture if they have a substantial portion of what they own invested in it.

The most common sources of *debt* financing include:

1. *Financial institutions.* While commercial banks are the main providers of debt financing for established small businesses, it is usually difficult for a new business to borrow from a bank. Banks are risk averse, and loans to new businesses are considered very risky, largely because the business has yet to establish its ability to repay the loan. Typically, if an entrepreneur is able to get bank financing for a new venture it is because the loan is in the form of a personal loan (as opposed to a business loan). The most common way to obtain a personal loan is to mortgage a house or borrow against the cash value of a life insurance policy.

In addition to commercial banks, other sources of debt financing include trust companies, co-operatives, finance companies, equipment companies, credit unions, and government agencies. Since finance companies lend in high-risk situations, their interest rates tend to be high. The federal and provincial governments have a wide range of financial assistance programs for small businesses. Among the various forms of assistance are low-interest loans, loan guarantees, interest-free loans, and wage subsidies.

2. *Suppliers.* Another source of financing is suppliers who provide goods (such as inventory) or services to the entrepreneur with an agreement to bill them later. This is referred to as *trade credit*. Trade credit can be very helpful in getting started, as it means that inventory, for example, can be acquired without paying cash for it which, in turn, frees up money to pay for other start-up costs. This type of financing is short-term; 30 days is the usual payback period. The amount of trade credit available to a new firm depends on the type of business and the supplier's confidence in the firm. Frequently, though, a new business has trouble getting trade credit since its capacity to repay has yet to be demonstrated.

The most common sources of *equity* financing include:

1. **Personal savings.** New venture founders draw heavily on their own finances to start their businesses. Most try to save as much as they can in preparation for start-up.

2. **Love money.** This type of financing includes investments from friends, relatives, and business associates. It is called "love money" because it is often given more on the basis of the family relationship or friendship than on the merit of the business concept.

3. **Private investors.** One popular source of equity capital is informal capital from private investors, also known as *angels*. Usually, these investors are financially well off individuals, many of whom are successful entrepreneurs who wish to recycle their wealth by investing in new businesses. Typically, the investment does not exceed $100 000.

4. **Venture capitalists.** Investments by venture capitalists come from professionally managed pools of investor money (venture capital). Since the risk of receiving little or no return on investment is high, only deals that present an attractive, high-growth business opportunity with a return between 35 and 50 percent are considered. Very few new ventures meet this criterion. Compared to angels, venture capitalists finance fewer firms in Canada.

Besides these conventional sources of financing, the possibilities for bootstrap financing are endless. For example, an entrepreneur might require an advance payment from customers, in full or in part. Equipment can be leased rather than purchased (which reduces the risk of equipment becoming obsolete). Office furniture can be rented, premises can be shared, and the manufacture of products can be subcontracted, thereby avoiding the expense of procuring material, equipment, and facilities. All of these activities free up cash which can then be used for other purposes.

Other Resources

Businesses may be owned by one person, but entrepreneurship is not a solo process. There are various stakeholders who provide resources to the venture including partners, employees, customers, suppliers, professionals, consultants, government agencies, lenders, shareholders, and venture capitalists. Sometimes ownership is shared with one or more of these stakeholders in order to acquire the use of their resources. When ownership is shared, there are decisions to be made about who to share it with, how much each stakeholder will own, at what cost, and under what conditions. The form of legal organization chosen affects whether ownership can be shared and whether resources can be accessed. We discuss this important point later in the chapter.

Deciding whether to share ownership by forming a venture team involves considering whether having a team is desirable or necessary, and whether the aim is to build a company with high growth potential. Whether a team is *necessary* depends upon:

- *The size and scope of the venture:* How many people does the venture require? Is it a one-person operation or does it need contributions from others? Can people be hired to fill the key roles as they are required?

- *Personal competencies:* What are the talents, know-how, skills, track-record, contacts, and resources that the entrepreneur brings to the venture? How do these match up with what the venture needs to succeed? If gaps are identified, the entrepreneur needs to decide what competencies are needed to complement his or hers and when they are needed.

The nature of the team depends upon the match-up between the lead entrepreneur and the opportunity, and how fast and aggressively he or she plans to proceed. Most teams tend to be formed in one of two ways: (a) one person has an idea (or wants to start a business), and then several associates join the team over the first few years of the venture's operation, or (b) an entire team is formed at the outset based on such factors as a shared idea, a friendship, or an experience.

The ideal team consists of people with complementary skills covering the key success areas for the business (for example, marketing, finance, production, etc.). Small founding teams tend to work better than big ones. It is quite common for the initial team to consist of just two people—a craftsperson and a salesperson.

If the entrepreneur does not have his or her sights set on establishing a venture with high growth potential, going solo may be a realistic option. Some new venture founders bring on additional team members only as the business can afford them. Most successful solo businesses are simple types of ventures, such as small retail stores or services.[40] The odds for survival, growth, profitability, and attracting capital are increased by a team approach.[41]

Assessing the "Fit" Between Elements in the Entrepreneurial Process

Assessing the "fit" between the key elements in the entrepreneurial process is an ongoing task, since the shape of the opportunity, and consequently the resources and people needed to capitalize on it, typically changes as it is developed. It is the entrepreneur that stands to gain the most by attending to these "fits" and any changes they may require, although other stakeholders, such as investors, will be considering them as well.

The Entrepreneur–Opportunity Fit

The first assessment of fit is between the entrepreneur and the opportunity. The entrepreneur needs to decide whether the opportunity, as identified, is something he or she *can do* and *wants to do*. A realistic self-assessment is important. Prospective ventures that are of limited personal interest and require skills and abilities that do not fit well with those of the entrepreneur should be quickly eliminated. For example, it does little good to identify an opportunity for an ecotourism business in a wilderness area if the entrepreneur is a sedentary urban dweller.

Once the entrepreneur has chosen the opportunity he or she wants to pursue, the success of the venture depends heavily upon the individual or individuals involved. No matter how good the product or service concept is, as the opportunity changes shape, it may demand skills a single entrepreneur lacks. This may prompt a decision to acquire the needed skills either by forming a team or by getting further training.

The Opportunity–Resources Fit

Assessing the opportunity–resources fit involves determining whether the resources needed to capitalize on the opportunity can be acquired. As the opportunity changes shape, so too will the resource requirements. When challenges or risks arise, the aim is to determine whether they can be resolved, and if so, to deal with them as quickly as possible. For example, if the venture requires a greater financial investment than originally anticipated, this does not necessarily mean that the venture should be abandoned. Other options such as taking on partners or leasing rather than building a facility may be viable. Of course, some ventures may not be viable regardless of the alternatives considered.

The Entrepreneur–Resources Fit

Once the resource requirements of the venture have been determined, the entrepreneur needs to assess whether he or she has the capacity to meet those requirements. For example, an entrepreneur with a stellar reputation for software development will have an easier time attracting employees for a venture specializing in software than someone with no track record. If that same entrepreneur is well connected with people in the industry, he or she will be more likely to gain commitments from customers, and, in turn, investors.

START-UP AND BEYOND

Entrepreneurs must make the right start-up decisions, but they must also pay attention to how the business will be run beyond the start-up phase. In this section, we examine three important topics that are relevant to these issues. First, we describe the three main ways that entrepreneurs start up a small business. Next, we look at the four main organizing options that are available to entrepreneurs. We conclude the chapter with a look at the reasons for success and failure in small business.

Starting Up a Small Business

Most entrepreneurs start up a small business in one of three ways: they start a business from scratch, they buy an existing business, or they buy a franchise. We have already examined the "starting from scratch" alternative in detail in the preceding section, so we focus here on the latter two options.

Buying an Existing Business

About one-third of all new businesses that were started in the past decade were bought from someone else. Many experts recommend buying an existing business because the odds of success are better. An existing business has already proven its ability to attract customers. It has also established relationships with lenders, suppliers, and other stakeholders. Moreover, an existing track record gives potential buyers a much clearer picture of what to expect than any estimate of a new business's prospects.

Describe two alternative strategies for becoming a business owner— *buying an existing business* and *buying a franchise*.

4

But an entrepreneur who buys someone else's business may not be able to avoid certain problems. For example, the business may have a poor reputation, its location may be poor, it may be difficult to determine an appropriate purchase price, and there may be uncertainty about the exact financial shape the business is in.

Taking Over a Family Business. A special case of buying an existing business involves family businesses. Taking over a family business poses both challenges and opportunities. On the positive side, a family business can provide otherwise unobtainable financial and management resources because of the personal sacrifices of family members. Family businesses often have a strong reputation or goodwill that can result in important community and business relationships. As well, employee loyalty is often high, and an interested, unified family management and shareholders group may emerge.

Toronto-based hosiery manufacturer Phantom Industries Inc. is an example of a family-owned business that has been successful through three generations of family members.[42] Another example is Irving Oil Ltd., the giant New Brunswick-based company, which now has fifth-generation members running businesses that are part of its empire.[43]

On the other hand, major problems can arise in family businesses. There may be disagreements over which family members assume control. If the parent sells his or her interest in the business, the price to be paid may be an issue. The expectation of other family members may also be problematic. Some family members may feel that they have a right to a job, promotion, and impressive title simply because they are part of the family.[44] Choosing an appropriate successor and ensuring that he or she receives adequate training and disagreements among family members about the future of the business are two other problem areas. Examples of family businesses that encountered serious problems are Saskatchewan-based Mitchell's Gourmet Foods (internal family feuding about who would control the company), Cuddy International Corp. (disagreements about which of the founder's sons were capable of running the business), and Eatons (inability to adapt to changing market conditions).[45]

Buying a Franchise

If you drive or walk around any Canadian town, you will notice retail outlets with names like McDonald's, Pizza Pizza, Swiss Chalet, Yogen Früz, 7-Eleven, Re/Max, Comfort Inn, Blockbuster Video, Sylvan Learning Centre, and Super Lube. What do all these businesses have in common? They are all franchises, operating under licences issued by parent companies to local entrepreneurs who own and manage them.

Franchising became very visible in the 1950s with fast-food franchisers like McDonald's, but it actually started in the early 1800s. In 1898, General Motors began franchising retail dealerships, and similar systems were created by Rexall (pharmacies) in 1902 and by Howard Johnson (restaurants and motels) in 1926. Franchising continues to increase in importance in the twenty-first century. Depending on how it is defined, franchising now accounts for 43 percent of retail sales in Canada.[46] There are thousands of franchise establishments in Canada, and they generate approximately $30 billion in annual sales revenue.

A franchise is an arrangement that gives franchisees (buyers) the right to sell the product of the franchiser (the seller). A **franchising agreement** outlines the duties and responsibilities of each party. For example, it stipulates the amount and type of payment that franchisees must make to the franchiser. Franchisees usually make an initial payment for the right to operate a local outlet of the franchise; they also make royalty payments to the franchiser ranging from 2 to 30 percent of the franchisee's annual revenues

franchising agreement Stipulates the duties and responsibilities of the franchisee and the franchiser.

or profits. The franchisee also pays an advertising fee so that the franchiser can advertise in the franchisee's local area. Franchise fees vary widely, from $30 000 for a Fantastic Sams's hair salon, to $1 million for a Burger King franchise, to hundreds of millions for a professional sports franchise.

The Advantages of Franchising. Both franchisers and franchisees benefit from the franchising way of doing business (see Table 4.3).

Is Franchising for You? Do you think you would be happy being a franchisee? The answer depends on a number of factors, including your willingness to work hard, your ability to find a good franchise to buy, and the financial resources you possess. If you are thinking seriously of going into franchising, you should consider several areas of costs that you will incur:

- the franchise sales price
- expenses that will be incurred before the business opens
- training expenses
- operational expenses for the first six months
- personal financial needs for the first six months
- emergency needs

ORGANIZING OPTIONS (FORMS OF BUSINESS OWNERSHIP)

Whether they intend to run a small farm, a large factory, an online retail business, a hair salon, or any one of many other types of business, entrepreneurs must decide which form of legal ownership best suits their needs.

Describe the four forms of *legal organization* for a business and discuss the advantages and disadvantages of each.

5

Table 4.3	The Benefits of Franchising

For the Franchiser	For the Franchisee
- The franchiser can attain rapid growth for the chain by signing up many franchisees in many different locations.	- Franchisees own a small business that has access to big business management skills.
- Franchisees share in the cost of advertising.	- The franchisee does not have to build up a business from scratch.
- The franchiser benefits from the investment money provided by franchisees.	- Franchisee failure rates are lower than when starting one's own business.
- Advertising money is spent more efficiently (the franchiser teams up with local franchisees to advertise only in the local area).	- A well-advertised brand name comes with the franchise and the franchisee's outlet is recognizable because it looks like all other outlets in the chain.
- The franchiser benefits because franchisees are motivated to work hard for themselves; the more revenue the franchisee generates, the more money the franchiser makes.	- The franchiser may send the franchisee to a training program run by the franchiser (e.g., the Canadian Institute of Hamburgerology run by McDonald's).
- The franchiser is freed from all details of a local operation, which are handled by the franchisee.	- The franchiser may visit the franchisee and provide expert advice on how to run the business.
	- Economies in buying allow franchisees to get lower prices for the raw materials they must purchase.
	- Financial assistance is provided by the franchiser in the form of loans; the franchiser may also help the franchisee obtain loans from local sources.
	- Franchisees are their own bosses and get to keep most of the profit they make.

Four options are available: the sole proprietorship, the partnership, the corporation, and the cooperative.

The Sole Proprietorship

sole proprietorship A business owned and operated by one person.

The **sole proprietorship** is a business owned and operated by one person. Legally, if you set up a business as a sole proprietorship, your business is considered to be an extension of yourself (and not a separate legal entity). Though usually small, a sole proprietorship may be as large as a steel mill or as small as a lemonade stand. While the majority of businesses in Canada are sole proprietorships, this form of ownership accounts for only a small proportion of total business revenues.

Advantages of a Sole Proprietorship

Freedom may be the most important benefit of a sole proprietorship. Sole proprietors answer to no one but themselves since they don't share ownership. A sole proprietorship is also easy to form. If you operate the business under your own name, with no additions, you don't even need to register your business name to start operating as a sole proprietor; you can go into business simply by putting a sign on the door. The simplicity of legal setup procedures makes this form appealing to self-starters and independent spirits, as do low start-up costs.

Another attractive feature is tax benefits. Most businesses suffer losses in their early stages. Since the business and the proprietor are legally one and the same, these losses can be deducted from income the proprietor earns from personal sources other than the business.

Disadvantages of a Sole Proprietorship

unlimited liability Personal liability for all debts of the business.

A major drawback is **unlimited liability**: A sole proprietor is personally liable (responsible) for all debts incurred by the business. If the business fails to generate enough cash, bills must be paid out of the owner's pocket. Another disadvantage is lack of continuity: A sole proprietorship legally dissolves when the owner dies. Finally, a sole proprietorship depends on the resources of one person whose managerial and financial limitations may constrain the business. Sole proprietors often find it hard to borrow money to start up or expand. Many bankers fear that they won't be able to recover loans if the owner becomes disabled.

The Partnership

partnership A form of organization established when two or more individuals agree to combine their financial, managerial, and technical abilities for the purpose of operating a business for profit.

general partners Partners who are actively involved in managing the firm and have unlimited liability.

limited partners Partners who don't participate actively in the business and whose liability is limited to the amount they invested in the partnership.

general partnership A type of partnership where all partners are jointly liable for the obligations of the business.

limited partnership A type of partnership with at least one general partner (who has unlimited liability) and one or more limited partners. The limited partners cannot participate in the day-to-day management of the business or they risk the loss of their limited liability status.

The **partnership**, frequently used by professionals like accountants and lawyers, is established when two or more individuals (partners) agree to combine their financial, managerial, and technical abilities for the purpose of operating a business for profit. Partnerships are often an extension of a business that began as a sole proprietorship. The original owner may want to expand, or the business may have grown too big for a single person to handle.

There are two basic types of partners in a partnership. **General partners** are actively involved in managing the firm and have unlimited liability. **Limited partners** don't participate actively in the business, and their liability is limited to the amount they invested in the partnership. A **general partnership** is the most common type of partnership and is similar in nature to the sole proprietorship in that all the (general) partners are jointly liable for the obligations of the business. The other type of partnership—a **limited partnership**—consists of at least one general partner (who has unlimited liability) and one or more limited partners. The limited partners can not participate in the day-to-day management of the business or they risk the loss of their limited liability status.

Advantages of a Partnership

The most striking advantage of a general partnership is the ability to grow by adding talent and money. Partnerships also have a somewhat easier time borrowing funds than do sole proprietorships because banks and other lending institutions prefer to make loans to enterprises that are not dependent on a single individual. Partnerships can also invite new partners to join by investing money.

Like a sole proprietorship, a partnership is simple to organize, with few legal requirements. Even so, all partnerships must begin with an agreement of some kind. It may be written, oral, or even unspoken. Wise partners, however, insist on a written agreement to avoid trouble later. This agreement should answer such questions as

- How will disagreements be resolved?
- Who invested what sums of money in the partnership?
- Who will receive what share of the partnership's profits?
- Who does what and who reports to whom?
- How will the partnership be dissolved?
- How would leftover assets be distributed among the partners?

The partnership agreement is strictly a private document. No laws require partners to file an agreement with some government agency. Nor are partnerships regarded as legal entities. In the eyes of the law, a partnership is nothing more than two or more persons working together. The partnership's lack of legal standing means that the partners are taxed as individuals.

Disadvantages of a Partnership

As with sole proprietorships, unlimited liability is the greatest drawback of a general partnership. By law, each partner may be held personally liable for all debts incurred in the name of the partnership. And if any partner incurs a debt, even if the other partners know nothing about it, they are all liable if the offending partner cannot pay up. Another problem with partnerships is lack of continuity. When one partner dies or pulls out, a partnership dissolves legally, even if the other partners agree to stay to continue the business.

A related drawback is the difficulty of transferring ownership. No partner may sell out without the other partners' consent. Thus, the life of a partnership may depend on the ability of retiring partners to find someone compatible with the other partners to buy them out. Finally, a partnership provides little or no guidance in resolving conflict between the partners. For example, suppose one partner wants to expand the business rapidly and the other wants it to grow slowly. If under the partnership agreement the two are equal, it may be difficult for them to decide what to do.

A practical illustration of the kinds of problems that can arise in partnerships is described in the Exercising Your Ethics feature found at the end of the chapter.

The Corporation

When you think of corporations you probably think of giant businesses such as Air Canada, Imperial Oil, or Nortel Networks. The very word "corporation" suggests bigness and power. Yet, the tiny corner newsstand has as much right to incorporate as does a giant oil refiner. And the newsstand and oil refiner have the same basic characteristics that all corporations share: legal status as a separate entity, property rights and obligations, and an indefinite lifespan. The Top 10 corporations in Canada are listed in Table 4.4.

A corporation has been defined as "an artificial being, invisible, intangible, and existing only in contemplation of the law."[47] As such, corporations may sue and be sued, buy, hold, and sell property, make and sell products to consumers, and commit crimes and be tried and punished for them. Simply defined, a **corporation** is a business that is a separate legal entity that is liable for its own debts and whose owners' liability is limited to their investment.

Stockholders—investors who buy shares of ownership in the form of stock—are the real owners of the corporation (the different kinds of stockholders are described in Chapter 18). Profits may be distributed to stockholders in the form of dividends, although corporations are not required to pay dividends. Instead, they often reinvest any profits in the business.

The **board of directors** is the governing body of a corporation. Its basic responsibility is to ensure that the corporation is run in a way that is in the best interests of the shareholders. The board chooses the president and other officers of the business and delegates the power to run the day-to-day activities of the business to those officers. The board sets policy on paying dividends, on financing major spending, and on executive salaries and benefits. Large corporations tend to have large boards with as many as 20 or 30 directors. Smaller corporations, on the other hand, tend to have no more than five directors. The Business Accountability box describes some recent issues that have arisen regarding boards of directors.

Inside directors are employees of the company and have primary responsibility for the corporation. That is, they are also top managers, such as the president and executive vice-president. **Outside directors** are not employees of the corporation in the normal course of its business. Attorneys, accountants, university officials, and executives from other firms are commonly used as outside directors.

corporation A business that is a separate legal entity that is liable for its own debts and whose owners' liability is limited to their investment.

stockholders A share of ownership in a corporation.

board of directors A group of individuals elected by a firm's shareholders and charged with overseeing, and taking legal responsibility for, the firm's actions.

inside directors Members of a corporation's board of directors who are also full-time employees of the corporation.

outside directors Members of a corporation's board of directors who are not also employees of the corporation on a day-to-day basis.

Table 4.4 Top 10 Corporations in Canada, 2005 (Ranked by Sales Revenue)

Corporation	Sales Revenue (billions of dollars)
1. General Motors of Canada	$34.9
2. Manulife Financial Corp.	32.0
3. George Weston Ltd.	31.3
4. Royal Bank of Canada	29.4
5. Imperial Oil Ltd.	27.9
6. Magna International Inc.	27.6
7. Power Corp. of Canada	26.6
8. Alcan Inc.	24.6
9. Sun Life Financial Inc.	21.9
10. DaimlerChrysler Canada Inc.	20.8

BUSINESS ACCOUNTABILITY

Getting on Boards

Boards of directors today are under pressure to become actively involved in planning and monitoring corporate activity. At WorldCom, Tyco, and other corporations, the boards were either unaware of the misdeeds taking place around them or, in some cases, actually were party to those activities. At Enron, for example, the board of directors several times voted to waive its policies regarding independence and arms-length transactions, allowing executives to continue their fraud unhampered. When the negligence of these boards was publicly exposed, investors cried out for reform.

Investors want boards to take a more active role in decision making and to provide more oversight. Most corporations, eager to distance themselves from scandal, are considering transformation of their boards of directors. The most effective boards are composed of more outsiders than insiders. This allows the directors to have independence from the powerful CEO. To enhance decision making ability, board members should come from diverse backgrounds and have top-level management experience. Directors should own a substantial amount of the company's stock. Boards should be actively involved in decision making, such as meeting regularly, setting the overall corporate strategy, and having access to confidential information. Boards that do not meet these criteria may be too cozy with corporate executives and thus fail to vigilantly safeguard the interests of shareholders.

Specific questions that should be asked are as follows:

- Are the majority of the board's members independent of the company (i.e., they are not part of the company's management, they don't work for another company that does business with the company, and they do not come from a parent company that controls the company)?
- Are the majority of the compensation committee's members independent (the compensation committee determines executive pay)?
- Are the majority of the nominating committee's members independent (the nominating committee recommends new board members)?
- Does the company have a system for formally evaluating the performance of its board of directors?
- Do the directors and the CEO own stock in the company?
- Do directors have to stand for re-election every year?
- Does the company have a written statement of its corporate governance practices?
- Does the company have only voting common shares and no non-voting shares?

Many high-tech companies are defying these guidelines. For example, the board of Amazon.com has just five members, is chaired by CEO Jeff Bezos, and lacks any real semblance of independence. Pat McGurn, a director at Institutional Shareholder Services, says, "People are coming to view Amazon's problems as the result of poor corporate governance rather than the effect of the economy in general. Unfortunately, the board doesn't seem to see governance as part of the solution."

This problem is not restricted to high-tech companies. In 2003, Gerald Schwartz, CEO of Onex Corporation, named his wife to sit on the board of directors of Onex. Institutional shareholders and corporate governance experts said such a move is contrary to the efforts of most public companies to increase the independence of their directors. One securities lawyer asked how a board member could evaluate a CEO's performance if the CEO is her husband.

Each year the *Report on Business* ranks Canadian corporations in terms of four key areas: board composition, board compensation, shareholder rights, and disclosure. In 2005, the top-ranked companies were SNC-Lavalin Group Inc., Bank of Montreal, Bank of Nova Scotia, and Suncor Energy (in that order). The lowest-ranked companies were Reitmans (Canada) Ltd., Duvernay Oil Corp., and Northern Orion Resources.

chief executive officer The person responsible for the firm's overall performance.

Corporate officers are the top managers hired by the board to run the corporation on a day-to-day basis. The **chief executive officer (CEO)** is responsible for the firm's overall performance. Other corporate officers typically include the president, who is responsible for internal management, and various vice-presidents, who oversee functional areas such as marketing or operations.

Types of Corporations

public corporation A business whose stock is widely held and available for sale to the general public.

There are two types of private sector corporations (corporations can also be found in the municipal, provincial, federal, and nonprofit sectors). The **public corporation** is a business whose shares of stock are widely held and available for sale to the general public. The shares of public corporations like George Weston, Air Canada, and Canadian Pacific are traded on securities exchanges and are widely available to the general public for purchase (see Chapter 19).

private corporation A business whose stock is held by a small group of individuals and is not usually available for sale to the general public.

By contrast, the shares of stock of a **private corporation** are held by only a few shareholders, are not widely available for purchase, and may have restrictions on their sale. For example, Kroeker Farms, a large agribusiness in Manitoba is owned by nine members of one family. Other private corporations are Para Paints of Canada and Bata Shoes. The vast majority of corporations are privately held.

initial public offering (IPO) Selling shares of stock in a company for the first time to the general investing public.

Most new corporations start out as private corporations, because few investors will buy an unknown stock. As the corporation grows and develops a record of success, it may issue shares to the public as a way of raising additional money. This is called its **initial public offering (IPO)**. In 2005, E.D. Smith, a maker of jams and pie fillings, went public with a $110 million IPO, and Tim Hortons announced plans for an IPO in 2006. IPOs were not very attractive to investors during the stock market decline of 2001–2003, but they became more popular as the stock market recovered. In 2001, for example, there were 1924 IPOs worth $26 billion, but in 2004 there were 2752 IPOs worth over $48 billion.[48]

A public corporation can also "go private," which is the reverse of going public. In 2004, Cara Operations Ltd.—the parent company of Harvey's, Swiss Chalet, and Second Cup—went private, and Magna International Inc. announced that would take its three publicly traded auto parts subsidiaries private.[49]

income trust The income trust structure involves corporations distributing all or most of their earnings to investors and thereby reduces the corporation's income tax liability.

During the last few years, many corporations converted to an **income trust** structure which allowed them to avoid paying corporate income tax if they distributed all or most of their earnings to investors. For example, Bell Canada Enterprises could have avoided an $800 million tax bill for 2008 by becoming an income trust. The federal government estimated that it was going to lose billions of dollars of tax revenue because so many corporations were becoming income trusts. In a surprise move in 2006, the government announced that it would begin taxing income trusts more like corporations by 2011. This announcement caused a significant decline in the market value of income trusts and it also means that very few corporations will now convert to an income trust structure.[50]

Formation of the Corporation

The two most widely used methods to form a corporation are federal incorporation under the Canada Business Corporations Act and provincial incorporation under any of the provincial corporations acts. The former is used if the company is going to operate in more than one province; the latter is used if the founders intend to carry on business in only one province. Except for banks and certain insurance and loan companies, any company can be federally incorporated under the Canada Business Corporations Act. To do so, articles of incorporation must be drawn up. These articles include such information as the name of the corporation, the type and number of shares to be issued, the number of directors the corporation will have, and the location of the company's operations. The specific procedures and information required for provincial incorporation vary from province to province.

All corporations must attach the word "Limited" (Ltd./Ltée), "Incorporated" (Inc.), or "Corporation" (Corp.) to the company name to indicate clearly to customers and suppliers that the owners have limited liability for corporate debts. The same sorts of rules apply in other countries. British firms, for example, use PLC for "public limited company" and German companies use AG for "Aktiengesellschaft" (corporation).

Advantages of Incorporation

The biggest advantage of the corporate structure is **limited liability**, which means that the liability of investors is limited to their personal investment in the corporation. In the event of failure, the courts may seize a corporation's assets and sell them to pay debts, but the courts cannot touch the investors' personal possessions. If, for example, you invest $1000 in a corporation that goes bankrupt, you may lose your $1000, but no more. In other words, your liability is limited to $1000.

> **limited liability** The liability of investors is limited to their personal investments in the corporation.

Another advantage of a corporation is continuity. Because it has a legal life independent of its founders and owners, a corporation can, in theory, continue forever. Shares of stock may be sold or passed on to heirs, and most corporations also benefit from the continuity provided by professional management. Finally, corporations have advantages in raising money. By selling **stock**, they expand the number of investors and the amount of available funds. The term stock refers to a share of ownership in a corporation. Continuity and legal status tend to make lenders more willing to grant loans to corporations.

> **stock** A share of ownership in a corporation.

Disadvantages of Incorporation

One of the disadvantages for a new firm in forming a corporation is the cost (approximately $2500). Corporations also need legal help in meeting government regulations because they are far more heavily regulated than are proprietorships or partnerships. Some people say that **double taxation** is another problem with the corporate form of ownership. By this they mean that a corporation must pay corporate income taxes on its profits, and then shareholders must also pay personal income taxes on the **dividends** they receive from the corporation. The dividend a corporation pays is the amount of money, normally a portion of the profits, which is distributed to the shareholders. Since dividends paid by the corporation are not tax deductible for the corporation, this amounts to double taxation. Others point out that shareholders get a "dividend tax credit," which largely offsets the effect of double taxation.

> **double taxation** A corporation must pay income taxes on its profits, and then shareholders must also pay personal income taxes on the dividends they receive from the corporation.

> **dividends** The amount of money, normally a portion of the profits, which is distributed to the shareholders.

The Co-operative

A **co-operative** is an incorporated form of business that is organized, owned, and democratically controlled by the people who use its products and services, and whose earnings are distributed on the basis of their use of the co-operative rather than their level of investment. As such, it is formed to benefit its owners in the form of reduced prices and/or the distribution of surpluses at year-end. The process works like this: suppose some farmers believe they can get cheaper fertilizer prices if they form their own company and purchase in large volumes. They might then form a co-operative, which

> **co-operative** An incorporated form of business that is organized, owned, and democratically controlled by the people who use its products and services, and whose earnings are distributed on the basis of use of the co-operative rather than level of investment.

can be either federally or provincially chartered. Prices are generally lower to buyers and, at the end of the fiscal year, any surpluses are distributed to members on the basis of how much they purchased. If Farmer Jones bought 5 percent of all co-op sales, he would receive 5 percent of the surplus.

The co-operative's start-up capital usually comes from shares purchased by the co-operative's members. Sometimes all it takes to qualify for membership in a co-operative is the purchase of one share with a fixed (and often nominal) value. Federal co-operatives, however, can raise capital by issuing investment shares to members or non-members. Co-operatives, like investor-owned corporations, have directors and appointed officers.

Voting rights are different from those in a corporation. In a co-operative, each member is entitled to one vote, regardless of how many shares he or she owns.

Types of Co-operatives

There are hundreds of different co-operatives, but they generally function in one of six main areas of business:

- *Consumer co-operatives.* These organizations sell goods to both members and the general public (e.g., co-op gasoline stations, agricultural implement dealers).

- *Financial co-operatives.* These organizations operate much like banks, accepting deposits from members, giving loans, and providing chequing services (e.g., credit unions).

- *Insurance co-operatives.* These organizations provide many types of insurance coverage, such as life, fire, and liability (for example, the Co-operative Hail Insurance Company of Manitoba).

- *Marketing co-operatives.* These organizations sell the produce of their farm members and purchase inputs for the production process (e.g., seed and fertilizer). Some, like Federated Co-operatives, also purchase and market finished products.

- *Service co-operatives.* These organizations provide members with services, such as recreation.

- *Housing co-operatives.* These organizations provide housing for members, who purchase a share in the co-operative, which holds the title to the housing complex.

In terms of numbers, co-operatives are the least important form of ownership. However, they are of significance to society and to their members since they may provide services that are not readily available, or that cost more than the members would otherwise be willing to pay. Table 4.5 compares the various forms of business ownership using different characteristics.

Advantages of a Co-operative

Co-operatives have many of the same advantages of investor-owned corporations such as limited liability of owners and continuity. A key benefit of a co-operative relates to its structure. As noted above, each member has only one vote in the affairs of the co-operative, regardless of how many shares he or she holds. This system prevents voting and financial control of the business by a few wealthy individuals. This is particularly attractive to members who are less wealthy than other members of the co-operative.

Table 4.5	A Comparison of Four Forms of Business Ownership			
Characteristic	Sole Proprietorship	Partnership	Corporation	Co-operative
Protection against liability for bad debts	low	low	high	high
Ease of formation	high	high	medium	medium
Permanence	low	low	high	high
Ease of ownership transfer	low	low	high	high
Ease of raising money	low	medium	high	high
Freedom from regulation	high	high	low	medium
Tax advantages	high	high	low	high

Whereas investor-owned corporations are typically exposed to double taxation because dividends to shareholders are distributed out of after-tax corporate income, co-operatives are allowed to deduct patronage refunds to members out of before-tax income. Thus, income may only be taxed at the individual member level rather than at both the co-operative and member level. In other words, a co-operative does not pay tax on income that it distributes as patronage dividends.[51]

Disadvantages of a Co-operative

One of the main disadvantages of co-operatives relates to attracting equity investment. Since the benefits from being a member of a co-operative arise through the level of use of the co-operative rather than the level of equity invested, members do not have an incentive to invest in equity capital of the co-operative. Another drawback is that democratic voting arrangements and dividends based purely on patronage turn off some entrepreneurs from forming or joining a co-operative.

SUCCESS AND FAILURE IN SMALL BUSINESS

Why do some ventures succeed while others fail? This question is difficult to answer since most of what we know is based on businesses that may under- or over-represent firms that succeed or fail. As outlined earlier, when the focus is on businesses with employees, as is the case with a great deal of research, businesses run by the self-employed (with no employees) are ignored. Much of what we know about business "failure" is based upon all firms that simply stopped operating, even though a business can cease operations for a variety of reasons other than failure, such as retirement or a decision by the entrepreneur to move on to something else.[52] Keeping these considerations in mind, we now outline the factors that have typically been associated with success and failure.

A 2005 study conducted by CIBC World Markets found that small businesses with above-average revenue growth were run by owners who had more education, used professional advisors, adopted the corporate form of ownership, did outsourcing work for other companies, had a high level of internet connectivity, and used the internet to sell outside of Canada.[53]

Identify four key reasons for success in small businesses and four key reasons for failure.

6

Reasons for Success

Beyond the specific findings like the CIBC study, four general factors typically explain the success of small business owners:

1. *Hard work, drive, and dedication.* Small business owners must be committed to succeeding and be willing to put in the time and effort to make it happen. Long hours and few vacations generally characterize the first few years of new business ownership.

2. *Market demand for the product or service.* Careful analysis of market conditions can help small business people assess the probable reception of their products. If the area around a college has only one pizza parlour, a new pizzeria is more likely to succeed than if there are already 10 in operation.

3. *Managerial competence.* Successful small business people have a solid understanding of how to manage a business. They may acquire competence through training (taking courses), experience, or by using the expertise of others. Few, however, succeed alone or straight out of university or college. Most spend time in successful companies or partner with others to bring expertise to a new business.

4. *Luck.* Luck also plays a role in the success of some firms. For example, after one entrepreneur started an environmental clean-up firm, he struggled to keep his business afloat. Then the government committed a large sum of money for toxic waste clean-up. He was able to get several large contracts, and his business is now thriving.

Reasons for Failure

Small businesses collapse for a number of reasons (see Table 4.6). Entrepreneurs may have no control over some of these factors (for example, weather, fraud, accidents), but they can influence most items on the list. Four general factors are particularly important:

1. *Managerial incompetence or inexperience.* Some entrepreneurs put their faith in common sense, overestimate their own managerial skills, or believe that hard work alone ensures success. If managers don't know how to make basic business decisions or don't understand basic management principles, they aren't likely to succeed in the long run.

2. *Neglect.* Some entrepreneurs try to launch ventures in their spare time, and others devote only limited time to new businesses. But starting a small business demands an overwhelming time commitment. If you aren't willing to put in the time and effort that a business requires, you aren't likely to survive.

3. *Weak control systems.* Effective control systems keep a business on track and alert managers to potential trouble. If your control systems don't signal impending problems, you may be in serious trouble before you spot more obvious difficulties.

4. *Insufficient capital.* Some entrepreneurs are overly optimistic about how soon they'll start earning profits. In most cases, it takes months or even years. Amazon.com didn't earn a profit for 10 years but obviously still required capital to pay employees and to cover other expenses. Experts say you need enough capital to operate at least six months without earning a profit; some recommend enough to last a year.[54]

Table 4.6	Causes of Small Business Failure

Poor management skills
- poor delegation and organizational ability
- lack of depth in management team
- entrepreneurial incompetence, such as a poor understanding of finances and business markets
- lack of experience

Inadequate marketing capabilities
- difficulty in marketing product
- market too small, nonexistent, or declines
- too much competition
- problems with distribution systems

Inadequate financial capabilities
- weak skills in accounting and finance
- lack of budgetary control
- inadequate costing systems
- incorrect valuation of assets
- unable to obtain financial backing

Inadequate production capabilities
- poorly designed production systems
- old and inefficient production facilities and equipment
- inadequate control over quality
- problems with inventory control

Personal reasons
- lost interest in business
- accident, illness
- death
- family problems

Disasters
- fire
- weather
- strikes
- fraud by entrepreneur or others

Other
- mishandling of large project
- excessive standard of living
- lack of time to devote to business
- difficulties with associates or partners
- government policies change

Summary of Learning Objectives

1. **Explain the meaning of and interrelationship among the terms** *small business, new venture creation,* **and** *entrepreneurship.* A small business has less than 100 employees. A new firm is one that has become operational within the previous 12 months, has adopted any of four main organizational forms—*sole proprietorship, partnership, corporation,* or *co-operative*—and sells goods or services. Entrepreneurship is the *process* of identifying an opportunity in the marketplace and accessing the resources needed to capitalize on it. In relation to small and/or new businesses, entrepreneurship is the process by which a small business or a new business is created.

2. **Describe the role of small and new businesses in the Canadian economy.** While 98 percent of employer businesses in Canada are small (they have less than 100 employees), 49 percent of the total private sector labour force works for small businesses. The distribution of employment by size of firm varies across industries. The small business sector's capacity for entrepreneurship and innovation accounts for much of the job creation this sector contributes to the economy, with start-ups accounting for most of the growth. On average, the number of businesses increased by 9300 each year during the 1991–2003 period, with most of the growth occurring in the services-producing sector. As the number of businesses has increased, so too has the number of women-led firms.

3. **Explain the** *entrepreneurial process* **and describe its three key elements.** The entrepreneurial process occurs within a social, political, and economic context and consists of three key elements: the entrepreneur, the opportunity, and resources. The *entrepreneur* is the driving force in identifying an opportunity and accessing the resources to capitalize on it. Opportunities don't simply materialize, entrepreneurs create them. *Opportunity* identification involves generating ideas, screening them to determine their potential, and developing the ones that remain. Entrepreneurs typically access the various *resources* needed by *bootstrapping*—doing more with less. These resources are both financial and non-financial. Two types of financing—*debt* and *equity*—can be accessed from a range of sources.

4. **Describe two alternative strategies for becoming a business owner**—*buying an existing business* and *buying a franchise.* It is necessary to work through the entrepreneurial process when *starting a business from scratch.* Whether start-up efforts will result in a new business

often depends upon how well matched the entrepreneur's skills and abilities are with the opportunity and the resources required, as well as how well matched the opportunity and resources are. Of the ventures that are brought to fruition, some will grow, while others will decline, die, or remain stable. Generally, when someone buys an existing business, the odds of success are better. An existing business has already proven its ability to attract customers. It has also established relationships with lenders, suppliers, and other stakeholders. Moreover, an existing track record gives potential buyers a much clearer picture of what to expect than any estimate of a new business's prospects. On the other hand, there may be uncertainty about the exact financial shape the business is in, the business may have a poor reputation, the location may be poor, or it may be difficult to determine an appropriate purchase price. A special case of buying an existing business involves family businesses, which pose both opportunities and challenges. In buying a *franchise* the buyer (franchisee) purchases the right to sell the product or service of the seller (franchiser) according to the terms of the franchising agreement. In return the franchiser provides assistance with the business's start-up as well as with ongoing operations once the business opens its doors.

5. **Describe four forms of** *legal organization* **for a business and discuss the advantages and disadvantages of each.** A *sole proprietorship* is a business owned and operated by one person. Answering only to themselves, sole proprietors enjoy considerable freedom in running the business. The ease of setting up a sole proprietorship makes it appealing to self-starters, as do the low start-up costs and the tax benefits. A major drawback is unlimited liability. A sole proprietor is personally liable for all debts incurred by the business. Another disadvantage is lack of continuity: A sole proprietorship dissolves when the owner dies. Finally, a sole proprietorship depends on the resources of a single individual.

A *general partnership* is similar to a sole proprietorship in that all partners have unlimited liability for the obligations of the business. The biggest advantage is its ability to grow by adding new talent and money. Because banks prefer to make loans to enterprises that are not dependent on single individuals, it's easier for partnerships to borrow money. They can also invite new partners to join by investing. Although a partnership is easy to form and has few legal requirements, all partnerships should have a partnership agreement. Partners are taxed as individuals, and unlimited liability is a drawback. Each partner may be liable for all partnership debts. Partnerships may lack continuity, and transferring ownership may be hard. No partner may sell out without the consent of the others.

All *corporations* share certain characteristics: They are separate legal entities, they have property rights and obligations, and they have indefinite lifespans. They may sue and be sued; buy, hold, and sell property; make and sell products; and be tried and punished for crimes committed. The biggest advantage of incorporation is limited liability: Investor liability is limited to one's personal investments in the corporation. If the business fails, the courts may sell a corporation's assets but cannot touch the personal possessions of investors. Another advantage is continuity—a corporation can continue forever. Shares can be sold or passed on to heirs, and most corporations benefit from the continuity of professional management. Finally, corporations have advantages in raising money. By selling stock, they expand the number of investors and the amount of available funds. Legal protections tend to make lenders more willing to grant loans.

Start-up costs and complexity are among the disadvantages of incorporating. Corporations are heavily regulated and must meet complex legal requirements in the provinces in which they're chartered. A potential drawback to incorporation is *double taxation*. A corporation pays income taxes on company profits, and its stockholders pay taxes on income returned by their investments. Thus, corporate profits are taxed twice—at the corporate and at ownership levels (but the dividend tax credit given to owners may offset the effects of double taxation). Of the two types of private-sector corporations—public and privately held—the vast majority are privately held. In forming a corporation, a business will incorporate feder-

ally if it is going to operate in more than one province and provincially if it is going to operate in only one province.

A *co-operative* is an organization that is formed to benefit its owners in the form of reduced prices and/or the distribution of surpluses at year-end. It is an incorporated business that is organized, owned, and democratically controlled by the people who use its products and services. The distribution of its earnings (or surpluses) is based upon the use of the co-operative rather than the level of investment. In addition to the two main advantages co-operatives share with corporations—limited liability and continuity—they also have two benefits that corporations don't have. Since all members have one vote, this democratic control ensures a few people cannot dominate the decision making. Additionally, co-operatives aren't subject to double taxation since surpluses are distributed to members from pre-tax profits. Co-operatives are not without disadvantages. The main drawback is that co-operatives often have difficulty raising equity, since members gain financial benefit according to their use of the co-operative, not according to the amount they have invested. While there are hundreds of different co-operatives, they usually function in one of six areas of business: consumer co-operatives, financial co-operatives, insurance co-operatives, marketing co-operatives, service co-operatives, or housing co-operatives.

6. **Identify four key reasons for success in small businesses and four key reasons for failure.** Four basic factors explain most small-business success: (1) hard work, drive, and dedication; (2) market demand for the product or service; (3) managerial competence; and (4) luck. Four factors contribute to small-business failure: (1) managerial incompetence or inexperience; (2) neglect; (3) weak control systems; and (4) insufficient capital.

KEY TERMS

board of directors, 124
bootstrapping, 116
business plan, 115
chief executive officer, 126
collateral, 116
co-operative, 127
corporation, 124
dividends, 127
double taxation, 127
entrepreneurs, 105
entrepreneurship, 105
franchise, 114

franchising agreement, 120
general partners, 122
general partnership, 122
income trust, 126
initial public offering (IPO), 126
inside directors, 124
intrapreneurs, 105
limited liability, 127
limited partners, 122
limited partnership, 122
nascent entrepreneurs, 104
new venture/firm, 105

outside directors, 105
partnership, 122
private sector, 107
private corporation, 126
public corporation, 126
sales forecast, 114
small business, 105
sole proprietorship, 122
stock, 127
stockholders, 124
unlimited liability, 122

QUESTIONS FOR ANALYSIS

1. What are some of the problems that are encountered when we try to define the term "small business"?

2. Why are new ventures the main source of job creation and new product/service ideas?

3. Do you think that you would be a successful entrepreneur? Why or why not?

4. Consider a new product or service that has recently become available for purchase by consumers. To what extent did this product or service possess the "screening" characteristics that are described in the chapter (adding value, providing competitive advantage, etc.)?

5. Using the product or service you described in Question 4, analyze the extent to which there is a good "fit" between the various elements in the entrepreneurial process.

6. Why might a corporation choose to remain private? Why might it choose to "go public"?

APPLICATION EXERCISES

1. Identify three trends—whether in fashion, lifestyle, or something else—and generate three ideas for capitalizing on each one of them.

2. Find a newspaper or magazine article that describes someone who is an entrepreneur. Use the information provided to explain what makes this person an entrepreneur.

3. Spend some time watching what people do and how they do it, and then (a) identify two ways to make what they do easier, and (b) describe two problems you observed and identify strategies for resolving those problems.

4. Interview the owner/manager of a sole proprietorship or general partnership. What characteristics of that business form led the owner to choose it? Does the owner ever contemplate changing the form of ownership of the business? Why or why not?

BUILDING YOUR BUSINESS SKILLS

Working the Internet

Goal

To encourage students to define opportunities and problems for small companies doing business on the internet.

The Situation

Suppose you and two partners own a gift basket store, specializing in special-occasion baskets for individual and corporate clients. Your business is doing well in your community, but you believe there may be opportunity for growth through a virtual storefront on the internet.

Assignment

Step 1

Join with two other students and assume the role of business partners. Start by researching internet businesses. Look at books and articles at the library and contact the following websites for help:

- Canada Business—Services for Entrepreneurs: www.cbsc.org
- U.S. Small Business Administration: www.sba.gov
- IBM Small Business Center: www.businesscenter.ibm.com
- Apple Small Business Home Page: www.apple.com/business/

These sites may lead you to other sites, so keep an open mind.

Step 2

Based on your research, determine the importance of the following small business issues:

- an analysis of changing company finances as a result of expansion to the internet
- an analysis of your new competitive marketplace (the world) and how it affects your current marketing approach, which focusses on your local community
- identification of sources of management advice as the expansion proceeds
- the role of technology consultants in launching and maintaining the website
- customer service policies in your virtual environment

Follow-Up Questions

1. Do you think your business would be successful on the internet? Why or why not?

2. Based on your analysis, how will internet expansion affect your current business practices? What specific changes are you likely to make?

3. Do you think that operating a virtual storefront will be harder or easier than doing business in your local community? Explain your answer.

EXERCISING YOUR ETHICS

Breaking Up Is Hard to Do

The Situation

Connie and Mark began a 25-year friendship after finishing college and discovering their mutual interest in owning a business. Established as a general partnership, their home-furnishings centre is a successful business sustained for 20 years by a share-and-share-alike relationship. Start-up cash, daily responsibilities, and profits have all been shared equally. The partners both work four days each week except when busy seasons require both of them to be in the store. Shared goals and compatible personalities have led to a solid give-and-take relationship that helps them overcome business problems while maintaining a happy interpersonal relationship.

The division of work is a natural match and successful combination because of the partners' different but complementary interests. Mark buys the merchandise and maintains up-to-date contacts with suppliers; he also handles personnel matters (hiring and training employees). Connie manages the inventory, buys shipping supplies, keeps the books, and manages the finances. Mark does more selling, with Connie helping out only during busy seasons. Both partners share in decisions about advertising and promotions.

The Dilemma

Things began changing two years ago, when Connie became less interested in the business and got more involved in other activities. While Mark's enthusiasm remained high, Connie's time was increasingly consumed by travel, recreation, and community-service activities.

At first, she reduced her work commitment from four to three days a week. Then she indicated that she wanted to cut back further, to just two days. "In that case," Mark replied, "we'll have to make some changes."

Mark insisted that profit sharing be adjusted to reflect his larger role in running the business. He proposed that Connie's monthly salary be cut in half (from $4000 to $2000). Connie agreed. He recommended that the $2000 savings be shifted to his salary because of his increased workload, but this time Connie balked, arguing that Mark's current $4000 salary already compensated him for his contributions. She proposed to split the difference, with Mark getting a $1000 increase and the other $1000 going into the firm's cash account. Mark said no and insisted on a full $2000 raise. To avoid a complete falling out, Connie finally gave in, even though she thought it unfair for Mark's salary to jump from $4000 per month to $6000. At that point, she made a promise to herself: "To even things out, I'll find a way to get $2000 worth of inventory for personal use each month."

Questions for Discussion

1. Identify the ethical issues, if any, regarding Mark's and Connie's respective positions on Mark's proposed $2000 salary increase.

2. What kind of salary adjustments do you think would be fair in this situation? Explain why.

3. There is, of course, another way for Mark and Connie to solve their differences: Because the terms of participation have changed, it might make sense to dissolve the existing partnership. What do you recommend in this regard?

CONCLUDING CASE 4-1

The Big Cheese

People familiar with the business landscape in Vermont point with justifiable pride to Ben Cohen and Jerry Greenfield, founders of Ben and Jerry's Homemade Holdings Inc., as the state's foremost entrepreneurs. But the ice cream boys are getting some competition these days from another pair of entrepreneurs who are making a popular line of cheese products the cream of local business.

The story starts in 1919, when 94 Vermont dairy farmers banded together to create a co-operative to make and market cheese. The initial membership fee was

$5.00 per cow and a cord of wood to fuel the boiler. Cabot Creamery (www.cabotcheese.com) is now a multi-million-dollar dairy-products company with a membership of 1500 farm families. Its cheeses have won numerous awards, including Best Cheddar in the World at the World Cheese Championship in Green Bay, Wisconsin.

Cabot has always built its brand on quality. Whereas many companies use enzymes to speed up the cheese-making process, Cabot uses only natural methods. Naturally processing high-quality cheese means that a 640-pound block of cheddar might have to sit in a warehouse for a year before it gets its rich, full-bodied flavour.

▶ ▶ ▶

At any time, therefore, Cabot might have 25 million pounds of cheese in the warehouse. And because costs are pegged to the price of milk when the cheese is first manufactured, profit margins are hard to predict. Managers have to forecast both the price of milk and the demand for cheese as much as a year in advance. Furthermore, the price of milk fluctuates just as much as the price of crude oil. "There's a pretty good temptation to play around with enzymes," admits Cabot CEO Richard Stammer. "If you can put out an extra-sharp cheddar in 5 months instead of 12, you're less likely to get stung by a spread in the price of milk."

In the early 1990s, Cabot was in danger of going under. Even with revenues of $35 million a year, annual profits were less than $1 million. Members were getting restless, and there was talk of abandoning Cabot and launching a new co-operative. But because a new venture would have been a big risk, members decided on another approach: In 1992, Cabot agreed to be taken over by Agri-Mark Inc., a dairy co-op based in Methuen, Massachusetts. Agri-Mark (www.agrimark.net) was the fourteenth largest dairy co-op in the United States and wanted to expand. Given the obvious fit between a dairy co-op and a cheese maker, the move seemed like a good one.

After Agri-Mark took control of Cabot in 1992, parent-company president Paul Johnston decided to install a new CEO. He didn't have to look far. His choice was Richard Stammer, Agri-Mark's chief economist. While Johnston was working his way up the ladder at an Agri-Mark milk-producing plant, Stammer had been an economics professor at Rutgers, where he had developed a strong understanding of the dynamics of prices in agricultural markets.

Johnston and Stammer couldn't have been more different, but they worked well together. Johnston is a demanding boss known for his bluntness and, occasionally, lack of tact. Stammer is reserved, polite, and gracious. But the two executives have managed to set aside their differences and focus on a common goal: running an efficient business that earns profits for its owners.

Among the first things they did was improve forecasting methods. The process is never perfect, but Cabot now does a much better job of predicting demand and prices for milk and cheese. They also set about to make Cabot a national brand by concentrating more heavily on product marketing. So far, the plan seems to be paying off: Profits have topped $8 million on annual revenues of $175 million.

Questions for Discussion

1. Why do you think Cabot is organized as a co-operative?

2. What role has entrepreneurship played in the history and success of Cabot?

3. Under what circumstances might it make sense for Cabot to reorganize as a corporation?

4. What issues of taxation and legal liability might be especially pertinent for Cabot and Agri-Mark?

CONCLUDING CASE 4-2

Getting in on the Ground Floor

Larry Gibson, 51, oversees a business empire that employs 80 people full time, (plus 110 under contract) and is projected to have sales of $30 million this year. But things didn't start out that way. Gibson got into the flooring business after finding university too slow for his liking. After working as a flooring installer in Halifax, he went west in the late 1970s and worked in Calgary and in the Arctic, honing his commercial estimating skills before returning to Nova Scotia in 1983.

After five years of managing Eaton's flooring business in Halifax, he got word that his division was closing in May, 1988. At the time Eaton's still had contracts and warranties outstanding. "So they came to me and said, 'Will you take these contracts on and go out on your own?'" Using personal savings, he and his wife Patricia bought a dilapidated Halifax building from which to launch a floor-covering business and took over the chain's local flooring accounts, setting up shop under the Install-A-Flor name.

The weekend before opening the doors in July 1988, Patricia started to cry, wondering if they were doing the right thing. Reassurance was not long in coming. Gibson's phone rang at 8:30 opening day, and on the line— unaware that Gibson's phone was resting on a sawhorse, since his office wasn't furnished yet—was Atlantic property developer Armour Construction. Gibson's earlier bid to install flooring in a 185-unit complex had been accepted. The deal was worth $440 000 over 15 months.

He says that first sale taught him that "if you believe you can do something, then put your mind and heart to it. There's always an element of surprise and the unforeseen, and it can be good or it can be bad. In my case, it was good and lucky." Indeed, Larry Gibson is known for his commitment to hard work, providing the best possible service, and

▶▶▶

delivering a quality product at a competitive price. He credits the nuns at the convent school in Herring Cove for instilling discipline in him and says the unexpected death of his father when he was 10 helped give him drive.

Mr. Gibson said the first few years of heads-down, all-out work took its toll on his health. "I was gritting my teeth at night and my stomach had a big knot in it, basically, because we started with nothing and always worried about turning that dollar and getting financial institutions and suppliers to believe in me," he recalled. "It was always tight."

Mr. Gibson credits his wife, who handles the business's finances and administration, with helping him through the early days. "I'd go home, we'd sit at the table—most people have salt shakers; we had a calculator. We would do quantity measures on plans and I would bid, bid, bid." That effort resulted in a 633 percent growth over the company's first five years. "When we first started, it was difficult to convince suppliers to sell us their products," recalls Patricia, "because selling to a newcomer is sometimes a bit of a risk. But Larry and I have a policy of 'Never take no for an answer. There's always another way.' We stuck with it and gained people's confidence."

Today, the business includes seven Floors Plus retail stores in Nova Scotia and New Brunswick, as well as specialty and contract divisions that operate internationally and have specialties such as clean room technology—on-site thermal welding and moulding of plastics—that is used in medical operating theatres and food-processing facilities. "Right now we're doing a school in Bermuda," said Mr. Gibson, adding that the business has opened offices in China and Ontario.

Contracting represents 40 percent of the company's business, with retail accounting for another 40 percent and the growing wholesale business, named Dantra (after his two children Daniel and Tracy, who both work in the family firm), representing 20 percent.

"We have a lack of supply here of specialty products," Mr. Gibson said in explaining the company's diversification. "Nobody's going to come in here and say, 'Listen, I want you to do clean rooms.' You've got to search this stuff out and find a market for it. It's not just about money, it's about service, being a leader and having knowledge about the market."

Market knowledge is market power, and Mr. Gibson has gained that by going all over the world in search of new business opportunities. "We know from traveling the styles that are coming," he said, noting that he is largely in the business of selling fashion. "The (Atlantic) area is a couple of years behind Toronto, New York, and even European or Asian markets. So we know we've got time to react if we react quickly."

Questions for Discussion

1. According to Statistics Canada's Business Register, would Install-a-Flor be considered a small business? Why or why not?

2. Assess the fit between Larry Gibson and the opportunity when Install-a-Flor was started. What personal characteristics contributed most to his success?

3. To what extent did Larry Gibson use bootstrapping in getting his business started? Explain.

4. Assess Larry Gibson's capacity for identifying opportunities according to the characteristics outlined in the opportunity screening section of the chapter.

5. What benefits or drawbacks are evident in this family business?

6. Would you recommend that Install-a-Flor go public?

7. Clearly, Install-a-Flor is no longer a new business. But is it entrepreneurial?

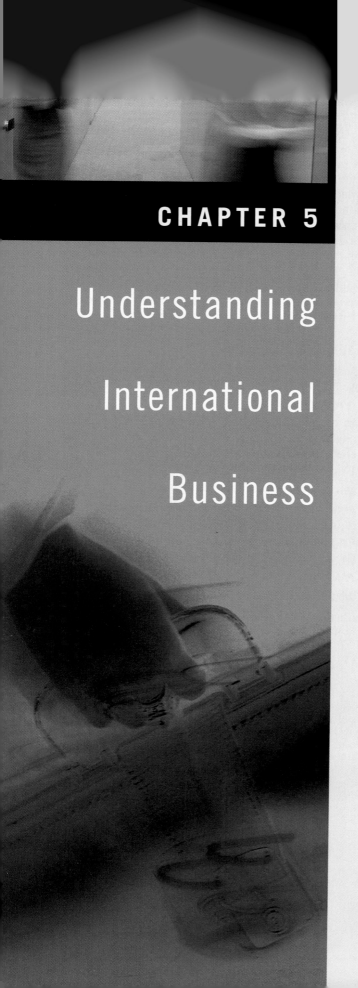

CHAPTER 5

Understanding International Business

After reading this chapter, you should be able to:

1 Describe the rise of international business and identify the *major world marketplaces*.

2 Explain how different forms of *competitive advantage*, *import-export balances*, *exchange rates*, and *foreign competition* determine the ways in which countries and businesses respond to the international environment.

3 Discuss the factors involved in deciding to do business internationally and in selecting the appropriate *levels of international involvement* and *international organizational structure*.

4 Describe some of the ways in which *social*, *cultural*, *economic*, *legal*, and *political differences* act as barriers to international trade.

5 Explain how *free trade agreements* assist world trade.

Corporate Espionage

Spying, intrigue, and shredded documents are activities we normally associate with countries spying on one another. But these activities are also evident in the business world. And make no mistake about it, Canada is just as likely a place for shenanigans as the United States. Norman Inkster, who helps companies fight off corporate spies, says that business firms engage in corporate espionage much more often than we ever hear about. And, he says, "getting a leg up" can be "low down and dirty." Consider the case of Air Canada versus WestJet.

It all started when a WestJet executive got a password that allowed him to access an Air Canada website that was supposed to be confidential and available only to Air Canada employees. This website gave the WestJet executive access to Air Canada's "load factor" on each one of its routes. This was critical information that allowed WestJet to identify Air Canada's strong and weak flights and then to develop a competitive strategy based on that information.

Air Canada learned that someone at WestJet was accessing their website only after someone tipped them off. In an attempt to find out just what WestJet knew, Air Canada hired private investigators to steal the WestJet executive's garbage. The garbage contained a lot of shredded paper, which was sent to Church Street Technology, a company that has developed a system for reassembling shredded pages. Owner Cody Ford first sorts the strips of shredded paper, then tapes them to a blank sheet of paper and scans them. A specialized computer program then reassembles the original document. Ford says that he can easily reassemble shredded documents.

While this was going on, WestJet was not idle. When the WestJet executive's garbage was stolen, a neighbour noticed and phoned the police. They informed the executive, so he took pictures of the investigators the next time they came for his garbage. The pictures appeared in the *Globe and Mail*.

Once Air Canada had determined what WestJet knew, and once WestJet knew that Air Canada had stolen one of their executive's garbage, the rivalry between the two companies moved from the boardroom to the courtroom, and the companies sued each other over allegations of corporate espionage. Air Canada filed a $220 million lawsuit against WestJet, accusing it of using the website information to schedule competing flights. WestJet counter-sued Air Canada, accusing it of trespassing and stealing private property.

The lawsuit was settled in 2006. WestJet apologized to Air Canada and said that its conduct was both unethical and unacceptable, and that WestJet accepted full responsibility for its misconduct. WestJet agreed to pay $5 million to Air Canada for the expenses Air Canada incurred while investigating the unauthorized accessing of its website. WestJet also agreed to contribute $10 million to children's charities. Clive Beddoe, CEO of WestJet, also apologized to WestJet shareholders and said this shouldn't have happened. WestJet's lawsuit against Air Canada was dismissed.

Questions for Discussion

1. Do you think that WestJet behaved in an unethical fashion? Why or why not? Do you think that Air Canada behaved in an unethical fashion? Why or why not?

2. Analyze this problem using the model in Figure 3.1 on p. 77. Work through the model step-by-step and explain your conclusions at each step in the process. What conclusions do you reach at the end of the process about the behaviour of WestJet and Air Canada?

3. Suppose that you are confronted with a situation where you strongly believe that another person acted in an unethical fashion, but that person totally disagreed with you. How would you go about convincing that person that their behaviour was unethical?

4. *"The WestJet executive who gained access to Air Canada's website did not behave in an unethical fashion. He simply used the information he was given to gather information from Air Canada's website. He then analyzed Air Canada's business activity and developed a strategy for WestJet that took advantage of that knowledge. This is simply an example of a person using information to his advantage."* Do you agree or disagree with this statement? Explain.

Sources: "Under the Radar," *Venture*, October 31, 2004; www.cbc.ca/canada/calgary/story/2006/05/29/ca-westjet-settlement-20060529.html.

The Business

of Managing

Corporate strategy, organizational structure, workforce diversity, labour–management relations, and employee motivation and satisfaction are five issues you will read about in the opening cases of Chapters 6 to 10. These and many other issues must be dealt with if companies hope to grow and prosper. Managers in all business firms—indeed, in any kind of organization—must carry out the basic management functions of planning, organizing, leading, and controlling. These important functions are the focus of this section of the text.

Part Two, The Business of Managing, provides an overview of business management today. It includes a look at the importance of managers in business firms, how businesses are structured to achieve their goals, the management of the firm's human resources, labour–management relations, and the importance of motivating and leading employees.

- We begin in **Chapter 6, Managing the Business Enterprise**, by describing how managers set goals and choose corporate strategies. The basic functions of management—planning, organizing, leading, and controlling—are examined, as are the different types and levels of managers that are found in business firms, and the corporate culture that is created in each firm.

- In **Chapter 7, Organizing the Business Enterprise**, we look at the basic organizational structures that companies have adopted, and the different kinds of authority that managers can have. The impact of the informal organization is also analyzed.

- In **Chapter 8, Managing Human Resources**, we explore the activities that are necessary to effectively manage employees, including assessing employee needs, training, promoting, and compensating employees.

- In **Chapter 9, Understanding Labour–Management Relations**, we look at the development of the union movement in Canada, why and how workers organize, and how government legislation has affected workers' rights to organize into unions.

- Finally, in **Chapter 10, Motivating and Leading Employees**, we examine the reasons why firms should establish good relationships with their employees, and how managers' attempts to maintain productivity can affect their relations with employees.

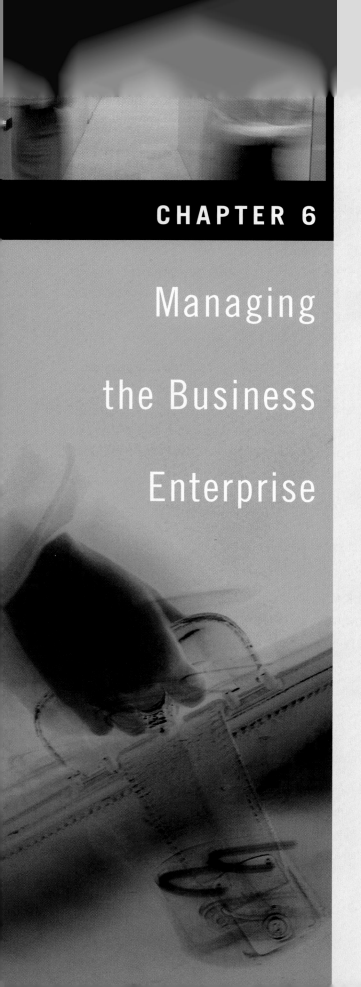

CHAPTER 6

Managing the Business Enterprise

After reading this chapter, you should be able to:

1 Explain the importance of setting *goals* and formulating *strategies* as the starting points of effective management.

2 Describe the four activities that constitute the *management process*.

3 Identify *types of managers* by level and area.

4 Describe the five basic *management skills*.

5 Describe the development and explain the importance of *corporate culture*.

Looking for Redemption?

Edgar Bronfman Jr. is the chairman of Warner Music Group, which includes record labels such as Warner Bros., Atlantic, Electra, and the Christian music producer Word Records. He is the son of Edgar Bronfman Sr., who was CEO of the Seagram Company. Seagram was started in the 1920s by Sam Bronfman, who sold liquor by mail order. Sam's son, Edgar Bronfman Sr. became CEO in 1957, and for the next 40 years the company focussed on the production of wine and distilled spirits. In the process, it became a household name in Canada.

In the mid-1990s, Edgar Bronfman Jr. took over leadership of Seagram from his father and made some dramatic strategic moves that turned the company away from its traditional products and moved it toward the high-risk entertainment business. For example, the company bought MCA Inc. (now Universal) and Polygram NV. These moves caused some people to recall founder Sam Bronfman's observation that third-generation family members often dissipate the family fortune. Edgar Jr. was well aware of this criticism, and he was determined not to fulfill his grandfather's prophecy.

Things seemed to go well for a time under Edgar Jr.'s leadership. In 2000, he sold Seagram to the French conglomerate Vivendi SA for $33 billion in Vivendi stock. This looked like a good deal because Seagram was paid the equivalent of $75 for each of its shares, even though Seagram's shares were trading at less than $50 at the time. But things soon turned sour. By the end of 2001, Vivendi was in deep financial trouble, and its stock price had declined from $130 to $50 per share. The Seagram fortune declined along with Vivendi's decline because Bronfman had taken Vivendi stock instead of cash when he sold Seagram. When the merger with Vivendi was originally announced, the Seagram family fortune was worth about U.S.$7 billion, but by 2003, it had declined to less than U.S.$1 billion. People started thinking Sam Bronfman was right after all.

In spite of these setbacks, Edgar Bronfman Jr. was determined to get back on the winning track. In 2003, he was unsuccessful in his attempt to buy Vivendi's film and TV assets, but in 2004 he and several partners were successful in purchasing Warner Music Group. Bronfman has adopted a corporate strategy based on the assumption that consumers will increasingly bypass traditional music stores and instead buy online digital music. He wants Warner Music Group to be a major player in emerging markets such as ringtones and ringbacks (where cellphones are programmed to play different tunes depending on who is calling the cellphone). He also thinks that music will be distributed through many more distribution channels than has historically been the case. He predicts that by 2009 about one-quarter of music revenue will come from digital music.

To pursue this strategy, Bronfman has borrowed a lot of money. So far, he is using some of this borrowed money to reward his shareholder partners. The partners have already taken more than $1 billion out of the firm. Standard & Poor's Corp., a bond rating firm, criticized this distribution, saying that it put the company's balance sheet at risk. For the 10 months ending September 30, 2004, Warner Music lost $136 million. Industry observers feel that Bronfman is counting far too much on future revenue, particularly since the music industry's attempts to defeat online piracy have not been very successful.

It is too early to tell if Bronfman's strategy is going to work. If it does, he will be seen as a top manager who had the vision and insight to position Warner Music Group so that it could capitalize on a major trend. If the strategy doesn't work, critics will keep saying that old Sam Bronfman was right. ◆

WHO ARE MANAGERS?

All corporations depend on effective management. Regardless of the type of business they work in, managers like Edgar Bronfman perform many of the same functions, are responsible for many of the same tasks, and have many of the same responsibilities. The work of all managers involves developing strategic and tactical plans. They must also analyze their competitive environments and plan, organize, direct, and control day-to-day operations.

Although our focus is on managers in *business* settings, remember that the principles of management apply to all kinds of organizations. Managers work in charities, churches, social organizations, educational institutions, and government agencies. The prime minister of Canada, the president of the University of Toronto, the executive director of the United Way, the dean of your business school, and the chief administrator of your local hospital are all managers. Remember, too, that managers bring to small organizations many of the same kinds of skills—the ability to make decisions and respond to a variety of challenges—that they bring to large ones. Regardless of the nature and size of an organization, managers are among its most important resources.

SETTING GOALS AND FORMULATING STRATEGY

goals Objectives that a business hopes and plans to achieve.

1 Explain the importance of setting *goals* and formulating *strategies* as the starting points of effective management.

The starting point in effective management is setting **goals**, objectives that a business hopes (and plans) to achieve. Every business needs goals, and we begin by discussing the basic aspects of organizational goal setting. However, deciding what it *intends* to do is only step one for an organization. A company's managers must also make decisions about *actions* that will and will not achieve its goals. From this perspective, *strategy* is the broad program that underlies those decisions; the basic steps in formulating strategy are discussed later in the chapter.

Setting Goals

Goals are performance targets, the means by which organizations and their managers measure success or failure at every level. In this section, we identify the main purposes for which organizations establish goals, classify the basic levels of business goals, and describe the process by which goals are commonly set.

The Purposes of Goal Setting

An organization functions systematically because it sets goals and plans accordingly. Indeed, an organization functions as such because it commits its resources on all levels to achieving its goals. Specifically, we can identify four main purposes in organizational goal setting:

1. *Goal setting provides direction, guidance, and motivation for all managers.* If managers know precisely where the company is headed, there is less potential for error in the different units of the company. Starbucks, for example, has a goal of increasing capital spending by 15 percent, with all additional expenditures devoted to opening new stores. This goal clearly informs everyone in the firm that expansion into new territories is a high priority for the firm.

2. *Goal setting helps firms allocate resources.* Areas that are expected to grow will get first priority. The company allocates more resources to new projects with large sales potential than it allocates to mature prod-

ucts with established but stagnant sales potential. Thus, Starbucks is primarily emphasizing new store expansion, while its ecommerce initiatives are currently given a lower priority. "Our management team," says CEO Howard Schultz, "is 100 percent focused on growing our core business without distraction...from any other initiative."

3. *Goal setting helps to define corporate culture.* General Electric's goal, for instance, is to push each of its divisions to number one or number two in its industry. The result is a competitive, often stressful, environment and a culture that rewards success and has little tolerance for failure. At the same time, however, GE's appliance business, television network (NBC), aircraft engine unit, and financial services business are each among the very best in their respective industries.

4. *Goal setting helps managers assess performance.* If a company sets a goal to increase sales by 10 percent in a given year, managers in units who attain or exceed the goal can be rewarded. Units failing to reach the goal will also be compensated accordingly. GE has a long-standing reputation for stringently evaluating managerial performance, richly rewarding those who excel—and getting rid of those who do not. Each year, the lower 10 percent of GE's managerial force are informed that either they make dramatic improvements in performance or consider alternative directions for their careers.

Kinds of Goals

Naturally, goals differ from company to company, depending on the firm's purpose and mission. Every enterprise, of course, has a *purpose*—a reason for being. Businesses seek profit, universities work to discover and transmit new knowledge, and government agencies exist to provide service to the public. Most enterprises also have a **mission statement**—a statement of how it will achieve its purpose. Bell Canada's mission, for example, is to be a world leader in helping communicate and manage information. DaimlerChrysler's mission statement emphasizes "delighted customers." Atco Ltd.'s mission is to provide products and services to the energy and resource industries, and to invest principally in energy-related assets in North America. The mission of Investor's Group is to satisfy clients who need general and comprehensive financial planning. Mission statements

mission statement An organization's statement of how it will achieve its purpose in the environment in which it conducts its business.

National leaders are managers, too, and those at the highest levels, like Russian President Vladimir Putin (centre), set goals for overall economic growth. When Economic Minister German Gref (left) announced an anticipated growth rate of 5.2 percent for the coming year, Putin publicly admonished his entire cabinet for setting their economic sights too low. Applauding his boss's policy (and responding to his management style), Gref quickly revised his estimate to a rosier 6.4 percent, citing the likelihood that oil prices would be higher than he had originally thought.

should also include some statement about the company's core values and its commitment to ethical behaviour.

Two business firms can have the same purpose—for example, to sell watches at a profit—yet they have very different missions. Timex sells low-cost, reliable watches in outlets ranging from department stores to corner drugstores. Rolex, on the other hand, sells high-quality, high-priced fashion watches through selected jewellery stores.

Regardless of a company's purpose and mission, every firm needs long-term, intermediate, and short-term goals:

long-term goals Goals set for extended periods of time, typically five years or more into the future.

- **Long-term goals** relate to extended periods of time—typically five years or more into the future. MasterCard, for example, might set a long-term goal of doubling the number of participating merchants during the next 10 years. Similarly, Sony might adopt a long-term goal to increase its share of the digital SLR market by 10 percent during the next five years.

intermediate goals Goals set for a period of one to five years.

- **Intermediate goals** are set for a period of one to five years into the future. Companies usually have intermediate goals in several areas. For example, the marketing department's goal might be to increase sales by 3 percent in two years. The production department might want to decrease expenses by 6 percent in four years. Human resources might seek to cut turnover by 10 percent in two years. Finance might aim for a 3 percent increase in return on investment in three years.

short-term goals Goals set for the very near future, typically less than one year.

- Like intermediate goals, **short-term goals**—which are set for one year or less—are developed for several different areas. Increasing sales by 2 percent this year, cutting costs by 1 percent next quarter, and reducing turnover by 4 percent over the next six months are all short-term goals.

Formulating Strategy

Planning is concerned with the nuts and bolts of setting goals, choosing tactics, and establishing schedules. In contrast, strategy tends to have a wider scope. It is by definition a "broad program" that describes an organization's intentions. A business strategy outlines how it intends to meet its goals, and includes the organization's responsiveness to new challenges and new needs. **Strategy formulation** involves three basic steps, as shown in Figure 6.1.

strategy formulation Creation of a broad program for defining and meeting an organization's goals.

Setting Strategic Goals

strategic goals Long-term goals derived directly from a firm's mission statement.

Strategic goals are long-term goals derived directly from the firm's mission statement. For example, Bernd Pischetsrieder, CEO of Volkswagen, has clear strategic goals for the European automaker. When he took over, Volkswagen was only marginally profitable, was regarded as an also-ran in

Figure 6.1 Strategy formulation.

the industry, and was thinking of pulling out of the U.S. market because its sales were so poor. Over the next few years, however, Pischetsrieder totally revamped the firm and now it is making big profits. Volkswagen is now a much more formidable force in the global automobile industry.[1]

SWOT Analysis. After strategic goals have been established, organizations usually go through a process called a **SWOT analysis** as they continue to formulate their strategy. This process involves assessing organizational *Strengths* and *Weaknesses* (the *S* and the *W*) and environmental *Opportunities* and *Threats* (the *O* and the *T*). Note that strengths and weaknesses are internal to the company, while opportunities and threats are external. In formulating strategy, companies attempt to capitalize on organizational strengths and take advantage of environmental opportunities. During this same process, they seek ways to overcome organizational weaknesses and cope with environmental threats.[2]

SWOT analysis Identification and analysis of organizational strengths and weaknesses and environmental opportunities and threats as part of strategy formulation.

Analyzing the Organization and Its Environment

The term **environmental analysis** means scanning the environment for threats and opportunities. Changing consumer tastes and hostile takeover offers are *threats*, as are new government regulations. Even more important threats come from new products and new competitors. *Opportunities*, meanwhile, are areas in which the firm can potentially expand, grow, or take advantage of existing strengths.

environmental analysis The process of scanning the environment for threats and opportunities.

Consider, for example, the case of British entrepreneur Richard Branson and his company, Virgin Group Ltd. Branson started the firm in 1968, when he was 17, naming it in acknowledgment of his own lack of experience in the business world. Over the years, he has built Virgin into one of the world's best-known brands, comprising a conglomeration of over 200 entertainment, media, and travel companies worldwide. Among the best known of his enterprises are Virgin Atlantic (an international airline), Virgin Megastores (retailing), and V2 Music (record labels). Branson sees potential threats from other competitors such as British Airways and KLM for Virgin Atlantic, Tower Records for retailing, and the EMI Group for recorded music.

But he also sees significant opportunities because of his firm's strong brand name (especially in Europe). Indeed, one of his most recent ventures is a new ecommerce firm. The business is called Virgin Mobile and operates like a cellular telephone company. But in addition to providing conventional cellular service, the Virgin telephone permits the user to press a red button to go directly to a Virgin operator who can sell products, make airline and hotel reservations, and provide numerous other services. A companion website complements the cellular service and its related programs. Virgin Mobile signed up more than one million new customers during its first year of operation and is one of the market leaders in Great Britain.[3]

In addition to performing environmental analysis, which is analysis of *external* factors, managers must examine *internal* factors. The purpose of **organizational analysis** is to better understand a company's strengths and weaknesses. Strengths might include surplus cash, a dedicated workforce, an ample supply of managerial talent, technical expertise, or weak competition. The absence of any of these strengths could represent an important weakness.

organizational analysis The process of analyzing a firm's strengths and weaknesses.

Branson, for example, started up Virgin Mobile in part because he saw so many of his current operations as old-line, traditional businesses that might be at future risk from new forms of business and competition. One strength he has employed has been the widespread name recognition that his businesses enjoy. Another strength relates to finances. Branson sold 49 percent of Virgin Atlantic to Singapore Airlines for almost $1 billion in cash, retaining ownership control but raising all of the funds he needed to launch his new venture. On the other hand, he also admits that neither he nor most of his senior managers have much experience in or knowledge about ecommerce, which may be a significant weakness.

Matching the Organization and Its Environment

The final step in strategy formulation is matching environmental threats and opportunities with corporate strengths and weaknesses. The matching process is the heart of strategy formulation: More than any other facet of strategy, matching companies with their environments lays the foundation for successfully planning and conducting business.

ENTREPRENEURSHIP AND NEW VENTURES

Best in Show

When Mark Warren, a Toronto investment banker, returned to Canada from London a few years ago with his four dogs, he was confronted with an underdeveloped market for pet insurance in North America. Pet insurance was sold mainly through veterinary clinics, and coverage was riddled with loopholes and exceptions. Seeing an opportunity to bring increased innovation and customer service to the market, Warren launched Pethealth in March 1999.

As people pour emotional equity into their pets (seven in 10 pet owners say their pets have the same rights to health as humans, according to a 2001 Ipsos-Reid study), they're more willing to consider complex medical procedures to extend their lives. With such operations costing in the thousands, pet insurance starts to make sense. "You're effectively replacing the high cost of the unexpected and the unforeseen with a budgetable monthly premium," says Warren.

His strategy has been to avoid the commoditization of Pethealth's insurance services, working hard to out-innovate the competition on all fronts: price, service, sales channels, and technology. Pethealth has led the market by, for example, introducing bigger and faster payouts than its competitors; by partnering with trusted retailers such as U.S. giant Petco to sell its pet insurance; and by befriending the fast-growing channel of animal shelters by providing them with free shelter management software. It also offers free 30-day health insurance on pets adopted from participating pounds—reassuring buyers, eliminating costly liabilities for the shelters, and creating low-cost trial customers, of which a significant percentage renew their policies once the trial ends.

According to Warren, "In 2005, we consolidated our position as Canada's largest provider of pet health insurance and are now the second largest provider in North America. 2005 also marked a watershed year in

our journey towards completing our vision of becoming the leading provider of integrated health-related information services to the companion animal industry, bringing unique products and services to veterinarians, shelters, and pet owners."

The transition from a single-service pet insurance provider began with the creation in 2003 of 24PetWatch (www.24petwatch.com), a microchip and lost pet recovery network. Pethealth is now the largest provider of RFID (radio frequency identification) technology and related services to veterinary clinics and animal shelters in Canada, and one of the top providers in the U.S. market.

In 2005, Pethealth rolled out additional innovative new services, 24PetMedInfo and 24PetMedAlert, that offer pet owners the ability to both track their pets' medical records online and also to allow emergency veterinary personnel to access the information in a lost pet emergency. 2005 also marked the launch of the Company's suite of .NET-based software solutions for veterinary clinics and animal welfare organizations throughout North America.

PetPoint™ (www.petpoint.com) is the first web-hosted management software program for animal welfare organizations in North America. In addition to providing a more efficient platform for shelters to manage their day-to-day operations, PetPoint also allows shelters to easily provide Pethealth's ShelterCare insurance and 24PetWatch microchip programs electronically at the point of adoption. PetPoint is now the leading management software solution to animal welfare organizations in North America.

EVE™ (www.eveforclinics.com), is the first web-based claims adjudication software for veterinary clinics. This program, the first of its kind in the pet insurance industry in North America, allows claims to be processed online at the veterinary clinic, thus enhancing the clinic/client relationship.

Over the long term, this process may also determine whether a firm typically takes risks or behaves more conservatively. Either strategy can be successful. Blue Bell, for example, is one of the most profitable ice-cream makers in the world, even though it sells its products in only about a dozen U.S. states. Based in Brenham, Texas, Blue Bell controls more than 50 percent of the market in each state where it does business. The firm has resisted the temptation to expand too quickly. Its success is based on product freshness and frequent deliveries—strengths that may suffer if the company grows too large.

A Hierarchy of Plans

Plans can be viewed on three levels: strategic, tactical, and operational. Managerial responsibilities are defined at each level. The levels constitute a hierarchy because implementing plans is practical only when there is a logical flow from one level to the next.

- **Strategic plans** reflect decisions about resource allocations, company priorities, and the steps needed to meet strategic goals. They are usually set by the board of directors and top management. General Electric's decision that viable products must be number one or number two within their respective categories is a matter of strategic planning.

- **Tactical plans** are shorter-range plans concerned with implementing specific aspects of the company's strategic plans. They typically involve upper and middle management. Coca-Cola's decision to increase sales in Europe by building European bottling facilities is an example of tactical planning.

- **Operational plans**, which are developed by middle- and lower-level managers, set short-term targets for daily, weekly, or monthly performance. McDonald's, for example, establishes operational plans when it explains precisely how Big Macs are to be cooked, warmed, and served.

Levels of Strategies

There are three levels of strategy in a business firm (see Figure 6.2). A **corporate-level strategy** identifies the various businesses that a company will be in, and how these businesses will relate to each other. A **business-level (competitive) strategy** identifies the ways a business will compete in its chosen line of products or services. **Functional strategies** identify the

strategic plans Plans that reflect decisions about resource allocations, company priorities, and steps needed to meet strategic goals.

tactical plans Generally, short-range plans concerned with implementing specific aspects of a company's strategic plans.

operational plans Plans setting short-term targets for daily, weekly, or monthly performance.

corporate-level strategy Identifies the various businesses that a company will be in, and how these businesses will relate to each other.

business-level (competitive) strategy Identifies the ways a business will compete in its chosen line of products or services.

functional strategies Identify the basic courses of action that each department in the firm will pursue so that it contributes to the attainment of the business's overall goals.

In the wake of a disastrous industry-wide slump in 2001, Cisco Systems, a giant maker of communications equipment, was forced to radically revise its strategic plans. Where engineers once pursued their own pet projects, engineering is now centralized under a group of top managers. Where individual units once chose their own suppliers, a committee now oversees all partnerships. Where the product line once consisted solely of networking apparatus, the company has branched out into a variety of new high-tech markets.

basic courses of action that each department in the firm will pursue so that it contributes to the attainment of the business's overall goals. Each of these strategies is discussed below.

Corporate-Level Strategies

There are several different corporate-level strategies that a company might pursue, including concentration, growth, integration, diversification, and investment reduction.

Concentration. A **concentration strategy** involves focussing the company on one product or product line. Organizations that have successfully pursued a concentration strategy include McDonald's and Canadian National Railway. The main advantage of a concentration strategy is that the company can focus its strengths on the one business it knows well. The main disadvantage is the risk inherent in putting all of one's eggs in one basket.

Growth. Companies have several growth strategies available to them, all of which focus on *internal* activities that will result in growth. These strategies include **market penetration** (boosting sales of present products by more aggressive selling in the firm's current markets), **product development** (developing improved products for current markets), and **geographic expansion** (expanding operations in new geographic areas or countries). CanJet, for example, is using a geographic expansion strategy, since it started by offering service in Eastern Canada but has now added flights to cities in Western Canada.[4]

Integration. There are two basic integration strategies, both of which focus on *external* activities that will result in growth. **Horizontal integration** means acquiring control of competitors in the same or similar markets with the same or similar products. For example, Hudson's Bay Company purchased Kmart and Zellers. **Vertical integration** means owning or controlling the inputs to the firm's processes and/or the channels through which the products or services are distributed. Thus, major oil companies like Shell not only drill and produce their own oil, but refine the oil into different products and then sell those products through company-controlled outlets across Canada. Another example of vertical integration is Irving Forest Products' purchase of Royale Tissue from Procter & Gamble.

Diversification. **Diversification** means expanding into related or unrelated products or market segments. Diversification helps the firm avoid the problem of having all of its eggs in one basket by spreading risk among several products or markets. *Related diversification* means adding new, but related, products or services to an existing business. For example, CN diversified into trucking, an activity that is clearly related to railway operations. Maple Leaf Gardens Ltd., which already owned the Toronto Maple Leafs, also acquired the Toronto Raptors basketball team. *Conglomerate diversification* means diversifying into products or markets that are not related to the firm's present businesses. For example, Brascan Ltd. owns companies in the mining, real estate, electric power generation, and financial services businesses. Conglomerate diversification is not nearly as popular as it was a few years ago.

concentration strategy Involves focussing the company on one product or product line.

market penetration Boosting sales of present products by more aggressive selling in the firm's current markets.

product development Developing improved products for current markets.

geographic expansion Expanding operations in new geographic areas or countries.

horizontal integration Acquiring control of competitors in the same or similar markets with the same or similar products.

vertical integration Owning or controlling the inputs to the firm's processes and/or the channels through which the products or services are distributed.

diversification Expanding into related or unrelated products or market segments.

Figure 6.2 Hierarchy of strategy.

Investment Reduction.   **Investment reduction** means reducing the company's investment in one or more of its lines of business. One investment-reduction strategy is *retrenchment*, which means the reduction of activity or operations. For example, Federal Industries formerly was a conglomerate with interests in trucking, railways, metals, and other product lines, but it retrenched and now focusses on a more limited set of customers and products. *Divestment* is another investment-reduction strategy; it involves selling or liquidating one or more of a firm's businesses. For example, BCE sold its Yellow Pages and White Pages for $4 billion.

investment reduction Reducing the company's investment in one or more of its lines of business.

Business-Level (Competitive) Strategies

Whatever corporate-level strategy a firm decides on, it must also have a competitive strategy. A competitive strategy is a plan to establish a profitable and sustainable competitive position against the forces that determine industry competition.[5] Michael Porter identifies three competitive strategies: cost leadership, differentiation, and focus.

Cost Leadership.   **Cost leadership** means becoming the low cost leader in an industry. Wal-Mart is an industry cost leader. Its distribution costs are minimized through a satellite-based warehousing system, its store-location costs are minimized by placing stores on low-cost land, and the stores themselves are very plain. Montreal-based Gildan Activewear is dedicated to achieving the lowest possible costs in producing its T-shirts. The company has captured 29 percent of the U.S. imprinted T-shirt market with this strategy.[6]

cost leadership Becoming the low cost leader in an industry.

Differentiation.   In a **differentiation strategy**, a firm seeks to be unique in its industry along some dimension that is valued by buyers. For example, Caterpillar Tractor emphasizes durability, Volvo stresses safety, Apple Computer stresses user-friendly products, and Mercedes-Benz emphasizes quality.

differentiation strategy A firm seeks to be unique in its industry along some dimension that is valued by buyers.

Focus.   A **focus strategy** means selecting a market segment and serving the customers in that market niche better than competitors. Before it was acquired by Nexfor, Fraser Inc. focussed on producing high-quality, durable, lightweight paper that is used in bibles. While it still has a good reputation in the production of bible paper, Nexfor Fraser Papers is more diversified now and produces papers for a variety of uses, including dog food bags and doughnut boxes.

focus strategy Selecting a market segment and serving the customers in that market niche better than competitors.

Functional Strategies

Each business's choice of competitive strategy (cost leadership, differentiation, or focus) is translated into supporting functional strategies for each of its departments to pursue. A functional strategy is the basic course of action that each department follows so that the business accomplishes its overall goals. To implement its cost-leadership strategy, for example, Wal-Mart's distribution department pursued a functional strategy of satellite-based warehousing that ultimately drove distribution costs down to a minimum.

CONTINGENCY PLANNING AND CRISIS MANAGEMENT

Because business environments are often difficult to predict, and because the unexpected can create major problems, most managers recognize that even the best-laid plans sometimes become impractical. For instance, when

Walt Disney Co. announced plans to launch a cruise line replete with familiar Disney characters and themes, managers also began aggressively developing and marketing packages linking three- and four-day cruises with visits to Disney World in Florida. The first sailing was scheduled for early 1998, and the company began to book reservations a year in advance. However, the shipyard constructing Disney's first ship (the *Disney Magic*) notified the company in October 1997 that it was behind schedule and that the ship would be delivered several weeks late. When similar problems befall other cruise lines, they can offer to rebook passengers on alternative itineraries. But because Disney had no other ship, it had no choice but to refund the money it had collected as prebooking deposits for its first 15 cruises.

The 20 000 displaced customers were offered substantial discounts if they rebooked on a later cruise. Many of them, however, could not rearrange their schedules and requested full refunds. Moreover, quite a few blamed Disney, and a few expressed outrage at what they perceived to be poor planning by the entertainment giant. Fortunately, *Disney Magic* was eventually launched and has now become both very popular and very profitable.[7]

Because managers know that such things can happen, they often develop alternative plans in case things go awry. Two common methods of dealing with the unknown and unforeseen are *contingency planning* and *crisis management*.

Contingency Planning

Contingency planning takes into account the need to find solutions for specific aspects of a problem. By its very nature, a contingency plan is a hedge against changes that might occur. **Contingency planning**, then, is planning for change: It attempts to identify in advance important aspects of a business or its market that might change. It also identifies the ways in which a company will respond to changes. Today, many companies use computer programs for contingency planning.

Suppose, for example, that a company develops a plan to create a new business. It expects sales to increase at an annual rate of 10 percent for the next five years and develops a marketing strategy for maintaining that level. But suppose that sales have increased by only 5 percent by the end of the first year. Does the company abandon the business, invest more in advertising, or wait to see what happens in the second year? Any of these alter-

contingency planning Identifying aspects of a business or its environment that might entail changes in strategy.

Commercial airlines have contingency plans to deal with problems like major snowstorms. These contingency plans involve making sure that planes are not stranded at airports that are experiencing snow delays.

natives is possible. However, things will go more smoothly if managers have decided in advance what to do in the event of lower sales. Contingency planning can help them do exactly that.

Disney learned from its mistake with its first ship, and when the second ship (the *Disney Wonder*) was launched a year later, managers did several things differently. First, they allowed for an extra two weeks between when the ship was supposed to be ready for sailing and its first scheduled cruise. They also held open a few cabins on *Disney Magic* as a backup for any especially disgruntled customers who might need to be accommodated due to unexpected delays launching *Disney Wonder*.

Crisis Management

Crisis management involves an organization's methods for dealing with emergencies that require an immediate response. The terrorist attack on the World Trade Center on September 11, 2001, was an extreme example of the need for crisis management. In the attack, all business firms in the World Trade Center lost the place where they conducted business, and some firms also lost hundreds of their employees.

crisis management An organization's methods for dealing with emergencies.

When Italian food giant Parmalat Finanziaria S.p.A. couldn't account for $11.7 billion in funds, its Canadian division, headed by CEO Marc Caira, faced a major crisis. Caira responded by auditing the Canadian operation's accounting practices to make sure his division wasn't part of the problem. After he had determined it wasn't, he then took a variety of actions to reassure customers, employees, and investors that everything was fine in the Canadian division. He did this by continuously communicating with the company's key constituents. Caira's actions worked. The year after the Parmalat scandal broke in Italy, the Canadian division recorded its highest sales and profits ever.[8]

McDonald's faced a different kind of crisis—slowly declining sales. Top management decided on some major strategy changes, including a de-emphasis on growth and more emphasis on healthy food offerings, improved service, and more attention to customer needs. The change was successful. The company now serves 2 million more customers each day than it did in 2003, and its stock price is up 148 percent since 2003.[9]

To prepare for emergencies, many organizations develop crisis plans. In recent years, a new technology called *disruption management* (DM) has emerged. It stresses internal self-reliance in planning for and preparing response to disruptions in an organization's external environment. Consider a shutdown caused by a snowstorm at Toronto's Pearson International Airport. An airline's least costly solution would be to simply cancel all incoming flights immediately. This approach cuts the airline's operating costs, but it is a terrible option for passengers who can't get where they're going. A DM approach would consider alternatives such as rescheduling flights into neighbouring airports and providing ground transportation into Toronto. A DM model would quickly simulate the costs and benefits of these and other options to help managers make an effective decision.

Describe the four activities that constitute the *management process*.

2

THE MANAGEMENT PROCESS

Management is the process of planning, organizing, leading, and controlling an enterprise's financial, physical, human, and information resources to achieve the organization's goals of supplying various products and services. Thus, the CEO of Walt Disney Productions is a manager because he regularly carries out these four functions as films are being made. Actors

management The process of planning, organizing, leading, and controlling a business's financial, physical, human, and information resources in order to achieve its goals.

such as Julia Roberts or Tom Cruise, while they may be the stars of the movies, are not managers because they don't carry out the four functions of management. The Business Accountability box explains the dynamic nature of managerial jobs.

The planning, organizing, leading, and controlling aspects of a manager's job are interrelated. While these activities generally follow one another in a logical sequence, sometimes they are performed simultaneously or in a different sequence altogether. In fact, a manager is likely to be engaged in all these activities during the course of a business day.

BUSINESS ACCOUNTABILITY

What Do Managers Actually Do?

Henry Mintzberg of McGill University conducted a detailed study of the work of five chief executive officers and found the following:

1. Managers work at an unrelenting pace.
2. Managerial activities are characterized by brevity, variety, and fragmentation.
3. Managers have a preference for "live" action, and emphasize work activities that are current, specific, and well-defined.
4. Managers are attracted to the verbal media.

Mintzberg believes that a manager's job can be described as 10 roles (in three categories) that must be performed. The manager's formal authority and status give rise to three *interpersonal roles*: (1) *figurehead* (duties of a ceremonial nature, such as attending a subordinate's wedding); (2) *leader* (being responsible for the work of the unit); and (3) *liaison* (making contact outside the vertical chain of command). These interpersonal roles give rise to three *informational roles*: (1) *monitor* (scanning the environment for relevant information); (2) *disseminator* (passing information to subordinates); and (3) *spokesperson* (sending information to people outside the unit).

The interpersonal and informational roles allow the manager to carry out four *decision-making roles*: (1) *entrepreneur* (improving the performance of the unit); (2) *disturbance handler* (responding to high-pressure disturbances, such as a strike at a supplier); (3) *resource allocator* (deciding who will get what in the unit); and (4) *negotiator* (working out agreements on a wide variety of issues, such as the amount of authority an individual will be given).

Managers in a 2005 study conducted by Toronto's Pace Productivity felt that they should have spent about half their time on activities such as managing staff, providing direction, and coaching, but that they

actually were able to spend only 18 percent of their time on "people management." Managers also thought that they should have spent about 6 percent of their time on administrative tasks, but they actually spent 25 percent of their time on those activities. The time managers thought they should spend on planning was about the same as what they actually spent. Consistent with Mintzberg's original findings, the Pace data also showed that managers' lives are very hectic, and their focus shifts rapidly from activity to activity. For example, for the average manager, 43 different activities lasted an average of just 16 minutes each.

Insight into what managers actually do can also be gained by looking at the so-called *functions* of management (planning, organizing, leading, and controlling). Consider the work of Marina Pyo, who is publisher, School Division, at Pearson Education Canada, a publisher of textbooks for elementary and secondary schools, colleges, and universities. Her job is to manage the activities that are necessary to develop resources in math and science for the Canadian elementary school market. Her work is at times intense, fragmented, rewarding, frustrating, and fast-paced. In short, she is a typical manager.

Pyo carries out the *planning* function when she drafts a plan for a new book. She is *organizing* when she develops a new organization chart to facilitate goal achievement. She is *leading* when she meets with a subordinate to discuss that person's career plans. And she is *controlling* when she checks sales prospects for a book before ordering a reprint.

Some of Pyo's activities do not easily fit into this "functions of management" model. For example, it is not clear which function she is performing when she negotiates the size of a reprint run with the manager of the sales division, or when she talks briefly with the president of her division about recent events in Pyo's area of responsibility.

Planning

Determining what the organization needs to do and how best to get it done requires planning. **Planning** has three main components. As we have seen, it begins when managers determine the firm's goals. Next, they develop a comprehensive strategy for achieving those goals. After a strategy is developed, they design tactical and operational plans for implementing the strategy.

The planning process has five basic steps. In *step 1*, goals are established for the organization. A commercial airline, for example, may set a goal to fill every seat on every flight. In *step 2*, managers identify whether a gap exists between the company's desire and actual position. For example, a year-end financial analysis will reveal whether a company met its profitability objectives. In *step 3*, managers develop plans to achieve the desired objectives. Objectives indicate *what* results are desired, while plans indicate *how* these objectives are to be achieved. In *step 4*, the plans that have been decided upon are implemented. This is the point in the planning process where thinking is converted into action. In *step 5*, the effectiveness of the plan is assessed. This requires comparing actual results with planned performance.

When Yahoo! was created, for example, the company's top managers set a strategic goal of becoming a top firm in the then-emerging market for internet search engines. But then came the hard part—figuring out how to do it. They started by assessing the ways in which people actually use the web. They also studied ways in which they would probably use it in the future, analyzed the successful strategies of other growing firms, and assessed the ways in which big companies were using the internet. They concluded that people wanted an easy-to-understand web interface. They also wanted to be able to satisfy a wide array of needs, preferences, and priorities by going to as few sites as possible to find what they were looking for.

One key component of Yahoo!'s strategy, therefore, was to foster partnerships and relationships with other companies so that potential web surfers could draw upon several sources through a single portal—which would, of course, be Yahoo! Thus, the goal of partnering emerged as one set of tactical plans for moving forward. Yahoo! managers then began fashioning alliances with such diverse partners as Reuters, Standard & Poor's, and the Associated Press (for news coverage), RE/MAX (for real estate information), and a wide array of information providers specializing in sports, weather, entertainment, shopping, travel, and so forth.

planning That portion of a manager's job concerned with determining what the business needs to do and the best way to achieve it.

Organizing

The portion of a manager's job that is concerned with mobilizing the necessary resources to complete a particular task is known as **organizing** (we examine this topic further in Chapter 7). The importance of the organizing function of management can be seen by considering what happened at Hewlett-Packard, which lost some of its lustre a few years ago. One of the major reasons for its slide could be traced back to what had once been a major strength. Specifically, HP had long prided itself on being little more than a corporate confederation of individual businesses. Sometimes these businesses even ended up competing against themselves. This approach had been beneficial for much of the firm's history: It was easier for each business to make its own decisions quickly and efficiently, and the competition kept each unit on its toes. By 1998, however, problems started to become apparent, and no one could quite figure out what was going on.

Enter Ann Livermore, then head of the firm's software and services business. Livermore realized that it was the structure that had served so well in the past that was now holding the firm back. Specifically, to regain

organizing That portion of a manager's job concerned with mobilizing the necessary resources to complete a particular task.

its competitive edge HP needed an integrated, organization-wide internet strategy. Unfortunately, the company's highly decentralized organization made that impossible. Livermore led the charge to create one organization to drive a single internet plan. "I felt we could be the most powerful company in the industry," she says, "if we could get our hardware, software, and services aligned." In fact, a reorganized HP has bounced back and is quickly regaining its competitive strength.[10]

Leading

leading That portion of a manager's job concerned with guiding and motivating employees to meet the firm's objectives.

The activities involving interactions between managers and their subordinates to meet the firm's objectives are known as **leading** (or directing). By definition, managers have the power to give orders and demand results. Leading, however, goes beyond merely giving orders. Leaders attempt to guide and motivate employees to work in the best interests of the organization. At discount airline WestJet, for example, CEO Clive Beddoe has been very successful in motivating employees to go above and beyond normal work practices to ensure the company's (and their own) financial success. We discuss leadership more fully in Chapter 10.

Controlling

controlling That portion of a manager's job concerned with monitoring the firm's performance and, if necessary, acting to bring it in line with the firm's goals.

Controlling is the process of monitoring a firm's performance to make sure that the firm is meeting its goals.

Figure 6.3 illustrates the control process that begins when management establishes standards, often for financial performance. If, for example, a company wants to increase sales by 20 percent over the next 10 years, then an appropriate standard might be an increase of about 2 percent a year. Managers then measure actual performance against standards. If the two amounts agree, the organization continues along its present course. If they vary significantly, however, one or the other needs adjustment. If sales have increased 2.1 percent by the end of the first year, things are probably fine. If sales have dropped 1 percent, some revision in plans may be needed. Perhaps the original goal should be lowered or more money should be spent on advertising.

Japanese organizations don't usually like radical restructuring, but when Senichi Hoshino took over the hapless Hanshin Tigers, he axed 24 of the team's 70 players and replaced them with free agents. He required everyone on the roster to compete for a position, tracked performance daily, and made individual coaches directly responsible for seeing that players executed certain skills. Soon after that, the Tigers won the pennant—a particularly important achievement, because superstition says that when the Tigers win, Japan will soon enjoy a period of prolonged prosperity.

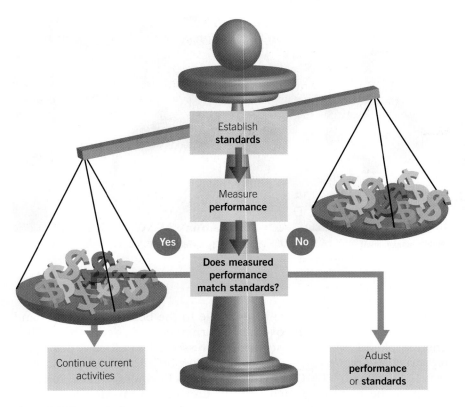

Figure 6.3 The control process.

Control can also show where performance is running better than expected and, thus, can serve as a basis for providing rewards or reducing costs. For example, when Ford introduced its Explorer SportsTrac (an SUV with a pickup bed), initial sales were so strong that the firm was able to delay a major advertising campaign for three months because it was selling all the vehicles it could make anyway.

TYPES OF MANAGERS

Although all managers plan, organize, lead, and control, not all managers have the same degree of responsibility for each activity. Moreover, managers differ in the specific application of these activities. Thus we can divide managers by their *level* of responsibility or by their *area* of responsibility.

Identify *types of managers* by level and area.

3

Levels of Management

The three basic levels of management are top, middle, and first-line management. In most firms there are more middle managers than top managers and more first-line managers than middle managers. Moreover, as the categories imply, the power of managers and the complexity of their duties increase as we move up the pyramid.

Top Managers

The small number of executives who guide the fortunes of most companies are **top managers**. Common titles for top managers include president, vice-president, treasurer, chief executive officer (CEO), and chief financial

top managers Those managers responsible for a firm's overall performance and effectiveness and for developing long-range plans for the company.

First-line management

Middle management

Top management

Organizations have three basic levels of management.

officer (CFO). Top managers are responsible to the board of directors and shareholders of the firm for its overall performance and effectiveness. They set general policies, formulate strategies, oversee all significant decisions, and represent the company in its dealings with other businesses and government.[11] Each year, KPMG/Ipsos-Reid surveys business leaders and asks them to pick the most respected CEO in Canada. Gwyn Morgan, retired CEO of EnCana, won the award for 2005.[12]

Middle Managers

middle managers Those managers responsible for implementing the decisions made by top managers.

Although below the ranks of the top executives, **middle managers** occupy positions of considerable autonomy and importance. Titles such as plant manager, operations manager, and division manager are typical of middle-management jobs. In general, middle managers are responsible for implementing the strategies, policies, and decisions of the top managers. For example, if top management decides to bring out a new product in 12 months or to cut costs by 5 percent, middle management will have to decide to increase the pace of new product development or to reduce the plant's workforce. With companies increasingly seeking ways to cut costs, the job of middle manager has lately become precarious in many large companies.

First-Line Managers

first-line managers Those managers responsible for supervising the work of employees.

Those who hold titles such as supervisor, office manager, and group leader are **first-line managers**. Although they spend most of their time working with and supervising the employees who report to them, first-line managers' activities are not limited to that arena. At a building site, for example, the project manager not only ensures that workers are carrying out construction as specified by the architect, but also interacts extensively with materials suppliers, community officials, and middle and top managers at the home office. The manager of a Canadian Tire store and the flight-services manager for a specific Air Canada flight would also be considered first-line managers.

Areas of Management

Within any large company, the top, middle, and first-line managers work in a variety of areas, including marketing, finance, operations, human resources, and information.

Marketing Managers

Marketing includes the development, pricing, promotion, and distribution of a product or service. *Marketing managers* are responsible for getting products and services to buyers. Marketing is especially important for firms dealing in consumer products, such as Procter & Gamble, Coca-Cola, and Roots. These firms often have large numbers of marketing managers at various levels. For example, a large firm will probably have a vice-president for marketing (top manager), regional marketing managers (middle managers), and several district sales managers (first-line managers). A marketing person often rises to the top of this type of corporation. In contrast, firms that produce industrial products such as machinery and janitorial supplies tend to put less emphasis on marketing and to have fewer marketing managers. However, these firms do not ignore marketing altogether. In recent years, law firms and universities have also come to recognize the value and importance of marketing. We look at marketing in detail in Chapters 15 to 17.

Financial Managers

Management of a firm's finances, including its investments and accounting functions, is extremely important to its survival. Nearly every company has *financial managers* to plan and oversee its financial resources. Levels of financial management may include a vice-president for finance (top), division controller (middle), and accounting supervisor (first-line). For large financial institutions, effective financial management is the company's reason for being. No organization, however, can afford to ignore the need for management in this area. Chapters 18 to 20 cover financial management in detail.

Operations Managers

A firm's operations are the systems by which it creates goods and services. *Operations managers* are responsible for production control, inventory control, and quality control, among other duties. Manufacturing companies like Steelcase, Bristol Aerospace, and Sony need operations managers at many levels. Such firms typically have a vice-president for operations (top), plant managers (middle), and foremen or supervisors (first-line). In recent years, sound operations management practices have also become increasingly important to service organizations, hospitals, universities, and the government. Operations management is the subject of Chapters 11 and 12.

Human Resource Managers

Every enterprise uses human resources. Most companies have *human resource managers* to provide assistance to other managers when they are hiring employees, training them, evaluating their performances, and determining their compensation level. In many companies, human resource managers are involved in negotiations with labour unions. Large firms may have several human resource departments, each dealing with specialized activities. Imperial Oil, for example, has separate departments to deal with recruiting and hiring, wage and salary levels, and labour relations. Smaller firms may have a single department, while very small organizations may have a single person responsible for all human resource activities. Chapters 8 to 10 address issues involved in human resource management.

Information Managers

A new type of managerial position appearing in many organizations is that of *information manager*. These managers are responsible for designing and implementing various systems to gather, process, and disseminate information. Dramatic increases in both the amount of information available to managers and the ability to manage it have led to the emergence of this important function. While relatively few in number now, the ranks of information managers are increasing at all levels. Federal Express, for example, has a chief information officer. Middle managers engaged in information management help design information systems for divisions or plants. Computer systems managers within smaller businesses or operations are first-line managers. Information management is discussed in Chapter 13.

Other Managers

Some firms have more specialized managers. Chemical companies such as CIL have research and development managers, for example, whereas companies such as Petro-Canada and Apple have public relations managers. The range of possibilities is endless; the areas of management are limited only by the needs and imagination of the firm.

BASIC MANAGEMENT SKILLS

4 Describe the five basic *management skills.*

While the range of managerial positions is almost limitless, the success that people enjoy in those positions is often limited by their skills and abilities. Effective managers must possess several skills: *technical, human relations, conceptual, decision-making,* and *time management skills.*

Technical Skills

technical skills Skills associated with performing specialized tasks within a firm.

human relations skills Skills in understanding and getting along with people.

Skills associated with performing specialized tasks within a company are called **technical skills**. A secretary's ability to type, an animator's ability to draw a cartoon, and an accountant's ability to audit a company's records are all technical skills. People develop their technical skills through education and experience. The secretary, for example, probably took a keyboarding course and has had many hours of practice both on and off the job. The animator may have had training in an art school and probably learned a great deal from experienced animators on the job. The accountant earned a university degree and, possibly, professional certification.

As Figure 6.4 shows, technical skills are especially important for first-line managers. Most first-line managers spend considerable time helping employees solve work-related problems, monitoring their performance, and training them in more efficient work procedures. Such managers need a basic understanding of the jobs they supervise.

As a manager moves up the corporate ladder, however, technical skills become less and less important. Top managers, for example, often need only a cursory familiarity with the mechanics of basic tasks performed within the company. Michael Eisner, for example, freely admits that he can't draw Mickey Mouse or build a ride for Disney World.

Meg Whitman, the CEO of eBay, understands the importance of human relations in a business whose model is helping sellers find buyers and buyers find sellers. At conventions where 10 000 of eBay's 28 million customers gather to communicate without the medium of cyberspace, Whitman autographs (collectible) eBay trading cards of herself and depends on ordinary users to tell her what works and what doesn't work at the online auction company.

Human Relations Skills

Effective managers must have good **human relations skills**—the skills that enable them to understand and get along with other people. A manager with poor human relations skills will have trouble getting along with subordinates, which will, in turn, cause valuable employees to quit or transfer, and contribute to poor morale. When Development Dimensions International (DDI) asked 944 human resource professionals to state the reasons why newly promoted managers fail, 53 percent said it was because of poor people skills.[13]

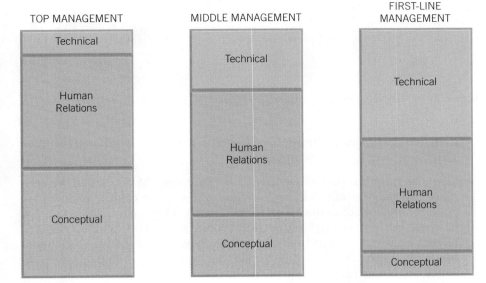

Figure 6.4 Different levels in an organization require different combinations of managerial skills.

While human relations skills are important at all levels, they are probably most important for middle managers, who must often act as bridges between top managers, first-line managers, and managers from other areas of the organization. Managers should possess good communication skills. Many managers have found that being able to understand others—and to get them to understand—can go far toward maintaining good relations in an organization.

Conceptual Skills

Conceptual skills refer to a person's ability to think in the abstract, to diagnose and analyze different situations, and to see beyond the present situation. Conceptual skills help managers recognize new market opportunities (and threats). They can also help managers analyze the probable outcomes of their decisions. The need for conceptual skills differs at various management levels: Top managers depend most on conceptual skills, first-line managers least. Although the purposes and everyday needs of various jobs differ, conceptual skills are needed in almost any job-related activity.

In many ways, conceptual skills may be the most important ingredient in the success of executives in ecommerce businesses. For example, the ability to foresee how a particular business application will be affected by or can be translated to the internet is clearly conceptual in nature.

conceptual skills Abilities to think in the abstract, diagnose and analyze different situations, and see beyond the present situation.

Decision-Making Skills

Decision-making skills include the ability to define problems and select the best course of action. Figure 6.5 illustrates the basic steps in decision making.

decision-making skills Skills in defining problems and selecting the best courses of action.

1. *Define the problem, gather facts, and identify alternative solutions.* Vivendi Universal is a large French entertainment and media company. The firm's top managers recently decided that they needed a stronger presence in the United States if they were to continue their quest to become a global media powerhouse. Thus, they defined their problem as how to best enter the U.S. media market. They subsequently determined

Figure 6.5 The decision-making process.

that there were two alternatives: starting a new media business from scratch or buying an existing one.

2. *Evaluate each alternative and select the best one.* Managers at Vivendi realized that it would take many years and a huge cash investment to launch a new media enterprise from scratch. They also recognized that because there was ongoing consolidation in the U.S. media industry, buying an existing firm might be relatively easy. Further analysis identified Houghton Mifflin, one of the last remaining independent publishers, as an attractive acquisition target.

3. *Implement the chosen alternative, periodically following up and evaluating the effectiveness of that choice.* Vivendi executives quietly began negotiating with senior managers at Houghton Mifflin in mid-2001. Within a matter of weeks, the two firms had reached an agreement: Vivendi Universal would acquire 100 percent of Houghton Mifflin, thus providing the French company with exactly what it had been seeking— a viable entry into U.S. markets.[14] Unfortunately, Vivendi subsequently fell on hard times, and on August 14, 2002, it announced that it would attempt to sell Houghton Mifflin to raise much-needed cash.

As this example demonstrates, decision making can be a complicated activity for managers. The Exercising Your Ethics box at the end of the chapter presents another decision-making opportunity for a manager.

Time Management Skills

time management skills Skills associated with the productive use of time.

Time management skills refer to the productive use that managers make of their time. In 2005, for example, Talisman Energy CEO James Buckee was paid a total of $23.3 million (including bonuses and options).[15] Assuming that he worked 50 hours a week and took two weeks vacation, Burton earned about $9200 per hour, or about $153 per minute. Any time that Buckee wastes represents a large cost to Talisman Energy and its stockholders.

To manage time effectively, managers must address four leading causes of wasted time:

■ *Paperwork.* Some managers spend too much time deciding what to do with letters and reports. Most documents of this sort are routine and can be handled quickly. Managers must learn to recognize those documents that require more attention.

■ *The telephone.* Experts estimate that managers are interrupted by the telephone every five minutes. To manage time more effectively, they suggest having a secretary screen all calls and setting aside a certain block of time each day to return the important ones.

■ *Meetings.* Many managers spend as much as four hours per day in meetings. To help keep this time productive, the person handling the meeting should specify a clear agenda, start on time, keep everyone focussed on the agenda, and end on time.

■ *Email.* More and more managers are also relying heavily on email and other forms of electronic communication. Like memos and telephone calls, many email messages are not particularly important; some are even trivial. As a result, time is wasted when managers have to sort through a variety of electronic folders, in-baskets, and archives. As the average number of electronic messages grows, the potential time wasted also increases.

Management Skills for the Twenty-First Century

Managers face some major challenges in the twenty-first century. We will touch on two of the most significant challenges: *global management* and *technology*.

Global Management Skills

Tomorrow's managers must equip themselves with the special tools, techniques, and skills necessary to compete in a global environment. They will need to understand foreign markets, cultural differences, and the motives and practices of foreign rivals.

On a more practical level, businesses will need managers who are capable of understanding international operations. In the past, most Canadian businesses hired local managers to run their operations in the various countries in which they operated. More recently, however, the trend has been to transfer Canadian managers to foreign locations. This practice helps firms better transfer their corporate cultures to foreign operations. In addition, foreign assignments help managers become better prepared for international competition as they advance within the organization.[16]

Management and Technology Skills

Another significant issue facing tomorrow's manager is technology, especially as it relates to communication. Managers have always had to deal with information. In today's world, however, the amount of information has reached staggering proportions. New forms of technology have added to a manager's ability to process information while simultaneously making it even more important to organize and interpret an ever-increasing amount of input.

Technology has also begun to change the way the interaction of managers shapes corporate structures. Computer networking, for example, exists because it is no longer too expensive to put a computer on virtually every desk in the company. In turn, this elaborate network controls the flow of the firm's lifeblood—information. Information no longer flows strictly up and down through hierarchies. It now flows to everyone at once. As a result, decisions are made more quickly—and more people are directly involved. With email, teleconferencing, and other forms of communication, neither time nor distance—nor such corporate "boundaries" as departments and divisions—can prevent people from working more closely together. More than ever, bureaucracies are breaking down, while planning, decision making, and other activities are beginning to benefit from group building and teamwork.

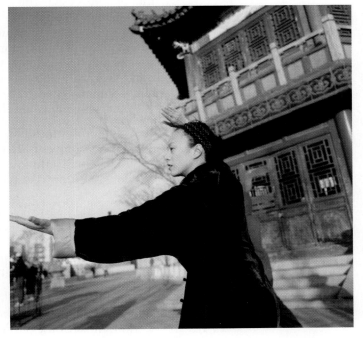

MTV needed someone to run its operation in China who understood both conservative Chinese television regulators and China's young urban elite. The company chose Li Yifei, a former UN intern, public relations consultant, and tai chi champion. Li has already brought the Chinese equivalent of the MTV awards to state-owned television, and the show had 150 million viewers.

MANAGEMENT AND THE CORPORATE CULTURE

5 Describe the development and explain the importance of *corporate culture*.

corporate culture The shared experiences, stories, beliefs, norms, and ethical stance that characterize a firm.

Every organization—big or small, more successful or less successful—has an unmistakable "feel" to it. Just as every individual has a unique personality, every company has a unique identity, called **corporate culture**—the shared experiences, stories, beliefs, norms, and ethical stance that characterize an organization. This culture helps define the work and business climate that exists in an organization.

A 2005 survey of executives at 107 Canadian companies revealed the following views among managers:

■ The three companies with the most admired corporate cultures were WestJet Airlines, Tim Hortons, and Royal Bank of Canada.

■ Over 80 percent of the executives surveyed said that corporate culture had an impact on financial performance.

■ Nearly two-thirds of those surveyed said their company did not monitor its corporate culture.

■ Nearly three-quarters of those surveyed said their firm's corporate culture was not what they wanted it to be.[17]

A strong corporate culture directs employees' efforts and helps everyone work toward the same goals. Some cultures, for example, stress financial success to the extreme, while others focus more on quality of life. A strong corporate culture also helps newcomers learn accepted behaviours. If financial success is the key to a culture, newcomers quickly learn that they are expected to work long, hard hours and that the "winner" is the one who brings in the most revenue. But if quality of life is more fundamental, newcomers learn that it's more acceptable to spend less time at work and that balancing work and non-work is encouraged. The survey mentioned above found that only 36 percent of executives felt that the corporate culture of their company was strong.

The following examples illustrate how culture differs across firms:

■ Magna International, a large Canadian producer of auto parts, is a firm with a strong culture. Its founder, Frank Stronach, is well known for his views about employees, working conditions, daycare centres, unions, the free enterprise system, and profit distribution.[18]

■ Four Seasons Hotels and Resorts has a different, but equally strong, culture. Managers are judged by deeds, not words, and act as role models; employees take their cues from the managers.[19]

■ At Toyota's Cambridge, Ontario, plant the corporate culture stresses values, principles, and trust. The culture is one of continuous improvement.[20]

■ At WestJet Airlines the corporate culture emphasizes profit maximization. Most of the employees own shares in the company, and all of them get to keep some of the profits. This is a powerful incentive for them to work productively.[21]

Forces Shaping Corporate Culture

A number of forces shape corporate cultures. First, the values held by top management help set the tone of the organization and influence its business goals and strategies. Frank Stronach (Magna International), Timothy

Eaton (Eaton's), Max Ward (Wardair), Larry Clark (Spar Aerospace), and Jean de Grandpre (BCE) are just a few of the leaders who have had a profound impact on the culture of their respective organizations. Even a large, long-time firm like Ford still bears the traces of founder Henry Ford.

The firm's history also helps shape its culture. The championship banners that line the arena where the Montreal Canadiens play signify that they are winners. Maintaining a corporate culture draws on many dimensions of business life. Shared experiences resulting from norms sustain culture. Thus, working long hours on a special project becomes a shared experience for many employees. They remember it, talk about it among themselves, and wear it as a badge of their contribution to the company.

Stories and legends are also important. Walt Disney has been dead for many years now, but his spirit lives on in the businesses he left behind. Quotations from Disney are affixed to portraits of him throughout the company's studios. And Disney's emphasis on family is still visible in corporate benefits such as paying for spouses to accompany employees on extended business trips. In fact, employees are often called "the Disney family."

Finally, strong behavioural norms help define and sustain corporate cultures. For example, a strong part of the culture at Hewlett-Packard Canada is that everyone wears a name tag and that everyone is called by his or her first name. And at Sony Corporation every employee wears a corporate smock.

Mainframe Entertainment of Vancouver has one of the lowest turnover rates in the animation business. Its culture emphasizes giving young artists and designers opportunities to acquire new skills and develop leadership potential—opportunities not available in the bigger Los Angeles studios.

Communicating the Culture and Managing Change

Corporate culture influences management philosophy, style, and behaviour. Managers, therefore, must carefully consider the kind of culture they want for their organization, then work to nourish that culture by communicating with everyone who works there. Wal-Mart, for example, is acutely conscious of the need to spread the message of its culture as it opens new stores in new areas. One of the company's methods is to regularly assign veteran managers to lead employees in new territories. At Continental Airlines, Gordon Bethune delivers weekly messages to all employees to update them on what's going on in the firm; the employees can either listen to Bethune's message on a closed-circuit broadcast or else call a toll-free telephone number and hear a recorded version at their own convenience.

Communicating the Culture

To use its culture to a firm's advantage, managers must accomplish several tasks, all of which hinge on effective communication. First, managers themselves must have a clear understanding of the culture. Second, they must transmit the culture to others in the organization. Communication is thus one aim in training and orienting newcomers. A clear and meaningful statement of the organization's mission is also a valuable communication tool. Finally, managers can maintain the culture by rewarding and promoting those who understand it and work toward maintaining it.

Managing Change

Organizations must sometimes change their cultures. Ontario Hydro, for example, had an "engineering" culture for many years. This meant that everything was planned and analyzed down to the last detail before any action was taken. But Ontario Hydro's culture has changed to a more consumer-oriented, risk-taking culture as it tries to cope with large debt and changes in its markets. The RCMP is also much different now than it was in the days when military tradition dominated the organization. It completed a "visioning process" that resulted in a new mission statement, a new set of core values, and a commitment to the communities in which it works.[22]

Until recently, CIBC has had an aggressive, deal-making culture that caused it to go head-to-head with large Wall Street companies in the United States. But after several major failures in the United States, CIBC's culture has become much more conservative. It is so conservative that it is alone among big Canadian banks in not having a foreign growth strategy. Outgoing president John Hunkin said that he was pleased that people now think that CIBC is the most conservative bank in Canada.[23]

When cultural change is required, the process usually goes through three stages:

1. At the highest level, analysis of the company's environment highlights extensive change as the most effective response to its problems. Conflict and resistance typically characterize this period.

2. Top management begins to formulate a vision of a new company. Whatever that vision is, it must include renewed focus on the activities of competitors and the needs of customers.

3. The firm sets up new systems for appraising and compensating employees that enforce its new values. The purpose is to give the new culture solid shape from within the firm.

Sometimes this three-stage process is never completed. Consider what happened at Nortel Networks, which hired a new president and a new chief technology officer in 2005 in an attempt to resolve some of the company's problems. Both of these individuals had worked at Cisco Systems Inc., and it was thought that they would be a great addition to a troubled company like Nortel. But Cisco has a hard-driving sales culture, while Nortel's culture is much less intense. Within three months, both new managers resigned from Nortel. CEO Bill Owens said their departure was due to different management styles and a different vision for the future of the company. In short, there was a culture clash that caused the new hires to leave the company, and the culture they envisioned will not be implemented at Nortel.[24]

Summary of Learning Objectives

1. **Explain the importance of setting _goals_ and formulating _strategies_ as the starting points of effective management.** _Goals_—the performance targets of an organization—can be _long-term, intermediate,_ and _short-term._ They provide direction for managers, they help managers decide how to allocate limited resources, they define the corporate culture, and they help managers assess performance. _Strategies_—the methods that a company uses to meet its stated goals—involve three major activities: setting strategic goals, analyzing the organization and its environment, and matching the organization and its environment. These strategies are translated into _strategic, tactical,_ and _operational plans._ To deal with crises or major environmental changes, companies develop _contingency plans_ and plans for _crisis management._

2. Describe the four activities that constitute the *management process*. *Management* is the process of planning, organizing, leading, and controlling an organization's financial, physical, human, and information resources to achieve the organization's goals. *Planning* means determining what the company needs to do and how best to get it done. *Organizing* means determining how best to arrange a business's resources and the necessary jobs into an overall structure. *Leading* means guiding and motivating employees to meet the firm's objectives. *Controlling* means monitoring the firm's performance to ensure that it is meeting its goals.

3. Identify *types of managers* by level and area. Managers can be differentiated in two ways: by level and by area. By level, *top managers* set policies, formulate strategies, and approve decisions. *Middle managers* implement policies, strategies, and decisions. *First-line managers* usually work with and supervise employees. Management areas include marketing, financial, operations, human resources, and information. Managers at all levels may be found in every area of a company.

4. Describe the five basic *management skills*. Most managers agree that five basic management skills are necessary for success. *Technical skills* are associated with performing specialized tasks ranging from typing to auditing. *Human relations skills* are associated with understanding and getting along with other people. *Conceptual skills* are the abilities to think in the abstract, to diagnose and analyze different situations, and to see beyond present circumstances. *Decision-making skills* allow managers to define problems and to select the best course of action. *Time management skills* refer to managers' ability to make productive use of the time available to them.

5. Describe the development and explain the importance of *corporate culture*. *Corporate culture* is the shared experiences, stories, beliefs, norms, and ethical stance that characterize an organization. A strong, well-defined culture can help a business reach its goals and can influence management styles. Culture is determined by several factors, including top management, the organization's history, stories and legends, and behavioural norms. If carefully communicated and flexible enough to accommodate change, corporate culture can be managed for the betterment of the organization.

KEY TERMS

business-level (competitive) strategy, 181
concentration strategy, 182
conceptual skills, 193
contingency planning, 184
controlling, 188
corporate culture, 196
corporate-level strategy, 181
cost leadership, 183
crisis management, 185
decision-making skills, 193
differentiation strategy, 183
diversification, 182
environmental analysis, 179
first-line managers, 190

focus strategy, 183
functional strategies, 181
geographic expansion, 182
goals, 176
horizontal integration, 182
human relations skills, 192
intermediate goals, 178
investment reduction, 183
leading, 188
long-term goals, 178
management, 185
market penetration, 182
middle managers, 190
mission statement, 177
operational plans, 181

organizational analysis, 179
organizing, 187
planning, 187
product development, 182
short-term goals, 178
strategic goals, 178
strategic plans, 181
strategy formulation, 178
SWOT analysis, 179
tactical plans, 181
technical skills, 192
time management skills, 194
top managers, 189
vertical integration, 182

QUESTIONS FOR ANALYSIS

1. How are the five basic management *skills* related to the four *functions* of management?

2. What is the relationship between Mintzberg's *roles* of management and the more traditional *functions* of management? Use examples to clarify your answer.

3. Select any group of which you are a member (your company, your family, or a club or organization, for example). Explain how planning, organizing, directing, and controlling are practised in that group.

4. Identify managers by level and area at your school, college, or university.

5. In what kind of company would the technical skills of top managers be more important than human relations or conceptual skills? Are there organizations in which conceptual skills are not important?

6. What differences might you expect to find in the corporate cultures of a 100-year-old manufacturing firm based in Winnipeg and a 2-year-old ecommerce firm in Ottawa?

7. Perform a SWOT analysis for the school you are currently attending.

8. Consider the various corporate-level strategies discussed in the text (concentration, growth, integration, diversification, investment reduction). What is the relationship between these various strategies? Are they mutually exclusive? Are they complementary? Explain.

APPLICATION EXERCISES

1. Interview a manager at any level of a local company. Identify that manager's job according to level and area. Show how planning, organizing, directing, and controlling are part of this person's job. Inquire about the manager's education and work experience. Which management skills are most important for this manager's job?

2. Compare and contrast the corporate cultures of two companies that do business in most communities. Be sure to choose two companies in the same industry—for example, a Bay department store and a Wal-Mart discount store.

BUILDING YOUR BUSINESS SKILLS

Speaking with Power

Goal

To encourage students to appreciate effective speaking as a critical human relations skill.

Background

A manager's ability to understand and get along with supervisors, peers, and subordinates is a critical human relations skill. At the heart of this skill, says Harvard University professor of education Sarah McGinty, is the ability to speak with power and control. McGinty defines "powerful speech" in terms of the following characteristics:

- the ability to speak at length and in complete sentences

- the ability to set a conversational agenda

- the ability to deter interruption

- the ability to argue openly and to express strong opinions about ideas, not people

- the ability to make statements that offer solutions rather than pose questions

- the ability to express humour

Taken together, says McGinty, "all this creates a sense of confidence in listeners."

Assignment

Step 1

Working alone, compare your own personal speaking style with McGinty's description of powerful speech by taping yourself as you speak during a meeting with classmates or during a phone conversation. (Tape both sides of the conversation only if the person to whom you are speaking gives permission.) Listen for the following problems:

- unfinished sentences

- an absence of solutions

- too many disclaimers ("I'm not sure I have enough information to say this, but…")

- the habit of seeking support from others instead of making definitive statements of personal conviction (saying, "As Emily stated in her report, I recommend consolidating the medical and fitness

▶▶▶

▶▶▶

functions," instead of "I recommend consolidating the medical and fitness functions")

■ language fillers (saying, "you know," "like," and "um" when you are unsure of your facts or uneasy about expressing your opinion)

Step 2

Join with three or four other classmates to evaluate each other's speaking styles. Finally,

■ Have a 10-minute group discussion on the importance of human relations skills in business.

■ Listen to other group members, and take notes on the "power" content of what you hear.

■ Offer constructive criticism by focussing on what speakers say rather than on personal characteristics (say, "Bob, you sympathized with Paul's position, but I still don't know what you think," instead of, "Bob, you sounded like a weakling").

Follow-Up Questions

1. How do you think the power content of speech affects a manager's ability to communicate? Evaluate some of the ways in which effects may differ among supervisors, peers, and subordinates.

2. How do you evaluate yourself and group members in terms of powerful and powerless speech? List the strengths and weaknesses of the group.

3. Do you agree or disagree with McGinty that business success depends on gaining insight into your own language habits? Explain your answer.

4. In our age of computers and email, why do you think personal presentation continues to be important in management?

5. McGinty believes that power language differs from company to company and that it is linked to the corporate culture. Do you agree, or do you believe that people express themselves in similar ways no matter where they are?

EXERCISING YOUR ETHICS

Making Room for Alternative Actions

The Situation

Assume that you are the manager of a large hotel adjacent to a medical centre in a major city. The medical centre itself consists of 10 major hospitals and research institutes. Two of the hospitals are affiliated with large universities and two with churches. Three are public and three are private. The centre has an international reputation and attracts patients from around the world.

Because so many patients and their families travel great distances to visit the medical centre and often stay for days or weeks, there are also eight large hotels in the area, including three new ones. The hotel that you manage is one of the older ones and, frankly, is looking a bit shabby. Corporate headquarters has told you that the hotel will either be closed or undergo a major remodelling in about two years. In the meantime, you are expected to wring every last cent of profit out of the hotel.

The Dilemma

A storm has just struck the area and brought with it major flooding and power outages. Three of the medical centre hospitals have been shut down indefinitely, as have six of the nearby hotels. Fortunately,

your hotel sustained only minor damage and is fully functional. You have just called a meeting with your two assistant managers to discuss what actions, if any, you should take.

One assistant manager has urged you to cut room rates immediately for humanitarian reasons. This manager also wants you to open the hotel kitchens 24 hours a day to prepare free food for rescue workers and meals to donate to the hospitals, whose own food service operations have been disrupted. The other assistant manager, meanwhile, has urged just the opposite approach: raise room rates by at least 20 percent and sell food to rescue workers and hospitals at a premium price. Of course, you can also choose to follow the advice of neither and continue doing business as usual.

Questions for Discussion

1. What are the ethical issues in this situation?

2. What do you think most managers would do in this situation?

3. What would you do?

4. Once you have made your decision, how would you implement it, given the short time frame that is available?

5. How would you measure the success of your decision?

The Business of Bagging Customers

Fickle customers and rapid changes make planning difficult in the high-fashion end of the apparel industry. Most fashion designers—Ralph Lauren, Donna Karan, Prada, Gucci, Fendi—have adopted a design-driven business model, in which the designer dictates style to the customers. Coach, however, has taken a different approach. The company asks the customers what they want and then provides it. Coach's customer focus has created a competitive advantage for the firm, which annually sells $865 of merchandise for every square foot of store space, compared to an industry average of $200–$300.

Coach started out in 1941 making virtually indestructible, high-quality handbags. In the 1970s it was bought by Sara Lee Corp., a big company pursuing a strategy of diversification. However, Coach's products were not stylish and sales languished. Moreover, because it was just one of literally dozens of businesses owned by Sara Lee at the time, the company suffered from the lack of focussed management attention. CEO Lew Frankfort knew the company was failing and said, "We were about to hit a wall." Frankfort also knew that the company's success depended on finding the right industry niche. Finally, in 2000 he convinced Sara Lee to spin off Coach as an independent company. And he wanted to retain the job of turning it around.

Frankfort wanted to attract high fashion's elite customers but remain an affordable luxury for customers who must save for a $200 bag. But how could Coach find and maintain that delicate balance? For help, he first turned to planning and forecasting. He said, "To be successful you need to live your business. You have to understand it organically and thoroughly."

He introduced many new analytical tools for tracking market trends, evaluating effectiveness, and managing risk. The firm's leaders look at sales data for each store and each product type on a daily basis, and during busy seasons, several times daily. But extensive and intensive customer research remains the cornerstone of his planning. Indeed, the company spends $2 million per year on surveys. The surveys are supplemented with one-on-one interviews with customers from locations around the world, to quiz them on everything from appearance and quality to the correct length for a shoulder strap.

"The tremendous amount of testing they do differentiates them from a lot of other fashion companies," says industry analyst Robert Ohmes. Analyst Bob Drbul says, "Their execution and business planning is in the league of a Wal-Mart or a Target" (two much larger firms known for their effective business planning). To test new products, they are first shown to selected buyers in 12 worldwide markets, to gauge initial customer reaction. An initial demand forecast is then made, and six months before introduction, they are tested in another 12 markets. At launch time, sales are monitored closely and adjustments made quickly.

For example, an unexpected spike in sales was investigated, and managers found that buying by Hispanic customers was on the increase. Within a week, the firm had moved up the opening date of a South Miami store and begun advertising in Spanish for the first time. Frankfort understands that, to be effective, plans must be translated into appropriate actions. "Not only do you need to know your business and your customers...you also need to be nimble to adapt," he claims.

A host of other changes have also aided Coach in its rapid rise. Lew Frankfort hired a former Tommy Hilfiger designer, Reed Krakoff, to update the firm's classic but clunky styles. "Something was missing," says Krakoff. "I had to take these ideas and make them fun—young in spirit." Instead of introducing new products twice a year, a common practice in the fashion industry, Coach releases new styles monthly. Customers now have a reason to visit the stores more often. Outsourcing the production function allowed the company to increase gross profit margins by 24 percent over five years. The firm has diversified into many other related lines of business, including shoes, jewellery, furniture, and more. There is even a Coach car, a co-branded Lexus, with a Coach leather interior.

Women's Wear Daily, the bible of the fashion industry, recently named Coach as the "most splurgeworthy luxury brand." Customers agree. Since the firm was spun off, its revenues have doubled and profits have grown at an average annual compound rate of 55 percent. Investors, too, like Coach. The firm's share price rose an astonishing 900 percent during its first four years as an independent firm. Krakoff gives the credit for the firm's achievements to Frankfort's planning skills, saying, "The key to Lew's success...is his ability to orchestrate a decision-making process that is both inclusive and incisive."

Questions for Discussion

1. Describe examples of each of the management functions illustrated in this case.

2. Which management skills seem to be most exemplified in Lew Frankfort?

3. What role have goals and strategy played in the success of Coach?

4. What corporate culture issues might exist when a former division of a big company is spun off?

Remaking BCE

BCE, Canada's largest phone company, held its annual business conference on December 15, 2004. At the conference, CEO Michael Sabia announced that BCE was making good progress on its strategic plan to achieve one of corporate Canada's biggest makeovers. The makeover involves harnessing new revenue streams as old ones decline. Sabia says that his management team will have to blow up the old culture of the company to make it competitive in the new world where technological boundaries between television, wireless networks, and landline phones will disappear. There are two parts to Sabia's vision: (1) Use internet technology to provide seamless communication across a variety of high-tech devices such as laptops, cellphones, personal digital assistants, televisions, etc., and (2) put together an array of business, information, and entertainment applications to send to all those electronic devices.

To date, the investment community has been skeptical that BCE can achieve its goals, given the rapid pace of change that is occurring in the industry. BCE has long relied on the stable revenue stream from traditional local and long-distance phone service it provides. But recently the profitability of that business has declined. BCE thinks that the growing demand for new services such as high-speed delivery of wireless data, broadband internet access, and digital television will increase its profitability. Sabia predicted that during 2005, subscribers to video and wireless service would increase by 10 and 15 percent, and internet subscribers would grow between 15 and 20 percent.

At present, 60 percent of BCE's revenue comes from providing traditional local and long-distance telephone service, and 40 percent comes from the new, high-growth services. The plan is to increase the proportion of revenue coming from new services to 55 percent by the end of 2006. Sabia used a baseball analogy to describe BCE's current position: "We're in the fourth inning," he said. He thought the pattern of the game had been set and BCE was on course to achieve good things down the road.

Analysts attending the business conference were also told that BCE has two other initiatives as part of its strategic plan. First, the company will invest over $1 billion to upgrade its high-definition network so that 85 percent of Quebec homes will have access to high-definition television by 2008. That investment is important since competitors like Canada's cable companies are preparing to enter the telephone business with internet-based calling. Second, BCE has embarked on an aggressive cost-cutting program to improve profit margins. BCE hopes to save approximately $1 billion by the end of 2006.

Michael Sabia has been focussing on corporate strategy since he became CEO in 2002. At that time, he was faced with a difficult decision, namely what kind of company would BCE be? Would it be a television company, a telecommunications company, a media company, or a New Economy company? A strategic decision was necessary because under former CEO Jean Monty, BCE had been acquiring companies in many different businesses, but several of them were not performing well. A CIBC World Markets research note said that BCE's strategy appeared to be in disarray.

To see why Sabia had a difficult strategic decision to make, consider the makeup of BCE in 2002. It had been pursuing a strategy that was often characterized by industry observers as "commerce, content, and connectivity." The *commerce* part of the equation included BCE Emergis (electronic commerce in the health and financial services industries) and CGI Group Inc. (information technology consulting). The *content* part of the equation was represented by Bell Globemedia, which included CTV (television stations), ROBTv (business reporting), the *Globe and Mail* (a national newspaper), and Sympatico-Lycos (internet portals). The connectivity part of the equation included Bell Canada (telephones), Bell ExpressVu (satellite broadcasting), Teleglobe (international voice and data networks), and Bell Canada International (telecom services in emerging markets).

The economic performance of these diverse holdings varied widely. Bell Canada was the most successful and CGI Group was also doing well. But there were problems in each of the other areas. BCE Emergis, for example, had difficulty reaching revenue projections because new customers simply hadn't materialized. In spite of that, Sabia said that BCE was very committed to making Emergis a success. The same sorts of problems existed with Teleglobe and BCI. Bell Globemedia (BGM) was also losing money, and in 2005 BCE reduced its stake in BGM by selling a 40 percent share to Woodbridge Co. Ltd., a 20 percent share to Torstar Corp., and a 20 percent share to the Ontario Teachers Pension Plan. This reduced BCE's stake in the company to 20 percent. BCE received $1.3 billion as part of the deal.

Questions for Discussion

1. Describe the various corporate-level strategies that a company can pursue. What strategy has BCE been pursuing until recently? What strategy is it pursuing now? To what extent is there a change?

2. What are the main steps in the decision-making process? How do they apply in this case?

3. Describe the skills of management. What skills are particularly important to a person like Michael Sabia? Defend your answer.

4. What is corporate culture? How might the corporate culture have changed at BCE over the last decade? Explain your reasoning.

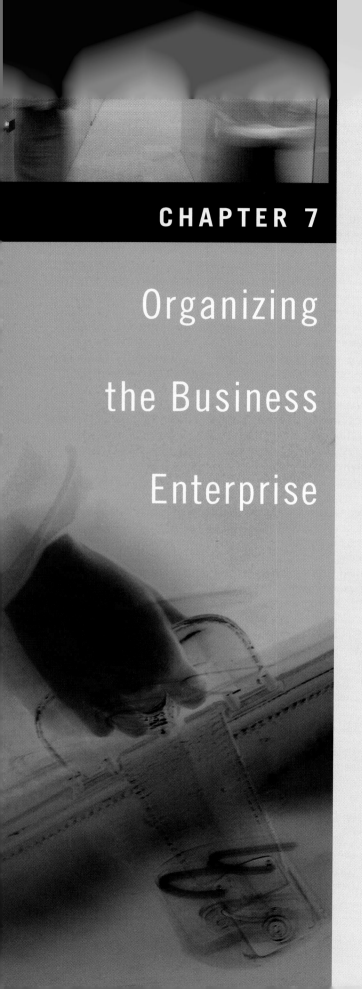

CHAPTER 7

Organizing the Business Enterprise

After reading this chapter, you should be able to:

1 Discuss the elements that influence a firm's *organizational structure*.

2 Explain how *specialization* and *departmentalization* are the building blocks of organizational structure.

3 Distinguish between *responsibility* and *authority* and explain the differences in decision making in *centralized* and *decentralized organizations*.

4 Explain the differences between *functional*, *divisional*, *project*, and *international organizational structures*, and describe the most popular new forms of organizational design.

5 Describe the *informal organization* and discuss *intrapreneuring*.

Frantic Films is a Winnipeg-based film and TV production company. Founded in 1997, the company has grown rapidly and now has more than 100 employees in four different locations. Shortly after its founding, it was named one of Canada's Hottest 50 Start-Ups by *Profit Magazine*. By 2004, it ranked #23 on the list of Canada's fastest-growing companies, and in 2005 it ranked #5 on the list of Manitoba's fastest-growing companies. In addition to being a fast-growing company, Frantic has also received numerous awards. A partial list includes the following:

- National Research Council recognition as a Canadian innovation leader
- Lions Gate Innovative Producers Award
- New Media Visionary Award nomination
- Blizzard Award (for the documentary series "Quest for the Bay")
- Finalist in the Ernst & Young Entrepreneur Of The Year award competition (multiple years)

Frantic Films is a private corporation that is owned and managed by three principal shareholders—Jamie Brown (chief executive officer), Chris Bond (president), and Ken Zorniak (chief operating officer). With its rapid growth, the company's organization chart has been revised several times, but its three original divisions—Visual Effects, Live Action, and TV Commercials—continue to be very important (see Figure 7.1).

The *visual effects* division (Frantic Films VFX Services Inc.) produces visual effects for TV and movies. Using visual effects software packages such as Maya, Houdini, Digital Fusion, and 3Dstudio Max, the division has established a reputation as one of the top visual effects providers in North America. The majority of the employees at Frantic are in this division. Its output includes visual effects for films like *Superman Returns*, *Stay*, *X-Men 3*, *The Italian Job*, *Catwoman*, *The Core*, and *Swordfish*. The division uses a matrix structure to complete film projects. This means that a project team, made up of specialists in areas like 3D animation, 2D animation, compositing, and hardware/software support, is put together. When the project is completed, the team disbands and its members are assigned to other projects. These teams are typically given specific goals that must be achieved, and then the team members use their technical expertise to decide how they can best achieve the goal.

The *TV commercial* division (Frantic Films Commercial Projects Inc.) produces television commercials for local Winnipeg companies, as well as for national and international clients. It also provides visual effects for commercials produced by other companies. The writers, producers, designers, compositors, animators, and editors have created award-winning spots for local, national, and international companies as diverse as the Royal Winnipeg Ballet, the Disney Channel, and Procter & Gamble Canada.

Figure 7.1 Organization chart for Frantic Films.

The *live action* division (Frantic Films Live Action Productions Inc.) produces and owns programs that have been broadcast around the world in over 40 countries. The division first develops the ideas for a program, then promotes the idea to broadcasters and financiers. If there is a strong interest, a budget is provided and the division produces the program. Frantic has produced documentary programs such as *Pioneer Quest* (one of the highest rated documentary series ever broadcast on a Canadian specialty channel), lifestyle series, ('*Til Debt Do Us Part*), television movies (*Zeyda* and the *Hitman*), and feature films (*Lucid*). Once a program is completed, rights are transferred to the releasing company and the individual, single-purpose production companies created for each show are wound up.

Recently, a software division has been created (Frantic Films Software Inc.). It employs seven individuals with specialized expertise, some of whom are computer science grads. When software division employees discovered that off-the-shelf software did not meet their needs, they began creating their own new stand-alone software to enhance certain visual effects like virtual water and smoke. This software was used to create the fluid-based character Tar Monster in the movie *Scooby-Doo II*.

Each of the divisions at Frantic Films operates fairly independently, but the company is still small enough that individuals from one division sometimes get involved in decisions in other divisions. For example, since the company does not have a marketing vice-president, marketing decisions are often made jointly by Brown, Bond, and Zorniak for each of the divisions. This means that Frantic Films does not have a "pure" functional or divisional structure.

When the company was first formed, the authority structure of the company was quite centralized because the principal shareholders had both the expertise to make decisions and the motivation to do so. But Brown thinks it is important to increase the involvement of lower-level workers in decisions, so he is trying to delegate more authority to them. Some progress has been

made in this area. For example, managers in some of the divisions were recently given the authority to spend up to $5000 without having to get the approval of top management. This change was made because the top managers found that they were spending too much time discussing whether to approve requests for relatively small amounts of money. So, they essentially delegated more authority to division managers by giving them the discretion to spend up to $5000. Brown also encourages employees to make recommendations on various issues to top management. He recognizes that giving employees more discretion can sometimes lead to less-than-optimal decisions, but he also wants to give people more experience in making decisions that affect the company.

Like all rapidly growing companies, Frantic Films has experienced certain "growing pains" with regard to its organizational structure. For example, offices were set up in California and British Columbia to get more visual effects business in those local areas, but until recently, there have not been dedicated sales people responsible for generating work there. While employees in those offices have been fully employed, they are more costly. The original idea was to have them obtain work that could be sent to the lower-cost Winnipeg office, but more work is being done by a growing workforce in the satellite offices. Top management is now in the process of determining the changes that are needed to make the organization's structure more effective.

The other structural problem concerns the division of duties between Brown, Bond, and Zorniak. When the company first formed, all three principals were involved in decision making for all the divisions. But as the company has grown, each individual has gradually become more focussed. For example, Brown has primary responsibility for the live action division, while Zorniak and Bond have primary responsibility for the visual effects division. There have been some discussions among the three principals about having one person be responsible for all three divisions so that work can be better coordinated, but so far they have not been able to agree on a course of action. ◆

WHAT IS ORGANIZATIONAL STRUCTURE?

1 Discuss the elements that influence a firm's *organizational structure*.

What do we mean by the term *organizational structure*? In many ways, a business is like an automobile. All automobiles have an engine, four wheels, fenders and other structural components, an interior compartment for passengers, and various operating systems including those for fuel, braking, and climate control. Each component has a distinct purpose but must also work in harmony with the others. Automobiles made by competing firms all have the same basic components, although the way they look and fit together may vary.

Similarly, all businesses have common structural and operating components, each of which has a specific purpose. Each component must fulfill its own purpose while simultaneously fitting in with the others. And, just like automobiles made by different companies, how these components look and fit together varies from company to company. Thus, **organizational structure** is the specification of the jobs to be done within a business and how those jobs relate to one another.

Every institution—be it a for-profit company like Frantic Films, a not-for-profit organization like the University of Saskatchewan, or a government agency like the Canadian Wheat Board—must develop the most appropriate structure for its own unique situation. What works for Air Canada will not work for Canada Revenue. Likewise, the structure of the Red Cross will not work for the University of Toronto.

organizational structure The specification of the jobs to be done within a business and how those jobs relate to one another.

Determinants of Organizational Structure

How is an organization's structure determined? Does it happen by chance or is there some logic that managers use to create structure? Does it develop by some combination of circumstance and strategy? Ideally, managers carefully assess a variety of important factors as they plan for and then create a structure that will allow their organization to function efficiently.

Many elements work together to determine an organization's structure. Chief among these are the organization's *purpose, mission,* and *strategy*. A dynamic and rapidly growing enterprise, for example, achieved that position because of its purpose and successful strategies for achieving it. Such a firm will need a structure that contributes to flexibility and growth. A stable organization with only modest growth will function best with a different structure.

Size, technology, and changes in environmental circumstances also affect structure. A large manufacturer operating in a strongly competitive environment requires a different structure than a local barbershop or video store. Moreover, even after a structure has been created, it is rarely free from tinkering—or even outright re-creation. Indeed, most organizations change their structures almost continually.

Since it was first incorporated in 1903, for example, Ford Motor Co. has undergone literally dozens of major structural changes, hundreds of moderate changes, and thousands of minor changes. In the last decade alone, Ford has initiated several major structural changes. In 1994, the firm announced a major restructuring plan called *Ford 2000*, which was intended to integrate all of Ford's vast international operations into a single, unified structure by 2000. By 1998, however, midway through implementation of the plan, top Ford executives announced major modifications, indicating that (1) additional changes would be made, (2) some previously planned changes would not be made, and (3) some recently realigned operations would be changed again. In 1999, managers announced another sweeping set of changes intended to eliminate corporate bureaucracy, speed decision making, and improve communication and working relationships among people at different levels of the organization.[1] In 2001, still more changes were announced that were intended to boost the firm's flagging bottom line and stem a decline in product quality.[2]

The Chain of Command

Most businesses prepare **organization charts** that illustrate the company's structure and show employees where they fit into the firm's operations. Figure 7.2 shows the organization chart for a hypothetical company. Each

organization chart A physical depiction of the company's structure showing employee titles and their relationship to one another.

chain of command Reporting relationships within a business; the flow of decision-making power in a firm.

box represents a job within the company. The solid lines that connect the boxes define the chain of command, or the reporting relationships within the company. For example, the plant manager reports directly to the vice-president for production who, in turn, reports to the president. When the **chain of command** is not clear, many different kinds of problems can result.

THE BUILDING BLOCKS OF ORGANIZATIONAL STRUCTURE

2 Explain how *specialization* and *departmentalization* are the building blocks of organizational structure.

The first step in developing the structure of any business, large or small, is twofold:

- *Specialization*: determining who will do what
- *Departmentalization*: determining how people performing certain tasks can best be grouped together

These two tasks are the basic building blocks of all business organization.

Specialization

job specialization The process of identifying the specific jobs that need to be done and designating the people who will perform them.

The process of identifying the specific jobs that need to be done and designating the people who will perform them leads to **job specialization**. In a sense, all organizations have only one major "job"—for example, making a profit by manufacturing and selling men's and boys' shirts. But this job, of

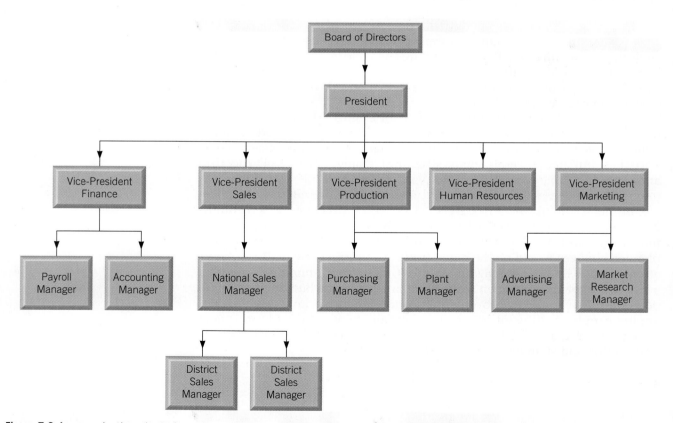

Figure 7.2 An organization chart shows key positions in the organization and interrelationships among them. An actual organization chart would, of course, be far more complex and include individuals at many more levels. Indeed, because of their size, larger firms cannot easily draw a diagram with everyone on it.

Organizational and industry-wide growth don't always result in greater job specialization. Animated feature films like *Toy Story 2* are now created by small teams of people who use point-and-click techniques to perform just about every job required by a project. The *Toy Story* movies, as well as *Finding Nemo* and *The Incredibles*, were made by Pixar Animation Studios, which works solely with computer-created animation. According to many experts, Pixar may soon take over industry leadership from Disney.

course, is broken into smaller components. In turn, each component is assigned to an individual. Consider the manufacture of men's shirts. Because several steps are required to produce a shirt, each job is broken down into its component parts—that is, into a set of tasks to be completed by a series of individuals or machines. One person, for example, cuts material for the shirt body, another cuts material for the sleeves, and a third cuts material for the collar. Components are then shipped to a sewing room, where a fourth person assembles the shirt. In the final stage, a fifth person sews on the buttons.[3]

Specialization and Growth

In a very small organization, the owner may perform every job. As the firm grows, however, so does the need to specialize jobs so that others can perform them. To see how specialization can evolve in an organization, consider the case of Mrs. Fields Cookies. When Debbi Fields opened her first store, she did everything herself: bought the equipment, negotiated the lease, baked the cookies, operated the store, and kept the records. As the business grew, however, Fields found that her job was becoming too much for one person. She first hired a bookkeeper to handle her financial records. She then hired an in-store manager and a cookie baker. She herself concentrated on advertising and promotions. Her second store required another set of employees—another manager, another baker, and some salespeople. While Fields focussed her attention on other expansion opportunities, she turned promotions over to a professional advertising director. Thus the job that she once did all by herself was increasingly broken down into components and assigned to different individuals.

Job specialization is a natural part of organizational growth. It is neither a new idea nor limited to factory work. In the ancient art of winemaking, for example, a high degree of specialization has existed for centuries. The activities necessary to make wine—picking and crushing grapes, fermenting the juice, aging and clarifying the wine, and selling it through specialized intermediaries—are performed by individuals who can draw on the knowledge and experience of their predecessors.

Job specialization has certain advantages: Individual jobs can be performed more efficiently, the jobs are easier to learn, and it is easier to replace people who leave the organization. On the other hand, if job specialization is carried too far and jobs become too narrowly defined, people get bored, derive less satisfaction from their jobs, and often lose sight of how their contributions fit into the overall organization.

Departmentalization

departmentalization The process of grouping jobs into logical units.

After jobs are specialized, they must be grouped into logical units. This process is called **departmentalization**. Departmentalized companies benefit from the division of activities. Control and coordination are narrowed and made easier, and top managers can see more easily how various units are performing. Departmentalization allows the firm to treat a department as a **profit centre**—a separate unit responsible for its own costs and profits. Thus, by assessing profits from sales in a particular area—for example, men's clothing—Sears can decide whether to expand or curtail promotions in that area.

profit centre A separate company unit responsible for its own costs and profits.

Managers do not group jobs randomly. They group them logically, according to some common thread or purpose. In general, departmentalization may occur along *functional, customer, product, geographic,* or *process* lines (or any combination of these).

Functional Departmentalization

functional departmentalization Departmentalization according to functions or activities.

Many service and manufacturing companies develop departments according to a group's functions or activities—a form of organization known as **functional departmentalization**. Such firms typically have production, marketing and sales, human resource, and accounting and finance departments. Departments may be further subdivided. For example, the marketing department might be divided geographically or into separate staffs for market research and advertising.

Customer Departmentalization

customer departmentalization Departmentalization according to the types of customers likely to buy a given product.

Stores like HMV are divided into departments—a classical music department, an R&B department, a pop department, and so on. Each department targets a specific customer category (people who want to buy different genres of music). **Customer departmentalization** makes shopping easier by providing identifiable store segments. Thus, a customer shopping for Shania Twain's latest CD can bypass World Music and head straight for Country. Stores can also group products in locations designated for deliveries, special sales, and other service-oriented purposes. In general, when it is departmentalized the store is more efficient and customers get better service—in part because salespeople tend to specialize and gain expertise in their departments.[4]

Product Departmentalization

product departmentalization Departmentalization according to the products being created or sold.

Both manufacturers and service providers often opt for **product departmentalization**—dividing an organization according to the specific product or service being created. A bank, for example, may handle consumer loans in one department and commercial loans in another. On a larger scale, 3M Corp., which makes both consumer and industrial products, operates different divisions for Post-it brand tape flags, Scotch-Brite scrub sponges, and the Sarns 9000 perfusion system for open-heart surgery.

Geographic Departmentalization

geographic departmentalization Departmentalization according to the area of the country or world supplied.

Some firms may be divided according to the area of the country—or even the world—they serve. This is known as **geographic departmentalization**. The Personal Services division of Montreal Trust, for example, is organized

Many department stores are departmentalized by product. Concentrating different products in different areas of the store makes shopping easier for customers.

around four regions—Atlantic, Quebec, Central, and BC/Western. Levi Strauss has one division for the United States, one for Europe, and one for the Asia-Pacific region.

The Business Accountability box describes some difficulties that companies can encounter when they try to choose between product and geographic departmentalization.

Process Departmentalization

Other manufacturers favour **process departmentalization**, in which the organization is divided according to production processes. This principle, for example, is logical for the pickle maker Vlasic, which has separate departments to transform cucumbers into fresh-packed pickles, pickles cured in brine, and relishes. Cucumbers destined to become fresh-packed pickles must be packed into jars immediately, covered with a solution of water and vinegar, and prepared for sale. Those slated for brined pickles must be aged in brine solution before packing. Relish cucumbers must be minced and combined with a host of other ingredients. Each process requires different equipment and worker skills.

Because different forms of departmentalization have different advantages, larger companies tend to adopt different types of departmentalization for various levels. For example, the company illustrated in Figure 7.3 uses functional departmentalization at the top level. At the middle level, production is divided along geographic lines. At a lower level, departmentalization is based on product groups.

process departmentalization
Departmentalization according to the production process used to create a good or service.

ESTABLISHING THE DECISION-MAKING HIERARCHY

After jobs have been appropriately specialized and grouped into manageable departments, the next step in organizing is to establish the decision-making hierarchy. That is, managers must explicitly define *reporting relationships* among positions so that everyone will know who has responsibility for various decisions and operations. The goal is to figure out how to structure and stabilize the organizational framework so that everyone works together to achieve common goals.

BUSINESS ACCOUNTABILITY

Product Versus Geographical Departmentalization: What's the Right Choice?

Geographic departmentalization ensures quick, responsive reaction to the needs of the company's customers in certain geographic areas. On the other hand, it may also lead to duplicate production and other facilities, and compartmentalization of knowledge in those same geographic areas. So, it's not easy to decide whether to organize geographically or around products.

Organizing geographically grew in popularity as globalization occurred and firms expanded across national borders. Years ago, when relatively limited communications made it difficult to take the pulse of consumer needs or monitor operations abroad, it made sense to let local managers in foreign countries run their regional or country businesses as more or less autonomous companies. However, two trends are making this structure less popular today. First, information technology is reducing the impediments to cross-border communication. Second, global competition is so intense that firms can't afford to miss an opportunity to quickly transfer product improvements from one region to another.

Many firms are therefore switching from geographic to product departmentalization. For example, food company Heinz abandoned geographical departmentalization and is now organized by products. Managers in the United States work with those in Europe, Asia, and other regions to apply the best ideas from one region to all the others.

The Canadian Imperial Bank of Commerce (CIBC) also reorganized to break down the walls between the conservative and traditional retail/commercial banking side, and the more volatile investment banking side. The company is now organized around product lines.

Exide Corp., the world's largest producer of automotive and industrial batteries, has also shifted from geographical to product departmentalization. Previously, Exide's structure consisted of about 10 "country organizations." The head of each country organization had considerable latitude to make decisions that were best for that person's country. It also meant that each country manager focussed on products that were marketable in that country. Under the new product system, global business units have been formed to oversee the company's various product lines such as car and industrial batteries. But the change has not been without problems. For example, when Exide made an acquisition, some top executives got upset when their unit was made subordinate to the newly acquired unit. It wasn't long before Exide was tinkering with its organization chart again.

Either approach—products or geography—can cause problems if taken to an extreme. If a company organizes by products, it can standardize manufacturing, introduce new products around the world faster, and eliminate overlapping activities. But if too much emphasis is placed on product and not enough on geography, a company is likely to find that local decision making is slowed, pricing flexibility is reduced, and products are not tailored to meet the needs of a specific country's customers.

Ford Motor Co. experienced exactly these problems when it decided to move toward the product model. The reorganization saved the company $5 billion in its first few years of operation, but Ford's market share declined during the same period. This is what we would expect to happen when too much emphasis is placed on product departmentalization. Ford responded to this drop in market share by giving executives in various regions more authority to decide what types of vehicles were best for their local market. In other words, it moved back a bit toward the geographical model.

Procter & Gamble also encountered problems after it replaced country organizations with global business units in an attempt to globalize P&G brands like Tide, Pampers, and Crest. The reorganization caused great upheaval within the company as thousands of employees shifted into new jobs. As many as half of all company executives took on new roles. The CEO who ordered the change left the company just 17 months into his job.

A major question that must be asked about any organization is this: *Who makes which decisions?* The answer almost never focusses on an individual or even on a small group. The more accurate answer usually refers to the decision-making hierarchy. The development of this hierarchy generally results from a three-step process:

1. *Assigning tasks*: determining who can make decisions and specifying how they should be made

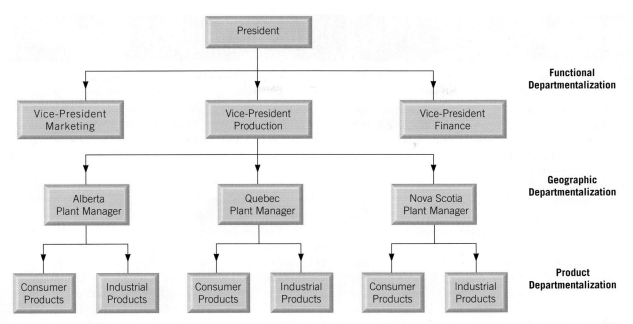

Figure 7.3 Most organizations use multiple bases of departmentalization. This organization, for example, is using functional, geographic, and product departmentalization.

2. *Performing tasks*: implementing decisions that have been made

3. *Distributing authority*: determining whether the organization is to be centralized or decentralized

To see this process in action, consider what has been happening at McDonald's, where executives have been systematically changing the firm's decision-making hierarchy. McDonald's has always been—and continues to be—highly centralized. But executives recently restructured both the company's decision-making processes and its operations. For instance, they reduced staff at corporate headquarters in Illinois, and established five regional offices throughout the United States. Now, many decisions are made at the regional level. They also clamped a lid on domestic growth and increased international expansion. In addition, they purchased stakes in three new restaurant chains with an eye on expansion: Donatos Pizza; Chipotle Mexican Grill; and Aroma, a British coffee chain. Four new managers have been installed, one to head up international operations and the others to oversee the three new restaurant partner groups. All four of these executives reported directly to the CEO.[5]

Assigning Tasks

The question of who is supposed to do what and who is entitled to do what in an organization is complex. In any company with more than one person, individuals must work out agreements about responsibilities and authority. **Responsibility** is the duty to perform an assigned task. **Authority** is the power to make the decisions necessary to complete the task.

For example, imagine a mid-level buyer for The Bay who encounters an unexpected opportunity to make a large purchase at an extremely good price. Let's assume that an immediate decision is absolutely necessary—but that this decision is one that this buyer has no authority to make without confirmation from above. The company's policies on delegation and authority are inconsistent, since the buyer is responsible for purchasing the clothes that will be sold in the upcoming season but lacks the authority to make the needed purchases.

Distinguish between *responsibility* and *authority* and explain the differences in decision making in *centralized* and *decentralized organizations*.

3

responsibility The duty to perform an assigned task.

authority The power to make the decisions necessary to complete a task.

ENTREPRENEURSHIP AND NEW VENTURES

The Techie Trio

When the three young owners of Triotech Amusement Inc. (Frederic Lachance, 35, David Lachance, 27, and Ernest Yale, 34) took their video game prototype to a trade show in Atlanta in 1999, it was their "make it or break it" chance. On the last day of the show, they made a sale, and from that first success have gone on to build a business that now has sales of close to $8 million.

Brothers David and Frederic Lachance were operating an internet café in Joliette, Quebec, in 1998 when they started providing "cabins" where people could play games over a network. This led to the idea of creating and selling closed cabins for game playing. With the help of software developer Ernest Yale they came up with their first product, Cyberpod. The three invested everything they had in the machine, and rented a truck and drove it to the Atlanta tradeshow where it was sold to an American distributor. "That's how Triotech got started," says Frederic. "We sold about 100 units through that distributor." In 2001, with their second product ready for launching, they hired their own sales representatives. They now have some 30 employees in Quebec and sales offices in Los Angeles and Texas.

The products Triotech Amusement develops and manufactures include video games, arcade machines, and multi-seat 3D theatres. The business is known for its technologically-advanced motion system and the sleek design of its products. Trademark products include Mad Wave Motion Theater, a two-seat coin-operated ride simulator; Wasteland Racer 2071, a driving simulator; and the XD Theater, a multi-seat motion-simulated thrill ride with 3D films. Known internationally, Triotech sells its products to amusement parks, entertainment centres, and arcade operators in the United States, England, Mexico, Russia, India, Australia, and Saudi Arabia. "Nothing beats watching people playing one of our games or enjoying one of our thrill rides," says Ernest. "Seeing their reactions makes it all worthwhile."

Frederic, David, and Ernest combine their complementary skills to run Triotech. Ernest, a video game developer since he was 12, heads the R&D unit in Montreal where he and his team develop software for new products. Frederic, president of the company, designs the actual machines that house the games and theatres and is responsible for sales and marketing strategy from Lavaltrie, outside of Montreal. David uses his technical skills in overseeing the day-to-day operations of manufacturing the units and designing the technology behind the hardware. Triotech has assembled a team of passionate people who care as much about the company as they do. "If there is anything that we're proud of it's our team," says Frederic.

As the company has grown, the three partners have faced the challenges of managing a larger organization and learning to delegate tasks. Frederic says the secret to handling growth is seeking out information, learning from others, and building a solid network of contacts. "There is no equivalent for our company in Canada," says Frederic, "and we operate in a sector that is virtually unknown in Quebec. But we've shown great growth potential; we're young and we've only touched the tip of what the possibilities are." "Since the beginning, we have dreamed of success," says Frederic. "But it's surprising how fast the business has grown. Dreams don't always come true, but for us this one has."

Performing Tasks

delegation Assignment of a task, a responsibility, or authority by a manager to a subordinate.

accountability Liability of subordinates for accomplishing tasks assigned by managers.

Trouble occurs when appropriate levels of responsibility and authority are not clearly spelled out in the working relationships between managers and subordinates. Here, the issues become delegation and accountability. **Delegation** begins when a manager assigns a task to a subordinate. **Accountability** falls to the subordinate, who must then complete the task. If the subordinate does not perform the assigned task properly and promptly, he or she may be reprimanded or punished, possibly even dismissed.

Fear of Delegating

Unfortunately, many managers have trouble delegating tasks to others. When this happens, subordinates may not be able to complete a task because their manager has not delegated sufficient authority to them. Such employees face a dilemma: They cannot do what the boss demands, but that boss will probably still hold them accountable. Effective managers surround themselves with a team of strong subordinates, and then delegate sufficient authority to those subordinates to get the job done. There are four things to keep in mind when delegating:

- Decide on the nature of the work to be done.

- Match the job with the skills of subordinates.

- Make sure the person chosen understands the objectives he or she is supposed to achieve.

- Make sure subordinates have the time and training necessary to do the task.

Experts pinpoint certain indicators that managers (particularly those in small businesses) are having trouble delegating effectively:

- the feeling that employees can never do anything as well as they can

- the fear that something will go wrong if someone else takes over a job

- the lack of time for long-range planning because they are bogged down in day-to-day operations

- the sense of being in the dark about industry trends and competitive products because of the time they devote to day-to-day operations

To overcome these tendencies, small business owners must admit that they can never go back to running all aspects of the business and that they can, in fact, prosper—with the help of their employees—if they learn to let go. But this problem isn't confined just to small businesses. Some managers in big companies also don't delegate as much or as well as they should. There are several reasons for this problem:

- the fear that subordinates don't really know how to do the job

- the fear that a subordinate might "show the manager up" in front of others by doing a superb job

- the desire to keep as much control as possible over how things are done

- a simple lack of ability as to how to effectively delegate to others

The remedies in these instances are a bit different. First, managers should recognize that they cannot do everything themselves. Second, if subordinates cannot do a job, they should be trained so that they can assume more responsibility in the future. Third, managers should recognize that if a subordinate performs well, it reflects favourably on that employee's manager. Finally, a manager who simply does not know how to delegate might need specialized training in how to divide up and assign tasks to others.

Distributing Authority

Delegation involves a specific relationship between managers and subordinates. Most businesses must also make decisions about general patterns of authority throughout the company. This pattern may be largely *centralized* or *decentralized* (or, usually, somewhere in between).

Centralized Organizations

In a **centralized organization**, top management retains the right to make most decisions, and top management must approve most lower-level decisions before they can be implemented.[6] McDonald's practises centralization as a way to maintain standardization. All restaurants must follow precise steps in buying products and making and packaging burgers and other

centralized organization Top managers retain most decision-making rights for themselves.

menu items. Most advertising is handled at the corporate level, and a regional manager must approve any local advertising. Restaurants even have to follow prescribed schedules for facilities' maintenance and upgrades like floor polishing and parking lot cleaning.[7]

Decentralized Organizations

decentralized organization Lower- and middle-level managers are allowed to make significant decisions.

As a company gets larger, more decisions must be made, and there is usually a move to a more decentralized pattern. In a **decentralized organization**, much of the decision-making authority is delegated to levels of management at various points below the top level. The purpose of decentralization is to make a company more responsive to its environment by breaking the company into more manageable units, and giving those units more autonomy. Reducing top-heavy bureaucracies is also a common goal of decentralization.

Determining the Optimum Level of Decentralization. Deciding just how centralized or decentralized a company should be is something of an art. Jack Welch, the former CEO of General Electric and a long-time proponent of decentralized management, says, "If you don't let managers make their own decisions, you're never going to be anything more than a one-person business." The logic of giving manager's more decision making autonomy is also behind the decentralizing strategy of cereal maker Kellogg Co. Top managers at Kellogg realized that to keep pace with today's eat-on-the-run lifestyles, lower-level managers had to have more autonomy to make decisions so they could rush new products to market.[8]

The idea of autonomy for managers sounds pretty reasonable, but decentralization can also cause difficulties for companies, as the story of Home Depot illustrates. Home Depot was founded in the early 1980s by Bernie Marcus and Arthur Blank. They encouraged store managers to think for themselves and to do what was best for their particular store. Authority was decentralized. Marcus and Blank said that they hired people who were actually more suited for self-employment or for running their own business. Time passed, and Marcus and Blank left the company. A new CEO—Robert Nardelli—came in and moved the company toward a much more centralized structure by emphasizing operating efficiencies, expense controls, and head office directives to store managers. He felt that operations were too loosely controlled under the founders. Nardelli loved the entrepreneurial spirit, but said that it had to be compliant more often.[9]

The advantages and disadvantages of decentralization can clearly be seen in the long history of General Motors. In the 1920s, GM's legendary president, Alfred Sloan, introduced a decentralized structure that gave each car division considerable autonomy to produce cars that would attract whatever market segment the division was pursuing. This decentralized structure continued in use as the company expanded from the United States into international markets. It worked so well that GM became the largest automobile manufacturer in the world. Although the company was large, in many parts of the world it operated more like a small regional company because its executives were given a great deal of autonomy over issues like car design. This helped GM offer cars that appealed to people in local markets.

But all this autonomy resulted in widely differing car designs that were very expensive to produce. As GM costs soared, and as competition from cost-conscious Japanese car makers became ferocious, GM's sales and overall profitability plummeted. Something had to be done. So GM *re*centralized and head office took away much of the autonomy that managers in various international divisions had. Now, GM requires its worldwide units to work much more closely together to design cars that can be sold (with modest variations) worldwide. This will reduce GM's cost per car.

The new, more centralized structure, means that engineers in various regions have less authority than they used to have when they are designing cars and the parts that will be used in those cars. A "Global Council" in Detroit now makes key decisions about how much will be spent on new car development. And the council can say "no" to proposed new car designs. For example, when GM engineers at its Daewoo joint venture with South Korea wanted to develop a sport utility vehicle especially suited for the South Korean market, the request was denied.

Another example: When the Saab 9-3 was being developed, GM asked its subsidiary to work from the same "Epsilon" architecture as the Opel Vectra (which was made in Germany) and the Chevrolet Malibu (which was made in the United States). This would allow GM to build any Epsilon vehicle at any of their production facilities around the world. But Saab's engineers changed some things like the electrical system and the engine cradle, and that meant that the Saab 9-3 couldn't easily be built at other production facilities. After that fiasco, GM transferred most of Saab's engineers to its European technical development centre, and Saab no longer has an independent engineering organization.[10]

Tall and Flat Organizations

Related to the concept of centralized or decentralized authority is the concept of tall or flat organizational structures. With relatively fewer layers of management, decentralized firms tend to have a **flat organizational structure** such as the one shown in Figure 7.4. In contrast, companies with centralized authority systems typically require multiple layers of management and thus have a **tall organizational structure**. The Canadian Forces is an example of such an organization. Because information, whether upward or downward bound, must pass through so many organizational layers, tall structures are prone to delays in information flow.

As organizations grow in size, it is both normal and necessary that they become at least somewhat taller. For instance, a small firm with only an owner-manager and a few employees is likely to have two layers—the owner-manager and the employees who report to that person. But as the firm grows, more layers will be needed. Born Information Services, for instance, is a small consulting firm created and run by Rick Born. At first, all employees reported to him. But when his firm grew to more than 20 people, he knew he needed help in supervising and coordinating projects. As a result, he added a layer of management consisting of what he called "staff managers" to serve as project coordinators. This move freed him up to seek new business clients.[11] Like other managers, however, Born must ensure that he has only the number of layers his firm needs. Too few layers can create chaos and inefficiency, while too many layers can create rigidity and bureaucracy.

Span of Control

As you can see from Figure 7.4, the distribution of authority in an organization also affects the number of people who work for any individual manager. In a flat organizational structure, the number of people managed by one supervisor—the manager's **span of control**—is usually wide. In tall organizations, span of control tends to be relatively narrow. Span of control, however, depends on many factors. Employees' abilities and the supervisor's managerial skills help determine whether span of control is wide or narrow, as do the similarity and simplicity of those tasks performed under the manager's supervision and the extent to which they are interrelated.[12]

If lower level managers are given more decision-making authority, their supervisors will have less work to do because some of the decisions they

flat organizational structure An organization with relatively few layers of management.

tall organizational structure An organization with many layers of management.

span of control The number of people managed by one manager.

previously made will be transferred to their subordinates. By the same token, these managers may then be able to oversee and coordinate the work of more subordinates, resulting in an increased span of control. At McDonald's, the creation of regional offices freed up time for the CEO. In turn, reorganization allowed him to then create four new executive positions, one to oversee international expansion and the others to work with new restaurant partners.

Similarly, when several employees perform either the same simple task or a group of interrelated tasks, a wide span of control is possible and often desirable. For instance, because all the jobs are routine, one supervisor may well control an entire assembly line. Moreover, each task depends on another. If one station stops, everyone stops. Having one supervisor ensures that all stations receive equal attention and function equally well.

In contrast, when jobs are more diversified or prone to change, a narrow span of control is preferable. At Case Corp., farm tractors are made to

Figure 7.4 Organizational structure and span of control.

order in five to six weeks. Farmers can select from among a wide array of options, including engines, tires, power trains, and even a CD player. A wide assortment of machines and processes is used to construct each tractor. Although workers are highly skilled operators of their assigned machines, each machine is different. In this kind of set-up, the complexities of each machine and the advanced skills needed by each operator mean that one supervisor can oversee only a small number of employees.[13]

Downsizing refers to the planned reduction in the scope of an organization's activity. It usually means cutting substantial numbers of managers and workers, and reducing the number and variety of products the company produces. Downsizing may eliminate entire layers of management (creating a "flatter" corporate structure), and the remaining managers end up with larger spans of control.

downsizing The planned reduction in the scope of an organization's activity.

Three Forms of Authority

In an organization, it must be clear who will have authority over whom. As individuals are delegated responsibility and authority in a firm, a complex web of interactions develops. These interactions may take one of three forms of authority: *line, staff,* or *committee and team*. In reality, like departmentalization, all three forms may be found in a given company, especially a large one.

Line Authority

Line authority is authority that flows up and down the chain of command (refer back to Figure 7.2 on p. 208). Most companies rely heavily on **line departments**—departments directly linked to the production and sales of specific products. For example, Clark Equipment Corp. has a division that produces forklifts and small earthmovers. In this division, line departments include purchasing, materials handling, fabrication, painting, and assembly (all of which are directly linked to production) along with sales and distribution (both of which are directly linked to sales).

Each line department is essential to an organization's success. Line employees are the "doers" and producers in a company. If any line department fails to complete its task, the company cannot sell and deliver finished goods. Thus, the authority delegated to line departments is important. A bad decision by the manager in one department can hold up production for an entire plant. For example, say that the painting department manager at Clark Equipment changes a paint application on a batch of forklifts, which then show signs of peeling paint. The batch will have to be repainted (and perhaps partially reassembled) before the machines can be shipped.

line authority An organizational structure in which authority flows in a direct chain of command from the top of the company to the bottom.

line department A department directly linked to the production and sales of a specific product.

Staff Authority

Most companies also rely on **staff authority**, which is based on special expertise and usually involves counselling and advising line managers. Common **staff members** include specialists in areas such as law, accounting, and human resource management. A corporate attorney, for example, may be asked to advise the marketing department as it prepares a new contract with the firm's advertising agency. Legal staff, however, do not actually make decisions that affect how the marketing department does its job. Staff members, therefore, aid line departments in making decisions but do not have the authority to make final decisions.

Suppose, for example, that the fabrication department at Clark Equipment has an employee with a drinking problem. The manager of the department could consult a human resource staff expert for advice on handling the situation. The staff expert might suggest that the worker stay on

staff authority Authority that is based on expertise and that usually involves advising line managers.

staff members Advisers and counsellors who aid line departments in making decisions but do not have the authority to make final decisions.

the job but enter a counselling program. But if the line manager decides that the job is too dangerous to be handled by a person whose judgment is often impaired by alcohol, that decision will most likely prevail.

Typically, the separation between line authority and staff responsibility is clearly delineated. As Figure 7.5 shows, this separation is usually shown in organization charts by solid lines (line authority) and dotted lines (staff responsibility). It may help to understand this separation by remembering that while staff members generally provide services to management, line managers are directly involved in producing the firm's products.

Committee and Team Authority

committee and team authority
Authority granted to committees or work teams involved in a firm's daily operations.

Recently, more and more organizations have started to use **committee and team authority**—authority granted to committees or work teams that play central roles in the firm's daily operations. A committee, for example, may consist of top managers from several major areas. If the work of the committee is especially important, and if the committee will be working together for an extended time, the organization may even grant it special authority as a decision-making body that goes beyond the individual authority possessed by each of its members.

At the operating level, many firms today are also using *work teams*—groups of operating employees empowered to plan and organize their own work and to perform that work with a minimum of supervision. As with permanent committees, the organization will usually find it beneficial to grant special authority to work teams so that they may function more effectively.[14]

BASIC ORGANIZATIONAL STRUCTURES

4 Explain the differences between *functional*, *divisional*, *project*, and *international organizational structures*, and describe the most popular new forms of organizational design.

A glance at the organization charts of many organizations reveals what appears to be an infinite variety of structures. However, closer examination shows that it is possible to identify four basic forms: functional, divisional, project, and international. These structures are described below.

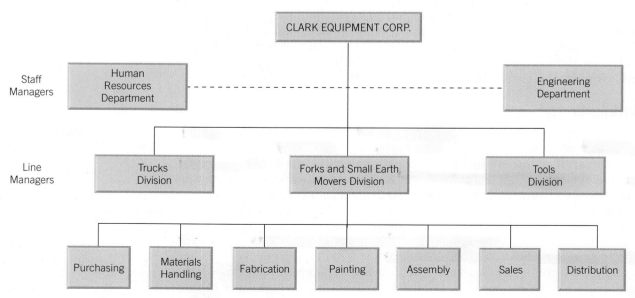

Figure 7.5 Line and staff organization: Clark Equipment Corp.

The Functional Structure

The **functional structure** is the oldest and most commonly used. In the functional organization, the various units in the organization are formed based on the functions that must be carried out to reach organizational goals. The functional structure makes use of departmentalization by function. An example of a functional structure is shown in Figure 7.2 (see p. 208). The advantages and disadvantages of the functional structure are summarized in Table 7.1.

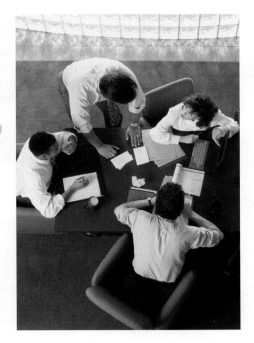

Business firms are increasingly using work teams and allowing groups of employees to plan and organize their own work with a minimum of supervision. This contributes to employee empowerment.

The Divisional Structure

The functional structure's disadvantages can make it inappropriate for some companies. Many companies have found that the **divisional structure**—which divides the organization into several divisions, each of which operates as a semi-autonomous unit and profit centre—is more suited to their needs. Divisions in organizations can be based on products, customers, or geography. In 2002, for example, Bell Canada created three divisions based on which customers were being served: consumers, small- and medium-sized businesses, and large corporations. This new structure replaces the former divisional structure that was geographically based.[15]

H.J. Heinz, one of the world's largest food-processing companies, is divisionalized along seven product lines: food service (selling small packaged products such as mustard and relish to restaurants); infant foods; condiments (Heinz ketchup, steak sauce, and tomato sauce); Star-Kist tuna; pet foods; frozen foods; and miscellaneous products, including both new lines being test-marketed and soups, beans, and pasta products. Because of its divisional structure, Heinz can evaluate the performance of each division independently. Until recently, for example, Heinz also had a division for its Weight Watchers business. But because this business was performing poorly, the company sold the Weight Watchers classroom program and folded its line of frozen foods into its existing frozen-foods division.[16]

functional structure Various units are included in a group based on functions that need to be performed for the organization to reach its goals.

divisional structure Divides the organization into divisions, each of which operates as a semi-autonomous unit.

Table 7.1	Advantages and Disadvantages of a Functional Structure

Advantages	Disadvantages
1. It focusses attention on the key activities that must be performed.	1. Conflicts may arise among the functional areas.
2. Expertise develops within each function.	2. No single function is responsible for overall organizational performance.
3. Employees have clearly defined career paths.	3. Employees in each functional area have a narrow view of the organization.
4. The structure is simple and easy to understand.	4. Decision making is slowed because functional areas must get approval from top management for a variety of decisions.
5. It eliminates duplication of activities.	5. Coordinating highly specialized functions may be difficult.

Because divisions are relatively autonomous, a firm can take such action with minimal disruption to its remaining business operations.

Like Heinz, other divisionalized companies are free to buy, sell, create, and disband divisions without disrupting the rest of their operations. Divisions can maintain healthy competition among themselves by sponsoring separate advertising campaigns, fostering different corporate identities, and so forth. They can also share certain corporate-level resources (such as market research data). Of course, if too much control is delegated to divisional managers, corporate managers may lose touch with daily operations. Competition between divisions has also been known to become disruptive, and efforts of one division may be duplicated by those of another.

The advantages and disadvantages of the divisional structure are summarized in Table 7.2.

Project Organization

A typical line or line-staff organization is characterized by unchanging vertical authority relationships. It has such a set-up because the organization produces a product or service in a repetitive and predictable way. Procter & Gamble, for example, produces millions of tubes of Crest toothpaste each year using standardized production methods. The company has done this for years and intends to do so indefinitely.

But some organizations find themselves faced with new product opportunities or with projects that have a definite starting and end point. These organizations often use a project structure to deal with the uncertainty encountered in new situations. **Project organization** involves forming a team of specialists from different functional areas of the organization to work on a specific project.[17] A project structure may be temporary or permanent; if it is temporary, the project team disbands once the project is completed and team members return to their regular functional area or are assigned to a new project.

project organization An organization that uses teams of specialists to complete specific projects.

Project organization is used extensively by Canadian firms, for example, in the construction of hydroelectric generating stations like those developed by Hydro-Québec on La Grande River and by Manitoba Hydro on the Nelson River. Once the generating station is complete, it becomes part of the traditional structure of the utility. Project organization is also used at Genstar Shipyards Ltd. in Vancouver. Each ship that is built is treated as a project and supervised by a project manager; the project manager for a given ship is responsible for ensuring that the ship is completed on time and within budget.[18] Project organization has also proven useful for coordinating the many elements needed to extract oil from the tar sands. Project management is also used in other kinds of tasks, including construction, military weapons, aerospace, and health-care delivery.[19]

matrix organization A project structure in which the project manager and the regular line managers share authority until the project is concluded.

A **matrix organization** is a variation of project structure in which the project manager and the regular line managers share authority. Ford, for example, used a matrix organization to design the Ford Thunderbird that

---

Table 7.2   Advantages and Disadvantages of a Divisional Structure

Advantages	Disadvantages
1. It accommodates change and expansion.	1. Activities may be duplicated across divisions.
2. It increases accountability.	2. A lack of communication among divisions may occur.
3. It develops expertise in the various divisions.	3. Adding diverse divisions may blur the focus of the organization.
4. It encourages training for top management.	4. Company politics may affect the allocation of resources.

was launched in 2001. A design team composed of people from engineering, marketing, operations, and finance was created to design the new car. During the time the team was working on the Thunderbird project, the engineering, marketing, operations, and finance experts reported primarily to the project manager, but the line managers of the departments they came from also had some say about what work they did. After the team's work was done, team members moved back to their permanent functional jobs.

In other companies, the matrix organization is a semi-permanent fixture. Figure 7.6 shows how Martha Stewart Living Omnimedia Inc. has created a permanent matrix organization for its burgeoning lifestyle business. The company is organized broadly into media and merchandising groups, each of which has specific product and product groups. Layered on top of this structure are teams of lifestyle experts organized into groups such as cooking, crafts, weddings, and so forth. Although each group targets specific customer needs, they all work across all product groups. A wedding expert, for example, might contribute to an article on wedding planning for a Martha Stewart magazine, contribute a story idea for a Martha Stewart cable television program, and supply content for a Martha Stewart website. This same individual might also help select fabrics suitable for wedding gowns that are to be retailed.[20]

This is a General Electric aircraft test engine site. Developed at a cost of $2 billion, the GE90-115B is the biggest and most powerful engine ever to lift a plane off the ground. GE's Aircraft Engine business is a division of GE Transportation, one of the company's primary business units.

International Organization

As we saw in Chapter 5, many businesses today manufacture, purchase, and sell in the world market. As a result, several different **international organizational structures** have emerged. Moreover, as competition on a

international organizational structure An organizational structure that is designed to help a company succeed in international markets. International departments, international divisions, or an integrated global organization are all variations of the international organizational structure.

Figure 7.6 Matrix organization at Martha Stewart.

global scale becomes more complex, companies often find that they must experiment with the ways in which they respond.

For example, when Wal-Mart opened its first store outside the United States in 1992, it set up a special projects team to handle the logistics. As more stores were opened abroad in the mid-1990s, the firm created a small international department to handle overseas expansion. By 1999, however, international sales and expansion had become such a major part of Wal-Mart's operations that the firm created a separate international division headed up by a senior vice-president. And by 2002, international operations had become so important to Wal-Mart that the international division was further divided into geographic areas where the firm does business, such as Mexico and Europe.

Wal-Mart typifies the form of organization outlined in Figure 7.7. Other firms have also developed a wide range of approaches to international organization structure. The French food giant Danone Group, for instance, has three major product groups: dairy products (Danone yogourt), bottled water (Evian), and cookies (Pim's). Danone's structure does not differentiate internationally, but rather integrates global operations within each product group.[21]

Finally, some companies adopt a truly global structure in which they acquire resources (including capital), produce goods and services, engage in research and development, and sell products in whatever local market is appropriate, without any consideration of national boundaries. Until a few years ago, for example, General Electric kept its international business operations as separate divisions. Now, however, the company functions as one integrated global organization. GE businesses around the world connect and interact with each other constantly, and managers freely move back and forth among them. This integration is also reflected in the top management team: The head of its audit team is French, the head of quality control is Dutch, and a German runs one of GE's core business groups.[22]

Organizational Design for the Twenty-First Century

As the world grows increasingly complex and fast paced, organizations continue to seek new forms of organization that permit them to compete effectively. Among the most popular of these new forms are the *boundaryless*

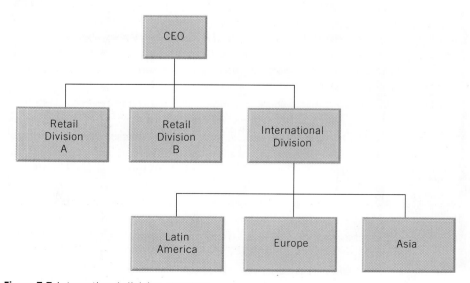

Figure 7.7 International division structure.

All the signs at this 85 000-square-foot store in Numazu identify it as a Seiyu outlet run by Japan's fifth-largest supermarket chain. However, Wal-Mart owns 38 percent of Seiyu, and this giant store is part of Wal-Mart's effort to enter the world's second-largest retail market.

organization, the *team organization*, the *virtual organization*, and the *learning organization*.

Boundaryless Organization

The *boundaryless organization* is one in which traditional boundaries and structures are minimized or eliminated altogether. For example, General Electric's fluid organization structure, in which people, ideas, and information flow freely between businesses and business groups, approximates this concept. Similarly, as firms partner with their suppliers in more efficient ways, external boundaries disappear. Some of Wal-Mart's key suppliers are tied directly into the retailer's vaunted information system. As a result, when Wal-Mart distribution centres start running low on, say, Wrangler blue jeans, the manufacturer receives the information as soon as the retailer. Wrangler proceeds to manufacture new inventory and restock the distribution centre without Wal-Mart having to place a new order.

Team Organization

Team organization relies almost exclusively on project-type teams, with little or no underlying functional hierarchy. People "float" from project to project as dictated by their skills and the demands of those projects. At Cypress Semiconductor, units or groups that become large are simply split into smaller units. Not surprisingly, the organization is composed entirely of small units. This strategy allows each unit to change direction, explore new ideas, and try new methods without having to deal with a rigid bureaucratic superstructure. Although few large organizations have actually reached this level of adaptability, Apple Computer and Xerox are among those moving toward it.

Virtual Organization

Closely related to the team organization is the virtual organization. A *virtual organization* has little or no formal structure. Typically, it has only a handful of permanent employees, a very small staff, and a modest administrative facility. As the needs of the organization change, managers bring in temporary workers, lease facilities, and outsource basic support services to meet the demands of each unique situation. As the situation changes, the temporary workforce changes in parallel, with some people leaving the organization and others entering it. Facilities and subcontracted services also change. In other words, the virtual organization exists only in response to its own needs.

Global Research Consortium (GRC) is a virtual organization that offers research and consulting services to firms doing business in Asia. As clients request various services, GRC's staff of three permanent employees subcontracts the work to an appropriate set of several dozen independent consultants and/or researchers with whom it has relationships. At any given time, therefore, GRC may have several projects underway and 20 or 30 people working on various projects. As the projects change, so too does the composition of the organization. Figure 7.8 illustrates a hypothetical virtual organization.

Learning Organization

The so-called *learning organization* works to integrate continuous improvement with continuous employee learning and development. Specifically, a learning organization works to facilitate the lifelong learning and personal development of all of its employees while continually transforming itself to respond to changing demands and needs.

While managers might approach the concept of a learning organization from a variety of perspectives, the most frequent goals are improved quality, continuous improvement, and performance measurement. The idea is that the most consistent and logical strategy for achieving continuous improvement is constantly upgrading employee talent, skill, and knowledge. For example, if each employee in an organization learns one new thing each day and can translate that knowledge into work-related practice, continuous improvement will logically follow. Indeed, organizations that wholeheartedly embrace this approach believe that only through constant employee learning can continuous improvement really occur.

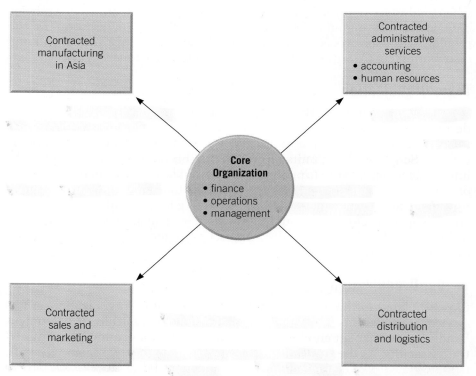

Figure 7.8 A virtual organization.

In recent years, many different organizations have implemented this approach on various levels. Shell Oil Co., for example, recently purchased an executive conference centre called the Shell Learning Center. The facility boasts state-of-the-art classrooms and instructional technology, lodging facilities, a restaurant, and recreational amenities, such as a golf course, swimming pool, and tennis courts. Line managers at the firm rotate through the centre and serve as teaching faculty. Teaching assignments last anywhere from a few days to several months. At the same time, all Shell employees routinely attend training programs, seminars, and related activities, all the while gathering the latest information they need to contribute more effectively to the firm. Recent seminar topics have included time management, balancing work and family demands, and international trade theory.

THE INFORMAL ORGANIZATION

Much of our discussion so far has focussed on the organization's *formal* structure—its "official" arrangement of jobs and job relationships. In reality, however, all organizations also have another dimension—an informal organization within which people do their jobs in different ways and interact with other people in ways that do not follow formal lines of communication. The Exercising Your Ethics box at the end of the chapter presents an interesting situation that illustrates the informal organization.

Describe the *informal organization* and discuss *intrapreneuring*.

5

Formal Versus Informal Organizational Systems

The formal organization of a business is the part that can be seen and represented in chart form. The structure of a company, however, is by no means limited to the organization chart and the formal assignment of authority. Frequently, the **informal organization**—everyday social interactions among employees that transcend formal jobs and job interrelationships—effectively alters a company's formal structure. Indeed, this level of organization is sometimes just as powerful, if not more powerful, than the formal structure.

On the negative side, the informal organization can reinforce office politics that put the interests of individuals ahead of those of the firm. Likewise, a great deal of harm can be caused by distorted or inaccurate information communicated without management input or review. For example, if the informal organization is generating false information about impending layoffs, valuable employees may act quickly (and unnecessarily) to seek other employment. Among the more important elements of the informal organization are *informal groups* and the *organizational grapevine*.

informal organization A network of personal interactions and relationships among employees unrelated to the firm's formal authority structure.

Informal Groups

Informal groups are simply groups of people who decide to interact among themselves. They may be people who work together in a formal sense or who simply get together for lunch, during breaks, or after work. They may talk about business, the boss, or non-work-related topics such as families, movies, or sports. For example, at the New York Metropolitan Opera, musicians and singers play poker during the intermissions. Most pots are in the $30 to $40 range. Luciano Pavarotti, the famed tenor, once played and lost big.

The impact of informal groups on the organization may be positive (if they work together to support the organization), negative (if they work together in ways that run counter to the organization's interests), or neutral (if what they do is unrelated to the organization).

Organizational Grapevine

grapevine An informal communications network that carries gossip and other information throughout an organization.

The **grapevine** is the informal communication network that runs through an entire organization.[23] Grapevines are found in all organizations except the very smallest, but they do not always follow the same patterns as formal channels of authority and communication, nor do they necessarily coincide with them. The internet is a worldwide grapevine. When people gather around the water cooler or on the golf course to exchange gossip and pass on information, they have names and faces. But with the internet, you may not know whom you are talking to and how reliable the person is who is providing the information.[24]

Because the grapevine typically passes information orally, messages often become distorted in the process. But most office gossip has at least some kernel of truth to it. Those passing on news may deliberately alter it, either to advance their own goals or to submarine someone else's chances. Listening to and passing on information damaging to someone's reputation can backfire, harming your credibility and making you a target for similar gossip.

In general, the more detailed the information, the less likely it is to be true. Likewise, beware the hush-hush "don't quote me on this" rumour. (Cynics claim that the better the news, the less likely it is to be true, too.) The higher the source, the greater the likelihood that the grapevine has the real story. Don't reject information from "lower" sources, however. Many an executive assistant can provide valuable insights into a corporation's plans.

Attempts to eliminate the grapevine are fruitless, but managers do have some control over it. By maintaining open channels of communication and responding vigorously to inaccurate information, they can minimize the damage the grapevine can do. In fact, the grapevine can actually be an asset. By getting to know the key people in the grapevine, for example, the manager can partially control the information they receive and use the grapevine to determine employee reactions to new ideas (e.g., a change in human resource policies or benefit packages). The manager can also receive valuable information from the grapevine and use it to improve decision making.

The grapevine is a powerful communications network in most organizations. These workers may be talking about any number of things—an upcoming deadline on an important project, tonight's football game, the stock market, rumours about an impending takeover, gossip about forthcoming promotions, or the weather.

Wise managers will tune in to the grapevine's message because it is often a corporate early warning system. Ignoring this valuable source of information can cause managers to be the last to know that they are about to get a new boss, or that they have a potentially fatal image problem. The grapevine is not infallible, however. In addition to miscommunication and attempts by some people to manipulate it for their own ends, it may carry rumours with absolutely no basis in fact. Such rumours are most common when there is a complete lack of information (apparently, human nature abhors such a vacuum and fills it). Unfortunately, baseless rumours can be very hard to kill.

Intrapreneuring

Sometimes organizations actually take steps to encourage the informal organization. They do so for a variety of reasons, two of which we have already discussed. First, most experienced managers recognize that the informal organization exists whether they want it or not. Second, many managers know how to use the informal organization to reinforce the formal organization. Perhaps more important, however, the energy of the informal organization can be harnessed to improve productivity.

Many firms, including Compaq Computer, Rubbermaid, 3M, and Xerox, are supporting a process called **intrapreneuring**—creating and maintaining the innovation and flexibility of a small-business environment within the confines of a large, bureaucratic structure. The concept is basically sound. Historically, most innovations have come from individuals in small businesses (see Chapter 4). As businesses increase in size, however, innovation and creativity tend to become casualties in the battle for higher sales and profits. In some large companies, new ideas are even discouraged, and champions of innovation have been stalled in mid-career.

Compaq, which is now part of Hewlett-Packard, is an excellent example of how intrapreneuring works to counteract this trend. The firm has one major division called the New Business Group. When a manager or engineer has an idea for a new product or product application, he or she takes it to the New Business Group and "sells" it. The managers in the group are then encouraged to help the innovator develop the idea for field testing. If the product takes off and does well, it is then spun off into its own business group or division. If it doesn't do as well as hoped, it may be maintained as part of the New Business Group or phased out.

intrapreneuring The process of creating and maintaining the innovation and flexibility of a small business environment within the confines of a large organization.

Summary of Learning Objectives

1. **Discuss the elements that influence a firm's *organizational structure*.** Every business needs structure to operate. *Organizational structure* varies according to a firm's mission, purpose, and strategy. Size, technology, and changes in environmental circumstances also influence structure. In general, while all organizations have the same basic elements, each develops the structure that contributes to the most efficient operations.

2. **Explain how *specialization* and *departmentalization* are the building blocks of organizational structure.** The building blocks of organizational structure are *job specialization* and *departmentalization*. As a firm grows, it usually has a greater need for people to perform specialized tasks (specialization). It also has a greater need to group types of work into logical units (departmentalization). Common forms of departmentalization are *customer*, *product*, *process*, *geographic*, and *functional*. Large businesses often use more than one form of departmentalization.

3. **Distinguish between *responsibility* and *authority* and explain the differences in decision making in *centralized* and *decentralized organizations*.** *Responsibility* is the duty to perform a task; *authority* is the power to make the decisions necessary to complete tasks. *Delegation* begins when a manager assigns a task to a subordinate; *accountability* means that the subordinate must complete the task. *Span of control* refers to the number of people who work for any individual manager. The more people supervised by a manager, the wider his or her span of control. Wide spans are usually desirable when employees perform simple or unrelated tasks. When jobs are diversified or prone to change, a narrower span is generally preferable.

   In a *centralized organization*, only a few individuals in top management have real decision-making authority. In a *decentralized organization*, much authority is delegated to lower-level management. Where both *line* and *line-and-staff systems* are involved, *line departments* generally have authority to make decisions while *staff departments* have a responsibility to advise. A relatively new concept, *committee and team authority*, empowers committees or work teams involved in a firm's daily operations.

4. **Explain the differences between *functional*, *divisional*, *project*, and *international organizational structures*, and describe the most popular new forms of organizational design.** In a *functional organization*, authority is usually distributed among such basic functions as marketing and finance. In a *divisional organization*, the various divisions of a larger company, which may be related or unrelated, operate in a relatively autonomous fashion. In *project organization*, in which individuals report to more than one manager, a company creates teams to address specific problems or to conduct specific projects. A company that has divisions in many countries may require an additional level of *international organization* to coordinate those operations. Four of the most popular new forms of organizational design are (a) boundaryless organizations (traditional boundaries and structures are minimized or eliminated), (b) team organizations (rely on project-type teams, with little or no functional hierarchy), (c) virtual organizations (have little formal structure and only a handful of permanent employees, a small staff, and a modest administrative facility), and (d) learning organizations (work to facilitate employees' lifelong learning and personal development while transforming the organization to meet changing demands and needs).

5. **Define the *informal organization* and discuss *intrapreneuring*.** The *informal organization* consists of the everyday social interactions among employees that transcend formal jobs and job interrelationships. To foster innovation and flexibility, some large companies encourage *intrapreneuring*—creating and maintaining the innovation and flexibility of a small business environment within the confines of a large bureaucratic structure.

KEY TERMS

QUESTIONS FOR ANALYSIS

1. Explain the significance of size as it relates to organizational structure. Describe the changes that are likely to occur as an organization grows.

2. Why do some managers have difficulties in delegating authority? Why does this problem tend to plague smaller businesses?

3. Draw up an organization chart for your college or university.

4. Describe a hypothetical organizational structure for a small printing firm. Describe changes that might be necessary as the business grows.

5. Compare and contrast the matrix and divisional approaches to organizational structure. How would you feel personally about working in a matrix organization in which you were assigned simultaneously to multiple units or groups?

6. If a company has a formal organizational structure, why is the informal organization so important?

7. Consider the organization where you currently work (or one where you have previously worked). Which of the four basic structural types was it most consistent with? What was the basis of departmentalization in the company? Why was that particular basis of departmentalization used?

8. What kinds of problems might develop in a matrix organization? *Why* would these problems develop?

APPLICATION EXERCISES

1. Interview the manager of a local service business—a fast-food restaurant. What types of tasks does this manager typically delegate? Is the appropriate authority also delegated in each case?

2. Using books, magazines, or personal interviews, identify a person who has succeeded as an intrapreneur. In what ways did the structure of the intrapreneur's company help this individual succeed? In what ways did the structure pose problems?

BUILDING YOUR BUSINESS SKILLS

Getting with the Program

Goal

To encourage students to understand the relationship between organizational structure and a company's ability to attract and keep valued employees.

The Situation

You are the founder of a small but growing high-technology company that develops new computer software. With your current workload and new contracts in the pipeline, your business is thriving except for one problem: You cannot find computer programmers for product development. Worse yet, current staff members are being lured away by other high-tech firms. After suffering a particularly discouraging personnel raid in which competitors captured three of your most valued employees, you schedule a meeting with your director of human resources to plan organizational changes designed to encourage worker loyalty. You already pay top dollar, but the continuing exodus tells you that programmers are looking for something more.

Method

Working with three or four classmates, identify some ways in which specific organizational changes might improve the working environment and encourage employee loyalty. As you analyze the following factors, ask yourself the obvious question: If I were a programmer, what organizational changes would encourage me to stay?

Level of job specialization. With many programmers describing their jobs as tedious because of the focus on detail in a narrow work area, what changes, if any, would you make in job specialization? Right now, for instance, few of your programmers have any say in product design.

Decision-making hierarchy. What decision-making authority would encourage people to stay? Is expanding employee authority likely to work better in a centralized or decentralized organization?

Team authority. Can team empowerment make a difference? Taking the point of view of the worker, describe the ideal team.

Intrapreneuring. What can your company do to encourage and reward innovation?

Follow-Up Questions

1. With the average computer programmer earning nearly $70 000 per year, and with all competitive firms paying top dollar, why might organizational issues be critical in determining employee loyalty?

2. If you were a programmer, what organizational factors would make a difference to you? Why?

3. As the company founder, how willing would you be to make major organizational changes in light of the shortage of qualified programmers?

EXERCISING YOUR ETHICS

Minding Your Own Business

The Situation

Assume that you have recently gone to work for a large high-tech company. You have discovered an interesting arrangement in which one of your co-workers is engaging. Specifically, he blocks his schedule for the hour between 11:00 a.m. and 12:00 noon each day and does not take a lunch break. During this one-hour interval, he is actually running his own real estate business.

The Dilemma

You recently asked him how he manages to pull this off. "Well," he responded, "the boss and I never talked about it, but she knows what's going on. They know they can't replace me, and I always get my work done. I don't use any company resources. So, what's the harm?" Interestingly, you also have a business opportunity that could be pursued in the same way.

Questions for Discussion

1. What are the ethical issues in this situation?

2. What do you think most people would do in this situation?

3. What would you do in this situation?

Cooking Up a New Structure

A few years ago, Sara Lee CEO John H. Bryan realized that he had a problem. During the 25 years of his tenure, the firm had grown beyond its foundation in food products to encompass dozens of lines of business—everything from cake mixes to insecticide to lingerie. The new businesses were acquisitions, and the original managers controlled each one as if it were a separate company. Calculating the cost of all this duplication, Bryan reached the conclusion that the company could not afford high costs at a time when price competition was heating up.

In an effort to fix things, starting in 1997, Bryan sold or eliminated about one-quarter of the firm's 200 products. He cut redundant factories and the workforce, reduced the number of products, and standardized company-wide processes. He called his extensive restructuring program "deverticalization," and his goal was to remove Sara Lee from manufacturing while strengthening its focus and effectiveness as a marketer. In the meantime, however, he continued to acquire rival firms to sustain the company's growth. Despite Bryan's efforts, Sara Lee continued to suffer from high costs and remained unfocussed and inefficient. Said one industry analyst about Bryan's strategy: "Sometimes, the more chairs you move around, the more dust you see behind the chairs."

In 2000, C. Steven McMillan took over from Bryan at Sara Lee, and in the immortal words of Yogi Berra, "It was déjà vu all over again." McMillan quickly realized that Bryan's moves had had little impact on the firm's performance and that he himself would need to start making some big changes. Borrowing a page from rival Kraft Foods, he began by merging the sales forces that specialized in various brands to create smaller, customer-focussed teams. In meats alone, for instance, Sara Lee had 10 different brands, including Ball Park, Hillshire Farms, Bryan, and Jimmy Dean. "So if you're a Safeway," explained McMillan, "you've got to deal with 10 different organizations and multiple invoices." Teams reduced duplication and were more convenient for buyers—a win-win situation. National retailers like Wal-Mart responded by increasing their orders for Sara Lee products.

McMillan also centralized decision making at the firm by shutting down 50 weaker regional brands and reorganizing the firm into three broad product categories: Food and Beverage, Intimates and Underwear, and Household Products. He abolished several layers of corporate hierarchy, including many of the middle managers the firm had inherited from its acquisitions. He created category managers to oversee related lines of business, and the flattened organizational structure led to improved accountability and more centralized control over Sara Lee's far-flung operations.

McMillan also borrowed some tactics from his predecessor, divesting 15 businesses, including Coach leather goods, and laying off 10 percent of his workers. In another move that was widely questioned by industry observers, he paid $2.8 billion for breadmaker Earthgrains. The move increased Sara Lee's market share in baked goods, but many observers felt that McMillan paid too much for a small potential return.

McMillan still had a few tricks up his sleeves. One bold move was developing a chain of retail stores named Inner Self. Each store features a spa-like atmosphere in which to sell Sara Lee's Hanes, Playtex, Bali, and Wonderbra products. Susan Nedved, head of development for Inner Self, thinks that the company-owned stores provide a more realistic and comforting environment for making underwear purchases than do some specialty outlets. "There seems to be an open void for another specialty concept that complements Victoria's Secret," says Nedved. "There was a need for shopping alternatives that really cater to the aging population."

McMillan remains confident that his strategy—more centralization, coordination, and focus—will do the trick at Sara Lee. "I do believe the things we're doing will enhance the growth rate of our company," he says. But many observers are less optimistic. As for Inner Self and underwear, one analyst points out that "even if you fix that business, it's still apparel, and it's not really viewed as a high-value-added business."

Even if McMillan's strategy does manage to cut costs and increase market share, skeptics point out that there is no logic behind the idea of housing baked goods, meats, coffee, underwear, shoe polish, and household cleaners under one corporate roof. Unless McMillan can find some as-yet-undiscovered synergy among such disparate units, Sara Lee is probably headed for a breakup into several smaller, more focussed, more profitable companies.

Questions for Discussion

1. Describe the basic structural components at Sara Lee.
2. What role does specialization play at Sara Lee?
3. What kinds of authority are reflected in this case?
4. What kind of organizational structure does Sara Lee seem to have?
5. What role has the informal organization played in Sara Lee's various acquisitions and divestitures?

Jersak Holdings

Vaclav Jersak was born in Prague, Czechoslovakia, in 1930. His family had long been active in the retail trade in that city. The Jersak family was very close, but the 1930s and 1940s were a time of great turbulence in central Europe. In 1938, Hitler's troops invaded Czechoslovakia and five years of war followed. After the war, Czechoslovakia came under the influence of the Soviet Union, and capitalistic ventures that had been such an integral part of the Jersak family were severely restricted. By the early 1960s, there were some hints of a return to a more capitalistic economy. To Jersak's dismay, these were snuffed out by the Soviet Union's invasion of Czechoslovakia in 1968.

The invasion was the last straw for Jersak, who had felt for some years that the environment for private business activity was very poor. At age 38, he decided to leave Czechoslovakia for a better life in Canada. He arrived in Toronto in December 1968, determined to apply his entrepreneurial talents in a more promising business environment. Jersak quickly discovered the freedom that entrepreneurs had in Canada. He started a small gas station, and over the next three years he opened several more. In 1971, he purchased a franchise of a major fast-food outlet, and by 1977 he owned four fast-food restaurants. His entrepreneurial instincts led him into a wide variety of business operations after that. From 1977 to 1991, he expanded his activity into the manufacture of auto parts, microcomputers, textiles, and office furniture. He purchased five franchises of a retail auto parts store, two automobile dealerships, and a carpet business that sells to both residential and commercial users. A mining company, a soft drink bottling plant, and a five-store chain of shoe stores are also part of Jersak Holdings Ltd.

As each new business venture was added, Jersak hired a person to manage the operating company. He also added individuals with expertise in accounting, finance, marketing, and production in his head office. Currently, Jersak Holdings Ltd. contains 17 operating companies, each headed by a manager (see Figure 7.9). Employment ranges from five to ten people in each company. In 2005, sales totalled $37 million and profits were $4.7 million.

Head office staff make most of the strategic decisions in the firm. Jersak and the other top executives have frequent informal meetings to discuss matters of importance to the firm. Discussions usually continue until a consensus is reached on a course of action. The operating managers are expected to put into practice the strategic plans that are made at head office.

Vaclav Jersak is now 76. As he looks back on the last 35+ years, he feels a great sense of satisfaction that he has accomplished so much. He has been thinking that the top management group operates smoothly because the people have worked together for many years. But he feels that areas of authority should be more clearly defined so that when changes occur in top management because of retirements, the new people will know exactly what they are responsible for.

Some of Jersak's business acquaintances are of the view that he should delegate considerably more authority to the managers of the operating companies. In effect, they recommend that he turn these operating managers into presidents of their own firms, each of them being responsible for making a profit in their particular enterprise. His acquaintances point out that giving the man-

Figure 7.9 Organization of Jersak Holdings Ltd.

agers of the operating companies this level of responsibility will motivate them to achieve much more than they are now. Also, it should motivate the employees in these firms because they will have more discretion as well. Jersak sees some real benefits in this approach, but worries that the current managers of the operating companies haven't had much experience in making important decisions. He also fears that head office will lose control of the operating companies. Jersak feels that it is important for head office staff to know some of the details of each operating company. Without this knowledge, he feels that the head office staff will be unable to make good decisions regarding the operating companies.

Other friends of Jersak argue that the time has come to centralize control at head office because the firm has gotten so large and is so diverse. Only in this way, they argue, will top management be able to effectively control all the activities of Jersak Holdings Ltd.

Jersak is uncertain about what to do, but he feels he must do something to ensure that his life's work will not disappear when he retires next year.

Questions for Discussion

1. Discuss the advantages and disadvantages of centralization and decentralization as they relate to Jersak Holdings Ltd.

2. Which basic approach—centralization or decentralization—should Jersak Holdings Ltd. adopt? Defend your answer.

3. What problems are evident in the current organizational structure of Jersak Holdings Ltd.? Design a new organization chart for the company that will solve these problems.

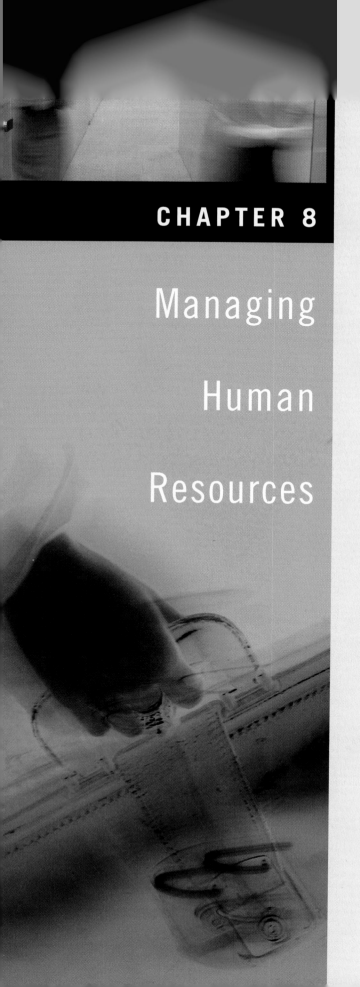

CHAPTER 8

Managing

Human

Resources

After reading this chapter, you should be able to:

1 Define *human resource management*, discuss its strategic significance, and explain how managers plan for human resources.

2 Identify the issues involved in *staffing* a company, including *internal* and *external recruiting* and *selection*.

3 Discuss different ways in which organizations go about developing the capabilities of employees and managers.

4 Explain ways in which organizations evaluate employee performance.

5 Discuss the importance of *wages and salaries*, *incentives*, and *benefit programs* in attracting and keeping skilled workers.

6 Describe some of the key legal issues involved in hiring, compensating, and managing workers.

7 Discuss *workforce diversity*, the management of *knowledge workers*, and the use of *contingent and temporary workers* as important changes in the contemporary workplace.

The following facts about visible minorities show just how important the issue of workforce diversity has become:

- 73 percent of the people who immigrated to Canada during the 1990s were visible minorities.
- 18 percent of Canada's population was born outside Canada.
- 20 percent of Saskatchewan's population will be Aboriginal by 2015.
- In 2001, approximately 4 million Canadians were visible minorities; by 2017, that number could increase to as much as 8.5 million.
- The largest visible minority group in Canada in 2001 was the Chinese, but the South Asian population is expected to grow more quickly during the next decade.
- Visible minorities currently make up 40 percent of the population of Vancouver.
- By 2017, visible minorities will form more than 50 percent of the populations of Toronto and Vancouver.
- By 2017, 22 percent of the total Canadian population will be visible minorities.

Changes of this magnitude simply cannot be ignored, either by Canadian politicians or by Canadian business firms. Procter & Gamble Canada is one of the many Canadian businesses that are taking steps to deal with the challenges and opportunities that come with a rapidly changing population demographic.

Thirty years ago, P&G was like a lot of other Canadian companies—most of its employees were white males. But that's changing rapidly. In 2005, for example, the 800 people who are employed at P&G's Toronto headquarters organized a major social gathering to celebrate the diverse nature of the P&G workforce (employees come from 40 different countries and speak at least 30 different languages). But the event wasn't just for fun. Like other companies, P&G has learned that employees are more productive when their differences are respected in the work environment. And that translates into increased corporate success. Since the top management positions at P&G are still predominantly held by white males, the company has set a strategic goal to diversify its workforce.

P&G thinks that a diverse workforce also helps the company market its well-known brands—Pampers, Crest, Tide, Mr. Clean, etc.—to a diverse group of consumers. And the facts reported above clearly show that Canadian consumers are becoming more diverse at a dizzying pace. As consumer demographics change, it is important to get more diverse people involved in making marketing decisions. The president of P&G Canada, Tim Penner, says that a diverse workforce enriches everyone in the company because they are exposed to other cultures; also, the diversity gives employees a better understanding of P&G's customers.

There are multiple "affinity groups" at P&G, such as the Women's Leadership Council, the French Canadian Network, the Asian Professional Network, the Christian Network, and the Jewish Network. The goal of these networks is to help employees feel comfortable about participating in corporate life, and to act as resource groups for employees who want insights about how to target certain specific markets.

Western Union is another company that is focussing on diversity, and it may be further along than most companies given the nature of its business—moving money overseas to the families of new Canadians who are working here and want to help their families back in their home country. The potential customers of Western Union are not easily reached by traditional marketing methods, so the company hires people who speak the language of their target market and who know what it feels like to be an immigrant in Canada. When recruiting new employees, Western Union does not demand "Canadian experience" as many other companies do. Rather, they want employees with international experience because of the nature of the company's business. After Western Union hires these people, they seek out local business operators to act as Western Union agents for their own ethnic community.

Marketing Manager Marco Amoranto is typical of the kind of employees that are hired at Western Union. He was born in the Philippines and originally worked for Colgate-Palmolive. He wanted to work in Canada but had trouble landing a job because he didn't have Canadian experience. At Western Union, he is responsible for marketing to Asian and Europeans. He recently returned from a "road show" where the company sponsored concerts featuring several top Philippine entertainers, including Freestyle, Basil Valdez, and Jaya.

The Western Union approach has yielded some interesting benefits. In one area of Toronto, for example, customers who wanted to transfer money back to the Philippines got a free loaf of Pan de Sel bread from a local Filipino baker. Thus, the results were positive for Western Union, its customers, and the baker. Western Union also brings in entertainers from its customers' home countries and then gives these customers free tickets to the concerts.

In the current, rapidly changing demographic environment, companies are discovering that they cannot be unconcerned about workforce (and customer) diversity. One company that has had some bad press recently in this area is Wal-Mart, which has been confronted with a class-action sex discrimination lawsuit, as well as a lot of nega-tive publicity about the alleged low wages and lack of health care available to its employees. In response to these concerns, the company has hired a director of diversity.

Lee Scott, the CEO of Wal-Mart, says that Wal-Mart is a "pretty good company," but with 1.5 million employees, there are bound to be some racists and sexists among them. The company has also developed incentives to motivate top managers to reach certain diversity goals. If the goals are not met, for example, Scott could forfeit up to $600 000 of his salary. Scott says that in the past, if an employee made a racist or sexist remark, the person might just be transferred. But in today's more enlightened environment, that kind of behaviour can no longer be tolerated and the person will be terminated. With Wal-Mart opening more stores in areas where a larger proportion of customers are Hispanic and black, there will be less tolerance of unacceptable behaviour among employees. ◆

THE FOUNDATIONS OF HUMAN RESOURCE MANAGEMENT

human resource management (HRM) Set of organizational activities directed at attracting, developing, and maintaining an effective workforce.

Human resource management (HRM) is the set of organizational activities directed at attracting, developing, and maintaining an effective workforce. Human resource management takes place within a complex and ever-changing environmental context and is increasingly being recognized for its strategic importance.[1]

1   Define *human resource management*, discuss its strategic significance, and explain how managers plan for human resources.

The Strategic Importance of HRM

Human resources are critical for effective organizational functioning. HRM (or *personnel*, as it is sometimes called) was once relegated to second-class status in many organizations, but its importance has grown dramatically in the last two decades. This new importance stems from increased legal complexities, the recognition that human resources are a valuable means for improving productivity, and the awareness today of the costs associated with poor human resource management.

Indeed, managers now realize that the effectiveness of their HR function has a substantial impact on a firm's bottom-line performance. Poor human resource planning can result in spurts of hiring followed by layoffs—costly in terms of unemployment compensation payments, training expenses, and morale. Haphazard compensation systems do not attract, keep, and motivate good employees, and outmoded recruitment practices can expose the firm to expensive and embarrassing legal action. Consequently, the chief human resource executive of most large businesses is a vice-president directly accountable to the CEO, and many firms are developing strategic HR plans that are integrated with other strategic planning activities.

Human Resource Planning

The starting point in attracting qualified human resources is planning. In turn, HR planning involves *job analysis* and *forecasting* the demand for and supply of labour (see Figure 8.1).

Job Analysis

Job analysis is a systematic analysis of jobs within an organization. A job analysis is made up of two parts:

- The **job description** lists the duties of a job, its working conditions, and the tools, materials, and equipment used to perform it.

- The **job specification** lists the skills, abilities, and other credentials needed to do the job.

Job analysis information is used in many HR activities. For instance, knowing about job content and job requirements is necessary to develop appropriate selection methods and job-relevant performance appraisal systems and to set equitable compensation rates.

job analysis A detailed study of the specific duties in a particular job and the human qualities required for that job.

job description The objectives, responsibilities, and key tasks of a job; the conditions under which it will be done; its relationship to other positions; and the skills needed to perform it.

job specification The specific skills, education, and experience needed to perform a job.

Forecasting HR Demand and Supply

After managers fully understand the jobs to be performed within an organization, they can start planning for the organization's future HR needs. The manager starts by assessing trends in past HR usage, future organizational plans, and general economic trends. A good sales forecast is often the foundation,

Figure 8.1 Planning for human resources.

ENTREPRENEURSHIP AND NEW VENTURES

The Guru for Fun Takes a Meeting With the V.P. of Buzz

Rather than dictating standard job titles, some new ventures and entrepreneurial firms now allow incumbents to name their own jobs. Others even let employees *create* their own jobs. Not surprisingly, some interesting twists have emerged.

It started with the internet bubble. For example, Amy Berkus, a marketing coordinator at a small dot-com, changed her job title to "marketing mechanic." "Everyone was creating new titles in Internet-speak," recalls Berkus. "We wanted titles that conveyed team spirit and a fun atmosphere.... It just fit the time." Other catchy designations included "V.P. of Buzz," "Chief People Officer," "Guru of Fun," "Gladiator," and "Chief Evangelist." Under the right circumstances, such titles encouraged creativity and got employees to think differently about their jobs. They also let everyone know that the company was hip. "It was a matter of doing away with everything that seemed to reek of the old," explains business professor Donna Hoffman. "The feeling was, 'We're going to make new rules. We need new titles.'"

But the times, of course, have changed. Executive recruiter Marc Lewis observes that "as the market has cooled, the interest in creative and unusual job titles has diminished." Smaller companies (as well as some larger ones) are now trying to create images of legitimacy, respectability, and honesty. Berkus admits that "the traditional titles [like 'customer care manager' and 'production supervisor'] lend themselves more to the image of a stable company that is driving toward profitability."

Does a return to confidence-inspiring, snooze-inducing job titles mean that companies have abandoned the effort to encourage employee creativity? By no means. Innovation is just as important during tough times as during boom times. The method, however, has changed. Today, entrepreneurial firms that want to encourage and reward creativity aren't willing to settle for window dressing. They're changing the jobs themselves.

Employers are finding, for instance, that basing positions on employee interests can be more effective than trying to fit unique individuals into predetermined job slots. Often a customized job is a reward for high performance. Steve Gluckman, a bicycle designer for REI (www.rei.com), a small supplier of outdoor gear, worked his way up from service manager to designer over 13 years. An avid cyclist, he says, "Some people sing. Some people paint. I ride my bike. Like a ballet dancer, like a gymnast, like a skateboarder, I express myself in my job." Starbucks's coffee education manager, Aileen Carrell, travels around the world educating employees about coffee. "I was hired as temporary Christmas help in 1990," explains Carrell, "and I fell madly in love with the fact that coffees came from the most amazing places, like Sulawesi." After working as a store manager for several years, Carrell herself proposed the creation of her new position. Of course, organizations will always have to define most of the jobs that have to be performed, but many are discovering that a little flexibility can lead to a lot of productivity.

especially for smaller organizations. Historical ratios can then be used to predict demand for types of employees, such as operating employees and sales representatives. Large organizations, of course, use much more complicated models to predict HR needs.

Forecasting the supply of labour involves two tasks:

■ forecasting *internal supply*—the number and type of employees who will be in the firm at some future date

■ forecasting *external supply*—the number and type of people who will be available for hiring from the labour market at large

The simplest approach merely adjusts present staffing levels for anticipated turnover and promotions. Large organizations use extremely sophisticated models to keep track of the present and future distributions of professionals and managers. This allows the company to spot areas where there will eventually be too many qualified professionals competing for too few promotions or, conversely, too few good people available to fill important positions.

Replacement Charts. At higher levels of the organization, managers make plans for specific people and positions. The technique most commonly used is the **replacement chart**, which lists each important managerial position, who occupies it, how long he or she will probably stay in it before moving on, and who (by name) is now qualified or soon will be qualified to move into it. This technique allows ample time to plan developmental experiences for people identified as potential successors to critical managerial jobs.

Skills Inventories. To facilitate both planning and identifying people for transfer or promotion, some organizations also have **employee information systems**, or **skills inventories**. These systems are usually computerized and contain information on each employee's education, skills, work experience, and career aspirations. Such a system can quickly locate every employee who is qualified to fill a position requiring, say, a degree in chemical engineering, three years of experience in an oil refinery, and fluency in French.

Forecasting the external supply of labour is a different problem altogether. How does a manager, for example, predict how many electrical engineers will be seeking work in Ontario or British Columbia three years from now? To get an idea of the future availability of labour, planners must rely on information from outside sources, such as government reports and figures supplied by colleges and universities on the number of students in major fields.

Matching HR Supply and Demand

After comparing future demand and internal supply, managers can make plans to manage predicted shortfalls or overstaffing. If a shortfall is predicted, new employees can be hired, present employees can be retrained and transferred into understaffed areas, individuals approaching retirement can be convinced to stay on, or labour-saving or productivity-enhancing systems can be installed.

If the organization needs to hire, the external labour-supply forecast helps managers plan how to recruit according to whether the type of person needed is readily available or scarce in the labour market. The use of temporary workers also helps managers in staffing by giving them extra flexibility. If overstaffing is expected to be a problem, the main options are transferring the extra employees, not replacing individuals who quit, encouraging early retirement, and laying people off.

STAFFING THE ORGANIZATION

Once managers have decided what positions they need to fill, they must find and hire individuals who meet the job requirements. A study by the Canadian Federation of Independent Business found that the top three characteristics employers are looking for when they hire people are a good work ethic, reliability, and willingness to stay on the job.[2] Staffing of the corporation is one of the most complex and important aspects of good human resource management. The top 10 employers by number of employees in Canada are listed in Table 8.1.

In this section, we will describe both the process of acquiring staff from outside the company (*external staffing*) and the process of promoting staff from within (*internal staffing*). Both external and internal staffing, however, start with effective recruiting.

replacement chart An HR technique that lists each important managerial position, who occupies it, how long he or she will probably stay in it before moving on, and who (by name) is now qualified or soon will be qualified to move into it.

employee information systems (skills inventories) Computerized systems that contain information on each employee's education, skills, work experience, and career aspirations.

Identify the issues involved in *staffing a company*, including *internal* and *external recruiting* and *selection*.

2

| Table 8.1 | The Top 10 Employers in Canada, 2005 |

Company	Employees
1. George Weston Ltd.	150 000
2. Onex Corp.	138 000
3. Magna International Inc.	82 000
4. McDonald's Restaurants of Canada Ltd.	77 000
5. Wal-Mart Canada Corp.	70 000
6. Alcan Inc.	69 000
7. Metro Inc.	65 000
8. Royal Bank of Canada	60 012
9. BCE Inc.	60 001
10. Canada Post Corp.	60 000

Recruiting Human Resources

recruiting The phase in the staffing of a company in which the firm seeks to develop a pool of interested, qualified applicants for a position.

Once an organization has an idea of its future HR needs, the next phase is usually recruiting new employees. **Recruiting** is the process of attracting qualified persons to apply for the jobs that are open. Where do recruits come from? Some recruits are found internally; others come from outside the organization.

Internal Recruiting

internal recruiting Considering present employees as candidates for job openings.

Internal recruiting means considering present employees as candidates for openings. Promotion from within can help build morale and keep high-quality employees from leaving. In unionized firms, the procedures for notifying employees of internal job-change opportunities are usually spelled out in the union contract. For higher-level positions, a skills inventory system may be used to identify internal candidates or managers may be asked to recommend individuals who should be considered.

External Recruiting

external recruiting Attracting people outside the organization to apply for jobs.

External recruiting involves attracting people outside the organization to apply for jobs. External recruiting methods include advertising, campus interviews, employment agencies or executive search firms, union hiring halls, referrals by present employees, and hiring "walk-ins" or "gate-hires" (people who show up without being solicited). Of course, a manager must select the most appropriate method for each job. Private employment agencies can be a good source of clerical and technical employees, and executive search firms specialize in locating top-management talent. Newspaper ads are often used because they reach a wide audience and thus allow minorities "equal opportunity" to learn about and apply for job openings.

The old-fashioned *job fair* has survived in spite of internet career postings and the proliferation of employment agencies and headhunters. At a job fair, candidates browse through the positions available and employers can see a sample of the skills candidates have. While job postings on the internet are impersonal, at job fairs candidates and recruiters can talk to each other face-to-face. Job fairs are also cheaper than posting jobs with an employment agency or headhunter. Non-traditional recruiting methods are also used. For example, Nortel Networks recruited at a rock concert that was held near one of its manufacturing facilities. Recruiters handed out lip balm, ran a raffle, and talked about Nortel to people who were arriving to hear Counting Crows and Live.[3]

At job fairs, students and recruiters can talk face-to-face about jobs that are available. Here, recruiters talk to students about the opportunities at the company.

Internships. One method of external recruiting involves offering college and university students **internships**—short-term paid positions where students focus on a specific project. If the individual works out well, the company often hires the student full-time after they graduate. At IBM Canada's "Extreme Blue" internship program, for example, students are responsible for turning an idea into a marketable product. They also network with industry leaders and develop their professional skills.[4]

internship A short-term paid position where students focus on a specific project.

Selecting Human Resources

Once the recruiting process has attracted a pool of applicants, the next step is to select someone to hire. The intent of the selection process is to gather information from applicants that will predict their job success and then to hire the candidates likely to be most successful. Of course, the organization can only gather information about factors that are predictive of future performance. The process of determining the predictive value of information is called **validation**.

validation The process of determining the predictive value of information.

To reduce the element of uncertainty, managers use a variety of selection techniques, the most common of which are shown in Figure 8.2. Each organization develops its own mix of selection techniques and may use them in almost any order.

Application Forms

The first step in selection is usually asking the candidate to fill out an application form. An application form is an efficient method of gathering information about the applicant's previous work history, educational background, and other job-related demographic data. It should not contain questions about areas unrelated to the job, such as gender, religion, or national origin. Application-form data are generally used informally to decide whether a candidate merits further evaluation, and interviewers use application forms to familiarize themselves with candidates before interviewing them.

Tests

Tests of ability, skill, aptitude, or knowledge relevant to a particular job are usually the best predictors of job success, although tests of general intelligence or personality are occasionally useful as well. In addition to being validated,

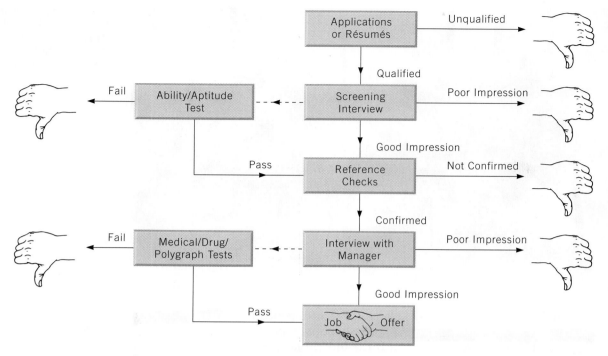

Figure 8.2 General steps in the selection process.

tests should be administered and scored consistently. All candidates should be given the same directions, allowed the same amount of time, and offered the same testing environment (e.g., temperature, lighting, distractions).

A survey conducted by Development Dimensions International found that 83 percent of hiring managers use some sort of testing as part of the hiring process. At Astral Media Inc. of Montreal, for example, job candidates are required to take a series of tests that measure verbal and numerical skills, as well as psychological traits. This testing increases the chance that Astral will hire high-performing employees who will fit in with the company's culture.[5]

An **assessment centre** is a series of exercises in which candidates perform realistic management tasks under the watchful eye of expert appraisers. A typical assessment centre might be set up in a large conference room and go on for two or three days. During this time, potential managers might take selection tests, engage in management simulations, make individual presentations, and conduct group discussions. Assessors check to see how each participant reacts to stress or to criticism by colleagues. A relatively new type of test that evolved from assessment centres is **video assessment**. Here, potential hires are shown videos of realistic work situations and then asked to choose a course of action to deal with the situation. Video assessment is fast, reliable, cheap, and versatile.

Regardless of the type of test that is used, it must be job-related (that is, it must not serve as a basis for discriminating against anyone for reasons unrelated to the job) and it must be a valid predictor of performance (that is, it must provide evidence that people who score well on it are more likely to perform well in the job than are people who score poorly on it).

Interviews

The interview is a popular selection device, but it is sometimes a poor predictor of job success because biases that are inherent in the way people perceive and judge others on first meeting affect subsequent evaluations. David

assessment centre A series of exercises in which management candidates perform realistic management tasks while being observed by appraisers.

video assessment Involves showing potential hires videos of realistic work situations and asking them to choose a course of action to deal with the situation.

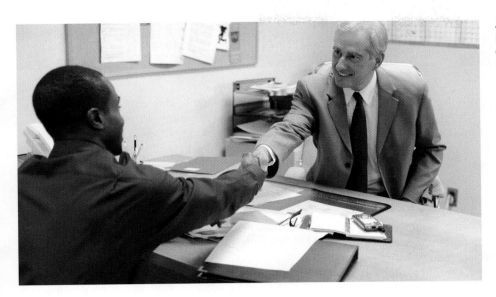

An in-depth interview with a prospective employee is often part of the recruiting process, particularly for managerial jobs.

Towler, the director of creative marketing for Kitchener, Ontario-based Creative Organizational Design, says that many companies are placing more emphasis on testing and less emphasis on interviewing because job candidates are becoming very clever at interviewing and giving all the "right" answers.[6]

Interview validity can be improved by training interviewers to be aware of potential biases and by increasing the structure of the interview. In a structured interview, questions are written in advance and all interviewers follow the same question list with each candidate. Such structure introduces consistency into the interview procedure and allows the organization to validate the content of the questions. For interviewing managerial or professional candidates, a somewhat less structured approach can be used. Although question areas and information-gathering objectives are still planned in advance, specific questions vary with the candidates' backgrounds.

Interviewers can also increase interview validity by asking "curveball" questions—that is, questions that job applicants would never expect to be asked—to see how well they think on their feet. Questions such as "How would you move Mount Fuji?" or How would you sell me a glass of water?" are curveball questions. Candidate answers to seemingly off-the-wall questions like these give interviewers additional insights into a candidate's strengths and weaknesses.[7] The Business Accountability box describes further actions that interviewers can take to make interviews useful.

Other Techniques

Organizations also use other selection techniques that vary with the circumstances. A manufacturer afraid of injuries to workers on the job might require new employees to have a physical examination. This gives the company some information about whether the employees are physically fit to do the work and what (if any) pre-existing injuries they might have.

Polygraph (lie detector) tests are largely illegal now, and drug tests are also coming under fire. In 1998, for example, the Ontario Divisional Court decided that Imperial Oil Ltd.'s drug policy (which included pre-employment drug testing that made offers of work conditional on a negative result) was unlawful because Imperial Oil failed to prove that a positive drug test would indicate a failure to perform essential duties. Imperial Oil's policy also required random drug and alcohol testing, but that was also judged to be discriminatory because the company could not prove that such testing was necessary to deter alcohol or drug impairment on the job.[8]

BUSINESS ACCOUNTABILITY

Behaviour-Based Interviewing

Behaviour-based interviewing assumes that your past behaviour is a pretty good predictor of your future behaviour. Specifically, it assesses how you reacted to difficult and/or important job situations in the past, and assumes that these are a good indicator of how you will react to similar job situations in the future. The approach can be used to test for technical skills (e.g., accounting, welding, or computer programming), management skills (e.g., organizing, motivating others, or communicating), and individual skills (e.g., dependability, discipline, or the ability to work on a team).

Instead of asking a traditional interviewing question like "Do you often take the initiative?" behaviour-based interviewing asks "Tell me about a situation where you became aware of a problem. What did you do?" Asking questions like this focusses the interview much more on your *behaviour* than on what you *say* you would do if the problem arose in the future. Other typical questions that interviewers ask in behaviour-based interviewing are as follows:

- Think of a time when you were asked to analyze information and then make a specific recommendation. What kind of reasoning and thought processes did you use?
- Think of a time when you had to deal with a customer that you thought was being unreasonable. How did you deal with that person?
- Think of a time when you had to cope with a major change in your job. What did you do?
- Think of a time when you had to work with a person that was not "pulling their weight." What, if anything, did you do?

Behaviour-based interviewing requires the person who is interviewing candidates to first identify the characteristics, skills, and behaviours that are important in the job that needs to be filled. The interviewer then constructs open-ended questions that will determine if the interviewee possesses those characteristics, skills, and behaviours.

Behaviour-based interviewing is becoming more common because companies are facing increasingly competitive environments. These competitive environments have meant downsizing, which places increasing demands on the workers who remain. There is also more emphasis on working in teams. These changing work situations have motivated companies to be much more focussed in their hiring because they want workers who are more skilled and motivated than previously.

The increasing use of behaviour-based interviewing means that you are likely to be exposed to it at some point in your job search. What should you do to prepare for a behaviour-based interview? The main thing is to think about the job you are interviewing for and the skills that will be required to do it. Try to tell an interesting story (from a previous paid or volunteer position) that succinctly describes a situation you faced, the actions you took, and the outcome that resulted from your actions. If the outcome was good, the interviewer will likely be favourably impressed with your logical thinking and actions. Even if the outcome wasn't so good, you can indicate what you learned from the experience and how that experience will benefit your new employer.

The Toronto-Dominion Bank wanted to give drug tests to all new employees because it wanted to have the public's trust. However, a federal court ruled that the bank's policy was discriminatory and that it wasn't related closely enough to job performance.[9]

DEVELOPING HUMAN RESOURCES

3 Discuss different ways in which organizations go about developing the capabilities of employees and managers.

Regardless of how effective a selection system is, most employees need additional training if they are to grow and develop in their jobs. This process begins with *orientation* and then proceeds to the *assessment of training and development needs* (including the performance of a *needs analysis*) and the selection of the best *training techniques and methods*.

New Employee Orientation

An important part of an organization's training and development program is new employee orientation. **Orientation** is the process of introducing new employees to the company's policies and programs, personnel with whom they will interact, and the nature of the job so that they can more quickly become effective contributors. Poor orientation can result in disenchantment, dissatisfaction, anxiety, turnover, and other employee problems. But effective orientation can play a key role in job satisfaction, performance, and retention. An effective orientation program will help newcomers feel like part of a team, introduce them quickly to co-workers, supervisors, and other new employees, and in a variety of other ways ease the transition from outsider to insider.

Some organizations also find it appropriate to include as a part of their orientation a general overview of and introduction to the business itself. This introduction may include such things as information about the firm's history, its evolution, its successes, and perhaps even some of its failures. Organizations with strong corporate cultures are especially likely to include such information because it is a quick and efficient way to provide information about the firm's culture to new hires. This makes it easier for them to understand the culture and to know how to function within it.

orientation The initial acquainting of new employees with the company's policies and programs, personnel with whom they will interact, and the nature of the job.

Training and Development

Beyond orientation for new employees, most organizations also find it effective to continue training and development on a regular basis. In other words, employees must be continually trained and developed to enhance and otherwise improve the quality of the contributions they make to the organization.

The starting point in assessing training and development needs is conducting a *needs analysis*—determining the organization's true needs and the training programs necessary to meet them. This analysis generally focusses on two things: the organization's job-related needs and the capabilities of the current workforce. The organization's needs are determined by the nature of the work that the organization needs to be done. That is, what knowledge, skills, and abilities does the organization need to compete? What skills must its workforce possess to perform the organization's work effectively?

Depending on both the content of the program and the instructors selected to present it, a number of techniques and methods can be used for the actual delivery of information. We examine some of the more popular techniques and methods in this section.

Work-Based Programs

One major family of techniques and methods consists of various **work-based programs** that tie training and development activities directly to task performance. The most common method of work-based training is **on-the-job training**. The employee is placed in the actual work situation and is shown how to perform a task by a supervisor or an experienced employee. Much on-the-job training is informal, as when one employee shows another how to operate the photocopy machine.

Another work-based program is **vestibule training**, which is a work simulation in which the job is performed under conditions closely simulating the actual work environment. At Montreal-based CAE Inc., engineers built a simulator for the world's largest passenger jet, the Airbus A380. Pilots use the simulator to learn how to fly the new jet without ever leaving the ground.[10]

work-based programs A technique that ties training and development activities directly to task performance.

on-the-job training Those development programs in which employees gain new skills while performing them at work.

vestibule training A work simulation in which the job is performed under conditions closely simulating the actual work environment.

systematic job rotations and transfers A technique in which an employee is systematically rotated or transferred from one job to another.

Another method of work-based training program is **systematic job rotations and transfers**. This method is most likely to be used for lower level managers or for operating employees being groomed for promotions to supervisory management positions. As the term suggests, the employee is systematically rotated or transferred from one job to another. The employee thus learns a wider array of tasks, acquires more abilities, and develops a more comprehensive view of the work of an organization or a particular sub-unit.

Instructional-Based Programs

instructional-based programs Training workers through the use of classroom-based programs such as the lecture approach.

lecture or discussion approach An instructional-based program in which a trainer presents material in a descriptive fashion to those attending a trainee program.

A second family of techniques and methods involves **instructional-based programs**. The most commonly used of these programs is the **lecture or discussion approach**. In these situations, a trainer presents material in a descriptive fashion to those attending a trainee program. Just as a professor lectures students on a particular subject matter, an organizational trainer "lectures" trainees. Depending on the situation and the size of the training class, the instructor may opt for a pure lecture method or may include discussion with trainees. Sometimes lectures are on video or audio tapes so that various individuals in the organization can receive the same training at different times and/or at different locations.

off-the-job training Those development programs in which employees learn new skills at a location away from the normal work site.

Off-the-job training is performed at a location away from the work site. It may be at a classroom within the same facility or at a different location altogether. For example, refresher courses are offered to managers of McDonald's 1375 Canadian restaurants at the Canadian Institute of Hamburgerology; in addition, training videotapes are shown to restaurant workers.[11] Coffee College is a two-week cram course run by Second Cup Ltd., Canada's largest retailer of specialty coffee. During their stay at Coffee College, franchisees and managers learn how to hire workers, keep the books, detect employee theft, and boost Christmas sales.[12]

Another instructional-based program is computer-assisted instruction. A trainee sits at a personal computer and operates software that has been specifically developed to teach certain material. The actual training materials are stored on the computer's hard drive, a CD-ROM, or a website. One major advantage of this method is that it allows self-paced learning and immediate feedback.

Video conferencing has become an important part of the training function in organizations because significant interaction is possible between the trainer and trainees.

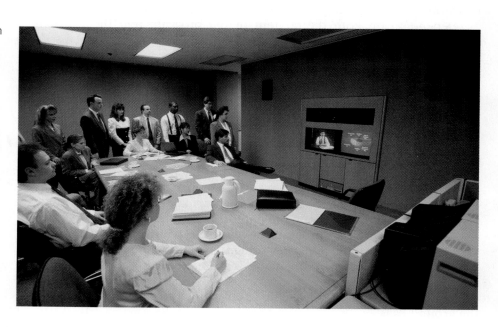

Team Building and Group-Based Training

Also increasingly popular in recent years are various team-building and group-based methods of training. As more and more organizations are using teams as a basis for doing their jobs, it should not be surprising that many of the same companies are developing training programs specifically designed to facilitate intragroup co-operation among team members.

One popular method involves various outdoor training exercises. Some programs, for example, involve a group going through a physical obstacle course that requires climbing, crawling, and other physical activities. Outward Bound and several other independent companies specialize in offering these kinds of programs, and their clients include such firms as General Foods, Xerox, and Burger King. Participants, of course, must see the relevance of such programs if they are to be successful. Firms don't want employees returning from team-building programs to report merely that the experience "was childlike and fun and fairly inoffensive."[13]

EVALUATING EMPLOYEE PERFORMANCE

Another important part of human resource management is **performance appraisal**—the specific and formal evaluation of an employee to determine the degree to which he or she is performing effectively. Appraisals are important because they provide a benchmark to assess the extent to which recruiting and selection processes are adequate. In other words, performance appraisals help managers assess the extent to which they are recruiting and selecting the best employees. They also contribute to effective training, development, and compensation.

performance appraisal A formal program for evaluating how well an employee is performing the job; helps managers to determine how effective they are in recruiting and selecting employees.

Explain ways in which organizations evaluate employee performance.

4

The Performance Appraisal Process

Several questions must be answered as part of the performance appraisal process. These questions generally relate to who conducts the performance appraisal and provides feedback to the individual whose performance is being evaluated.

Conducting the Performance Appraisal

The individual's supervisor is the person most likely to conduct a performance appraisal. Supervisors usually have both the most knowledge of the job requirements and the most opportunity to observe employees performing their jobs. In addition, the supervisor is usually responsible for the performance of his or her subordinates. Thus, the supervisor is both responsible for employees' high performance and accountable for their inadequate performance.

Sources of Information. One possible source of information in the performance appraisal process is the subordinates of the individual being appraised. Subordinates are an especially important source of information when the performance of their own managers is being evaluated. Their input is perhaps most useful when the performance appraisal focusses on the manager's leadership potential. Another source of information is self-evaluation. In many professional and managerial situations, individuals occasionally may be asked to evaluate their own performance. A final source of information is customers. Restaurants such as Red Lobster, for example, place feedback forms in the envelopes in which customers receive their bills. These types of forms typically ask customers to evaluate their experience at the restaurant by asking questions about the service, the food, and the restaurant itself.

Managers must recognize that each source of information is subject to various weaknesses and shortcomings. As a result, many organizations find it effective to rely on a variety of different information sources in the conduct of appraisals. They may, for example, gather information not merely from supervisors or peers, but from both. Indeed, some organizations gather information from every source described in this section. This comprehensive approach is called **360-degree feedback**.

360-degree feedback Gathering information from a manager's subordinates, peers, and superiors when assessing the manager's performance.

Providing Performance Feedback

After the performance appraisal, the next major activity is providing feedback, coaching, and counselling. Many managers do a poor job in this area, in part because they don't understand how to do it properly and in part because they don't enjoy it. Almost by definition, performance appraisal in many organizations tends to focus on negatives. As a result, managers may have a tendency to avoid giving feedback because they know that an employee who receives negative feedback may be angry, hurt, discouraged, or argumentative. But clearly, if employees are not told about their shortcomings, they will have no concrete reason to try to improve and receive no guidance as to how to improve. It is critical, therefore, that managers follow up on appraisals by providing feedback.

Methods for Appraising Performance

Because of the nature of many jobs today, especially managerial work, most methods for appraising performance rely on judgments and ratings. A great deal of effort has therefore been expended trying to make relatively subjective evaluations as meaningful and useful as they can be. While some of the methods are based on relative rankings, others are based on ratings. In this section, we examine a few of the more popular methods, which we have categorized as either *ranking* or *rating methods*.

Ranking Methods

simple ranking method A method of performance appraisal that requires a manager to rank-order from top to bottom or from best to worst each member of a particular work group or department.

forced distribution method A method of performance appraisal that involves grouping employees into predefined frequencies of performance ratings.

The **simple ranking method** requires a manager to rank-order from top to bottom or from best to worst each member of a particular work group or department. The individual ranked first is the top performer, the individual ranked second is the second-best performer, and so forth. The basis for the ranking is generally global or overall performance. Another ranking method, the **forced distribution method**, involves grouping employees into predefined frequencies of performance ratings. Those frequencies are determined in advance and are imposed on the rater. A decision might be made, for instance, that 10 percent of the employees in a work group will be grouped as "outstanding," 20 percent as "very good," 40 percent as "average," 20 percent as "below average," and the remaining 10 percent as "poor." The forced distribution method is familiar to many students because it is the principle used by professors who grade on a so-called "bell curve" or "normal curve."

Rating Methods

graphic rating scale A statement or question about some aspect of an individual's job performance for which the rater must select the response that fits best.

One of the most popular and widely used methods is the **graphic rating scale**, which consists simply of a statement or question about some aspect of an individual's job performance. Following the statement or question is a series of answers or possible responses from which the rater must select the one that fits best. For example, one common set of responses to a graphic rating scale with five possible alternatives is *strongly agree, agree, neither agree nor disagree, disagree,* and *strongly disagree.* These responses, or "descriptors," are usually arrayed along a bar, line, or similar visual representation marked with numbers or letters corresponding to each descriptor. Figure 8.3 shows a sample graphic rating scale.

Graphic rating scales are appealing because they are relatively easy to develop. A manager simply "brainstorms" or otherwise develops a list of statements or questions that are presumably related to relevant indicators of performance. Moreover, a wide array of performance dimensions can be tapped with various rating scales on the same form. As we noted, a number or a letter accompanies each descriptor on the rating form. Most rating scales have ranges of one to five or one to seven. To develop a performance measure, the manager simply adds up the "points" for a particular employee's responses to obtain an overall index of performance.

Somewhat different is the **critical incident method**. A critical incident is simply an example of especially good or poor performance on the part of the employee. Organizations that rely on this method often require raters to recall such instances and then describe what the employee did (or did not do) that led to success or failure. This technique not only provides information for feedback but also defines performance in fairly clear, behavioural terms. In other cases, managers keep logs or diaries in which they record examples of critical incidents.

critical incident method A technique of performance appraisal in which raters recall examples of especially good or poor performance by an employee and then describe what the employee did (or did not do) that led to success or failure.

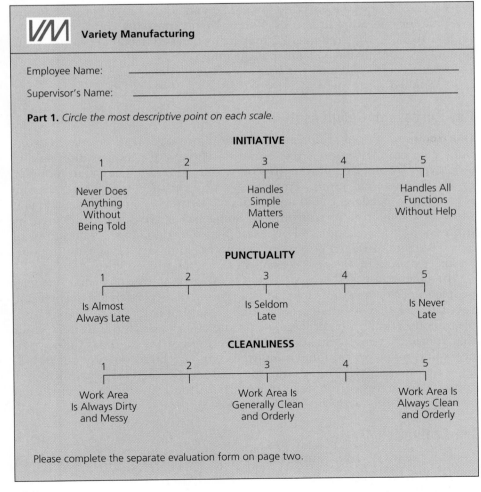

Figure 8.3 Performance rating scale.

PROVIDING COMPENSATION AND BENEFITS

5 Discuss the importance of *wages and salaries*, *incentives*, and *benefit programs* in attracting and keeping skilled workers.

compensation What a firm offers its employees in return for their labour.

Employees do not work for free—they expect to be compensated for the time, talent, and effort they devote to their jobs and to helping the organization achieve its goals. In this section, we explore basic compensation, incentives and performance-based rewards, and employee benefits and services. **Compensation** is the set of rewards that organizations provide to individuals in return for their willingness to perform various jobs and tasks within the organization. As we shall see, compensation includes a number of different elements, including base salary, incentives, bonuses, benefits, and other rewards. Compensation should never be a random decision, but rather the result of a careful and systematic strategic process.

The compensation received by CEOs can be extremely large, especially when bonuses and options are included. The most highly paid managers in the 2005 *Globe and Mail* Survey of Compensation were Hank Swartout of Precision Drilling Trust (who earned $74.8 million), Hunter Harrison of Canadian National Railway ($56.2 million), Frank Stronach of Magna International ($40.3 million), and Mike Zafirovski of Nortel Networks ($37.4 million).[14]

Determining Basic Compensation

wages Dollars paid based on the number of hours worked.

salary Dollars paid at regular intervals in return for doing a job, regardless of the amount of time or output involved.

Basic compensation means the base level of wages or salary paid to an employee. **Wages** generally refer to hourly compensation paid to operating employees. Most of the jobs that are paid on an hourly wage basis are lower-level and/or operating-level jobs. Rather than expressing compensation on an hourly basis, the organization may instead describe compensation on an annual or monthly basis. Many college and university graduates, for example, compare job offers on the basis of annual **salary**, such as $36 000 versus $38 000 a year.

Pay Surveys in Compensation

pay survey A survey of compensation paid to employees by other employers in a particular geographic area, an industry, or an occupational group.

One common source of information that many organizations use to determine base compensation is **pay surveys**—surveys of compensation paid to employees by other employers in a particular geographic area, an industry, or an occupational group. Pay surveys provide the information that an organization needs to avoid an imbalance between its own pay scale and those of comparable organizations. Some pay surveys are conducted by professional associations. For example, the Canadian Federation of Business School Deans publishes an annual summary of salaries for professors teaching in business schools in Canadian universities.

In general, a pay survey simply asks other organizations what they pay people to perform various jobs. Most organizations participate in such surveys because they will have access to the resulting data. There is, for example, a consortium of eight large electronic companies in the United States that routinely survey one another to determine what each pays new engineers and other professional employees who are hired directly out of college or university. The companies alternate the responsibility for conducting surveys from year to year, with the responsible organization sharing its results with the other members.

Job Evaluation

Another means of determining basic compensation is *job evaluation*, which should not be confused with job analysis. Recall that managers use job analysis to understand the requirements and nature of a job and its performance so that appropriate individuals can be recruited and selected. **Job evaluation** is a method for determining the relative value or worth of a job to the organization so that individuals who perform it can be appropriately compensated. In other words, it is mostly concerned with establishing internal pay equity.

job evaluation A method for determining the relative value or worth of a job to the organization so that individuals who perform it can be appropriately compensated.

Establishing a Pay Structure

A third method for determining basic compensation is establishing a *pay structure*. Compensation for different jobs is based on the organization's assessment of the relative value to the organization of each job class. Thus, there should be a logical rank ordering of compensation levels from the most valuable to the least valuable jobs throughout the organization. The organization, of course, may also find it necessary to group certain jobs together; thus, two or more jobs that are valued relatively equally will be compensated at approximately the same level. In addition, the organization decides on minimum and maximum pay ranges for each job or job class. Managers might use performance, *seniority* (a system that gives priority in promotions to employees with greater length of service), or a combination of the two to determine how much a person can be paid within the pay range for doing a particular job.

The internet allows job seekers and current employees to more easily get a sense of what their true market value is. If they can document the claim that their value is higher than what their current employer now pays or is offering, they may be in a position to demand higher salaries. One manager who met with a subordinate to discuss her raise was surprised when she produced data from five different websites to support her request for a bigger raise than he had intended to offer.

Performance-Based Compensation

Besides basic compensation, many organizations also offer performance-based rewards. The reason is obvious: When rewards are associated with higher levels of performance, employees will presumably be motivated to work harder in order to reap those awards.

Merit Pay Plans

Merit pay refers to pay awarded to employees according to the relative value of their contributions. Employees who make greater contributions receive higher pay than those who make lesser contributions. **Merit pay plans**, then, are compensation plans that base at least some meaningful portion of compensation on merit. The most general form of a merit pay plan is the raise—an annual salary increase granted to an employee because of his or her relative merit. In such plans, merit is usually determined or defined according to individual performance and overall contribution to the organization.

merit pay Pay awarded to employees according to the relative value of their contributions.
merit pay plans Compensation plans that formally base at least some meaningful portion of compensation on merit.

Skill- and Knowledge-Based Pay Systems. Although these systems are usually not strictly viewed as merit systems, it is worth noting how **skill-based pay** or **knowledge-based pay** systems focus employee attention on different areas but still rely on similar motivational processes. Instead of rewarding employees for increased performance, such systems reward them for the acquisition of more skills or knowledge. Skill-based pay systems reward employees for the acquisition of job-related skills. Knowledge-based pay systems reward employees for learning, because presumably, as they acquire more and more skills and knowledge, employees become more valuable to the organization.

skill-based pay Pay awarded to employees not for any specific level of performance, but for the acquisition of job-related skills.
knowledge-based pay Pay awarded to employees for learning.

Incentive Compensation Systems

Incentive compensation systems are among the oldest forms of performance-based rewards. Indeed, some companies were using individual piece-rate incentive plans over 100 years ago. Under a **piece-rate incentive plan**, the organization pays an employee a certain amount of money for every unit produced. An employee might, for example, be paid $1 for every 12 units of a product successfully completed. But such simplistic systems fail to account for such factors as minimum wage levels and rely on two questionable assumptions: (1) that performance is totally under an individual's control, and (2) that the individual employee does a single task continuously during the course of his or her work time. Today, therefore, incentive compensation systems tend to be much more sophisticated.

piece-rate incentive plan A compensation system in which an organization pays an employee a certain amount of money for every unit produced.

Incentive Pay Plans. Generally speaking, **individual incentive plans** reward individual performance on a real-time basis. That is, rather than increasing a person's base salary at the end of the year, an employer gives an individual a salary increase or some other financial reward for outstanding performance immediately or shortly after the performance occurred. For example, many baseball players have clauses in their contracts that pay them bonuses for hitting more than .300 over a season.

individual incentive plans A compensation system in which an employer gives an individual a salary increase or some other financial reward for outstanding performance immediately or shortly after the performance occurred.

Individual incentive systems are most common where performance can be assessed objectively (for example, by the number of units of output) rather than subjectively by a superior. Perhaps the most common form of individual incentive is the **sales commission** paid to people engaged in sales work. Salespeople "on commission" are paid based on the number of units they sell or the dollar value of sales they generate for the company.

sales commission Paying salespeople based on the number of units they sell or the dollar value of sales they generate for the company.

Other Forms of Incentives. Occasionally organizations use other forms of incentives. For example, a non-monetary incentive, such as additional time off or a special perk, might be useful. At some companies, recognition is given to employees in the form of special points that are awarded on the recommendation of a supervisor. Recipients can convert their points into money or they can use them to buy merchandise or trips from a special online catalogue.[15]

Individual incentive plans have been a big part of professional sports for many years. Some players receive multi-million dollar annual compensation for outstanding individual performance.

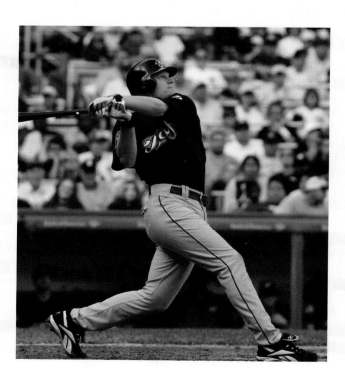

Team and Group Incentive Systems

The merit compensation and incentive compensation systems described in the preceding sections deal primarily with reward plans for individuals. There are also performance-based reward programs for teams and groups. Given today's increasing trend toward team- and group-based methods of work, such programs are growing in importance.

Gain Sharing. Many organizations use **gain-sharing programs**, which are designed to share with employees the cost savings from productivity improvements. Palliser Furniture Ltd., for example, introduced a gain-sharing plan that rewards employees for increasing production. Any profit resulting from production above a certain level is split 50-50 between the company and the employees.[16] The underlying assumption is that employees and the employer have the same goals and should therefore share in incremental economic gains. In general, organizations start by measuring team- or group-level productivity. The team or work group itself is then charged with lowering costs and otherwise improving productivity through any measures that members develop and their manager approves. Any resulting cost savings or productivity gains are then quantified and translated into dollar values. According to a predetermined formula, these dollar savings are then allocated to both employer and employees.

gain-sharing program An incentive program in which employees receive a bonus if the firm's costs are reduced because of greater worker efficiency and/or productivity.

Performance Increases. Some companies use incentives at the team or group level. Just like individual incentives, some team or group incentives tie rewards directly to performance increases. Like individual incentives, team or group incentives are also paid as they are earned rather than added to base salaries.

Profit Sharing. Other team- or group-level incentives go beyond the contributions of a specific work group. These are generally organization-wide incentives. One long-standing type of incentive program is called a **profit-sharing plan**. At the end of the year, some portion of the company's profits is paid into a profit-sharing pool that is then distributed to all employees. In 2000, Dofasco's profit-sharing plan gave each worker $7906 beyond his or her regular pay. Dofasco annually contributes 14 percent of its pre-tax profits to the profit-sharing plan.[17] Ipsco Steel of Regina introduced a profit-sharing plan that gives all workers an identical year-end bonus. In one recent year, over $9 million was distributed to employees.[18]

profit-sharing plan An incentive program in which employees receive a bonus depending on the firm's profits.

Benefits

In addition to financial compensation, most organizations provide employees with an array of other indirect compensation in the form of benefits. **Benefits** generally refer to various rewards, incentives, and other things of value that an organization gives employees in addition to wages, salaries, and other forms of direct financial compensation. Because these benefits have tangible value, they represent a meaningful form of compensation even though they are not generally expressed in financial terms.

benefits What a firm offers its workers other than wages and salaries in return for their labour.

Canada's universal health care system is a real advantage to doing business in Canada because business firms do not have to pay to provide this coverage. Rather, its cost is supported largely from general tax revenues. A study of the cost of employee benefits as a percentage of wages and salaries in nine industrialized countries found that Canada's percentage (25 percent) was the lowest, and Germany's was the highest (70 percent). The other seven countries (United States, United Kingdom, Japan, the Netherlands, Austria, Italy, France) were somewhere between these two extremes.[19]

Mandated Protection Plans

protection plan A plan that protects employees when their income is threatened or reduced by illness, disability, death, unemployment, or retirement.

employment insurance A protection plan that provides a basic subsistence payment to employees who are between jobs.

Protection plans protect employees when their income is threatened or reduced by illness, disability, death, unemployment, or retirement. A number of these plans are required by law, but others are optional. One mandated benefit is **employment insurance**, which provides a basic subsistence payment to employees who are between jobs. It is intended for people who have stopped working for one organization but who are assumed to be actively seeking employment with another. Both employers and employees pay premiums to an employment insurance fund.

Also mandated are Canada Pension Plan payments. The original purpose of this program was to provide some limited income to retired individuals to supplement personal savings, private pensions, part-time work, and so forth. It is funded through employee and employer taxes that are withheld from payroll.

workers' compensation Mandated insurance that covers individuals who suffer a job-related illness or accident.

Workers' compensation is mandated insurance that covers individuals who suffer a job-related illness or accident. Employers bear the cost of workers' compensation insurance. The exact premium is related to each employer's past experience with job-related accidents and illnesses. For example, a steel company might pay $20 per $100 of wages, while an accounting firm might pay only 10 cents per $100 of wages.

Optional Protection Plans

Another major category of employee benefits consists of various optional protection plans. Health insurance has become the most important type of coverage, and has expanded in recent years to include vision care, mental health services, dental care, and prescription drugs. Employee prescription drug plan costs are doubling about every five years, and companies are increasingly concerned about their ability to offer this kind of coverage.[20]

Pension liabilities are also a problem. A 2005 study by the Certified General Accountants of Canada found that the shortfall in pension funding at Canada's largest corporate defined benefit plans was $29 billion. A shortfall means that the assets in the pension plan are not sufficient to meet future pension promises.[21] In 2005, 72 percent of all federally regulated pension plans had a shortfall, compared to only 53 percent at the end of 2004.[22] Employers also face mounting liabilities for *benefits* for retired workers. A study of 71 of Canada's largest companies showed that their liabilities for retiree benefits (not pensions) amounted to $16 billion. In one recent year at Suncor Energy Inc., for example, the company's benefits liability was $98 million (almost as much as its pension liability of $99 million).[23]

Paid Time Off

Paid vacations are usually for periods of one, two, or more weeks during which an employee can take time off from work and continue to be paid. Most organizations vary the amount of paid vacation with an individual's seniority, but some companies are reducing the time required to qualify for paid vacations. At Carlson Wagonlit Travel Canada, employees get four weeks of paid vacation after working at the company for just five years. Formerly, 10 years of service was required.[24]

Another common paid time off plan is *sick leave*. This benefit is provided when an individual is sick or otherwise physically unable to perform his or her job. Most organizations allow an individual to accumulate sick time according to a schedule, such as one sick day per month. Sometimes an organization will allow an employee to take off a small number of days simply for "personal business." This benefit is usually called *personal leave*. Occasions might include funerals, religious observances, weddings, birthdays, or simply personal holidays. The Catholic Children's Aid Society, for example, provides its child protection workers with time off when they need it because the workers face high-stress situations.[25]

Some companies go even further and offer their employees paid or unpaid sabbaticals. They do so to help workers rejuvenate themselves and increase their enthusiasm for their job. At Bertelsmann AG, for example, full-time employees who have 20 years of service get a 5-week, full pay sabbatical, while employees who have 10 years get 4 weeks. Employees at Procter & Gamble are eligible for a 12-week unpaid sabbatical after they have worked for the company for 1 year.[26]

Other Types of Benefits

In addition to protection plans and paid time off, many organizations offer a growing number of other benefit programs. **Wellness programs**, for example, concentrate on preventing illness in employees rather than simply paying their expenses when they become sick. In some organizations, these programs are simple and involve little more than organized jogging or walking during lunch breaks. More elaborate programs include smoking cessation, blood pressure and cholesterol screening, and stress management. Some organizations maintain full-fledged health clubs on-site and provide counselling and programs for fitness and weight loss.

Childcare benefits are also becoming extremely popular. In fact, any organization that wants to be considered "family friendly" must have some type of childcare benefits, and being a "family-friendly" company is increasingly becoming a competitive advantage. These plans might include scheduling help, referrals to various types of services, or reimbursement accounts for childcare expenses. In many cases, they actually include company-paid daycare. Eldercare is also going to become increasingly common as the population ages and workers care for their elderly parents. Over 300 Canadian companies sponsor childcare centres at the work site. The childcare centre run by Husky Injection Molding Systems in Bolton, Ontario provides on-site haircuts, music lessons, and a pajama party on Valentine's Day so parents can spend time together. If an employee has to work late, the staff will feed the employee's child at no cost.[27]

Cafeteria-Style Benefit Plans

Most benefit programs are designed for all employees in an organization. Although the exact benefits may vary according to the employee's level in the organization, within those levels plans are generally "one size fits all." In contrast, **cafeteria-style benefit plans** allow employees to choose the benefits they really want. Under these plans, the organization typically establishes a budget, indicating how much it is willing to spend, per employee, on benefits. Employees are then presented with a list of possible benefits and the cost of each. They are free to put the benefits together in any combination they wish. Employees at Toyota's Cambridge, Ontario, plant are given the opportunity once each year to restructure their benefit packages. For example, they can give more weight to dental coverage if they have young children, or to life insurance or disability coverage, depending on their circumstances.[28]

wellness program A program that concentrates on preventing illness in employees rather than simply paying their expenses when they become sick.

cafeteria-style benefit plans A flexible approach to providing benefits in which employees are allocated a certain sum to cover benefits and can "spend" this allocation on the specific benefits they prefer.

THE LEGAL CONTEXT OF HRM

As much or more than any area of business, HRM is heavily influenced by federal law, provincial law, and judicial review. In this section, we summarize some of the most important and far-reaching areas of HR regulation. These include *equal employment opportunity, comparable worth, sexual harassment, employee safety and health,* and *retirement.*

Describe some of the key legal issues involved in hiring, compensating, and managing workers.

6

Equal Employment Opportunity

equal employment opportunity regulations Regulations to protect people from unfair or inappropriate discrimination in the workplace.

The basic goal of all **equal employment opportunity regulations** is to protect people from unfair or inappropriate discrimination in the workplace. Let's begin by noting that discrimination in itself is not illegal. Whenever one person is given a pay raise and another is not, or when one person is hired and another is not, the organization has made a decision to distinguish one person from another. As long as the basis for this discrimination is purely job-related (made, for instance, on the basis of performance or qualifications) and is applied objectively and consistently, the action is legal and appropriate. Problems arise when distinctions among people are not job-related. In such cases, the resulting discrimination is illegal.

Anti-Discrimination Laws

Canadian Human Rights Act Ensures that any individual who wishes to obtain a job has an equal opportunity to apply for it.

When recruiting, firms must be careful not to violate anti-discrimination laws. The key federal anti-discrimination legislation is the **Canadian Human Rights Act** of 1977. The goal of this act is to ensure that any individual who wishes to obtain a job has an equal opportunity to compete for it. The act applies to all federal agencies, federal Crown corporations, any employee of the federal government, and business firms that do business interprovincially. Thus, it applies to such firms as the Bank of Montreal, Air Canada, Telecom Canada, Canadian National Railways, and many other public and private sector organizations that operate across Canada. Even with such wide application, the act affects only about 10 percent of Canadian workers; the rest are covered under provincial human rights acts.

The Canadian Human Rights Act prohibits a wide variety of practices in recruiting, selecting, promoting, and dismissing personnel. The act specifically prohibits discrimination on the basis of age, race and colour, national and ethnic origin, physical handicap, religion, gender, marital status, or prison record (if pardoned). Some exceptions to these blanket prohibitions are permitted. Discrimination cannot be charged if a blind person is refused a position as a train engineer, bus driver, or crane operator. Likewise, a firm cannot be charged with discrimination if it does not hire a deaf person as a telephone operator or as an audio engineer.

These situations are clear-cut, but many others are not. For example, is it discriminatory to refuse women employment in a job that routinely requires carrying objects with a mass of more than 50 kilograms? Difficulties in determining whether discrimination has occurred are sometimes dealt with by using the concept of **bona fide occupational requirement**. An employer may choose one person over another based on overriding characteristics of the job in question. If a fitness centre wants to hire only women to supervise its women's locker room and sauna, it can do so without being discriminatory because it established a bona fide occupational requirement.

bona fide occupational requirement When an employer may choose one applicant over another based on overriding characteristics of the job.

The Canadian Human Rights Commission carries out enforcement of the federal act. The commission can either respond to complaints from individuals who believe they have been discriminated against, or launch an investigation on its own if it has reason to believe that discrimination has occurred. During an investigation, data are gathered about the alleged discriminatory behaviour and, if the claim of discrimination is substantiated, the offending organization or individual may be ordered to compensate the victim.

Each province has also enacted human rights legislation to regulate organizations and businesses operating in that province. These provincial regulations are similar in spirit to the federal legislation, with many minor variations from province to province. All provinces prohibit discrimination on the basis of race, national or ethnic origin, colour, religion, sex, and marital status, but some do not address such issues as physical handicaps, criminal record, or age. Provincial human rights commissions enforce provincial legislation.

The **Employment Equity Act** of 1986 addresses the issue of discrimination in employment by designating four groups as employment disadvantaged—women, visible minorities, Aboriginal people, and people with disabilities. Companies covered by the act are required to publish statistics on their employment of people in these four groups.

The Bank of Montreal recently became the first company outside the United States to win a prestigious award for promoting women's careers. The Bank of Montreal has introduced initiatives such as flexible working hours, a mentoring program, a national career information network, and a gender awareness workshop series.[29]

Companies are increasingly making provisions for disabled employees. At Rogers Cablevision, a division of Rogers Communications Inc., a large workplace area was completely redesigned to accommodate workers who were either visually disabled or in wheelchairs. Special equipment was also installed—a large-print computer for workers with partial sight, and a device that allows blind workers to read printed materials.[30]

Employment Equity Act Federal legislation that designates four groups as employment disadvantaged—women, visible minorities, Aboriginal people, and people with disabilities.

Comparable Worth

In spite of recent advances, the average woman still earns only about three-quarters of what the average man earns. (The average *single* woman, however, earns 99 percent of what the average man earns.[31]) The average woman also spends a lower proportion of her potential years of work actually working. For example, for men aged 55–64, the proportion of potential years of work spent actually working is 92.3 percent; for women of that age, the ratio is only 64.2 percent.[32]

Various research studies show that compared to men, the average woman has less actual labour market experience, is less likely to work full time, and is more likely to leave the labour force for long periods of time. These factors very likely cause companies to differentiate between men and women in terms of salaries.

Comparable worth is a legal concept that addresses paying equal wages for jobs that are of comparable value to the employer. This might mean comparing dissimilar jobs, such as those of nurses and mechanics or secretaries and electricians. Proponents of comparable worth say that all the jobs in a company must be evaluated and then rated in terms of basic dimensions such as the level of skill they require. All jobs could then be compared based on a common index. People in different jobs that rate the same on this index would be paid the same. Experts hope that this will help to reduce the gap between men's and women's pay.

comparable worth A legal idea that aims to pay equal wages for work of equal value.

In a long-standing comparable worth dispute, the Supreme Court of Canada ruled in 2006 that flight attendants at Air Canada—who have been trying for years to achieve pay equity with male-dominated groups of employees—could compare their pay with the pay of ground crews and pilots because all these employees work for the same company. In spite of this ruling, the president of the Air Canada Canadian Union of Public Employees was concerned that it might take many years before the flight attendants actually saw a wage increase.[33]

Critics of comparable worth object on the grounds that it ignores the supply and demand aspects of labour. They say, for example, that legislation forcing a company to pay people more than the open market price for their labour (which may happen in jobs where there is a surplus of workers) is another example of unreasonable government interference in business activities. They also say that implementing comparable worth will cost business firms too much money. A study prepared for the Ontario Ministry of Labour estimated that it would cost approximately $10 billion for the public and private sectors in Ontario to establish equitable payment for jobs of equal value. Yet the cost defence cannot be easily used. In 2005, the Canadian Human Rights Tribunal ruled that a wage gap between male and female clerical workers at Canada Post was the result of systemic sex discrimination. It ordered the company to pay a total of $150 million in back pay to 6000 female clerical workers.[34] In an earlier case, the tribunal ruled that the federal government must pay a total of more than $3 billion to thousands of civil servants because it discriminated against workers in female-dominated job classifications. About 85 percent of these workers were women.

There is one very interesting fact in this debate about comparable worth: Male earning power has been declining for decades. Young males who are now entering the labour market, regardless of their education, will likely earn dramatically less than their predecessors did. Young, female university graduates, on the other hand, have recently earned more than their predecessors.[35]

Sexual Harassment

sexual harassment Requests for sexual favours, unwelcome sexual advances, or verbal or physical conduct of a sexual nature that creates an intimidating or hostile environment for a given employee.

Within the job context, **sexual harassment** refers to requests for sexual favours, unwelcome sexual advances, or verbal or physical conduct of a sexual nature that creates an intimidating or hostile environment for a given employee. The Canadian Human Rights Act takes precedence over any policies that a company might have developed on its own to deal with sexual harassment problems.

quid pro quo harassment Form of sexual harassment in which sexual favours are requested in return for job-related benefits.

hostile work environment Form of sexual harassment deriving from off-colour jokes, lewd comments, and so forth.

Quid pro quo harassment is the most blatant form of sexual harassment. It occurs when the harasser offers to exchange something of value for sexual favours. A male supervisor, for example, might tell or suggest to a female subordinate that he will recommend her for promotion or give her a raise in exchange for sexual favours. The creation of a **hostile work environment** is a subtler form of sexual harassment. A group of male employees who continually make off-colour jokes and lewd comments and perhaps decorate the work environment with questionable photographs may create a hostile work environment for a female colleague. Regardless of the pattern, the same bottom-line rules apply: Sexual harassment is illegal, and the organization is responsible for controlling it.

Verbal comments by prominent managers are also problematic. For example, when Neil French, a legendary advertising executive and the creative director of WPP Group PLC, gave a speech in Toronto in 2005, he was asked why there were so few women who were creative advertising directors. He replied that women focus too much on their family duties and this usually prevents them from succeeding in management. His comments caused quite a stir, and French soon resigned from his position. It is interesting to note that the Toronto office of Ogilvy & Mather (a subsidiary of WPP) is headed by two creative directors, both of whom are women.[36]

If a manager is found guilty of sexual harassment, the company is also liable because the manager is an agent of the company. In fact, even if one employee makes another employee feel uncomfortable, the instigator may be guilty of sexual harassment. To deal effectively with the potential for sexual harassment, managers should

■ develop clear and enforceable policies dealing with sexual harassment

■ inform all employees about the existence of these policies

■ train employees to recognize and refrain from sexual harassment

- take complaints about sexual harassment seriously
- establish a procedure for dealing with harassment complaints
- take action against those who are involved in sexual harassment

Employee Safety and Health

Employee safety and health programs help to reduce absenteeism and turnover, raise productivity, and boost morale by making jobs safer and more healthful. Government regulations about employee safety are becoming stricter. Ontario, which loses more than seven million working days yearly because of on-the-job injuries, has passed amendments to the Ontario Occupational Health and Safety Act. Officers and directors of companies are held personally responsible for workplace health and safety and are punishable by jail terms and fines for permitting unsafe working conditions.[37]

Some industrial work—logging, construction, fishing, and mining—can put workers at risk of injury in obvious ways. But other types of work—such as typing or lifting—can also cause painful injuries. **Repetitive strain injuries (RSIs)** occur when workers perform the same functions over and over again. These injuries disable more than 200 000 Canadians each year and account for nearly half of all work-related time loss claims.

repetitive strain injuries (RSIs) Injuries that occur when workers perform the same functions over and over again.

In Canada, each province has developed its own workplace health and safety regulations. The purpose of these laws is to ensure that employees do not have to work in dangerous conditions. These laws are the direct result of undesirable conditions that existed in many Canadian businesses at the close of the nineteenth century. While much improvement is evident, Canada still has some problems with workplace health and safety. In one study of six Western industrialized nations, Canada had the worst safety record in mining and construction and the second-worst record in manufacturing and railways.

The Ontario Occupational Health and Safety Act illustrates current legislation in Canada. It requires all employers to ensure that equipment and safety devices are used properly. Employers must also show workers the proper way to operate machinery. At the job site, supervisors are charged with the responsibility of ensuring that workers use equipment properly. The act also requires workers to behave appropriately on the job. Employees have the right to refuse to work on a job if they believe it is unsafe; a legal procedure exists for resolving any disputes in this area.

In most provinces, the Ministry of Labour appoints inspectors to enforce health and safety regulations. If the inspector finds a sufficient hazard, he or she has the authority to clear the workplace. Inspectors can usually arrive at a firm unannounced to conduct an inspection.

Retirement

Until the 1990s, Canadian courts generally upheld 65 as the mandatory retirement age, but most Canadian provinces have now abolished mandatory retirement. Even though mandatory retirement is now out of favour, workers are actually retiring earlier than they used to. In the late 1970s, the average retirement age in Canada was 65, but by 2003 it had dropped to 62.3 years.[38] A Statistics Canada study showed that "boomer" couples are unlikely to retire at the same time. Often women stay in the work force longer than their husbands.[39] Some managers fear that the abolition of mandatory retirement will result in less productive employees remaining at work after age 65, but research shows that the employees who stay on the job past 65 are usually the most productive ones.

NEW CHALLENGES IN THE CHANGING WORKPLACE

7 Discuss *workforce diversity*, the management of *knowledge workers*, and the use of *contingent and temporary workers* as important changes in the contemporary workplace.

As we have seen throughout this chapter, HR managers face several ongoing challenges in their efforts to keep their organizations staffed with effective workers. To complicate matters, new challenges arise as the economic and social environments of business change. We conclude this chapter with a discussion of several of the most important HRM issues facing business today: *managing workforce diversity, managing knowledge workers,* and *managing contingent and temporary workers.*

Managing Workforce Diversity

workforce diversity The range of workers' attitudes, values, beliefs, and behaviours that differ by gender, race, age, ethnicity, physical ability, and other relevant characteristics.

As we saw in the opening case, one extremely important set of human resource challenges centres on **workforce diversity**—the range of workers' attitudes, values, beliefs, and behaviours that differ by gender, race, age, ethnicity, physical ability, and other relevant characteristics. In the past, organizations tended to work toward homogenizing their workforces, getting everyone to think and behave in similar ways. Partly as a result of affirmative action efforts, however, many organizations are now creating more diverse workforces by embracing more women, ethnic minorities, and foreign-born employees than ever before.

Organizations are increasingly recognizing that diversity can be a competitive advantage. For example, by hiring the best people available from every group rather than hiring from just one or a few groups, a firm can develop a higher-quality workforce. Similarly, a diverse workforce can bring a wider array of information to bear on problems and can provide insights on marketing products to a wider range of consumers. Says the head of workforce diversity at IBM: "We think it is important for our customers to look inside and see people like them. If they can't...the prospect of them becoming or staying our customers declines."

Managing Knowledge Workers

Traditionally, employees added value to organizations because of what they did or because of their experience. In the "information age," however, many employees add value because of what they know.[40]

The Nature of Knowledge Work

knowledge workers Workers who are experts in specific fields like computer technology and engineering, and who add value because of what they know, rather than how long they have worked or the job they do.

These employees are usually called **knowledge workers**, and the skill with which they are managed is a major factor in determining which firms will be successful in the future. Knowledge workers, including computer scientists, engineers, and physical scientists, provide special challenges for the HR manager. They tend to work for high-tech firms and are usually experts in some abstract knowledge base. They often prefer to work independently and tend to identify more strongly with their professions than with any organization—even to the extent of defining performance in terms recognized by other members of their professions.

As the importance of information-driven jobs grows, the need for knowledge workers continues to grow as well. But these employees require extensive and highly specialized training, and not every organization is willing to make the human capital investments necessary to take advantage of these jobs. In fact, even after knowledge workers are on the job, training updates are critical to prevent their skills from becoming obsolete. It has been suggested, for example, that the "half-life" of a technical education in engineering is about three years. The failure to update such skills will not only result in the loss of competitive advantage but also increase the likeli-

This worker has the extensive training and highly specialized skills that are needed in this high-tech manufacturing process. Management of such knowledge workers is increasingly important for business success.

hood that the knowledge worker will move to another firm that is more committed to updating his or her knowledge.

Knowledge Worker Management and Labour Markets

In recent years, the demand for knowledge workers has been growing at a dramatic rate. As a result, organizations that need these workers must introduce regular market adjustments (upward) to pay them enough to keep them. This is especially critical in areas in which demand is growing, as even entry-level salaries for these employees are skyrocketing. Once an employee accepts a job with a firm, the employer faces yet another dilemma. Once hired, workers are subject to the company's internal labour market, which is not likely to be growing as quickly as the external market for knowledge workers as a whole. Consequently, the longer an employee remains with a firm, the further behind the market his or her pay falls—unless, of course, it is regularly adjusted upward.

Not surprisingly, the growing demand for these workers has inspired some fairly extreme measures for attracting them in the first place.[41] High starting salaries and sign-on bonuses are common. British Petroleum Exploration was recently paying starting petroleum engineers with under-sea platform-drilling knowledge—not experience, just knowledge—salaries in the six figures, plus sign-on bonuses of over U.S.$50 000 and immediate profit sharing. Even with these incentives, HR managers complain that they cannot retain specialists because young engineers soon leave to accept sign-on bonuses from competitors. Laments one HR executive: "We wind up six months after we hire an engineer having to fight off offers for that same engineer for more money."[42]

Managing Contingent and Temporary Workers

A final contemporary HR issue involves the use of contingent and/or temporary workers. Indeed, recent years have seen an explosion in the use of such workers by organizations.

Trends in Contingent and Temporary Employment

A **contingent worker** is a person who works for an organization on something other than a permanent or full-time basis. Categories of contingent workers include independent contractors (freelancers), on-call workers, temporary employees (usually hired through outside agencies), and contract

contingent worker A person who works for an organization on something other than a permanent or full-time basis.

and leased employees. Another category is part-time workers. The financial services giant Citigroup, for example, makes extensive use of part-time sales agents to pursue new clients.

Managing Contingent and Temporary Workers

Given the widespread use of contingent and temporary workers, HR managers must understand how to use such employees most effectively. That is, they need to understand how to manage contingent and temporary workers. One key is careful planning. Even though one of the presumed benefits of using contingent workers is flexibility, it still is important to integrate such workers in a coordinated fashion. Rather than having to call in workers sporadically and with no prior notice, organizations try to bring in specified numbers of workers for well-defined periods of time. The ability to do so comes from careful planning.

A second key is understanding contingent workers and acknowledging both their advantages and their disadvantages. That is, the organization must recognize what it can and cannot achieve by using contingent and temporary workers. Expecting too much from contingent workers, for example, is a mistake that managers should avoid.

Third, managers must carefully assess the real cost of using contingent workers. Many firms adopt this course of action to save labour costs. The organization should be able to document precisely its labour-cost savings. How much would it be paying people in wages and benefits if they were on permanent staff? How does this cost compare with the amount spent on contingent workers? This difference, however, could be misleading. Contingent workers might be less effective performers than permanent and full-time employees. Comparing employees on a direct-cost basis, therefore, is not necessarily valid. Organizations must learn to adjust the direct differences in labour costs to account for differences in productivity and performance.

Finally, managers must fully understand their own strategies and decide in advance how they intend to manage temporary workers, specifically focussing on how to integrate them into the organization. On a very simplistic level, for example, an organization with a large contingent workforce must make some decisions about the treatment of contingent workers relative to the treatment of permanent, full-time workers. Should contingent workers be invited to the company holiday party? Should they have the same access to such employee benefits as counselling services and childcare? Managers must understand that they need to develop a strategy for integrating contingent workers according to some sound logic and then follow that strategy consistently over time.[43]

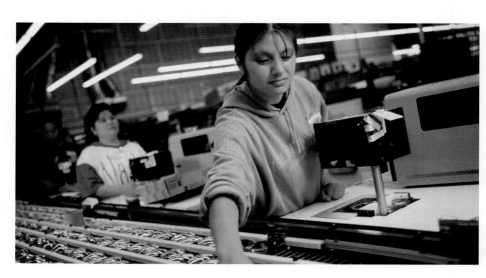

This young woman is one of 1500 temporary workers at Sola Optical. Sola keeps at least 100 temps working at all times, because it gives human resource managers both scheduling flexibility and the opportunity to try potential permanent employees.

Summary of Learning Objectives

1. **Define *human resource management*, discuss its strategic significance, and explain how managers plan for human resources.** *Human resource management*, or *HRM*, is the set of organizational activities directed at attracting, developing, and maintaining an effective workforce. HRM plays a key strategic role in organizational performance. Planning for human resource needs entails several steps. Conducting a *job analysis* enables managers to create detailed, accurate job descriptions and specifications. After analysis is complete, managers must forecast demand and supply for both the numbers and types of workers they will need. Then they consider steps to match supply with demand.

2. **Identify the issues involved in *staffing* a company, including *internal* and *external recruiting* and *selection*.** *Recruiting* is the process of attracting qualified persons to apply for jobs that an organization has open. *Internal recruiting* involves considering present employees for new jobs. This approach helps build morale and rewards an organization's best employees. *External recruiting* means attracting people from outside the organization to apply for openings. When organizations are actually selecting people for jobs, they generally use such selection techniques as *application forms*, *tests*, *interviews*, and other techniques. Regardless of what selection techniques are used, they must be valid predictors of an individual's expected performance in the job.

3. **Discuss different ways in which organizations go about developing the capabilities of employees and managers.** If a company is to get the most out of its workers, it must develop both those workers and their skills. Nearly all employees undergo some initial *orientation* process that introduces them to the company and to their new jobs. Many employees are given the opportunity to acquire new skills through various *work-based* and/or *instructional-based programs*.

4. **Explain ways in which organizations evaluate employee performance.** *Performance appraisals* help managers decide who needs training and who should be promoted. Appraisals also tell employees how well they are meeting expectations. Although a variety of alternatives are available for appraising performance, employee supervisors are most commonly used. No matter who does the evaluation, however, feedback to the employee is very important. Managers can select from a variety of ranking and rating methods for use in performance appraisal.

5. **Discuss the importance of *wages and salaries*, *incentives*, and *benefit programs* in attracting and keeping skilled workers.** *Wages and salaries*, *incentives*, and *benefit packages* may all be parts of a company's compensation program. By paying its workers as well as or better than competitors, a business can attract and keep qualified personnel. *Incentive programs* can also motivate people to work more productively. *Indirect compensation* also plays a major role in effective and well-designed compensation systems.

6. **Describe some of the key legal issues involved in hiring, compensating, and managing workers.** In hiring, compensating, and managing workers, managers must obey a variety of federal and provincial laws. *Equal employment opportunity* and *equal pay* laws forbid discrimination other than action based on legitimate job requirements. The concept of *comparable worth* states that equal wages should be paid for jobs that are of comparable value to the employer. Firms are also required to provide employees with safe working environments, as set down by the guidelines of provincial occupational health and safety acts. *Sexual harassment* is another key contemporary legal issue in business.

7. **Discuss *workforce diversity*, the management of *knowledge workers*, and the use of *contingent and temporary workers* as important changes in the contemporary workplace.** *Workforce diversity* refers to the range of workers' attitudes, values, beliefs, and behaviours that differ by gender, race, ethnicity, age, physical ability, and other relevant characteristics. Many firms think that having a diverse workforce creates a competitive advantage, so they have set a goal to have a workforce that reflects the growing diversity of the population as it enters the labour pool.

Many firms today also face challenges in managing *knowledge workers*. The recent boom in high-tech companies has led to rapidly increasing salaries and high turnover among the workers who are best prepared to work in those companies. *Contingent workers* are temporary and part-time employees hired to supplement an organization's permanent workforce. Their numbers have grown significantly since the early 1980s and are expected to rise further. The practice of hiring contingent workers is gaining in popularity because it gives managers more flexibility and because temps are usually not covered by employers' benefit programs.

KEY TERMS

360-degree feedback, 250
assessment centre, 244
benefits, 255
bona fide occupational
    requirement, 258
cafeteria-style benefit plans, 257
Canadian Human Rights Act, 258
comparable worth, 259
compensation, 252
contingent worker, 263
critical incident method, 251
employee information systems
    (skills inventories), 241
Employment Equity Act, 259
employment insurance, 256
equal employment opportunity
    regulations, 258
external recruiting, 242
forced distribution method, 250
gain-sharing program, 255
graphic rating scale, 250
hostile work environment, 260

human resource management
    (HRM), 238
individual incentive plans, 254
instructional-based programs, 248
internal recruiting, 242
internship, 243
job analysis, 239
job description, 239
job evaluation, 253
job specification, 239
knowledge workers, 262
knowledge-based pay, 253
lecture or discussion approach,
    248
merit pay, 253
merit pay plans, 253
off-the-job training, 248
on-the-job training, 247
orientation, 247
pay survey, 252
performance appraisal, 249
piece-rate incentive plan, 254

profit-sharing plan, 255
protection plan, 256
quid pro quo harassment, 260
recruiting, 242
repetitive strain injuries (RSIs),
    261
replacement chart, 241
salary, 252
sales commission, 254
sexual harassment, 260
simple ranking method, 250
skill-based pay, 253
systematic job rotations and
    transfers, 248
validation, 243
vestibule training, 247
video assessment, 244
wages, 252
wellness program, 257
work-based programs, 247
workers' compensation, 256
workforce diversity, 262

QUESTIONS FOR ANALYSIS

1. Why is a good employee–job match important? Who benefits more, the organization or the employee? Explain.

2. Why is the formal training of workers so important to most employers? Why don't employers simply let people learn about their jobs as they perform them?

3. What are your views on drug testing in the workplace? What would you do if your employer asked you to submit to a drug test?

4. Have you or anyone you know ever suffered discrimination in a hiring decision? Did you or the person you know do anything about it?

5. What training do you think you are most likely to need when you finish school and start your career?

6. What benefits do you consider most and least important in attracting workers? In keeping workers? In motivating workers to perform their jobs well?

7. Select a job currently held by you or a friend. Draw up a job description and job specification for this position.

8. How much will benefit considerations (as opposed to salary) affect your choice of an employer after graduation?

APPLICATION EXERCISES

1. Interview an HR manager at a local company. Focus on a position for which the firm is currently recruiting applicants and identify the steps in the selection process.

2. Obtain a copy of an employment application. Examine it carefully and determine how useful it might be in making a hiring decision.

BUILDING YOUR BUSINESS SKILLS

Getting Online for a Job

Goal

To introduce students to career-search resources available on the internet.

The Situation

If companies are on one side of the external staffing process, people looking for work are on the other. Companies need qualified candidates to fill job openings and candidates need jobs that are right for them. The challenge, of course, is to make successful matches. Increasingly, this matchmaking is being conducted on the internet. Companies are posting jobs in cyberspace, and job seekers are posting résumés in response. The number of job postings has grown dramatically in recent years. On a typical Sunday, you might find as many as 50 000 postings on the Monster Board, a leading job site. With so many companies looking for qualified candidates online, it makes good business sense to learn how to use the system.

Assignment

Using internet career resources means locating job databases and preparing and posting a résumé. (You will therefore need access to the internet to complete this exercise.)

Step 1

Team up with three classmates to investigate and analyze specific job databases. In each case, write a short report describing the database (which you and other group members may use during an actual job search). Summarize the site and its features as well as its advantages, disadvantages, and costs. Start with the following sites and add others you may find on your own:

The Monster Board, www.monster.com

Careerbuilder.com, www.careerbuilder.ca

College Grad Job Hunter, www.collegegrad.com

Step 2

Investigate the job opportunities listed on the home pages of various companies. Consider trying the following companies:

Air Canada, www.aircanada.com

Dofasco, www.dofasco.ca

Royal Bank, www.royalbank.com

IBM, www.ibm.com/ca/

Wal-Mart, www.walmartstores.com

McDonald's, www.mcdonalds.com

Bombardier, www.bombardier.com

Write a summary of the specific career-related information you find on each site.

Step 3

Working with group members, research strategies for composing effective cyber résumés. The following websites provide some helpful information on formats and personal and job-related information that should be included in your résumé. They also offer hints on the art of creating a scannable résumé:

Workopolis, www.workopolis.com

Career Magazine, www.careermag.com

Two books by Joyce Lain Kennedy, *Electronic Job Search Revolution* and *Electronic Résumé Revolution*, also contain valuable information.

Step 4

Working as a group, create an effective electronic résumé for a fictitious college or university graduate looking for a first job. Pay attention to format, language, style, and the effective communication of background and goals.

Step 5

Working as a group, learn how to post your résumé online. (Do not submit the résumé you created for this exercise, which is, after all, fictitious.) The databases provided will guide you in this process.

Follow-Up Questions

1. Why is it necessary to learn how to conduct an electronic job search? Do you think it will be more or less necessary in the years ahead?

2. Why do you think more computer-related jobs than non-technical jobs are posted online? Do you think this situation will change?

3. Why is it a waste of time to stylize your résumé with different fonts, point sizes, and centred headings?

4. What is the advantage of emailing your résumé directly to a company rather than applying for the same job through an online databank?

EXERCISING YOUR ETHICS

Taking Advantage of Contingent Workers

The Situation

You are a store manager in a large retail organization. Your job is full-time, and you receive good benefits from the company. However, many people in your store (cashiers, shelf-stockers, greeters, etc.) work only part-time for the company. You know that many of them want to work full-time but the company does not allow it. One of the reasons is that part-time workers are not eligible for benefits and this reduces the company's human resource expenses. Top management has emphasized on several occasions that it is imperative that costs be controlled so your store can remain competitive, and reducing human resource costs is one obvious way to do that.

The Dilemma

You have become increasingly concerned that the human resource management policies of your organization leave something to be desired. In the past few months, several workers have expressed their deep concerns to you that they are having extreme financial difficulty because they are not given enough hours of work each week. You know these workers, and they are hard-working, reliable people. You have great sympathy for them, particularly the ones who have families. You also know, however, that competition from competitors like Wal-Mart is intense, and that keeping costs low is absolutely imperative if your firm hopes to compete. You know that if the prices you charge are not competitive, customers will shop elsewhere. If that happens, there won't be any jobs for anybody, full-time or otherwise.

Questions for Discussion

1. What are the ethical issues in this situation?

2. What do you think most managers would do in this situation?

3. What would you do? Defend your answer.

CONCLUDING CASE 8-1

Las Vegas Gambles Online

Imagine this assignment: Your boss tells you that you are responsible for hiring almost 10 000 new workers. But that's the easy part. You have to have them all prepared to start working on the same day, their job skills have to be impeccable, and there can be no mistakes. Oh, and just to make it interesting, you are not allowed to use a single sheet of paper! Sound impossible? Well, that's just what a team of Las Vegas executives was asked to do.

In the few short years since it opened, Bellagio hotel and casino in Las Vegas has become one of the gambling mecca's most popular destinations. But before it opened, and behind the scenes, Bellagio also gave human resource (HR) managers new insights into how to staff a new organization. The task facing the resort's HR executives was daunting. They had to hire 9600 workers in 24 weeks and have everyone trained and on the payroll when the first customer walked through the door. The firm's HR team not only pulled this feat off without a hitch, it did it without using a single sheet of paper!

With the precision of a full-scale military operation, the Bellagio team designed and implemented one of the most sophisticated HR selection systems ever devised. To apply for a position, applicants called and requested an appointment. They were then scheduled in batches to arrive at the resort's hiring centre, where they filled out an application at a computer terminal. One hundred terminals were kept busy 12 hours a day, 6 days a week. As applications were submitted, employees at the checkout desk conducted unobtrusive assessments of the applicants' communication skills and overall demeanour, eliminating about 20 percent of the applicants.

Next came 27 000 interviews. For example, a hiring manager could sit at a PC and call up the highest-rated desk clerk candidates. The database system would rank order the candidates according to predetermined criteria. The manager could then call in, say, three applicants for each open position for face-to-face interviews. An interview consisted of a set of structured questions. During an interview, the manager would discreetly evaluate the responses to each question on a hidden keypad. These data were then fed back into the database.

If a manager wanted to hire a particular applicant, he or she could pull up a software screen and check "Conduct background check." A team of investigators would then verify employment, military, and education history; for some jobs, a drug test was mandatory. About 8 percent of applicants were rejected at this stage because of falsified information on their applications.

▶▶▶

If a manager was ready to offer a job to a particular individual, another screen was used to check "Yes." When this happened, the applicant was invited to a job-offer meeting, which is when people were actually offered jobs. If they accepted, they then completed various required documents—again, in electronic form—for benefits and income tax purposes. They were also scheduled for relevant training sessions. And when the big day came and the Bellagio officially opened its doors, 9600 new employees were in place and ready to work.

The massive hiring job at Bellagio staggers the imagination. But in reality, many firms must routinely plan to hire large numbers of people in a coordinated fashion. Las Vegas itself reflects a microcosm of this task with each massive new casino that is opened. The Mandalay Bay, the Venetian, and similar mega-resorts have had to do the same thing as Bellagio. In other outposts, Disney must hire thousands of new employees to staff each new theme park it opens, Toyota must hire thousands of workers for each new factory it builds, and Royal Caribbean must hire thousands of service staff for each new cruise ship it launches.

Wal-Mart is in the midst of a hiring explosion that may eventually make these examples truly passé. It has announced a goal of hiring one million new people over the next five years. About 800 000 of these will be to fill newly created jobs, while the other 200 000 will be replacements for retirees and other employees forecasted to leave the firm. That's like hiring the entire city of Mississauga, Ontario.

So what does the giant retailer plan to do? For one thing, it may need to up its pay grades a bit and offer more benefits. For another, it plans to step up its university recruiting for potential new store managers. And it hopes to entice the spouses, children, and other relatives of its current employees to join its ranks. If Wal-Mart is successful, it may end up revolutionizing not only the retailing industry but the human resource management function as well.

Questions for Discussion

1. What are the unique challenges of hiring massive numbers of people?

2. Identify at least five factors that might disrupt a firm's massive hiring plans.

3. Compare and contrast the challenges faced by Bellagio and Wal-Mart.

4. What other employment situations might be able to use Bellagio's model?

5. Suppose a firm had to reduce its staff by several thousand workers in a short period of time. What might it learn from Bellagio?

CONCLUDING CASE 8-2

Galt Contracting

Galt Contracting is a small B.C.-based company that plants trees for lumber companies like Canfor, Gorman Brothers, and Riverside. In the spring of each year, Donald Galt, the owner-manager of Galt Contracting, bids on tree-planting contracts that will be available during the upcoming summer. He visits the block of land that is up for bid and looks it over with a lumber company representative. He then develops a bid and submits it to the lumber company. If he is awarded the job, Galt's profit is determined by the amount of the lumber company contract minus the amount he pays his workers.

The Business of Tree Planting

Once Galt knows that he has gotten a contract, he hires tree planters to do the actual tree planting. Galt usually hires university students who are looking for good-paying summer jobs. The work is hard, but tree planters can make very good money because they are paid on a piece-rate system, that is, they are paid a certain amount of money for each tree that they plant. The amount usually varies between 16 and 32 cents per tree, depending on the terrain and the kind of tree that is being planted. The more difficult the terrain is, the higher the piece rate that planters receive.

A tree planter may plant as few as 1000 trees or as many as 2500 each day, depending on the terrain and the planter's skill. On an average day, a reasonably experienced planter can put 1300 seedlings in the ground. Planters don't have a set lunch break, but eat on the run. They usually leave their lunch boxes at the main cache, and eat about halfway through the day on one of their return trips to the cache to pick up more seedlings.

Each planter is assigned a "piece" to plant for the day, usually an area equal in size to a football field, but not necessarily symmetrical. The limits of each planter's area are marked with flags by the planters as they begin planting in the morning. Planters leave the main cache and begin planting trees in a straight line. As they plant, they "flag a line" which indicates the boundaries of their piece. This involves staking out strips of brightly coloured tape close to the line of trees. This line helps each planter determine where their piece begins and ends. Planting is then done in a back-and-forth pattern within each piece as planters work back toward the main cache as their bag gradually empties. They monitor the number trees left in their planting bags so they can end up near the main cache when they run out of trees.

Trees must be planted in different concentrations on different pieces, and a certain jargon has arisen to describe this activity. For example, if spacing is "2.9," this means that trees must be planted 2.9 metres apart; if spacing is "3.1," this means that trees must be planted 3.1 metres apart. Planters prefer "2.9" days over "3.1" days because they don't have to cover as much ground and can therefore plant more trees and make more money.

Quality Control

A checker—who works for the lumber company—inspects the work of the planters to ensure that they are planting properly. Checkers use a cord to inscribe a circle on a randomly chosen part of a piece. On "2.9" days, the checker will ensure that 7 trees are contained in the circle within the cord. The checker also determines whether the trees are planted properly. Trees must not have any air pockets around the roots, there must be no "j-rooted" (crooked) roots, and trees must be planted on the south (sunny) side of any obstacles on the piece. Trees must also be planted close to obstacles so that they are not trampled by the cattle that sometimes graze in the area. If a planter consistently plants too many or too few trees on a piece, the checker can demand that the piece be replanted. This happens infrequently, but when it does, the planter's pay is sharply reduced.

Galt sometimes checks workers himself, especially if he has reason to believe that they are doing a sloppy job. The biggest problem he has encountered is workers who plant large numbers of trees, but do so very poorly. Planters know that if Galt is following them around for any significant period of time, that he is suspicious about the quality of their planting. Planters are very hard on each other in terms of quality. They become very upset if one of their group tries to make more money by planting large numbers of trees by cutting corners. Planters put pressure on each other to do a good job because the reputation of the whole group suffers if one or two planters do poor quality work. As well, planters resent those among them who make more money simply by planting large numbers of trees in a poor quality way. A planter who is known to do a sloppy job or who is

forced to replant an area might, for example, be nick-named "j-root."

Planters don't know when the checker will come by. If a planter "gets in good" with a checker, the checker may go easy when checking the planter's work. The checkers are themselves checked by other lumber company employees to ensure that they are doing reasonable quality control work. In turn, the lumber company is checked by the provincial government to see that trees are planted properly.

The Problem

Galt has been paying planters on a piece-rate basis for many years, but recently he has become very concerned about it because too many trees are improperly planted and die soon after planting. Galt thinks this is happening because planters are focussing on quantity at the expense of quality (they are so motivated by the money they can earn if they plant a lot of trees that they are doing sloppy work). At the end of last year's planting season, Galt was told in no uncertain terms by one lumber company that if he did not improve the quality of his tree planting, he would not get any more jobs.

The problem is significant enough that Galt has been thinking about dropping the piece-rate system and moving toward a "flat rate" system which would give planters a fixed amount of pay for each day's work. Galt thinks that this would cause planters to take more time and care when planting each tree since they would not have to worry about how much money they were going to make for the day. In the past, Galt has occasionally paid workers on a flat rate, particularly when the terrain was uneven. But this system is not problem-free either. For example, Galt gets the impression that when he pays on a flat-rate basis that planters don't work as hard, and they take more breaks. Galt also knows that planters *like* the piece rate system because they can make good money. The piece-rate system generates friendly competition among planters to see who can be the most productive. Those who plant the most trees have higher status among their peers, and they also earn more money. Overall, Galt thinks that this friendly competition increases the number of trees that are planted.

When the piece rate system is used, there is not much socializing among workers on the site, except when they are bagging up at the main cache at various times throughout the day. Socializing is generally seen as counterproductive because workers who stand around and talk aren't planting trees, and this reduces their pay.

As Galt considered all these facts, he wondered what he should do regarding the payment system he uses for planters.

▶▶▶

Questions for Discussion

1. What are the advantages and disadvantages of paying tree planters on a piece-rate system? On a flat-rate system?

2. Review the motivation theories in Chapter 10. What does each of those theories say (or imply) about Galt's idea of dropping the piece-rate system and paying planters a flat rate for each day of work?

3. Devise a payment system for tree planters that minimizes negative consequences. Describe the impact of your proposal on each of the following factors:

    - the motivation levels of the planters
    - the activities of the quality control checkers
    - the level of quality needed in tree planting
    - the needs of the lumber companies
    - Donald Galt's need to run a profitable company

4. What should Donald Galt do?

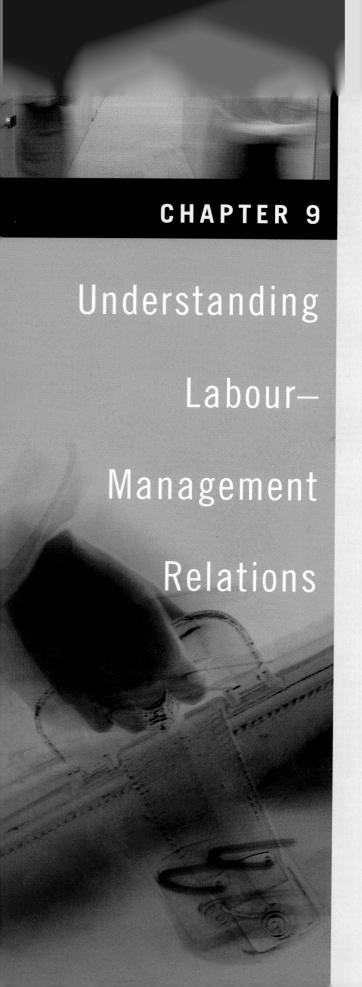

CHAPTER 9

Understanding Labour–Management Relations

After reading this chapter, you should be able to:

1 Explain why workers organize into *labour unions*.

2 Trace the evolution of unions and discuss *trends in unionism* in Canada.

3 Describe *the major laws governing labour–management relations*.

4 Describe the union *certification* and *decertification processes*.

5 Identify the steps in the *collective bargaining process*.

The Big Switcheroo

Vancouver City Savings Credit Union (Van City for short) is Canada's biggest credit union. With 41 branches, 2000 employees, and $9 billion in assets, it is hard to miss the Van City signs around Vancouver.

Dave Mowat is the CEO of the company, and he is a powerful man. Lisa Paille, who is a front-line worker in a suburban Van City branch, doesn't have any of Mowat's responsibilities, and she isn't so powerful. A company-wide contest picks Lisa Paille as the person who will switch jobs with Mowat. Here is the story of what happened when these two people switched jobs. Who will get the bigger reality check?

On her first day as CEO, Paille finds that her day is booked solid. Her first duty is conducting the head office manager's meeting. As Lisa conducts the meeting, she really feels that she has been put on the spot. She isn't doing well, and she keeps nervously looking at her notes as she speaks. Afterwards, her vice-presidents line up to meet with her, but by the time the finance vice-president shows up, she is running 30 minutes behind schedule. She is already looking weary and it's not even 1 p.m. Lisa doesn't have time to contact her family during the day, and when she arrives home, it is past her kids' bedtime.

Mowat isn't having an easy time of it on his first day, either. His first job is as a teller. He discovers that he is breaking dress rules by not wearing a tie (this violates the dress code which states that business attire is required). He is also experiencing front-line stress at the branch. The people who are waiting in line are impatient, and Mowat gets flustered trying to deal with them. He doesn't work fast enough. He doesn't get to go home until his money balances. He comes close (just 10 cents out). His day ends early, and he gets to eat dinner with his family while it is still daylight. That doesn't often happen when he stays late at work to attend to CEO duties.

On day 2, it's more of the same for Paille. It is difficult keeping the top executives in line, running meetings, and doing everything on time, but she is doing a little better today, and she actually finishes one meeting ahead of schedule. But later she gets behind schedule again. Lunch is sent in to save time, but Paille doesn't feel comfortable eating in front of the other managers. As she deals with her work backlog, she is learning that there is never an early end to a CEOs day. She heads to a company hockey game to boost morale, and talks on the phone during the game trying to reduce her work backlog.

On his second day, Mowat is answering the phones at the call centre. He has to act quickly and move on to other calls. But he spends about twice as long on each call as he is supposed to spend. He also discovers the stress of having his supervisor monitor his calls. Later in the day, he hustles business at Save-On Foods, a partner of Van City. His job is to sign up new customers.

On day 3, Lisa arrives at 8:45 a.m. and her day is again filled with appearances, ending with another speech to a group of managers. She also gladhands at the Vancouver Board of Trade (the Van City CEO is a member of the board). She is beginning to understand the importance of networking. She also speaks at an employee's anniversary party and presents him with a gift.

On his third day, Mowat starts at 6 a.m. in the Van City mail room. He delivers mail to all the offices, including the CEOs (where he observes that Paille is not yet in her office). He also does some information technology work by changing backup tapes. He finds that the process is complicated, and comments on how important the person doing that work is. Mowat does maintenance duties in the afternoon.

At the end of the three days, Lisa leaves the executive suite and returns to the front lines. Mowat puts down his tools and resumes his CEO duties. They both report on what they learned from their job switch. Paille says she enjoyed the experience, but she is glad it is over because she had to wear a lot of different hats. She has a new appreciation for how hectic and complex the work of a top manager is. Mowat feels that he did pretty well during the switch, but his productivity was judged as too low. He says he is impressed at how well the company's systems work.

Questions for Discussion

1. Briefly describe the four functions of management. Give several examples from the case of how the four functions of management are evident at Van City. Using the four functions of management as a basis, show how the jobs of Lisa Paille and Dave Mowat are different.

2. How are technical skills, human relations skills, and conceptual skills different? Explain the relative importance of each of these skills for a CEO like Dave Mowat and for a front-line worker like Lisa Paille. Give examples from the case to demonstrate the use of these skills.

3. Briefly summarize what Henry Mintzberg discovered about the work of CEOs. Was Lisa Paille's experience as the CEO consistent with what Mintzberg found? Give examples of how Lisa Paille performed some of the roles that Mintzberg identified.

4. What kind of insights do you think Mowat and Paille gained as a result of their switching jobs? To what extent will these insights make each of them more effective in their jobs? Defend your answer.

Source: "The Big Switcheroo," *Venture*, January 16, 2005.

Managing

Operations

and

Information

To be effective, Canadian business firms must produce high-quality goods and services. They must also have good information on which to base business decisions. The opening cases in the chapters in this section show how business firms do this.

Part Three, Managing Operations and Information, provides an overview of four aspects of business that are important to a firm's survival: the efficient production of goods and services, increasing productivity and quality, managing information systems, and understanding principles of accounting.

- We begin in **Chapter 11, Producing Goods and Services**, by examining how firms manage the production of goods and services, and how they control both the cost and the quality of their output.

- Then, in **Chapter 12, Increasing Productivity and Quality**, we consider the various approaches companies take to improve the productivity and the quality of their output, and thus their competitive position.

- Next, in **Chapter 13, Managing Information Systems and Communication Technology**, we describe the concept of management information systems, and how modern electronic technologies have revolutionized the work of managers. Included in this discussion is an analysis of the key elements of the information system, the concept of databases and application programs, and the importance of telecommunications and networks in the effective management of information.

- Finally, in **Chapter 14, Understanding Accounting Issues**, we examine the role of accountants in gathering, assembling, and presenting financial information about a firm. We also look at the tools accountants use and the statements they prepare to report a firm's financial standing.

CHAPTER 11

Producing

Goods and

Services

After reading this chapter, you should be able to:

1 Explain the meaning of the terms *production* and *operations*.

2 Describe the four kinds of *utility* provided by production and explain the two classifications of *operations processes*.

3 Identify the characteristics that distinguish *service operations* from *goods production* and explain the main differences in the *service focus*.

4 Describe the factors involved in *operations planning*.

5 Explain some factors in *operations scheduling* and describe some activities involved in *operations control*, including *materials management* and the use of certain *operations control tools*.

▶▶▶

Why are these non–Big Three carmakers moving to the southern United States? There are two key reasons. First, automakers want to reduce their overall costs. Since wage rates are a big consideration in overall costs, automakers have been looking for places where wages are lower. One of the places they have found is the southern United States. Almost all of these states also happen to have "right-to-work" laws. This means that no worker can be forced to join a union or pay union dues.

Second, the auto companies are receiving large financial incentives to move to the southern United States. For example, South Carolina shelled out $135 million in incentives to attract BMW, Mississippi gave incentives of $295 million to Nissan, and Alabama gave $253 million to Mercedes to locate there. These incentives include free land, infrastructure improvements, income tax deferrals, and money for training workers. Canadian unions and Canadian automobile executives say that Canadian provinces are being left behind because they won't give the kinds of incentives that are necessary to attract carmakers. Buzz Hargrove, the Canadian Auto Workers president, is upset that DaimlerChrysler decided to cancel plans for a new assembly plant in Windsor, which would have created 2500 jobs. He blamed the federal and Ontario governments for failing to provide monetary incentives that would have convinced DaimlerChrysler to build the new plant in Canada. In February 2003, the province of Ontario did set aside $625 million to help win investments in the province from DaimlerChrysler and Ford.

Late in 2005, the federal government announced that it would give hundreds of millions of dollars in new incentives to automobile companies if they would locate in Canada. After many years of largely resisting the provision of incentives, the government may now see them as a necessary evil. Even so, in early 2006 a Conservative minority government was elected, replacing the Liberals as the governing party. What effect this will have on the incentives strategy is unclear.

The movement of manufacturing to the southern United States isn't the only move south that is evident. Automakers have also set up assembly plants in South Africa, Brazil, and Thailand. The cars produced in these plants will supply markets in Japan, Europe, and North America. Until now, automakers thought that cars produced in these areas would not be well received by consumers in industrialized countries, but that is changing. BMW, for example, has poured hundreds of millions of dollars into its South African production facility. It says the cost of land, electricity, and labour is much lower there than in industrialized countries. A survey by J.D. Power & Associates found that the quality of cars produced at BMW's South African plant beat the quality of their cars produced in Germany and the United States.

Honda has begun making cars in Thailand and will ship them to its home market in Japan. Honda is also planning to build a new plant in China that will export much of its output. GM also builds a car in Thailand for export to Europe. Ford has built a plant in northeastern Brazil that will export mini-sport utility vehicles to the United States. All of these new plants have the latest technology and quality control systems. So far, the number of cars exported from these new plants is only a small proportion of total world car production, but that will increase steadily during the next decade.

Because the wages paid to workers in these overseas locations can be as little as one-tenth that paid to North American workers, the automakers have a strong incentive to move their operations. The low wages more than make up for the cost of shipping parts to these plants and then shipping the finished cars back to North America, Japan, or Europe.

Unions in North America and Europe are increasingly concerned that this trend will mean fewer high-paying jobs for their members. Buzz Hargrove is angry that Ford is planning to import the Fusion from Brazil when it is also planning to close a pickup truck plant in Canada. Ford says the numbers are so small that they won't reduce the number of union jobs. But Ford also notes that its plant in Brazil is its lowest-cost plant, and its quality is high; that could mean much higher production and export of vehicles in the future. Ford also noted that it will produce two new SUVs at a plant in Oakville, Ontario, beginning in 2006. These vehicles were originally scheduled to be produced in Atlanta, Georgia.

Questions for Discussion

1. Explain in your own words how trends in the worldwide automobile market are causing employment problems in automobile manufacturing in Ontario and Quebec. Can anything be done to reverse the trend? If not, explain why not. If something can be done, explain what that might be.

2. Explain how problems at companies like GM have impacted the operations of parts suppliers in Canada.

3. What do the problems in the automobile business (for both manufacturers and parts suppliers) imply for other parts of the economy that are not directly related to the automobile business? Explain.

4. Southern U.S. states like Alabama have given hundreds of millions of dollars in incentives to companies that agree to set up manufacturing plants there. Should the provinces of Ontario and Quebec be more active in giving the same type of incentives to maintain employment in automobile manufacturing in Canada? Defend your answer.

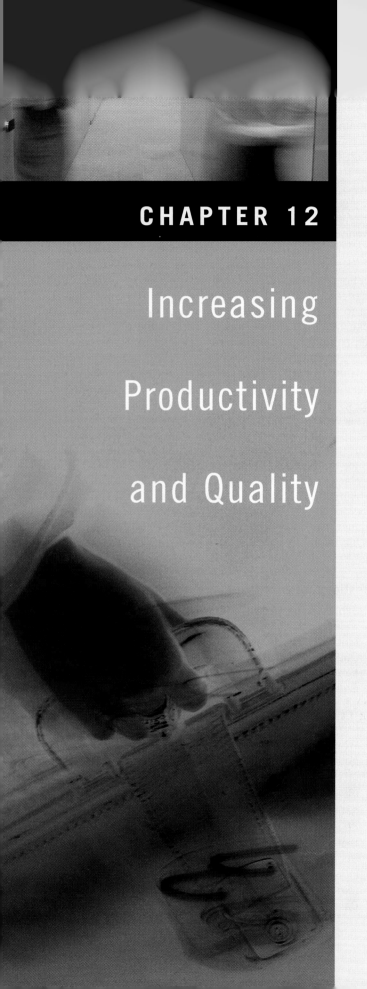

CHAPTER 12

Increasing Productivity and Quality

After reading this chapter, you should be able to:

1 Describe the connection between *productivity* and *quality*.

2 Understand the importance of increasing productivity.

3 Identify the activities involved in *total quality management* and describe six tools that companies can use to achieve it.

4 Identify three trends in productivity and quality management, including *supply chain management*.

5 Explain how a supply chain strategy differs from traditional strategies for coordinating operations among firms.

6 Discuss four strategies that companies use to improve productivity and quality.

During the past few years, considerable publicity has been given to the economic revolution that is taking place in China. With wage rates that are far below those in Canada, China has become a formidable competitor because it is such a low-cost producer of goods. The most obvious way to cope with this competitive threat is to reduce the number of hours of labour that are required to make a product, and thereby reduce the

product's cost. This is another way of saying that Canadian companies must increase labour productivity.

Growth rates in labour productivity (GDP per hour worked) vary across countries, and Canada has not fared well in recent years. In 2004, for example, Canadian labour productivity did not increase at all, while many other countries increased their labour productivity by 1.5–2.5 percent.

The productivity news is not all bad. In some industries—primary metals, wood products, construction, transport equipment, paper, and chemicals—Canadian productivity actually exceeds that of the United States. But in many other industries—including computers and electronics, fabricated metal products, textiles, furniture, retail trade, financial services, and electrical equipment—Canadian productivity lags far behind the United States.

Consider the case of the automobile industry. In 2005, Harbour Consulting ranked GM Canada's Oshawa no. 1 plant at the top of its list of most productive plants in North America. The plant, which makes Chevrolet Impalas and Monte Carlos, takes 15.85 hours to produce one car. The second most productive plant is a Nissan plant in Tennessee, which takes 15 minutes longer. Oshawa no. 2 plant was in fourth place at 17.47 hours.

But car manufacturing is a worldwide phenomenon, and car makers in Japan are even more efficient (productive) than North American car makers. In a worldwide comparison, using another benchmark, Nissan led the way, earning $1603 on the average vehicle, followed by Toyota ($1488), and Honda ($1250). Ford earned $620 and Chrysler just $186. GM *lost* $2311 on each vehicle it sold because of declining demand from consumers and high pension and health care costs.

But how can labour productivity be increased? As we saw in the Opening Case in Chapter 2, a variety of approaches have been suggested, including changes in tax policies that would encourage manufacturers to invest in more productive equipment. Consider the issue of capital cost allowance (CCA). In the United States, manufacturers are allowed to write off equipment much faster than in Canada. This means that U.S. companies pay less tax than Canadian companies. In Canada, Standen's Ltd. is a clear example of the disincentive that tax policy can create. The company, which produces truck springs, was considering buying an automotive springs plant in Wallaceburg, Ontario, but eventually decided it wouldn't make the purchase because the after-tax cost of the investment was too high. If Canadian tax laws allowed greater deductions for investment in machinery, the purchase would have been feasible.

But these suggestions are not without controversy. The Canadian Labour Congress, for example, accepts the importance of productivity and the need to increase it, but says there are good and bad ways to do that. A "bad" way, in their view, is to cut jobs, while a "good" way is to invest in innovation and employee training. The Information Technology Association of Canada says that U.S. companies in the information and communications technology sector spend more than twice as much per worker than Canadian companies do.

There is also debate about the role that managers play in this problem. Some people argue that Canadian managers are not expending enough energy or do not have enough imagination, and that is why Canadian productivity is lagging. But Jack Mintz, the head of the C.D. Howe Institute, says that Canadian managers are very good and are simply responding to their environment—in this case, the tax environment. Specifically, he notes that Canadian managers invest outside Canada because of lower tax rates on capital investment in other countries. He says that a comparison of 36 industrialized countries shows that Canada has the second-highest marginal tax rate on capital investment.

Of particular importance to Canadian businesses is the productivity comparison with their U.S. counterparts. While productivity comparisons with the much larger U.S. economy may seem unfair, Canada's immense trade with the United States makes such comparisons important. Output per hour in Canadian manufacturing was about 14 percent below the United States for the period 1977–94. Since 1994, the situation has actually worsened—output per hour in Canada was 29 percent lower than the United States in 2000 and 32 percent lower in 2001. Put another way, labour productivity growth was 3.8 *percentage points* higher in the United States than in Canada during the period 1994–2000.

To catch up to the United States, Canada will have to exceed the rate of productivity growth in the United States each year by about one percentage point for the next 15 years. One percentage point might not sound like much, but it would require Canadian industry to achieve an annual productivity growth rate of over 3 percent. That rate of productivity growth has been achieved only twice in Canada in the last 25 years.

When making productivity comparisons, we must be careful that we consider certain factors which may give one country an inherent advantage over another. For example, Canadian oil and gas producers are less productive than their U.S. counterparts. This is so partly because Canadian companies are spending large amounts of money developing expensive offshore and non-conventional oil sands deposits, while U.S. oil and gas producers continue to extract energy from wells that use technology that was developed long ago. Another example: Canadian retailers are less productive than U.S. retailers, partly because Wal-Mart has forced its U.S. competitors to cut costs to survive. This cost cutting does raise productivity and benefits *consumers*, but *employees* often suffer. One study showed that Wal-Mart workers earned 31 percent less than the average wage paid by large retailers, and that less than half of Wal-Mart's workers had health insurance.

A delicate balancing act is required to achieve higher productivity while not reducing worker well-being. Companies need to foster a competitive climate (which drives productivity growth) and at the same time promote social, environmental, and employee welfare. ◆

It is no secret that productivity and quality are watchwords in today's business. Companies are not only measuring productivity and insisting on improvements, but also insisting on quality so they can bring to market products that satisfy customers, improve sales, and boost profits. By focussing on the learning objectives of this chapter, you will better understand the increasingly important concepts of productivity and quality.

THE PRODUCTIVITY–QUALITY CONNECTION

1 Describe the connection between *productivity* and *quality*.

productivity A measure of efficiency that compares how much is produced with the resources used to produce it.

quality A product's fitness for use in terms of offering the features that consumers want.

Productivity is a measure of economic performance. It measures how much is produced relative to the resources used to produce it. The more we are able to produce the right things while using fewer resources, the more productivity grows and everyone—the economy, businesses, and workers—benefits.

Productivity considers both the amounts and the quality of what is produced. By using resources more efficiently, the quantity of output will be greater. But unless the resulting goods and services are of satisfactory quality (the "right things"), consumers will not want them. **Quality**, then, means fitness for use—offering features that consumers want.

Responding to the Productivity Challenge

As the opening case clearly shows, productivity has both international and domestic ramifications. Obviously, when one country is more productive than another, it will accumulate more wealth. Similarly, a nation whose productivity fails to increase as rapidly as that of competitor nations will see its standard of living fall.

It is important to understand the true meaning of *productivity* and to devise ways to measure it. Since *quality* must be defined in terms of value to the customer, companies must design their marketing efforts to cultivate a more customer-oriented focus. As quality-improvement practices are implemented, more and more firms will receive payoffs from these efforts. Four factors interact in this process: *customers*, *quality*, *productivity*, and *profits*.

Workers at this call centre in Bangalore, India, operated by ICICI OneSource, field calls from the customers of multinational firms headquartered in the United States and Europe. Global broadband makes this business model possible, so many of these jobs (30 000 in Canada) are outsourced to Indian service suppliers because workers get paid only a fraction of what Canadian workers would get. Even at that, they earn eight times as much as the average Indian earns per year ($450).

Measuring Productivity

How do we know how productive a country is? Most countries use **labour productivity** to measure their level of productivity:

$$\text{labor productivity of a country} = \frac{\text{gross domestic product}}{\text{total number of workers}}$$

labour productivity Partial productivity ratio calculated by dividing gross domestic product by total number of workers.

This equation reflects the general idea of productivity. It compares a country's total annual output of goods and services with the resources used to produce that output. The focus on labour, rather than on other resources (such as capital or energy), is preferred because most countries keep accurate records on employment and hours worked.

A 2005 Statistics Canada report showed that foreign-controlled manufacturing plants in Canada accounted for two-thirds of the growth in labour productivity during the period 1980–99. But the study emphasized that it wasn't the fact that the plants were foreign-controlled that led to higher productivity; rather, it was the extent to which the companies had an international orientation. In other words, Canadian producers that had foreign units were just as productive as foreign-owned plants. It seems that firms that compete internationally have more incentive to be more productive.[1]

Productivity Among Global Competitors

A study by the Organisation for Economic Co-operation and Development (OECD) reported on productivity levels in 23 participating countries. Figure 12.1 compares productivity among several OECD countries. As you can see, output per hour worked in Belgium is about 28 percent higher than the average for OECD members. At 31 percent below average, output in New Zealand is lowest among the nations listed in Figure 12.1.

A 2006 study by the U.S. Bureau of Labour Statistics showed that during 2003–04, Canada's output per hour increased by 2.9 percent. That was far less than the productivity growth in Korea (12.1 percent), Sweden (9.8 percent), and the United States (5.2 percent). The study also showed that over the longer-term (1979–2004), annual increases in Canadian productivity (2.6 percent) were less than annual productivity increases in other

Figure 12.1 International productivity comparisons.

countries such as the United States (4.1 percent), Sweden (4.7 percent), and Taiwan (5.7 percent).[2]

Why such differences from nation to nation? The answer lies in many factors: technologies, human skills, economic policies, natural resources—and even in traditions. Consider, for example, just one industrial sector—food production. In Japan, the food-production industry employs more workers than the automotive, computer, consumer electronics, and machine-tool industries combined. It is a fragmented, highly protected industry—and, compared with U.S. food production, it is extremely inefficient. The average U.S. worker produces 3.5 times as much food as his or her Japanese counterpart. Overall, data show that in the time it takes a U.S. worker to produce $100 worth of goods, Japanese workers produce about $68 worth. Belgian workers, on the other hand, produce $107 worth.[3]

According to Michael Porter, a Harvard University expert on international competitiveness, Canada's competitiveness is a concern because we have been living off our rich diet of natural resources. In Porter's view, Canada will have to start emphasizing innovation and develop a more sophisticated mix of products if it hopes to be successful in international markets. Porter criticizes Canadian business, government, and labour for failing to abandon outdated ways of thinking regarding productivity and innovation.[4]

Domestic Productivity

Nations must be concerned about domestic productivity regardless of their global standing. A country that improves its ability to make something out of its existing resources can increase the wealth of all its inhabitants. Conversely, a decline in productivity shrinks a nation's total wealth. When that happens, an increase in one person's wealth comes only at the expense of others with whom he or she shares an economic system.

For example, additional wealth from higher productivity can be shared among workers (as higher wages), investors (as higher profits), and customers (as stable prices). When productivity drops, however, wages can be increased only by reducing profits (penalizing investors) or by increasing prices (penalizing customers). It is understandable, then, that investors, suppliers, managers, and workers are all concerned about the productivity of specific industries and companies.

Manufacturing Versus Service Productivity

Manufacturing productivity is higher than service productivity. For many years, it was widely believed that the service sector suffered from "Baumol's disease," named after economist William Baumol who argued that since the service sector focussed more on hands-on activity that machines couldn't replace, it would be more difficult to increase productivity in services. Baumol, noted, for example, that it would always require four musicians to play a Mozart quartet. But the Opera company of Brooklyn is challenging Baumol's basic assumption. It now puts on the opera *The Marriage of Figaro* without the usual full orchestra. Instead, it uses just 12 musicians and a technician who oversees a computer program that plays all the other musical parts. The orchestra's productivity has increased sharply because it does not have to pay for the usual complement of musicians.[5]

Productivity gains are starting to appear among a wide array of service providers such as airlines, pet stores, package delivery companies, providers of financial services, and retail establishments. Many of these organizations have increased their productivity by becoming more like factories, and they use modern information technology to eliminate inefficiencies. Automated check-in kiosks in airports are a good example. Two-thirds of Northwest's passengers now check in using the kiosks.

Industry Productivity

In addition to differences between the manufacturing and service sectors, industries within these sectors differ vastly in terms of productivity. Agriculture is more productive in Canada than in many other nations because we use more sophisticated technology and superior natural resources. Technological advances have also given the computer industry a productivity edge in many areas. Steel manufacturing, which experienced significant problems in the 1970s and 1980s, has improved recently. For example, in the early 1980s, about 10 hours of labour were required to produce a tonne of steel. Now, only about four hours of labour are needed. One reason for the improvement is a new technology called continuous casting. Today, machines can turn molten metal into slabs that can be processed while still red-hot. It is no longer necessary to cool the steel, strip off the moulding, and then reheat it for processing. This new process has meant immense savings in both labour and energy.[6]

In an effort to increase productivity, Canfor Corp. developed a system called Genus, which it is using to manage its forestry operations. Genus, a computerized database containing geographic information and other essential data about Canfor's vast lumber and pulp operations in British Columbia and Alberta, will be used as a strategic planning tool to determine how the company should adjust its logging plans to reflect both market demand and logging regulations laid down by the Forest Practices Code of British Columbia Act.[7]

The productivity of specific industries concerns many people for different reasons. Labour unions need to take it into account in negotiating contracts, since highly productive industries can give raises more easily than can less productive industries. Investors and suppliers consider industry

Understand the importance of increasing productivity.

2

On the left, workers assemble a truck the old way, manually lowering and bolting frames onto axles. On the right, the process is highly automated (and safer), with robotic grippers to flip and align the bulky frames.

productivity when making loans, buying securities, and planning their own future production.

Company Productivity

High productivity gives a company a competitive edge because its costs are lower. As a result, it can offer its product at a lower price (and gain more customers), or it can make a greater profit on each item sold. Increased productivity also allows companies to pay workers higher wages without raising prices.

The productivity of individual companies is also important to investors, workers, and managers. Comparing the productivity of several companies in the same industry helps investors in buying and selling stocks. Employee profit-sharing plans are often based on the company's productivity improvements each year. And managers use information about productivity trends to plan for new products, factories, and funds to stay competitive in the years ahead.

TOTAL QUALITY MANAGEMENT

It is no longer enough for businesses to simply measure productivity in terms of the numbers of items produced. They must also take quality into account. In the decades after the Second World War, business consultant W. Edwards Deming tried to persuade firms in North America that they needed to improve quality at least as much as quantity. He wasn't very successful, but his arguments won over the Japanese. Through years of meticulous hard work, Japan's manufacturers have changed "Made in Japan" from a synonym for cheap, shoddy merchandise into a hallmark of reliability. More recently, North American firms have been doing much better in the quality area. In 2006, for example, J.D. Power & Associates ranked GM's

Oshawa No. 2 plant—which produces the Buick Allure and the Pontiac Grand Prix—as highest in quality out of 80 assembly plants in North America. The Oshawa No. 2 plant has won this award several times. Another example of an attempt to convey quality and accountability to consumers is described in the Business Accountability box.

Quality advocates such as Joseph Juran and Kaoru Ishikawa introduced methods and tools for implementing quality. Juran's "Quality Trilogy"—quality planning, quality control, and quality improvement—was the first structured process for managing quality. It identifies management steps for ensuring quality. In addition to management actions, Juran, like Deming and Ishikawa, championed the idea of company-wide employee participation. These theorists also developed quality tools for day-to-day work activities because they knew that without employee participation, real quality improvement would never happen. Ishikawa, for example, developed so-called "fishbone diagrams," also known as "cause-and-effect diagrams" or "Ishikawa

BUSINESS ACCOUNTABILITY

Rating the Quality of Diamonds

How do you rate the quality of diamonds? Historically, diamond quality has been assessed by reference to 4 C's: *cut*, *colour*, *clarity*, and *carat*. But perhaps a fifth C is emerging, and that is "country of origin." Better yet, the fifth C may also stand for "Canada."

Until just a few years ago, Canada was not even a player in the international diamond business. But in 1991, a promising diamond field was located in the Northwest Territories and the race was on to exploit the possibilities. Skeptics said that even if diamonds were found in commercial quantities in Canada, the diamonds would have to be sold to DeBeers, the company that controlled the world diamond trade. But once diamond wholesalers were shown the first Canadian diamonds, they realized that the quality was as high as that from the best diamond mines in the world, and they eagerly bought them. The myth of DeBeers control soon evaporated.

The first Canadian diamond mine was opened in the Northwest Territories in 1998, and by 2003 it was already producing 6 percent of the total world's supply of rough diamonds. A second mine opened in 2003, and another is scheduled for 2006. By that time, Canada will produce 12 percent of the world's diamonds. There are also promising developments in diamond mining in Saskatchewan, where core samples drilled by Shore Gold show that high quality diamonds exist there.

In recent years, there has been much negative press about so-called "blood diamonds," that is, diamonds that were mined by armed workers in war-torn African countries like Botswana. These diamonds were then exported, and the money used to support further military campaigns. The developing Canadian diamond industry has no such image problems. Diamonds in Canada are mined under very ethical and environmentally strict conditions. And there's one added advantage: The quality of Canadian diamonds is very high. Canadian rough diamonds average $170 per carat in value, far above the $100 level at which diamonds are considered precious. The new samples from Saskatchewan are valued at about U.S.$135 per carat.

But is country of origin important enough to influence consumers when they purchase a diamond? In the minds of many consumers, the quality of certain products *is* associated with the product's country of origin. Think, for example, of Swiss watches, Italian leather, and French wines. Oren Sofer, CEO of diamond wholesaler Beny Sofer & Sons LLC, says that if you can brand water, you certainly should be able to brand diamonds. He wants consumers to eventually recognize "Canadian diamonds" as an important brand name.

This is not an impossible goal. The move is already underway to establish a high quality reputation for Canadian diamonds. Sirius Diamond Inc., a Vancouver diamond wholesaler, engraves a tiny polar bear on the Canadian diamonds it sells, and Birks & Sons Inc. engraves a maple leaf on its diamonds. The government of the Northwest Territories provides a certificate for each diamond that has come from its mines. This ensures that diamonds from other countries cannot be passed off as Canadian stones.

diagrams," that help teams of employees investigate and track down causes of quality problems in their work areas. The diagram in Figure 12.2, for instance, was designed to help an airport manager find out why his facility had so many delayed departures. Focussing on five major categories of possible causes, he then noted several potential causes of the problem in each. (It turns out that there weren't enough tow trucks to handle baggage transfers.)[8]

Managing for Quality

total quality management (TQM)
A concept that emphasizes that no defects are tolerable and that all employees are responsible for maintaining quality standards.

Total quality management (TQM) (sometimes called *quality assurance*) includes all the activities necessary for getting high-quality goods and services into the marketplace. It must consider all parts of the business, including customers, suppliers, and employees. TQM emphasizes that no defects are tolerable, and that employees are responsible for maintaining quality standards. At Toyota's Cambridge, Ontario, plant, for example, workers can push a button or pull a rope to stop the production line when something is not up to standard.[9]

The strategic approach to TQM begins with leadership and the desire for TQM. This approach involves getting people's attention, getting them to think in an entirely new way about what they do, and then getting them to improve both processes and products.[10]

Customer focus is the starting point. Companies must develop methods for determining what customers want, and then direct all their resources toward fulfillment of those needs to gain greater customer satisfaction. Total participation is mandatory. Unless all employees are working toward improved quality, the firm is wasting potential contributions from its human resources, and is missing a chance to become a stronger competitor in the marketplace. TQM in today's competitive markets demands unending and continuous improvement of products, after-sales services, and all of the company's internal processes, such as accounting, delivery, billing, and information flow.

Says John Kay, director of Oxford University's School of Management: "You can't run a successful company if you don't care about customers and

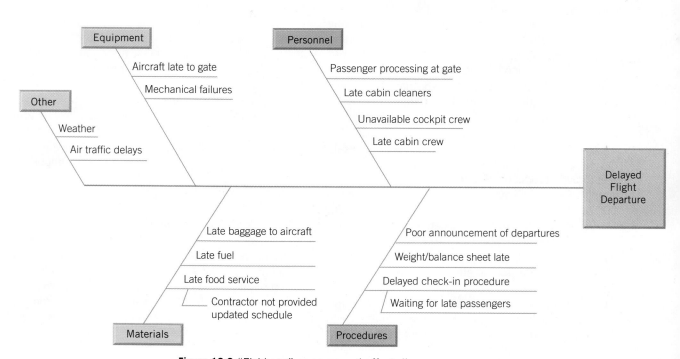

Figure 12.2 "Fishbone" or cause-and-effect diagram.

employees, or if you are systematically unpleasant to suppliers."[11] To bring the interests of all these stakeholders together, TQM involves planning, organizing, directing, and controlling.

Successful use of TQM requires a high level of commitment from all members of the organization. Consider the case of Standard Aero in Winnipeg, which is in the business of aircraft overhaul. When the company instituted TQM, the process began with the formation of a "change council" consisting of the CEO and five senior managers. This council ensured that the TQM initiative received the money, equipment, and support it needed for success. Next, a nine-person task force was formed that consisted of employees who had done the full range of jobs on one of Standard's major overhaul contracts. Its first job was to find out what the customer wanted. It did this by designing a questionnaire and visiting customer plants around the world to gather information. The task force also worked within Standard Aero to determine exactly how the company did its aircraft overhaul work. After weeks of analysis, the task force was able to significantly reduce the time required for overhaul work. For example, the number of times a certain gearbox was handled as it moved through the repair process was reduced by 84 percent.[12]

Planning for Quality

Planning for quality should begin before products are designed or redesigned. Managers need to set goals for both quality levels and quality reliability in the beginning. **Performance quality** refers to the features of a product and how well it performs. For example, Maytag gets a price premium because its washers and dryers offer a high level of performance quality. Customers perceive Maytag as having more advanced features and being more durable than other brands. (Everyone knows that the Maytag repairman is a lonely and idle person.)

performance quality The overall degree of quality; how well the features of a product meet consumers' needs and how well the product performs.

Performance quality may or may not be related to quality reliability in a product. **Quality reliability** refers to the consistency or repeatability of performance. Toyota's small cars may not equal the overall quality level or have the luxury features of Rolls Royce; consequently, Toyota's prices are much lower. But Toyotas have high quality reliability. The firm has a reputation for producing very few "lemons."

quality reliability The consistency of quality from unit to unit of a product.

Organizing for Quality

Perhaps most important to the quality concept is the belief that producing quality goods and services requires an effort from all parts of the organization. The old idea of a separate "quality control" department is no longer enough. Everyone—from the chairperson of the board to the part-time clerk-purchasers, engineers, janitors, marketers, machinists, and other personnel—must work to ensure quality. In Germany's Messerschmitt-Boelkow-Blohm aerospace company, for example, all employees are responsible for inspecting their own work. The overall goal is to reduce eventual problems to a minimum by making the product correctly from the beginning. The same principle extends to teamwork practice at Heinz Co., where teams of workers are assigned to inspect virtually every activity in the company. Heinz has realized substantial cost savings by eliminating waste and rework.

At Motorola, the concept of teamwork as a key to organizational quality has resulted in an international event called the Total Customer Satisfaction Team Competition. Teams are composed of Motorola employees and also include customers and outside suppliers. Teams are judged on their success not only in promoting productivity but also in sharing innovative ideas with people both inside and outside the company.

Although everyone in a company contributes to product quality, responsibility for specific aspects of total quality management is often assigned to specific departments and jobs. In fact, many companies have quality assurance, or quality control, departments staffed by quality experts. These people may be called in to help solve quality-related problems in any of the firm's other departments. They keep other departments informed of the latest developments in equipment and methods for maintaining quality. In addition, they monitor all quality control activities to identify areas for improvement.

Leading for Quality

Too often, firms fail to take the initiative to make quality happen. Leading for quality means that managers must inspire and motivate employees throughout the company to achieve quality goals. They need to help employees see how they affect quality and how quality affects their jobs and their company. Leaders must continually find ways to foster a quality orientation by training employees, encouraging their involvement, and tying wages to quality of work. If managers succeed, employees will ultimately accept **quality ownership**—the idea that quality belongs to each person who creates or destroys it while performing a job.

> **quality ownership** The concept that quality belongs to each employee who creates or destroys it in producing a good or service; the idea that all workers must take responsibility for producing a quality product.

General Electric Co. embarked on a strong quality control initiative a few years ago. Top management commitment to the program was ensured by tying executive bonuses to actual implementation of the quality control program. The program involves training managers to be "Black Belts" in quality improvement. These Black Belts then spent their time in GE plants setting up quality improvement projects. Young managers were told that they wouldn't have much of a future at GE unless they became Black Belts.

Controlling for Quality

By monitoring its products and services, a company can detect mistakes and make corrections. To do so, however, managers must first establish specific quality standards and measurements. Consider the following control system for a bank's teller services. Observant supervisors periodically evaluate transactions against a checklist. Specific aspects of each teller's work—appearance, courtesy, efficiency, and so on—are recorded. The results, reviewed with employees, either confirm proper performance or indicate changes that are needed to bring performance up to standards.

In the auto industry, a key measure of quality is the number of recalls. By this standard, there's room for improvement in total quality management at General Motors, which recalled 7.5 million vehicles in the first quarter of 2004 alone. GM says that it is being proactive and dealing with potential problems to build consumer confidence.

TOOLS FOR TOTAL QUALITY MANAGEMENT

In managing for quality, many leading companies rely on assistance from proven tools. Often, ideas for improving both the product and the production process come from **competitive product analysis**. For example, Toshiba will take apart a Xerox photocopier and test each component. Test results help Toshiba's managers decide which Toshiba product features are satisfactory (in comparison to the competition), which product features need to be upgraded, or whether Toshiba's production processes need improvement.

There are many specific tools that can be used to achieve TQM. Here, we briefly describe the following: *value-added analysis, statistical process control, quality/cost studies, quality improvement teams, benchmarking, getting closer to the customer, ISO 9000, re-engineering,* and *adding value through supply chains.*

competitive product analysis Process by which a company analyzes a competitor's products to identify desirable improvements.

Value-Added Analysis

Value-added analysis refers to the evaluation of all work activities, material flows, and paperwork to determine the value that they add for customers. It often reveals wasteful or unnecessary activities that can be eliminated without jeopardizing customer service. The basic tenet is so important that Tootsie Roll Industries, the venerable candy company, employs it as a corporate principle: "We run a trim operation and continually strive to eliminate waste, minimize cost, and implement performance improvements.[13]

value-added analysis The evaluation of all work activities, material flows, and paperwork to determine the value they add for customers.

Statistical Process Control

Although every company would like complete uniformity in its outputs, all firms experience unit-to-unit variations in their products. Companies can gain better control, however, by understanding the sources of variation. **Statistical process control (SPC)** methods—especially process variation studies and control charts—allow managers to analyze variations in production data.

statistical process control (SPC) Statistical analysis techniques that allow managers to analyze variations in production data and to detect when adjustments are needed to create products with high quality reliability.

process variation Any change in employees, materials, work methods, or equipment that affects output quality.

Process Variation

Variations in a firm's products may arise from the inputs in its production process. As people, materials, work methods, and equipment change, so do production outputs. While some amount of **process variation** is acceptable, too much can result in poor quality and excessive operating costs. Consider the box-filling operation for Honey Nuggets cereal. Each automated machine fills two 400-gram boxes per second. Even under proper conditions, slight variations in cereal weight from box to box are normal. Equipment and tools wear out, the cereal may be overly moist, and machinists make occasional adjustments. But how much variation is occurring? How much is acceptable?

Information about variation in a process can be obtained from a *process capability study.* Boxes are taken from the filling machines and weighed. The results are plotted, as in Figure 12.3, and compared with the

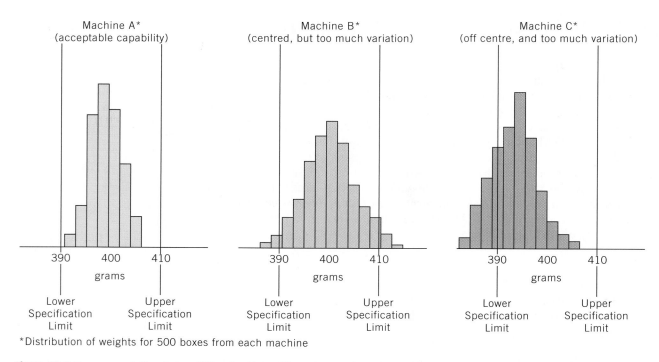

Machine A*
(acceptable capability)

Machine B*
(centred, but too much variation)

Machine C*
(off centre, and too much variation)

*Distribution of weights for 500 boxes from each machine

Figure 12.3 Process variation in box filling for Honey Nuggets cereal.

upper and lower specification limits (quality limits) for weight. These limits define good and bad quality for box filling. Boxes with more than 410 grams are a wasteful "giveaway." Underfilling has a cost because it is unlawful.

The chart in Figure 12.3 reveals that Machine A's output is acceptable because none of its boxes violate the quality limits. Machine A, then, is fully capable of meeting the company's quality standards. Machines B and C, however, have problems. In their present condition, they are not "capable" because they cannot reliably meet Honey Nuggets' quality standards. The company must take special—and costly—actions to sort the good from the bad boxes before releasing the cereal for shipment. Unless machines B and C are renovated, substandard production quality will plague Honey Nuggets.

Control Charts

Knowing that a process is capable of meeting quality standards is not enough. Managers must still monitor the process to prevent its drifting astray during production. To detect the beginning of bad conditions, managers can check production periodically and plot the results on a **control chart**. For example, several times a day a machine operator at Honey Nuggets might weigh several boxes of cereal together to ascertain the average weight.

Figure 12.4 shows the control chart for machine A, in which the first five points are randomly scattered around the centre line, indicating that the machine was operating well. However, the points for samples 5 through 8 are all above the centre line, indicating that something was causing the boxes to overfill. The last point falls outside the upper *control limit*, confirming that the process is out of control.

At this point, the machine must be shut down so that a manager and/or the operator can investigate what is causing the problem—equipment, people, materials, or work methods. Control is completed by correcting the problem and restoring the process to normal.

control chart A statistical process control method in which results of test sampling of a product are plotted on a diagram that reveals when the process is beginning to depart from normal operating conditions.

Figure 12.4 Honey Nuggets cereal process control chart for machine A.

Quality/Cost Studies

Statistical process controls help keep operations up to existing capabilities. But in today's competitive environment, firms must consistently raise quality capabilities. However, any improvement in products or production processes means additional costs, whether for new facilities, equipment, training, or other changes. Managers thus face the challenge of identifying those improvements that offer the greatest promise. **Quality/cost studies** are useful because they not only identify a firm's current costs but also reveal areas with the largest cost-savings potential.[14]

Quality costs are associated with making, finding, repairing, or preventing defective goods and services. All of these costs should be analyzed in a quality/cost study. For example, Honey Nuggets must determine its costs for **internal failures**. These are expenses—including the costs of overfilling boxes and the costs of sorting out bad boxes—incurred during production and before bad products leave the plant. Studies indicate that many manufacturers incur very high costs for internal failures—up to 50 percent of total costs.

Despite quality control procedures, however, some bad boxes may get out of the factory, reach the customer, and generate complaints from grocers and cereal eaters. These are **external failures** that occur outside the factory. The costs of correcting them—refunds to customers, transportation costs to return bad boxes to the factory, possible lawsuits, factory recalls—should also be tabulated in the quality/cost study.

Quality Improvement Teams

Quality improvement (QI) teams are groups of employees from various work areas who meet regularly to define, analyze, and solve common production problems. Their goal is to improve both their own work methods and the products they make.[15] Many QI teams organize their own work, select leaders, and address problems in the workplace. Motorola sponsors company-wide team competitions to emphasize the value of the team approach, to recognize outstanding team performance, and to reaffirm the team's role in the company's continuous-improvement culture. Teams get higher marks for dealing with projects closely tied to Motorola's key

quality/cost study A method of improving product quality by assessing a firm's current quality-related costs and identifying areas with the greatest cost-saving potential.

internal failures Expenses incurred during production and before bad products leave the plant.

external failures Allowing defective products to leave the factory and get into consumers' hands.

quality improvement (QI) team TQM tool in which groups of employees work together to improve quality.

initiatives. Over the years, competing teams have increased cellular phone production by 50 percent and cut electronic-circuit defects by 85 percent (for a one-year savings of $1.8 million).[16]

Benchmarking

benchmarking Comparing the quality of the firm's output with the quality of the output of the industry's leaders.

A powerful TQM tool that has been effective for some firms is called **benchmarking**. To improve its own products or its business procedures, a company compares its current performance against its own past performance, or one company finds and implements the best practices of others. With *internal benchmarking*, a firm tracks its own performance over time to evaluate its progress and to set goals for further improvement. As an example, the percentage of customer phone calls with more than two minutes of response time may be 15 percent this month. Compared with past months, this percentage may be high or low. In short, past performance is the benchmark for evaluating recent results.

External benchmarking begins with a critical review of competitors (or even companies in other lines of business) to determine which goods or services perform the best; these activities and products are called *best practices*. For example, Toronto Hospital gathered performance data on 26 indicators from various Canadian hospitals so that it could determine how well it was performing compared with other organizations in the health-care industry.[17] Executives from Ford, DaimlerChrysler, and General Motors frequently tour Toyota manufacturing facilities as they try to figure out how Toyota makes cars so efficiently.

Getting Closer to the Customer

As one advocate of quality improvement has put it, "Customers are an economic asset. They're not on the balance sheet, but they should be." One of the themes of this chapter has been that struggling companies have often lost sight of customers as the driving force for all business activity. Perhaps they waste resources designing products that customers do not want.

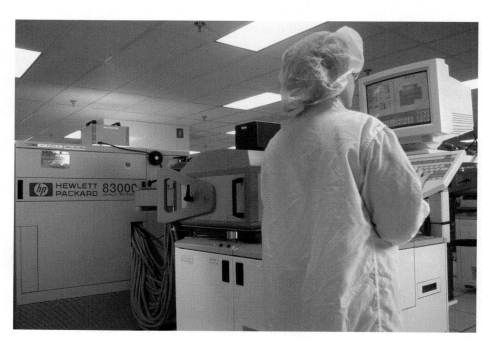

At Hewlett-Packard, testing machines use tiny probes to ensure that the electronic characteristics of every semiconductor are correct. Such systems are designed to check primarily for so-called "class defects"—problems that can affect a whole range of products on the assembly line. One bad wafer at the end of the line can represent a waste of $10 000 in costs, and its commercial value is zero.

Sometimes they ignore customer reactions to existing products or fail to keep up with changing consumer tastes. By contrast, the most successful businesses keep close to their customers and know what they want in the products they consume.

Some years ago at Greyhound Lines of Canada, the marketing and operations vice-president wanted to drive home the point to managers that clean restrooms were important to customers. He warned regional managers that he would visit bus depots on one-hour's notice to see if the restrooms were clean enough to eat dinner in. Within weeks, photos of regional managers having dinner in spotless restrooms began pouring in to the vice-president's office.[18]

Caterpillar Financial Services won the 2003 Malcolm Baldrige National Quality Award for high ratings by its customers, including dealers and buyers of Caterpillar equipment. Construction companies buying and financing equipment from Cat Financial are better satisfied, as Cat has moved its services increasingly online. Customers, who buy equipment costing anywhere from $30 000 to $2 million, now have 24-hour-a-day access to information on how much they owe and they can make payments around the clock, too. In the past, any of the 60 000 customers had to phone a Cat representative who was often unavailable, resulting in customer delays and wasted time on unsuccessful calls. Praise for the improved online system, and announcement of the quality award, is testimony to Cat Financial's dedication in knowing what customers want, and then providing it.[19]

| Identify three trends in productivity and quality management, including *supply chain management*. | **4** |

ISO 9000:2000 and ISO 14000

After the terrorist attacks in the United States in 2001, the U.S. Transportation Security Administration embarked on a mission to prevent terrorist attacks on U.S transportation systems. A unit known as AAR-500 was given responsibility for bolstering security at American airports. AAR-500 recognized a major quality problem: the need to train and certify individual employees to perform specific tasks in a revamped screening system. To train 28 000 new airport security personnel, AAR-500 turned to international quality standards that had been applied successfully in private service businesses. To instill public confidence in the new screening system, AAR-500 also adopted the principle of independent third-party certification of the system.[20]

Both the training and certification systems were based on the world-class standards of **ISO 9000**—a certification program attesting to the fact that a factory, a laboratory, or an office has met the rigorous quality management requirements set by the International Organization for Standardization. ISO 9000 (pronounced *ICE-o nine thousand*) originated in Europe to standardize materials received from suppliers in such high-technology industries as electronics, chemicals, and aviation. Today, more than 140 countries have adopted ISO 9000 as a national standard. More than 400 000 certificates have been issued in 160 countries.[21]

ISO 9000 Program certifying that a factory, laboratory, or office has met the quality management standards of the International Organization for Standardization.

The latest version, *ISO 9000:2000*, indicates that it was revised in 2000. Revised standards allow firms to show that they follow documented procedures for testing products, training workers, keeping records, and fixing defects. To become certified, companies must document the procedures followed by workers during every stage of production. The purpose is to ensure that a manufacturer's product is exactly the same today as it was yesterday and as it will be tomorrow. Ideally, standardized processes would ensure that goods are produced at the same level of quality even if all employees were replaced by a new set of workers.

ISO 14000 Certification program attesting to the fact that a factory, laboratory, or office has improved environmental performance.

The **ISO 14000** program certifies improvements in *environmental* performance. Extending the ISO approach into the arena of environmental protection and hazardous waste management, ISO 14000 requires a firm to develop an *environmental management system (EMS)*: a plan documenting how the company has acted to improve its performance in using resources (such as raw materials) and in managing pollution. A company must not only identify hazardous wastes that it expects to create, but it must also stipulate plans for treatment and disposal. ISO 14000 covers practices in environmental labelling—the use of such terms as *energy efficient* and *recyclable*—and assesses the total environmental impact of the firm's products, not just from manufacturing, but also from use and disposal.

Process Re-engineering

Every business consists of *processes*—activities that it performs regularly and routinely in conducting business. Examples abound: receiving and storing materials from suppliers, billing patients for medical treatment, filing insurance claims for auto accidents, inspecting property for termites, opening chequing accounts for new customers, filling customer orders from internet sales. Any business process can add value and customer satisfaction by performing processes well. By the same token, any business can disappoint customers and irritate business partners by managing them poorly.

business process re-engineering Redesigning of business processes to improve performance, quality, and productivity.

Business process re-engineering focusses on improving both the productivity and quality of business processes—rethinking each step of an organization's operations by starting from scratch. *Re-engineering* is the fundamental rethinking and radical redesign of business processes to achieve dramatic improvements in measures of performance, such as cost, quality, service, and speed.[22] The calling-services company GTE, for example, found that its over-the-phone service was not user-friendly for customers wanting to correct service or billing problems. To provide fast, accurate one-stop service, GTE re-engineered the whole service process by improving equipment, retraining employees, and connecting software to formerly inaccessible corporate databases.

The Re-engineering Process

Figure 12.5 shows the six steps involved in the re-engineering process. It starts with a statement of the benefits envisioned for customers and the company and then flows logically through the next five steps:

1. Identify the business activity that will be changed.

2. Evaluate information and human resources to see if they can meet the requirements for change.

3. Diagnose the current process to identify its strengths and weaknesses.

4. Create the new process design.

5. Implement the new design.

As you can see, re-engineering is a broad undertaking that requires know-how in technical matters, depends on leadership and management skills, and calls upon knowledge about customer needs and how well they are being met by the company and its competition. The bottom line in every re-engineering process is adopting a company-wide, customer-first philosophy. Redesign is guided by a desire to improve operations so that goods and services are produced at the lowest possible cost and at the highest value for the customer.

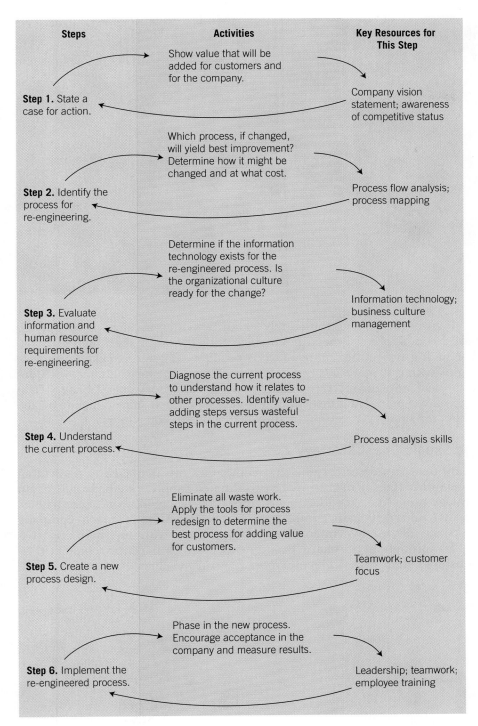

Figure 12.5 Re-engineering process.

Explain how a supply chain strategy differs from traditional strategies for coordinating operations among firms.

5

Adding Value Through Supply Chains

Managers sometimes forget that a company belongs to a network of firms that must coordinate their activities. The term *supply chain* refers to the group of companies and stream of activities that work together to create a product. A **supply chain** for any product is the flow of information, materials, and services that starts with raw-materials suppliers and continues through other stages in the operations process until the product reaches the end customer.[23]

supply chain Flow of information, materials, and services that starts with raw materials suppliers and continues through other stages in the operations process until the product reaches the end customer.

Seagate Technology, a maker of computer hard drives, used to build everything itself—disks, motors for spinning disks, and tracking mechanisms for reading and writing on disks. But it needed factories in Malaysia, Ireland, and the United States, each with its own supplies of inventory. Seagate wasn't flexible enough to respond to changes required by customers until it teamed up with a consulting firm called DesignShop and figured out how to reorganize itself. Now, company-wide operations are run by a computer-based planning system, the supplier list has been slashed, and even important components are being outsourced.

Figure 12.6 shows the supply chain activities involved in supplying baked goods to consumers. Each stage adds value for the final customer. Although a typical beginning stage is product design, our bakery example begins with raw materials (grain harvested from the farm). It also includes additional storage and transportation activities, factory operations for baking and wrapping, and distribution to retailers. Each stage depends on the others for success in getting fresh-baked goods to consumers.

The Supply Chain Strategy

Traditional strategies assume that companies are managed as individual firms rather than as members of a coordinated supply system. Supply chain strategy is based on the idea that members of the chain, working as a coordinated unit, will gain competitive advantage. Although each company looks out for its own interests, it works closely with suppliers and customers throughout the chain. Everyone focusses on the entire chain of relationships rather than on just the next stage in the chain.[24]

Figure 12.6 Supply chain for baked goods.

A traditionally managed bakery, for example, would focus simply on getting production inputs from flour millers and paper suppliers and supplying baked goods to distributors. Unfortunately, this approach limits the chain's performance and doesn't allow for possible improvements when activities are more carefully coordinated. Supply chain management can improve performance and, as a result, provide higher quality at lower prices.

Supply Chain Management

Supply chain management (SCM) looks at the chain as a whole to improve the overall flow through a system composed of companies working together. Because customers ultimately get better value, SCM gains competitive advantage for each supply-chain member.[25] Dell Computer's supply chain, for example, improves performance by allowing people to share information. Dell shares long-term production plans and up-to-the-minute sales data with suppliers via the internet. The process starts when customer orders are automatically translated into updated production schedules on the factory floor. These schedules are used not only by operations managers at Dell but also by such parts suppliers as Sony, which adjust their own production and shipping activities to better meet Dell's production needs. In turn, parts suppliers' updated schedules are transmitted to their materials suppliers, and so on. As Dell's requirements

supply chain management (SCM) Principle of looking at the chain as a whole to improve the overall flow through the system.

ENTREPRENEURSHIP AND NEW VENTURES

Ship Shape

Twice a year, Vanguard Global Services Inc. conducts a formal review of each of its customers' logistics processes in a search for greater efficiencies. And chances are the review will save clients time or money. "We're in a dynamic environment," says Richard Court, CEO of the cross-border logistics firm based in Mississauga, Ont. "Our capabilities and resources change, our customers' needs change, and the marketplace changes." For example, by harnessing economies of scale created by one client's fast-growing shipment volume, Vanguard was able to offer a $300 000 price reduction. While some might say Vanguard left money on the table, Court says, "The customer was thrilled."

Such initiative has won Vanguard the hearts and wallets of such customers as Sony, Hitachi, and Psion Teklogix, helping Vanguard's sales climb from $212 894 in 2000 to $12.5 million in 2005—an increase of 5774 percent in the face of trade-stifling events such as the September 11 terrorist attacks and the rise of the Canadian dollar.

Court and his two partners, Mark Bates and Edward Ayranto—who together have more than 50 years in the shipping business—launched Vanguard in 1999 to provide customized cross-border transportation services. Their focus is high-volume shippers in the automotive and electronics sectors. And their timing has been perfect: As trade between Canada and the United States gets more complicated, companies are

becoming more likely to outsource shipping. Those same companies can hardly ignore Vanguard's promise of customized service for 10 percent to 50 percent less than its rivals charge.

Such savings result partly from Vanguard's preference for long-term relationships with clients. It gives Vanguard the option of performing a complex analysis of a customer's supply chain, which leads to a formal report that explains how the movement of goods can be streamlined and that quantifies the benefits.

Court says learning the ins and outs of a customer's operation typically takes three months to a year, but the effort seems to be worth it. Vanguard recently applied its magic to a handheld electronics manufacturer that had no control over shipping costs or when parts would arrive, due to its dependence on a multitude of suppliers that controlled their own shipping. Vanguard cut the firm's transportation costs by 30 percent by assuming responsibility for all shipments, leveraging economies of scale, and even providing pre-printed labels and waybills to the suppliers.

Not content to rest on its laurels, Vanguard is accelerating growth. The firm recently moved from a 40 000-sq.-ft. warehouse to a state-of-the-art 65 000-sq.-ft. facility, and is investing in warehousing systems and technology that will improve the visibility and control of shipments. "We are expanding our capabilities and increasing our capacity," says Court. "It's all part of moving to provide the whole product for our customer."

Before too long, you will be able to pick up an item from a Wal-Mart shelf and scan it automatically on to your debit card, skipping the checkout line altogether. The same technology—called radio frequency identification (RFID)—will signal the Wal-Mart storeroom to restock the item you bought.

change, suppliers synchronize their schedules to produce the right materials and parts efficiently.

Because the smooth flow of accurate information along the chain reduces unwanted inventories, avoids delays, and cuts supply times, materials move faster to business customers and individual consumers. For both, the efficiency of SCM means faster deliveries and lower costs than customers could get if each member acted only according to its own operations requirements.

Re-engineering Supply Chains for Better Results

By lowering costs, speeding up service, or coordinating flows of information and materials, process improvements and re-engineering often improve supply chains. Consider, for example, the supply chain for transistor radios. For a long time, Li & Fung, the largest export trading company in Hong Kong, imported radio components made in both the United States and Asia. After supplying these components to a Hong Kong assembly factory, Li & Fung shipped finished radios to U.S. and European distributors. Gradually, however, rising wage rates in Hong Kong became a threat to Li & Fung. Increases in assembly costs would cut into its profits and market share. The company thus re-engineered its supply chain. First, it added a new stage. It created little kits—plastic bags filled with all the components needed to make a radio. Second, one supply-chain link was replaced. The kits were shipped to a new assembler in southern China instead of to the old Hong Kong factory. Finally, another stage was added. After the Chinese supplier had completed the labour-intensive, low-wage assembly process, finished radios were shipped back to Hong Kong for final inspection and testing by Li & Fung before being shipped to customers. The result: lower prices and increased business for companies throughout the chain.

PRODUCTIVITY AND QUALITY AS COMPETITIVE TOOLS

6 Discuss four strategies that companies used to improve productivity and quality.

A company's ability to compete by improving productivity and quality depends on participation by all parts of the firm. And total firm involvement stems from having company-wide strategies that we consider in this section: the company's willingness to invest in innovation, its long-run perspective on its goals, its concern for the quality of work life, and the improving of its service operations.

Invest in Innovation and Technology

Many firms that have continued to invest in innovative technology have enjoyed rising productivity and rising incomes. For example, while Steinway & Sons' piano factory is just as concerned as ever about maintaining the highest quality in its products, it's using newer technology to help the woodworkers do their jobs more efficiently and precisely. "It still takes us a year to craft one of these things," says Steinway president Bruce Stevens, "but technology is assisting us in making more precise parts that our people can assemble. It's helping us create a better instrument."[26]

Adopt a Long-Run Perspective

Instead of emphasizing short-run results, many quality-oriented firms are committed to a long-run perspective for **continuous improvement**—the ongoing commitment to improving products and processes, step by step, in pursuit of ever-increasing customer satisfaction. Motorola is a good example. In 1996, its Six Sigma program set a target of 3.4 defects per million parts. By 2003, the company's production-monitoring software—Manufacturing Intellitrak—had helped to reduce errors in some applications to two defects per *billion* parts.[27]

The Six Sigma program, which is used by many other companies besides Motorola, continuously captures, measures, and eliminates defects in every company-wide process, from financial transactions and accounting practices, to R&D and production processes, to marketing and human resources activities. The earliest adopters of Six Sigma in Canada have been full-service brokerages such as Royal LePage Commercial who have international clients.[28]

continuous improvement The ongoing commitment to improve products and processes, step by step, in pursuit of ever-increasing customer satisfaction.

Emphasize Quality of Work Life

The products and services of businesses represent such a large part of total national output that the well-being and participation of their workers is central to improving national productivity. How can firms make their employees' jobs more challenging and interesting? Many companies are enhancing workers' physical and mental health through recreational facilities, counselling services, and other programs. In addition, more and more firms have started programs to empower and train employees.

Employee Empowerment

Many firms are replacing the work environments of yesterday, based on the principle of management-directed mass production, with worker-oriented environments that foster loyalty, teamwork, and commitment. Trident Precision Manufacturing has a program for full employee involvement. Over 95 percent of employee recommendations for process improvements have been accepted since the program started. As a result, employee turnover has fallen from 41 percent to less than 5 percent. Sales per employee have more than doubled.

As we saw in Chapter 10, firms using this approach have found success in the concept of *employee empowerment*—the principle that all employees are valuable contributors to a business and should be entrusted with certain decisions regarding their work. The Hampton Inns motel chain, for example, initiated a program of refunds to customers who were dissatisfied with their stays for any reason. Managers were pleased, and the refund policy created far more additional business than it cost. A surprise bonus was the increased morale when employees—everyone from front-desk personnel to maids—were empowered to grant refunds. With greater participation and job satisfaction, employee turnover was reduced to less than one-half its previous level. Such confidence in employee involvement contrasts sharply with the traditional belief that managers are the primary source of decision making and problem solving.

Employee Training

Employee involvement is effective when it is implemented with preparation and intelligence. *Training* is a key method of preparing employees for productivity-improvement programs. In fact, a recent American Management Association survey found a direct relationship between training and greater productivity profitability: Firms that increased training activities were 66 percent more likely to report improved productivity and three times more likely to report increased profits. Moreover, after training, waste diminishes and quality increases. Finally, team training not only teaches employees to work in groups, but it also acquaints them more fully with the company's markets and operations.[29]

Improve the Service Sector

As important as employee attitudes are to goods production, they are even more crucial to service production, since employees often *are* the service. The service sector has grown rapidly, but this growth has often come at a cost of high inefficiency. Many newly created service jobs have not been streamlined. Some companies operate effectively, but many others are very inefficient, dragging down overall productivity. As new companies enter these markets, however, the increased need to compete should eventually force service producers to operate more productively.

Quality begins with listening to customers to determine what services they want. Companies in the temporary-services industry, for example, have long emphasized the needs of clients for clerical and light-industrial employees. More recently, however, temp services have realized the need for highly skilled, specialized temps such as nurses, accountants, and scientists.

In trying to offer more satisfactory services, many providers have discovered five criteria that customers use to judge service quality:[30]

- *Reliability*: Perform the service as promised, both accurately and on time.

- *Responsiveness*: Be willing to help customers promptly.

- *Assurance*: Maintain knowledgeable and courteous employees who will earn the trust and confidence of customers.

- *Empathy*: Provide caring, individualized attention to customers.

- *Tangibles*: Maintain a pleasing appearance of personnel, materials, and facilities.

Summary of Learning Objectives

1. **Describe the connection between *productivity* and *quality*.** *Productivity* is a measure of economic performance; it compares how much is produced with the resources used to produce it. *Quality* is a product's fitness for use. However, an emphasis solely on productivity or solely on quality is not enough. Profitable competition in today's business world demands high levels of both productivity and quality.

2. **Understand the importance of increasing productivity.** It is important that Canadian business firms increase their rate of productivity growth so that they can be competitive in world markets. As Canadian business firms increase productivity, they will be able to produce a greater quantity of goods without using more resources.

3. **Identify the activities involved in *total quality management*, and describe six tools that companies can use to achieve it.** *Total quality management (TQM)* (sometimes called *quality assurance*) includes all the activities necessary for getting high-quality goods and services into the marketplace. The strategic approach to TQM begins with customer focus. It includes methods for determining what customers want and then directing all the company's resources toward satisfying those wants and needs. Total participation is mandatory, and TQM is more than part-time. It demands continuous improvement of products, services, and improvement in all of the company's internal processes, such as accounting, delivery, billing, and information flows. Six tools that are used to achieve TQM include (1) *Value-added analysis* (the evaluation of all work activities, material flows, and paperwork to determine the value that they add for customers); (2) *statistical process control (SPC)* (methods by which employees can gather data and analyze variations in production activities to determine when adjustments are needed); (3) *quality/cost studies* (identify a firm's current costs but also reveal areas with the largest cost-savings potential); (4) *quality improvement (QI) teams* (groups of employees from various work areas who meet regularly to define, analyze, and solve common production problems); (5) *benchmarking* (improving business products or procedures by comparing them to either the firm's own past performance or the best practices of others); and (6) *getting closer to the customer* (know what customers want in the products they consume).

4. **Identify three trends in productivity and quality management, including *supply chain management*.** (1) *ISO 9000* is a certification program attesting to the fact that a factory, a laboratory, or an office has met the rigorous quality-management requirements set by the International Organization for Standardization. It allows firms to show that they follow documented procedures for testing products, training workers, keeping records, and fixing product defects. *ISO 14000* certifies improvements in *environmental* performance. (2) *Business process re-engineering* focusses on improving both the productivity

and quality of business processes—rethinking each step of an organization's operations by starting from scratch. *Re-engineering* is the fundamental rethinking and redesign of processes to achieve dramatic improvements in measures of performance. (3) The *supply chain* refers to the group of companies and stream of activities that operate together to create a product. Traditional strategies assume that companies are managed as individual firms rather than as members of a coordinated supply chain. *Supply chain management (SCM)* looks at the chain as a whole to improve the overall flow through a system composed of companies working together. Because customers ultimately get better value, SCM gives chain members a competitive advantage.

5. **Explain how a supply chain strategy differs from traditional strategies for coordinating operations among firms.** The supply chain strategy is based on the idea that members of the supply chain can gain competitive advantage by working together as a coordinated system of units. For example, sharing information allows companies to reduce inventories, improve quality, and speed delivery of products to consumers. In contrast, traditional strategies assume that companies are managed as individual firms, with each one acting in its own interest.

6. **Discuss four strategies that companies use to improve productivity and quality.** (1) *Invest in innovation and technology*: Many firms that have continued to invest in innovative technology have enjoyed rising productivity and rising incomes. Increasingly, investments in the internet and information technology are rising, with new applications in every major industry. (2) *Adopt a long-run perspective*: Many quality-oriented firms are committed to long-term efforts at continuous improvement: the ongoing commitment to improving products and processes, step by step, in pursuit of ever-increasing customer satisfaction. (3) *Emphasize quality of work life*: Business products and services represent such a large part of total national output that the well-being and participation of workers is crucial to improving national productivity. (4) *Improve the service sector*: As important as employee attitude is to goods production, it is even more crucial to service production, where employees often are the service. In trying to offer more satisfactory services, many companies have discovered five criteria that customers use to judge service quality: *reliability*, *responsiveness*, *assurance*, *empathy*, and *tangibles*.

KEY TERMS

QUESTIONS FOR ANALYSIS

1. What is the relationship between productivity and quality?

2. High productivity in the service sector has historically been difficult to achieve. Why was this so? What might be changing in this area that will cause service productivity to increase during the next decade?

3. Explain how inputs and outputs relate to each other in the basic equation for measuring labour productivity.

4. What are the costs and benefits for a company that is in the process of deciding to pursue quality and productivity as competitive tools?

5. Explain how the functions of management (planning, organizing, leading, and controlling) relate to one another in the pursuit of quality.

6. How might benchmarking be used to increase productivity in the service sector?

7. Why is employee empowerment essential to the success of quality improvement teams?

APPLICATION EXERCISES

1. Interview a production manager in a local firm and determine which of the tools for total quality management the company is currently using. Also determine why the company has chosen not to use some of the tools.

2. Using a local company as an example, show how you would conduct a quality/cost study. Identify the cost categories and give some examples of the costs in each category. Which categories do you expect to have the highest and lowest costs? Why?

3. Select a company of interest to you and consider the suggestions for competing that are detailed in this chapter. Which of these suggestions apply to this company? What additional suggestions would you make to help this company improve its overall quality and productivity?

BUILDING YOUR BUSINESS SKILLS

Making Your Benchmark in the Business World

Goal

To encourage students to understand ways in which benchmarking can improve quality and productivity.

The Situation

As the director of maintenance for a regional airline, you are disturbed to learn that the cost of maintaining your 100-plane fleet is skyrocketing. A major factor is repair time; when maintenance or repairs are required, work often proceeds slowly. As a result, additional aircraft must be pressed into service to meet the schedule. To address the problem, you decide to use a powerful total quality management tool called *benchmarking*: You will approach your problem by studying ways in which other companies have successfully managed similar problems. Your goal is to apply the best practices to your own maintenance and repair operation.

Assignment

Step 1

Working with three or four other students, choose your benchmarking target from among the following choices:

▶▶▶

▶▶▶

- the maintenance and repair operations of a competing airline

- the pit crew operations of an Indianapolis 500 race car team

- the maintenance and repair operations of a nationwide trucking company

Write a memo explaining the reasons for your choice.

Step 2

Write a list of benchmarking questions that will help you learn the best practices of your targeted company. Your goal is to ask questions that will help you improve your own operation. These questions will be asked during on-site visits.

Step 3

As part of a benchmarking project, you will be dealing with your counterparts in other companies. You have a responsibility to prepare for these encounters, and you must remember that what you learn during the exchange process is privileged information. Given these requirements, describe the steps that you would take before your first on-site visit, and outline your benchmarking code of ethics.

Follow-Up Questions

1. Why is benchmarking an important method for improving quality?

2. Why did you make your benchmarking choice? Explain why the company you selected holds more promise than other companies in helping you solve your internal maintenance problems.

3. What kind of information would help you improve the efficiency of your operations? Are you interested in management information, technical information, or both?

4. In an age of heightened competition, why do you think companies are willing to benchmark with each other?

EXERCISING YOUR ETHICS

Calculating the Cost of Conscience

The Situation

Product quality and cost affect every firm's reputation and profitability as well as the satisfaction of customers. This exercise will expose you to some ethical considerations that pertain to certain cost and service decisions that must be made by operations managers.

The Dilemma

As director of quality for a major appliance manufacturer, Ruth was reporting to the executive committee on the results of a recent program for correcting problems with a newly redesigned rotary compressor that the company had recently begun putting in its refrigerators. After receiving several customer complaints, the quality lab and the engineering department had determined that some of the new compressor units ran more loudly than expected. Some remedial action was needed. One option was simply waiting until customers complained and responding to each complaint if and when it occurred. Ruth, however, had decided that this approach was inconsistent with the company's policy of offering the highest quality in the industry. Deciding that the firm's reputation called for a proactive, "pro-quality" approach, Ruth had initiated a program for contacting all customers who had purchased refrigerators containing the new compressor.

Unfortunately, her "quality-and-customers-first" policy was expensive. Local service representatives had to phone every customer in each area of the country, make appointments for home visits, and replace original compressors with a newer model. But because replacement time was only one-half hour, customers were hardly inconvenienced, and food stayed refrigerated without interruption. Customer response to the replacement program was overwhelmingly favourable.

Near the end of Ruth's report, an executive vice-president was overheard to comment, "Ruth's program has cost this company $400 million in service expenses." Two weeks later, Ruth was fired.

Questions for Discussion

1. What are the underlying ethical issues in this situation?

2. What are the respective roles of profits, obligations to customers, and employee considerations for the firm in this situation?

3. Suppose you were an employee who realized that your company was selling defective appliances. Suppose that the cost of correction might put the firm out of business. What would you do?

Keeping Track of German Engineering

For auto enthusiasts, the first faint signs of criticism seemed an anomaly, a false blip on the radar screen, rather than the beginning of the full-scale trend that was to follow. Results of a secret European poll on car quality were leaked to the press in 2002, and Mercedes—for decades the pride of German engineering—was not at the top of the list. The poll, conducted by Europe's auto makers, showed Mercedes quality and customer satisfaction slipping since 1999 to levels even below Opel, the German-made General Motors brand with a not-so-good image in the European market. A more recent German study of durability during the first three years of ownership rated six Toyota models and five other cars ahead of the MLK, the highest-rated Mercedes model. And contrary to expectations, the quality rankings for Mercedes were nose-diving in North America as well: A 2001 J.D. Power & Associates study of vehicle dependability found Mercedes tumbling to eleventh place from sixth place the year before, leaving it alongside Jaguar, Lincoln, and Cadillac.

"Being Mercedes, quality is absolutely the highest priority," said company spokeswoman Donna Boland. "It's what our brand is based on. We will use every resource at our disposal to bring those numbers up," she added at the time. But the J.D. Power numbers indicated that a challenging climb lay ahead for this industry icon. The survey of some 156 000 car owners reported that five-year-old Mercedes cars had grown to 296 problems per 100 vehicles, versus 285 for other luxury brands. When questioned about specific problem areas, drivers gave Mercedes the biggest markdown of all premium brands for quality of "transmission" and "features/controls." J.D. Power then downgraded the overall quality of Mercedes from "good" to "fair" in 2002. "It's becoming more evident that Mercedes-built quality isn't as bullet-proof as it used to be," said Al Bedwell, research manager at J.D. Power in Oxford, England.

Oddly enough, the quality downslide started when Mercedes decided to shift away from its traditional orientation of "making what the engineers want" and, instead, began focussing more on "making what consumers want." Executives insisted that engineers design cars to meet a certain price point. The idea was to increase sales with a broader range of cars, especially with smaller and less expensive models such as the A-Class. For most firms such a decision makes sense, but the long-standing reputation for engineering and precision workmanship had been a unique competitive asset in the industry for Mercedes.

Although the new consumer strategy worked—worldwide sales and profits increased—quality ratings have taken a beating. By 2003, the quality reputation suffered further with problems in advanced electronic features, and a J.D. Power survey showed customer satisfaction only slightly above the industry average and below Chrysler. Meanwhile, as sales of its upscale models began to slump, a new study announced that Mercedes had lost its first-place ranking as the car model retaining the greatest percentage of its value over time. According to *Automotive Lease Guide*, the 2004 models retained 52 percent of their value after a three-year lease, down from 54.5 percent a year earlier. Rival BMW moved into first place, followed by Honda, Lexus, Toyota, and Acura, then Mercedes. Even so, *Automotive Lease Guide* President Raj Sundaram points out that the Mercedes brand still has a strong resale: "This residual [value] that Mercedes has, a lot of other brands would love to have it." Still, that's not consolation enough for the folks at Mercedes. In one of the few times executives have publicly commented on the quality issue, DaimlerChrysler Chief Executive Jurgen Schrempp admitted the company's concern about Mercedes quality.

Customers willingly pay a premium price—up to $126 000 for a CL600 sedan—because Mercedes cars are engineered to higher standards, are in the forefront with advanced technology features, and are assembled with greater care than other cars. At least that has been the belief of luxury car-lovers—until recently. Owners and company executives alike have watched in disbelief as the Mercedes quality ranking among car brands sold in the United States tumbled from number one in 1993 to number three in 1999 to twenty-sixth place in 2003 (based on problems reported after three years). The brand's dignified top-of-the-line reputation in past years is contradicted today by angry comments—about leaky roofs, faulty electronics, non-inflating air bags, and other failed expectations—posted publicly on websites such as troublebenz.com and lemonmb.com.

The quality downslide is having its effects on profitability, too. Mercedes sold fewer cars in Europe and Japan in 2002 than in 2001, and sales were off another 2 percent in 2003. Although U.S sales were up more than 3 percent for 2003, rival BMW's sales surpassed Mercedes, and market research revealed the number of drivers wanting a Lexus is growing twice as fast as those wanting a Mercedes. In contrast to a decade or more ago, when Mercedes was one of few genuinely fine products for luxury car fans, today's drivers are not so kind to any one brand. "The market is less and less forgiving," says Garel Rhys, director of the Center for Automotive Industry Research at the University of Cardiff in Wales. "People don't have to wait for Mercedes to sort itself out. They're going to buy a BMW or Lexus."

Mercedes is taking drastic steps to keep customers happy and restore confidence in the company's once-pristine reputation. To remedy one recent problem, nearly 2000 owners were offered new E-class cars—at no charge—with factory-installed navigation systems to replace cars with failed navigation systems that had been installed after purchase. In a more strategic outreach for customer satisfaction, Mercedes executives are urging U.S. dealers to invest $500 million for expanded service facilities to handle complaints, including training for 1000 new service technicians. Meanwhile, back at Mercedes headquarters in Stuttgart, Germany, CEO Jurgen Hubbert is reorganizing the company's electronics engineering to prevent premature introduction of the latest technology in its high-end cars. In their haste to catch up with Asian car makers, over-eager engineers sometimes push for new gadgets, such as navigation, phone, radio, satellite, and computer diagnostics without first testing them as a unified system to ensure they work together reliably.

Radical redesign is high on the agenda for the M-class sport-utility vehicle, the Mercedes product receiving, perhaps, more customer complaints than any other since its introduction in 1998. With malfunctions on nearly every part of the car, dealers have been unable to keep pace with its service requirements. The 2005 model was completely re-engineered with a car-like unibody frame instead of the original truck-like body-on-frame structure. Similarly, the smallest Mercedes model—the A-Class, with a short wheel base and high roof—needed expensive re-engineering for the suspension system after the car failed a safety test conducted by a Swedish car magazine. These recent failures have revealed a recurring Mercedes problem: The company is unable to design a car right the first time, and that causes customer complaints, lower quality, expensive repairs, and a tarnished image. But it also points to an area that, if improved, could lead to the company's revival as the industry's quality leader.

Questions for Discussion

1. How would you define "quality" and how is quality measured in this industry? Are some measurements more useful than others? Explain.

2. Think about Mercedes products, the company, and its customers. What are the basic causes that led to declining quality?

3. Consider the costs that Mercedes has incurred from declining quality. What are the kinds (categories) of costs resulting from poor quality? Give examples from the case illustrating each category in your list. Which category do you suppose is most costly? Explain.

4. What further steps or actions (in addition to those listed in the case) would you recommend for restoring the quality reputation of Mercedes? What priority ordering would you assign for those steps?

5. In hindsight, what actions could have been taken at Mercedes to maintain its top quality position and prevent deterioration of quality? For each action you identify, explain how it would have prevented the company's quality downfall.

CONCLUDING CASE 12-2

Supply Chain Management at Loblaw

Loblaw Companies Limited is Canada's biggest seller of groceries, and its Real Canadian Superstores—which sell both groceries and general merchandise—are a prominent feature on the Canadian retail scene. Because price-conscious consumers are always looking for the best prices, and because Wal-Mart announced that it was poised to open its own superstores, Loblaw decided that it must improve its supply chain system to compete.

In 2005, Loblaw had come to the conclusion that it was taking too long for its products to get from its warehouses to its retail grocery stores. To fight off Wal-Mart, and to better serve customers, Loblaw embarked on a $62 million restructuring project, which involved improving its supply chain network, reorganizing grocery merchandising, procurement, and operations groups, updating its information technology systems, consolidating work formerly done in regional offices into its new Ontario head office building, reducing the number of warehouses from 32 to 26, consolidating operations in state-of-the-art facilities, and cutting 1400 jobs.

If Loblaw cannot effectively sell both groceries and general merchandise, it will be at a disadvantage compared to Wal-Mart. Loblaw must compete with Wal-Mart's legendary supply chain management system (described in the Opening Case in Chapter 13). To do so, it must develop its own system for keeping in-demand products on its shelves. Such a system will also allow Loblaw to lower its prices and compete with Wal-Mart. Loblaw has hired a supply chain expert from Wal-Mart to spearhead the resolution of its distribution problems.

Loblaw is wise to not underestimate the Wal-Mart threat. In the United States, Wal-Mart went from a zero share in groceries to become that country's largest grocer in less than a decade. If Wal-Mart has that kind of success in Canada, it will obviously have a detrimental effect on Canadian retailers like Loblaw and Sobeys.

Problems developed as system implementation began, and Loblaw president John Lederer admitted to financial analysts that the company had moved too fast in trying to implement too many different changes. For example, the company experienced problems as it tried to move 2000 administrative employees to the company's new headquarters in Brampton, Ontario. When about 75 general merchandise product buyers decided to quit the company rather than move, this turnover made it difficult to maintain continuity with suppliers. These missteps not only cost the company millions, they set back its plans for implementation by at least a year.

As well, too many distribution facilities were closed before the newer, high-tech ones were ready to cope with increased volume. One supplier shipped merchandise to the Calgary warehouse, but the shipment was refused. Many weeks passed before the shipment was finally accepted and the supplier was paid. These distribution problems forced the company to pull back on marketing its general merchandise offerings. Since it is well known in the retail business that customers get very unhappy when advertised items are not on the shelf, it made little sense to spend money on marketing if the company couldn't guarantee product availability.

Loblaw also incurred some other not-so-obvious costs because of distribution problems. For example, it had to mark down many toys because they were received too late for the Christmas season. Loblaw discovered that it isn't only groceries that are perishable.

Further problems arose in Loblaw's retail stores, where shelves were sometimes empty. Because customers don't know all the products that the superstores carry, there are often noticeably fewer people in the non-grocery sections. In 2005, Loblaw's store productivity declined 2.4 percent.

Not all of Loblaw's problems are logistical. In an attempt to compete with Wal-Mart—which is well-known for its anti-union stance (see the Business Accountability box in Chapter 9)—Loblaw is trying to reduce labour costs by getting the union to agree to wage cuts. Its employees are represented by the United Food and Commercial Workers union.

The news is not all bad for Loblaw. Even though it missed financial analysts' estimates for three straight quarters, and even though the price of the company's shares has dropped, it appears that analysts are willing to give Loblaw a break because they realize that even strong retailers occasionally encounter problems. The general consensus is that Loblaw is making the right moves to strengthen their long-term competitive position. This is particularly important given Wal-Mart's plans in Canada.

Questions for Discussion

1. What is a supply chain? Why is efficiency in its supply chain so crucial to Loblaw?

2. What is supply chain management? How is it relevant for Loblaw?

3. What is the relationship between supply chain management, productivity, and quality?

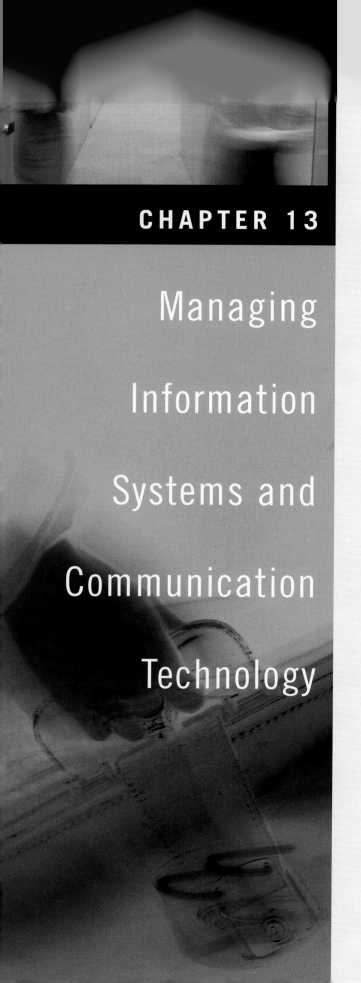

CHAPTER 13

Managing Information Systems and Communication Technology

After reading this chapter, you should be able to:

1 Explain why businesses must manage *information* and show how computer systems and communication technologies have revolutionized *information management*.

2 Identify and briefly describe three elements of *data communication networks*—the internet, the World Wide Web, and intranets.

3 Describe five *new options for organizational design* that have emerged from the rapid growth of information technologies.

4 Discuss different information-systems *application programs* that are available for users at various organizational levels.

5 Identify and briefly describe the *main elements of an information system*.

6 Briefly describe the content and role of a *database* and the purpose of *database software* for information systems.

We hear it all the time: "Information is power." And that's true. But it's also true that information is critical for business success, especially in the rapidly changing globalized economy that has emerged during the past decade or so. To survive in this "new world," managers need accurate information about not only the internal workings of their business, but also about how their business is connecting with the external environment. It is especially

important that businesses connect with their customers. Some of the recent developments in inventory management, retailing, and forestry that are helping companies connect with their customers are described below.

INVENTORY MANAGEMENT

It could be the biggest new thing in inventory management since the invention of the bar code 30 years ago. It's called Radio Frequency Identification (RFID), and it allows information encoded on small tags to be transmitted by radio signal to scanners and computer networks. The tags can be "read" even when they are out of sight and on the move.

RFID is expected to eventually replace the bar code, and will allow public- and private-sector organizations to accurately keep track of people and products in real time. It will, for example, allow companies to speed up the rate at which products get to the store shelf so that in-demand products are available when customers want them. This is important because retail studies suggest that a store typically loses 4 percent of its potential sales because of out-of-stock items. The RFID tags can also give customers information they may be interested in. For example, RFID tags are used on Japanese Kobe beef. Customers can scan the tag at the retail store and find out exactly which farm the beef came from, what it was fed, and if it was treated with antibiotics.

Two Canadian companies are providing RFID products to interested businesses. Samsys Technologies Inc. of Richmond Hill, Ontario, has focussed on developing "readers" for supply chain management applications. It has already delivered an automatic tracking system to the U.S. Army Joint Munitions Command, and its readers are

being used in a pilot program at Pacific Cycle LLC, the largest bicycle manufacturer in the United States. The second company is Sirit Inc. of Mississauga, Ontario, which focusses on selling transponders for vehicles using highway tolls.

RETAILING

With sales of nearly $300 billion annually, Wal-Mart has taken the retail world by storm and is the world's largest company. How has Wal-Mart accomplished this feat? First and foremost is Wal-Mart's policy of everyday low prices. But there is another important reason: product availability. Wal-Mart is a master at providing products that are virtually always in stock. Its customers are therefore confident that they can find what they want at Wal-Mart.

But exactly *how* has Wal-Mart been able to ensure product availability? The answer is a space-age information system that keeps track of every single item sold in every Wal-Mart store around the world. The system puts into practice founder Sam Walton's belief that to be successful in retailing, you have to keep an eye on what is selling at each retail store, and why it is selling.

The information system works like this. When a customer in a Wal-Mart store buys a certain item, its Uniform Product Code (UPC) is scanned. The information is first beamed to Wal-Mart's own satellite, and then to Wal-Mart's Computer Data Processing Center in Bentonville, Arkansas. All sales are recorded and put into the database that allows Wal-Mart to track the shopping and spending patterns of its customers. In each retail store, Wal-Mart employees can get the same information by reading the UPC bar code with their Telxon wireless device.

Next, orders are sent to suppliers when restocking of an item is needed. These suppliers respond by shipping the required products to the appropriate Wal-Mart distribution centre. Supplier trucks pull up on one side of the building to unload, and Wal-Mart trucks load up on the other side. Each Wal-Mart store that the distribution centre serves has its own loading door. Once loaded, the trucks race off to the local Wal-Mart to deliver the goods to re-supply the shelves.

Wal-Mart's information system not only keeps shelves of Wal-Mart stores stocked, it also he costs because products are not sent to individual stores until they are actually needed. It is really just-in-time retailing. The information system also provides an added benefit: It allows Wal-Mart's suppliers to better plan their production schedules because they know almost instantaneously what is going on at the retail level.

Wal-Mart is adopting the RFID system because it wants to have accurate information about the location of its vast amount of inventory. In 2005, 137 of its largest suppliers tagged pallets of products. Nearly two-thirds of items are currently tagged, and the number is growing. The data are shared with Wal-Mart's suppliers and allow them to see where their products are going. Wal-Mart thinks the RFID system will help reduce product returns and recalls.

The RFID idea sounds like a good thing. But consumer and privacy advocates have raised concerns about the RFID technology because they fear that embedded chips will lead to a "Big Brother" situation where companies will be tempted to misuse the detailed information they have about consumers. This is not idle speculation. Benetton Group was going to implant RFID chips in the clothes it sells, but dropped the idea when consumers said they didn't like the fact that the company could track them after they left the store. Ontario's privacy commissioner says that RFID makers and users will have to adopt privacy safeguards if they want to avoid a consumer backlash.

FORESTRY

Something even more sophisticated than RFID technology is being contemplated by forestry companies. Canfor Corp. has a vision of the future that includes sensors attached to trees that would indicate whether the tree is ready to be harvested and how it should be cut up. These sensors (called *motes*) would provide information on the tree's growth rate and size, the soil conditions, the amount of light the tree is receiving, and other things that influence tree growth. This information would then be transmitted to a central computer. With this system of information gathering, timber companies would know exactly how much lumber inventory they have while their trees are still in the ground.

John Tolkamp, Canfor's general manager for information technology, foresees the day when a customer puts in an order and the tree that is needed to make the lumber for that customer is harvested within a few minutes. He says it will be "the Dell model of forestry." He also speculates that in the future, a house builder could give Canfor an electronic copy of the house's specifications, and then Canfor could send the builder a pre-cut house that's ready to put together. It would be a "build-by-the-numbers" system, a more sophisticated version of the old "paint-by-the-numbers" product. The technology already exists to do these things, but the cost of implementing it is prohibitive at the moment (imagine the cost of attaching sensors to millions of trees). ◆

INFORMATION MANAGEMENT: AN OVERVIEW

1 | Explain why businesses must manage *information* and show how computer systems and communication technologies have revolutionized *information management*.

information manager The manager responsible for the activities needed to generate, analyze, and disseminate information that a company needs to make good decisions.

information management An internal operation that arranges the firm's information resources to support business performance and outcomes.

As the opening case shows, today's businesses rely on information management in ways that we could not foresee as recently as a decade ago. Managers now turn to digital technology as an integral part of organizational resources and as a means of conducting everyday business. Every major firm's business activities—designing services, ensuring product delivery and cash flow, evaluating personnel, creating advertising—is linked to information systems. Thus the management of information systems is a core business activity that can no longer be delegated to technical personnel.

Most businesses regard their information as a private resource—an asset that they plan, develop, and protect. It is not surprising, then, that companies have **information managers**, just as they have production, marketing, and finance managers. **Information management** is an internal operation that arranges the firm's information resources to support business performance and outcomes.

To find the information they need to make critical decisions, managers must often sift through a virtual avalanche of reports, memos, magazines, and phone calls. Thus the question that faces so many businesses today is how to get useful information to the right people at the right time. In this section, we will explore the ways in which companies manage information with computers and related information technologies.

Data Versus Information

Although business people often complain that they receive too much information, they usually mean that they get too much **data**—raw facts and figures. **Information** is usefully interpreted data (see Figure 13.1).

Consider the following data:

- Fifty million tubes of toothpaste were sold last year.

- The birth rate is rising slowly.

- Forty-four million tubes of toothpaste were sold the year before last.

- Advertising for toothpaste increased 23 percent last year.

- A major dentists' group recently came out in favour of brushing three times a day.

If all these data can be put together in a meaningful way, they may produce information about what sells toothpaste and whether manufacturers should build new plants. The challenge for businesses is to turn a flood of data into information and to manage that information to their best advantage.

data Raw facts and figures.

information A meaningful, useful interpretation of data.

Information Systems

One response to this challenge has been the growth of the **information system (IS)**—a system for transforming raw data into information and transmitting it for use in decision making. IS managers must first determine what information is needed. Then they must gather the data and apply the technology to convert data into information. They must also control the flow of information so that it goes only to those people who need it.[1]

Supplied information varies according to such factors as the functional areas in which people work (say, accounting or marketing) and their management levels. At all levels, informational quality depends on an organization's

information system (IS) An organized method of transforming data into information that can be used for decision making.

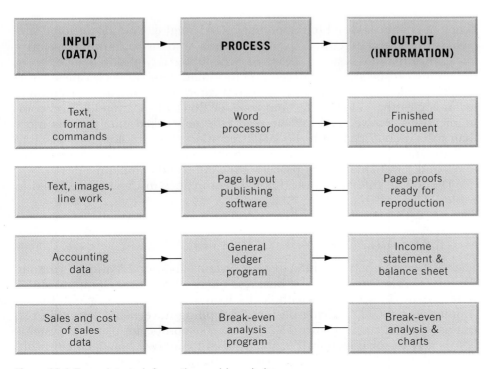

Figure 13.1 From data to information and knowledge.

Information systems are becoming increasingly important as managers try to cope with the flood of data they are confronted with each day.

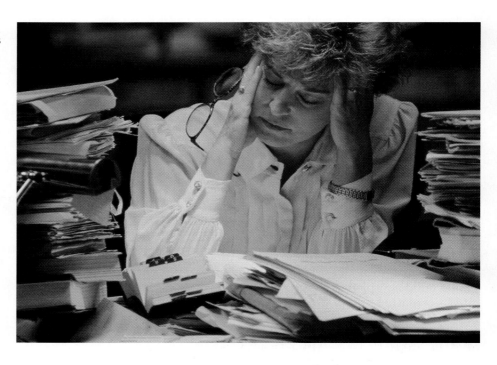

technological resources and on the people who manage them. In the following section, we discuss the evolution of information-processing technology and then describe the information requirements of today's organization.

NEW BUSINESS TECHNOLOGIES IN THE INFORMATION AGE

Employees at every level in the organization, ranging from operational specialists to the top executive, use information systems to improve performance. Information systems assist in scheduling day-to-day vehicle trips, evaluating prospective employees, and formulating the firm's business strategy. The widening role of IS results from rapid developments in electronic technologies that allow faster and broader flows of information and communications. As we shall see, however, the networked enterprise is more than a firm equipped with the latest technology. Technology has inspired new organizational designs, innovative relationships with other organizations, and new management processes for improved competitiveness.

The top 10 information technology companies in Canada are listed in Table 13.1.

The Expanding Scope of Information Systems

The relationship between information systems and organizations is among the fastest-changing aspects of business today. At one time, IS applications were narrow in scope and technically focussed—processing payroll data, simulating new engineering designs, compiling advertising expenditures. But as you can see in Figure 13.2, managers soon began using IS systems not merely to solve technical problems, but to analyze management problems, especially for control purposes—applying quality-control standards to

Table 13.1	The Top 10 Information Technology Companies in Canada, 2005
Company	**Annual Revenues (in billions of $)**
1. CGI Group Inc.	$3.6
2. Microsoft Canada Co.	1.2
3. Cognos Inc.	1.0
4. MacDonald, Dettwiler and Associates Ltd.	0.8
5. Creo Inc.	0.8
6. Accenture Inc.	0.6
7. Geac Computer Corporation Ltd.	0.5
8. EDS Canada Inc.	0.5
9. Open Text Corp.	0.5
10. Oracle Corp. Canada Inc.	0.3

production, comparing costs against budgeted amounts, keeping records on employee absences and turnover.

Today, information systems are also crucial in planning. Managers routinely use IS to decide on a firm's products and markets for the next 5 to 10 years. The same database that helps marketing analyze demographics for millions of customers is also used for such higher-level applications as financial planning, managing materials flows, and setting up electronic funds transfers with suppliers and customers.

Another basic change in organizations is an increased interdependence between a company's business strategy and its IS. Today, the choice of a business strategy—say, to be the low-cost provider or the most flexible provider or the high-quality provider—requires an information system that can support that strategy. To effectively support a strategy, the system's software, hardware, and other components must be integrated (see Figure 13.3).

Electronic Business and Communications Technologies

The pressures to maintain better communications and information systems are increasing as competition intensifies and as organizations expand into global and ebusiness operations. Firms like Ralston Purina Co., for instance, need instantaneous communications among managers in those countries in which they either sell products or buy raw materials, including Canada,

Scope of IS Application

Isolated technical problems | Low-level management problems | Higher level management questions | Organization-wide planning and implementation

1950s–1960s   1960s–1970s   1970s–1980s   1990s–2000s

Figure 13.2 Evolution of IS scope.

Figure 13.3 Aligning business strategy and the IS.

China, Colombia, Brazil, and the United States. New electronic information technologies and more advanced data communication networks are meeting the needs of such companies.

Electronic Information Technologies

electronic information technologies (EIT) IS applications based on telecommunications technologies.

Electronic information technologies (EIT) are IS applications based on telecommunications technologies. EITs use networks of appliances or devices (such as cellphones and computers) to communicate information by electronic means. EITs enhance the performance and productivity of general business activities by performing two functions:

1. Providing coordination and communication within the firm

2. Speeding up transactions with other firms

Six of the most widely used innovations in today's digital business systems are as follows:

fax machine A machine that can quickly transmit a copy of documents or graphics over telephone lines.

- The **fax machine** (short for *facsimile machine*) can transmit and receive digitized images of text documents, drawings, and photographs over telephone lines in a matter of seconds, thus permitting written communication over long distances. Fax machines are popular with both large and small firms because of speed and low cost.

voice mail A computer-based system for receiving and delivering incoming telephone calls.

- **Voice mail** refers to a computer-based system for receiving and delivering incoming telephone calls. Incoming calls are never missed because a voice responds to the caller, invites a message, and stores it for later retrieval. A company with voice mail networks each employee's phone for receiving, storing, and forwarding calls.

electronic mail (email) system Electronic transmission of letters, reports, and other information between computers.

- An **electronic mail** (or **email**) **system** electronically transmits letters, reports, and other information between computers, whether in the same building or in another country. It is also used for voice transmission and for sending graphics and videos from one computer to another. Email thus substitutes for the flood of paper and telephone calls that threatens to engulf many offices.

electronic conferencing Allows people to communicate simultaneously from different locations via telephone, video, or email group software.

- **Electronic conferencing** is becoming increasingly popular because it eliminates travel and thus saves money. It is also increasingly accessible and speeds up information flows. Teleconferencing allows people to communicate simultaneously from various locations via email group software or via telephone. One form of electronic conferencing, *data conferencing*, allows people in remote locations to work simultaneously on the same document. Working as a team, they can modify part of a database, revise a marketing plan, or draft a press release. Another form of electronic conferencing, *videoconferencing*, allows participants to see one another on a video screen while the teleconference is in progress.

- Collaborative work by teams and other groups is facilitated by **groupware**—software that connects members of the group for email distribution, electronic meetings, message storing, appointments and schedules, and group writing. Linked by groupware, members can work together on their own desktop computers even if they are remotely located. Groupware is especially useful when members work together regularly and rely on intensive information sharing. Groupware products include Lotus Development Corp.'s Lotus Notes, Netscape Communicator, and Microsoft's Office 2000 software suite, which uses web technology.

groupware A system that allows two or more individuals to communicate electronically between desktop PCs.

- Information from outside a company can be linked to its electronic network, and the information can be made available at every workstation. Commercial *digital information services* provide online information for both special-purpose and general topics. Lexis, for example, is specifically a source for legal-research information. In contrast, America Online offers a variety of business information as well as general-interest information.

More and more companies are turning to videoconferencing as a means of holding meetings among people located in distant places. The technology allows people to analyze each other's body language in addition to what they are saying. This helps create richer communication.

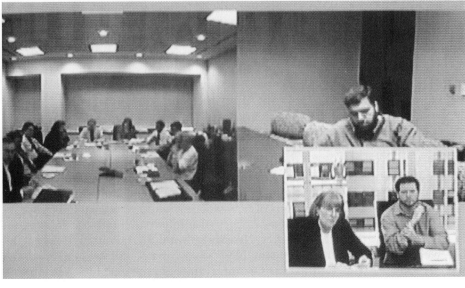

Data Communication Networks

Data communication networks carry streams of digital data (electronic messages, documents, and other forms of video and sound) back and forth quickly and economically on telecommunication systems. The most prominent network, the internet, and its companion system, the World Wide Web, have emerged as powerful communication technologies. Let's look a little more closely at each of these networks.

2 Identify and briefly describe three elements of *data communication networks*—the internet, the World Wide Web, and intranets.

data communication networks Global networks that permit users to send electronic messages quickly and economically.

internet A gigantic network of networks that serves millions of computers, offers information on business, science, and government, and provides communication flows among more than 170 000 separate networks around the world.

The Internet. The **internet**—the largest public data communications network—is a gigantic network of networks that serves millions of computers, offers information on business, science, and government, and provides communication flows among more than 170 000 separate networks around the world. Originally commissioned by the U.S. military as a communication tool for use during war, the internet allows personal computers in virtually any location to be linked together. The internet has gained in popularity because it is an efficient tool for information retrieval that makes available an immense wealth of academic, technical, and business information. Because it can transmit information quickly and at low cost—lower than long-distance phone service, postal delivery, and overnight delivery—the internet has also become the most important email system in the world. For thousands of businesses, therefore, the internet has joined—and is even replacing—the telephone, fax machine, and express mail as a standard means of communication.

Although individuals cannot connect directly to the internet, for small monthly usage fees they can subscribe to the internet via an **internet service provider (ISP)**, such as Prodigy, America Online, or Earthlink. An ISP is a commercial firm that maintains a permanent connection to the internet and sells temporary connections to subscribers.[2] Nearly one billion internet users are active in more than 180 countries. The most intensive internet usage is in Malaysia, where 30 percent of the country's population is online.

internet service provider (ISP) A commercial firm that maintains a permanent connection to the internet and sells temporary connections to subscribers.

World Wide Web A system with universally accepted standards for storing, retrieving, formatting, and displaying information on the internet.

The World Wide Web. Thanks to the **World Wide Web** (or simply "the web"), the internet is easy to use and allows users around the world to communicate electronically with little effort. The World Wide Web is a system with universally accepted standards for storing, retrieving, formatting, and displaying information.[3] It provides the "common language" that enables us to "surf" the internet and makes the internet available to a general audience, rather than merely to technical users such as computer programmers. To access a website, for example, the user must specify the *Uniform Resource Locator (URL)* that points to the resource's unique address on the web. For example, Air Canada's URL is *www.aircanada.ca*—a designation that specifies the storage location of Air Canada's web pages.

Each website opens with a *home page*—a screen display that welcomes the visitor with a greeting that may include graphics, sound, and visual enhancements introducing the user to the site. Additional *pages* provide details on the sponsor's products and explain how to contact help in using the site. Often, sites furnish URLs for related websites that the user can link to by simply pointing and clicking. The person responsible for maintaining an organization's website is usually called a *webmaster*. Large websites use dedicated workstations—large computers—known as **web servers** that are customized for managing, maintaining, and supporting websites.

web servers Dedicated workstations—large computers—that are customized for managing, maintaining, and supporting websites.

browser Software that enables a user to access information on the web.

With hundreds of thousands of new webpages appearing each day, cyberspace is now serving up billions of pages of publicly accessible information. Sorting through this maze would be frustrating and inefficient without access to a web **browser**—software that enables the user to access information on the web. A browser runs on the user's PC and supports the graphics and linking

ENTREPRENEURSHIP AND NEW VENTURES

When to Put Your Incubator on Life Support

Is Bill Gross a new-venture visionary or just a scoundrel? Once touted as an internet superstar, Gross is often credited with popularizing the concept of the incubator when, in 1996, he founded Idealab (www.idealab.com), a Pasadena-based firm for generating new companies from scratch. Gross's master plan for mass-producing start-ups sounds simple enough: Find good ideas, turn them into internet companies, recruit executives to run them, and raise start-up capital. In return for these services, Idealab takes an ownership stake in the new firms.

As CEO, Gross himself is a serial entrepreneur whose endless stream of start-up ideas forms the basis of Idealab's current portfolio, which includes more than 15 companies, including CarsDirect.com, Cooking.com, Overature, Evolution Robotics, and a host of legacy companies—CitySearch, eToys, GoTo.com, HomesDirect, Tickets.com, and PETsMART.com—that are no longer part of the Idealab network.

Gross, testifies business journalist Joseph Nocera, is "the most amazing entrepreneur I've met in 20 years covering business." Unfortunately, adds Nocera, he's also "a stupendously poor manager." Nocera isn't alone in having observed Gross's unorthodox, sometimes nonsensical business style: According to some, he always seems to have more ideas than he knows what to do with. Others say that he knows far more about starting a business than running one. Still others find him a captivating talker who has a habit of shifting from topic to topic but who is willing to try things—sometimes seemingly loony ideas—that others wouldn't dream of touching.

In any case, Gross emerged as a hero in the heyday of the internet, and his impact on the incubator industry has been profound: Since 1996, hosts of wannabe imitators have converged on Pasedena to observe Idealab in operation and copy its business model. Between 1996 and 2001, Gross's success inspired dozens of new incubator firms, including eCompanies, CMGI Inc., Internet Capital Group, and DivineInterVentures.

At the height of the tech boom, investors were enthusiastic, too: Idealab attracted $35 million in 1996, $70 million in 1997, $170 million in 1999, and a whopping $1 billion more in 2000. Dell Computer ventured $100 million, as did T. Rowe Price and the Japanese wireless company Hikari Tsushin. Five ex-Microsoft executives contributed $2.5 to $5 million each, while Travelers Insurance invested $15 million. When Hollywood talent agents, excited about Idealab's entertainment site (Z.com), insisted that they be allowed to invest, the William Morris Agency's $1.9 million was quickly overshadowed by United Talent Agency's $2.5 million. Other Hollywood notables pitched in various sums ranging from $100 000 to $4.2 million each.

But then the ebusiness bubble burst and many of Idealab's start-ups were on the fast track to failure. In early 2002, Gross's reputation took another hit when he was charged with squandering $800 million of investors' money in just eight months. Angry investors say he used their money to buy controlling interest in losing propositions such as cosmetics etailer Eve.com (not to mention Z.com itself).

Some accuse Gross and Idealab president Marcia Goodstein with mismanagement of the company's funds. So bad are so many of Idealab's current companies that investors are pressuring Gross to liquidate Idealab; most are willing to accept 35 cents on the dollar. (Gross has made a counteroffer of 10 cents on the dollar.) A group that includes Dell Computer and T. Rowe Price has filed suit to liquidate and distribute the $500 million remaining in Idealab's account. The litigation is still pending. Responds Teresa Bridwell, Idealab vice president of corporate communications: "Our belief is that there is much unrealized value in Idealab today that we would like to mature and return [funds] to all investors." Bridwell adds that the internet market went sour for everyone and that Idealab isn't the only business incubator on life support. New ventures, she suggests, are risky, and perhaps the faint of heart should consider investments other than internet incubators.

---

capabilities needed to navigate the web. Popular browsers include Netscape, Mozilla Firefox, and Microsoft Internet Explorer.

The web browser offers additional tools—website directories and search engines—for navigating the web. Among the most successful cyberspace enterprises are companies such as Yahoo! that maintain free-to-use **directories** of web content. When Yahoo! is notified about new websites, it classifies them in its directory. The user enters one or two key words (for

directories Features that help people find the content they want on the web. The user types in key words and the directory retrieves a list of websites with titles containing those words.

search engine Software for searching webpages that does not pre-classify them into a directory.

example, "compact disc"), and the directory responds by retrieving a list of websites with titles containing those words.

In contrast to a directory, a **search engine** will search cyberspace's millions of webpages without pre-classifying them into a directory. It searches for webpages that contain the same words as the user's search terms. Then it displays addresses for those that come closest to matching, those that are the next closest, and so on. A search engine, such as AltaVista or Lycos, may respond to millions of inquiries each day. It is thus no surprise that both directories and search engines are packed with paid ads.

Intranets. The success of the internet has led some companies to extend its technology internally, so that employees can browse internal websites containing information. These private networks, or **intranets**, are accessible only to employees via entry through electronic firewalls. **Firewalls** are hardware and software security systems that ensure that internal computer systems are not accessible to outsiders.[4] Compaq Computer Corp.'s intranet allows employees to shuffle their retirement savings among various investment funds. Ford Motor Co.'s intranet connects 120 000 workstations in Asia, Europe, and the United States to thousands of Ford websites containing private information on Ford activities in production, engineering, distribution, and marketing. Sharing such information has helped reduce the lead time for getting new models into production from 36 to 24 months. The savings to Ford, of course, will be billions of dollars in inventory and fixed costs.[5]

intranet A company's private network that is accessible only to employees via entry through electronic firewalls.

firewall Hardware and software security systems that ensure that internal computer systems are not accessible to outsiders.

Extranets. Sometimes firms allow outsiders access to their intranets. These so-called **extranets** allow outsiders limited access to a firm's internal information system. The most common application allows buyers to enter the seller's system to see which products are available for sale and delivery, thus providing product-availability information quickly to outside buyers. Industrial suppliers, too, are often linked to their customers' intranets so that they can see planned production schedules and ready supplies as needed for customers' upcoming operations.

extranet A network that allows outsiders limited access to a firm's internal information system.

Larry Page (left) and Sergey Brin started the search engine Google

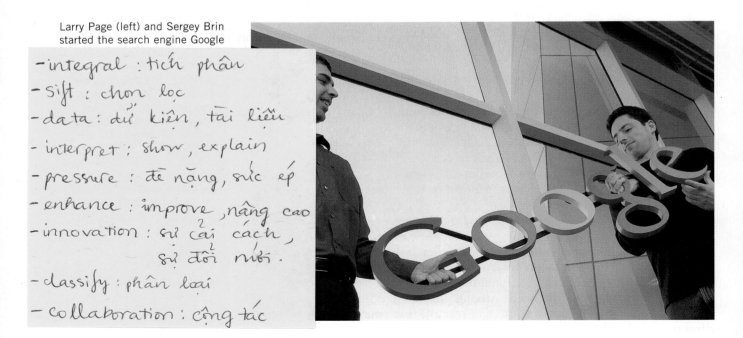

-integral : tích phân
-sift : chọn lọc
-data : dữ kiện, tài liệu
- interpret : show, explain
- pressure : đè nặng, sức ép
- enhance : improve, nâng cao
- innovation : sự cải cách, sự đổi mới.
- classify : phân loại
- collaboration : cộng tác

New Options for Organizational Design: The Networked Enterprise

The rapid growth of information technologies has changed the very structure of business organizations. We begin this section with a discussion of changes wrought by technology in the workforce and organizational structures of many organizations. We then examine ways in which electronic networks are contributing to greater flexibility in dealing with customers. After discussing the growing importance of collaboration in the workplace, we look at the ways in which information networks can help make the workplace independent of a company's physical location. Finally, we describe new management processes inspired by the availability of electronic networks.

Describe five *new options for organizational design* that have emerged from the rapid growth of information technologies.

3

Leaner Organizations

Information networks are leading to leaner companies with fewer employees and simpler organizational structures. Because today's networked firm can maintain information linkages among both employees and customers, more work can be accomplished with fewer people. As a bank customer, for example, you can dial into a 24-hour information system and find out your current balance from a digital voice. You no longer need bank tellers or phone operators. In the industrial sector, assembly workers at an IBM plant used to receive instructions from supervisors or special staff. Now instructions are delivered electronically to their workstations.

Widespread reductions in middle-management positions and the shrinkage of layers in organizational structure are possible because information networks now provide direct communications between the top managers and workers at lower levels. Electronic information networks are replacing the operating managers who formerly communicated company policies, procedures, or work instructions to lower-level employees.

More Flexible Operations

Electronic networks allow businesses to offer customers greater variety and faster delivery cycles. Products such as cellular phones, PCs, and audio systems can be custom-ordered, too, with your choice of features and options and next-day delivery. The principle is called **mass-customization**: Although companies produce in large volumes, each unit features the unique variations and options that the customer prefers. As you can see in Figure 13.4, flexible production and fast delivery depend on an integrated network to coordinate all the transactions, activities, and process flows necessary to make quick adjustments in the production process. The ability to organize and store massive volumes of information is crucial, as are the electronic linkages among customers, manufacturers, materials suppliers, and shippers.

mass-customization Producing large volumes of products or services, but giving customers the choice of features and options they want.

Increased Collaboration

Collaboration, not only among internal units but with outside firms as well, is on the rise because networked systems make it cheaper and easier to contact everyone, whether other employees or outside organizations. Aided by intranets, more companies are learning that complex problems can be solved better by means of collaboration, either in formal teams or through spontaneous interaction. In the new networked organization, decisions that were once the domain of individuals are now shared as both people and departments have become more interdependent. The design of new products, for example, was once an engineering responsibility. Now, in contrast,

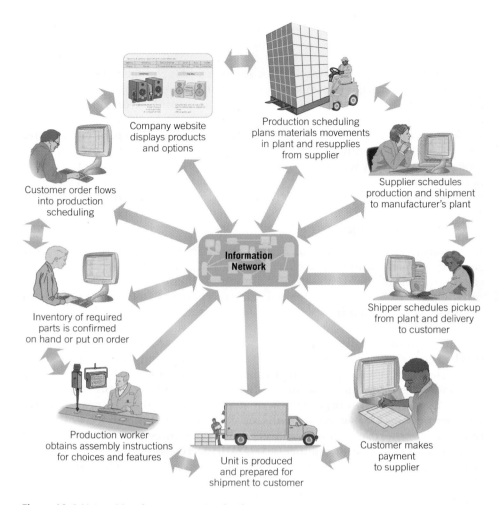

Figure 13.4 Networking for mass-customization.

it can be a shared responsibility because so much information is accessible for evaluation from various perspectives. Marketing, finance, production, engineering, and purchasing can share their different stores of information and determine a best overall design.

Networking and the Virtual Company. Networked systems can also improve collaboration between organizations through the so-called *virtual company*. This can be a temporary team assembled by a single organization, but a virtual company can also be created by several allied firms.[6] Each contributes different skills and resources that collectively result in a competitive business that wouldn't be feasible for any one of them working alone. A company with marketing and promotional skills, for example, may team up with firms with expertise in warehousing and distribution, engineering, and production. Networking lets collaborators exchange ideas, plan strategy, share customer information, and otherwise coordinate efforts, even if their respective facilities are far apart.

Greater Independence of Company and Workplace

Geographic separation of the workplace from the company headquarters is more common than ever because of networked organizations. Employees no longer work only at the office or the factory, nor are all of a company's operations performed at one location. The sales manager for an advertising agency may visit the company office in Toronto once every two weeks, preferring instead to work over the firm's electronic network from her home office in Montreal. A medical researcher for the Calgary Clinic may work at a home office networked into the clinic's system.

A company's activities may also be geographically scattered but highly coordinated, thanks to a networked system. Many ebusinesses, for example, do not conduct any activities at one centralized location. When you order products from an internet storefront—say, a chair, a sofa, a table, and two lamps—the chair may come from a co-operating warehouse in Windsor and the lamps from a manufacturer in Toronto, while the sofa and table may be direct-shipped from two manufacturers in North Carolina. All of these activities are launched instantaneously by the customer's order and coordinated through the network, just as if all of them were being processed at one location.

Improved Management Processes

Networked systems have changed the very nature of the management process. The activities, methods, and procedures of today's manager differ significantly from those that were common just a few years ago. Once, for example, upper-level managers did not concern themselves with all the detailed information that filtered upward in the workplace. Why? Because it was expensive to gather and slow in coming and quickly became out of date. Workplace management was delegated to middle and first-line managers.

With networked systems, however, instantaneous information is accessible in a convenient and usable format. Consequently, more and more upper managers use it routinely for planning, leading, directing, and controlling operations. Today, a top manager can find out the current status of any customer order, inspect productivity statistics for each workstation, and analyze the delivery performance of any driver and vehicle. More importantly, managers can better coordinate company-wide performance. They can identify departments that are working well together and those that are creating bottlenecks.

Enterprise Resource Planning. One type of networked system is **enterprise resource planning (ERP)**—a large information system for integrating the activities of all of a company's units.[7] It is supported by one large database through which everyone shares the same information when any transaction occurs. The biggest supplier of commercial ERP packages is Germany's SAP AG, followed by Oracle. Hershey Foods uses the SAP system. It identifies the status of any order and traces its progress from order entry through customer delivery and receipt of payment. Progress and delays at intermediate stages—materials ordering, inventory availability, production scheduling, packaging, warehousing, distribution—can be checked continuously to determine which operations should be more closely coordinated with others to improve overall performance.

enterprise resource planning (ERP) Large information systems for integrating all the activities of a company's business units.

TYPES OF INFORMATION SYSTEMS

In a sense, the phrase *information system* may be a misnomer. It suggests that there is one system when, in fact, a firm's employees will have different interests, job responsibilities, and decision-making requirements. One information system cannot accommodate such a variety of information requirements. Instead, "the information system" is a complex of several

Discuss different information-systems *application programs* that are available for users at various organizational levels.

4

information systems that share information while serving different levels of the organization, different departments, or different operations.

User Groups and System Requirements

Four user groups, each with different system requirements, are identified in Figure 13.5, which also indicates the kinds of systems best suited to each user level. Among users we include **knowledge workers**—employees whose jobs involve the use of information and knowledge as the raw materials of their work. Knowledge workers are specialists, usually professionally trained and certified—engineers, scientists, information technology specialists, psychologists—who rely on information technology to design new products or create new business processes.

Managers at Different Levels

Because they work on different kinds of problems, top managers, middle managers, knowledge workers, and first-line managers have different information needs. First-line (or operational) managers, for example, need information to oversee the day-to-day details of their departments or projects. Knowledge workers need special information for conducting technical projects. Meanwhile, middle managers need summaries and analyses for setting intermediate and long-range goals for the departments or projects under their supervision. Finally, top management analyzes broader trends in the economy, the business environment, and overall company performance to conduct long-range planning for the entire organization.

Consider the various information needs of a flooring manufacturer. Sales managers (first-level managers) supervise salespeople, assign territories to the sales force, and handle customer service and delivery problems.

knowledge workers Employees whose jobs involve the use of information and knowledge as the raw materials of their work.

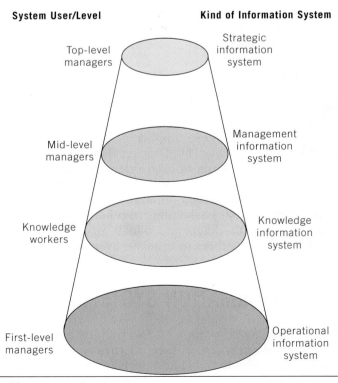

Figure 13.5 Matching users and systems.

They need current information on the sales and delivery of products: lists of incoming customer orders and daily delivery schedules to customers in their territories. Regional managers (middle managers) set sales quotas for each sales manager, prepare budgets, and plan staffing needs for the upcoming year. They need information on monthly sales by product and region. Knowledge workers developing new flooring materials need information on the chemical properties of adhesives and compression strengths for floor structures. Finally, top managers need both external and internal information. Internally, they use sales data summarized by product, customer type, and geographic region, along with comparisons to previous years. Equally important is external information on consumer behaviour patterns, the competition's performance, and economic forecasts.

Functional Areas and Business Processes

Each business *function*—marketing, human resources, accounting, production, and finance—has its own information needs. In addition, in businesses organized according to business processes, process groups need special information. Each user group and department is represented by an IS. Now add to these systems the four systems needed by the four levels of users that we just discussed: The total number of systems and applications increases significantly.

Each cell on the left side of Figure 13.6 represents a potential IS associated with a given functional group. Top-level finance managers, for instance, plan long-range spending for facilities and equipment, and they determine sources of capital. The arrows on the right side of Figure 13.6 show that a business-process group will include users, both managers and employees, drawn from all organizational levels. The supply chain management group, for instance, may need to cut the number of suppliers. The IS supporting this project would contain information cutting across different functions and management levels. The group will need information on and expertise in marketing, warehousing and distribution, production, communications technology, purchasing, and finance. It will also need input on operational, technical, and managerial issues—say, technical requirements for new suppliers and future financial requirements.

	Organization Function			Business Process			
	Marketing	Finance	Production	Strategic Planning	Product Development	Order Fulfilment	Supply Chain Management
Top-level managers							
Mid-level managers							
Knowledge workers							
First-level managers							

Figure 13.6 Matching user levels with functional areas and business processes.

Major Systems by Level

In this section, we discuss different kinds of systems that provide applications at some organizational levels but not at others. For any routine, repetitive, highly structured decision, a specialized application will suffice. System requirements for knowledge workers, however, will probably vary because knowledge workers often face a variety of specialized problems. Applications of information systems for middle or top-level management decisions must also be flexible, though for different reasons. In particular, they will use a broader range of information collected from both external and internal sources.

Transaction Processing Systems

transaction processing systems (TPS) Applications of information processing for basic day-to-day business transactions.

Transaction processing systems (TPS) are applications of information processing for basic day-to-day business transactions. Customer order-taking by online retailers, approval of claims at insurance companies, receiving and confirming reservations by airlines, payroll processing and bill payment at almost every company—all are routine business processes. Typically, the TPS for first-level (operational) activities is well defined, with predetermined data requirements, and follows the same steps to complete all transactions in the system.

A diagram representing the TPS for a customer-billing process is shown in Figure 13.7. The process begins when finished products for a customer's order are packed and ready for shipment. Using data stored in the company's master files, billing staffers match the customer's identification number (from the billing master file) with code numbers for products (from the products master file). The system instantly tallies the payment amount due (including the bill of the current shipment plus any past-due payments), creates the billing document (invoice), and provides status reports to first-level managers and other system users with online access. Information from the billing and products master files flows electronically to the accounting system for updating accounts receivables and inventory accounts.

Systems for Knowledge Workers and Office Applications

Systems for knowledge workers and office applications support the activities of both knowledge workers and employees in clerical positions. They provide assistance for data processing and other office activities, including the creation of communications documents. Like other departments, the IS department includes both knowledge workers and data workers.

IS Knowledge Workers. IS knowledge workers include both systems analysts (and designers) and application (or systems) programmers:

- *Systems analysts and designers* deal with the entire computer system. They represent the IS group in working with users to learn users' requirements and to design systems that meet them. Generally, they decide on the types and sizes of computers and on how to set up links among computers to form a network of users.

- *Programmers* write the software instructions that tell computers what to do. Application programmers, for example, write instructions to address particular problems. Systems programmers ensure that a system can handle the requests made by various application programs.

system operations personnel People who run a company's computer equipment.

Operations Personnel (Data Workers). People who run the company's computer equipment are called **system operations personnel**. They ensure that the right programs are run in the correct sequence and monitor

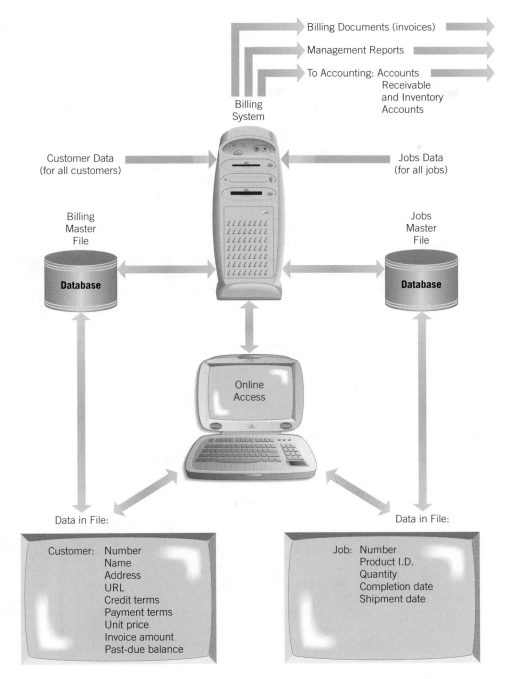

Billing Documents (invoices)

Management Reports

To Accounting: Accounts
Receivable
and Inventory
Accounts

Billing
System

Customer Data
(for all customers)

Jobs Data
(for all jobs)

Billing
Master
File

Jobs
Master
File

Database

Database

Online
Access

Data in File:

Data in File:

Customer: Number
Name
Address
URL
Credit terms
Payment terms
Unit price
Invoice amount
Past-due balance

Job: Number
Product I.D.
Quantity
Completion date
Shipment date

Figure 13.7 Flow diagram for customer-billing TPS.

equipment to ensure that it is operating properly. Many organizations also have personnel for entering data into the system for processing.

Knowledge-Level and Office Systems

New support systems—word processing, document imaging, desktop publishing, computer-aided design, simulation modelling—have increased the productivity of both office and knowledge workers. We will discuss word processing—systems for formatting, editing, and storing documents—later in this chapter. Desktop publishing, also discussed later, combines graphics and word-processing text to publish professional-quality print and web documents. Document imaging systems can scan paper documents and images, convert them into digital form for storage on disks, retrieve them, and transmit them electronically to workstations throughout the network.

World-class firms are using system applications for knowledge workers to reduce product-design times, reduce production-cycle times, and make faster deliveries to customers.

computer-aided design (CAD) Computer analysis and graphics programs that are used to create new products.

- **Computer-aided design (CAD)** assists in designing products by simulating the real product and displaying it in three-dimensional graphics. Immersion's MicroScribe-3D software, for example, uses a pen-like tool to scan the surface of any three-dimensional object, such as a football helmet, and electronically transforms it into a 3D graphic. The helmet designer can then try different shapes and surfaces in the computer and analyze the new designs on a video monitor.[8] Products ranging from cellphones to auto parts are created using CAD because it creates faster designs at lower cost than manual modelling methods. The older method—making handcrafted prototypes (trial models) from wood, plastic, or clay—is replaced with *rapid prototyping (RP)*: the CAD system electronically transfers instructions to a computer-controlled machine that then automatically builds the prototype.[9]

computer-aided manufacturing (CAM) Computer systems used to design and control all the equipment and tools for producing goods.

- **Computer-aided manufacturing (CAM)** is used to design the manufacturing equipment, facilities, and plant layouts for better product flows and productivity. *Computer operations control* refers to any system for managing the day-to-day production activities for either goods or service production. Hospitals, for instance, use computer-based scheduling for preparing patients' meals, just as manufacturers do for making cars, clocks, and paper products.

Management Information Systems

management information systems (MIS) Systems that support an organization's managers by providing daily reports, schedules, plans, and budgets.

Management information systems (MIS) support an organization's managers by providing daily reports, schedules, plans, and budgets. Each manager's information activities vary according to his or her functional area (say, accounting or marketing) and management level. Whereas mid-level managers focus mostly on internal activities and information, higher-level managers are also engaged in external activities. Middle managers, the largest MIS user group, need networked information to plan such upcoming activities as personnel training, materials movements, and cash flows. They also need to know the current status of the jobs and projects being carried out in their departments: What stage is it at now? When will it be finished? Is there an opening so the next job can be started? Many of a firm's management information systems—cash flow, sales, production scheduling, and shipping—are indispensable for helping managers find answers to such questions.

Decision Support Systems (DSS)

decision support system (DSS) Computer systems used to help managers consider alternatives when making decisions on complicated problems.

Middle- and top-level managers receive decision-making assistance from a **decision support system (DSS)**—an interactive system that locates and presents information needed to support the decision-making process. Whereas some DSSs are devoted to specific problems, others serve more general purposes, allowing managers to analyze different types of problems. Thus a firm that often faces decisions on plant capacity, for example, may have a *Capacity DSS* in which the manager inputs data on anticipated levels of sales, working capital, and customer-delivery requirements. Then the system's built-in transaction processors manipulate the data and make recommendations on the best levels of plant capacity for each future time period.

Executive Support Systems

An **executive support system (ESS)** is a quick-reference, easy-access application of information systems specially designed for upper-level managers. ESSs are designed to assist with executive-level decisions and problems, ranging from "What lines of business should we be in five years from now?" to "Based on forecasted developments in electronic technologies, to what extent should our firm be globalized in five years? In 10 years?" An ESS also uses a wide range of both internal information and external sources, such as industry reports, global economic forecasts, and reports on competitors.

Artificial Intelligence and Expert Systems

Artificial intelligence (AI) is the construction of computer systems to imitate human behaviour—in other words, systems that perform physical tasks, use thought processes, and learn. In developing AI systems, business specialists, modellers, and information-technology experts try to design computer-based systems capable of reasoning so that computers, instead of people, can perform certain activities. A credit-evaluation system may decide which loan applicants are creditworthy and which are too risky, and it may then compose acceptance and rejection letters accordingly.[10]

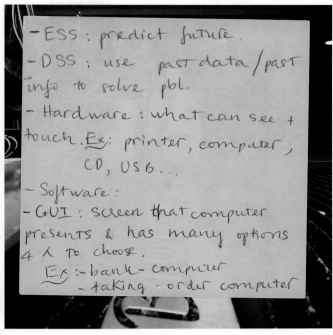

   Robotics—the combination of computers with industrial robots—is a category of AI. With certain "reasoning" capabilities, robots can "learn" repetitive tasks such as painting, assembling components, and inserting screws. They also avoid repeating mistakes by "remembering" the causes of past mistakes and, when those causes reappear, adjusting or stopping until adjustments are made.

   There are also AI systems that possess sensory capabilities, such as lasers that "see," "hear," and "feel." In addition, as machines become more sophisticated in processing natural languages, humans can give instructions and ask questions merely by speaking to a computer. AND Corporation, based in Toronto, Ontario, has developed a software program—called HNeT—that can learn to recognize faces. This may seem like a simple thing, but millions of dollars had been spent on this problem without success until AND Corporation developed the software. The system can be used to improve airport security and to track terrorists.[11]

Expert Systems. A special form of AI program, the **expert system**, is designed to imitate the thought processes of human experts in a particular field.[12] Expert systems incorporate the rules that an expert applies to specific types of problems, such as the judgments a physician makes when diagnosing illnesses. In effect, expert systems supply everyday users with "instant expertise."

   Nortel Networks uses an expert system called Engineering Change Manager, which simplifies and speeds up product design changes by suggesting redesigns to meet product requirements. Campbell Soup developed an expert system to mimic complex decision processes and save the expert knowledge that was going to be lost when a long-time expert soup maker announced his intention to retire.[13]

As late as the 1980s, computers hadn't had much impact on industrial automation, largely because there were no good software programs for computer-operated manufacturing. Myron Zimmerman recognized a need, and he founded VenturCom, which develops programs for controlling industrial production equipment like this metal cutting machine.

executive support system (ESS) A quick-reference, easy-access application of information systems specially designed for upper-level managers.

artificial intelligence (AI) The construction and/or programming of computers to imitate human thought processes.

robotics The use of computer-controlled machines that perform production tasks.

expert system A form of artificial intelligence in which a program draws on the rules an expert in a given field has laid out to arrive at a solution for a problem.

Robotics is a category of artificial intelligence. Robots can "learn" repetitive tasks and "remember" the causes of past mistakes.

ELEMENTS OF THE INFORMATION SYSTEM

5 Identify and briefly describe the *main elements of an information system.*

computer network A form of computer system architecture in which computers at different locations can function independently but are also interconnected and able to exchange information with one another.

We now know that an *information system* is a group of interconnected devices at several different locations that can exchange information. We also know that *networking*—connecting these devices—allows otherwise decentralized computers to exchange data quickly and easily. Obviously, a key component of the information system is its **computer network**—all of the computer and information technology devices that, working together, drive the flow of digital information throughout the system.

The computer is a powerful machine, but it is only one part of the information system. Every system has six components: (1) hardware, (2) software, (3) control, (4) database, (5) people, and (6) telecommunications. We will describe each of the first four components in detail. We have already described the fifth element, the people at various levels who use and prepare the system. We will reserve our discussion of telecommunications for the next section. Remember that all six of these components must be present and properly coordinated for a networked information system to function effectively.

Hardware

hardware The physical components of a computer system.

Figure 13.8 shows the various systems and components that make up IS **hardware**—the physical components of a computer system. The functioning of a computer's hardware is not as complicated as it looks. To get a bird's-eye view of how the system works, suppose that you are a very simple piece of data (say, the number 3).

input device Hardware that gets data into the computer in a form the computer can understand.

central processing unit (CPU) Hardware in which the actual transforming of data into information takes place; contains the primary storage unit, the control unit, and the arithmetic logic unit.

- To get into the computer, data must be entered by an **input device**. Optical scanners, voice pickups, CD drives, and computer mice are all input devices, but let's assume that you are entered by a friend using the most common input device, a keyboard. When your friend presses the number 3 on the keyboard, an electronic signal is sent to the computer's **central processing unit (CPU)**, where the actual processing of data takes place.

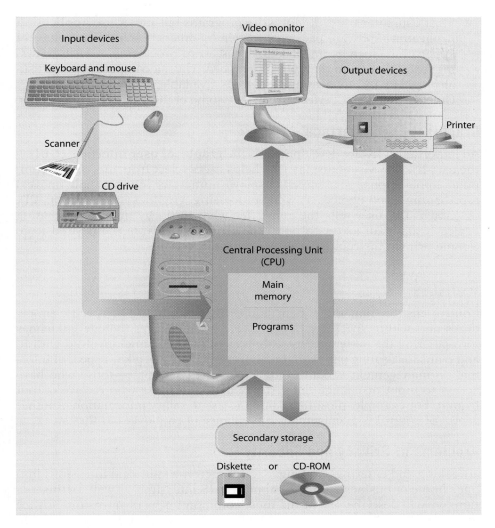

Figure 13.8 Hardware components of an IS.

■ You are now inside the CPU in a form that the computer can understand. What happens now? As a piece of data, you must go first to **main memory**—the part of the computer's CPU that stores those programs that it needs to operate.

main memory The part of a computer's CPU that stores those programs that it needs to operate.

■ Now the CPU searches through its memory for instructions—**programs**—on what to do with you. Using the appropriate instructions, it then performs the calculations (addition, subtraction, multiplication, and division) and comparisons as directed by the program. Then, the CPU sends the results to one or more **output devices**: a video monitor, a printer, or a speaker.

program Any sequence of instructions to a computer.

output device That part of a computer's hardware that presents results to users; common forms include printers and video monitors.

Software

Although hardware is a vital component, it needs programs—**software**—to function. There are two types of software programs:

software Programs that instruct the computer in what to do and how to do it.

■ **System programs** tell the computer what resources to use and how. For example, an operating system program tells the computer how and when to transfer data from secondary to primary storage and return information to the user.

system program A program that tells a computer what resources to use and how to use them.

■ Most computer users do not write programs but rather use **application programs**—software packages written by others. Each different type of application (such as financial analysis, word processing, or web browsing) uses a program that meets that need. Thus, a computer system usually has many application programs available, such as Lotus 1-2-3, Quicken, and WordPerfect. We review some of these later in this chapter.

Graphical User Interface

An important software development is the **graphical user interface (GUI)**—the user-friendly visual display that helps users select from among the computer applications. The screen displays numerous **icons** (small images) representing such choices as word processing, graphics, fax, printing, CD, or games. The user tells the computer what to do by moving a pointing device (usually an arrow) around the screen to activate the desired icon. Simple printed instructions explain activated features.

Control

Control ensures that the system is operating according to specific procedures and within specific guidelines. These procedures include guidelines for operating the system, responsibilities of the personnel involved with it, and plans for dealing with system failure. For example, a key aspect of information management is controlling two groups of people—those who have access to input or change the system's data and those who receive output from it. For example, most firms limit access to salary information. Another aspect of control is management surveillance of employees as they work.

Problems of Privacy and Security

"Breaking and entering" no longer refers merely to physical intrusions into one's home or business. Today, it applies to IS intrusions as well. In this section, we will describe one of the most common forms of intrusion: *privacy invasion*. We will also discuss some of the methods that companies use to provide *security* for their information systems.[14]

Privacy Invasion. With information systems, privacy invasion occurs when intruders (hackers) gain unauthorized access, either to steal information, money, or property or to tamper with data. You have probably read or heard about computer enthusiasts who have gained access to school systems to change grades.

At Equifax Canada, computer hackers breached its system and gained access to personal information on hundreds of Canadians.[15] In the United States, a computer hacker is on trial for allegedly stealing more than one billion records from Acxiom, a data-selling company. The company admitted that the stolen data could include information about millions of people. It also admitted that it didn't even know its system had been hacked into until it was contacted by investigators in the case. Another company, CardSystems Solutions, said hackers may have obtained information on 200 000 credit card holders.[16]

Computer experts are becoming increasingly concerned that the large number of hacker attacks in recent years is causing people to question the security of the internet. If people have security concerns, they will be less likely to use the electronic medium, and this will have a negative effect on thousands of businesses that sell over the internet. Law enforcement agencies around the world are trying to catch hackers, but the criminals often stay one step ahead.

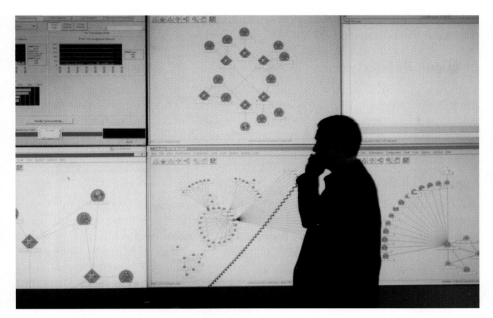

At Acxiom, computer systems track consumer data provided by nearly every credit-card issuer, bank, and insurance company in North America. The company is currently improving its computer-security models, but many people who worry about the potential for abuse point out that Acxiom itself has been successfully "hacked" more than once in the past couple of years.

Security. As we have seen, security measures for protection against intrusion are a constant challenge. To gain entry into most systems, IS users have protected passwords that guard against unauthorized access, but many firms rely on additional protective software for safeguards. To protect against intrusions by unauthorized outsiders, companies use security devices, called electronic *firewalls*, in their systems. Firewalls allow employees access to both the internet and the company's internal computer network while barring entry by outsiders. Since its system was hacked into, Acxiom has beefed up its password protocols and its encryption, and has also conducted many security audits.

Security for electronic communications is an additional concern. Electronic transmissions can be intercepted, altered, and read by intruders. To prevent unauthorized access, many firms rely on **encryption**—the use of a secret numerical code to scramble the characters in the message, so that the message is not understandable during transmission. Only personnel with the deciphering codes can read them. Protection for preserving data files and databases is not foolproof and typically involves making backup copies to be stored outside the computer system, usually in a safe. Thus, damaged system files can be replaced by backup.

The most important security factor is the people in the system. At most firms, personnel are trained in the responsibilities of computer use and warned of the penalties for violating system security. For example, each time a computer boots up, a notice displays the warning that software and data are protected and spells out penalties for unauthorized use.

Montreal-based La Senza Corp. understands how important people are to computer security. It blocks its staff from accessing instant message services and email sites such as Hotmail because these may compromise the company's network security. Sometimes staff become frustrated with these restrictions because they do not appreciate the importance of network security.[17]

encryption The use of a secret numerical code to scramble characters in a message, so that the message is not understandable during transmission.

Databases and Application Programs

Briefly describe the content and role of a *database* and the purpose of *database software* for information systems.

6

All computer processing is the processing of data. It is carried out by programs—instructions that tell the system to perform specified functions. In this section we begin by briefly describing the nature of computer data and databases. We then discuss a few of the specialized applications programs designed for business use.

Data and Databases

Computers convert data into information by organizing them in some meaningful manner. Within a computer system, chunks of data—numbers, words, and sentences—are stored in a series of related collections called fields, records, and files. Taken together, all of these data files constitute a **database**—a centralized, organized collection of related data.

database A centralized, organized collection of related data.

Application Programs

Most computer users don't write programs. Programs are available for a huge range of business-related tasks. Some address such common, long-standing needs as accounting and inventory control, while others have been developed for an endless variety of specialized needs. Most business programs fall into one of four categories: *word processing*, *spreadsheets*, *database management*, and *graphics*. Of all PC software applications, 70 percent are designed for the first three types of programs.[18]

Word Processing. Popular **word-processing programs**, such as Microsoft Word for Windows and Lotus's Word Pro, allow computer users to store, edit, display, and print documents. Sentences and paragraphs can be added or deleted without retyping or restructuring an entire document, and mistakes are easily corrected.

word-processing programs Application programs that allow the computer to act as a sophisticated typewriter to store, edit, and print letters and numbers.

Spreadsheets. **Electronic spreadsheets** spread data across and down the page in rows and columns. Users enter data, including formulas, at row and column intersections, and the computer automatically performs the necessary calculations. Payroll records, sales projections, and a host of other financial reports can be prepared in this manner.

electronic spreadsheets Application programs that allow the user to enter categories of data and determine the effect of changes in one category (e.g., sales) on other categories (e.g., profits).

Spreadsheets are good planning tools because they let managers see how making a change in one item affects related items. For example, you can insert operating-cost percentages, tax rates, or sales revenues into the spreadsheet. The computer will automatically recalculate all the other figures and determine net profit. Popular spreadsheet packages include Lotus 1-2-3, Quattro Pro, and Microsoft Excel for Windows.[19]

Database Management. Another popular type of personal-productivity software is a **database management program**. Such programs as Microsoft Access for Windows and Borland's InterBase are popular for desktop applications. Oracle9i is a popular database for internet computing. These systems can create, store, sort, and search through data and integrate a single piece into several different files.

database management programs Application programs that keep track of and manipulate the relevant data of a business.

Figure 13.9 shows how a database management program might be used at a company called Artists' Frame Service. In this case, the program is integrating the file for customer orders with the company's inventory file. When sales to Jones and Smith are entered into the customer orders file, the database system automatically adjusts the frame inventory file; the quantities of materials B5 and A3 are reduced because those materials were used to make the frames for Jones and Smith.

Graphics. **Computer graphics programs** convert numeric and character data into pictorial information, such as charts and graphs. They make computerized information easier to use and understand in two ways. First, graphs and charts summarize data and allow managers to detect problems, opportunities, and relationships more easily. Second, graphics contribute to clearer and more persuasive reports and presentations.

computer graphics programs Application programs that convert numerical and character data into pictorial forms.

Customer Orders File					Frame Inventory File		
Job Order Number	Customer Name	Quantity Ordered (inches)	Frame Material Number		Frame Material Number	Description	Quantity on Hand
12345	Jones, John	42	B5		A3	Italian Olive	500
25974	Smith, Mary	89	A3		B2	Plastic Black	010
					B5	Plastic Green	272

Figure 13.9 Artists' Frame Service.

Two of the most common graphics displays are the pie chart and the bar graph. As Figure 13.10 shows, both types of graphics can convey different kinds of information—in this case, the types of materials that should be ordered by a framing shop like Artists' Frame Service. Both types of graphs are more likely to help a manager make decisions than the raw numbers on which they are based.

Presentation graphics software, such as CorelDRAW, Microsoft PowerPoint for Windows, and Microsoft Visio 2002, lets users assemble graphics for visual displays, slides, video, and even sound splices for professional presentations. By varying colours and size, and using pictures and charts with three-dimensional effects and shading, animation, and sound users can make more interesting presentations.

Computer graphics capabilities go beyond data presentation. They also include stand-alone programs for artists, designers, and special effects engineers. Everything from simple drawings to motion picture special effects are now created by computer graphics software. The sinking ship in *Titanic*, the aliens in *Men in Black II*, and the dog in *Scooby-Doo* were all created with computer graphics.

Some software allows firms to publish sales brochures, in-house magazines, and annual reports. The latest **desktop publishing** packages for the PC combine word processing and graphics to produce typeset-quality text with stimulating visual effects. They also eliminate printing costs for

presentation graphics software Application programs that offer choices for assembling graphics for visual displays, slides, video, and even sound splices for professional presentations.

desktop publishing Combines word processing and graphics capability in producing typeset-quality text from personal computers.

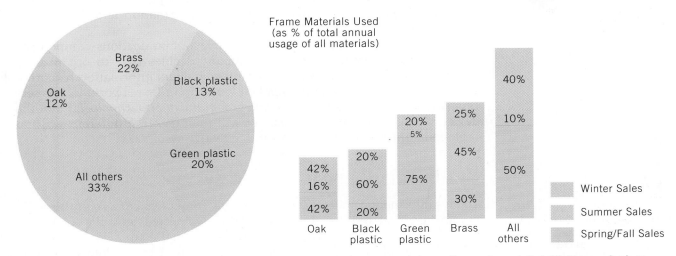

Figure 13.10 Both the pie chart and the bar graph show that four frame materials are the most used, but the bar graph also shows that brass and oak are most popular in winter.

The realism of the space creatures and alien environments in Star Wars is due to special effects created with computer graphics.

reports and proposals. QuarkXPress, which can manipulate text, tables of numbers, graphics, and full-colour photographs, is used by ad agencies such as J. Walter Thompson because its computer-generated designs offer greater control over colour and format. Other packages include Microsoft Publisher and Adobe Systems PageMaker.

software piracy The unauthorized use of software such as word processing and spreadsheets.

Software piracy—the unauthorized use of software such as word processing and spreadsheets—is a worldwide problem. The Canadian Alliance Against Software Theft (CAAST) estimates that 33 percent of software that is installed on computers in Canada is pirated. The piracy rate in countries like Vietnam and China is over 90 percent. CAAST estimates that software piracy has resulted in sales losses of $41 billion worldwide for companies that sell software.[20]

TELECOMMUNICATIONS AND NETWORKS

Although communications systems are constantly evolving (see the Business Accountability box), some of the fundamental elements are well established: computers, communications devices, and networking. The most powerful vehicle for using these elements to their full potential is the marriage of computers and communication technologies. Thanks to lower-cost, higher-capacity networks, the joining of computers, communication, and mass media is changing the nature of information and the ways in which business is conducted.

A *network* is a means of organizing telecommunications components into an effective system. When a company decides how to organize its equipment and facilities, it also determines how its information resources will be shared, controlled, and applied for users in its network. In this section, we will first discuss *multimedia communication technologies* and the devices found in today's systems. We will then describe different ways of organizing information resources into effective systems.

Multimedia Communication Systems

multimedia communication systems Connected networks of communication appliances such as faxes, televisions, sound equipment, cellphones, printers, and photocopiers that may also be linked by satellite with other remote networks.

Today's information systems include not only computers but also **multimedia communication systems**. These systems are connected networks of communication appliances such as faxes, televisions, sound equipment, cellphones, printers, and photocopiers that may also be linked by satellite with other remote networks. Not surprisingly, the integration of these elements is changing the ways in which we live our lives and manage our businesses.

Sharing the Wealth

Janus Friis and Niklas Zennstrom are the Baltic programmers who invented Kazaa—the most downloaded file-sharing program in the world—which provides a free market for videos, music, and porn. With lawyers tracking them, these elusive internet pirates move quietly into London, then secretly to a favourite hangout—the NoKu bar—in Tallinn (Estonia's capital) for a moment of relaxation, and further to Sweden under cover of darkness for secret strategy meetings. "They've resulted in significant damage to the record industry," says Matt Oppenheim, head legal officer for the Recording Industry Association of America (RIAA). While Oppenheim—the chief Kazaa hunter—doggedly tries to serve them legal papers, Friis and Zennstrom have launched an even grander startup, called Skype, that's going to revolutionize telephoning.

Skype—Zennstrom's unique version of what the industry calls "Voice Over Internet Protocol" (VOIP)—is software that provides nearly costless PC-to-PC telephoning. Once it's downloaded onto your computer, a window pops up so you can search the directory for other registered users. Crystal-clear calls are possible so long as both parties have microphones and are hooked up on the internet. In a recent six-month period more than 6 million users in 170 countries downloaded Skype. Zennstrom hopes for and—frighteningly for competitors—is likely to get another 25 million downloads very soon. Why? The download is free and Skype's cost to add a new user is just one-tenth of a cent, compared to $400 to add a new customer at Vonage—the biggest independent VOIP service provider in the United States. Skype's cost advantage stems from tricks Friis and Zennstrom learned while experimenting with Kazaa. It uses peer-to-peer technology in which digital files are stored on subscribers' computers rather than storing millions of files on the company's central computer, allowing Skype to grow without adding much infrastructure.

What impact, then, is in store for the telecom industry? "I knew it was over when I downloaded Skype," says Michael Powell, chairman of the U.S. Federal Communications Commission. "When the inventors of Kazaa are distributing for free a little program that you can use to talk to anybody else, and the quality is fantastic, and it's free—it's over. The world will change now inevitably." Once millions of callers get used to the idea of free phone calling, it will be a hard habit to reverse. So, Friis and Zennstrom's business plan has a global reach with a system capable of handling 6 billion customers. "We're building the next great communications platform," says Skype's product manager Andreas Sjolund.

But with no geographic or political boundaries, who is accountable for how the system is used, its growth, control over competition, and regulation of the technology? In the absence of uniform international regulations, does accountability reside with the technology's users, or the service providers? For answers, we'll have to wait because accountability issues aren't keeping pace with Skype's catch-us-if-you-can, fast-paced technology.

A good example is the modern grocery store. The checkout scanner reads the bar code on the product you buy. Data are then transmitted to the store's inventory-control system, which updates the number of available units. If inventory falls below a given level, more product is ordered electronically. Meanwhile, the correct price is added to your bill and checkout coupons are printed automatically according to the specific product you bought. Your debit card transfers funds, sales reports are generated for the store's management, and all the while, satellite transmissions are dispatching a truck to begin loading replacement supplies for the store.

Communication Devices

Today's technology lets people conduct business across large distances and from places where communications were once unavailable. *Global positioning systems (GPSs),* for example, use satellite transmissions to track the geographic locations of targets, such as boats or even people. When you're linked to a GPS network, your firm can know your whereabouts at all times. *Personal digital assistants (PDAs)* are tiny hand-held computers with wireless telecommunications capabilities. Many can access the internet, even receiving and sending email messages from the most primitive locations. *Paging systems* and *cellular telephones* connect us instantly with distant networks.

Communication Channels

Communication channels, including wired and wireless transmission, are the media that make all these transmissions possible.[21] Most of us use communication channels when we use wired telephone systems, but today most telephone transmissions are data, not conversations. Fax data account for 90 percent of all telephone signals between the United States and Japan.

Meanwhile, microwave systems transmit wireless radio signals between transmission stations. Satellite communications have also gained popularity with the growth in demand for wireless transmission. Accessible through satellite networks built by McCaw, Hughes, Motorola, AT&T, and Loral, the net is available in remote areas where underground cable isn't feasible.

Broadband Channels. Today's broadband channels, also called ADSL connections, are replacing traditional transmission lines that, until recently, have been the mainstay for connections between computers. In contrast with traditional lines (wires), broadband channels can carry multiple signals—voice, data, audio, visual—simultaneously, rather than carrying just one kind of signal at a time. The result is faster download speed and internet access for multimedia communications.

System Architecture

There are several ways to organize the components in computer and communications networks. One way to classify networks is according to *geographic scope*. Another is according to the *pattern of connections* among the system's devices.

Local and Wide Area Networks

Networked systems classified according to geographic scope may be either local or wide area networks. Computers may be linked province-wide or even nationwide through telephone lines, microwave, or satellite communications, as in a **wide area network (WAN)**. Firms can lease lines from communications vendors or maintain private WANs. Wal-Mart, for example, depends heavily on a private satellite network that links more than 2000 retail stores to its Bentonville, Arkansas, headquarters.

Internal networks covering limited distances may link all of a firm's nearby computers, as in a **local area network (LAN)**. Computers within a building, for example, can be linked by cabling (fibre optic, coaxial, or twisted wire) or by wireless technology. Internally networked computers share processing duties, software, storage areas, and data. On the Home Shopping Network, hundreds of operators seated at monitors in a large room are united by a LAN to enter call-in orders from customers. This arrangement allows the use of a single computer system with one database and software system.

Wireless Networks. Wireless technologies use airborne electronic signals for linking network appliances. In addition to mobile phones, wireless technology extends to laptops, hand-held computers, and applications in cars (including internet access and music players, map terminals, and game machines). Businesses benefit by avoiding webs of wires crisscrossing facilities. Ford, for example, uses an innovative industrial information system—WhereNet—for tracking inventory by means of identification tags that transmit radio waves. Antennas mounted on the factory ceiling receive

wide area network (WAN) A system to link computers across the country through telephone wires or satellites.

local area network (LAN) A system to link computers in one building or in a small geographical area by cabling or wireless technology.

transmissions and send information to a central computer that locates tags in the plant. The system saves time and money by coordinating the delivery of hundreds of parts to assembly lines.[22]

Client–Server Systems. An obvious advantage of networks is the sharing of resources—thus avoiding costly and unnecessary duplication. In a **client–server network**, **clients** are the users of services. They are the points of entry, usually laptop computers, workstations, or desktop computers. The **server** provides the services shared by network users. The powerful minicomputer at the network hub, for example, which is larger and more sophisticated than your PC or *microcomputer*, may be the server for the surrounding client PCs in an office network.

More specifically, the server may act as a file server, a print server, and a fax server. As a *file server*, the minicomputer has a large-capacity disk for storing the programs and data shared by all the PCs in the network. It contains customer files plus the database, word-processing, graphics, and spreadsheet programs that may be used by clients. As a *print server*, the minicomputer controls the printer, stores printing requests from client PCs, and routes jobs to the printer as it becomes available. As the *fax server*, the minicomputer receives, sends, and otherwise controls the system's fax activities. Only one disk drive, one printer, and one fax, therefore, are needed for an entire system of users. Internet computing uses the client–server arrangement.

client–server network A network composed of both clients (users) and servers that allows the clients to access various services without costly and unnecessary duplication.

client A point of entry in a client–server network.

server A computer that provides the services shared by network users.

Summary of Learning Objectives

1. **Explain why businesses must manage *information* and show how computer systems and communication technologies have revolutionized *information management*.** Because businesses are faced with an overwhelming amount of *data* and *information* about customers, competitors, and their own operations, the ability to manage this input can mean the difference between success and failure. The management of its information system is a core activity because all of a firm's business activities are linked to it. New digital technologies have taken an integral place among an organization's resources for conducting everyday business.

2. **Identify and briefly describe three elements of *data communication networks*—the internet, the World Wide Web, and intranets.** *Data communication networks*, both public and private, carry streams of digital data (electronic messages) back and forth quickly and economically via *telecommunication systems*. The largest public communications network, the *internet*, is a gigantic network of networks linking millions of computers and offering information on business around the world. The internet is the most important email system in the world. Individuals can subscribe to the internet via an *internet service provider (ISP)*. The *World Wide Web* is a system with universally accepted standards for storing, formatting, retrieving, and displaying information. It provides the common language that enables users around the

world to "surf" the internet using a common format. *Intranets* are private networks that any company can develop to extend internet technology internally—that is, for transmitting information throughout the firm. Intranets are accessible only to employees, with access to outsiders prevented by hardware and software security systems called *firewalls*.

3. **Describe five *new options for organizational design* that have emerged from the rapid growth of information technologies.** Information networks are leading to *leaner* organizations—businesses with fewer employees and simpler organizational structures—because networked firms can maintain electronic, rather than human, information links among employees and customers. Operations are *more flexible* because electronic networks allow businesses to offer greater product variety and faster delivery cycles. Aided by intranets and the internet, *greater collaboration* is possible, both among internal units and with outside firms. *Geographic separation* of the workplace and company headquarters is more common because electronic links are replacing the need for physical proximity between the company and its workstations. *Improved management processes* are feasible because managers have rapid access to more information about the current status of company activities and easier access to electronic tools for planning and decision making.

4. **Discuss different information-systems *application programs* that are available for users at various organizational levels.** *Transaction processing systems (TPS)* are applications for basic day-to-day business transactions. They are useful for routine transactions, such as taking reservations and meeting payrolls, that follow predetermined steps. Systems for knowledge workers and office applications include *personal productivity tools* such as word processing, document imaging, desktop publishing, computer-aided design (CAD), and simulation modelling. *Management information systems (MIS)* support an organization's managers by providing daily reports, schedules, plans, and budgets. Middle managers, the largest MIS user group, need networked information to plan upcoming activities and track current activities. *Decision support systems (DSSs)* are interactive applications that assist the decision-making processes of middle and top-level managers. *Executive support systems (ESSs)* are quick-reference, easy-access programs to assist upper-level managers. *Artificial intelligence (AI)* and *expert systems* are designed to imitate human behaviour and provide computer-based assistance in performing certain business activities.

5. **Identify and briefly describe the *main elements of an information system*.** *Hardware* is the physical devices and components, including the computer, in the *information system (IS)*. It consists of an input device (such as a keyboard), a central processing unit (CPU), a main memory, disks for data storage, and output devices (such as video monitors and printers). *Software* includes the computer's operating system, application programs (such as word processing, spreadsheets, and web browsers), and a graphical user interface (GUI) that helps users select among the computer's many possible applications.

Control is important to ensure not only that the system operates correctly but also that data and information are transmitted through secure channels to people who really need them. Control is aided by the use of electronic security measures, such as firewalls, that bar entry to the system by unauthorized outsiders. The *database* is the organized collection of all the data files in the system. *People* are also part of the information system. IS *knowledge workers* include systems analysts who design the systems and programmers who write software instructions that tell computers what to do. System users, too, are integral to the system. *Telecommunications* components include multimedia technology that incorporates sound, animation, video, and photography along with ordinary graphics and text. Electronic discussion groups, videoconferencing, and other forms of interactive dialogue are possible with communication devices (such as global positioning systems and personal digital assistants) and communication channels (such as satellite communications).

6. **Briefly describe the content and role of a *database* and the purpose of *database software* for information systems.** The *database* is a centralized, organized collection of related data, in digital form, within a computer system. The database is the storehouse of all the system data that are classified into fields, records, and files having numerical storage locations. The purpose of the database and *database software* is to make the data accessible on demand for system users. *Database management programs* are software applications that enable data to be conveniently stored, retrieved, sorted, and searched. This software allows system users to integrate a single piece of data into several different files within the system so that useful information is created.

KEY TERMS

QUESTIONS FOR ANALYSIS

1. Why must a business manage information as a resource?

2. How can an electronic conferencing system increase productivity and efficiency?

3. Why do the four levels of user groups in an organization need different kinds of information from the IS?

4. In what ways are local area networks (LANs) different from or similar to wide area networks (WANs)?

5. Give two examples (other than those in this chapter) for each of the major types of business application programs.

6. Describe three or four activities in which you regularly engage that might be made easier by multimedia technology.

7. Give three examples (other than those in this chapter) of how a company can become leaner by adopting a networked IS.

APPLICATION EXERCISES

1. Visit a company and interview an individual who is knowledgeable about the firm's management information system. Determine what problems and opportunities exist because of the system.

2. Describe the IS at your school. Identify its components and architecture. What features either promote or inhibit collaboration?

3. Visit a small business in your community to investigate the ways it's using communication technologies and the ways it plans to use them in the future. Prepare a report for class presentation.

BUILDING YOUR BUSINESS SKILLS

The Art and Science of Point-and-Click Research

Goal
To introduce students to World Wide Web search sites.

Background
In a recent survey of nearly 2000 web users, two-thirds said they used the web to obtain work-related information. With an estimated 320 million pages of information on the web, the challenge for business users is fairly obvious: how to find what they're looking for.

Assignment
You'll need a computer and access to the World Wide Web to complete this exercise.

Step 1
Get together with three classmates and decide on a business-related research topic. Choose a topic that interests you—for example, "Business Implications of the Most Recent Census," "Labour Disputes in Professional Sports," or "Marketing Music Lessons and Instruments to Parents of Young Children."

►►►

Step 2

Search the following sites for information on your topic (dividing them among group members to speed the process):

Alta Vista www.altavista.com
Ask.com www.ask.com
Dogpile www.dogpile.com
Excite www.excite.com
Google www.google.ca
Hotbot www.hotbot.com
Go go.com
Lycos www.lycos.com
Metacrawler www.metacrawler.com
Northern Light www.northernlight.com
Yahoo! www.yahoo.com

Take notes as you search so that you can explain your findings to other group members.

Step 3

Working as a group, answer the following questions about your collective search:

1. Which sites were the easiest to use?

2. Which sites offered the most helpful results? What specific factors made these sites better than the others?

3. Which sites offered the least helpful results? What were the problems?

4. Why is it important to learn the special code words or symbols, called operators, that target a search? (Operators are words like AND, OR, and NOT that narrow search queries. For example, using AND in a search tells the system that all words must appear in the results-for example, American AND Management AND Association.)

Follow-Up Questions

1. Research the differences between search engines and search directories. Then place the sites listed in Step 2 in the proper category. Did you find search engines or directories more helpful in this exercise?

2. Why is it important to learn how to use the search-site "Help" function?

3. Based on your personal career goals, how do you think that mastering web-research techniques might help you in the future?

4. How has the web changed the nature of business research?

EXERCISING YOUR ETHICS

Supplying the Right Answers

The Situation

Networked systems facilitate information sharing among companies and often involve sensitive customer data. This exercise asks you to consider ethical issues that might arise when firms are developing information technologies for use in networked systems.

The Dilemma

Home Sweet Home-e (HSH-e) was an ebusiness start-up that sold virtually everything in home furnishings—from linens and towels to cleaning supplies and furniture. From home computers, HSH-e members could shop in virtual storefronts, chat online with other shoppers, talk live with virtual store clerks, and pay electronically at a one-stop website. In reality, HSH-e was a virtual store: a network of numerous suppliers located around the country, each specializing in a particular line of goods. The network was connected by a centrally controlled information technology that HSH-e developed, owned, and operated. Once a customer's order was placed, suppliers instantaneously received information on what to ship, where to ship it, and how much to charge.

HSH-e chose only suppliers who guaranteed fast, reliable deliveries and promised to supply HSH-e exclusively. The linen supplier, for example, could not supply products to other home-furnishings ebusinesses. In return, the supplier was guaranteed all HSH-e orders for linen products. As HSH-e grew, suppliers stood to gain more business and prosper in an expanding etail industry. As it turns out, some prospective suppliers refused to join the network and others in the network were discontinued by HSH-e for failing to expand fast enough to keep up with demand.

Questions for Discussion

1. For a potential HSH-e supplier of a specialized product line, what are the ethical issues in this situation?

2. Consider past suppliers who have been discontinued or have withdrawn from the HSH-e network. Do they face any ethical issues involving HSH-e customers? Involving HSH-e operations? Involving other HSH-e suppliers?

3. Suppose you work at HSH-e and discover a non-network supplier that is more attractive than one of the company's existing suppliers. What ethical considerations do you face in deciding whether or not to replace an existing supplier?

CONCLUDING CASE 13-1

The Point of Cashing In

Who would expect a 120-year-old company to lead a high-tech revolution for the emerging self-service economy? When John H. Patterson founded the National Cash Register Company in 1884, he had little notion of the power of electricity, let alone the potential of employee-less digital technologies for linking buyers with sellers. Yet, this sometimes oddball and paternalistic guru spear-headed development of the mechanical cash register that was a high-tech marvel of its day. In doing so, Patterson set the tone for the company's innovative culture that persists even today. NCR, the world's largest maker of automated teller machines (ATMs), is now headed by Mark Hurd, a cyber-age visionary with aspirations of becoming the leading developer of equipment—hi-tech point-of-sale (POS) machines—for the soon-to-be self-service economy.

NCR's vision for its biggest-selling POS—the ATM—goes far beyond the cash-dispensing machines we think of today. Take cheque clearing and cash depositing, for example. Instead of inserting an envelope of cheques and waiting three days for them to clear, you insert the endorsed cheque into the ATM, where it's scanned and deposited to an account immediately. The deposit receipt will include an image of the cheque. Similarly, when the customer inserts a stack of bills, the ATM will count them and credit them immediately to the account, instead of waiting to unbundle and count the bills the next day. Both cheque clearing and bill counting are among the bank's most labour-intensive activities, so banks stand to reduce labour costs and human errors.

Looking beyond banking, Hurd expects new POS applications from a complete changeover to self-service in every kind of retailing that currently involves buyer-seller interaction. His idea is to get customers to do more themselves—and like it, just as they do for everyday tasks such as self-dialing long distance phone calls (versus operator assistance, which was dominant in an earlier age), self-service/payment at the gas pump (instead of paying inside), and message writing (typing, filing, and sending your own correspondence on a PC, rather than a secretary doing it). "There will be a continual drive to get consumers to do more of the work—and enjoy it—at places where we shop," says Hurd.

Retailers, banks, and other labour-intense service companies haven't taken advantage of POS devices and, moreover, their customer data contain a wealth of potential information that lies fallow. If companies fully utilized customer data, it would allow shoppers to buy via self-service, with nearly instant access to recommended products based on personal buying patterns. Digital assistance in everything from browsing available products

to scanning, weighing, and paying in less time would eliminate the need for costly clerks and cashiers. This futuristic view of a technology-based, self-service economy is not just an illusion—for NCR, it's the core of the company's business strategy.

Dundee, Scotland, is the site of NCR's research centre for ATMs of the future. Visitors get a smiling welcome from Timmy—NCR's cheery young greeter—followed by demonstrations of the latest ATM technology. Speaking in any language, she shows visitors the newest developments: solar-power machines, anti-theft protection that stains money with ink if the machine is violated, radio-frequency identification for loading money electronically into a cellphone, and machines that can accept stacks of cheques and cash without envelopes. The most imaginative innovation, perhaps, is Timmy herself. She's an avatar—a computer-generated character driven by NCR's text-to-speech software—that you'll be seeing soon on the screen of your favourite ATM. This digital sales clerk strokes her hair as she greets customers by name, offers special promotions based on the customer's profile from NCR's data-mining software, then explains how to use various features on the new machine. NCR hopes she'll be the digital jack-of-all-trades that provides everything you need in a self-service mode that reduces expensive human labour costs. "I can be whatever and whoever you want me to be," says Timmy.

CEO Mark Hurd believes his company is uniquely positioned for endless new POS applications beyond ATMs, because there's more to such equipment than just the POS server that meets the customer's eye. Behind the scenes, sophisticated software is prowling through gigantic data warehouses, combing mounds of consumer data for clues about buying patterns and trends for the future. NCR has it all, with its lineup of automated checkout systems and digital salesclerks linked with data warehousing software. The automated checkout system, for example, is already in use at Home Depot. NCR's powerful data warehousing/mining software—the company's biggest source of revenue—is used by the U.S. Air Force to track planes, parts, and pilots, while data-driven giants SBC Communications and Wal-Mart use it for logistics and customer support. By linking those technologies to digital salesclerks-such as "Timmy"—POS applications can revolutionize retailing. Yet, Hurd believes, most companies are unaware of what NCR's technologies can enable them to do, especially in lowering costs and customizing services for individuals. Transactions that rely on employees for interfacing with customers—hotel check-ins, patient check-ins at the doctor's office, student academic advising, airport check-ins, and retail shopping to name a few—are ripe for changeover to self-service.

▶▶▶

In today's digital world, it's hard to believe that commonplace tools like the cash register and the sales receipt—both NCR inventions—revolutionized retailing more than a century ago. In like fashion, Mark Hurd wants today's retailers to get the most from NCR's POS technologies: The supermarket shopper enters a loyalty card number into a small electronic cart recorder—much like a purse-size portable kiosk—that accompanies the cart and tracks the shopper's location, aisle-by-aisle, using infrared beacons from the ceiling. In each section of the store, data-mining software reviews the shopper's history to create special offers, customized to the individual's preferences, gives directions for finding specific items, and reminds them of items they might have forgotten. The shopping trip ends with self-service checkouts where customers don't have to empty their cart. All this is happening now, with consumers doing more of the work while creating mounds of new information. NCR, says Hurd, will "help companies ingest and dispatch that data very quickly."

Questions for Discussion

1. Do you think Mark Hurd might be too optimistic about the rise of self-service in the near future? Identify some technology and economic forces that will determine the rise or decline of self-service.

2. What industries, in addition to those mentioned in the case, are good prospects for adopting NCR's POS technologies? For at least three such industries, identify reasons why you believe they are good prospects.

3. From past experiences as a shopper, what weaknesses, if any, can you think of in NCR's POS technologies? What is your assessment of the seriousness of those weaknesses?

4. Suppose you were designing a "digital salesclerk." What are the operational features that you consider most important for customer satisfaction? Explain.

5. Do you see any potential ethical issues in the use of NCR's POS technologies? Explain.

CONCLUDING CASE 13-2

Internet Wars

There is an international drug war going on. No, not the one against heroin and cocaine. This drug war pits manufacturers of cigarettes and prescription drugs against internet companies that sell these products at cut-rate prices. Here's the story, first for cigarettes, and then for prescription drugs.

Cigarettes

During the last few years, many companies have begun selling cigarettes on the internet. Italian brothers Gianpaolo and Carlo Messina, who operate Yesmoke.ch in a duty-free customs location in Balerna, near the Italian border, are typical. They buy name-brand cigarettes like Camels and Marlboros from duty-free airport retailers for less than $1 a pack, then ship them to customers (mostly in the United States) who have placed orders on their internet site. Although it is illegal for U.S. citizens to buy cigarettes without paying taxes, anyone with a credit card can buy these cigarettes. Customers get their cigarettes at far below normal retail costs because the Messinas don't pay any cigarette taxes to U.S. jurisdictions and can therefore charge much lower prices than retailers do.

In an attempt to stop Yesmoke's activities, Philip Morris filed a lawsuit against the company, charging unfair business practices and patent infringement. Yesmoke ignored the suit and a judge ruled against Yesmoke in a default judgment. But Yesmoke says it is not breaking Swiss law by simply exporting cigarettes, and since it does not operate in the United States, it is not bound by U.S. law. An interesting twist to the story is Yesmoke's claim that Philip Morris is actually selling cigarettes to Yesmoke from one of its factories in the Philippines that produces too much for the local market there. Yesmoke claims it buys the excess cigarettes at a deep discount. Philip Morris denies that it is selling cigarettes to Yesmoke, but the European Union recently charged Philip Morris with complicity in smuggling by intentionally overproducing cigarettes at some of its European factories. As part of a larger anti-smuggling agreement with the EU, Philip Morris agreed to pay $1.25 billion (over 12 years), and the charges were dropped.

In 2004, New York City also filed a lawsuit against Yesmoke, saying that the company owed the city $17 million in back taxes on sales to residents of New York. Whether the city will ever be able to collect those back taxes is doubtful. U.S. states are very concerned that internet sales of cigarettes will prevent them from collecting millions of dollars in cigarette taxes, money which they badly need. Traditional retailers are also concerned, since internet retailers will cut into their business.

Prescription Drugs

For many years, Americans who live in border cities have been coming to Canada to purchase prescription drugs because these drugs are cheaper in Canada. When only a relatively small number of Americans came across the border to buy drugs, not much of a fuss was made. But the internet has suddenly made it possible for Americans living anywhere in the United States to purchase Canadian drugs without even coming to Canada. Instead, they can simply go online and order the drugs (they must provide a U.S. doctor's prescription).

In 2003, the U.S. House of Representatives approved a bill that allowed Americans to import drugs from 25 different nations (including Canada). This gave a big boost to Canadian internet pharmacies. All this demand for Canadian drugs has created a group of Canadian entrepreneurs who want to satisfy it (and, of course, make a profit doing so). Both the big drug companies and the Canadian Pharmacists Association (CPhA) oppose internet pharmacies. Depending on who you talk to, their reasons are either selfish (they fear loss of profit) or because they are concerned about the health and safety of others.

The big drug companies say that there are several problems with respect to internet pharmacies:

■ The safety of drugs is compromised when they are sold over the internet because the internet pharmacist doesn't know if the patient is taking other drugs that might interfere with the patient's prescription request.
■ The internet system can't easily verify that the person wanting the prescription filled hasn't already had it filled from some other internet pharmacy as well.
■ The internet system can't verify whether the prescription is authentic.
■ When drugs are shipped, they can be exposed to various hazards that might reduce their effectiveness.

The internet pharmacies respond to these claims with several counter-arguments:

■ The drug companies won't sell to Canadian-based internet pharmacies because the drug companies will make lower profit margins than if they sold to U.S. pharmacies.
■ Internet pharmacies are providing patients with more affordable prescription drugs; without these drugs, the quality of life of these patients would be much lower.
■ Traditional pharmacists oppose internet pharmacies simply because they are resisting new ways of doing things.

Most of the big drug companies now refuse to sell any of their products to internet pharmacies, and the Canadian Competition Bureau concluded that no laws were violated by this decision. When the drug companies refused to ship their products to internet pharmacies or to the wholesalers who were supplying them, it was assumed that internet pharmacies would have great trouble getting supplies of prescription drugs. But they have continued to get access to drugs and sell those drugs to people in the United States.

How do they do it? By being very entrepreneurial and establishing elaborate supply networks, that's how. More specifically, internet pharmacies are getting their supplies from hundreds of traditional neighbourhood Canadian pharmacies. But since the big drug companies carefully examine orders from pharmacies looking for suspicious "spikes" in demand, the internet pharmacies are very careful about ordering only small amounts from traditional pharmacies. They also pay these traditional pharmacies a "commission" to supply them. These commissions range from 5 to 15 percent.

Late in 2004, Health Minister Ujjal Dosanjh announced that the government was considering shutting down internet pharmacies to protect both the pricing regime and the supply of prescription drugs for Canadians. If the internet pharmacies were shut down, it would cause the loss of thousands of jobs that were created in the industry. In June 2005, however, Dosanjh backed off from his earlier threats and instead announced that legislation would be introduced to protect Canada's drug supply by allowing the government to shut down bulk exports of prescription medicines from internet pharmacies. The legislation would allow Canadian internet pharmacies to continue to fill prescriptions from individuals in the United States. The internet pharmacies breathed a sigh of relief upon hearing this announcement, because it was a much less threatening decision than the one that Dosanjh had been considering in late 2004.

Questions for Discussion

1. Explain how the internet has facilitated the growth of companies selling cigarettes and prescription drugs.

2. Should internet cigarette sellers and internet pharmacies be allowed to operate? What regulations, if any, should the Canadian government put on these companies?

3. Would you buy cigarettes from an internet seller? Would you buy prescription drugs from an internet pharmacy? Why or why not?

4. Critique each of the arguments that are being made by the drug companies and the Canadian Pharmacists Association. Then do the same for each of the arguments being made by the internet pharmacies. On balance, which arguments do you think are the most compelling? Explain.

5. Develop arguments for and against selling cigarettes on the internet.

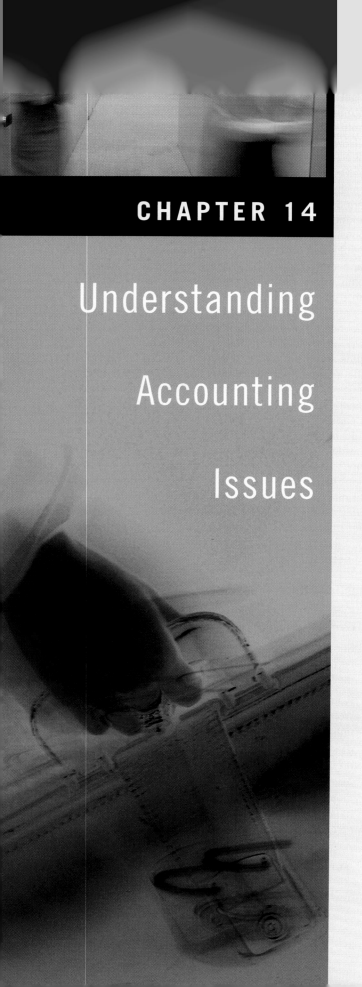

CHAPTER 14

Understanding Accounting Issues

After reading this chapter, you should be able to:

1 Explain the role of accountants and distinguish between the kinds of work done by *public* and *private* *accountants*.

2 Explain how the *accounting equation* and *double-entry accounting* are used in record keeping.

3 Describe the three basic *financial statements* and show how they reflect the activity and financial condition of a business.

4 Explain the key standards and principles for reporting financial statements.

5 Show how computing key *financial ratios* can help in analyzing the financial strengths of a business.

6 Explain some of the special issues that arise in *international accounting*.

Do We Need to Audit the Auditors?

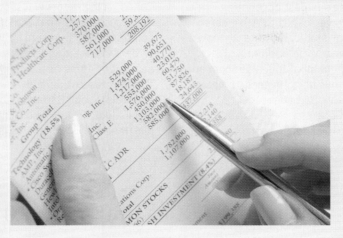

The large amount of negative publicity that has been given to firms like Enron and WorldCom during the last few years makes for very interesting reading, but it is also making accountants very nervous. More and more investors are asking questions like, "How much confidence can I really have when I read an auditor's statement that a company's practices adhere to generally accepted accounting principles?" or "How can a company go bankrupt shortly after having their books audited by an independent auditor?" In 2002, NFO WorldGroup, a market research firm, gave outside auditors a "D" grade for their overall performance.

The case of Livent Inc., a live theatre company that formerly had theatres in Vancouver, Toronto, and New York, illustrates the problems the auditing profession is facing. Livent went bankrupt in the late 1990s amid charges of questionable accounting practices, and two of its executives—Garth Drabinsky and Myron Gottlieb—are now on trial for allegedly defrauding investors and creditors out of $500 million. Investors lost 95 percent of their investment after Livent disclosed accounting irregularities in 1998.

In 2000, the Institute of Chartered Accountants of Ontario (ICAO) took disciplinary action against Livent's senior vice president of finance, who was a Chartered Accountant. He was fined $25 000 and expelled from the ICAO after admitting that he had filed false financial statements and fraudulently manipulated Livent's books. After that, the ICAO began investigating the role of Deloitte & Touche, the accounting firm that was Livent's auditors, and in 2004, the ICAO laid charges of professional misconduct against four partners at Deloitte & Touche. (A few years earlier, in a U.S. court, a judge concluded that Deloitte had not participated in the fraud.) Deloitte is also facing several other lawsuits, including one resulting from the collapse of the Italian dairy firm Parmalat. In that case, investors are suing Parmalat executives and two partners in Deloitte's Italian branch for allegedly conspiring to hide nearly $17 billion of debt.

At a disciplinary hearing in April 2004, Deloitte's lawyer argued that the ICAO charges were "rubbish," and that the allegations were simply differences of opinion regarding the application of generally accepted accounting principles. He pointed out that Livent managers had admitted lying to Deloitte auditors to prevent them from finding out about Livent's real financial condition. The lawyer indicated that his clients were angry that they had been charged, and criticized the long delay in bringing the ICAO charges forward. He also filed an application with the Ontario Superior Court to drop the charges and prevent the ICAO from pursuing the case further.

William Parrett, the CEO of Deloitte, says that there is an "expectation gap" between what the investing public expects and what external auditors can possibly deliver. While auditors simply certify the accuracy of a company's financial statements (based on information provided by the company), investors want auditors to certify that a company is actually financially healthy. Parrett also says that it is not reasonable to hold auditing firms accountable for the illegal and secretive behaviour of corporate executives. Parrett does agree that auditing firms will have to improve the rigour of their audits, and he said that Deloitte has been working hard to overcome any existing deficiencies. The company has appointed an ethics officer in each of its national companies, has added more resources to audit teams, and re-checks initial audit results.

Parrett's explanation sounds pretty reasonable, but people still want to know how cases like Livent, Parmalat, and Enron happen even after the companies' financial statements have been audited by an independent accounting firm. One answer is that auditors are sometimes tempted to "look the other way" when they encounter questionable practices. But *why* would accounting firms not point out questionable accounting practices when they find them? One reason is that many accounting firms have historically also done management consulting for the firms they are auditing. The fees generated from this management consulting can be very lucrative, and often exceed the auditing fees the accounting firm receives. Accountants are human beings, so we should not be surprised if they worry that their clients will be upset if auditors question certain accounting practices. And if clients get upset enough, they may not give the accounting firm any more management consulting contracts. The obvious solution to this problem is to prohibit accounting firms from doing both auditing and management consulting for a given client. In 2002, the Canadian Imperial Bank of Commerce announced that it would no longer allow its auditors to do any management consulting for CIBC.

One very specific Canadian response so far is the establishment of a new Canadian Public Accountability Board (CPAB), which will oversee supervision, inspection, and discipline of Canada's largest accounting firms. The accounting firms will have to get CPAB clearance before their clients' financial statements are accepted. In short, the auditors are going to be audited.

We should not conclude from all of this that doom and gloom reigns in the auditing business. In fact, things are looking up, partly because the Sarbanes-Oxley Act was passed in 2002 by the U.S. Congress. Section 404 of the Act requires U.S.-listed companies to analyze their reporting controls and to make any improvements that are necessary. At each year-end, auditors must certify these controls. Many people in the accounting field believe that Canadian legislators will soon introduce similar legislation. And guess what? That will affect over 4000 Canadian corporations, which in turn will create a substantial increase in demand for the services of auditors. Canadian public accounting firms have already begun recruiting more staff. The increased demand for accountants who are knowledgeable about Sarbanes-Oxley is particularly evident in places like Calgary, the home of many Canadian companies that are listed on U.S. stock exchanges. ◆

WHAT IS ACCOUNTING AND WHO USES IT?

accounting A comprehensive system for collecting, analyzing, and communicating financial information.

bookkeeping Recording accounting transactions.

accounting information system (AIS) An organized procedure for identifying, measuring, recording, and retaining financial information so that it can be used in accounting statements and management reports.

Accounting is a comprehensive information system for collecting, analyzing, and communicating financial information. As such, it is a system for measuring business performance and translating those measures into information for management decisions. **Bookkeeping** is just one phase of accounting—the recording of accounting transactions. Clearly, accounting is much more comprehensive than bookkeeping because accounting involves more than just the recording of information.

Accounting also uses performance measures to prepare performance reports for owners, the public, and regulatory agencies. To meet these objectives, accountants keep records of such transactions as taxes paid, income received, and expenses incurred, and they analyze the effects of these transactions on particular business activities. By sorting, analyzing, and recording thousands of transactions, accountants can determine how well a business is being managed and how financially strong it is. As the opening case shows, the accounting system can produce distorted results that, in turn, can create huge problems for both owners and managers.

Because businesses engage in many thousands of transactions, ensuring consistent, dependable financial information is mandatory. This is the job of the **accounting information system (AIS)**: an organized procedure for identifying, measuring, recording, and retaining financial information so that it can be used in accounting statements and management reports. The system includes all the people, reports, computers, procedures, and resources for compiling financial transactions.[1]

There are numerous users of accounting information:

- *Business managers* use accounting information to set goals, develop plans, set budgets, and evaluate future prospects.

- *Employees and unions* use accounting information to get paid and to plan for and receive such benefits as health care, insurance, vacation time, and retirement pay.

- *Investors and creditors* use accounting information to estimate returns to stockholders, to determine a company's growth prospects, and to decide if the company is a good credit risk before investing or lending.

- *Taxing authorities* use accounting information to plan for tax inflows, to determine the tax liabilities of individuals and businesses, and to ensure that correct amounts are paid in a timely fashion.

■ *Government regulatory agencies* rely on accounting information to fulfill their duties; the provincial securities commissions, for example, require firms to file financial disclosures so that potential investors have valid information about a company's financial status.

WHO ARE ACCOUNTANTS AND WHAT DO THEY DO?

At the head of the AIS is the **controller**, who manages all the firm's accounting activities. As chief accounting officer, the controller ensures that the accounting system provides the reports and statements needed for planning, controlling, and decision-making activities. This broad range of activities requires different types of accounting specialists. In this section, we will begin by distinguishing between the two main fields of accounting, *financial* and *managerial*. Then we will discuss the different functions and activities of the three professional accounting groups in Canada.

controller The individual who manages all the firm's accounting activities.

Financial and Managerial Accounting

In any company, two fields of accounting—financial and managerial—can be distinguished by the different users they serve. As we have just seen, it is both convenient and accurate to classify users of accounting information as users outside the company and users inside the company. This same distinction allows us to categorize accounting systems as either *financial* or *managerial*.

Financial Accounting

A firm's **financial accounting system** is concerned with external users of information—consumer groups, unions, shareholders, and government agencies. It prepares and publishes income statements and balance sheets at regular intervals. All of these documents focus on the activities of *the company as a whole*, rather than on individual departments or divisions.

In reporting data, financial accountants must conform to standard reporting formats and procedures imposed by both the accounting profession and government regulatory agencies. This requirement helps ensure that users can clearly compare information, whether from many different companies or from the same company at different times. The information in such reports is mostly *historical*: That is, it summarizes financial transactions that have occurred during past accounting periods.

financial accounting system The process whereby interested groups are kept informed about the financial condition of a firm.

Managerial Accounting

In contrast, **managerial** (or **management**) **accounting** serves internal users. Managers at all levels need information to make decisions for their departments, to monitor current projects, and to plan for future activities. Other employees, too, need accounting information. Engineers, for instance, want to know costs for materials and production so they can make product or operations improvements. To set performance goals, salespeople need data on past sales by geographic region. Purchasing agents use information on materials costs to negotiate terms with suppliers.

Reports to these users serve *the company's individual units*, whether departments, projects, plants, or divisions. Internal reports may be designed in any form that will assist internal users in planning, decision making, and controlling. Furthermore, as *projections* and *forecasts* of both

managerial (management) accounting Internal procedures that alert managers to problems and aid them in planning and decision making.

financial data and business activities, internal reports are an extremely important part of the management accounting system: They are forward-looking rather than historical in nature.

Professional Accountants

Users of financial statements want to be confident that the accountants who have prepared them have a high level of expertise and credibility. Three professional accounting organizations have developed in Canada to certify accounting expertise.

Chartered Accountants

chartered accountant (CA) An individual who has met certain experience and education requirements and has passed a licensing examination; acts as an outside accountant for other firms.

The Canadian Institute of Chartered Accountants (CICA) grants the **chartered accountant (CA)** designation. To achieve this designation, a person must earn a university degree, then complete an educational program and pass a national exam. About half of all CAs work in CA firms that offer accounting services to the public; the other half work in government or industry. CA firms typically provide audit, tax, and management services (see Table 14.1 for a list of the 10 largest CA firms in Canada). CAs focus on external financial reporting, that is, certifying for various interested parties (shareholders, lenders, Canada Customs and Revenue Agency, etc.) that the financial records of a company accurately reflect the true financial condition of the firm. In 2006, there were about 70 000 CAs in Canada.[2]

Certified General Accountants

certified general accountant (CGA) An individual who has completed an education program and passed a national exam; works in private industry or a CGA firm.

The Certified General Accountants Association of Canada grants the **certified general accountant (CGA)** designation. To become a CGA, a person must complete an education program and pass a national exam. To be eligible, a person must have an accounting job with a company. Formerly, CGAs were not allowed to audit the financial statements of publicly held companies, but this is rapidly changing, and now CGAs can audit corporate financial statements in most provinces. Most CGAs work in private companies, but there are a few CGA firms. Some CGAs also work in CA firms. CGAs also focus on external financial reporting, and emphasize the use of the computer as a management accounting tool. From time to time, CGA-Canada

Table 14.1	The Top 10 Accounting Firms in Canada, 2005
Company	**Annual Revenues (in millions of $)**
1. Deloitte & Touche LLP	$1151
2. KPMG LLP	885
3. PricewaterhouseCoopers LLP	876
4. Ernst & Young LLP	788
5. Grant Thornton Canada	361
6. BDO Dunwoody LLP	260
7. Meyers Norris Penny LLP	143
8. Collins Barrow National Cooperative Inc.	109
9. RSM Richter LLP	95
10. HLB/Schwartz Levitsky Feldman LLP	37

BUSINESS ACCOUNTABILITY

The Pension Crisis

Traditional pension plans are typically defined benefit plans, that is, the company promises to pay a certain defined amount of money to employees when they retire. But a CGA-Canada report showed that the total deficit of the country's largest pension plans at the end of 2004 was $26 billion. If the indexation of pension benefits is taken into account, the number soars to $190 billion. In terms of proportions, 59 percent of traditional pension plans were experiencing pension shortfalls; this number jumps to 96 percent if the indexation of benefits is taken into account.

There are also problems in funding retiree *bene-fits* (not pensions). A study of 71 of Canada's largest companies showed that their liabilities for retiree *benefits* amounted to $16 billion. In one recent year at Suncor Energy Inc., for example, the company's benefits liability was $98 million (almost as much as its pension liability of $99 million). With baby boomers living longer, and with large numbers of them heading into retirement, the situation for both retiree pensions and retiree benefits is likely to get worse before it gets better.

The problems in pension plans have been caused by a variety of factors, but two factors stand out. First, there have been lower than anticipated returns on investments held by the pension plans. In the 1990s, returns on pension plan investments averaged 11 percent. This rate of return was higher than the 7.5 percent that had been predicted. But during the period 2001–03, the average rate of return for pension plan investments was just 3.1 percent. This was far below the 7 percent that had been assumed. This situation was made even worse because companies began to invest more heavily in equities as a result of their positive experience in the stock market boom of the 1990s. In 1990, 64 percent of pension assets were invested in fixed-income securities and only 36 percent in the more risky equities. By 2004, however, 56 percent of pension assets were invested in equities and only 37 percent in fixed-income securities.

Second, because pension plan investments had achieved such high returns during the 1990s, many companies took pension plan contribution "holidays" and did not contribute anything to the plans they were sponsoring. When the lower investment returns of the twenty-first century started showing up, pension surpluses quickly became pension deficits. In retrospect, companies should not have taken contribution holidays.

The crisis in defined benefit pension plans has caused employers to examine alternative ways to deal with pensions. The simplest solution is to drop defined *benefit* pension plans and instead offer employees defined *contribution* pension plans. When the latter is used, the company's liability is known, but the value of the pension plan when a person retires is unknown (its value is determined solely by the rate of return that the investments in the plan have achieved). Defined contribution plans obviously reduce the uncertainty for the company, but create more uncertainty for retirees.

Companies are, in fact, shifting to defined contribution pension plans. In the United States, for example, there were 112 000 defined benefit plans in 1985, but now there are only about 29 000. The move away from defined benefit plans is also occurring in Canada, although at a slower rate. But that is likely to change, since Canadian legislation requires the company to bear the full financial burden of pension deficits. The current crisis in defined benefit plans means that over the next five years, $15 billion extra dollars will have to be put into those plans to make up for past investment losses. Companies therefore have an incentive to move away from defined benefit plans and toward defined contribution plans, because with the latter they at least know what their contribution requirements are.

Canadian accounting rules may also need to be re-examined. Under current rules, companies can delay recognizing changes in the value of their pension plans. Using a practice called "smoothing," companies can spread the reporting of changes over several years. When stock markets were booming, no one scrutinized pension plans much because their value was going up. But when stock markets started dropping in 2000, large liabilities began building up (but companies kept that information off their balance sheets). National Bank Financial studied 79 Canadian companies—representing 80 percent of the capitalization of the S&P/TSX—and found that their off-balance sheet pension deficits totalled $21 billion.

Canadian and international accounting regulators are working on changes to accounting rules that will bring more realism to pension reporting. The most obvious change involves ending the practice of smoothing and reporting pension fund returns as they actually take place. This means that income from the pension fund would be reported as investment income and the costs of running the pension fund would be reported as expenses. Regulators recognize that a change like this will increase the volatility in the earnings that corporations report, but they point out that investors will be able to more clearly see what is happening (good or bad) in a company's pension fund.

commissions reports on important issues such as pensions (see the Business Accountability box). In 2006, there were about 41 000 CGAs in Canada.[3]

Certified Management Accountants

certified management accountant (CMA) An individual who has completed a university degree, passed a national examination, and completed a strategic leadership program; works in industry and focusses on internal management accounting.

The Society of Management Accountants of Canada grants the **certified management accountant (CMA)** designation. To achieve the designation, a person must a have university degree, pass a two-part national entrance examination, and complete a strategic leadership program while gaining practical experience in a management accounting environment. CMAs work in organizations of all sizes, and focus on applying best management practices in all the operations of a business. CMAs bring a strong market-focus to strategic management and resource deployment, synthesizing and analyzing financial and non-financial information to help organizations maintain a competitive advantage. CMAs emphasize the role of accountants in the planning and overall strategy of the firm in which they work. In 2006, there were about 37 000 CMAs in Canada.[4]

Accounting Services

CAs and CGAs usually perform several accounting services for their clients. The most common of these are auditing, tax services, and management services.

Auditing

audit An accountant's examination of a company's financial records to determine if it used proper procedures to prepare its financial reports.

In an **audit**, the accountant examines a company's AIS to determine whether the company's financial reports fairly present its financial operations. Companies normally must provide audited financial reports when applying for loans or when selling stock. The audit will determine if the firm has controls to prevent errors or fraud from going undetected. Auditors also examine receipts such as shipping documents, cancelled cheques, payroll records, and cash receipts records. In some cases, an auditor may physically check inventories, equipment, or other assets, even if it means descending 200 metres underground in a lead mine.

A financial report is an integral component of the financial accounting system.

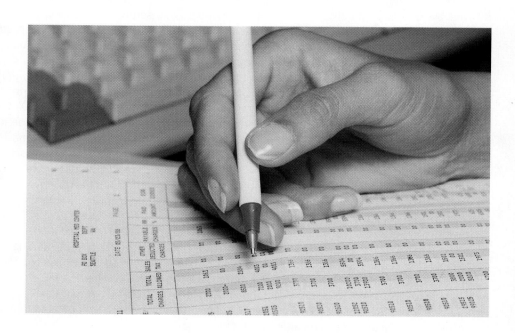

Detecting fraud is not the primary purpose of audits, but in recent years there has been much publicity about the alleged failure of auditors to detect fraud. Therefore, when audits are being conducted, sometimes **forensic accountants** are used to track down hidden funds in business firms. Because white-collar crime is on the increase, the number of forensic accountants has increased in recent years. Forensic accountants were used to examine Swiss bank accounts for assets deposited by victims of Nazi persecution during the Second World War.[5] Al Rosen, who writes articles about accounting practices, is a well-known Canadian forensic accountant.

forensic accountant An accountant who tracks down hidden funds in business firms, usually as part of a criminal investigation.

One of the auditor's responsibilities is to ensure that the client's accounting system adheres to **generally accepted accounting principles (GAAP)**—the body of theory and procedure developed and monitored by the CICA. At the end of an audit, the auditor will certify whether the client's financial reports comply with GAAP. Recently, some non-profit organizations such as churches and universities have said that they felt pressured by their auditors to use GAAP. They argue, however, that GAAP principles are designed for profit-seeking business firms, not non-profit organizations. Non-profits should be judged on how well they meet their goals—for example, helping people—rather than on a financial criterion like profit.[6]

generally accepted accounting principles (GAAP) Standard rules and methods used by accountants in preparing financial reports.

Tax Services

Tax services include helping clients not only with preparing their tax returns but also in their tax planning. Tax laws are complex. A CA's advice can help a business structure (or restructure) its operations and investments and save millions of dollars in taxes. To serve their clients best, of course, accountants must stay abreast of changes in tax laws—no simple matter.

Management Consulting Services

Management consulting services range from personal financial planning to the planning of corporate mergers. Other services include plant layout and design, marketing studies, production scheduling, computer feasibility studies, and design and implementation of accounting systems. Some accounting firms even assist in executive recruitment. Small wonder that the staffs of accounting firms may include engineers, architects, mathematicians, and even psychologists.

management consulting services Specialized accounting services to help managers resolve a variety of problems in finance, production scheduling, and other areas.

Private Accountants

To ensure the fairness of their reports, CAs and CGAs must be independent of the firms they audit. They are employees of accounting firms and provide services for many clients. But businesses also hire their own **private accountants** as salaried employees to deal with the company's day-to-day accounting needs.

private accountant An accountant hired as a salaried employee to deal with a company's day-to-day accounting needs.

Private accountants perform a variety of accounting jobs. An internal auditor at Petro-Canada, for example, might fly to the Hibernia site to confirm the accuracy of oil-flow meters on the offshore drilling platform. But a supervisor responsible for $200 million in monthly accounts payable to vendors and employees may travel no further than the executive suite. The nature of the accounting job thus depends on the specific business and the activities needed to make that business a success. Large businesses employ specialized accountants in such areas as budgets, financial planning, internal auditing, payroll, and taxation. Each accounting area has its own challenges and excitement. In small businesses, a single individual may handle all accounting tasks.

TOOLS OF THE ACCOUNTING TRADE

All accountants, whether public or private, rely on record keeping. Private accountants use journals and ledgers to enter and keep track of business transactions for their company. Underlying these records are the two key concepts of accounting: the *accounting equation* and *double-entry bookkeeping*.

The Accounting Equation

At various points in the year, accountants use the following equation to balance the data pertaining to financial transactions:

$$\text{Assets} = \text{Liabilities} + \text{Owners' equity}$$

To understand the importance of this equation, we must first understand the terms *assets*, *liabilities*, and *owners' equity*.[7]

Assets and Liabilities

asset Anything of economic value owned by a firm or individual.

liability Any debt owed by a firm or individual to others.

An **asset** is any economic resource that is expected to benefit a firm or an individual who owns it. Assets include land, buildings, equipment, inventory, and payments due the company (accounts receivable). A **liability** is a debt that the firm owes to an outside party.

Owners' Equity

owners' equity Any positive difference between a firm's assets and its liabilities; what would remain for a firm's owners if the company were liquidated, all its assets were sold, and all its debts were paid.

You may have heard of the equity that a homeowner has in a house—that is, the amount of money that could be made by selling the house and paying off the mortgage. Similarly, **owners' equity** is the amount of money that owners would receive if they sold all of a company's assets and paid all of its liabilities. We can rewrite the accounting equation to highlight this definition:

$$\text{Assets} - \text{Liabilities} = \text{Owners' equity}$$

If a company's assets exceed its liabilities, owners' equity is *positive*; if the company goes out of business, the owners will receive some cash (a gain) after selling assets and paying off liabilities. If liabilities outweigh assets, owners' equity is *negative*; assets are insufficient to pay off all debts. If the company goes out of business, the owners will get no cash and some

The inventory at this car dealership is part of the company's assets. The cars constitute an economic resource because the firm will benefit financially as it sells them. When they are sold, at the end of the company's accounting period, the dealership will convert the cost of the cars as expenses and show them as costs of goods sold.

creditors won't be paid. Owners' equity is meaningful for both investors and lenders. Before lending money to owners, for example, lenders want to know the amount of owners' equity in a business. Owners' equity consists of two sources of capital:

1. The amount that the owners originally invested

2. Profits earned by and reinvested in the company

When a company operates profitably, its assets increase faster than its liabilities. Owners' equity, therefore, will increase if profits are retained in the business instead of paid out as dividends to stockholders. Owners' equity also increases if owners invest more of their own money to increase assets. However, owners' equity can shrink if the company operates at a loss or if owners withdraw assets.

Double-Entry Accounting

If your business buys inventory with cash, you decrease your cash and increase your inventory. Similarly, if you buy supplies on credit, you increase your supplies and increase your accounts payable. If you invest more money in your business, you increase the company's cash and increase your owners' equity. In other words, *every transaction affects two accounts*. Accountants thus use a **double-entry accounting system** to record the dual effects of transactions.[8] This practice ensures that the accounting equation always balances.

double-entry accounting system A bookkeeping system, developed in the fifteenth century and still in use, that requires every transaction to be entered in two ways—how it affects assets and how it affects liabilities and owners' equity—so that the accounting equation is always in balance.

FINANCIAL STATEMENTS

As we noted earlier, the job of accounting is to summarize the results of a firm's transactions and to issue reports to help managers make informed decisions. Among the most important reports are **financial statements**, which fall into three broad categories—*balance sheets, income statements,* and *statements of cash flows.*[9] In this section, we will discuss these three types of financial statements, as well as the function of the budget as an internal financial statement. We'll conclude by explaining the most important reporting practices and the standards that guide accountants in drawing up financial statements.

Describe the three basic *financial statements* and show how they reflect the activity and financial condition of a business.

3

financial statement Any of several types of broad reports regarding a company's financial status; most often used in reference to balance sheets, income statements, and/or statements of cash flows.

Balance Sheets

Balance sheets supply detailed information about the accounting equation factors: assets, liabilities, and owners' equity. Because they also show a firm's financial condition at one point in time, balance sheets are sometimes called *statements of financial position.* Figure 14.1 shows the balance sheet for Perfect Posters.

balance sheet A type of financial statement that summarizes a firm's financial position on a particular date in terms of its assets, liabilities, and owners' equity.

Assets

As we have seen, an asset is any economic resource that a company owns and from which it can expect to derive some future benefit. From an accounting standpoint, most companies have three types of assets: *current, fixed,* and *intangible.*

Current Assets. **Current assets** include cash and assets that can be converted into cash within a year. They are normally listed in order of **liquidity**—the ease with which they can be converted into cash. Business

current assets Cash and other assets that can be converted into cash within a year.

liquidity The ease and speed with which an asset can be converted to cash; cash is said to be perfectly liquid.

☐☐☐☐☐☐☐☐☐ **Perfect Posters, Inc.**
555 Riverview, Toronto, Ontario

Perfect Posters, Inc.
Balance Sheet
As of December 31, 2006

Assets

Current Assets:

Cash		$7,050
Marketable securities. . . .		2,300
Accounts receivable.	$26,210	
Less: Allowance of.		
doubtful accounts.	(650)	25,560
Merchandise inventory.		21,250
Prepaid expenses		1,050
Total current assets		**$57,210**

Fixed Assets:

Land		18,000
Building	65,000	
Less: Accumulated		
depreciation	(22,500)	42,500
Equipment	72,195	
Less: Accumulated		
depreciation	(24,815)	47,380
Total fixed assets. . .		**107,880**

Intangible Assets:

Patents	7,100	
Trademarks	900	
Total intangible		
assets		**8,000**
Total assets		**$173,090**

Liabilities and Owners' Equity

Current liabilities:

Accounts payable.	$16,315	
Wages payable.	3,700	
Taxes payable.	1,920	
Total current liabilities		**$21,935**

Long-term liabilities:

Notes payable, 8%		
due 2009	10,000	
Bonds payable, 9%		
due 2011	30,000	
Total long-term		
liabilities		**40,000**
Total liabilities		**$61,935**

Owners' Equity

Common stock, $5 par	40,000	
Additional paid-in capital	15,000	
Retained earnings	56,155	
Total owners' equity		**111,155**
Total liabilities and owners' equity . . .		**$173,090**

Figure 14.1 Perfect Posters' balance sheet shows clearly that the firm's total assets equal its total liabilities and owners' equity.

debts, for example, can usually be satisfied only through payments of cash. A company that needs but cannot generate cash (in other words, a company that is not liquid) may thus be forced to sell assets at sacrifice prices or even go out of business.

By definition, cash is completely liquid. *Marketable securities* purchased as short-term investments are slightly less liquid but can be sold quickly if necessary. Marketable securities include stocks or bonds of other companies, government securities, and money market certificates. There are three other important non-liquid assets held by many companies: *accounts receivable*, *merchandise inventory*, and *prepaid expenses*.

accounts receivable Amounts due to the firm from customers who have purchased goods or services on credit; a form of current asset.

Accounts receivable are amounts due from customers who have purchased goods on credit. Most businesses expect to receive payment within 30 days of a sale. In our hypothetical example, the entry labelled *Less: Allowance of doubtful accounts* in Figure 14.1 indicates $650 in receivables that Perfect Posters does not expect to collect. Total accounts receivable assets are decreased accordingly.

merchandise inventory The cost of merchandise that has been acquired for sale to customers but is still on hand.

Following accounts receivable on the Perfect Posters balance sheet is **merchandise inventory**—the cost of merchandise that has been acquired for sale to customers and is still on hand. Accounting for the value of inventories on the balance sheet is difficult because inventories are flowing in and out throughout the year. Therefore, assumptions must be made about which ones were sold and which ones remain in storage.

prepaid expense Includes supplies on hand and rent paid for the period to come.

Prepaid expenses include supplies on hand and rent paid for the period to come. They are assets because they have been paid for and are available to the company. In all, Perfect Posters' current assets as of December 31, 2006, totalled $57 210.

Fixed Assets. **Fixed assets** (for example, land, buildings, and equipment) have long-term use or value. But as buildings and equipment wear out or become obsolete, their value decreases. To reflect decreasing value, accountants use **depreciation** to spread the cost of an asset over the years of its useful life. Depreciation means calculating an asset's useful life in years, dividing its worth by that many years, and subtracting the resulting amount each year. Each year, therefore, the asset's remaining value decreases on the books. In Figure 14.1, Perfect Posters shows fixed assets of $107 880 after depreciation.

Intangible Assets. Although their worth is hard to set, intangible assets have monetary value. **Intangible assets** usually include the cost of obtaining rights or privileges such as patents, trademarks, copyrights, and franchise fees. **Goodwill** is the amount paid for an existing business beyond the value of its other assets. Perfect Posters has no goodwill assets; however, it does own trademarks and patents for specialized storage equipment. These are intangible assets worth $8000. Larger companies, of course, have intangible assets that are worth much more.

Liabilities

Like assets, liabilities are often separated into different categories. **Current liabilities** are debts that must be paid within one year. These include **accounts payable**—unpaid bills to suppliers for materials as well as wages and taxes that must be paid in the coming year. Perfect Posters has current liabilities of $21 935.

Long-term liabilities are debts that are not due for at least one year. These normally represent borrowed funds on which the company must pay interest. Perfect Posters' long-term liabilities are $40 000.

Owners' Equity

The final section of the balance sheet in Figure 14.1 shows owners' equity broken down into *common stock, paid-in capital,* and *retained earnings.* When Perfect Posters was formed, the declared legal value of its common stock was $5 per share. By law, this $40 000 ($5 × 8000 shares) cannot be distributed as dividends. **Paid-in capital** is additional money invested in the firm by its owners. Perfect Posters has $15 000 in paid-in capital.

Retained earnings are net profits minus dividend payments to stockholders. Retained earnings accumulate when profits, which could have been distributed to stockholders, are kept instead for use by the company. At the close of 2006, Perfect Posters had retained earnings of $56 155.

Income Statements

The **income statement** is sometimes called a **profit-and-loss statement**, because its description of revenues and expenses results in a figure showing the firm's annual profit or loss. In other words,

Revenues – Expenses = Profit (or loss)

Popularly known as "the bottom line," profit or loss is probably the most important figure in any business enterprise. Figure 14.2 shows the 2006 income statement for Perfect Posters, whose bottom line that year was $12 585. The income statement is divided into three major categories: *revenues, cost of goods sold,* and *operating expenses.*

---

fixed assets Assets that have long-term use or value to the firm such as land, buildings, and machinery.

depreciation Distributing the cost of a major asset over the years in which it produces revenues; calculated by each year subtracting the asset's original value divided by the number of years in its productive life.

intangible assets Non-physical assets such as patents, trademarks, copyrights, and franchise fees that have economic value but whose precise value is difficult to calculate.

goodwill The amount paid for an existing business beyond the value of its other assets.

current liabilities Any debts owed by the firm that must be paid within one year.

accounts payable Amounts due from the firm to its suppliers for goods and/or services purchased on credit; a form of current liability.

long-term liabilities Any debts owed by the firm that are not due for at least one year.

paid-in capital Any additional money invested in the firm by the owners.

retained earnings A company's net profits less any dividend payments to shareholders.

income (profit-and-loss) statement A type of financial statement that describes a firm's revenues and expenses and indicates whether the firm has earned a profit or suffered a loss during a given period.

□□□□□□□□□□□ **Perfect Posters, Inc.**
555 Riverview, Toronto, Ontario

Perfect Posters, Inc.
Income Statement
Year ended December 31, 2006

Revenues (gross sales)...........			**$256,425**
Costs of goods sold:			
Merchandise inventory,			
January 1, 2006..............	$22,380		
Merchandise purchases			
during year................	103,635		
Goods available for sale........		$126,015	
Less: Merchandise inventory,			
December 31, 2006.........		21,250	
Cost of goods sold			**104,765**
Gross profit			**151,660**
Operating expenses:			
Selling and repackaging expenses:			
Salaries and wages........	49,750		
Advertising...............	6,380		
Depreciation—warehouse and ..			
repackaging equipment......	3,350		
Total selling and repackaging			
expenses.................		59,480	
Administrative expenses:			
Salaries and wages..........	55,100		
Supplies..................	4,150		
Utilities....................	3,800		
Depreciation—office equipment .	3,420		
Interest expense..................	2,900		
Miscellaneous expenses..........	1,835		
Total administration expenses......		71,205	
Total operating expenses......			**130,685**
Operating income (income before taxes)...			20,975
Income taxes...................			8,390
Net income....................			**$12,585**

Figure 14.2 Perfect Posters' income statement. The final entry on the income statement, the bottom line, reports the firm's profit or loss.

Revenues

revenues Any monies received by a firm as a result of selling a good or service or from other sources such as interest, rent, and licensing fees.

When a law firm receives $250 for preparing a will or when a supermarket collects $65 from a customer buying groceries, both are receiving **revenues**—the funds that flow into a business from the sale of goods or services. In 2006, Perfect Posters reported revenues of $256 425 from the sale of art prints and other posters.

Cost of Goods Sold

cost of goods sold Any expenses directly involved in producing or selling a good or service during a given time period.

In Perfect Posters' income statement, the **cost of goods sold** category shows the costs of obtaining materials to make the products sold during the year. Perfect Posters began 2006 with posters valued at $22 380. Over the year, it spent $103 635 to purchase posters. During 2006, then, the company had $126 015 worth of merchandise available to sell. By the end of the year, it had sold all but $21 250 of those posters, which remained as merchandise inventory. The cost of obtaining the goods sold by the firm was thus $104 765.

gross profit (gross margin) A firm's revenues (gross sales) less its cost of goods sold.

Gross Profit (or Gross Margin). To calculate **gross profit** (or **gross margin**), subtract cost of goods sold from revenues obtained from goods sold. Perfect Posters' gross profit in 2006 was $151 660 ($256 425 – $104 765). Expressed as a percentage of sales, gross profit is 59.1 percent ($151 660 ÷ $256 425).

Gross profit percentages vary widely across industries. In retailing, Home Depot reports 30 percent. In manufacturing, Harley-Davidson reports 34 percent; and in pharmaceuticals, Wyeth reports 75 percent. For companies with low gross margins, product costs are a big expense. If a company has a high gross margin, it probably has low cost-of-goods-sold but high selling and administrative expenses.

Operating Expenses

In addition to costs directly related to acquiring goods, every company has general expenses ranging from erasers to the president's salary. Like cost of goods sold, **operating expenses** are resources that must flow out of a company for it to earn revenues. As you can see in Figure 14.2, Perfect Posters had operating expenses of $130 685 in 2006. This figure consists of $59 480 in selling and repackaging expenses and $71 205 in administrative expenses.

Selling expenses result from activities related to selling the firm's goods or services. These may include salaries for the sales force, delivery costs, and advertising expenses. General and administrative expenses, such as management salaries, insurance expenses, and maintenance costs, are expenses related to the general management of the company.

Operating Income and Net Income. Sometimes managers must determine **operating income**, which compares the gross profit from business operations against operating expenses. This calculation for Perfect Posters ($151 660 – $130 685) reveals an operating income, or income before taxes, of $20 975. Subtracting income taxes from operating income ($20 975 – $8390) reveals **net income** (also called **net profit** or **net earnings**). In 2006, Perfect Posters' net income was $12 585.

Statement of Cash Flows

Some companies prepare only balance sheets and income statements. However, many firms also report a **statement of cash flows**. This statement describes a company's yearly cash receipts and cash payments. It shows the effects on cash of three business activities:

- *Cash flows from operations.* This part of the statement is concerned with the firm's main operating activities: the cash transactions involved in buying and selling goods and services. It reveals how much of the year's profits result from the firm's main line of business (for example, Jaguar's sales of automobiles) rather than from secondary activities (for example, licensing fees a clothing firm paid to Jaguar for using the Jaguar logo on shirts).

operating expenses Costs incurred by a firm other than those included in cost of goods sold.

operating income Compares the gross profit from business operations against operating expenses.

net income (net profit or net earnings) A firm's gross profit less its operating expenses and income taxes.

statement of cash flows A financial statement that describes a firm's generation and use of cash during a given period.

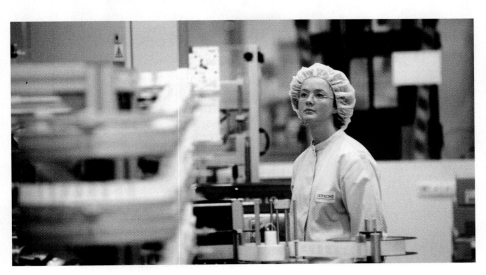

At the end of its accounting period, this pharmaceuticals company will subtract the cost of making the goods that it sold from the revenues received from sales. The difference will be its gross profit (or gross margin). Cost of goods sold does not include the firm's operating expenses, including such selling expenses as advertising and sales commissions. In part, gross margins in the pharmaceuticals industry are high because they do not account for high selling expenses.

- *Cash flows from investing.* This section reports net cash used in or provided by investing. It includes cash receipts and payments from buying and selling stocks, bonds, property, equipment, and other productive assets.

- *Cash flows from financing.* The final section reports net cash from all financing activities. It includes cash inflows from borrowing or issuing stock as well as outflows for payment of dividends and repayment of borrowed money.

The overall change in cash from these three sources provides information to lenders and investors. When creditors and stockholders know how firms obtained and used their funds during the course of a year, it is easier for them to interpret the year-to-year changes in the firm's balance sheet and income statement. The importance of cash flow is noted in the Entrepreneurship and New Ventures box.

The Budget: An Internal Financial Statement

budget A detailed financial plan for estimated receipts and expenditures for a period of time in the future, usually one year.

For planning, controlling, and decision making, the most important internal financial statement is the **budget**—a detailed statement of estimated receipts and expenditures for a period of time in the future. Although that period is usually one year, some companies also prepare budgets for three- or five-year periods, especially when considering major capital expenditures.

Budgets are also useful for keeping track of weekly or monthly performance. Procter & Gamble, for example, evaluates all of its business units monthly by comparing actual financial results with monthly budgeted amounts. Discrepancies in "actual versus budget" totals signal potential problems and initiate action to get financial performance back on track.

Although the accounting staff coordinates the budget process, it requires input from many people in the company regarding proposed activities, needed resources, and input sources.[10] Figure 14.3, for example, is a sample sales budget. In preparing such a budget, the accounting department must obtain from the sales group both its projections for units to be sold and expected expenses for each quarter of the coming year. Accountants then draw up the final budget, and throughout the year, the accounting department compares the budget with actual expenditures and revenues.

This concession stand at Rogers Centre is operated by the Toronto Blue Jays. It sells products manufactured mostly by members of the Sporting Goods Manufacturers Association (SGMA), which makes apparel, footwear, and equipment. Much of this merchandise is licensed from Major League Baseball Properties Inc., which distributes licensing revenues to the sport's 30 franchises. MLB Teams (who own logos and uniform designs) and MLB Properties treat sales of licensed products as cash flows from operations.

ENTREPRENEURSHIP AND NEW VENTURES

How Can You Account for a Good Beer?

Denison's, lamented in an article in the Canadian trade journal *World of Beer,* "has closed, and with it has gone our sole opportunity to enjoy Canada's finest Bavarian-style wheat beer and some of the best lagers in the land." The failure of Denison's Brewing Co., a favourite among brewpub aficionados in Toronto, Ontario, issued a stark warning to all local brewers: Even a great-tasting beer will go sour if you can't produce and sell it profitably.

The lesson of Denison's rise and fall has been studied seriously at Black Oak Brewing Co., where founders Ken Woods and John Gagliardi may be the perfect pair to survive in Canada's highly competitive beer market. Although each brings different skills to the joint venture, they share a vision: to make—and sell—the highest-quality beer possible. Gagliardi, certified as a brewmaster by the world-renowned Siebel Institute in 1993, is the quality-control expert whose responsibilities include ensuring the consistency and character of every batch of Black Oak. He admits that as a businessman, he is "first and foremost" a beer lover, and he continues to refresh the company's brand mix by releasing seasonal brews, such as Oktoberfest and Christmas Nutcracker—a practice that permits him to conduct brewing experiments without too much risk. "We're bent on making the highest-quality beer possible," says Gagliardi. "It's got to have the right taste and the perfect clarity and quality. We won't settle for anything less than the best, because we know our customers are going to be expecting a high-quality beer."

Woods, meanwhile, is a Certified Management Accountant (CMA) and a member of the Society of Management Accountants of Canada, but he shares his partner's enthusiastic interest in beer and brewing.

For 10 years, he devoted his evenings to developing both his bartending skills and his business contacts, while both would-be entrepreneurs refined their concepts of beers and brewery operations. Since opening Black Oak in 1999, they've managed to develop award-winning beers such as Black Oak Nut Brown Ale, Pale Ale, and Premium Lager, which *The Bar Towel,* a website for Toronto beer lovers, calls "fine, flavourful brews."

Just as importantly, they've also managed to cultivate successful business operations. Woods's accounting background enables him to set up and monitor management and financial procedures, such as the cost controls that made it possible for the company to buy a vintage 1940s labelling machine. "It doesn't matter that it's old," explains Woods. "It's a great piece of equipment and we got it at the right price." Woods and Gagliardi also take care to buy high-quality raw materials at the right price. That's why toasted wheat comes from the nearby town of Fergus while malt is imported from western Canada.

Accounting expertise is especially important because the company's cash flows are affected by the terms of payment negotiated with suppliers and by its procedures for collecting sales revenues. Working in finance and purchasing departments while earning his CMA credentials, Woods learned a lot about payables and receivables. He also produced staff expense reports and tax documents and set up standards for keeping operating costs under control. Finally, his management-accountant training has been especially useful in dealing with the numerous guidelines and rafts of government forms that characterize Ontario's highly regulated beer industry. Being a CMA, says Woods, "is really helpful because it firms up everything you need to know in the marketplace."

Reporting Standards and Practices

Accountants follow numerous standard reporting practices and principles when they prepare external reports, including financial statements. The common language dictated by standard practices is designed to give external users confidence in the accuracy and meaning of the information in any financial statement. Spelled out in great detail in GAAP, these principles cover a wide range of issues, such as when to recognize revenues from operations, the so-called "matching" of revenues and expenses, and full public disclosure of financial information to the public. Without agreed-upon practices in these and many other accounting categories, users of financial statements would be unable to compare financial information from different companies and thus misunderstand—or be led to misconstrue—a given company's true financial status.

> Explain the key standards and principles for reporting financial statements.
>
> **4**

🞏🞏🞏🞏🞏🞏🞏🞏🞏🞏🞏🞏   **Perfect Posters, Inc.**
555 Riverview, Toronto, Ontario

Perfect Posters, Inc.
Sales Budget
First Quarter, 2007

	January	February	March	Quarter
Budgeted sales (units)	7,500	6,000	6,500	20,000
Budgeted selling price per unit	$3.50	$3.50	$3.50	$3.50
Budgeted sales revenue	**$26,250**	**$21,000**	**$22,750**	**$70,000**
Expected cash receipts:				
From December sales	$26,210[a]			$26,210
From January sales	$17,500[b]	$8,750		26,250
From February sales		14,000	$7,000	21,000
From March sales			15,200	15,200
Total cash receipts:	**$43,710**	**$22,750**	**$22,200**	**$88,660**

[a] This cash from December sales represents a collection of the Account Receivable appearing on the December 31, 2006, Balance Sheet.
[b] The company estimates that two-thirds of each month's sales revenues will result in cash receipts during the same month. The remaining one-third is collected during the following month.

Figure 14.3 Perfect Posters, Inc. sales budget, First Quarter, 2007.

Revenue Recognition

As we noted earlier, revenues are funds that flow into a business as a result of its operating activities during the accounting period. *Revenue recognition* is the formal recording and reporting of revenues in the financial statements. Although any firm earns revenues continuously as it makes sales, earnings are not reported until the earnings cycle is completed. This cycle is complete under two conditions:

1. The sale is complete and the product has been delivered

2. The sale price to the customer has been collected or is collectable (accounts receivable)

The completion of the earning cycle, then, determines the timing for revenue recognition in the firm's financial statements. Revenues are recorded for the accounting period in which sales are completed and collectable (or collected). This practice assures the reader that the statement gives a fair comparison of what was gained for the resources that were given up.

Matching

Net income is calculated by subtracting expenses from revenues. The *matching principle* states that expenses will be matched with revenues to determine net income for an accounting period.[11] Why is this principle important? It permits the user of the statement to see how much net gain resulted from the assets that had to be given up to generate revenues during the period covered in the statement. Consequently, when we match revenue recognition with expense recognition, we get net income for the period.

Consider the hypothetical case of Little Red Wagon Co. Let's see what happens when the books are kept in two different ways:

1. Correct Method: Revenue recognition is matched with expense recognition to determine net income when the earnings cycle is *completed*.

2. Incorrect Method: Revenue recognition occurs *before* the earnings cycle is completed.

Suppose that 500 red wagons are produced and delivered to customers at a sales price of $20 each during 2005. In 2006, 600 red wagons are produced and delivered. In part (A) of Table 14.2, the correct matching method has been used: Revenues are recorded for the accounting period in which sales are completed and collectable from customers, as are the expenses of producing and delivering them. The revenues from sales are matched against the expenses of completing them. By using the matching principle, we see clearly how much better off the company is at the end of each accounting period as a result of that period's operations: It earned $2000 net income for 2005 and $3000 for 2006.

In part (B) of Table 14.2, revenue recognition and the matching principle have been violated. Certain activities of the two accounting periods are disguised and mixed together rather than separated for each period. The result is a distorted performance report that incorrectly shows that 2005 was a better year than 2006. Here's what Little Red Wagon's accountants did wrong: The sales department sold 200 red wagons (with revenues of $4000) to a customer late in 2005. Those *revenues* are included in the $14 000 for 2005. But because the 200 wagons were produced and delivered to the customer in 2006, the *expenses* are recorded, as in (A), for 2006. The result is a distorted picture of operations. It looks as if expenses for 2006 are out of line for such a low sales level, and it looks as if expenses (as compared with revenues) were kept under better control during 2005.

The firm's accountants violated the matching principle by ignoring *the period during which the earnings cycle was completed.* Although $4000 in sales of wagons occurred in 2005, the earnings cycle for those wagons was not completed until they were produced and delivered, which occurred in 2006. Accordingly, both the revenues and expenses for those 200 wagons should have been reported in the same period—namely, in 2006, as was reported in part (A). There, we can see clearly what was gained and what was lost on activities that were completed *in an accounting period.* By requiring this practice, the matching principle provides consistency in reporting and avoids financial distortions.

Full Disclosure

Full disclosure means that financial statements should include not just numbers, but also interpretations and explanations by management so that external users can better understand information contained in the statements.

Table 14.2	Revenue Recognition and the Matching Principle

(A) The correct method reveals each accounting period's activities and results

	Year ended December 31, 2005	Year ended December 31, 2006
Revenues	$10,000	$12,000
Expenses	8,000	9,000
Net income	2,000	3,000

(B) The incorrect method disguises each accounting period's activities and results

	Year ended December 31, 2005	Year ended December 31, 2006
Revenues	$14,000	$8,000
Expenses	8,000	9,000
Net income	6,000	(1,000)

Because they know more about inside events than outsiders, management prepares additional useful information that explains certain events or transactions or discloses the circumstances underlying certain financial results.

ANALYZING FINANCIAL STATEMENTS

5 Explain how computing key *financial ratios* can help in analyzing the financial strengths of a business.

Financial statements present a great deal of information, but what does it all mean? How, for example, can statements help investors decide what stock to buy or help managers decide whether to extend credit? Statements provide data, which in turn can be applied to various ratios (comparative numbers). These ratios can then be used to analyze the financial health of one or more companies. They can also be used to check a firm's progress by comparing current and past statements.

Ratios are normally grouped into three major classifications:

solvency ratios Ratios that estimate the financial risk that is evident in a company.

profitability ratios Measures of a firm's overall financial performance in terms of its likely profits; used by investors to assess their probable returns.

activity ratios Measures of how efficiently a firm uses its resources; used by investors to assess their probable returns.

- **Solvency ratios**, both short-term and long-term, estimate risk.
- **Profitability ratios** measure potential earnings.
- **Activity ratios** reflect management's use of assets.

Depending on the decisions to be made, a user may apply none, some, or all the ratios in a particular classification.

Short-Term Solvency Ratios

liquidity ratios Measures of a firm's ability to meet its immediate debts; used to analyze the risks of investing in the firm.

In the short run, a company's survival depends on its ability to pay its immediate debts. Such payments require cash. Short-term solvency ratios measure a company's relative liquidity and thus its ability to pay immediate debts. The higher a firm's **liquidity ratios**, then, the lower the risk involved for investors.

Current Ratio

current ratio A form of liquidity ratio calculated as current assets divided by current liabilities.

The current ratio has been called the "banker's ratio" because it focusses on a firm's creditworthiness. The **current ratio** measures a company's ability to meet current obligations out of current assets. It thus reflects a firm's ability to generate cash to meet obligations through the normal, orderly process of selling inventories and collecting accounts receivable. It is calculated by dividing current assets by current liabilities.

As a rule, a current ratio is satisfactory if it is 2:1 or higher—that is, if current assets are more than double current liabilities. A smaller ratio may indicate that a company will have difficulty paying its bills. Note, however, that a larger ratio may imply that assets are not being used productively and should be invested elsewhere.

How does Perfect Posters measure up? Look again at the balance sheet in Figure 14.1 (see page 444). Judging from its current assets and current liabilities at the end of 2006, we see that

$$\frac{\text{Current assets}}{\text{Current liabilities}} = \frac{\$57\ 210}{\$21\ 935} = 2.61$$

How does Perfect Posters' ratio compare with those of other companies? It's lower than O'Reilly Automotive's ratio (2.94) and higher than those of Gillette (1.56), Cisco Systems (2.14), and Starwood Hotels & Resorts Worldwide (0.23). Although Perfect Posters may be holding too much uninvested cash, it looks like a good credit risk.

working capital The difference between a firm's current assets and current liabilities.

Working Capital. A related measure is **working capital**—the difference between the firm's current assets and its current liabilities. Working capital indicates the firm's ability to pay off short-term debts (liabilities) that it owes to outsiders. At the end of 2006, Perfect Posters' working capital was $35 275 ($57 210 – $21 935). Because current liabilities must be paid off within one year, current assets are more than enough to meet current obligations.

Long-Term Solvency Ratios

To survive in the long run, a company must be able to meet both its short-term (current) debts and its long-term liabilities. These latter debts usually involve interest payments. A firm that cannot meet them is in danger of collapse or takeover—a risk that makes creditors and investors quite cautious.

Debt-to-Owners'-Equity Ratio

To measure the risk that a company may encounter this problem, analysts use long-term solvency ratios called **debt ratios**. The most commonly used debt ratio is the **debt-to-owners'-equity ratio** (or debt-to-equity ratio), which describes the extent to which a firm is financed through borrowed money. It is calculated by dividing **debt**—total liabilities—by owners' equity. Companies with debt-to-equity ratios above 1.0 are probably relying too much on debt. Such firms may find themselves owing so much that they lack the income needed to meet interest payments or to repay borrowed money.

debt ratios Measures of a firm's ability to meet its long-term debts; used to analyze the risks of investing in the firm.

debt-to-owners'-equity ratio A form of debt ratio calculated as total liabilities divided by owners' equity.

debt A company's total liabilities.

In the case of Perfect Posters, we can see from the balance sheet in Figure 14.1 that the debt-to-equity ratio calculates as follows:

$$\frac{\text{Debt}}{\text{Owners' equity}} = \frac{\$61\ 935}{111\ 155} = \$0.56$$

Leverage. Note that a fairly high debt-to-equity ratio may sometimes be not only acceptable but desirable. Borrowing funds provides **leverage**—the ability to make otherwise unaffordable purchases. In leveraged buyouts (LBOs), firms have willingly taken on huge debt to buy out other companies. When the purchased company allows the buying company to earn profits above the cost of the borrowed funds, leveraging makes sound financial sense, even if it raises the buyer's debt-to-equity ratio. Unfortunately, many buyouts have led to financial trouble when actual profits fell short of anticipated levels or when rising rates increased interest payments on the debt acquired by the buyer.

leverage Using borrowed funds to make purchases, thus increasing the user's purchasing power, potential rate of return, and risk of loss.

Profitability Ratios

Although it is important to know that a company is solvent in both the long term and the short term, safety or risk alone is not an adequate basis for investment decisions. Investors also want some measure of the returns they can expect. *Return on equity* and *earnings per share* are two commonly used profitability ratios.

Return on Equity

Owners are interested in the net income earned by a business for each dollar invested. **Return on equity** measures this performance by dividing net income (recorded in the income statement, Figure 14.2) by total owners' equity (recorded in the balance sheet, Figure 14.1).[12] For Perfect Posters, the return-on-equity ratio in 2006 can be calculated as follows:

return on equity A form of profitability ratio calculated as net income divided by total owners' equity.

$$\frac{\text{Net income}}{\text{Total owners' equity}} = \frac{\$12\ 585}{\$111\ 155} = 11.3\%$$

Is this figure good or bad? There is no set answer. If Perfect Posters' ratio for 2006 is higher than in previous years, owners and investors should be encouraged. But if 11.3 percent is lower than the ratios of other companies in the same industry, they should be concerned.

Earnings per Share

earnings per share A form of profitability ratio calculated as net income divided by the number of common shares outstanding.

Defined as net income divided by the number of shares of common stock outstanding, **earnings per share** determines the size of the dividend a company can pay to its shareholders. Investors use this ratio to decide whether to buy or sell a company's stock. As the ratio gets higher, the stock value increases, because investors know that the firm can better afford to pay dividends. Naturally, stock will lose market value if the latest financial statements report a decline in earnings per share. For Perfect Posters, we can use the net income total from the income statement in Figure 14.2 to calculate earnings per share as follows:

$$\frac{\text{Net income}}{\text{Number of common shares outstanding}} = \frac{\$12\ 585}{8000} = \$1.57 \text{ per share}$$

As a baseline for comparison, note that Kraft Food's recent earnings were $2.01 per share, while ConocoPhillips earned $10.21.

Activity Ratios

The efficiency with which a firm uses resources is linked to profitability. As a potential investor, then, you want to know which company gets more mileage from its resources. Activity ratios measure this efficiency. For example, suppose that two firms use the same amount of resources or assets. If Firm A generates greater profits or sales, it is more efficient and thus has a better activity ratio.

Inventory Turnover Ratio

inventory turnover ratio An activity ratio that measures the average number of times inventory is sold and restocked during the year.

Certain specific measures can be used to explain how one firm earns greater profits than another. One of the most important measures is the **inventory turnover ratio**, which calculates the average number of times that inventory is sold and restocked during the year—that is, how quickly inventory is produced and sold.[13] First, a company needs to know its average inventory: the typical amount of inventory on hand during the year. Average inventory can be calculated by adding end-of-year inventory to beginning-of-year inventory and dividing by two. The company can then calculate the inventory turnover ratio, which is expressed as the cost of goods sold divided by average inventory:

$$\frac{\text{Cost of goods sold}}{\text{Average inventory}} = \frac{\text{Cost of goods sold}}{(\text{Beginning inventory} + \text{Ending inventory}) \div 2}$$

High inventory turnover ratio means efficient operations. Because a smaller amount of investment is tied up in inventory, the company's funds can be put to work elsewhere to earn greater returns. However, inventory turnover must be compared with both prior years and industry averages. An inventory turnover rate of 5, for example, might be excellent for an auto supply store, but it would be disastrous for a supermarket, where a rate of about 15 is common. Rates can also vary within a company that markets a variety of products. To calculate Perfect Posters' inventory turnover ratio for 2006, we take the merchandise inventory figures for the income statement in Figure 14.2. The ratio can be expressed as follows:

$$\frac{\$104\ 765}{(\$22\ 380\ +\ \$21\ 250) \div 2} = 4.8 \text{ times}$$

The inventory turnover ratio measures the average number of times that a store sells and restocks its inventory in one year. The higher the ratio, the more products that get sold and the more revenue that comes in. Supermarkets must have a higher turnover ratio than, say, auto supply or toy stores. In almost all retail stores, products with the highest ratios get the shelf spaces that generate the most customer traffic and sales.

In other words, new merchandise replaces old merchandise every 76 days (365 days divided by 4.8). The 4.8 ratio is below the average of 7.0 for comparable wholesaling operations, indicating that the business is slightly inefficient.

INTERNATIONAL ACCOUNTING

As we saw in Chapter 5, many companies, such as McCain Foods, Sabian Cymbals, and Electrovert Ltd., receive large portions of their operating revenues from foreign sales. Canadian companies also purchase components from foreign countries. Retailers such as the Bay and Sears buy merchandise from other countries for sale in Canada. In addition, more and more companies own subsidiaries in foreign countries. With all this international activity, there is obviously a need to keep track of foreign transactions. One of the most basic accounting needs is translating the values of the currencies of different countries.

Explain some of the special issues that arise in *international accounting*.

6

Foreign Currency Exchange

A unique consideration in international accounting is the value of currencies and their exchange rates. As we saw in Chapter 5, the value of any country's currency is subject to occasional change. Political and economic conditions, for instance, affect the stability of a nation's currency and its value relative to the currencies of other countries.

As it's traded around the world, market forces determine a currency's value—what buyers are willing to pay for it. The resulting values are called **foreign currency exchange rates**. When a currency becomes unstable—that is, when its value changes frequently—it is regarded as a *weak currency*. The value of the Brazilian real, for example, fluctuated between 0.416 and 0.957—a variation of 130 percent in U.S. dollars—during the period from 1997 to 2002. On the other hand, a *strong currency* historically rises or holds steady in comparison to other currencies.

As changes in exchange rates occur, they must be considered by accountants when recording international transactions. They will affect, perhaps

foreign currency exchange rate
What buyers are willing to pay for a given currency.

"It's up to you now, Miller. The only thing that can save us is an accounting breakthrough."

profoundly, the amount that a firm pays for foreign purchases and the amount it gains from sales to foreign buyers.

International Transactions

International purchases, credit sales, and accounting for foreign subsidiaries all involve transactions affected by exchange rates. When a Canadian company imports Bordeaux wine from the French company Pierre Bourgeois, the Canadian company's accountant must be sure that the company's books reflect its true costs. The amount owed to Pierre Bourgeois changes daily along with the exchange rate between euros and Canadian dollars. Thus, the accountant must identify the actual rate *on the day that payment in euros is made* so that the correct Canadian-dollar cost of the purchase is recorded.

International Accounting Standards

Professional accounting groups from about 80 countries are members of the International Accounting Standards Board (IASB), which is trying to eliminate national differences in financial reporting procedures.[14] Bankers, investors, and managers want procedures that are comparable from country to country and applicable to all firms regardless of home nation. Standardization is occurring in some areas but is far from universal. IASB financial statements include an income statement, balance sheet, and statement of cash flows similar to those issued by Canadian and U.S. accountants. International standards, however, do not require a uniform format, and variety abounds.

Summary of Learning Objectives

1. **Explain the role of accountants and distinguish between the kinds of work done by *public* and *private* accountants.** *Accounting* is a comprehensive system for collecting, analyzing, and communicating financial information. It measures business performance and translates the results into information for management decisions. It also prepares performance reports for owners, the public, and regulatory agencies. To meet these objectives, accountants keep records of income, expenses, and taxes, and they analyze the effects of these transactions on particular business activities. *Bookkeeping* (just one phase of accounting) is the recording of transactions. Ensuring consistent, dependable financial information is the job of the *accounting information system (AIS)*—an organized procedure for identifying, measuring, recording, and retaining financial information so that it can be used in accounting statements and management reports. Users of such information include (1) business managers, (2) employees and unions, (3) investors and creditors, (4) taxing authorities, and (5) government regulatory agencies.

   There are two main fields in accounting: (1) A *financial accounting system* deals with external information users (consumer groups, unions, stockholders, and government agencies). It regularly prepares income statements, balance sheets, and other financial reports published for shareholders and the public. (2) *Managerial (or management) accounting* serves internal users, such as managers at all levels.

2. **Explain how the *accounting equation* and *double-entry accounting* are used in record keeping.** Accountants use the *accounting equation* to balance the data pertaining to financial transactions:

   Assets = Liabilities + Owners' equity

   (1) An *asset* is any economic resource that is expected to benefit its owner (such as buildings, equipment, inventory, and payments due the company). (2) A *liability* is a debt that the firm owes to an outside party. (3) *Owners' equity* is the amount of money that owners would receive if they sold all of a company's assets and paid all of its liabilities.

   Because every transaction affects two accounts, accountants use a *double-entry accounting system* to record the dual effects. Because the double-entry system requires at least two bookkeeping entries for each transaction, it keeps the accounting equation in balance.

3. **Describe the three basic *financial statements* and show how they reflect the activity and financial condition of a business.** Accounting summarizes the results of a firm's transactions and issues reports to help managers make informed decisions. The class of reports known as *financial statements* are divided into three categories—balance sheets, income statements, and statements of cash flows. *Balance sheets* (sometimes called *statements of financial position*) supply detailed information about the accounting-equation factors: assets, liabilities, and owners' equity. The *income statement* (sometimes called a profit-and-loss statement) describes revenues and expenses to show a firm's annual profit or loss. The *statement of cash flow* reports cash receipts and payments from operating, investing, and financing activities.

4. **Explain the key standards and principles for reporting financial statements.** Accountants follow standard reporting practices and principles when they prepare financial statements. Otherwise, users wouldn't be able to compare information from different companies, and they might misunderstand—or be led to misconstrue—a company's true financial status. The following are three of the most important standard reporting practices and principles: (1) *Revenue recognition* is the formal recording and reporting of revenues in the financial statements. All firms earn revenues continuously as they make sales, but earnings are not reported until the earnings cycle is completed; (2) The *matching principle* states that expenses will be matched with revenues to determine net income. It permits users to see how much net gain resulted from the assets that had to be given up to generate revenues; (3) Because they have inside knowledge, management prepares additional information that explains certain events or transactions or discloses the circumstances behind certain results. *Full disclosure* means that financial statements include management interpretations and explanations to help external users understand information contained in statements.

5. **Show how computing key *financial ratios* can help in analyzing the financial strengths of a business.** Financial statements provide data that can be applied to *ratios* (comparative numbers). Ratios can then be used to analyze the financial health of one or more companies. They can also be used to check a firm's progress by comparing current with past statements. Ratios are grouped into three major classifications:

(1) *Solvency ratios* estimate risk. *Short-term solvency ratios* measure relative liquidity and thus a company's ability to pay immediate debts. The higher a firm's liquidity ratios, the lower the risk for investors. The most common liquidity ratio is the current ratio, which measures ability to meet current obligations out of current assets. It thus reflects a firm's ability to generate cash to meet obligations through the normal process of selling inventories and collecting accounts receivable. Working capital is the difference between current assets and current liabilities. It indicates ability to pay off short-term debts (liabilities) owed to outsiders. *Long-term solvency ratios* measure ability to meet long-term liabilities consisting of interest payments. Debt ratios are long-term solvency ratios. The most common debt ratio is the debt-to-owners' equity ratio (or debt-to-equity ratio), which describes the extent to which a firm is financed through borrowed money. A fairly high debt-to-equity ratio may sometimes be desirable because borrowing funds provides leverage—the ability to make otherwise unaffordable purchases.

(2) *Profitability ratios* measure potential earnings. Return on equity measures income earned for each dollar invested. Earnings per share determines the size of the dividend that a company can pay shareholders. Investors use it when deciding whether to buy or sell a company's stock. As it gets higher, stock value increases, because investors know that the firm can better afford to pay dividends.

(3) *Activity ratios* reflect management's use of assets by measuring the efficiency with which a firm uses its resources. The inventory turnover ratio measures the average number of times that inventory is sold and restocked annually—that is, how quickly it is produced and sold. A high inventory turnover ratio means efficient operations: Because a smaller amount of investment is tied up in inventory, the firm's funds can be put to work elsewhere to earn greater returns.

6. **Explain some of the special issues that arise in *international accounting*.** Accounting for foreign transactions involves special procedures, such as translating the values of different countries' currencies and accounting for the effects of exchange rates. Moreover, currencies are subject to change: As they're traded each day around the world, their values are determined by market forces—what buyers are willing to pay for them. The resulting values are *foreign currency exchange rates*, which can be fairly volatile. When a currency becomes unstable—when its value changes frequently—it is called a weak currency. The value of a strong currency historically rises or holds steady in comparison with the U.S. dollar.

International purchases, sales on credit, and accounting for foreign subsidiaries all involve transactions affected by exchange rates. When a Canadian company imports a French product, its accountant must be sure that its books reflect its true costs. The amount owed to the French seller changes daily along with the exchange rate between euros and dollars. The Canadian accountant must therefore identify the actual rate on the day that payment in euros is made so that the correct Canadian-dollar cost of the product is recorded.

With accounting groups from about 80 countries, the International Accounting Standards Board (IASB) is trying to eliminate national differences in financial reporting. Bankers, investors, and managers want financial reporting that is comparable from country to country and across all firms regardless of home nation. Standardization governs some areas but is far from universal.

KEY TERMS

accounting, 436
accounting information system (AIS), 436
accounts payable, 445
accounts receivable, 444
activity ratios, 452
asset, 442
audit, 440
balance sheet, 443

bookkeeping, 436
budget, 447
certified general accountant (CGA), 438
certified management accountant (CMA), 440
chartered accountant (CA), 438
controller, 437
cost of goods sold, 446

current assets, 443
current liabilities, 445
current ratio, 452
debt, 453
debt ratios, 453
debt-to-owners'-equity ratio, 453
depreciation, 445
double-entry accounting system, 443

QUESTIONS FOR ANALYSIS

1. Balance sheets and income statements are supposed to be objective assessments of the financial condition of a company. But the accounting scandals of the last few years show that certain pressures may be put on accountants as they audit a company's financial statements. Describe these pressures. To what extent do these pressures make the audit more subjective?

2. If you were planning to invest in a company, which of the three types of financial statements would you want most to see? Why?

3. A business hires a professional accountant like a CA or CGA to assess the financial condition of the company. Why would the business also employ a private accountant?

4. How does the double-entry system reduce the chances of mistakes or fraud in accounting?

5. Explain how financial ratios allow managers to monitor their own efficiency and effectiveness.

6. Suppose that Inflatables Inc., makers of air mattresses for swimming pools, has the following transactions in one week:

- sale of three deluxe mattresses to Al Wett (paid cash—$75) on 7/16
- received cheque from Ima Flote in payment for mattresses bought on credit ($90) on 7/13
- received new shipment of 200 mattresses from Airheads Mfg. (total cost $2000) on 7/17

Construct a journal for Inflatables Inc.

7. Dasar Company reports the following data in its September 30, 2006, financial statements:

Gross sales $225 000

Current assets 40 000

Long-term assets 100 000

Current liabilities 16 000

Long-term liabilities 44 000

Owners' equity 80 000

Net income 7 200

a. Compute the current ratio.
b. Compute the debt-to-equity ratio.
c. Compute the return on sales.
d. Compute the return on owners' equity.

APPLICATION EXERCISES

1. Interview an accountant at a local manufacturing firm. Trace the process by which budgets are developed in that company. How does the firm use budgets? How does budgeting help its managers plan business activities? How does budgeting help them control business activities? Give examples.

2. Interview the manager of a local retail or wholesale business about taking inventory. What is the firm's primary purpose in taking inventory? How often is it done?

3. Interview the manager of a local business and ask about the role of ethics in the company's accounting practices. Is ethics in accounting an important issue to the manager? What steps are taken to ensure ethical practices internally?

BUILDING YOUR BUSINESS SKILLS

Putting the Buzz in Billing

Goal

To encourage students to think about the advantages and disadvantages of using an electronic system for handling accounts receivable and accounts payable.

Assignment

Step 1

Study Figure 14.4. The outside cycle depicts the seven steps involved in issuing paper bills to cus-

tomers, payment of these bills by customers, and handling by banks of debits and credits for the two accounts. The inside cycle shows the same bill issuance and payment process handled electronically.

Step 2

As the chief financial officer of a provincial hydroelectric utility, you are analyzing the feasibility of switching from a paper to an electronic system of billing and bill payment. You decide to discuss the ramifications of the choice with three business associates (choose three classmates to take on these roles). Your discussion

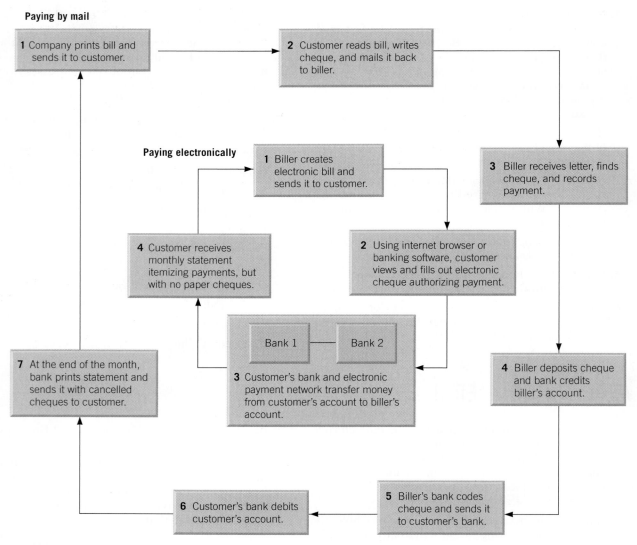

Figure 14.4 Managing operations and information.

▶▶▶

requires that you research electronic payment systems now being developed. Specifically, using online and library research, you must find out as much as you can about the electronic bill-paying systems being developed by Visa International, Intuit, IBM, and the Checkfree Corp. After you have researched this information, brainstorm the advantages and disadvantages of using an electronic bill-paying system in your company.

Follow-Up Questions

1. What cost savings are inherent in the electronic system for both your company and its customers? In your answer, consider such costs as handling, postage, and paper.

2. What consequences would your decision to adopt an electronic system have on others with whom you do business, including manufacturers of cheque-sorting equipment, Canada Post, and banks?

3. Switching to an electronic bill-paying system would require a large capital expenditure for new computers and computer software. How could analyzing the company's income statement help you justify this expenditure?

4. How are consumers likely to respond to paying bills electronically? Are you likely to get a different response from individuals than you get from business customers?

EXERCISING YOUR ETHICS

Confidentially Yours

The Situation

Accountants are often entrusted with private, sensitive information that should be used confidentially. In this exercise, you're encouraged to think about ethical considerations that might arise when an accountant's career choices come up against a professional obligation to maintain confidentiality.

The Dilemma

Assume that you're the head accountant in a large electronics firm. Your responsibilities include preparing income statements and balance sheets for financial reporting to stockholders. In addition, you regularly prepare confidential budgets for internal use by managers responsible for planning departmental activities, including future investments in new assets. You've also worked with auditors and supplied sensitive information to consultants from a CA firm that assesses financial problems and suggests solutions.

Now let's suppose that you're approached by another company—one of the electronics industry's most successful firms—and offered a higher-level position. If you accept, your new job will include developing financial plans and serving on the strategic planning committee. Thus, you'd be involved not only in developing strategy but also in evaluating the competition. You'll undoubtedly be called upon to use your knowledge of your previous firm's competitive strengths and weaknesses. You realize that your insider knowledge could be useful in your new job.

Questions for Discussion

1. What are the roles of financial accounting, managerial accounting, and accounting services in this scenario?

2. What are the chief ethical issues in this situation?

3. As the central figure in this scenario, how would you handle this situation?

What Numbers Can Be Crunched Offshore?

Planning on an accounting career for job security? If so, you might want to take a second look at what's happening with *business process outsourcing (BPO)*. Worldwide finance and accounting outsourcing exceeded $38 billion in 2004, up from $12 billion just five years earlier. BPO is the use of third parties to perform services (not manufacturing) that a company would otherwise do internally. Universities and hospitals, for example, outsource cafeteria operations to food service firms, retailers outsource human resources (HR) activities to HR firms, and manufacturing companies outsource shipping and delivery activities to UPS, FedEx, and other delivery specialists that do the job better, at lower cost.

The outsourcer's basic philosophy is that businesses do best when they focus on their core activities, rather than getting sidetracked into non-core activities that, for many firms, includes accounting. Offshore outsourcing *(offshoring)*—using third parties in other countries—is expected to grow rapidly, with the biggest growth expected in back-office professional services that have low customer contact and require little customization—basic accounting services, radiology analysis (for example, x-rays, CT scans, MRIs), computer software and information technology development, and engineering (for example, product design, testing, and analysis). Standardized processes are easily exported for service abroad, thanks to the internet's global reach. Accounting's basic number-crunching activities—payroll, accounts receivable, accounts payable, cash accounting, inventory valuation—are easily outsourced because the same accounting rules apply to all customers.

Not surprisingly, accounts payable, followed by accounts receivable, are the accounting functions most companies choose to outsource. These high-volume transactional activities are more likely to be outsourced than payroll and taxes, and far more likely to be outsourced than internal auditing, budgeting, and financial statement preparation. Some major companies, however, among them British Petroleum (BP), Delta Airlines, International Paper, and Nortel, are established outsourcers for various parts of their accounting. Accenture, the leading outsourcing provider with more than $3 billion in contract value, handles BP's processing for accounts payable, accounts receivable, cash and banking, and value-added-tax accounting. Safeway Stores in the United Kingdom uses outsourcing of accounting for accounts payable, stock accounting, cash accounts, payroll, and parts of its financial accounting.

In addition to cost savings, better reporting quality—more accurate, with improved delivery and increased speed of reporting—is a significant benefit from outsourcing because providers focus on specialized accounting activities using professional specialists for continuous improvement. As Peter Smith, a partner in the PricewaterhouseCoopers Business Process Outsourcing division, notes, "There's a different feeling when you're providing the service externally, as opposed to internally. There's a greater expectation from the client. They really do expect a much better service." On the downside, however, outsourcing increases the risk of data security. Placing private information in faraway hands, especially in the absence of clear-cut legislation on data privacy and security (as in India), increases chances of violating the client's trust in accounting integrity.

Beyond the basics, however, companies are beginning to outsource more intricate accounting activities, too, including stock and margin accounting, financial accounting, management accounting, real estate accounting, tax compliance, and even internal auditing. For these more customized processes, one of the outside company's employees may be co-located to the outsourcer's facility because good interaction with the client and thorough understanding of its business practices are needed. Data for these more customized accounting activities are transmitted for offshore processing, then results are transmitted back to the outsourcer.

While process-driven, high-volume transaction work is ripe for outsourcing, other accountancy work that depends on domestic-based knowledge is less susceptible. Some financial accounting activities, for example, rely on interpretation of corporate governance, and much of taxation requires in-depth knowledge of domestic tax policy and the regulatory environment. Philip Middleton, financial services partner at Ernst & Young, believes that the deciding factor on outsourcing is the depth of the accountant–client relationship. "If you look around our business and ask what kinds of tasks might go to Bangalore, for example, the answer is probably not a great deal. A lot of what we do requires proximity to clients—close client relationships," he says. But with fast-developing technologies, especially in multimedia communications systems and collaborative groupware, digital proximity might overcome physical remoteness and provide enough depth in the accountant–client relationship to allow even further outsourcing in accounting.

With its abundance of well-educated and highly skilled employees, India has become the back office of the world. In medical services, for example, x-ray images are digitally transmitted to India where skilled radiologists evaluate them, then transmit results back to North American client

▶▶▶

hospitals. Accounting skills, too, are plentiful, with average salaries just one-fifth of those in Western countries and, as a former British Colony, India has a widespread English-speaking culture. With over a third of its college graduates speaking more than two languages fluently, and many speaking as many as six, India is well positioned as an international outsourcing provider. Its Chartered Accountant designation for assuring professionalism is similar in rigor and esteem to the U.S. CPA certification. It comes as no surprise, then, that Deloitte & Touche forecasts that by 2008, India's financial and accounting services will be boosted by some one million new back-office jobs and technology-related positions, moved there by the world's top 100 financial companies.

While India holds the premier position today in offshore work, other countries—Australia, Ireland, Malaysia, the Philippines, and South Africa—are gearing up for the battle of accounting outsourcing destinations, with low-cost and high-technology expertise as primary weapons. Among the strongest contenders, if it can overcome a non–English-speaking tradition, is China, with its one billion population, rapid economic growth, low-cost labour, and serious investment in technical education. Its stated goal is to become the world's top outsourcing destination for accounting.

Questions for Discussion

1. What factors do you think are most important to consider in deciding which parts of a firm's accounting system, if any, are appropriate for outsourcing?

2. Suppose the accounting firm that prepares your income tax return outsources the work to a third-party tax-service provider. Do you think the accounting firm should get your permission before outsourcing the work? Why or why not?

3. Suppose you are hoping for an accounting career. To what extent does the trend toward offshore outsourcing threaten your career prospects? In what ways does it provide new opportunities?

4. What steps might a firm take to ensure that its private information is safeguarded by its offshore accounting provider?

5. What ethical issues, if any, are involved in a decision about outsourcing a firm's accounting activities? Explain.

CONCLUDING CASE 14-2

Continuing Concerns in the Accounting Profession

The corporate accounting and insider trading scandals of a few years ago have caused users of financial data to be increasingly concerned that the balance sheets and income statements of corporations may not be exactly what they seem. Those concerns prompted a Canadian Senate Banking Committee to analyze ways to restore investor confidence in financial data. The committee made several recommendations, including forcing CEOs to vouch for the truthfulness of their financial statements, passing new legislation governing the conflicts of interest faced by investment analysts, and requiring companies to have only independent directors on their audit committees.

Most of the really dramatic cases of corporate fraud have occurred in the United States, but Canada has the dubious distinction of having one of its own in the limelight. Canadian-born Bernard Ebbers had risen from Alberta milkman and nightclub bouncer to become CEO of WorldCom, one of the largest companies in the United States. It was alleged that Ebbers conspired with subordinates to "cook the books" when a business downturn occurred. These actions wiped out $100 billion of the company's market value, cost 17 000 people their jobs, and wiped out the life savings of investors. Scott Sullivan, one of Ebbers' subordinates, pled guilty and testified that Ebbers had ordered him to cook the books to hit earnings targets. In 2005, Ebbers was found guilty on nine charges of securities fraud and filing false documents. He was sentenced to 25 years in prison for his role in the collapse of WorldCom Inc.

In addition to outright accounting fraud, concerns have been expressed about the difficulty investors have in understanding what accounting statements really mean. In recent years, two issues in this area have received attention: overstating sales revenue and understating pension liabilities. The problem of overstating sales revenue is discussed below (see the Business Accountability box on p. 439 for a discussion of the pension liability issue).

Overstating Sales Revenue

Many companies are tempted to use "creative accounting" to inflate sales revenue, and this yields a distorted picture of how much product or service a company is actually selling. This is done so that the company will not disappoint the expectations of the stock market and then see their stock price drop. There are different ways that sales revenue can be overstated. For example, some software makers sell a lot of product at the end of a quarter and then count all those sales as revenue without taking into account the future costs the firm will incur to support the software or to provide the free upgrades they promised. Or, a company that acts as a sales agent for an airline might include the ticket price, plus the commission it earns, as revenue. When the airline firm is paid, the cost goes on the expense line. This approach vastly overstates revenue (but not profit). The company should have included only its sales commissions as revenue.

High-tech firms in particular are seen as too liberal in recording revenues on their financial statements. Because of this, the Ontario Securities Commission is shifting its emphasis from examining prospectuses to analyzing the way companies report income. It has set up a continuous disclosure team to review the financial reports of corporations in a systematic manner. To get a better understanding of the revenue problem, the OSC is also asking companies how they account for revenue from things like service contracts, and whether they benchmark their accounting practices against those used by other firms in their industry.

Other Concerns

A variety of other concerns have also been raised during recent years, including the following:

- There is sometimes a "chummy" relationship between auditors and their clients; this makes it more difficult for auditors to be completely objective.
- There is considerable "elasticity" in the application of generally accepted accounting principles; thus, companies have a lot of leeway in their accounting practices.
- If a person from an accounting firm takes a management position with a firm that is a client, future audits may be too "cozy" and fail to be objective.
- Self-regulation by the accounting industry doesn't work.
- There has been much fruitless debate in accounting firms about how to deal with stock options that are given to executives (if these are shown as expenses, they depress corporation earnings and lower the stock price).
- The accounting profession has moved away from establishing broad accounting principles and instead spent much of its time drafting detailed rules; even if these detailed rules are followed, the financial statements that are produced can present a distorted picture of a company's financial condition.

What should be done to resolve these problems? A few of the more commonly heard solutions are as follows:

- Auditors should clarify their language so that readers of financial statements will have a better idea of how a company is doing before they invest in it.
- Auditors should give more consideration to the users of financial statements, perhaps emphasizing different data for different user groups.
- Auditors should be charged with detecting fraud and reporting when they find it.
- Firms should be required to change their auditors on a regular basis (for example, once every five years), to prevent "chummy" relationships from developing.
- Auditors should not be allowed to take jobs with former clients until after a specified time period has passed (say, three to five years).
- A truly independent monitoring group should be formed that would assess the extent to which companies are meeting standards in their financial reporting.
- Stock options should be shown as expenses.
- When earnings forecasts are made, there must be a clear statement of how the forecasted numbers were arrived at.
- Companies should be required to show how much they paid for auditing services, and how much they paid for management consulting from the same auditor.
- Auditors should be required to rank a company's accounting practices in terms of how "aggressive" they are, rather than just saying the books are okay or not okay.

Questions for Discussion

1. Who are the various users of accounting information? How will each of these users be influenced if sales revenues are overstated and pension liabilities are understated?

2. What are the three basic financial statements that accountants generate for business firms? What does each one show? How will overstating sales revenue and understating pension liabilities affect each of these statements?

3. Read the sections in the chapter on revenue recognition and matching. How is the material in those sections helpful in dealing with the "overstating of sales revenue" problem noted in the case?

4. Consider the following statement: "*Since sales revenues and pension returns are measured in dollars, and since dollars are easy to quantify, it should be very clear what sales revenues and investment income a firm had in a given period. It is therefore unnecessary to have policies about how sales revenues and pension returns should be reported.*" Do you agree or disagree? Explain.

Presenting Yourself Online

We've seen that information and communication technology are valuable resources for increasing any firm's competitiveness, as discussed in Chapters 13 and 14. As you prepare for your career, you'll find that information and technology resources are also helpful for presenting yourself online to prospective employers. This exercise gives you the opportunity to look more closely at various online career information resources, including announcements of job vacancies, methods for job hunting, and hiring.

Assignment

Recall from Chapter 13 that geographic separation of the workplace from the company headquarters is more common than ever because of networked organizations. Similarly, job seekers, as well as businesses searching for employees, rely more and more on digital contact between applicants and employers, rather than face-to-face and land-mail communication. While the traditional method of sending out printed résumés is still effective, the online possibilities are too big to ignore. Your objective in this exercise is to evaluate online sources for career information and to explore ways you can use online technology for job hunting.

To complete this exercise, do the following:

1. Examine activities for online career planning that are presented in "Marketing Yourself Online" in Chapter 6 of *Beginning Your Career Search*, 3rd ed., by James S. O'Rourke IV.

2. Explore one of the internet's general-career sites, such as www.job.com, as discussed by O'Rourke. Identify three (or more) of the site's career-planning services that would be more difficult to obtain using offline sources.

3. Consider O'Rourke's suggestions for online job searches that might apply to a career field that interests you. Search in three ways for jobs in your career field: Use an online newspaper source, a general-career website, and any of the internet's general-purpose search engines. Which source provides the most useful information?

4. Using any means you choose, identify a potential employer for the career field that interests you. Explore that organization's career opportunities by visiting its website. Do its employment listings contain information that might help you adapt your résumé for a better match with opportunities at that organization?

5. Compare two methods for entering the job market: sending out printed résumés versus online postings. List the résumé-design skills for each method that are most important for job-search success. Explain differences in the skills requirements for the two methods.

6. O'Rourke cautions job seekers against using free web-hosting services that flash ads alongside your résumé. Explain the reasons for this warning.

 Visit the Companion Website at **www.pearsoned.ca /griffin** to view the CBC video segments that accompany the following cases.!

Handmaster

Dr. Terry Zachary is a chiropractor turned entrepreneur who has developed a product that is designed to strengthen all the muscles in the human hand. The product looks pretty simple (a polyurethane sponge ball and a plastic cord), but as Terry was looking into how to produce it, he discovered that if he had it manufactured in China he could cut the production cost by 50 percent compared to what it would cost to produce in Canada.

So, Zachary decided he had to make a trip to China to look at potential manufacturers. He wants to have different companies produce the ball and the cord to reduce the chance that his product will be counterfeited and copied. His plan was to visit eight potential manufacturers in five different Chinese cities so that he could determine who might be best to work with. His first visit is to a company called Changzhou Yuming. Zachary meets with the managers and shows them a sample of the cord that he might want them to produce. He tells them that the quality must be high. Zachary tours their production facilities and is impressed by what he sees. The Yuming managers are very aggressive in assuring him that they can do the work he wants. They clearly want him as a customer, but Zachary finds that communicating through an interpreter is difficult and frustrating.

His next meeting is with managers from Erison, the company that Zachary thinks might be able to make the foam ball for his product. He tells the Erison managers that he wants three different densities for the ball (firm, medium, soft), and that the density must be just right. Later, Zachary takes a bus to the Lelpro factory in Wuxi; that company makes various items including basketballs. Eventually, Zachary decides that Lelpro will make the foam ball for his product. He then heads home.

Six weeks later, Zachary is back in China to see how things are progressing. This is make-or-break time for him. His company has orders for the Handmaster, but he has had problems getting the Chinese manufacturing companies up to speed. At Yuming, the company that is making the cord, Zachary sees the machine that will make the cord. A test run is underway, and the Yuming production managers say they are getting close to what Zachary wants. Communication is still difficult, and Zachary feels that it is hard to pin down exact dates for when the product will be ready. He is also frustrated because there seems to be a difference between what is being promised and what is actually being delivered. Still, progress is being made, and Zachary feels that his manufacturer is actually getting close to what he wants.

Zachary then goes to check on the production of the foam ball at Lelpro. He checks the all-important density and finds it is good. He thinks that Lelpro is a pretty good company to deal with, but he is taking a chance that they can actually deliver the product in 20 days as required. He didn't put a penalty clause in the contract if they don't deliver on time, but thinks perhaps he should have.

Back at Yuming, there are still problems. Zachary wants to see a final product, but is having trouble conveying that to the Yuming managers. They say they are getting close. Zachary forcefully tells the interpreter to find out the exact time a crucial mould is supposed to arrive at the factory. He also continually asks the interpreter what the Chinese managers are saying. All of this is frustrating, but Zachary can do nothing but wait. Finally, just in time, he gets the final version of the cord for the product. All of the manufacturing jobs that Zachary's product will create will stay in China, but product packaging will be done in Canada.

In the end, Zachary is impressed with way that the Yuming managers worked through the problems that developed. He says a cordial goodbye to the people at Yuming and returns to Canada.

Questions for Discussion

1. What are the different kinds of utility? What kind of utility is being generated by these Chinese manufacturers?

2. What are the five types of transformation technology that are available? Which one is being used by the manufacturers in this situation?

3. What is the difference between analytic and synthetic processes? Which process is being used here?

4. What kind of layout is likely used in the manufacture of the Handmaster product?

5. Which of the total quality management techniques might be useful in the production of the Handmaster product?

Source: "Handmaster: Made in China," *Venture*, March 14, 2004.

African Accountants

In Canada's business jungle, all tracks lead to Bay Street, where lions of modern industry reign. Accountants keep Bay Street's books, but the heat is on to keep better books. Accountants don't like people who bring in shoeboxes full of receipts and then ask the accountant to organize them. Instead, accountants want the material organized before they try to do any calculations. But all this organizing costs money, and small- and mid-sized businesses don't usually have the money to pay for it.

For George Wall, of Wall & Associates, finding enough casual workers to do data organization and entry was a big challenge. He had to pay them up to $20 an hour, and that service was way too pricey for many of his clients. But what if Wall could find workers who would do this work for one-tenth the hourly wage he had to pay people in Toronto? He found the solution by adopting global outsourcing. It works like this: When that shoebox arrives, each piece of paper is first fed into a high-speed scanner and then stored on a server. While Bay Street sleeps, the material is sent to Kampala, Uganda, over the internet, where the data are keyed in by African accountants who are paid only about $1 a day.

In a freshly painted office in Kampala, a dozen computers have just been taken out of their boxes, and a dozen workers have just been hired. Their boss is 20-something Abu Luaga, a Ugandan with a commerce degree who has the contract to do accounting work for Wall & Associates. He teaches the new hires what to do. His start-up funds came from his family, and he got involved with Wall & Associates through his connections with a Canadian business consultant.

There is much competition from other developing countries to get this kind of business. But his workers are keen, and they're already trained as bookkeepers. They're eager to see what the developed world has to offer, but many have never had a computer before and need training so that they can recognize various financial documents and learn Canadian accounting jargon. They're also being trained to think the way Canadian businesses

do. As well, Luaga reminds them about deadlines and privacy. Because these workers are dealing with sensitive information, no cellphones are allowed in the office and the copying or saving of files or images is prohibited.

What are the implications of all this information flowing from the first world to the third world and back again? It may be just the kind of miracle Uganda needs. The telecommunications industry has been a bright spot in the Ugandan economy, but Ugandans still make only about $1 a day. The country still relies on money earned by exporting coffee, and the government is dependent on foreign donors for part of its budget. Officials admit that the technical skills of workers aren't as good as those of people in some Asian countries, but this system allows educated Ugandans to work in their home country.

Luaga's workers say the work has already changed their career prospects. But not all Canadian clients have jumped at the chance to zip their documents to Africa. George Wall is convinced they will eventually be comfortable with the idea, and Luaga is banking on it. He's leasing bigger and better office space because he thinks that a new office and clients in Canada will impress other potential clients in Africa.

Questions for Discussion

1. What is the difference between financial and managerial accounting? Is the work that the African accountants are doing financial or managerial accounting? Explain.

2. Why might Canadian clients be reluctant to have Wall & Associates send their data to Africa for organizing? What can George Wall do to respond to their concerns?

3. Suppose that you read a newspaper editorial condemning the practice of sending documents to Africa on the grounds that this was yet another example of exporting Canadian jobs overseas to low-wage countries. How would you respond?

Source: "African Accountants," *Venture*, February 16, 2003.

Managing

Marketing

What is the first thing you think of when you hear the names Coffee Crisp, Post-It, Crest, and Eno? If you grew up in Canada, you probably didn't hesitate at all before picturing candy, little slips of paper with one sticky edge, toothpaste, and something to calm your stomach. Your rapid association of company names and the goods or services they provide is a tribute to the effectiveness of the marketing managers of the firms that produce these goods. These and many other names have become household words because companies have developed the right products to meet customers' needs, have priced those products appropriately, have made prospective customers aware of the products' existence and qualities, and have made the products readily available.

Part Four, Managing Marketing, provides an overview of the many elements of marketing, including developing, pricing, promoting, and distributing various types of goods and services.

- We begin in **Chapter 15, Understanding Marketing Processes and Consumer Behaviour**, by examining the ways in which companies distinguish their products, determine customer needs, and otherwise address consumer buying preferences.

- Then, in **Chapter 16, Developing and Promoting Goods and Services**, we explore the development of different types of products, the effect of brand names and packaging, how promotion strategies help a firm meet its objectives, and the advantages and disadvantages of several promotional tools.

- Finally, in **Chapter 17, Pricing and Distributing Goods and Services**, we look at the strategies firms use to price their products. We also consider the various outlets business firms use to distribute their products, and we discuss the problems of storing goods and transporting them to distributors.

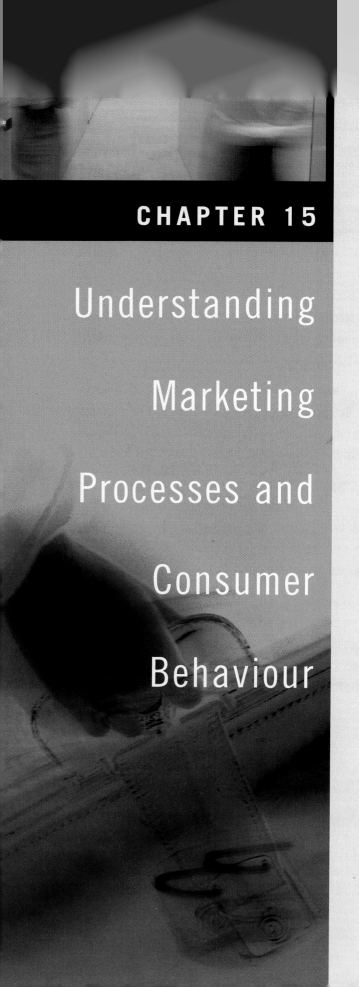

CHAPTER 15

Understanding Marketing Processes and Consumer Behaviour

After reading this chapter, you should be able to:

1 Explain the concept of *marketing* and describe the five forces that constitute the *external marketing environment*.

2 Explain the purpose of a *marketing plan* and identify the four components of the *marketing mix*.

3 Explain *market segmentation* and show how it is used in *target marketing*.

4 Explain the purpose and value of *marketing research*.

5 Describe the key factors that influence the *consumer buying process*.

6 Discuss the three categories of *organizational markets* and explain how *organizational buying behaviour* differs from consumer buying behaviour.

7 Describe the *international* and *small business marketing mixes*.

For many years, marketers directed their attention to consumers in the 18–35 age bracket because it was assumed that if they could get younger consumers to like their products, these consumers would continue to be loyal to it as they grew older. But this assumption has been called into question by marketing research data showing that customers are quite willing to switch brands if given the incentive to do so. Companies are also realizing that older consumers simply have a lot more money to spend than younger consumers do. For example, the net worth of people aged 65–69 is about 15 times the net worth of people aged 34 and younger.

Another factor is demographics: By 2010, about one-third of the population will be over 50 years of age. Between 2003 and 2016, the number of Canadians aged 55–64 will increase by 51 percent, and the number over 65 will increase by 41 percent. The number of Canadians aged 18–24 will increase by only 5 percent during that same period.

Is it possible for a company to attract older customers while still making younger ones think their products are cool? Sony thinks so. Its advertisement showing a grandmother taking underwater pictures of sharks scored well with younger viewers who liked the adventure aspect of the advertisement. Sony calls customers in the 50–64 age bracket "zoomers" to reflect the fact that they have more active lifestyles than their parents did. Here are several other examples of marketing to older people:

- Ford Motor Co. is introducing the Ford Five Hundred, a sedan (which older drivers like) that has some of the features of an SUV (it also has a roomy trunk for golf bags).
- Procter & Gamble has identified about 30 different products (including Puffs and Downey fabric softener) that can be marketed to people over 50; it has targeted older women with two new products (Rejuvenating Effects toothpaste and Olay Anti-Aging Cream), and has also developed Actonel, an osteoporosis drug, which is likely to do well in Japan, Italy, and France because of the aging populations there.

- Motorola introduced a new phone that should be of interest to older consumers because its zoom function allows the user to increase the font size so that it's more readable; the phone also has speakers that can be connected to a hearing aid.
- Vodafone introduced a new phone that shows a clear message that the batteries need recharging rather than a tiny icon that is hard for older folks to see.
- In Japan, Meiji Dairies Corp. started making a yogurt brand for people over 40.
- Walt Disney World developed a program aimed at people over 50 called "Magical Gatherings" that allows customers to use a website to plan trips with golf buddies or old schoolmates.
- Anheuser-Busch attracted older drinkers away from wine and other less-filling beverages by introducing a low-carb Michelob beer and calling it "Michelob Ultra"; it was introduced in three Florida retirement communities.
- Francine Tremblay launched Le Bel Age, a French-language magazine for "mature" Canadians; she also produced Good Times, an English-language magazine aimed at the same age group.

Of course, companies are not giving all their attention to older people. Rather, they are using demographics (studying characteristics of the population such as age, income, ethnic background, etc.) to determine how to best market to their customers. The age distribution of a country's population is important and it has a big impact on the marketing strategies of companies that are trying to sell everything from diapers to arthritis medicine. For example, the strategy of focussing on the youth market still looks pretty good in places like Brazil, Mexico, and Vietnam (because a large proportion of their population is young), but not so good in countries like Japan, Germany, and France (where a large proportion of the population is old).

In North America, the importance of demographics in marketing can be seen in a variety of situations. Consider the following:

- Ford Motor of Canada gives graduates a $750 rebate on their first-time purchase of a car.
- In 2003, the *Toronto Star* started a youth-oriented newspaper aimed at kids 9 to 14; this offering complements the existing *Starship* feature, which is aimed at kids 6 to 12 and the *boom!* feature (aimed at teenagers).
- Mattel Inc., the maker of the Barbie doll, formerly targeted girls aged 2 to 8 for this product, but

7- and 8-year-old girls are now less and less interested in Barbie dolls and see them as something that "little kids" play with.
- Major League Baseball Enterprises tracks demographic trends to set marketing goals for its $6 billion-a-year business; 20 years ago, the typical fan was a child, but today's average fan is about 37 years old. ◆

WHAT IS MARKETING?

1 Explain the concept of *marketing* and describe the five forces that constitute the *external marketing environment*.

marketing Planning and executing the development, pricing, promotion, and distribution of ideas, goods, and services to create exchanges that satisfy both buyers' and sellers' objectives.

marketing concept The idea that the whole firm is directed toward serving present and potential customers at a profit.

What do you think of when you hear the word "marketing"? If you are like most people, you probably think of advertising for something like detergent or soft drinks. But marketing is more than just advertising. **Marketing** is the "the process of planning and executing the conception, pricing, promotion, and distribution of ideas, goods, and services to create exchanges that satisfy individual and organizational goals."[1]

Because we are all consumers and because we all buy goods and services, we are influenced by the marketing activities of companies that want us to buy their products. But as consumers, we are in fact *the* essential ingredients in the marketing process. Every day, we express *needs* for such essentials as food, clothing, and shelter and *wants* for such nonessentials as entertainment and leisure activities. Our needs and wants are the forces that drive marketing.

The **marketing concept** means that the whole firm is coordinated to achieve one goal—to serve its present and potential customers and to do so at a profit. This concept means that a firm must get to know what customers really want and follow closely the changes in tastes that occur. The various departments of the firm—marketing, production, finance, and human resources—must operate as a system, well coordinated and unified in the pursuit of a common goal—customer satisfaction.

We begin our study of marketing by looking at how marketing focusses on providing value and utility for consumers. We then explore the marketing environment and the development of marketing strategy. Finally, we focus on the four activities that comprise the marketing mix: *developing, pricing, promoting,* and *placing products*.

Providing Value and Satisfaction

What attracts buyers to one product instead of another? While our desires for the many goods and services available to us may be unbounded, limited financial resources force most of us to be selective. Accordingly, consumers buy products that offer the best value when it comes to meeting their needs and wants.

Value and Benefits

value Relative comparison of a product's benefits versus its costs.

Value compares a product's benefits with its costs. The benefits of a *high-value* product are much greater than its costs. *Benefits* include not only the functions of the product, but also the emotional satisfactions associated with owning, experiencing, or possessing it. Every product has costs, including sales price, the expenditure of the buyer's time, and the emotional costs of making a purchase decision. The satisfied buyer perceives the benefits derived from the purchase to be greater than its costs. Thus the simple but important ratio for value:

$$Value = \frac{Benefits}{Costs}$$

Marketing strategies focus on increasing value for customers. Marketing resources are deployed to add value to products to satisfy customers' needs and wants. Satisfying customers may mean developing an entirely new product that performs better (provides greater benefits) than existing products. Or it may mean keeping a store open extra hours during a busy season (adding the benefit of greater shopping convenience). Some companies simply offer price reductions (the benefit of lower cost). Customers may also gain benefits from an informational promotion that explains how a product can be used in new ways.

Value and Utility

To understand how marketing creates value for customers, we need to know the kind of benefits that buyers get from a firm's goods or services. Products provide consumers with **utility**—the ability of a product to satisfy a human want or need. Marketing strives to provide four kinds of utility:

utility Ability of a product to satisfy a human want or need.

- When a company turns out ornaments in time for Christmas, it creates *time utility*: It makes products available when consumers want them.

- When a department store opens its annual Christmas department, it creates *place utility*: It makes products available where customers can conveniently purchase them.

- When the store sells ornaments, it provides *ownership utility* by conveniently transferring ownership from store to customer.

- By making products available in the first place—by turning raw materials into finished ornaments—the ornament maker creates *form utility*.

Marketing plays a role in all four areas—determining the timing, place, terms of sale, and product features that provide utility and add value for customers. Marketers, therefore, must begin with an understanding of customers' wants and needs. Their methods for creating utility are described in this and the following two chapters.

Goods, Services, and Ideas

The marketing of tangible goods is obvious in everyday life. You walk into a department store and are given a free scented paper strip as an initial product sample of a new perfume. A pharmaceutical company proclaims the virtues of its new cold medicine. Your local auto dealer offers to sell you an automobile with no interest charges for four years. These products—the perfume, the cold medicine, and the car—are all **consumer goods**: products that you, the consumer, buy for personal use. Firms that sell products to consumers for personal consumption are engaged in *consumer marketing*.

consumer goods Products purchased by individuals for their personal use.

Marketing is also important for **industrial goods**, which are products used by companies to produce other products. Surgical instruments and earthmovers are industrial goods, as are such components and raw materials as integrated circuits, steel, and unformed plastic. Firms that sell products to other manufacturers are engaged in *industrial marketing*.

industrial goods Products purchased by companies to use directly or indirectly to produce other products.

Marketing is also relevant for **services**—intangible products such as time, expertise, or some activity that you can purchase. *Service marketing* has become a major growth area in Canada. Insurance companies, airlines,

services Intangible products, such as time, expertise, or an activity that can be purchased.

Each of these advertisements provides information about a specific product, service, or idea. The soy milk, for example, is a tangible consumer product. The advertisement for the fitness club promotes a service that can be enjoyed. The public service ad promotes the idea of healthy behaviour.

investment counsellors, health clinics, and accountants all engage in service marketing, both to individuals and to other companies.

Finally, marketers also promote *ideas*. Television ads, for example, can remind us that teaching is an honourable profession and that teachers are "heroes." Other ads stress the importance of driving only when sober and the advantages of not smoking.

BUSINESS ACCOUNTABILITY

When Smoke Gets in Your Eyes

In Canada, government restriction on the advertising of cigarettes has a long history. Television advertising of cigarettes has been prohibited since 1971, and various other restrictions (including some rather dramatic label requirements) have come into force since then. Recently, for example, new legislation came into effect designed to discourage tobacco companies from sponsoring sports and cultural events so that they could get their brands prominently displayed to consumers. At a charity dinner in Toronto 2004, for example, the Rothmans Benson & Hedges table simply said "anonymous" in spite of the fact that the company had paid thousands of dollars to sponsor the table. Tobacco companies are still allowed to advertise in magazines and newspapers, but the rules are so restrictive they generally don't try anymore. Yves-Thomas Dorval, a spokesman for Imperial Tobacco Canada Ltd., says that since "promotion" is essentially prohibited by law, tobacco companies are focussing on the three other "Ps" of marketing (price, place, and product).

Clashes between stop-smoking groups and tobacco companies are common, particularly when tobacco companies appear to be ignoring the spirit of the restrictions that have been placed on them. For example, as part of the TD Canada Downtown Jazz Festival, Imperial Tobacco set up an outdoor smoking lounge in Toronto's Nathan Phillips Square. The lounge was criticized by the Ontario Free-Tobacco Network, which called on the mayor of Toronto to stop Imperial from using "scantily-clad girls" to promote cigarettes on city property.

All of these situations are interesting, but an important question remains: Who is accountable for the negative effects of tobacco use? Government agencies in both Canada and the United States (Health Canada and the American Public Health Association, respectively) seem to take the position that it is the companies who sell cigarettes that bear most of the responsibility. Not surprisingly, cigarette companies argue that because tobacco use is an individual behaviour choice for which potential health risks are well known, accountability falls to the consumer instead of the producer of the product. How accountable should tobacco firms be?

Coalitions of health advocacy groups—including the World Health Organization—and other grassroots public health organizations—are insisting that corporate accountability be formally acknowledged. In the United States, the $39 billion in settlement revenues that was given to states during a recent five-year period is cited as tangible recognition of the industry's accountability, but only for after-affects. Not far enough, insist the health advocates, arguing that the more than 400 000 tobacco-related deaths each year in North America are preventable: Companies should also be accountable for effective preventive measures that are absent now and are likely to remain so until more regulation is imposed on them. Tobacco firms, in response, point to several recent court rulings in the United States that denied more than $50 billion in claims brought by HMOs and insurance companies for reimbursement of tobacco-related health expenses. They point to these cases as supportive of the industry's argument that it is not accountable.

While the issue of accountability simmers, marketing finds itself on both sides of the controversy. Advertising expenditures by Canadian and U.S. tobacco's companies have soared to more than $11 billion each year. Health advocates cite "predatory marketing practices" as the industry advertises in youth magazines and develops advertising campaigns targeted at Hispanic, Asian, and other population groups that as yet may not be fully aware of health risks from smoking. Young adults with low incomes and lower education levels are representative of the target-market demographics of smoking. Consider the following statistics:

- The rate of smoking among people who did not complete high school is three times the rate for those with an undergraduate university degree.
- Smoking among pregnant women is 15 times greater for those who did not graduate from high school than it is for those with a university education.
- About one-third of people living below the poverty line are smokers, compared with only one-quarter of those above the poverty line.
- Low-wage workers smoke more than those with high wages.

Health advocates say that tobacco companies have increasingly paid retailers to display tobacco advertising, have used "buy one, get one free" promotions, and have set up promotional racks and giveaways that make cigarettes easier to buy for these targeted smokers.

Marketing by health advocacy groups has embraced "idea-and-information" messages to promote the stop-smoking idea and to appeal for more corporate accountability. The American Legacy Foundation's award-winning TV "truth" campaign debunks the idea that smoking is glamorous, and features information about the social costs and health consequences of tobacco. A report by the U.S. National Cancer Institute publicized the idea that "light" cigarettes don't reduce health risks and often simply lead to brand switching rather than quitting. Community-based and grassroots efforts include counter-marketing campaigns to educate higher risk groups—targeted by the tobacco industry—about tobacco's harmful effects. Media ads and promotional materials targeted at legislators and regulators are appealing for more regulation and explicit acknowledgement of industry's accountability for reducing the ill effects from tobacco. Meanwhile, both sides know that each day brings with it hundreds of new smokers, quitters, and tobacco-related deaths.

Relationship Marketing

Although marketing often focusses on single transactions for products, services, or ideas, marketers also take a longer-term perspective. Thus, **relationship marketing** emphasizes lasting relationships with customers and suppliers. Stronger relationships—including stronger economic and social ties—can result in greater long-term satisfaction and customer loyalty.[2]

Banks, for example, offer *economic* incentives to encourage longer-lasting relationships. Customers who purchase more of the bank's products (for example, chequing accounts, savings accounts, and loans) accumulate credits toward free or reduced-price services, such as free traveller's cheques. As another example, motorcycle manufacturer Harley-Davidson offers social incentives through the Harley Owners Group (H.O.G.). H.O.G. gives motorcyclists the opportunity to bond with other riders and to develop long-term friendships.

relationship marketing A type of marketing that emphasizes lasting relationships with customers and suppliers.

The Marketing Environment

Marketing plans, decisions, and strategies are not determined unilaterally by any business—not even by marketers as experienced and influential as Coca-Cola and Procter & Gamble. Rather, they are strongly influenced by powerful outside forces. As you can see in Figure 15.1, any marketing program must recognize the outside factors that comprise a company's **external environment**. In this section, we will describe five of these environmental factors: *the political/legal, social/cultural, technological, economic,* and *competitive environments.*

external environment Outside factors that influence marketing programs by posing opportunities or threats.

Political and Legal Environment

Political activities, both foreign and domestic, have profound effects on business (refer back to Chapter 1 for a discussion of how government influences business). Legislation on the use of cellphones in cars and pollution legislation can determine the destinies of entire industries. Marketing managers therefore try to maintain favourable political/legal environments in several ways. For example, to gain public support for their products and activities, marketing uses advertising campaigns for public awareness on issues of local, regional, or national importance. They also lobby and contribute to political candidates (although there are legal restrictions on how much they can contribute). Such activities sometimes result in favourable laws and regulations and may even open new international business opportunities.

Social and Cultural Environment

More people are working at home, more women are entering the workforce, the number of single-parent families is increasing, food preferences and physical activities reflect the growing concern for healthful lifestyles, and the growing recognition of cultural diversity continues. These and other issues reflect the values, beliefs, and ideas that form the fabric of Canadian society today. Obviously, these broad attitudes toward issues have direct effects on business. Today, for example, as we continue to insist on a

Figure 15.1 The external marketing environment.

"greener" Canada, we have seen the demise of freon in air conditioners and increased reliance on recycling materials in the goods that we consume.

Changing social values force companies to develop and promote new products for both individual consumers and industrial customers. For example, although most of us value privacy, web surfers are discovering that a loss of privacy is often a price for the convenience of internet shopping. Dot-com sites regularly collect personal information that they use for marketing purposes and which they often sell to other firms. Responding to the growing demand for better privacy protection, firms like iNetPrivacy offer such products as Anonymity 4 Proxy software, which allows you to surf the Net anonymously.

Technological Environment

New technologies affect marketing in several ways. Obviously, they create new goods (say, the satellite dish) and services (home television shopping). New products make some existing products obsolete (for example, compact discs are replacing audiotapes), and many of them change our values and lifestyles. In turn, they often stimulate new goods and services not directly related to the new technology itself. Cellular phones, for example, not only facilitate business communication, but also free up time for recreation and leisure.

Consider the phenomenon of DNA "fingerprinting." The O.J. Simpson trial (United States), the Guy Paul Morin case (Canada), and the television show *CSI: Crime Scene Investigation* have made just about everyone aware of its availability to law-enforcement officials. Bear in mind, however, that it is also the focal point of a new industry—one that involves biological science and laboratory analysis and instrumentation as well as criminology. DNA fingerprinting, then, is a product. Along with its technical developments, therefore, it involves marketing decisions—such as pricing and promotion. This has been the case with literally thousands of technological breakthroughs in such fields as genetics, electronics, aeronautics, medicine, information sciences, communications systems, transportation, the internet (which we discussed in Chapter 13), and emarketing (which we discuss in Chapter 17).

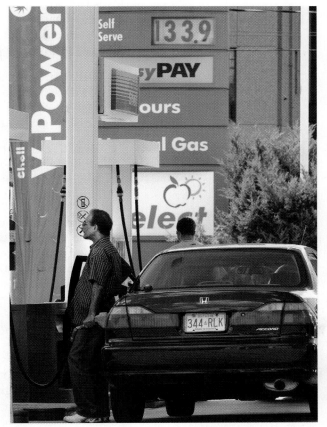

Economic Environment

Economic conditions determine spending patterns by consumers, businesses, and governments. Thus they influence every marketer's plans for product offerings, pricing, and promotional strategies. Among the more significant economic variables, marketers are concerned with inflation, interest rates, recession, and recovery. In other words, they must monitor the general business cycle, which typically features a pattern of transition from periods of prosperity to recession to recovery (return to prosperity). Not surprisingly, consumer spending increases as "consumer confidence" in economic conditions grows during periods of prosperity. Conversely it decreases during low-growth periods, when unemployment rises and purchasing power declines.

Traditionally, analysis of economic conditions focussed on the national economy and the government's policies for controlling or moderating it.

In 2006, gas prices exceeded $1 per litre in most locations in Canada. The price of a barrel of crude oil—more than $70—was the highest ever recorded. The jump in prices reflects a variety of circumstances in the global economic environment, including fears of terrorism in the Middle East and increased demand for oil in China and India.

478 PART FOUR Managing Marketing

Increasingly, however, as nations form more and more economic connections, the "global economy" is becoming more prominent in the thinking of marketers everywhere.[3] At U.S.-based Wal-Mart, for example, more than 18 percent of all sales revenue comes from the retailer's international division. Although international sales were up 17 percent for 2004, sales in some Latin American countries stalled. Why? Because economic conditions in such markets as Argentina and Brazil differ significantly from those in Mexico, which, in turn, differ from those in China, South Korea, and Germany.

Competitive Environment

In a competitive environment, marketers must convince buyers that they should purchase their products rather than those of some other seller. In a broad sense, because both consumers and commercial buyers have limited resources to spend, every dollar spent to buy one product is no longer available for other purchases. Each marketing program, therefore, seeks to make its product the most attractive; theoretically, a failed program loses the buyer's dollar forever (or at least until it is time for the next purchase decision).

By studying the competition, marketers determine how best to position their own products for three specific types of competition:

substitute product A product that is dissimilar from those of competitors but that can fulfill the same need.

- **Substitute products** are dissimilar from those of competitors but can fulfill the same need. For example, your cholesterol level may be controlled with either a physical-fitness program or a drug regimen; the fitness program and the drugs compete as substitute products.

brand competition Competitive marketing that appeals to consumer perceptions of similar products.

- **Brand competition** occurs between similar products, such as the auditing services provided by large accounting firms like Ernst & Young and KPMG Peat Marwick. The competition is based on buyers' perceptions of the benefits of products offered by particular companies.

international competition Competitive marketing of domestic against foreign products.

- **International competition** matches the products of domestic marketers against those of foreign competitors—say, a flight on Swissair versus Air Canada. The intensity of international competition has been heightened by the formation of alliances such as the European Union and NAFTA.

2 Explain the purpose of a *marketing plan* and identify the four components of the *marketing mix*.

Strategy: The Marketing Mix

As a business activity, marketing requires management. Although many individuals also contribute to the marketing of a product, a company's **marketing managers** are typically responsible for planning and implementing all the marketing-mix activities that result in the transfer of goods or services to its customers. These activities culminate in the **marketing plan**: a detailed and focussed strategy for gearing marketing activities to meet consumer needs and wants. Marketing, therefore, begins when a company identifies a consumer need and develops a product to meet it.

marketing managers Managers responsible for planning and implementing all the marketing-mix activities that result in the transfer of goods or services to customers.

marketing plan A detailed strategy for gearing the marketing mix to meet consumer needs and wants.

marketing mix The combination of product, price, place, and promotion strategies used in marketing a product.

In planning and implementing strategies, marketing managers develop the four basic components (often called the "Four Ps") of the **marketing mix** (see Figure 15.2). In this section, we briefly describe each of those components: *product, price, place,* and *promotion.*

Figure 15.2 Choosing the marketing mix for a business.

Product

Marketing begins with a **product**—a good, a service, or an idea designed to fill a consumer need or want. Conceiving and developing new products is a constant challenge for marketers, who must always consider the factor of change—changing technology, changing consumer wants and needs, and changing economic conditions. Meeting consumer needs, then, often means changing existing products to keep pace with emerging markets and competitors. *Mass-customization*, which was explained in Chapter 13, allows marketers to provide products that satisfy very specific needs of consumers.

Producers often promote particular features of products to distinguish them in the marketplace. **Product differentiation** is the creation of a feature or image that makes a product differ enough from existing products to attract consumers. For example, Volvo automobiles provide newer, better safety features to set them apart from competitors. Customers of E*Trade™, the online investment service, gain value from after-hours trading not offered by conventional investment-service firms.

product A good, service, or idea that satisfies buyers' needs and demands.

product differentiation The creation of a product or product image that differs enough from existing products to attract consumers.

Price

Price refers not only to the actual amount of money that consumers must pay for a product or service, but also to the total value of things that consumers are willing to give up in return for being able to have the benefits of the product or service. For example, if a person wants to own a Chrysler 300M, that person may have to take money out of a savings account to pay for the car. The value of the interest that would have been earned on the savings account is part of the value that the customer gives up to own the car. From the seller's perspective, determining the best **price** at which to sell a product is often a balancing act. On the one hand, prices must support a variety of costs—operating, administrative, research, and marketing costs. On the other hand, prices can't be so high that consumers turn to competitors products. Successful pricing means finding a profitable middle ground between these two requirements.

Both low- and high-price strategies can be effective in different situations. Low prices, for example, generally lead to larger sales volumes. High prices usually limit market size but increase profits per unit. High prices may also attract customers by implying that a product is of high quality. We discuss pricing in more detail in Chapter 17.

price That part of the marketing mix concerned with choosing the appropriate price for a product to meet the firm's profit objectives and buyers' purchasing objectives.

Jann Wenner started *Rolling Stone* magazine in 1967, and it's been the cash cow of Wenner Media ever since. In 1985, Wenner bought *Us* magazine and set out to compete with *People*, perhaps the most successful magazine ever published. Wenner's latest strategy calls for greater differentiation between the two products. *People* is news driven, reporting on ordinary people as well as celebrities, and Wenner intends to punch up *Us* with more coverage of celebrity sex and glitter. So far, he hasn't been successful. *People* reaches 3.7 million readers, *Us* about 900 000.

Place (Distribution)

distribution That part of the marketing mix concerned with getting products from the producer to the buyer, including physical transportation and choice of sales outlets.

In the marketing mix, *place* refers to **distribution**. Placing a product in the proper outlet—say, a retail store—requires decisions about several activities, all of which are concerned with getting the product from the producer to the consumer. Decisions about warehousing and inventory control are distribution decisions, as are decisions about transportation options.

Firms must also make decisions about the *channels* through which they distribute products. Many manufacturers, for instance, sell goods to other companies that, in turn, distribute them to retailers. Others sell directly to major retailers such as Sears, Wal-Mart, or Safeway. Still others sell directly to final consumers. We explain distribution decisions further in Chapter 17.

Promotion

promotion Techniques for communicating information about products.

The most highly visible component of the marketing mix is **promotion**, which refers to techniques for communicating information about products. The most important promotional tools include advertising, personal selling,

By providing both distribution and advertising for Grand & Toy, this truck plays a dual role in the company's marketing.

sales promotions, and public relations. We describe promotional activities more fully in Chapter 16.

Product, price, place, and promotion focus on the seller's perspective. From the buyer's perspective, each of the 4 Ps provides a certain benefit. In effect, the seller's 4 Ps are a mirror image of the buyer's 4 Cs: customer solution (product), customer cost (price), customer convenience (place), and customer communication (promotion).[4]

TARGET MARKETING AND MARKET SEGMENTATION

Marketing managers long ago recognized that they cannot be "all things to all people." People have different tastes, different interests, different goals, different lifestyles, and so on. The marketing concept's recognition of consumers' various needs and wants led marketing managers to think in terms of target marketing. **Target markets** are groups of people with similar wants and needs.

Target marketing clearly requires **market segmentation**, dividing a market into categories of customer types or "segments." For example, Mr. Big-and-Tall sells to men who are taller and heavier than average. Certain special interest magazines are oriented toward people with specific interests (see Table 15.1). Once they have identified market segments, companies may adopt a variety of product strategies. Some firms decide to provide a range of products to the market in an attempt to market their products to more than one segment. For example, General Motors of Canada offers compact cars, vans, trucks, luxury cars, and sports cars with various features and prices. Its strategy is to provide an automobile for nearly every segment of the market.

In contrast, some businesses restrict production to one market segment. Rolls-Royce understands that only a relatively small number of people are willing to pay $310 000 for exclusive touring limousines. Rolls, therefore,

Explain *market segmentation* and show how it is used in *target marketing*. **3**

target market Any group of people who have similar wants and needs and may be expected to show interest in the same product(s).

market segmentation Dividing a market into categories according to traits customers have in common.

| Table 15.1 | Magazines with Specific Target Audiences |

Accounting
- CAmagazine
- CGA Magazine
- CMA Management

Agriculture
- Agro-Nouvelles
- Meat & Poultry Magazine
- Country Life in B.C.

Sports
- Cycle Canada
- Chalk and Cue
- Athletics Canada

Gardening
- Canadian Gardening
- The Gardener for the Prairies
- Gardening Life

Fishing/Hunting
- Canadian Fly Fisher
- Outdoor Canada
- B.C. Outdoors Sport Fishing

Automotive
- Aftermarket Canada
- Bodyshop
- World of Wheels

Boating
- Boating Business
- Canadian Boating
- Porthole Magazine

Music
- CHART Magazine
- CODA Magazine
- Opus

makes no attempt to cover the entire range of possible products; instead, it markets only to a very small segment of the total automobile buyers market.

Table 15.2 shows how a marketer of home-electronic equipment might segment the radio market. Note that segmentation is a strategy for analyzing consumers, not products. The analysis in Table 15.2, for example, identifies consumer-users—joggers, commuters, and travellers. Only *indirectly*, then, does it focus on the uses of the product itself. In marketing, the process of fixing, adapting, and communicating the nature of the product itself is called *positioning*.

Identifying Market Segments

By definition, the members of a market segment must share some common traits or behaviours that will affect their purchasing decisions. In identifying market segments, researchers look at *geographic, demographic, psychographic,* and *product-use variables*.

Geographic Variables

In some cases, where people live affects their buying decisions. The heavy rainfall in British Columbia prompts its inhabitants to purchase more umbrellas than does Arizona's desert. Urban residents have less demand for pickup trucks than do their rural counterparts. Sailboats sell better along both coasts than they do in the prairie provinces. **Geographic variables** are the geographical units, from countries to neighbourhoods, that may be considered in a segmentation strategy.

These patterns affect marketing decisions about what products to offer, at what price to sell them, how to promote them, and how to distribute them. For example, consider the marketing of down parkas in rural Saskatchewan. Demand will be high, price competition may be limited, local newspaper advertising may be very effective, and the best location may be one easily reached from several small towns.

Although the marketability of some products is geographically sensitive, others enjoy nearly universal acceptance. Coke, for example, gets more than 70 percent of its sales from markets outside the United States. It is the market leader in Great Britain, China, Germany, Japan, Brazil, and Spain. By

geographic variables Geographical units that may be considered in a segmentation strategy.

Table 15.2	Possible Segmentation of the Radio Market
Segmentation	**Product/Target Market**
Age	Inexpensive, unbreakable, portable models for young children
	Inexpensive equipment—possibly portable—for teens
	Moderate-to-expensive equipment for adults
Consumer attitude	Sophisticated components for audio buffs
	All-in-one units in furniture cabinets for those concerned with room appearance
Product use	Miniature models for joggers and commuters
	"Boom box" portables for taking outdoors
	Car stereo systems for travelling
	Components and all-in-one units for home use
Location	Battery-powered models for use where electricity is unavailable
	AC current for North American users
	DC current for other users

contrast, Pepsi earns 78 percent of its income from the United States. Coke's chief competitor in most countries is not Pepsi, but some local soft drink.

Demographic Variables

Demographic variables describe populations by identifying characteristics such as age, income, gender, ethnic background, marital status, race, religion, and social class. These are objective criteria that cannot be altered. Marketers must work with or around them. Table 15.3 lists some demographic market segments. Depending on the marketer's purpose, a segment can be a single classification (*aged 20–34*) or a combination of categories (*aged 20–34, married with children, earning $25 000–$34 999*). Foreign competitors, for example, are gaining market share in auto sales by appealing to young buyers (*under age 30*) with limited incomes (*under $30 000*). While companies such as Hyundai, Kia, and Daewoo are winning entry-level customers with high-quality and generous warranties, Volkswagen targets under-35 buyers with its entertainment-styled VW Jetta.[5]

Another important demographic variable is ethnic diversity. Canada's great ethnic diversity requires companies to pay close attention to ethnicity as a segmentation variable. For example, Rogers Communication Inc.'s television advertising campaign for its Bollywood Oye! video-on-demand service is designed to promote its business to South Asian communities in Canada. Rogers currently has 32 multicultural channels and wants to be a leader in customizing services to suit specific ethnic groups. Visible minorities in Canada control $76 billion in annual buying power, and to be effective in multicultural marketing, companies must really understand the underlying values that ethnic minority customers hold.[6]

demographic variables
Characteristics of populations that may be considered in developing a segmentation strategy.

Psychographic Variables

Members of a market can also be segmented according to such **psychographic variables** as lifestyle, opinions, interests, and attitudes. One company that is using psychographic variables to revive its brand is Burberry, whose plaid-lined gabardine raincoats have been a symbol of

psychographic variables
Psychological traits that a group has in common, including motives, attitudes, activities, interests, and opinions.

Table 15.3	Demographic Market Segmentation
Age	Under 5; 5–11; 12–19; 20–34; 35–49; 50–64; 65+
Education	Grade school or less; some high school; graduated high school; some college or university; college diploma or university degree; advanced degree
Family life cycle	Young single; young married without children; young married with children; older married with children under 18; older married without children under 18; older single; other
Family size	1, 2–3, 4–5, 6+
Income	Under $9000; $9000–$14 999; $15 000–$25 000; over $25 000
Nationality	Including but not limited to African, Asian, British, Eastern European, French, German, Irish, Italian, Latin American, Middle Eastern, and Scandinavian
Race	Including but not limited to Inuit, Asian, black, and white
Religion	Including but not limited to Buddhist, Catholic, Hindu, Jewish, Muslim, and Protestant
Sex	Male, female
Language	Including but not limited to English, French, Inuktitut, Italian, Ukrainian, and German

British tradition since 1856. After a recent downturn in sales, Burberry is repositioning itself as a global luxury brand, like Gucci and Louis Vuitton. The strategy calls for luring top-of-the-line, fashion-conscious customers. Burberry pictures today's luxury-product shopper as a world traveller who identifies with prestige fashion brands and monitors social and fashion trends in *Harper's Bazaar*.[7]

Psychographics are particularly important to marketers because, unlike demographics and geographics, they can sometimes be changed by marketing efforts. For example, many companies have succeeded in changing at least some consumers' opinions by running ads highlighting products that have been improved directly in response to consumer desires. Many companies in Poland have succeeded in overcoming consumer resistance to buying on credit by promoting the safety and desirability of using credit rather than depending solely on cash for family purchases. One product of such changing attitudes is a booming economy and the emergence of a growing and robust middle class. The increasing number of Polish households that own televisions, appliances, automobiles, and houses is fuelling the status of Poland's middle class as the most stable in the former Soviet bloc.[8]

Product-Use Variables

product-use variables Consumer characteristics based on the use of a product, benefits expected from it, reasons for purchasing it, and loyalty to it.

The term **product-use variables** refers to the ways in which consumers use a product, the benefits they expect from it, their reasons for purchasing it, and their loyalty to it.[9] A women's shoemaker might identify three segments—wearers of athletic, casual, and dress shoes. Each segment is looking for different benefits in a shoe. A woman buying an athletic shoe may not care about its appearance but may care a great deal about arch support and traction in the sole. A woman buying a casual shoe will want it to look good and feel comfortable. A woman buying a dress shoe may require a specific colour or style and may even accept some discomfort. Consumers who always buy one brand are classified as *hard-core loyalists*, whereas *switchers* buy various brands.

Whatever basis is used for segmenting a market, care must be taken to position the product correctly. A product's position refers to the important attributes that consumers use to assess the product. For example, a low-

Although Nike leads the $15.5 billion athletic footwear industry, it still has a serious problem: Women's footwear accounts for about one-third of industry sales but generates only about one-fifth of Nike's. Nike is going after this demographic segment with a marketing campaign that focuses on differences between the way men and women think about sports and the way they shop for clothing. According to Nike marketers, for example, women are more interested in image trends and active lifestyles than in athletic competition and sports celebrities.

Figure 15.3 Product positioning.

priced car like a Ford Focus tends to be positioned on the basis of *economy*, while a Porsche is positioned in terms of *high performance*. In Figure 15.3, the product positioning chart shows that Tim Hortons emphasizes a standardized product and provides fast service to people in a hurry, while Starbucks provides more customized products in more leisurely surroundings.

Market Segmentation: A Caution

Segmentation must be done carefully. A group of people may share an age category, income level, or some other segmentation variable, but their spending habits may be quite different. Look at your friends in school. You may all be approximately the same age, but you have different needs and wants. Some of you may wear cashmere sweaters while others wear sweatshirts. The same holds true for income. University professors and truck drivers frequently earn about the same level of income. However, their spending patterns, tastes, and wants are generally quite different.

In Canada, the two dominant cultures—English and French—have historically shown significant differences in consumer attitudes and behaviour. Researchers have found, for example, that compared with English Canadians, French Canadians are more involved with home and family, attend ballet more often, travel less, eat more chocolate, and are less interested in convenience food. But this does not necessarily mean that companies must have different product offerings for Quebec. When Headspace Marketing Inc. asked 1000 Quebecers to rate how well 12 different retail brands had adapted to the needs and expectations of Quebecers, they found that the top three brands were Tim Hortons, Canadian Tire, and Bureau en gros (in that order). Interestingly, Tim Hortons ranked much higher than Starbucks (which ranked last) in spite of the fact that Tim Hortons did very little to adapt its product line to the Quebec market and Starbucks did a lot. What Tim Hortons did do well was get involved with community charities and activities that brought it closer to local residents. The company also used two Quebec actors in their ad campaigns. This apparently made the Tim Hortons brand "resonate" better with Quebecers. The situation is similar for second-ranked Canadian Tire. The chain sells pretty much the same product line in Quebec as in the rest of Canada, but it also got involved in local charities and used Quebec singer Jici Lauzon as a spokesperson.[10]

MARKET RESEARCH

4 Explain the purpose and value of *marketing research*.

market research The systematic study of what buyers need and how best to meet those needs.

Market research, which is the study of what buyers need and how best to meet those needs, can address any element in the marketing mix. Business firms spend millions of dollars each year as they try to figure out their customers' habits and preferences. Market research can greatly improve the accuracy and effectiveness of market segmentation.[11] Failure to do market research can lead to significant problems. For example, in 2004 the CEO of Coca-Cola admitted that the company had missed the change in consumer tastes away from carbonated drinks and toward healthier, non-carbonated drinks. PepsiCo Inc., on the other hand, capitalized on these trends with its Propel Fitness Water and Gatorade.[12]

The place of marketing research in the overall marketing process is shown in Figure 15.4. Ultimately, its role is to increase the firm's competitiveness by understanding the relationship among the firm's customers, its marketing variables, and its marketing decisions. Marketing researchers use a variety of methods to obtain, interpret, and use information about customers. They determine the kinds of information that are needed for decisions on marketing strategy, goal setting, and target-market selection. In doing so, they may conduct studies on how customers will respond to proposed changes in the current marketing mix. One researcher, for example, might study consumer response to an experimental paint formula (new

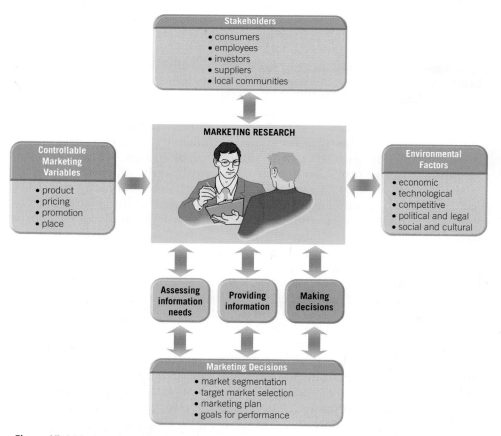

Figure 15.4 Market research and the marketing process.

product). Another might explore the response to a price reduction (new price) on calculators. A third might check response to a proposed advertising campaign (new promotion). Marketers can also try to learn whether customers are more likely to purchase a given product in a specialty shop or on the internet (new place).

Most companies will benefit from market research, but they need not do the research themselves. O-Pee-Chee Co. Ltd. of London, Ontario (the bubble gum and candy manufacturer) does no market research and no product testing, yet it continues to be successful in a market where products change at a dizzying pace. By signing a licensing agreement with two U.S. giants, O-Pee-Chee simply looks at what's hot in the United States and then starts manufacturing those lines in Canada.[13]

The Research Process

Market research can occur at almost any point in a product's existence. Most commonly, however, it is used when a new or altered product is being considered. These are the five steps in performing market research:[14]

1. *Study the current situation*. What is the need and what is being done to meet it at this point?

2. *Select a research method*. In choosing a method, marketers must bear in mind the effectiveness and costs of different methods.

3. *Collect data*. **Secondary data** is information already available as a result of previous research by the firm or other agencies. For example, Statistics Canada publishes a great deal of data that is useful for business firms. Using secondary data can save time, effort, and money. But in some cases secondary data are unavailable or inadequate, so **primary data**—new research by the firm or its agents—must be obtained. Hostess Frito-Lay, the maker of Doritos, spent a year studying how to best reach its target market—teenagers. The researchers hung around shopping malls, schools, and fast-food outlets to watch the teens.[15]

   secondary data Information already available to market researchers as a result of previous research by the firm or other agencies.

   primary data Information developed through new research by the firm or its agents.

4. *Analyze the data*. Data are not useful until they have been organized into information.

5. *Prepare a report*. This report should include a summary of the study's methodology and findings. It should also identify alternative solutions (where appropriate) and make recommendations for the appropriate course of action.

Research Methods

The four basic types of methods used by market researchers are *observation*, *surveys*, *focus groups*, and *experimentation*.

Observation

Probably the oldest form of market research is simple **observation** of what is happening. It is also a popular research method because it is relatively low in cost, often drawing on data that must be collected for some other reason, such as reordering. In earlier times, when a store owner notices that customers were buying red children's wagons, not green ones, the owner reordered more red wagons, the manufacturer's records showed high sales of red wagons, and the marketing department concluded that customers wanted red wagons. But observation is now much more sophisticated. For example, electronic scanners in supermarkets allow marketers to "observe" consumers' preferences rapidly and with tremendous accuracy.

observation A market research technique involving viewing or otherwise monitoring consumer buying patterns.

"I'd get out of children and into older people."

Another example: Procter & Gamble sent video crews into about 80 households in the United Kingdom, Germany, and China to capture people's daily routines and how they use products. By analyzing the tapes, P&G hoped to get insights into consumer behaviour. The company can use this information to develop new products to satisfy needs that consumers didn't even know they had.[16]

Using video equipment to observe consumer behaviour is called *video mining.* It is being adopted by many stores in North America who use hidden cameras to determine the percentage of shoppers that buy and the percentage that only browse. They do this by comparing the number of people taped with the number of transactions the store records. Some consumer organizations are raising privacy concerns, since shoppers are unaware that they are being taped.[17]

Surveys

Sometimes marketers need to ask questions about new marketing ideas or about how well the firm is doing its marketing tasks. One way to get answers is by conducting a **survey**. When United Parcel Service (UPS) surveyed customers to find out how it could improve service, it found that clients wanted more interaction with drivers because they can offer practical advice on shipping. UPS thus added extra drivers, freeing up some time for drivers to get out of their trucks and spend time with customers.[18]

> **survey** A market research technique based on questioning a representative sample of consumers about purchasing attitudes and practices.

Because no firm can afford to survey everyone, marketers must be careful to get a representative group of respondents when they do surveys. They must also construct the survey questions so that they get honest answers that address the specific issue being researched. Surveys can be expensive to carry out and may vary widely in their accuracy.

In the past, surveys have been mailed to individuals for their completion, but online surveys are now gaining in popularity because the company gets immediate results, and because the process is a less intrusive way of gathering data. At Hudson's Bay Co., customers can use online surveys to tell the company how happy or unhappy they are about the service they received at any of the Bay's department stores. The company can then make any changes that are needed to keep customers happy. The Bay used to hire mystery shoppers to find out how well it was serving the public, but that program ended when the online survey system was adopted.[19]

Focus Groups

Many firms also use **focus groups**, where 6 to 15 people are brought together to talk about a product or service. A moderator leads the group's discussion, and employees from the sponsoring company may observe the proceedings from behind a one-way mirror. The people in the focus group are not usually told which company is sponsoring the research. The comments of people in the focus group are taped, and then researchers go through the data looking for common themes.

focus group A market research technique involving a small group of people brought together and allowed to discuss selected issues in depth.

When Procter & Gamble was developing a new air freshener, it asked people in focus groups to describe their "desired scent experience." They discovered that people get used to a scent after about half an hour and no longer notice it. P&G used this information to develop a "scent player" called Febreze Scentstories that gives off five different scents every 30 minutes.[20] Focus groups at farm implement manufacturer John Deere have suggested many improvements in farm tractors, including different ways to change the oil filter and making the steps to the tractor cab wider.[21]

Experimentation

The last major form of market research, experimentation, also tries to get answers to questions that surveys cannot address. As in science, **experimentation** in market research attempts to compare the responses of the same or similar individuals under different circumstances. For example, a firm trying to decide whether to include walnuts in a new candy bar probably would not learn much by asking people what they thought of the idea. But if it made some bars with nuts and some without and then asked people to try both, the responses could be very helpful.[22]

experimentation A market research technique in which the reactions of similar people are compared under different circumstances.

Data Warehousing and Data Mining

Almost everything you do leaves a trail of information about you. Your preferences in movie rentals, television viewing, internet sites, and groceries; the destinations of your phone calls, your credit-card charges, your financial status; personal information about age, gender, marital status, and even health—these are just some of the items in a huge cache of data that are stored about each of us. The collection, storage, and retrieval of such data in electronic files is called **data warehousing**. For marketing researchers, the data warehouse is a gold mine of clues about consumer behaviour.[23]

data warehousing Process of collecting, storing, and retrieving data in electronic form.

As they watch a sitcom with six commercial breaks, these women are participating in a marketing research experiment. The researchers think that their results will be more accurate than questionnaire and focus-group responses because they're getting them straight from the subjects' brains. A spike in a subject's left prefrontal cortex means that she probably likes a product or an ad. A spike in the right prefrontal cortex is bad news for the advertiser. Using machines designed to detect brain tumours, researchers can even tell which part of an ad makes a dent in the subject's long-term memory.

data mining Application of electronic technologies for searching, sifting, and reorganizing data to collect marketing information and target products in the marketplace.

The Uses of Data Mining. After collecting information, marketers use **data mining**—the application of electronic technologies for searching, sifting, and reorganizing pools of data—to uncover useful marketing information and to plan for new products that will appeal to target segments in the marketplace.[24] Using data mining, for example, the insurance company Farmers Group discovered that a sports car is not an exceptionally high insurance risk if it's not the only family car. The company thus issued more liberal policies on Corvettes and Porsches and so generated more revenue without significantly increasing payout claims. Among retailers, Wal-Mart has long been a data-mining pioneer, maintaining perhaps the world's largest privately held data warehouse. Data include demographics, markdowns, returns, inventory, and other data for forecasting sales and the effects of marketing promotions.[25]

UNDERSTANDING CONSUMER BEHAVIOUR

Market research in its many forms can be of great help to marketing managers in understanding how the common traits of a market segment affect consumers' purchasing decisions. Why do people buy DVDs? What desire are they fulfilling? Is there a psychological or sociological explanation for why consumers purchase one product and not another? These questions and many others are addressed in the area of marketing known as **consumer behaviour**, which focusses on the decision process by which customers come to purchase and consume a product or service.

consumer behaviour The study of the process by which customers come to purchase and consume a product or service.

Influences on Consumer Behaviour

To understand consumer behaviour, marketers draw heavily on the fields of psychology and sociology. The result is a focus on four major influences on consumer behaviour: psychological, personal, social, and cultural. By identifying the four influences that are most active, marketers try to explain consumer choices and predict future purchasing behaviour:

- *Psychological influences* include an individual's motivations, perceptions, ability to learn, and attitudes.

- *Personal influences* include lifestyle, personality, economic status, and life-cycle stage.

- *Social influences* include family, opinion leaders (people whose opinions are sought by others), and reference groups such as friends, co-workers, and professional associates.

- *Cultural influences* include culture (the "way of living" that distinguishes one large group from another), subculture (smaller groups, such as ethnic groups, with shared values), and social class (the cultural ranking of groups according to criteria such as background, occupation, and income).

Although these factors can have a strong impact on a consumer's choices, their effect on actual purchases is sometimes weak or negligible. Some consumers, for example, regularly purchase certain products because they are satisfied with their performance. Such people (for example, users of Craftsman tools) are less subject to influence and stick with preferred brand names. On the other hand, the clothes you wear and the food you eat often reflect social and psychological influences on your consuming behaviour.

The Consumer Buying Process

Researchers who have studied consumer behaviour have constructed models that help marketing managers understand how consumers come to purchase products. Figure 15.5 presents one such model. At the heart of this and similar models is an awareness of the psychosocial influences that lead to consumption. Ultimately, marketing managers use this information to develop marketing plans.

Describe the key factors that influence the *consumer buying process*.

5

Problem/Need Recognition

The buying process begins when a consumer becomes aware of a problem or need. After strenuous exercise, you may recognize that you are thirsty and need refreshment. After the birth of twins, you may find your one-bedroom apartment too small for comfort. After standing in the rain to buy movie tickets, you may decide to buy an umbrella. Need recognition also occurs when you have a chance to change your purchasing habits. For example, the income from your first job after graduation will allow you to purchase items that were too expensive when you were a student. You may also discover a need for professional clothing, apartment furnishings, and cars. Visa and the Bay recognize this shift and market their credit cards to graduates.

Information Seeking

Having recognized a need, consumers seek information. This search is not always extensive. If you are thirsty, you may ask where the pop machine is, but that may be the extent of your information search. Other times you simply rely on your memory for information. Before making major purchases, most people seek information from personal sources, marketing sources, public sources, and experience. For example, if you move to a new town, you will want to find out who is the best local dentist, physician, hair stylist, butcher, or pizza maker. To get this information, you may check with personal sources such as acquaintances, co-workers, and relatives. Before buying an exercise bike, you may go to the library and read the latest *Consumer Reports*—a public source of consumer ratings—on such equipment.

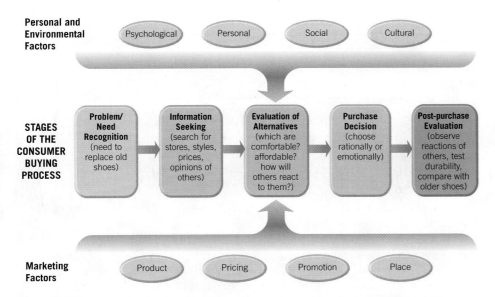

Figure 15.5 Consumer buying process.

You may also ask market sources such as the salesclerk or rely on direct experience. For example, you might test ride the bike to learn more before you buy. The internet has become an important source of information; one-third of consumers rely on the internet to gather information.[26]

Evaluation of Alternatives

If you are in the market for a set of golf clubs, you probably have some idea of who produces clubs and how they differ. You may have accumulated some of this knowledge during the information-seeking stage and combined it with what you knew before. Based on product attributes such as colour, taste, price, prestige, quality, and service record, you will decide which product best meets your needs.

Purchase Decisions

Ultimately, you make a purchase decision. You may decide to defer the purchase until a later time or you may decide to buy now. "Buy" decisions are based on rational and emotional motives. **Rational motives** involve a logical evaluation of a product's cost, quality, and usefulness. **Emotional motives** include fear, sociability, imitation of others, and aesthetics. You might buy mouthwash to avoid ostracism, or you might buy the same brand of jeans as your friends. Emotional motives can lead to irrational purchase decisions.

rational motives Those reasons for purchasing a product that involve a logical evaluation of product attributes such as cost, quality, and usefulness.

emotional motives Those reasons for purchasing a product that involve non-objective factors.

Post-Purchase Evaluations

Marketing does not stop with the sale of a product or service, but includes the process of consumption. What happens *after* the sale is therefore very important. Marketers know that consumers do not want to go through a complex decision process for every purchase, and that they often choose a product they have used and liked in the past. Therefore marketers are very motivated to keep consumers happy so they will make repeat purchases of the product. Unfortunately for marketers, when consumers are not satisfied with a purchase they typically complain to friends rather than to the company. This negative word-of-mouth advertising can be very harmful to a company. In more extreme cases, unhappy consumers may file a lawsuit or publicly criticize the product and the company.

What information is this shopper looking for to decide on his purchase? Marketers would like to know how and why consumers buy the products they buy. A better understanding of the customer buying process allows sellers to tailor their products to meet customer needs.

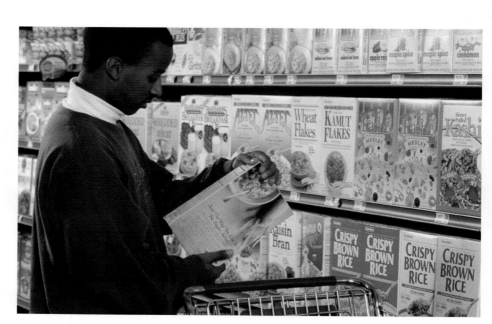

ORGANIZATIONAL MARKETING AND BUYING BEHAVIOUR

Buying behaviour is observable daily in the consumer market, where marketing activities, including buying–selling transactions, are visible to the public. Equally important, however, but far less visible, are *organizational* (or *commercial*) *markets*—organizations that buy goods and services to be used in creating and delivering consumer products. Marketing to these buyers involves different kinds of organizational markets and buying behaviours that are quite different from those found in consumer markets.

Discuss the three categories of *organizational markets* and explain how *organizational buying behaviour* differs from consumer buying behaviour.

6

Organizational Markets

Organizational or commercial markets fall into three categories: *industrial*, *reseller*, and *government/institutional markets*.

Industrial Market

The **industrial market** includes businesses that buy goods falling into one of two categories: goods to be converted into other products and goods that are used up during production. This market includes farmers, manufacturers, and some retailers. For example, Seth Thomas purchases electronics, metal components, and glass to make clocks for the consumer market. The company also buys office supplies, tools, and factory equipment—items never seen by clock buyers—to be used during production.

industrial market Businesses that buy goods to be converted into other products that will be sold to ultimate consumers.

Reseller Market

Before products reach consumers, they pass through a **reseller market** consisting of intermediaries, including wholesalers and retailers, who buy the finished goods and resell them (wholesalers and retailers are discussed in Chapter 17). Retailers like department stores, drugstores, and supermarkets buy clothing, appliances, foods, medicines, and other merchandise for resale to the consumer market. Retailers also buy such services as maintenance, housekeeping, and communications.

reseller market Intermediaries like wholesalers and retailers who buy finished products and resell them.

Government and Institutional Market

Federal, provincial, and municipal governments purchase millions of dollars worth of computer equipment, buildings, paper clips, and other items. The **institutional market** consists of non-governmental organizations, such as hospitals, churches, museums, and charitable organizations, which also comprise a substantial market for goods and services. Like organizations in other commercial markets, these institutions use supplies and equipment, as well as legal, accounting, and transportation services.

institutional market Non-government organizations such as hospitals, churches, and schools.

Organizational Buying Behaviour

In some respects, industrial buying behaviour bears little resemblance to consumer buying practices. Differences include the buyers' purchasing skills and an emphasis on buyer–seller relationships.

Differences in Buyers

Unlike most consumers, organizational buyers are professional, specialized, and expert (or at least well informed).

- As *professionals*, organizational buyers are trained in methods for negotiating purchase terms. Once buyer–seller agreements have been reached, they also arrange for formal contracts.

- As a rule, industrial buyers are company *specialists* in a line of items. As one of several buyers for a large bakery, for example, you may specialize in food ingredients. Another buyer may specialize in baking equipment (industrial ovens and mixers), while a third may buy office equipment and supplies.

- Industrial buyers are often *experts* about the products they buy. On a regular basis, organizational buyers study competing products and alternative suppliers by attending trade shows, by reading trade magazines, and by conducting technical discussions with sellers' representatives.

Differences in the Buyer–Seller Relationship

Consumer–seller relationships are often impersonal, short-lived, one-time interactions. In contrast, industrial situations often involve frequent and enduring buyer–seller relationships. The development of a long-term relationship provides each party with access to the technical strengths of the other as well as the security of knowing what future business to expect. Thus, a buyer and a supplier may form a design team to create products of benefit to both. Accordingly, industrial sellers emphasize personal selling by trained representatives who understand the needs of each customer.

THE INTERNATIONAL MARKETING MIX

7 Describe the *international* and *small business marketing mixes.*

Marketing products internationally means mounting a strategy to support global business operations. Obviously, this is no easy task since foreign customers may differ from domestic buyers in language, customs, business practices, and consumer behaviour. When companies decide to go global, marketers must consider how each element of the marketing mix might be affected.

International Products

Some products (for example, Budweiser, Coca-Cola, and Marlboros) can be sold in many different countries with virtually no changes, but often only a redesigned (or completely different) product will meet the needs of foreign buyers. To sell the Macintosh in Japan, for example, Apple Computer had to develop a Japanese-language operating system.

Mattel, the maker of Barbie dolls, is just one company that has learned some interesting lessons about the international market. When it conducted focus groups with kids in dozens of countries, it found that worldwide demand existed for many of the same products. Mattel discovered, in essence, that children have similar tastes no matter where they live. Mattel's experience with its famous Barbie doll is illustrative. The dolls sold in Japan, for example, had always had black hair and Asian features, not the blonde, blue-eyed appearance of Barbie dolls sold in North America. This seemed to make intuitive sense, but now Mattel is finding that the original Barbie doll is selling just as well in Asia as in North America.

Mattel's experience is not unique. Various other companies that sell products to international consumers have found the same phenomenon:

- The Harry Potter book series already had a global following when the first Harry Potter movie was released.

- Harlequin Enterprises, which sells millions of romance novels in many different countries, uses the same book covers around the world. The pictures of Caucasians on the book covers do not seem to deter customers in other countries from buying Harlequin romance novels.

- Sports is another universal language. Basketball stars like Michael Jordan and Shaquille O'Neal have high name recognition overseas. In a poll of Chinese students in rural Shaanxi province, Michael Jordan tied with former Chinese premier Zhou En-lai for the title "World's Greatest Man."

But there are still important differences between countries, and these cannot be ignored. For example, German children aren't attracted to action toys the way Canadian and U.S. children are. There are also differences even within basic product lines. U.S. kids, for example, want NASCAR toy cars, while European children want Formula One models.

ENTREPRENEURSHIP AND NEW VENTURES

When in Rome

When Art Aylesworth first tried to sell solar-powered LED lights for bus stops in Britain's capital, he was stymied. Oh, they might speak English in London, but the strategy he used to sell lights to the North American marine industry didn't translate to both a new country and sector.

Five years later, Aylesworth's Carmanah Technologies Corp. targets nine industries in 115 countries. Exports, which yield 92 percent of sales, powered five-year revenue growth of 1246 percent, with Carmanah now ranked number one in the world in sales of solar-powered LED lights. Its new winning strategy? Customizing sales and marketing to each industry and country.

That may sound daunting, but, like it or not, the rules of play are set by prospective clients. "You have to be a chameleon in the way you present your products and do business," says Aylesworth, Carmanah's CEO. "Figure out how they do things and join in."

Shape-shifting is hard and complicated work, but Aylesworth says it's worth it: "Had we stuck with the [original] strategy, the business would have grown about fivefold in five years. By adapting the way we have, it has grown about 35 times as big."

Rather than offer a single website, Carmanah has 11, tailored to various industries and subsectors (e.g., railwaylights.com and solarairportlights.com), with more in the works. Customers want to know you understand their world, says Aylesworth, and a customized site yields opportunities more easily and affordably than a sales rep. Carmanah has also added new sales channels to suit client preferences. It used to sell only through distributors, but now also uses its own salespeople, contracted sales agents, and strategic partnerships.

Geographically, it tailors its technology to each market as regulations or local practices require. But, Aylesworth says, Carmanah's main export challenge has been learning foreign cultures and business processes, which takes time and no small amount of trial and error. Deals in Europe and Asia, for example, require far more patience and relationship-building than in Canada. Indeed, Carmanah's five-year, $16-million deal with London's transit authority was four years in the making.

Carmanah crafts a strategy for each prospect by first asking a series of questions: which products they want and use, how and why they use them, how they buy or replace technology (including regulatory and approval procedures), who they partner with, and which sales channels they prefer. It's crucial to find the right "lead investigator" to gather such market feedback. The first senior manager Carmanah sent to the Middle East failed to earn the trust of locals, even after many trips and meetings. Aylesworth now stresses the importance of hiring a business-development manager who's hard to deter, astute, and "tough-natured but nice when they need to be."

Shape-shifting isn't cheap, either. Carmanah invested $5 million over five years to develop new products and markets. Still, the approach doesn't require vast resources: Carmanah had just 12 staff when it adopted this strategy.

What you do need, advises Aylesworth, is enough money to invest for the long haul. You should also hone your communication skills and hire people with relevant geographical or industry expertise to shorten the learning curve. Above all, weigh your decision to enter a market carefully so you don't misjudge your resources, opportunity, or desire. "If you ever walk away," warns Aylesworth, "you won't get back in easily."

International Pricing

When pricing for international markets, marketers must handle all the considerations of domestic pricing while also considering the higher costs of transporting and selling products abroad. Some products cost more overseas than in Canada because of the added costs of delivery. Due to the higher costs of buildings, rent, equipment, and imported meat, a McDonald's Big Mac that sells for $2.99 in Canada has a price tag of over $10 in Japan. In contrast, products like jet airplanes are priced the same worldwide because delivery costs are incidental; the huge development and production costs are the major considerations regardless of customer location.

International Promotion

Some standard Canadian promotional techniques do not always succeed in other countries. In fact, many Europeans believe that a product must be inherently shoddy if a company does any hard-sell advertising. International marketers must also be aware that cultural differences can cause negative reactions to products that are advertised improperly. Some Europeans, for example, are offended by television commercials that show weapons or violence. Advertising practices are regulated accordingly. Consequently, Dutch commercials for toys do not feature the guns and combat scenes that are commonplace on Saturday morning television in North America. Meanwhile, liquor and cigarette commercials that are banned from Canadian and U.S. television are thriving in many Asian and European markets.

Symbolism, too, is a sometimes-surprising consideration. In France, for instance, yellow flowers suggest infidelity. In Mexico, they are signs of death—an association made in Brazil by the colour purple. Clearly, product promotions must be carefully matched to the customs and cultural values of each country.

International Distribution

In some industries, delays in starting new distribution networks can be costly. Therefore, companies with existing distribution systems often enjoy

Feathercraft is a small British Columbia manufacturer that has been successful selling kayaks in the Japanese market.

an advantage over new businesses. Several companies have gained advantages in time-based competition by buying existing businesses. Procter & Gamble, for example, saved three years of start-up time by buying Revlon's Max Factor and Betrix cosmetics, both of which are well established in foreign markets. P&G can thus immediately use these companies' distribution and marketing networks for selling its own brands in the United Kingdom, Germany, and Japan.

Other companies contract with foreign firms or individuals to distribute and sell their products abroad. Foreign agents may perform personal selling and advertising, provide information about local markets, or serve as exporters' representatives. But having to manage interactions with foreign personnel complicates a marketing manager's responsibilities. In addition, packaging practices in Canada must sometimes be adapted to withstand the rigours of transport to foreign ports and storage under conditions that differ radically from domestic conditions.

SMALL BUSINESS AND THE MARKETING MIX

As we noted in Chapter 4, far more small businesses fail than succeed. Yet many of today's largest firms were yesterday's small businesses. McDonald's began with one restaurant, a concept, and one individual (Ray Kroc) who had tremendous foresight. Behind the success of many small firms lies a skilful application of the marketing concept and careful consideration of each element in the marketing mix.

Small-Business Products

Some new products—and firms—are doomed at the start simply because few consumers want or need what they have to offer. Too often, enthusiastic entrepreneurs introduce products that they and their friends like, but they fail to estimate realistic market potential. Other small businesses offer new products before they have clear pictures of their target segments and how to reach them. They try to be everything to everyone, and they end up serving no one well. In contrast, sound product planning has paid off for many small firms. "Keep it simple" is a familiar key to success—that is, fulfill a specific need and do it efficiently.

Small-Business Pricing

Haphazard pricing that is often little more than guesswork can sink even a firm with a good product. Most often, small-business pricing errors result from a failure to project operating expenses accurately. Owners of failing businesses have often been heard to utter statements like "I didn't realize how much it costs to run the business!" and "If I price the product high enough to cover my expenses, no one will buy it!" But when small businesses set prices by carefully assessing costs, many earn very satisfactory profits—sometimes enough to expand or diversify.

Small-Business Promotion

Successful small businesses plan for promotional expenses as part of start-up costs. Some hold down costs by taking advantage of less expensive promotional methods. Local newspapers, for example, are sources of publicity when they publish articles about new or unique businesses. Other small businesses have succeeded by identifying themselves and their products with associated groups, organizations, and events. Thus a custom-crafts gallery might join with a local art league and local artists to organize public showings of their combined products.

Small-Business Distribution

Problems in arranging distribution can make or break small businesses. Perhaps the most critical aspect of distribution is facility location, especially for new service businesses. The ability of many small businesses—retailers, veterinary clinics, and gourmet coffee shops—to attract and retain customers depends partly on the choice of location.

In distribution, as in other aspects of the marketing mix, however, smaller companies may have advantages over larger competitors, even in highly complex industries. They may be quicker, for example, in applying service technologies. Everex Systems Inc. sells personal computers to wholesalers and dealers through a system the company calls "Zero Response Time." Phone orders are reviewed every two hours so that the factory can adjust assembly to match demand.

Summary of Learning Objectives

1. **Explain the concept of *marketing* and describe the five forces that constitute the *external marketing environment*.** Marketing is "the process of planning and executing the conception, pricing, promotion, and distribution of ideas, goods, and services to create exchanges that satisfy individual and organizational goals." Products provide consumers with *utility*—the ability of a product to satisfy a human want or need. Marketing can be used to promote consumer and industrial goods and services, as well as ideas. The *external environment* consists of the outside forces that influence marketing strategy and decision making. The *political/legal environment* includes laws and regulations, both domestic and foreign, that may define or constrain business activities. The *social and cultural environment* is the context within which people's values, beliefs, and ideas affect marketing decisions. The *technological environment* includes the technological developments that affect existing and new products. The *economic environment* consists of the conditions, such as inflation, recession, and interest rates, that influence both consumer and organizational spending patterns. Finally, the *competitive environment* is the environment in which marketers must persuade buyers to purchase their products rather than their competitors'.

2. **Explain the purpose of a *marketing plan* and identify the four components of the *marketing mix*.** *Marketing managers* plan and implement all the marketing activi-

ties that result in the transfer of products to customers. These activities culminate in the *marketing plan*—a detailed strategy for focussing the effort to meet consumer needs and wants. Marketing managers rely on the "Four Ps" of marketing, or the *marketing mix*. (1) *Product*: Marketing begins with a product, a good, a service, or an idea designed to fill a consumer need or want. *Product differentiation* is the creation of a feature or image that makes a product differ from competitors. (2) *Pricing*: Pricing is the strategy of selecting the most appropriate price at which to sell a product. (3) *Place (Distribution)*: All distribution activities are concerned with getting a product from the producer to the consumer. (4) *Promotion*: Promotion refers to techniques for communicating information about products and includes advertising.

3. **Explain *market segmentation* and show how it is used in *target marketing*.** Marketers think in terms of *target markets*—groups of people who have similar wants and needs and who can be expected to show interest in the same products. Target marketing requires *market segmentation*—dividing a market into customer types or "segments." Four of the most important influences are: (1) *geographic variables* (the geographical units that may be considered in developing a segmentation strategy); (2) *demographic variables* (describe populations by identifying such traits as age, income, gender, ethnic background, marital status, race, religion, and social class); (3) *psychographic*

variables (such as lifestyles, interests, and attitudes); and (4) *product-use variables* (the ways in which consumers use a product, the benefits they expect from it, their reasons for purchasing it, and their loyalty to it).

4. **Explain the purpose and value of *marketing research*.** *Market research* is the study of what buyers need and of the best ways to meet those needs. This process involves a study of the current situation, the selection of a research method, the collection of data, the analysis of data, and the preparation of a report that may include recommendations for action. The four most common research methods are *observation*, *surveys*, *focus groups*, and *experimentation*.

5. **Describe the key factors that influence the *consumer buying process*.** *Consumer behaviour* is the study of the process by which customers decide to purchase products. The result is a focus on four major influences on consumer behaviour: (1) *Psychological influences* include motivations, perceptions, ability to learn, and attitudes. (2) *Personal influences* include lifestyle, personality, and economic status. (3) *Social influences* include family, opinion leaders, and such reference groups as friends, co-workers, and professional associates. (4) *Cultural influences* include culture, subculture, and social class. By identifying which influences are most active in certain circumstances, marketers try to explain consumer choices and predict future purchasing behaviour.

6. **Discuss the three categories of *organizational markets* and explain how *organizational buying behaviour* differs from consumer buying behaviour.** *Organizational* (or *commercial*) *markets*, in which organizations buy goods and services to be used in creating and delivering consumer products, fall into three categories. (1) The *industrial market* consists of businesses that buy goods to be converted into other products or goods that are used during production. (2) Before products reach consumers, they pass through a *reseller market* consisting of intermediaries that buy finished goods and resell them. (3) *Government and institutional market*: Federal, provincial, and local governments buy durable and non-durable products. The institutional market consists of non-governmental buyers such as hospitals, churches, museums, and charities. Organizational buying behaviour differs from consumer buyer behaviour in two major ways: (1) *Differences in buyers*: Organizational buyers are professionals trained in arranging buyer–seller relationships and negotiating purchase terms. They are usually specialists in a line of items and are often experts about the products they are buying. (2) *Differences in the buyer–seller relationship*: Whereas consumer–seller relationships are often fleeting, one-time interactions, industrial situations often involve frequent, enduring buyer–seller relationships.

7. **Describe the *international* and *small business marketing mixes*.** When they decide to go global, marketers must reconsider each element of the marketing mix. (1) *International products*: Whereas some products can be sold abroad with virtually no changes, sometimes only a redesigned product will meet the needs of foreign buyers. (2) *International pricing*: When pricing for international markets, marketers must consider the higher costs of transporting and selling products abroad. (3) *International distribution*: In some industries, companies have gained advantages by buying businesses already established in foreign markets. (4) *International promotion*: Occasionally, a good ad campaign can be transported to another country virtually intact. Quite often, however, standard Canadian promotional tactics do not succeed in other countries.

Behind the success of many small firms lies an understanding of each element in the marketing mix. (1) *Small-business products*: Understanding of what customers need and want has paid off for many small firms. (2) *Small-business pricing*: Haphazard pricing can sink even a firm with a good product. Small-business pricing errors usually result from failure to project operating expenses accurately. But when small businesses set prices by carefully assessing costs, many earn satisfactory profits. (3) *Small-business distribution*: Perhaps the most critical aspect of distribution is facility location: The ability of many small businesses to attract and retain customers depends partly on the choice of location. (4) *Small-business promotion*: Successful small businesses plan for promotional expenses as part of start-up costs. Some take advantage of less expensive promotional methods.

KEY TERMS

brand competition, 478
consumer behaviour, 490
consumer goods, 473
data mining, 490
data warehousing, 489
demographic variables, 483
distribution, 480
emotional motives, 492
experimentation, 489
external environment, 476
focus group, 489
geographic variables, 482
industrial goods, 473
industrial market, 493

institutional market, 493
international competition, 478
market research, 486
market segmentation, 481
marketing, 472
marketing concept, 472
marketing managers, 478
marketing mix, 478
marketing plan, 478
observation, 487
price, 479
primary data, 487
product, 478
product differentiation, 479

product-use variables, 484
promotion, 480
psychographic variables, 483
rational motives, 492
relationship marketing, 475
reseller market, 493
secondary data, 487
services, 473
substitute product, 478
survey, 488
target market, 481
utility, 473
value, 472

QUESTIONS FOR ANALYSIS

1. Why and how is market segmentation used in target marketing?

2. Select an everyday product (books, CDs, skateboards, dog food, or shoes, for example). Show how different versions of your product are aimed toward different market segments. Explain how the marketing mix differs for each segment.

3. Select another product and describe the consumer buying process that likely occurs before it is purchased.

4. Explain the key differences between consumer buying behaviour and organizational buying behaviour.

5. What is the value to consumers of things like loyalty cards and discount cards? Why would companies offer consumers such cards?

6. Why has the in-store use of hidden cameras become so popular? Is this "video mining" ethical? If not, how could it be made more acceptable?

7. If you were starting your own small business, what are the key marketing pitfalls you would try to avoid?

8. Select a product or service that you regularly use. Explain the relative importance of each of the four elements in the marketing mix (product, price, promotion, and place). Then select another product and determine the extent to which the relative emphasis changes. If it changed, why did it change?

APPLICATION EXERCISES

1. Interview the marketing manager of a local business. Identify the degree to which this person's job is focussed on each element in the marketing mix.

2. Select a product made by a foreign company and sold in Canada. What is the product's target market? What is the basis on which the target market is segmented? Do you think that this basis is appropriate? How might another approach, if any, be beneficial? Why?

BUILDING YOUR BUSINESS SKILLS

Dealing in Segments and Variables

Goal

To encourage students to analyze the ways in which various market segmentation variables affect business success.

The Situation

You and four partners are thinking of purchasing a heating and air conditioning (H/AC) dealership that specializes in residential applications priced between $2000 and $40 000. You are now in the process of deciding where that dealership should be. You are considering four locations: Miami, Florida; Toronto, Ontario; Vancouver, B.C.; and Dallas, Texas.

Assignment

Step 1

Working with four classmates (your partnership group), do library research to learn how H/AC makers market their residential products. Check for articles in *The Globe and Mail*, *Canadian Business*, *The Wall Street Journal*, and other business publications.

Step 2

Continue your research. This time, focus on the specific marketing variables that define each prospective location. Check Statistics Canada data at your library and on the internet and contact local chambers of

commerce (by phone and via the internet) to learn about the following factors for each location:

- geography
- demography (especially age, income, gender, family status, and social class)
- psychographic variables (lifestyles, interests, and attitudes)

Step 3

Meet with group members to analyze which location holds the greatest promise as a dealership site. Base your decision on your analysis of market segment variables and their effects on H/AC sales.

Follow-Up Questions

1. Which location did you choose? Describe the market segmentation factors that influenced your decision.

2. Identify the two most important variables you believe will have the greatest impact on the dealership's success. Why are these factors so important?

3. Which factors were least important in your decision? Why?

4. When equipment manufacturers advertise residential H/AC products, they often show them in different climate situations (in winter, summer, or high-humidity conditions). Which market segments are these ads targeting? Describe these segments in terms of demographic and psychographic characteristics.

EXERCISING YOUR ETHICS

Driving a Legitimate Bargain

The Situation

This exercise illustrates how ethical issues can become entwined with personal selling activities, product pricing, and customer relations.

The Dilemma

In buying his first-ever new car, Matt visited showrooms and websites for every make of SUV. After weeks of reading and test-driving, he settled on a well-known Japanese-made vehicle with a manufacturer's suggested retail price of $34 500 for the 2006 model.

The price included accessories and options that Matt considered essential. Because he planned to own the car for at least five years, he was willing to wait for just the right package rather than accept a lesser-equipped car already on the lot. Negotiations with Gary, the sales representative, continued for two weeks. Finally, a sales contract was signed for $32 600, with delivery due no more than two or three months later if the vehicle had to be special-ordered from the factory, earlier if Gary found the exact car when he searched other dealers around the country. On April 30, to close the deal, Matt had to write a cheque for $1000.

Matt received a call on June 14 from Angela, Gary's sales manager: "We cannot get your car before

October," she reported, "so it will have to be a 2007 model. You will have to pay the 2007 price." Matt replied that the agreement called for a stated price and delivery deadline for 2006, pointing out that money had exchanged hands for the contract. When asked what the 2007 price would be, Angela responded that it had not yet been announced. Angrily, Matt replied that he would be foolish to agree now on some unknown future price. Moreover, he didn't like the way the dealership was treating him. He told Angela to send back to him everything he had signed; the deal was off.

Questions for Discussion

1. Given the factors involved in the consumer buying process, how would you characterize the particular ethical issues in this situation?

2. From an ethical standpoint, what are the obligations of the sales rep and the sales manager regarding the pricing of the product in this situation?

3. If you were responsible for maintaining good customer relations at the dealership, how would you handle this matter?

CONCLUDING CASE 15-1

Dell-ivering on Consumer Electronics

There's a good reason why competitors don't match Dell's success in selling computers. From the outset, Michael Dell's vision recognized a market with different kinds of potential users—the business sector, non-business organizations such as schools and other institutions, as well as the growing segment of PC users in homes—each with different needs and resources. Choosing to focus more on the business and institutional segments, Dell envisioned an unheard-of combination of service features for PC customers: high-quality products, lowest cost, ease in ordering and receiving products, live interaction with expert technical assistance for building a PC "the way you like it," super-fast deliveries, and after-the-sale communications to ensure product performance and keep users informed about upgrades to enhance their PCs.

The market response has been overwhelming, resulting in Dell's dominant position as industry leader. Dell's unique vision for integrating all stages of marketing—development of the product and related services, pricing it, selling to consumers directly via telephone or the internet, delivering directly to customers from efficient manufacturing plants, and promotional messages for product awareness and use—are unmatched by competitors that are struggling to copy Dell's way of doing business.

As if that were not enough to cause headaches in the PC industry, Dell recently launched itself into the broader consumer electronics market for even greater revenue growth. Today's giant electronics retailers, such as Circuit City and Best Buy, may soon be looking over their shoulders if Dell's customer-friendly business model is successfully carried over into flat-panel TVs,

DVD recorders, MP3 players, and digital cameras. Plans even call for opening an online music-downloading store on the same popular website where PC users buy other Dell products. The potential range of products is enormous because music, movies, photos, and other entertainment are increasingly digital and, thus, are becoming compatible extensions of PCs. Commenting on the company's new thrust, Chairman Michael Dell states, "The whole new ballgame is these worlds [computing and consumer electronics] converging, and that's a world we're comfortable in."

But will they necessarily succeed? Some experts think the crossover into consumer products could be a problem because, unlike Gateway and Hewlett-Packard's focus on the consumer segment, Dell's primary PC focus has been on business and institutional markets. A classic example of a failed crossover is IBM's ill-fated attempt in the 1980s to woo consumers with its downsized PC Jr. computer. With hugely successful sales and technical support for business customers, IBM never understood the consumer market, and Big Blue's efforts proved a mismatch that ended with the withdrawal of the PC Jr. from the marketplace in the late 1990s. But Dell CEO Kevin Rollins says such risks are largely offset by Dell's brand familiarity in both business and consumer markets.

Price is equally important to consumers, says industry analyst Peter Kastner. "Dell's no-middleman model almost guarantees a value-based price," and that means more intense price-for-performance competition than exists now in consumer electronics. The bottom line for consumers will be lower prices while other firms in the industry try to imitate Dell's low-price–high-value business model.

But even if these improvements are made, some critics will not be happy. The vice-president at one advertising space-buying company, for example, says that the only thing that is important to measure is "live" viewing. That's because people who are watching a DVR program are probably not even watching the ads. Not surprisingly, TV companies disagree with that assessment. They argue that ad rates should be determined by the total viewership an ad gets.

Questions for Discussion

1. What are the various methods that are available to market researchers as they gather data about customers? Which method does Nielsen use?

2. The viewership data that Nielsen's develops is important in determining how much advertisers pay to place their ads on TV. What are the advantages and disadvantages of the system? Are there alternative systems that might work better? Explain.

3. The argument has been made that counting DVR viewing isn't useful because people either don't watch program advertisements when using a DVR, or that advertisements simply don't have the same urgency even if they are watched. Do you agree or disagree with this argument? Give reasons. Whatever your position, how does uncertainty over issues like this influence the value of marketing research data? What could be done to improve the data?

4. Suppose that you are buying advertising space on TV. Would you be more likely to accept Nielsen data for, say, sports programs than you would for dramas? Explain. What kind of biases might you have and why?

CHAPTER 16

Developing and Promoting Goods and Services

After reading this chapter, you should be able to:

1 Explain the definition of a product as a *value package*.

2 Describe the *new product development process* and trace the stages of the *product life cycle*.

3 Explain the importance of *branding*, *packaging*, and *labelling*.

4 Identify the important objectives of *promotion* and discuss the considerations in selecting a *promotional mix*.

5 Discuss the most important *advertising strategies* and describe the key *advertising media*.

6 Outline the tasks involved in *personal selling* and list the steps in the *personal selling process*.

7 Describe the various types of *sales promotions*, and distinguish between *publicity* and *public relations*.

8 Describe the development of *international promotion strategies*.

but the media attention it receives is very valuable for True North. The day after the discovery was reported on *The National*, over 1 million shares of True North were traded, and the stock jumped to $1.24 per share.

On the eve of the shareholders meeting two weeks later, the first results are in. The deeper underground the company digs, the better the quality and size of the emeralds. But the sample is small, and the company doesn't know how much the total deposit may be worth. But at least this year the company can show investors real emeralds. At its meeting last year, they didn't have any emeralds, and investors were not happy.

Just before the shareholders meeting, Andy meets with the company geologist in a strategy session. They need to figure out what message they want to give to investors. He can't hype the company too much or he will run into trouble with securities regulators. But he also can't be too negative or vague, because investors want to see some action. At the meeting, Smith reports that the emerald sector looks comparable to the diamond sector (although it is less well developed at the moment). He emphasizes that the company has found bigger stones underground in recent digging, and he tells the shareholders that True North's emerald deposit could eventually be worth billions of dollars. The company's geologist is more cautious, and simply says that that the results look interesting from an economic point of view.

The geologist then shows shareholders some real emeralds taken from the Yukon property. Investors are happy with this hard evidence that something real is happening.

Emerald fever is still alive, but until True North starts actually selling stones at the retail level, nothing is for sure. For now, shareholders seem willing to continue backing the company. But an operating mine is at least two years away, and many tasks remain to be completed: various permits are needed, more testing must be done at Regal Ridge, and there are environmental questions that must be answered.

Questions for Discussion

1. Explain the difference between par value, market value, and book value of a company's stock. Which of these values are investors of True North concerned about? Why?

2. What subjective factors influence the price of a company's stock? Which of these are relevant for this case? Explain.

3. Briefly describe the major sources of short- and long-term funds for businesses. Which of these sources would a firm like True North be most likely to use? Why?

4. What are the factors that a company must take into account when deciding between debt and equity financing? Explain which of these are relevant for True North, and the type of financing that the company would likely choose, given a consideration of these factors.

Source: "Canadian Emeralds," *Venture*, March 28, 2004.

BUSINESS LAW

THE ROLE OF LAW IN CANADIAN SOCIETY

law   The set of rules and standards that a society agrees upon to govern the behaviour of its citizens.

Law is the set of rules and standards that a society agrees upon to govern the behaviour of its citizens. Both the British and the French influenced the development of law in Canada. In 1867, the British North America (BNA) Act created the nation of Canada. The BNA Act was "patriated" to Canada in 1982 and is known as the Constitution Act. This act divides legislative powers in Canada between the federal and provincial governments.

Sources of Law

The law in Canada has evolved and changed in response to our norms and values. Our laws have arisen from three sources: (1) customs and judicial precedents (the source of common law), (2) the actions of provincial and federal legislatures (the source of statutory law), and (3) rulings by administrative bodies (the source of administrative law).

common law   The unwritten law of England, derived from precedent and legal judgments.

    Common law is the unwritten law of England, derived from ancient precedents and judges' previous legal opinions. Common law is based on the principle of equity, the provision to every person of a just and fair remedy. Canadian legal customs and traditions derive from British common law. All provinces except Quebec, which uses the French Civil Code, have laws based on British common law, and court decisions are often based on precedents from common law. That is, decisions made in earlier cases that involved the same legal point will guide the court.

statutory law   Written law developed by city councils, provincial legislatures, and parliament.

    Statutory law is written law developed by city councils, provincial legislatures, and parliament. Most law in Canada today is statutory law.

administrative law   Rules and regulations that government agencies develop based on their interpretations of statutory law.

    Administrative law is the rules and regulations that government agencies and commissions develop based on their interpretations of statutory laws. For example, Consumer and Corporate Affairs Canada develops regulations on false advertising using federal legislation.

The Court System

In Canada, the judiciary branch of government has the responsibility of settling disputes among organizations or individuals by applying existing laws. Both provincial and federal courts exist to hear both criminal and civil cases. The Supreme Court of Canada is the highest court in Canada. It decides whether to hear appeals from lower courts.

BUSINESS LAW

business law   Laws that specifically affect how businesses are managed.

Business firms, like all other organizations, are affected by the laws of the country. **Business law** refers to laws that specifically affect how business firms are managed. Some laws affect all businesses, regardless of size, industry, or location. For example, the Income Tax Act requires businesses to pay income tax. Other laws may have a greater impact on one industry than on others. For example, pollution regulations are of much greater concern to Inco than they are to Carlson Wagonlit Travel.

    Business managers must have at least a basic understanding of eight important concepts in business law:

- contracts
- agency
- bailment
- property
- warranty
- torts
- negotiable instruments
- bankruptcy

Contracts

Agreements about transactions are common in a business's day-to-day activity. A **contract** is an agreement between two parties to act in a specified way or to perform certain acts. A contract might, for example, apply to a customer buying a product from a retail establishment or to two manufacturers agreeing to buy products or services from each other. A valid contract includes several elements:

- *an agreement*—All parties must consciously agree about the contract.

- *consideration*—The parties must exchange something of value (e.g., time, products, services, money, etc.).

- *competence*—All parties to the contract must be legally able to enter into an agreement. Individuals who are below a certain age or who are legally insane, for example, cannot enter into legal agreements.

- *legal purpose*—What the parties agree to do for or with each other must be legal. An agreement between two manufacturers to fix prices is not legal.

The courts will enforce a contract if it meets the criteria described above. Most parties honour their contracts, but occasionally one party does not do what it was supposed to do. **Breach of contract** occurs when one party to an agreement fails, without legal reason, to live up to the agreement's provisions. The party who has not breached the contract has three alternatives under the law in Canada: (1) discharge, (2) sue for damages, or (3) require specific performance.

An example will demonstrate these three alternatives. Suppose that Barrington Farms Inc. agrees to deliver 100 dozen long-stemmed roses to the Blue Violet Flower Shop the week before Mother's Day. One week before the agreed-upon date, Barrington informs Blue Violet that it cannot make the delivery until after Mother's Day. Under the law, the owner of Blue Violet can choose among any of the following:

Discharge

Blue Violet can also ignore its obligations in the contract. That is, it can contract with another supplier.

Sue for Damages

Blue Violet can legally demand payment for losses caused by Barrington's failure to deliver the promised goods. Losses might include any increased price Blue Violet would have to pay for the roses or court costs incurred in the damage suit.

Require Specific Performance

If monetary damages are not sufficient to reimburse Blue Violet, the court can force Barrington's to live up to its original contract.

contract An agreement between two parties to act in a specified way or to perform certain acts.

breach of contract When one party to an agreement fails, without legal reason, to live up to the agreement's provisions.

AGENCY

In many business situations, one person acts as an agent for another person. Well-known examples include actors and athletes represented by agents who negotiate contracts for them. An **agency–principal relationship** is established when one party (the agent) is authorized to act on behalf of another party (the principal).

The agent is under the control of the principal and must act on behalf of the principal and in the principal's best interests. The principal remains liable for the acts of the agent as long as the agent is acting within the scope of authority granted by the principal. A salesperson for IBM, for example, is an agent for IBM, the principal.

Bailment

Many business transactions are not covered by the agency–principal relationship. For example, suppose that you take your car to a mechanic to have it repaired. Because the repair shop has temporary possession of something you own, it is responsible for your car. This is a **bailor–bailee relationship**. In a bailor–bailee relationship, the bailor (the car owner) gives possession of his or her property to the bailee (the repair shop) but retains ownership of the item. A business firm that stores inventory in a public warehouse is in a bailor–bailee relationship. The business firm is the bailor and the warehouse is the bailee. The warehouse is responsible for storing the goods safely and making them available to the manufacturer upon request.

The Law of Property

Property includes anything of tangible or intangible value that the owner has the right to possess and use. **Real property** is land and any permanent buildings attached to that land. **Personal property** is tangible or intangible assets other than real property. Personal property includes cars, clothing, furniture, money in bank accounts, stock certificates, and copyrights.

Transferring Property

From time to time, businesses and individuals need to transfer property to another person or business. A **deed** is a document that shows ownership of real property. It allows the transfer of title of real property.

A **lease** grants the use of an asset for a specified period of time in return for payment. The business or individual granting the lease is the lessor and the tenant is the lessee. For example, a business (the lessee) may rent space in a mall for one year from a real estate development firm (the lessor).

A **title** shows legal possession of personal property. It allows the transfer of title of personal property. When you buy a snowmobile, for example, the former owner signs the title over to you.

Warranty

When you buy a product or service, you want some assurance that it will perform satisfactorily and meet your needs. A **warranty** is a promise that the product or service will perform as the seller has promised it will.

There are two kinds of warranties—express and implied. An **express warranty** is a specific claim that the manufacturer makes about a product. For example, a warranty that a screwdriver blade is made of case-hardened

---

agency–principal relationship When one party (the agent) is authorized to act on behalf of another party (the principal).

bailor–bailee relationship When a bailor, a property owner, gives possession of the property to a bailee, a custodian, but retains ownership of the property.

property Anything of tangible or intangible value that the owner has the right to possess and own.

real property Land and any permanent buildings attached to that land.

personal property Tangible or intangible assets other than real property.

deed A document that shows ownership of real property.

lease A document that grants the use of an asset for a specified period of time in return for payment.

title A document that shows legal possession of personal property.

warranty A promise that the product or service will perform as the seller has promised it will.

express warranty A specific claim that a manufacturer makes about a product.

steel is an express warranty. An **implied warranty** suggests that a product will perform as the manufacturer claims it will. Suppose that you buy an outboard motor for your boat and the engine burns out in one week. Because the manufacturer implies by selling the motor that it will work for a reasonable period of time, you can return it and get your money back.

Because opinions vary on what is a "reasonable" time, most manufacturers now give limited time warranties on their products. For example, they will guarantee their products against defects in materials or manufacture for six months or one year.

> **implied warranty** An assumption that a product will perform as the manufacturer claims it will.

Torts

A **tort** is a wrongful civil act that one party inflicts on another and that results in injury to the person, to the person's property, or to the person's good name. An **intentional tort** is a wrongful act intentionally committed. If a security guard in a department store suspects someone of shoplifting and uses excessive force to prevent him or her from leaving the store, the guard might be guilty of an intentional tort. Other examples are libel, embezzlement, and patent infringement.

> **tort** A wrongful civil act that one party inflicts on another.
> **intentional tort** A wrongful act intentionally committed.

Negligence is a wrongful act that inadvertently causes injury to another person. For example, if a maintenance crew in a store mops the floors without placing warning signs in the area, a customer who slips and falls might bring a negligence suit against the store.

> **negligence** A wrongful act that inadvertently causes injury to another person.

In recent years, the most publicized area of negligence has been product liability. **Product liability** means that businesses are liable for injuries caused to product users because of negligence in design or manufacturing. **Strict product liability** means that a business is liable for injuries caused by their products even if there is no evidence of negligence in the design or manufacture of the product.

> **product liability** The liability of businesses for injuries caused to product users because of negligence in design or manufacture.
> **strict product liability** The liability of businesses for injuries caused by their products even if no evidence of negligence in the product's design or manufacture exists.

Negotiable Instruments

Negotiable instruments are types of commercial paper that can be transferred among individuals and business firms. Cheques, bank drafts, and certificates of deposit are examples of negotiable instruments.

> **negotiable instrument** Types of commercial paper that can be transferred among individuals and business firms.

The Bills of Exchange Act specifies that a negotiable instrument must

- be written
- be signed by the person who puts it into circulation (the maker or drawer)
- contain an unconditional promise to pay a certain amount of money
- be payable on demand
- be payable to a specific person (or to the bearer of the instrument)

Negotiable instruments are transferred from one party to another through an endorsement. An **endorsement** means signing your name to a negotiable instrument; this makes it transferable to another person or organization. If you sign only your name on the back of a cheque, you are making a *blank* endorsement. If you state that the instrument is being transferred to a specific person, you are making a *special* endorsement. A *qualified* endorsement limits your liability if the instrument is not backed up by sufficient funds. For example, if you get a cheque from a friend and want to use it to buy a new stereo, you can write "without recourse" above your name. If your friend's cheque bounces, you have no liability. A *restrictive* endorsement limits the negotiability of the instrument. For example, if you write "for deposit only" on the back of a cheque and it is later stolen, no one else can cash it.

> **endorsement** Signing your name to a negotiable instrument, making it transferable to another person or organization.

Bankruptcy

At one time, individuals who could not pay their debts were jailed. Today, however, both organizations and individuals can seek relief by filing for **bankruptcy**, which is the court-granted permission to not pay some or all of their debts.

bankruptcy Permission granted by the courts to individuals and organizations not to pay some or all of their debts.

Thousands of individuals and businesses file for bankruptcy each year. They do so for various reasons, including cash flow problems, reduced demand for their products, or some other problem that makes it difficult or impossible for them to resolve their financial problems. In recent years, large businesses like Eaton's, Olympia & York, and Enron have sought the protection of bankruptcy laws. Three main factors account for the increase in bankruptcy filings:

1. The increased availability of credit

2. The "fresh-start" provisions in current bankruptcy laws

3. The growing acceptance of bankruptcy as a financial tactic

insolvent person (or company) One who cannot pay current obligations to creditors as they come due, or whose debts exceed their assets.

bankrupt person (or company) One who has either made a voluntary application to start bankruptcy proceedings (voluntary bankruptcy) or has been forced by creditors into bankruptcy (involuntary bankruptcy) by a process referred to as a receiving order.

In Canada, jurisdiction over bankruptcy is provided by the Bankruptcy and Insolvency Act. An **insolvent person (or company)** is defined as one who cannot pay current obligations to creditors as they come due, or whose debts exceed their assets. A **bankrupt person (or company)** is one who has either made a voluntary application to start bankruptcy proceedings (voluntary bankruptcy) or has been forced by creditors into bankruptcy (involuntary bankruptcy) by a process referred to as a *receiving order*. A person who is insolvent may or may not be bankrupt, and a person who is bankrupt may or may not be insolvent, as there are other bases for bankruptcy under the act. Another procedure under the act is referred to as a *proposal*, which can delay or avoid liquidation by providing the debtor with time to reorganize affairs and/or propose a payment schedule to creditors.

On a practical basis, business bankruptcy under the act may be resolved or avoided by one of three methods:

- Under a *liquidation plan*, the business ceases to exist. Its assets are sold and the proceeds are used to pay creditors.

- Under a *repayment plan*, the bankrupt company works out a new payment schedule to meet its obligations. The time frame is usually extended, and payments are collected and distributed by a court-appointed trustee.

- *Reorganization* is the most complex form of business bankruptcy. The company must explain the sources of its financial difficulties and propose a new plan for remaining in business. Reorganization may include a new slate of managers and a new financial strategy. A judge may also reduce the firm's debts to ensure its survival. Although creditors naturally dislike debt reduction, they may agree to the proposal, since getting, say, 50 percent of what you are owed is better than getting nothing at all.

For many people, the goal of financial success isn't *being* wealthy: It's the things that they can *do* with wealth. That's why chapter one in so many financial success stories deals with a hard reality: Like it or not, dealing with personal finances is a life-long job. As a rule, it involves a life-altering choice between two options:

- committing to the rational management of your personal finances—controlling them as a way of life and helping them grow

- letting the financial chips fall where they may and hoping for the best (which seldom happens)

Not surprisingly, option 1 results in greater personal satisfaction and financial stability. Ignoring your finances, on the other hand, invites frustration, disappointment, and, quite often, acute financial distress.

TAKING YOUR FINANCES PERSONALLY

In Chapter 20, we explored some basic financial-management activities, including the role of financial managers in cash flow management, financial planning and control, and debt and equity financing. We discussed the activities of financial managers—clarifying financial goals, determining short-term and long-term funding needs, and managing risk. Many of the principles of organizational finance pertain to personal finance as well. Recall, for example, the principle of reducing organizational financial risk by diversifying investments. When Enron collapsed, many employees lost their entire savings because their retirement portfolios consisted of just one security—Enron common stock—instead of a broader selection of investments.

In managing your own finances and pursuing your own personal financial goals, you must consider the activities that we'll revisit in the following sections: cash management, financial planning and control, investment alternatives, and risk management. We start by describing a key factor in success: the personal financial plan. Then we'll detail the steps in the planning process and relate them to some core concepts and crucial decisions in personal financial management.

BUILDING YOUR FINANCIAL PLAN

Financial planning is the process of looking at your current financial condition, identifying your goals, and anticipating your requirements for meeting those goals. Once you've determined the assets you need to meet your goals, you'll then identify the best sources and uses of those assets for eventually reaching your goals. But remember: Because your goals and financial position will change as you enter different life stages, your plan should always make room for revision. Figure B.1 summarizes a step-by-step approach to personal financial planning.

Knowing Your Net Worth

Begin by assessing your current financial position. Your personal net worth is the value of all your assets minus all your liabilities or debts. Bear in

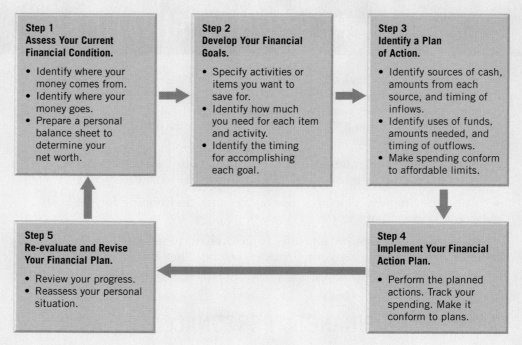

Figure B.1

mind that personal net worth doesn't refer to the resources that you plan to manage in the future (as in a budget): It's a measure of *your wealth at the present time.* The worksheet in Figure B.2 provides some sample calculations for developing your own personal "balance sheet." Because assets and liabilities change over time, updating your balance sheet not only allows you to monitor changes but also provides more accurate information for realistic budgeting and planning.

Using Your Net Worth to Set and Evaluate Goals

Your personal balance sheet lets you review your *current* overall financial condition. Once you know where you presently stand, you can move on to Step 2 in financial planning: setting specific goals for the future by calculating *changes in net worth.* The worksheet in Figure B.3 allows for goal setting in three time frames: *immediate* (within one year), *intermediate* (within five years), and *long term* (over more than five years). This kind of planning should encourage you to set measurable goals and completion times when calculating your future financial needs. It also lets you set priorities for rationing your resources if, at some point, you don't have the wherewithal to pursue all of your goals.

Because subsequent planning steps—beginning with Step 3 (identifying a plan of action) and including implementation—will affect assets and liabilities, your balance sheet will change over time. That's why it needs periodic updating to reflect your current net worth, to monitor your progress, and to help you start a new planning cycle.

The Time Value of Money

The time value of money is perhaps the single most important concept in personal finance. It's especially relevant for setting financial goals and evaluating investments. The concept of *time value* recognizes the basic fact that, while it's invested, money grows by earning interest or yielding some other form of return. Thus, whenever you make everyday purchases, you're giv-

Assets: What You Own		Example Numbers	Your Numbers
LIQUID ASSETS			
1. Cash.	$	300	_____
2. Savings.	+	3700	_____
3. Chequing	+	1200	_____
INVESTMENTS:			
4. RRSPs	+	12 400	_____
5. Securities	+	500	_____
6. Retirement Plan	+	—	_____
7. Real Estate (other than primary residence)	+	—	_____
HOUSEHOLD:			
8. Cars (market value).	+	18 000	_____
9. House (market value).	+	84 000	_____
10. Furniture.	+	3400	_____
11. Personal Property	+	6600	_____
12. Other assets		—	_____
13. Total Assets (add lines 1–12)		**= $130 100**	_____
Liabilities (Debt): What You Owe			
CURRENT LIABILITIES:			
14. Credit card balance.	$	1300	_____
15. Unpaid bills due.	+	1800	_____
16. Alimony and child support	+	—	_____
LONG-TERM LIABILITIES:			
17. Home mortgage	+	72 500	_____
18. Home equity loan	+	—	_____
19. Car loan	+	4100	_____
20. Student loan	+	3600	_____
21. Other liabilities	+	2400	_____
22. Total Liabilities (add lines 14–21)		**= $85 700**	_____
Net Worth			
23. Total Assets (line 13)	$	130 100	_____
24. Less: Total Debt (line 22)	+	85 700	_____
25. Results: Net Worth		**= $44 400**	_____

Figure B.2

ing up interest that you could have earned with the same money if you'd invested it instead. From a financial standpoint, "idle" or uninvested money—money that could be put to work earning more money—is a wasted resource.

Why Money Grows

The value of time stems from the principle of compound growth—the compounding of interest paid over given time periods. With each additional time period, interest payments accumulate and earn even more interest, thus multiplying the earning capacity of the investment. Let's say, for example, that you invest $1 today at 10 percent annual interest. As you can see from Table B.1, you'll have $1.10 at the end of one year (your $1 original investment plus $0.10 in interest). If you reinvest your whole $1.10, you'll earn interest on both your first year's interest and your original investment. During year 2, therefore, your savings will grow to $1.21 (your $1.10 reinvestment plus $0.11 in interest). Obviously, each year's interest will be

Name the Goal	Financial requirement (amount) for this goal	Time frame for accomplishing goal	Importance (1 = highest, 5 = lowest)
Immediate Goals:			
Live in a better apartment			
Obtain adequate life, disability, liability, property insurance			
Establish an emergency cash fund			
Pay off credit card debt			
Other			
Intermediate Goals:			
Save for wedding			
Save to buy new car			
Establish regular savings program (5% of gross income)			
Save for college for self			
Pay off major outstanding debt			
Make a major purchase			
Save for home remodeling			
Save for down payment on a home			
Other			
Long-Term Goals:			
Pay off home mortgage			
Save for college for children			
Save for vacation home			
Increase personal net worth to $ __ in __ years.			
Achieve retirement nest egg of $ __ in __ years.			
Accumulate fund for travel in retirement			
Save for long-term care needs			
Other			

Figure B.3

Table B.1 Calculating Compound Growth

Year	Beginning Amount	+	Annual Interest Earned	=	Ending Amount
1	$1.000	+	$0.100 [0.10 × $1.000 = $0.10]	=	$1.100
2	1.100	+	0.110 [0.10 × $1.100 = $0.11]	=	1.210
3	1.210	+	0.121 [0.10 × $1.210 = $0.121]	=	1.331
4	1.331	+	0.133 [0.10 × $1.331 = $0.133]	=	1.464
5	1.464	+	0.146 [0.10 × $1.464 = $0.146]	=	1.610
6	1.610	+	0.161 [0.10 × $1.610 = $0.161]	=	1.771
7	1.771	+	0.177 [0.10 × $1.771 = $0.177]	=	1.948
8	1.948	+	0.195 [0.10 × $1.948 = $0.195]	=	2.143

greater than the previous year's. The interest accumulated over a single time period may seem rather modest, but when you add it up over many periods, the growth can be impressive. After about 7½ years at 10 percent, your original $1 will have doubled. In other words, if you had invested $10 000, you'd have $20 000.

The Rule of 72

How long does it take to double an investment? A handy rule of thumb is called the "Rule of 72." You can find the number of years needed to double your money by dividing the annual interest rate (in percent) into 72. If, for example, you reinvest annually at 8 percent, you'll double your money in about 9 years:

$$\frac{72}{8} = 9$$

The Rule of 72 can also calculate how much interest you must get if you want to double your money in a given number of years: Simply divide 72 by the desired number of years. Thus, if you want to double your money in 10 years, you need to get 7.2 percent:

$$\frac{72}{10} = 7.2$$

Finally, the Rule of 72 highlights the downside as well as the upside of the compound-growth principle. The process means greater wealth for savers but increased indebtedness for borrowers. As we have seen, for example, an 8 percent rate doubles the principal every 9 years:

$$\frac{72}{8} = 9$$

Over a period of 36 years, the amount doubles four times:

$$\frac{36}{9} = 4$$

At 4 percent, by contrast, it doubles only twice over 36 years. Table B.2 charts the accumulation of the difference—$16 000 versus $4000—between investments (or loans) made at 8 percent versus 4 percent. The lesson for the personal-finance manager is clear: When investing (or saving), seek higher interest rates because money doubles more frequently; when borrowing, seek lower interest rates because indebtedness grows more slowly.

Table B.2	The Power of Doubling
Initial Investment (or Initial Unpaid Debt) = $1000	
Number of Times Doubled	**Value after Doubling**
1	$2000
2	$4000
3	$8000
4	$16 000

Making Better Use of Your Time Value

Most people want to save for the future, either for things they need (down payments on a house, university or college tuition, retirement nest eggs) or for nonessentials (luxury items and recreation). Needless to say, the sooner you get started, the greater your financial power will be. You will have taken advantage of the time value of money for a longer period of time.

Consider the following illustration. Co-workers Ellen and Barbara are both planning to retire in 25 years. Let's assume that they are planning for a 10 percent annual return on investment (stock markets in North America have averaged about 10 percent over the past 75 years, with higher returns in some years and lower returns in others). Their savings strategies, however, are different. Whereas Barbara begins saving immediately, Ellen plans to start later but invest larger sums. Barbara will invest $2000 annually for each of the next five years (years 1–5), for a total investment of $10 000. She'll let interest accumulate through year 25. Ellen, meanwhile, wants to live a little larger by spending rather than saving for the next 10 years. Then, for years 11–20, she'll start saving $2000 annually, for a total investment of $20 000. She, too, will allow annual returns to accumulate until year 25, when both she and Barbara retire. Will Ellen have a larger retirement fund in year 25 because she's ultimately contributing twice as much as Barbara?

Not by a long shot. Barbara's retirement wealth will be much larger— $90 358 versus Ellen's $56 468—even though she invested only half as much ($10 000 versus $20 000). We explain the disparity by crunching all the numbers in Figure B.4. As you can see, Barbara's advantage lies in timing

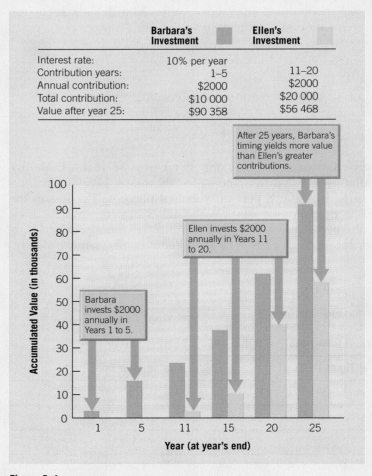

Figure B.4

—namely, the length of her savings program. Her money is invested longer—over a period of 21 to 25 years—with interest compounding over that range of time. Ellen's earnings are compounded over a shorter period— 6 to 15 years. Granted, Ellen may have had more fun in years 1 to 5, but Barbara's retirement prospects look brighter.

Time Value as a Financial-Planning Tool

How much must you set aside today to accumulate enough money for something you want tomorrow? By its very nature, financial planning takes into account not only future needs (retirement, vacations, a wedding, major purchases) but also sources of funds for meeting those needs. Timing, however, is important. The timing of financial transactions will determine whether your plan works or doesn't work the way you intend. Start by considering the time value of money at the outset of your planning cycle. In this respect, various time-based tables for financial calculations are quite useful.[1] Table B.3, for example, shows how much a $1 investment will grow over different lengths of time and at different interest rates. Let's see how we can use this tool for financial planning.

Having recently inherited $50 000, Jason wants to invest for his old age. Specifically, he wants to accumulate a $200 000 nest egg by the time he reaches 55 (30 years from now). He also wants to spend some of the money while he's young enough to enjoy it, but he doesn't know how much he'll have left to spend after he's determined the amount needed to meet his retirement goal.

To help Jason with his planning, we first need to focus on our 30-year investment; thus $n = 30$ in Table B.3. As you can see, the accumulated value of that investment depends on the annual interest rate. At 4 percent, for instance, the growth factor is 3.243. Over 30 years, therefore, $1 invested now will grow to $3.243. Our question, then, is this: If $1 invested now yields $3.243, how many dollars must we invest now to accumulate $200 000 in 30 years? The answer is fairly simple. If $1 provides $3.243 in 30 years, and if we want to accumulate $200 000, we divide $200 000 by $3.243 to determine Jason needs to invest $61 671 to reach his retirement goal.

Jason's worksheet, which is shown in Table B.4, reveals trial calculations made with three different interest rates—conservative, moderate, optimistic—available from alternative investments. As you can see, a 4 percent return on investment won't provide the desired $200,000. If he gets only 4 percent, Jason would have to invest $61 671; but, as we know, he has only $50 000. As a matter of fact, if he invested the entire $50 000 at 4 percent, he'd end up with just $162 150 ($50 000 × $3.243 = $162 150), which is well below his $200 000 goal.

Thus Jason has two choices: find a higher-paying investment or, if he's willing to settle for 4 percent, reduce the amount of his desired nest egg. To make his decision, Jason can use the trial data contained in Table B.4. Projecting an investment at 8 percent, he needs to allocate only about $20 000 to start his nest egg and still have more than $30 000 for other uses. If he considers the 8 percent investment too risky, he may opt for the safer 6 percent return; in that case, he'd still have $15 175 left ($50 000 – $34 825).

CONSERVING MONEY BY CONTROLLING IT

Several steps in the financial planning process call for conserving money by paying attention to where it goes—by keeping spending within affordable limits and understanding on what you're spending your money.[2] As too many people have found out the hard way, a major pitfall in any financial

Table B.3   Timetable for Growing $1

n	1%	2%	3%	4%	5%	6%	7%	8%	9%	10%
1	1.010	1.020	1.030	1.040	1.050	1.060	1.070	1.080	1.090	1.100
2	1.020	1.040	1.061	1.082	1.102	1.124	1.145	1.166	1.188	1.210
3	1.030	1.061	1.093	1.125	1.158	1.191	1.225	1.260	1.295	1.331
4	1.041	1.082	1.126	1.170	1.216	1.262	1.311	1.360	1.412	1.464
5	1.051	1.104	1.159	1.217	1.276	1.338	1.403	1.469	1.539	1.611
6	1.062	1.126	1.194	1.265	1.340	1.419	1.501	1.587	1.677	1.772
7	1.072	1.149	1.230	1.316	1.407	1.504	1.606	1.714	1.828	1.949
8	1.083	1.172	1.267	1.369	1.477	1.594	1.718	1.851	1.993	2.144
9	1.094	1.195	1.305	1.423	1.551	1.689	1.838	1.999	2.172	2.358
10	1.105	1.219	1.344	1.480	1.629	1.791	1.967	2.159	2.367	2.594
11	1.116	1.243	1.384	1.539	1.710	1.898	2.105	2.332	2.580	2.853
12	1.127	1.268	1.426	1.601	1.796	2.012	2.252	2.518	2.813	3.138
13	1.138	1.294	1.469	1.665	1.886	2.133	2.410	2.720	3.066	3.452
14	1.149	1.319	1.513	1.732	1.980	2.261	2.579	2.937	3.342	3.797
15	1.161	1.346	1.558	1.801	2.079	2.397	2.759	3.172	3.642	4.177
16	1.173	1.373	1.605	1.873	2.183	2.540	2.952	3.426	3.970	4.595
17	1.184	1.400	1.653	1.948	2.292	2.693	3.159	3.700	4.328	5.054
18	1.196	1.428	1.702	2.026	2.407	2.854	3.380	3.996	4.717	5.560
19	1.208	1.457	1.753	2.107	2.527	3.026	3.616	4.316	5.142	6.116
20	1.220	1.486	1.806	2.191	2.653	3.207	3.870	4.661	5.604	6.727
21	1.232	1.516	1.860	2.279	2.786	3.399	4.140	5.034	6.109	7.400
22	1.245	1.546	1.916	2.370	2.925	3.603	4.430	5.436	6.658	8.140
23	1.257	1.577	1.974	2.465	3.071	3.820	4.740	5.871	7.258	8.954
24	1.270	1.608	2.033	2.563	3.225	4.049	5.072	6.341	7.911	9.850
25	1.282	1.641	2.094	2.666	3.386	4.292	5.427	6.848	8.623	10.834
30	1.348	1.811	2.427	3.243	4.322	5.743	7.612	10.062	13.267	17.449
40	1.489	2.208	3.262	4.801	7.040	10.285	14.974	21.724	31.408	45.258
50	1.645	2.691	4.384	7.106	11.467	18.419	29.456	46.900	74.354	117.386

continued

Table B.3 *continued*

n	11%	12%	13%	14%	15%	16%	17%	18%	19%	20%
1	1.110	1.120	1.130	1.140	1.150	1.160	1.170	1.180	1.190	1.200
2	1.232	1.254	1.277	1.300	1.322	1.346	1.369	1.392	1.416	1.440
3	1.368	1.405	1.443	1.482	1.521	1.561	1.602	1.643	1.685	1.728
4	1.518	1.574	1.630	1.689	1.749	1.811	1.874	1.939	2.005	2.074
5	1.685	1.762	1.842	1.925	2.011	2.100	2.192	2.288	2.386	2.488
6	1.870	1.974	2.082	2.195	2.313	2.436	2.565	2.700	2.840	2.988
7	2.076	2.211	2.353	2.502	2.660	2.826	3.001	3.185	3.379	3.583
8	2.305	2.476	2.658	2.853	3.059	3.278	3.511	3.759	4.021	4.300
9	2.558	2.773	3.004	3.252	3.518	3.803	4.108	4.435	4.785	5.160
10	2.839	3.106	3.395	3.707	4.046	4.411	4.807	5.234	5.695	6.192
11	3.152	3.479	3.836	4.226	4.652	5.117	5.624	6.176	6.777	7.430
12	3.498	3.896	4.334	4.818	5.350	5.936	6.580	7.288	8.064	8.916
13	3.883	4.363	4.898	5.492	6.153	6.886	7.699	8.599	9.596	10.699
14	4.310	4.887	5.535	6.261	7.076	7.987	9.007	10.147	11.420	12.839
15	4.785	5.474	6.254	7.138	8.137	9.265	10.539	11.974	13.589	15.407
16	5.311	6.130	7.067	8.137	9.358	10.748	12.330	14.129	16.171	18.488
17	5.895	6.866	7.986	9.276	10.761	12.468	14.426	16.672	19.244	22.186
18	6.543	7.690	9.024	10.575	12.375	14.462	15.879	19.673	22.900	26.623
19	7.263	8.613	10.197	12.055	14.232	16.776	19.748	23.214	27.251	31.948
20	8.062	9.646	11.523	13.743	16.366	19.461	23.105	27.393	32.429	38.337
21	8.949	10.804	13.021	15.667	18.821	22.574	27.033	32.323	38.591	46.005
22	9.933	12.100	14.713	17.861	21.644	26.186	31.629	38.141	45.923	55.205
23	11.026	13.552	16.626	20.361	24.891	30.376	37.005	45.007	54.648	66.247
24	12.239	15.178	18.788	23.212	28.625	35.236	43.296	53.108	65.031	79.496
25	13.585	17.000	21.230	26.461	32.918	40.874	50.656	62.667	77.387	95.395
30	22.892	29.960	39.115	50.949	66.210	85.849	111.061	143.367	184.672	237.373
40	64.999	93.049	132.776	188.876	267.856	378.715	533.846	750.353	1051.642	1469.740
50	184.559	288.996	450.711	700.197	1083.619	1670.669	2566.080	3927.189	5988.730	9100.191

n = Number of time periods
% = Various interest rates

Table B.4   Nest Egg Worksheet

	Investment Returns (annual rate)			Your numbers
	Conservative 4%	Moderate 6%	Optimistic 8%	%
Ending amount after 30 years:	$200 000	$200 000	$200 000	_____
Growth factor (from table):	3.243	5.743	10.062	_____
Amount* to invest now (end amount/ growth factor):	$61 671**	$34 825	$19 877	_____
	($200 000/3.243)	($200 000/5.743)	($200 000/10.062)	

*Rounded to nearest whole dollar.
**This amount is greater than the available $50 000.

plan is the temptation to spend too much, especially when credit is so easy to get. Consumers often lose track of how much they spend, and, to make matters worse, some don't consider the costly finance charges associated with easy credit. Because many credit-card issuers target university and college students and recent graduates with tempting offers appealing to the desire for financial independence, we'll use the following section to explain the financial costs entailed by credit cards. Keep in mind, however, that the same lessons apply equally to home-equity loans, consumer finance agreements, and other sources of credit.

Credit Cards: Keys to Consumer Satisfaction or Fiscal Handcuffs?

Although some credit cards don't charge annual fees, all of them charge interest on unpaid (outstanding) balances. Because credit-card debt is one of the most expensive sources of funds, you need to understand the costs before you start charging instead of being surprised when you open the bill. For one thing, many card users don't realize how much interest they're paying or how long it will take them to pay off their bills.

Table B.5 reprints a page from California's "Minimum Payment Credit Card Calculation." Using the table as a guide, let's consider the following situation. Suppose you owe $5000 for credit-card purchases and your card company requires a minimum monthly payment of 5 percent of the unpaid balance. The interest rate is 18 percent APR (annual percentage rate) on the outstanding balance. (By the way, these aren't too high: Some rates are well above 20 percent.)

Thus, Table B.5 reflects an account with $5000 outstanding balance at the end of last month. This is the amount on which your interest of 18 percent APR is charged. Remember, too, that your card company requires a minimum monthly payment (minimum payment due—or MPD) of 5 percent (of the current balance). Let's assume that you pay only the monthly minimum and ask ourselves two questions:

1. How many months will it take to pay off the $5000?

2. How much interest will you have paid when you do pay it off?

In Table B.5, the column labelled "MPD 5%" reveals that at 18 percent APR it will take you 115 months to pay off $5000. That's approximately 9 1/2 years! And remember: This number assumes that your balance gradually diminishes to zero because you add no other purchases to the card. Your total payment of $7096.70 covers your $5000 debt plus interest charges. An immediate cash payoff, therefore, would avoid $2096.70 in interest payments.

Why does repayment take so long? In Table B.6, we run through some sample calculations for the first two months in your 115-month repayment process. As you can see, your minimum monthly payment decreases because your ending balance gets smaller with each monthly payment. Your $250 payment in February includes $75 in interest owed on the $5000 balance in the previous month. At 18 percent APR, interest on $5000 would be $900 for a year (0.18 × $5000), but for one month (January), it's only 1/12 of that amount—$75. You're paying the rest of your February instalment of $175 ($250 – $75) on the principal amount, thereby reducing the month-end balance to $4825. If we carry out these calculations over 115 months, we find that, when your account is paid in full, you've made "payments on principal" of $5000 and interest payments of $2096.70.

Table B.5	Paying Off Credit-Card Debt

Balance = $5000.00

APR	MPD 2%		MPD 3%		MPD 4%		MPD 5%		MPD 10%	
	Months	Cost	Months	Cost	Months	Cost	Months	Cost	Months	Cost
6%	211	$6,576.80	144	$5,965.56	111	$5,696.30	92	$5,544.58	50	$5,260.74
7%	221	$6,945.82	148	$6,164.85	114	$5,831.99	93	$5,647.25	50	$5,306.87
8%	233	$7,360.22	153	$6,378.23	116	$5,974.39	95	$5,753.83	51	$5,353.84
9%	246	$7,829.02	158	$6,607.24	119	$6,124.04	96	$5,864.56	51	$5,401.63
10%	262	$8,363.77	163	$6,853.67	122	$6,281.51	98	$5,979.70	52	$6,450.30
11%	279	$8,979.59	169	$7,119.61	125	$6,447.40	100	$6,099.50	52	$5,499.87
12%	299	$9,696.61	175	$7,407.50	128	$6,622.45	102	$6,224.26	53	$5,550.32
13%	323	$10,542.23	182	$7,720.16	131	$6,807.42	104	$6,354.29	53	$5,601.75
14%	351	$11,554.78	189	$8,060.94	134	$7,003.17	106	$6,489.94	53	$5,654.11
15%	385	$12,789.56	197	$8,433.88	138	$7,210.72	108	$6,631.59	54	$5,707.49
16%	428	$14,329.44	206	$8,843.78	142	$7,431.13	110	$6,779.63	54	$5,761.88
17%	482	$16,304.46	216	$9,296.40	146	$7,665.64	112	$6,934.49	55	$5,817.33
18%	553	$18,931.11	226	$9,798.89	150	$7,915.67	115	$7,096.70	55	$5,873.86
19%	652	$22,598.52	238	$10,359.98	155	$8,182.84	117	$7,266.77	56	$5,931.51
20%	799	$28,083.97	251	$10,990.60	160	$8,468.95	120	$7,445.32	56	$5,990.30
21%	1040	$37,198.63	266	$11,704.63	165	$8,776.09	123	$7,632.92	57	$6,050.28
22%	1518	$55,367.78	283	$12,519.87	171	$9,106.71	126	$7,830.38	58	$6,111.48
23%	2930	$109,673.97	303	$13,459.58	177	$9,463.60	129	$8,038.42	58	$6,173.93
24%	*	*	325	$14,554.76	184	$9,850.03	132	$8,257.96	59	$6,237.69
25%	*	*	352	$15,847.75	191	$10,269.86	135	$8,489.97	59	$6,302.77

Practise Paying Off Your Debt

Using the method illustrated in Table B.6, you should be able to answer the following questions about credit-card repayment (the answers appear at the end of this appendix):

1. According to the data in Table B.6, your minimum monthly payment for April would be which of the following? [select one] (a) $232.81; (b) $253.47; (c) $230.56; (d) $226.18.

2. According to the data in Table B.6, for April, the interest owed on your previous balance would be which of the following? [select one] (a) $70.43; (b) $71.94; (c) $69.84; (d) $68.32.

3. According to the data in Table B.6, for April, your ending balance owed on principal would be which of the following? [select one] (a) $4182.16; (b) $4493.16; (c) $4517.22; (d) $4334.97.

Save Your Money: Lower Interest Rates and Faster Payments

A closer look at Table B.5 confirms two principles for saving money that you can apply when borrowing from any source, not just credit cards: Look for lower interest rates and make faster repayments.

Seeking Lower Interest Rates

Because higher interest rates obviously mean more expensive money, you save money with lower interest rates (money that you can "stretch" by using it for other things). With a little research, you'll find that potential creditors charge different rates (ranging from below 10 percent to over 20 percent APR among credit-card issuers). How much can you save? Look again at Table B.5 and compare the cost of borrowing $5000 at 18 percent with the cost of borrowing it at 9 percent. If you assume the same 5 percent minimum monthly payment, how much interest does 9 percent save you over the life of the repayment? The answer is $1232.14 ($864.56 instead of $2096.70). That's a nearly 59 percent savings.

Making Faster Payments

Because money has a time value, lenders charge borrowers according to the length of time for which they borrow it. In general, longer lending periods increase the cost, while shorter periods are cheaper. Accordingly, borrowers often speed up payments to cut interest costs. Using Table B.5, for example, compare the costs of the "5% MPD" (required monthly payment of 5 percent

Table B.6 Calculating Minimum Monthly Payments				
Month	**Minimum Monthly Payment (5% of Previous Ending Balance)**	**= Interest Owed on Previous Balance* ($1/12 \times 18\%$) Previous Balance)**	**+ Payment on Principal**	**Ending Balance Owed on Principal**
January	—	—	—	$5000
February	$250 [0.05 × $5000]	= $75 [1/12 × 0.18 × $5000]	+ $175	$4825 [5000 − 175]
March	$241.25 [0.05 × 4825]	= $72.38 [1/12 × 0.18 × 4825]	+ $168.87	$4656.13 [4825 − 168.87]

*Monthly interest is calculated using 1/12 of annual interest rate.

on the remaining balance) with the faster "10% MPD." The faster schedule cuts the repayment period from 115 to 55 months and, at 18 percent APR, reduces interest costs by $1222.84 (7096.70 – 5873.86).

What if you combined both faster repayment and the lower interest rate (9 percent versus 18 percent)? You'd cut your total interest cost to just $450.30—a savings of $1695.07 over the amount you'd pay if you made slower repayments at the higher rate.

FINANCIAL COMMITMENTS OF HOME OWNERSHIP

Should you rent or buy the roof you need over your head? The answer to that question involves a variety of considerations, including life stage, family needs, career, financial situation, and preferred lifestyle. If you decide to buy, for example, you have to ask yourself how much house you can afford. To answer that question, you need to ask yourself a number of questions about your personal financial condition and your capacity for borrowing.

To Buy or Not to Buy: That Is the Question

Renting is attractive because you can move in without making an initial investment (or at least making a hefty down payment). That's why it's a popular choice among young adults, especially singles with limited budgets and people whose lifestyles aren't congenial to settling down in a fixed location. Flexibility, mobility, and freedom from obligations of maintenance and upkeep are important advantages. Financially speaking, however, rent payments are cash outflows that provide future financial benefits to owners instead of renters.

By the same token, first-time homebuyers cite the prospect of future financial gain as an attractive reason for buying. The financial inducements are in fact powerful, including home equity, increasing property values, and tax advantages. You can see if buying is a good idea for you by consulting a "rent-versus-buy calculator" on the Web, such as the one at www.ginniemae.gov/. By letting you try various interest rates, down payments, loan lengths, and rental costs, calculators specify the financial advantages of renting or buying under a wide range of financial circumstances.

Many younger adults with children report that they choose to buy because they want privacy, space, and the freedom to choose a neighbourhood. Finally, most home buyers say that they get satisfaction from a sense of ownership—from having their own property. Table B.7 summarizes the key considerations in deciding whether to rent or buy a place to live.

How Much House Can You Afford?

For most people, buying a home is the biggest investment they'll ever make. But even though ownership, as we've seen, bestows several benefits, many people make the regrettable mistake of buying a house that's too expensive for their pocketbooks. Don't saddle yourself with house payments that you can't afford. In addition, new homebuyers quickly discover that the typical demands of ownership—especially the demand on their time and other resources for maintaining and improving a home—tend to cut into the money left over for recreation, eating out, taking vacations, and buying new cars. You can reduce the financial pressure by calculating in advance a realistic price range—one that not only lets you buy a house but also lets you live a reasonably pleasant life once you're in it.

Most people need a loan to buy a house or a condominium. A mortgage loan is a loan that's secured by the property—the home—being purchased. Because the size of a loan depends on the cost of the property, both borrowers and lenders want to know whether the buyer can afford the house they want. How can you determine how much you can afford? One time-tested (though somewhat conservative) rule of thumb cautions the buyer to keep the price below 2 1/2 times his or her annual income. Thus, if your income is $48 000, look for a house priced below $120 000.

Any such calculation, however, will give you just a rough estimate of what you can afford. There are other considerations. What you can afford also depends on how much money you have for a down payment and how much you can borrow. Lending institutions use two guidelines for estimating a buyer's borrowing capacity: (1) the borrower's ability to meet the recurring costs of buying and owning, and (2) other long-term debt that the buyer has already incurred.

PITI

What are those recurring costs? Every month, the homeowner must pay principal, interest, taxes, and insurance—*PITI*, for short. Because all four costs are greater for more expensive homes, the buyer's monthly obligation depends on how much house he or she has bought. The size of principal and interest payments depends on the mortgage amount, the length of the mortgage loan, and the interest rate. Obviously, if you borrow a fixed amount, the larger your monthly payment, the faster you'll pay off your loan. As Table B.8 shows, monthly payments on conventional loans are lower for longer-term loans and higher for larger interest rates.

In evaluating loan applications, lenders use PITI calculations to estimate the buyer's financial capacity—his or her ability to meet monthly payments. To determine how much someone is likely to lend you, calculate 28 percent of your gross monthly income (that is, before taxes and other deductions). If your PITI costs don't exceed that figure, you'll probably get the loan. With a monthly gross income of $4000, for example, your PITI costs shouldn't exceed $1120 (28 percent of $4000). Figure B.5 gives a sample calculation, and you should be able to make step-by-step computations by plugging your own numbers into the worksheet.

Table B.7	To Buy or Not to Buy
Renting	**Buying**
• No down payment to get started	• Must make payments for mortgage, property taxes, and insurance
• Flexibility to leave	• Equity builds up over time
• No obligation for upkeep or improvements	• More privacy
• No groundskeeping	• Value of property may increase
• Easy cash-flow planning (a single monthly payment)	
• May provide access to recreation and social facilities	• Financial gains from selling house can be exempt from taxes
• Rental conditions may be changed by owner	• Greater control over use of property and improvements
• Timing for repairs controlled by owner	• The home can become a source of cash by refinancing with another mortgage loan or a home-equity loan

Other Long-Term Debt

In evaluating financial capacity, lenders also look at any outstanding debt that will take the borrower more than 10 months to pay off, such as car loans, child support and alimony payments, student loans, and credit-card bills. In general, they will accept long-term indebtedness (including PITI) that amounts to 36 percent of gross income. Remember: Because PITI itself can be up to 28 percent, you might be allowed as little as 8 percent in other long-term debt. With your $4000 monthly gross income, your total debt should be less than $1440 (which allows $1120 for PITI and $320 for other debt). If your total debt exceeds $1440, you may have to settle for a smaller loan than the one you calculated with the PITI method. Figure B.6 gives an example of such an alternative calculation; again, you can plug your own numbers into the worksheet.

Table B.8 Monthly Mortgage Payments on a $10 000 Loan

Interest Rate (%)	Length of Loan					
	10 Years	15 Years	20 Years	25 Years	30 Years	40 Years
5.0	$106.07	$79.08	$66.00	$58.46	$53.68	$48.22
5.5	108.53	81.71	68.79	61.41	56.79	51.58
6.0	111.02	84.39	71.64	64.43	59.96	50.22
6.5	113.55	87.11	74.56	67.52	63.21	58.55
7.0	116.11	89.88	77.53	70.68	66.53	62.14
7.5	118.71	92.71	80.56	73.90	69.93	65.81
8.0	121.33	95.57	83.65	77.19	73.38	69.53
8.5	123.99	98.48	86.79	80.53	76.90	73.31
9.0	126.68	101.43	89.98	83.92	80.47	77.14
9.5	129.40	104.43	93.22	87.37	84.09	81.01
10.0	132.16	107.47	96.51	90.88	87.76	84.91
10.5	134.94	110.54	99.84	94.42	91.48	88.86
11.0	137.76	113.66	103.22	98.02	95.24	92.83
11.5	140.60	116.82	106.65	101.65	99.03	96.83
12.0	143.48	120.02	110.11	105.33	102.86	100.85
12.5	146.38	123.26	113.62	109.04	106.73	104.89
13.0	149.32	126.53	117.16	112.79	110.62	108.95
13.5	152.27	129.83	120.74	116.56	114.54	113.03
14.0	155.27	133.17	124.35	120.38	118.49	117.11
14.5	158.29	136.55	128.00	124.22	122.46	121.21
15.0	161.33	139.96	131.68	128.08	126.44	125.32

If you want to go into more detail about your own payment capabilities, search for websites that provide mortgage calculators for testing interest rates, lengths of loans, and other personal financial information.

PROTECTING YOUR NET WORTH

With careful attention, thoughtful saving and spending, and skilful financial planning (and a little luck), you can build up your net worth over time. In addition to steps for accumulating net worth, therefore, every financial plan should consider steps for preserving it. One approach involves the risk–return relationship that we discussed in Chapter 20. Do you prefer to protect your current assets, or are you willing to risk them in return for greater growth? At various life stages, and whenever you reach a designated level of wealth, you should adjust your asset portfolio to conform to your risk and return preferences—conservative, moderate, or aggressive. Another approach is life insurance.

ASSUMPTIONS:

30-year mortgage
Closing costs (fees for property survey, credit report, title search,
    title insurance, attorney, interest advance, loan origination) = $5000
Funds available for closing costs and down payment = $25 000
Interest rate on mortgage = $6\frac{1}{2}$% per year
Estimated real estate taxes = $200 per month
Estimated homeowner's insurance = $20 per month

Example Numbers   Your Numbers

1. Monthly income, gross (before taxes or deductions)....... $4000   _____
2. Apply PITI ratio (0.28 x amount on line 1) to determine
    borrower's payment capacity:
    0.28 x $4000 = ...$1120   _____
3. Determine mortgage payment (principal and interest)
    by subtracting taxes and insurance from
    PITI (line 2):... – $ 220   _____
4. Result: Maximum mortgage payment
    (principal and interest).. $ 900   _____

5. Using Table B.8, find the monthly mortgage payment
    on a $10 000 loan at $6\frac{1}{2}$% interest for
    30 years..$63.21   _____
6. Since each $10 000 loan requires a $63.21 monthly payment,
    how many $10 000 loans can the borrower afford
    with the $900 payment capacity? The answer is
    determined as follows:
        $900.00/$63.21 =
        14.2382 loans of $10 000 each.

7. Result: Maximum allowable mortgage loan   _____
    calculated as follows:
        14.2382 loans (from line 6 above)
        x $10 000 per loan] = ...$142 382   _____

8. Result: Maximum house price borrower can afford
    using PITI (amount of house that can be bought with
    available funds):

        From loan...................$142 382   _____
        From down payment....$ 25 000   _____
        Less closing cost.......– $ 5 000   _____
                ....$162 382   _____

Figure B.5

Life Insurance

You can also think of life insurance as a tool for financial preservation. As explained in Chapter 20, a life insurance policy is a promise to pay beneficiaries after the death of an insured party. In return, of course, insurance companies collect *premiums*—payments from the insurance purchaser—during his or her lifetime.

What Does Life Insurance Do?

From a personal-finance perspective, the purpose of life insurance is to replace income upon the death of the policyholder. Accordingly, the amount of insurance you need depends on how many other people rely on your income. Insurance, for example, is crucial for the married parent who is a family's sole source of income. On the other hand, a single person with no

ASSUMPTIONS:

30-year mortgage
Closing costs = $5000
Funds available for closing costs and down payment = $25 000
Interest rate on mortgage = $6\frac{1}{2}$% per year
Estimated real estate taxes = $200 per month
Estimated homeowner's insurance = $20 per month

Example Numbers		Your Numbers
1. Monthly income, gross (before taxes or deductions)............$4000		_____
2. Apply debt ratio (0.36 x amount on line 1) to determine borrower's payment capacity:		
0.36 x $4000 = ... $1440		_____
3. Less current payments on non-mortgage debts that will last more than 10 months:		
car loan........................–$ 300		
student loan................–$ 100		
credit card debt...........–$ 100		
–$ 500		
4. Less taxes and insurance for house.................................–$ 220		_____
5. Result: Maximum mortgage payment		
** (principal and interest)..$ 720**		_____
6. Using Table B.8, find the monthly mortgage payment payment on a $10 000 loan at $6\frac{1}{2}$% interest for 30 years...$63.21		_____
7. Since each $10 000 loan requires a $63.21 monthly payment, how many $10 000 loans can the borrower afford with the $720 payment capacity? The answer is determined as follows:		
$720.00/$63.21 =		
11.3906 loans of $10 000 each		_____
8. Result: Maximum allowable mortgage loan		
[calculated as follows:		
11.3906 loans (from line 7 above)		
x $10 000 per loan]..**$113 906**		_____
9. Result: Maximum house price borrower		
** can afford** (amount of house that can be bought with available funds):		
From loan..................$113 906		_____
From down payment...$ 25 000		_____
Less closing costs.....–$ 5 000		_____
....**$133 906**		_____

Figure B.6

financial dependents needs little or no insurance and will probably prefer to put money into higher-paying investments.

How Much Should I Buy?

To estimate the amount you need, begin by adding up all of the annual expenses—rent, food, clothing, transportation, schooling, debts to be paid—that you pay for the dependents who would survive you. Then multiply the total by the number of years that you want the insurance to cover your dependents. Typically, this sum will amount to several times your current annual income. Thus many policyholders, especially during the life stages of highest need—are insured for 10 to 20 times their annual salaries.

Two Basic Types of Insurance

Term insurance pays a predetermined benefit when death occurs during the stipulated term—say, 10, 20, or 30 years—covered by the policy. If the insured outlives the term, the policy loses its value and simply ceases. When it is in force, however, the insured knows that it will provide funds to beneficiaries if he or she dies. Premiums for term life insurance are significantly lower than premiums for whole life insurance.

Unlike term life, *whole-life insurance*—also known as *cash-value insurance*—remains in force as long as premiums are paid. In addition to paying a death benefit, whole life accumulates cash value over time—a form of savings. Once the insured reaches a point at which he or she no longer needs the coverage, paid-in money can be withdrawn. Whole-life savings, however, earn less interest than most alternative forms of investment.

How Much Does It Cost?

The cost of insurance, of course, depends on how much you buy. But it also depends on your life expectancy and other risk factors that insurers determine statistically. Premiums are higher for people whose life expectancies are shorter, whether because of gender, age, weight, occupation, or preexisting health conditions.

The lower cost of term insurance is an important consideration, not just for people on limited incomes, but also for those seeking higher returns from other types of investment. A healthy, 30-year-old, non-smoking female, for example, can expect to pay about $360 a year for a $300 000 term policy and about $600 to $700 a year for a $1 million term policy. Depending on the insurer and the conditions of coverage, whole life may cost the same person up to 10 times as much as term. To get the best match between your policy and your personal situation, therefore, you should evaluate the terms and conditions of a variety of policies. You can get convenient comparisons on websites such as IntelliQuote.com (www.intelliquote.com).

Answers to "Practise Paying Off Your Debt"

1. Item (a) is the correct answer, obtained as follows:

   Minimum monthly payment
   (5% of previous ending balance):
   April $232.81 = (0.05 × $4656.13)

2. Item (c) is the correct answer, obtained as follows:

   Interest owed on previous balance
   ($1/12$ × 0.18 × previous balance):
   April $69.84 = ($1/12$ × 0.18 × $4656.13)

3. Item (b) is the correct answer, obtained as follows:

Payment on principal (monthly payment–monthly interest)	Ending balance owed on principal (previous balance–payment on principal)
April $162.97 = ($232.81 – $69.84)	$4493.16 = ($4656.13 – $162.97)

A Midsummer Day's Nightmare

Lindsay Sawyer and John Melnyk

DISCUSSION QUESTIONS/OBJECTIVES

1. What is the problem here? Why is it a problem?
2. To whom or to what do you have a responsibility in this situation? Why?
3. What fundamental purposes, principles, and potential consequences are relevant here? Construct consequential, principled, and purposive arguments, both for and against alternatives you consider relevant.
4. As the decision maker of this case, how would you proceed and why?

A Midsummer Day's Nightmare

I started work at a nationally known fast food restaurant when I was seventeen. I had had other jobs, but none of them was as much fun as this one. I reported for my first shift and was introduced to a new atmosphere that was unlike anything I had experienced before.

One of the first things I learned was that having fun was really encouraged. Smiles were the norm, and, in fact, expected. This friendly environment led to a lot of fast friendships with my co-workers, especially since we all went to neighbouring high schools. Our employer encouraged these ties and would organize activities for us outside of work.

We enjoyed these outings, but the best "perk" by far was the food, which was half price to employees, even outside of scheduled shifts! We could even informally extend this discount to friends once in a while, which made it an even more enviable privilege.

I loved my job and worked very hard at it. After fourteen months I got my first promotion. Six months later I was promoted again to a junior management position along with two of my co-workers.

We received very little preparation to deal with this move up to management. We were given a workbook covering topics such as food safety, employee relations, shift planning, scheduling, etc., and were supposed to get time on the job to work through it and then go to classes. But that never happened. However, we were all told immediately about the importance of management always presenting a united front. Most of our training was on the job—we were given a different colour shirt, a new nametag, and encouraged to do our best. My first shift as a manager I was left alone to supervise a busy dinner hour.

My promotions brought me into more frequent contact with Michael Roberts, area manager for the district. Michael was a scary figure to all store employees because whenever he came in he found faults. Heaven help you if your personal grooming wasn't perfect, if you didn't have your nametag on, or even if you weren't using the prescribed pattern to mop the floor!

Now that I was in a management position, Michael knew me by name, and made a point of talking to me every time he came in. I suddenly had to develop a working relationship with him and meet his high standards.

There were many benefits to this promotion though, the best of which was now, free food! The expensive items on the menu were now always available to us. We would take advantage of this whenever we could, sometimes eating three meals a day at our restaurant! We now also had the authority to reward our subordinates with free food.

Because we were a small branch, we rarely had more than one manager working at a time, which left me completely in charge during my shift. This meant that it was up to me to ensure that company standards were met and that all customers were satisfied, as well as to deal with any complaints. I also had to make sure everything was in place for the next shift; if there was something that I wasn't able to finish, I had to communicate it clearly to the manager of the next shift.

I also became privy to more knowledge about our store. I quickly learned that we had trouble making a profit because the restaurant was so small. As a result we had to be very careful about expenses, especially food wastage. We would order $5000 to $6000 of supplies every week to ten days, and try to be careful to order only what we would need. As a result sometimes we would run out of something, or several things, before the next order. I hated when that happened.

If it was just a little thing, like milk or tomatoes, we would buy some at retail to tide us over, although this was not encouraged. For more basic items, like hamburger patties and buns, I had to phone around to other outlets and "beg" to "borrow" some supplies. This was a real hassle, and irritating to the other managers too. Furthermore, we often had only two or three employees working at a time, so it was a huge inconvenience to send one to pick up supplies—that is, provided I could convince someone with a driver's licence and gas in their car to go. I once had to go myself on a busy Saturday during Christmas season to pick up eighty trays of buns. It took me three hours and my mom's SUV.

Most of the equipment in our restaurant was old and in bad repair. We couldn't get authorization to replace it, so we had to make do. When I complained, I was told to use the manuals and try to fix it myself! I had absolutely no idea how to service these temperamental machines that would often act up, especially when we were busy. I once had an ice cream machine explode goo all over me for my trouble trying to fix it.

The air conditioning didn't always work either, but the grills were by far the most troublesome. They would stop heating properly in the middle of the day and not cook the food thoroughly. I got to know several repairmen on a first-name basis; we spent many hours going over this problem together.

Nevertheless I persevered, and over the next ten months I gained valuable experience and completed all the necessary steps to be promoted again. Towards the end of this period I met with my restaurant manager several times, and she assured me that a promotion was in the works, subject to the approval of the area manager.

I was really looking forward to that... it would mean I would no longer have to wear a hat on the job!

ONE SUMMER DAY...

One summer day I came in to open the restaurant after a day off. It was 6:00 a.m. and already warm outside, even more so inside the store because the air conditioning didn't work well. I started getting the computer system up and counting the cash, and sent the open staff person, Jason, to start making the muffins and getting the tables ready for our 7:00 a.m. opening.

As I was counting the cash, Jason called to me from the back. He was young and somewhat excitable, so I didn't think anything of it as I went over to see what was the matter.

Jason gestured excitedly and directed me towards the large walk-in freezer, insisting I look inside. I went into the freezer to take a look. I didn't like going in there because it was always so cold. But not today!

The freezer was room temperature! It must have been off overnight!

"Oh NO!" I thought,

as I looked in an open box of chicken and picked up a piece. It was warm and squishy; the coating crumbled off on my hand. I opened a box of hamburger patties and touched one on top. It felt mushy, and was beginning to lose its shape. I leaned over and opened a box in the middle. It was cool, and the meat in the centre of the box seemed still frozen.

My mind started racing. I ran to the phone to call my restaurant manager; I knew she was opening at another location that morning. It was about 6:30 a.m. Pat picked up the phone after several rings.

"Hi Pat, it's me... umm... I have a really big problem. You see... uh... "

"Jennifer, I'm really busy! Hurry up!" she snapped.

"I came in this morning and the freezer has been off for hours. Everything is goopy and gross and I don't know what to do. It's disgusting!"

"WHAT! You've got to be kidding. Who the hell was working yesterday? I just don't believe this. Damn! I'm too busy to deal with this now. Call Mike." Click—she hung up.

I looked at my watch; it was 6:35 a.m. I had to call Michael at home.

"Hi Michael, it's Jennifer from 82nd West... Pat told me to call you!" I blurted out. *"Sorry about this, but I have a big problem. Our freezer has been off for several hours, the food's gross and mushy. I don't know what to do."*

There was a brief pause as Michael woke up.

"What? Are you joking? Why is the freezer off? Is it broken? Is it unplugged?"

"Umm... I don't really know."

In a panic I ran to the back room to figure out why the freezer wasn't on. The answer was at the fuse box, where I discovered the freezer circuits were in the "off" position. Quickly I reset them. I knew we had received a supply order the day before. In order to save energy in the heat of the day, the freezer was likely shut off while the order was carried in. This wouldn't have been a problem... if only someone had remembered to turn it back on.

I could tell Michael was seething, but he controlled it well.

"OK, as long as all the cooking temperatures are met, the food will be all right. You can still use everything there."

He went on, *"It's important that we don't cause a panic about this. Don't talk about it in the restaurant and make sure food temperatures are met. Everything will be OK. Continue your shift Jennifer."* *"Uh... OK... umm... "*

I hung up the phone in a daze. I couldn't quite bring myself to carry out those instructions right away. I felt confused and upset, as I stood lost in my thoughts searching for some instruction or part of my training for guidance. I knew what to do if there was a bomb threat, but nothing had prepared me for this.

I had about twenty minutes worth of food in our small freezers up front. Jason was waiting for my instructions. I looked at my watch—it was 6:45 a.m.

APPENDIX

Exhibit 1   **Excerpts from the Food and Drug Act, and Food and Drug Regulations, as Administered by Health Canada**

Interpretation
"Unsanitary conditions" means such conditions or circumstances as might contaminate with dirt or filth, or render injurious to health, a food, drug or cosmetic.

Food
4. No person shall sell an article of food that
   a) has in or on it any poisonous or harmful substance;
   b) is unfit for human consumption;
   c) consists in whole or in part of any filthy, putrid, disgusting, rotten, decomposed or diseased animal or vegetable substance;
   d) is adulterated; or
   e) was manufactured, prepared, preserved, packaged or stored under unsanitary conditions.

Sale of Barbecued, Roasted or Broiled Meat or Meat By-Products
B.14.072   No person shall sell meat or a meat by-product that has been barbecued, roasted or broiled and is ready for consumption unless the cooked meat or meat by-product
   (a) at all times
      (i)   has a temperature of 40° F (4.4° C) or lower, or 140° F (60° C) or higher,
      or
      (ii)   has been stored at an ambient temperature of 40° F (4.4° C) or lower, or 140° F (60° C) or higher
   (b) carries on the principal display panel of the label a statement to the effect that the food must be stored at a temperature of 40° F (4.4° C) or lower, or 140° F (60° C) or higher.

An Evaluation of the Parking Ticket Payment Processing System in the City of Waterloo

The City of Waterloo is aware of residents' complaints about the payment options available for paying parking tickets. This, compounded with the high costs and potential inefficiencies of their current processing systems, has prompted Carol Walker to investigate possible options. This case focuses on the evaluation of their current information system and three other possible options.

David Hemsworth, Loralee Nicol, Jon Mesquita, Cristóbal Sánchez-Rodriguez, Bettina Bosch, and Sarah Gage

Case Study Number: 050031-W
Copyright © 2004 Wilfrid Laurier University
While it is not permitted to copy this case, copies or permission to reproduce are available from The School of Business & Economics, Wilfrid Laurier University, Waterloo, Ontario N2L 3C5. Please contact The School of Business & Economics at 519-884-0710 ext. 6999. This material is not covered under authorization from CanCopy or any other reproduction rights organization.

DISCUSSION QUESTIONS/OBJECTIVES
QUESTIONS

1. Should Waterloo outsource the processing of parking tickets and get out of the parking ticket business entirely?

2. Which system(s) should they select, if any?

3. Should Waterloo hide the online patron ticket fee ($1.50) in the ticket costs to promote online or phone usage, or, alternately, should the city "eat" the patron online ticket fee since they will save money in administration, thus promoting use of the system? Should this cost be spread across all of the tickets or levied against only those who would use the new system? Remember, if people pay online, the lineups at the city centre will be shorter!

OBJECTIVES

1. *IT Project Selection:* Students will learn how to apply the tools and techniques that IT professionals use when assessing various project alternatives. This includes an in-depth financial analysis as well as an examination of the qualitative aspects involved in the decision.

2. *Technology:* Students will gain insights into the complexities, technology, and infrastructure of a typical city's manual parking ticket payment information system.

3. *IT Deployment:* Students will be able to identify and discuss how new technology can be implemented to increase customer satisfaction and automate the ticket payment process.

An Evaluation of the Parking Ticket Payment Processing System in the City of Waterloo

INTRODUCTION

Carol Walker sighed and shook her head as she hung up the phone. Yet another customer was complaining that they could not pay their ticket on the Web or by phone. It was only Tuesday afternoon, but already this week she had received five calls that made similar complaints, and expressed frustration with the current lack of choices available for parking ticket payment. Unfortunately, the City of Waterloo (population 100,000) had not upgraded its parking ticket system to include any of the new payment options, such as over the Internet, by phone, or at the bank. Tickets could be paid only in person at the Waterloo City Centre, or by mailing a cheque to the city. Each year the City of Waterloo issues 32,000 tickets. It was Carol's aspiration to provide more convenient methods of ticket payment, possibly through the web, telephone, kiosks, or banks.

Carol, the team leader for the Bylaw Enforcement Department, was as frustrated by this inefficient system as the ticket payers were. Under the current system, tickets were being paid very slowly and administrative costs to collect on overdue accounts were high. Carol was thinking that something had to be done to satisfy these needs as she quickly drafted an email to Jerry Filmore, the Director of Information Systems. She referred to the large number of phone calls she had received from annoyed patrons who were unimpressed with the current payment methods. In the past, Carol had spoken with Jerry regarding the possibility of enhancing the current payment system, however, the discussions never really evolved into a plan of action.

BACKGROUND

After sending an email to Jerry regarding the problem, Carol walked out of her office and towards the staff lounge. On her way there, she happened to pass the city's vision statement. It read, "The City of Waterloo is a progressive organization built on principles which anticipate and satisfy the requirements of our customers, achieved through a team of committed, highly skilled and valued people" (**www.city.waterloo.on.ca**). While reading this statement, she thought, "this sure doesn't describe the evolution of the parking ticket payment system in Waterloo."

Carol had begun researching on-line systems that had recently been implemented by nearby cities that were a similar size to Waterloo. Specifically, she had been looking at the City of Burlington's system for paying parking tickets on-line, because of its similar size and structure. Once Burlington had made the decision over what type of on-line ticket payment system was preferred, it took about six weeks to implement. It was implemented on September 3, 2002 and by November 2002, 10 percent of patrons were paying parking tickets through the Internet using a MasterCard or Visa credit card. To inform the public of this new payment option, the department posted signs at the Burlington City Centre, and a press release and article were featured in the local newspaper. The web address was printed on the back of the ticket as the first method of payment.

PARKING TICKET PAYMENT IN WATERLOO

Revenue

The City of Waterloo is expecting revenue of $500,000.00 this year (2003) from parking tickets. The city issues approximately 32,000 tickets per year, which translates to an average of $15.63 in revenue per ticket. In the past, the city has found that the number of tickets issued remain constant despite the rising ticket fines (the demand for tickets is inelastic!). The streets surrounding the city's two universities remain a hot spot to issue tickets.

Human Resources

There are currently thirteen people who are employed to service the administration of the parking ticket payment system at the City of Waterloo. Carol Walker is one of the primary workers involved in the parking ticket payment process at the City of Waterloo and supervises the system. Assisting her is Sherry Bell, the by-law administrative assistant. In addition, the city employs three tellers who process payments for the tickets that are paid on time; these tellers have direct customer contact. The department that issues tickets employs eight by-law enforcement officers, three of whom have fixed daytime routes they patrol: one daytime officer roams the city (s/he has a police radio and is in constant contact with the dispatcher) and four officers patrol at night. The approximate salaries and the percentage of time spent directly on parking-ticket-related activities, as well as the associated overhead costs, are summarized in Appendix A.

Current Information System

The City of Waterloo currently uses a system called "Autoprocess" to manage their parking ticket database and payments. When a ticket is issued, the by-law enforcement officer enters the information into a hand-held device. The information must be downloaded from the device at the end of the officer's shift, making it impossible for a customer who received a ticket in the morning to pay the same day. This adds to the frustration of patrons who find time to pay the ticket the same day, but are unable to because the ticket information is not yet recognized by the system.

Tickets can be paid by cheque, cash, or debit card in person at the city centre, or through the mail by cheque. Once the ticket payments have been processed, the tickets are stored in boxes for a period of two years.

One drawback of the current system is that it requires a lot of labour input. Tellers spend unnecessary time taking in-person payments that could be made without their involvement if there were alternative payment methods. Customers who pay in person are frequently inconvenienced due to long waits in large line-ups (at most there are only three tellers available) and in addition, the city centre is open only during normal working hours.

Ticket Aging Process

In the event that a ticket is not paid within the allotted fifteen-day period, a complicated process with many different steps is set in motion. The following is a systematic outline of the ticket aging process.

Day 1	Patron receives parking ticket.
Day 16–20	License plate number is sent to Ministry of Transportation. Patrons perso nals information is sent to the city the same day from the Ministry.
Day 22	Notice of impending conviction is sent to registered owner of the vehicle. Payment due date is set for Day 40.
Day 40	Parking ticket payment due date.
Day 41	City prints Certificate Requesting Conviction (on the nearest Tuesday to Day 41). Ticket fine rises by $16 ($4.75 goes to the City of Waterloo, $3.00 to Ontario Court of Justice, $8.25 to M.T.O. to get license plate ownership information).
Day 44	Certificate Requesting Conviction is sent to Waterloo. Provincial Court identifies ticket as not being contested or paid (on Friday closest to Day 44). After conviction is filed, customer receives a notice of Final Due Date. Patron has been convicted by the Courts and no longer has the ability to contest the ticket.
Day 120	Patron's license plate number is sent to the Ministry of Transportation for "plate denial" (customer cannot renew vehicle license unless fee is paid). Additional $20 added to ticket price for Ministry of Transportation fee for looking up license plate information and plate denial process (none of which goes to the City of Waterloo).

Cost Structure and Payment Details

An analysis of ticket payments is as follows:

- 25% of the tickets received are paid before the 15th day
- 25% of the tickets received are paid between the 15th day and the 40th day
- 25% of the tickets received are paid between the 40th day and 120th day
- 25% of the tickets received are not paid until the payer is subjected to a "plate denial"

The cost structure changes as the ticket aging process evolves. It begins with a standard cost to the city of $1.25 to process each ticket that is paid before the fifteenth day. These costs are in addition to the salaries paid to the teller staff mentioned earlier. If the ticket is not paid by the fifteenth day, an additional $1.25 cost is incurred to process a notice and send the notification to the registered owner of the vehicle. Ten percent of payments received after one notice arrive in an incorrect amount, and an additional notice is sent to the registered owner of the vehicle requesting that the correct payment be made. This results in an additional cost of $1.25. On Day 41, the city processes a "Certificate of Conviction" to be signed by the court, which leads to a processing and printing cost of $5. An additional $1 is incurred for delivery of this certificate to the court, while filing the signed version of this costs the City of Waterloo another $1. Out of all issued tickets, 5 percent are contested and presented in court. This costs an average $12.50 per ticket, reflecting the cost of having an officer present. For simplicity, ignore how this 5 percent is represented in the remainder of the ticket payments and just include it as an additional cost. See Appendix B for a table containing the cost structure of the ticket aging process.

DECISION CRITERIA FOR A NEW PAYMENT SYSTEM

The City of Waterloo has decision criteria that must be met in any ticket payment system they choose to implement. According to the city, the new system should:

- Be cost effective
- Increase convenience to their customers
- Reduce the average payment period
- Decrease manual labour for administrative staff
- Lower the costs incurred by the city per ticket issued
- Create possibilities for future expansion into other payment areas
- Be compatible with the current Oracle-based information system

ALTERNATIVES

The two alternatives that the City of Waterloo is considering are an online payment system and/or a phone-based system. Payment through the bank was ruled out because it causes difficulty in payment timing due to processing time delays in the bank (e.g., if payment is delayed by the bank, the ticket may "age" to the next step which would cause major complexities with the current system).

On-line Website System

The use of a website to facilitate on-line payments would increase the access to Waterloo's ticket payment system. Creating an on-line option could be implemented using the city's current website, adding a link on the home page to the new parking ticket payment system. Rather than using internal resources to develop this new system, Waterloo would contract either a company that specializes in on-line ticket payment or a programming company to design and customize a web-based system in accordance to the specific needs of the city. Both would include having a secure payment system, the required customer web interface, as well as a back-office system that would interface to current "Autoprocess" software. This integration would be required to verify and reconcile ticket information in the Autoprocess database with information being submitted by the on-line customer (e.g., current ticket payment amount, timing, name, address, etc.). In addition, a receipt/payment confirmation, which would either be printed out or e-mailed to the customer, would be necessary. Carol realized that it is often quite inefficient to build from scratch an information system rather than to use a product that already exists, has technical support and provides a wide range of features.

A favourable example for this alternative of a web-based application would be to employ the services provided by a third party such as "Paytickets.ca," rather than having it built from scratch. Paytickets.ca "is a service that allows individuals and businesses to pay their parking tickets online through an Internet portal. This is provided by a unique partnership between Royal Bank of Canada and Teranet Enterprise Inc." (**www.paytickets.ca**). To pay a ticket, a patron simply logs onto the website for the city, and clicks on the link to "Pay Parking Tickets." This then takes them to a screen where they enter the details of the ticket, including ticket number, infraction date, license plate, province of plate, and the ticket amount. Patrons must then re-enter the ticket number for validation. The system then shows an interim summary verifying information just entered. The next screen is the payment screen where the patron enters their credit card information and email address. They are then provided with a payment summary and a receipt with confirmation number.

Paytickets.ca requires a minimum contract term of five years, with a set fee of $3,000 per annum. The variable cost structure uses a progressive method. The first 5,000 tickets of the year paid on-line costs the city $1.50 per transaction; for between 5,001 and 12,000 tickets a fee of $1.25 per ticket is charged; and finally on any tickets above 12,001, a fee of $1.00 is charged to the city. There is an annual minimum fee charged of $2,000. The city will pay the greater of $2,000 or the result of the progressive payment system. See Appendix C for a table containing the fixed and variable costs of the website.

One benefit of using Paytickets.ca is its compatibility with the existing back-office system at the city. Implementing this system avoids the costs of raising the capital necessary to develop an in-house on-line payment system, and allows for a timelier implementation period. It would also decrease the workload for tellers because a percentage of people who would normally be served by tellers would now be automatically processed through the Internet.

Finally, payment within the first fifteen days is expected to rise to 30 percent of total tickets issued, an additional 30 percent by Day 40, which would further reduce costs. Between the 40th and 120th day, it is expected that 20 percent of the tickets will be paid and finally, the remaining 20 percent of the tickets will be paid when the owner is subject to a "plate denial." From the customer's perspective, it is a huge increase in convenience to be able to pay the ticket at any time during the day, instead of waiting to pay during city office hours. It is also expected that if it was implemented, 33 percent of the payments would go through the internet site, 33 percent through the mail, and the remaining 33 percent would be paid in person.

Unfortunately, one of the drawbacks to implementing the on-line system is the internal training needed to support residents that phone in for help accessing the system which might require a larger time commitment from staff. Furthermore, not all customers have access to computers or the Internet. However, for purposes of this case, assume the labour and capital expenses do not change from the current system with this or the phone-based system (described subsequently).

Phone System

Another alternative to the current payment system could be to implement a telephone-based system. A teller would be designated to answer phone calls from patrons who wish to pay their tickets over the phone. This would require an authorization procedure for credit cards. Tellers would manually input the information into the system and confirm that the credit card payment has been cleared. This would require the credit card authorization system to contact the credit company and confirm credit availability, while the patron is holding on the other line. This also has the benefit of allowing in-person payments to be accepted via credit card.

One of the benefits of implementing a phone-based payment system is the potential for a large number of patrons to utilize this method because of its ease of use and accessibility. Customers would be able to call from home or the workplace, making it easier to pay the ticket during the city centre's office hours. Additionally, a shorter implementation period and less up-front capital would be necessary since the city would use the existing Autoprocess system.

One of the negative aspects of establishing a phone-based payment system is that it would still involve a large time commitment for a teller to handle the patrons' phone calls. Patrons who elect to pay at the city centre may also be frustrated if they see a teller handling telephone calls while they wait in line. This has already been a source of customer aggravation in the past.

It is expected that use of the telephone system would increase the number of payments at each stage by the same amount as the Web-based system. It is also expected that if it was implemented, that one-third of the payments would go through the phone system, one third through the mail, and the remaining third would be paid in person.

Finally, it is expected that both of the new systems would increase the number of tickets paid earlier in the process; however, because of human nature and procrastination, it is not expected that the combination of two systems would together increase the number of ticket payments beyond the increase that would be seen if either system was individually implemented (i.e., beyond the 30 percent, 30 percent, 20 percent, and 20 percent seen at each of the four stages respectively). Since the number of tickets processed will not change, it is assumed that the amount of labour will remain constant.

Outsourcing

The City of Waterloo also has the option of outsourcing the processing and collection functions of the ticket business to a third party (see Appendix D). Although the city would still be responsible for handing out the parking tickets, they would not be required to send out notices or receive payments for the tickets. This would reduce Carol's involvement in the parking ticket area from 60 percent of her position to 30 percent. In addition, only 25 percent of one teller's position would be required to answer telephone questions. Finally, this alternative would also allow the City to retrieve the $60,000 opportunity cost of the building (i.e., potentially reduce costs associated with the leasing of equivalent space). If this option were chosen, a third party, such as MSB (**www.muniserv.com/gov_parking.html**), would charge the City $1.50 CDN per ticket, and an additional $1.25 CDN per ticket for each additional notice sent to the patron (i.e., the notice sent after 15 days if the ticket has not been paid).[1] Such companies claim that their payment collection methods and notice mailing system produce measurable savings and potentially increase the likelihood of quicker payment. Mail-in, phone-based, and online web-based payment options would be available to pay parking tickets, and ticket payment rates are expected to be similar to the phone-based and web-based projections discussed earlier.

PLANS FOR THE FUTURE

The City of Waterloo has a number of services it would like to examine in the future. First, if it decides to implement an on-line system to pay parking tickets, this investment would likely provide the experience to enable them to accommodate other city payments in the future. For example, currently patrons must pay for dog tags and facility bookings at the city office. The city wants the system to handle these payments, and in addition, eventually allow patrons to pay their taxes using the Internet. Another idea for the future is to establish kiosk units at specified locations in the city where patrons can pay their parking tickets, dog tag fees, and facility booking fees. These kiosks may be set up at the local mall or city centre. This would provide patrons who do not have access to the Internet with a means of paying city-related fees quickly and easily.

---

[1]Marjorie Fleming, Senior Vice President, MSB, Newport Beach, CA. Interviewed by Melissa Barfoot. June 26, 2003.

CONCLUSION

Carol shut Jerry's office door and sighed. "This is not going to be an easy decision," she thought to herself. She had just spent the last hour with Jerry discussing the issues of the current system and possible solutions to the problem. One of the stipulations that she and Jerry both agreed on was that whatever choice was made, it would have to be communicated effectively to the public. The solution would not be successful if customers are unaware of it. Some of the key questions that needed answering included what solution will satisfy the decision criteria set out by the city? Should they choose one or more of the available alternatives? And is it worth the costs to change the current system? These decisions must be made with careful consideration and in a timely fashion.

Appendix A — Employee Salaries and Overhead Expenses

Employee	Annual Salary	# Employed	% *	Total
Carol Walker	$45,000	1	60%	$27,000
Sherry Bell	$27,000	1	60%	$16,200
Tellers	$24,000	3	25%	$18,000
Day officers	$26,000	3	100%	$78,000
Night officers	$27,000	4	100%	$108,000
Roaming officer	$27,000	1	100%	$27,000
Total				**$274,200**

* Percentage of time spent on parking tickets

Note: The City must own four cars at $20 000/yr. (depreciation and operating costs). The cost of office overhead to house the parking ticket department can be assumed to be $60 000/yr.

Appendix B — Cost Structure of Ticket Aging Process

Costs	Timing	Cost per Transaction	Current system % of tickets incurring costs	Online % of tickets incurring costs
Processing costs	t ≤ 15 days	$1.25	100%	100%
First notice	t > 15 days	$1.25	75%	70%
Incorrect info after first notice		$1.25	25% × 10%	30% × 10%
Certificate of conviction	t > 40	5 + 1 + 1	50%	40%
5% Contested tickets		12.5	5%	5%

FIXED AND VARIABLE COSTS

Since the on-line payment system will be used only by those paying their fees within the first forty days, a maximum of 60 percent of the total number of tickets issued will be susceptible to on-line transaction costs. Moreover, it is estimated that 33 percent of those tickets will be paid on-line. Therefore, $(0.6 \times 32\ 000)\ 0.33 = $ **6336** tickets will incur online transaction costs. There is a fixed fee of $3000 in addition to the progressive ticket-processing costs.

Appendix C	Website Costs		

Website Costs—Variable Costs for the 6336 tickets that will be processed online

Progressive ticket structure	Cost per transaction	Transaction costs	Total transaction costs
First 5,000 tickets	$1.50	5,000 × $1.50 = $7,500	$7,500 + $1,670 = $9,170
5,001 – 12,000	$1.25	(6,336–5,000) × $1.25 = $1,670	
12,001 +	$1.00	0	

Note: An annual set fee of $3,000 + the greater of $2,000 or the result of the progressive payment system (above).

Appendix D	Outsourcing Costs	

Quantity of tickets being outsourced	Cost per ticket (US$)	Cost per ticket for each additional notice (US$)
32,000	$1.35	$1.00

Building Guanxi Between Red Dragon China and Hanover Chemical Company Limited (A)

Neil Remington Abramson and Hemant Merchant

Reprinted with permission from Dr. Hemant Merchant, Faculty of Business Administration, Simon Fraser University, Vancouver (Canada). Copyright held by Dr. Hemant Merchant. Note: Company and personal names have been changed.

It was near the end of September, 2002. Henry Chan stood at the window of his 21st floor office at the Red Dragon China Shipping Company Limited where he worked as the brokerage department manager. The autumn sun was rising and the towers of Pudong stood dark against the light, casting shadows over the Yangtze River that flowed between Shanghai and its newest business district. Henry felt confused. Soon the leaves of autumn would be flying down, and like them his hopes of building a guanxi relationship with Peter Woo, the logistics director of the Hanover Chemical Company (HCC), seemed destined to fall into ruin.

Ever since he had received the assignment to build guanxi with HCC from the Singapore head office of Red Dragon Limited almost exactly a year ago, he had been actively doing his best. Now Peter had been reassigned to one of HCC's small town sub-factories and it looked as if he might have been demoted. It was said that the transfer was part of the joint venture's manager training program. It was, however, highly unusual for a Chinese Communist Party (CCP) member to be promoted by first being transferred to a lower position.

HCC was the biggest producer of liquid chemical products coming on line in central China in the near future. Once it was up and running in 2005, HCC would be exporting 150 thousand metric tons of liquid chemical to the international chemical market every year. It was critical to Red Dragon's whole corporate strategy that it obtained HCC's export business. The Red Dragon China office could close without it. Henry felt sure that he would be in serious trouble in Singapore if he did not figure out how to successfully deal with this unexpected situation.

RED DRAGON AND THE SHIPBROKER INDUSTRY

Red Dragon was one of Asia's largest shipbrokers. With a team of thirty experienced brokers, sixty total personnel, and offices in Singapore, China,

North America and Europe, Red Dragon provided shipping services for petroleum, chemical, vegetable oil, and dry cargo, and had arranged 1.2 million metric tons of cargo in the last year. It had long-term business relationships with about one thousand ship owners and charters.[1] Red Dragon China had been established in 1995 with an office in Shanghai. It served as the gateway to the Chinese chemical market for the entire Red Dragon Group global network. Specializing in China chemical products spot chartering,[2] Red Dragon China maintained daily business contacts with approximately 200 ship owners and one hundred fifty charters. In 2000, twenty percent of the Red Dragon Group's total tonnage had been booked by Red Dragon China. In March, 2002, Red Dragon China expanded by opening a Nanjing subsidiary company. According to Martin Lee, Red Dragon Singapore's general manager, the Red Dragon Group's whole long-term strategy was to benefit from China's booming economy.[3]

Henry had been with Red Dragon China since it opened. Originally from Shandong Province, Henry had been responsible for ship chartering at the Shanghai office of Sunway Chemical Company Limited, an American chemical producer. He was headhunted by Red Dragon Singapore in 1994 because of his exceptional work performance. After a year of training in Singapore, he became the manager of Red Dragon China's brokerage department.

Henry's responsibility was to arrange water transportation for shippers (manufacturers) through shipping companies (ship owners and charters). He would arrange contracts of affreightment (COA) with shippers. These were agreements to book cargo space on vessels at specified times and prices. Once a COA was in place, he would notify the shipping companies, issue draft letters of indemnity/bills of lading, settle various issues related to freight, demurrage and claims, and provide whatever supporting services were required for vessel operations, ship arrivals and departures. For these services, Red Dragon China received a 2.5 percent commission of the value of the amount paid to the shipping companies. As Red Dragon China prospered, so did Henry who had three assistant brokers working for him by 2002.

Many at the Red Dragon Group believed that the Chinese subsidiary's success was to a large extent due to Henry's ability to build guanxi. Red Dragon China had become one of the largest liquid chemical products shipping service providers in China and in large part the company relied on the large network of government officials, ship owners, charters, port authority managers and port agents that he had built. It was his comprehensive knowledge of ships, direct access to some of China's largest fleets, and good connections with local small and medium sized ship owners that enabled Red Dragon China to provide first-class brokerage services.

Henry also believed that the secret of his success was his ability to build guanxi relationships. Guanxi, or personal connection, represented a reciprocal flow of transactions and benefits between two parties over the course of their relationship. While many Western managers believed that guanxi was tantamount to corruption because it involved offering and expecting gifts and favors, most Chinese believed that the essence of guanxi was trust, shared goals, and mutual benefits. Very few Chinese believed that guanxi was a corrupt practice. Mutual trust and a personal relationship were developed based on long-term reliability. As a relationship became more durable, both parties developed ganqing, or a positive emotional and

---

[1]Ship owners and charters would arrange their shipping schedules and routes to receive and deliver cargo arranged by brokers. Charters were companies that chartered ships from owners. Both were dependent on brokers because individual ships were unable to guarantee the comprehensive scheduling service requirements of shippers, and it was easier for shippers to arrange a schedule through a broker than deal with a host of individual ships.

[2]Arranging cargo and ship space on the spot market.

personal feeling for each other. The guanxi, or gifts and favors part, was just a series of symbolic or material exchanges that developed and signaled the ganqing feelings.

Guanxi was an important practice in China because the Chinese strongly preferred doing business through durable and trust-based relationships with those they regarded as insiders. The most durable relationships were with family who were always insiders. Next best were relationships with long time friends such as old school classmates. Least best were "meat and potatoes" friendships established solely for business purposes—often over lunches and dinners—with people regarded as outside the circle of true friendship. These "meat and potato relationships were secured with gifts and favors but the Chinese regarded them as producing only small and short-term obligations. To create a successful business relationship, you needed to establish durable insider friendship based on feelings of ganqing.

Henry had his own definition of guanxi based on the values he had learned growing up in Shandong Province where people were known to be especially hospitable, honest and candid with each other. Guanxi was a process for transforming an outsider into an insider. He said,

> Guanxi is an art. I heard many people say that guanxi was con-
> nection. However, I think connection touches only the surface
> part of guanxi. For me, it is not only connection. It is a special
> kind of relationship based on trust, reciprocity, common inter-
> ests and mutual obligations. The basic code of Confucianism—
> benevolence, righteousness and fidelity—taught me how to act
> and deal with the relationship with others. Great attention is
> paid to people's morality according to the proverb, 'learn to be a
> good man first, then learn how to do business.'

Morality issues were crucial and Henry believed that the key was building trust over time.

> If I'm not a man worthy of trust, I do not have the ability or
> willingness to repay my friends' favors anymore. Guanxi build-
> ing is a long-term investment of time, money and energy
> through social interactions such as gift-giving, voluntary favors
> and banquets.

Over the years Henry applied his principles to develop good guanxi with about seventy domestic ship owners and thirty-five cargo charters. He became known at Red Dragon China as "hui zuo ren" or, a person who is good at developing guanxi. In October, 2001, it was natural for Red Dragon China's management to appoint Henry to the task of building guanxi with HCC's logistics department in order to eventually obtain a COA for the shipment of HCC export production.

HANOVER CHEMICAL COMPANY

In the Chinese proverb of the fox and the tiger, the fox receives no respect in the woods because of his lack of physical size and strength. No one takes him seriously. His solution is to make friends with a strong and respectable tiger. Then, the fox can walk through the jungle with his friend and enjoy the same fearful respect accorded the tiger. For Red Dragon China, HCC was a tiger and if it shared Red Dragon's vision and point-of-view, Red Dragon China would have the presence of a tiger.

HCC was a 50-50 joint venture (JV) signed in 1998 between a German multinational corporation (MNC) and a Chinese state-owned company. Since the mid 1990s, China's chemical market had been growing at about nine percent per year, and the industry was considered one of the fastest growing in China. In 2000, total sales of petroleum and chemical products in China were US$172 billion and trade value was approximately US$ 72.2 billion. Many MNCs flocked to China hoping to set up JVs so as to be able to enter China with the help of local partners. The purpose of HCC was to build and operate a high technology and integrated petrochemical site producing LDPE, toluene, and xylene. While most product would be sold within China, about 150 thousand metric tons would be shipped to international chemical markets after full production started in 2005. In the meantime, German managers worked alongside Chinese counterparts with the expectation that by 2005, HCC would be primarily managed by local Chinese.

It was clear that HCC's chemical exports would have to be moved to market by bulk carrier ships. There was no pipeline planned and container ships were out of the question due to the liquid nature of the cargo. The only real transportation option was shipping brokerage because the product would not be available for at least two or three years and large bulk shipping companies could not commit to abandoning existing customers or build capacity for such an eventuality. The attention of many logistics service providers was attracted and all approached HCC's logistics department knowing that a service contract with HCC would guarantee a strong position in Jiangsu Province's liquid chemical transportation market. Of this multitude, only two companies had the size and international network to satisfy HCC's service and price requirements. Red Dragon China was one and the other was RKP. Other brokerage companies looked to be interested in setting up shop in China but it took as long as five years to build a credible network of local shipping companies. Henry observed,

> The ship owners in China are not qualified enough to meet
> HCC's standards. Most cargoes will need to be shipped by
> domestic shipping companies which are mainly small or
> medium sized companies. It will be difficult to meet HCC's serv-
> ice and price requirements. HCC will be required to investigate
> the options. They will have to establish regular contacts with the
> major players to get fully prepared for full production in 2005. If
> they can't find a carrier at that time, they will be in trouble.

RKP Shipping Company Limited was one of the world's largest and oldest independent ship brokering companies and it was the Red Dragon Group's greatest worldwide competitor. RKP was a European company with wholly owned offices in ten cities around the world including London, Jakarta, Singapore and Hong Kong. Rumor had it that RKP planned to open in Shanghai if it managed to obtain the HCC COA. Henry believed that the RKP Hong Kong office had already established contact with HCC. Brokering cargo space on ships was pretty much selling a commodity and because RKP was larger and had a more extensive worldwide network, Henry guessed that it might be able to offer slightly better service and prices than could the Red Dragon Group. They might be especially aggressive if HCC was the key to entering Jiangsu Province. If Henry could successfully build guanxi as a basis for doing business with HCC, then the relationship would differentiate Red Dragon's service. Henry observed,

> It's highly possible in a state-owned company that Chinese cus-
> tomers will pay more for reliable shipping. Also, if two parties
> have good guanxi, even though the shipping price is higher than
> somebody else, the guanxi partner will get the business.

If Red Dragon got the COA, then it would ensure that Red Dragon China was a long-term success and perhaps temporarily freeze RKP out of Jiangsu. If Red Dragon didn't get the COA, then the survival of Red Dragon China would depend on Henry's ability to keep his existing much smaller customers who might be tempted by RKP's success. Success was also personally important to Henry. Everyone at Red Dragon thought of Henry as the master of guanxi. If he failed, he would lose face among his colleagues and maybe also with his customers.

BUILDING GUANXI AT HCC

It took Henry three long months of careful investigation to identify the one key person that he needed build guanxi with. This was Peter Woo who was the logistics director at HCC. Peter seemed to have the authority to determine with whom HCC would sign its COA and there seemed not to be others inside or outside the HCC hierarchy that could, or would be able to direct the business elsewhere. Three months was not too long to invest in making a correct decision. Building guanxi was a long-term and time consuming investment of emotion, energy and financial resources. No quick returns were to be expected and if you picked the wrong target, there would never be the hoped for returns. Quoting a Chinese proverb, Henry said,

> 'You should use a long cord to catch a big fish.' Otherwise it is highly possible that you will be treated as a 'meat-and-potatoes' friend. Such a friendship can only be temporary. It is unreliable and shallow. They will not offer you precious support when you are in trouble.

Trying to learn more about Peter, Henry visited a friend in the Nanjing municipal government trying to access Peter's personnel file since he worked for a state-owned company. Sun Tzu had said in *The Art of War* that you needed to know both yourself and your enemy to ensure victory. The great Communist Leader Mao Zedong had said that business was war and that one had to have as much information as possible and think deeply before making every move. Henry's friend referred him to another friend in Beijing who used to work at the China United Chemical Company headquarters. Henry found out that Peter had been born in 1955 in Ningbo City, Zhejiang Province in southern China. This was important because people from north and south China often viewed guanxi differently. Henry explained,

> With North Chinese, more attention will be given to the emotional attachment of guanxi. Generally speaking, North Chinese treasure friendship very much. If you have good guanxi with them, they will give you the shirt off their back. South Chinese are more realistic and materialistic. As a result, mutual benefits or shared interests need to be emphasized. Favors should be tendered more frequently.

Peter was known to be an excellent CCP member. He had completed his executive MBA at Shanghai Fudan University. He was married to a Beijing woman, Lin, and she had refused to give up her work in Beijing when Peter had moved to Nanjing to work at HCC. As a result, Peter traveled to Beijing every two weeks to visit her. The couple had one son who was planning to take the College Entrance Examination in 2003. One frustration for Henry was that he could not determine what hobbies Peter had. He said,

> I like to collect information regarding friends' habits, hobbies and their ways of working, and adjust my methods of getting along with them accordingly. I'd like to focus on my friends' hobbies in order to arouse their interests before conducting business with them.

Henry's first chance to meet Peter occurred in February, 2002, at Peter's EMBA alumni reunion. One of Peter's classmates was the vice president of a Shanghai based state-owned shipping company. He had also been doing business with Henry for three years and the two shared a guanxi relationship. He introduced Henry to Peter. Henry commented,

> In my network, the guanxi with classmates, relatives and fellow villagers is the core. My relationship with classmates is extremely important. It's the most stable and valuable intangible asset I have. Pure and real friendship was developed between classmates because we were young and did not have conflicts of interest when we were at university. Alumni association meetings are a good way for me to expand my guanxi network.

Henry hoped that he could build a relationship with Peter based on classmate connections. This would already be one step higher than a "meat-and-potatoes" relationship. Henry and Peter exchanged business cards and Henry told Peter that he wanted to take an EMBA program and asked Peter for advice. He told Peter that he would be more than happy to go to Shanghai Fudan University if people like Peter had studied there. Peter seemed, however, uninterested in conversing with Henry and offered no advice. It was difficult to know what his real opinion was and his responses and reactions were not that positive. He only asked Henry how old he was and seemed surprised that a man of thirty would already be the manager of a department in a foreign company. Henry's impression of Peter was that he spent his time quietly watching and studying people. He said,

> It was difficult to tell if my endeavor was effective or not. Peter is composed and conservative. He is good at examining someone's words and observing their countenance. He's an excellent listener and much more cunning and conscious than I have imagined. Confucius said that a true gentleman speaks slowly but acts quickly. Peter follows this proverb strictly.

Trying to obtain more information, Henry directed Jiang, the general manager of the newly formed Red Dragon China subsidiary in Nanjing, to organize a dinner and karaoke party for Peter's subordinates. Jiang was a retired manager from China General Agency Company's Nanjing branch. This gathering was a big success for Henry because it turned out that one of Peter's subordinates, Zhang, was also from Shandong. Intimate personal relationships can be established quickly between Shandong people if they meet outside their own hometowns. Henry bonded easily with Zhang through constant personal visits and entertainments. When Zhang's sister needed a job in Shanghai, Henry got her one with one of his guanxi contacts. When Zhang's mother had a heart attack, Henry got her into the best hospital in Shanghai and put up Zhang's father in Red Dragon's Shanghai dormitory. Now, Henry could keep close contact with an "insider" in Peter's department at HCC and be able to obtain much more information about Peter and his predilections. Zhang told Henry that Peter spent most of his time writing a thesis called *Chemical Logistics in China* and that he had written other articles on the same subject. Henry also found out that Peter had been invited to give a thirty-minute presentation at a distribution logistics conference to be held in Shanghai in April.

Henry prepared carefully for this event. With Zhang's help, he gathered and studied all of Peter's articles. At the end of Peter's presentation, he asked several well-prepared questions. Peter was astonished by Henry's deep understanding of his subject. Peter gave detailed answers and recommended several references. He willingly agreed when Henry asked if he could come see Peter if he had any other questions. Subsequently, Henry visited Peter frequently to ask for assistance on logistics-related subjects. He prepared well-designed questions beforehand. He said,

> I called him Teacher Peter and found him much more talkative on such occasions. I seldom spoke and pretended to be a good student and listener during these meetings. On the one hand, what he said was meaningful and useful for my business. On the other hand, I was sure that Peter gained face when his study was appreciated by others.

At the end of April, Peter had a car accident. The accident was not serious but Peter was ordered by his doctor to rest at home for a week. Lin, Peter's wife, came from Beijing to take care of him. Henry decided to try to meet Lin and arrange some entertainment or sightseeing for her. He hoped that Peter would notice his friendly gesture and gain face. Henry followed the Chinese proverb that you must not only bow and scrape before the tiger. You must also seek every opportunity to ingratiate yourself with the tiger's relatives, friends, mistress or wife. Peter asked Sina Du, his general manager at the Red Dragon Shanghai office to accompany Lin. Sina was a tough, clear-minded and determined businesswoman. She invited Lin for a two-day shopping and relaxation trip in Shanghai in early May after Peter had recovered. She invited Peter as well but he declined due to the pent up demand for his return to work.

For those two days, Henry and Sina made themselves out to be the most warm-hearted hosts in the world. They booked Lin a five-star hotel suite and rented a luxury Mercedes Benz to show her around. All lunches and dinners were served either at first class restaurants or famous bars. At the end, they offered to pay for Lin's shopping bills as well but she declined. Henry confirmed that Peter and Lin's son was studying for the 2003 College Entrance Exam and discovered that Lin was afraid that her son would not do well. After checking with Singapore, Henry offered the full support of Red Dragon Singapore to help get Lin's son into a Singapore University. Lin said, "Henry, you are so nice! Peter should tell me beforehand that he has such a good friend like you in Shanghai." When Lin returned to Beijing, she gave gifts to Henry and Sina and invited them to visit she and her husband in Beijing.

A week later, Peter called Henry's cell to express his gratitude. Henry took it as a sign that Peter was touched by his friendship and understood the basic reciprocity principle of guanxi. "If you receive a favor, you need to repay it in the future but there is no need to repay it immediately," he said. In fact, it was a sign of greater trust and a stronger relationship when friends were willing to wait longer for a better return.

This gave Henry much hope. In a guanxi relationship, give-and-take is expected, and returns are balanced for both sides in the long term. What constitutes balance depends on the relative power and position of the two parties. Each is expected to give the best they can but the gifts of the tiger will be greater than anything the fox can offer. If the more powerful individual does not offer the greater gift, then he/she will be seen to lose face.

The favor Henry wanted from Peter was his support in coordinating the signing of a strategic COA with HCC. This COA contract would keep other competitors like RKP away. It would secure the cooperation between the shipbroker and the shipping companies for a certain period of time at a reasonable profit margin for both sides. At the very minimum, Henry hoped that Peter would promise to grant him first priority in the submission of quotations when HCC's cargo came to market. In the meantime, Henry hoped that Peter would signal his friendship by making frequent requests for market information and quotations. He said,

> At the beginning, he can only talk with me about the market, but gradually this increases intimacy with me and not with my competitors. This will be a sign that eventually the COA will come to me and not my competitors.

Now Henry wanted to give Peter "the big gift" to cement the relationship and to show his expectation of receiving a big favor. In guanxi, there were small gifts and big gifts. Small gifts represented friendship and it was not their small value that mattered but the emotional attachment that they symbolized. Small gifts, meals and drinks created a sense of obligation far exceeding their cost. Henry gave them to friends, and to the relatives and friends of those he hoped to influence, during traditional Chinese festivals, birthdays, and at weddings. Henry had given small gifts to Peter and none had ever been returned. Big gifts were intended to seal the deal and were only given to those with great influence. They were dangerous, however, because they could be interpreted as bribes and the Chinese central government had recently passed strict laws to prevent the spread of corruption. Many officials and senior managers at state-owned corporations had been jailed or even sentenced to death for taking bribes. Henry noted,

> I have been considering preparing some big gifts for Peter. However, I finally gave it up. From my point-of-view, the big gift is a double-edged sword because the line between bribery and gift-giving is really difficult to distinguish. The big gift should be used wisely according to different situations and people.

On the one hand, Peter was from the south and this suggested that he would be more pragmatic and be pleased to receive the big gift. On the other hand, his wife Lin was from Beijing where big gifts were especially dangerous. Also, Peter was an honored member of the CCP which indicated that he must cherish his political reputation and would want to stay away from even the hint of a corruption scandal. Zhang supported this view saying, "I saw Peter refuse many people's personal visits on weekends. He once threw a bag out in the corridor when one guest tried to leave it in his room." Henry concluded that it would definitely jeopardize his guanxi with Peter if he was indelicate about a big gift. "If I am not one hundred percent sure about the result, I would rather forget it," he dithered.

Henry observed that Peter would only do favors for "qualified friends". These were people who not only enjoyed a good relationship with Peter but who were also capable of fulfilling a contract and handling mutual business properly. Henry repeatedly stressed Red Dragon's competitive advantage as one of the biggest chemical shipping brokers in China, arguing to Peter that Red Dragon could reduce HCC's shipping costs and expand HCC's worldwide business contacts.

To help demonstrate Red Dragon's advantages, Henry arranged for David Lam, Red Dragon Singapore's managing director, to accompany him to visit Peter in June. Lam prepared a one-hour presentation about the history and key core competencies of Red Dragon and presented it for Peter's whole department. Peter was impressed and began to contact Henry asking for more information about the domestic and international liquid chemical marketplaces, and freight market trends. He also asked Henry to submit a quotation for regular spot ship chartering. Henry was excited by Peter's positive response and worked even harder to boost guanxi with Peter hoping to "strike while the iron is hot."

TERRIBLE NEWS

At the end of September, Henry was shocked to learn that Peter was being re-assigned to one of HCC's sub-factories in a small city outside Nanjing. It was claimed that this was part of a senior manager-training program that intended to fully qualify Chinese managers to run HCC by 2005. Henry had doubts. Ever since the Cultural Revolution in the 1960s and 1970s, being sent down to the countryside was considered an extreme punishment and very few ever came back. Henry recalled his feelings,

> I was so upset and surprised. The dilemma is what will happen next. If Peter won't come back after this program, then all my previous investments of time and money will be wasted. I have to start again from the very beginning with the new manager. I need to decide whether or not to stay with Peter. If I continue the guanxi building with him, my effort will become worthless if Peter leaves the logistics department.

Trying to figure things out, Henry visited Peter in the small city and tried to find out what had happened. It seemed to Henry that Peter was reluctant to talk about what had happened to him, and he didn't seem to want to say too much about his new assignment or status. Peter said, "Now I understand that what is out of sight is out of mind," and he joked that he was a dragon who went near the shallow water and got bullied by a fish. Henry terminated the meeting quickly. He simply didn't know what to say to help pacify Peter. There was already a new German expatriate, Mr. Mike Holt, who had been appointed the manager of the HCC logistics department.

Henry wondered what he should do. He could stick with Peter and hope for the best. If Henry kept building guanxi with Peter and Peter recovered his position, then he would be very grateful for Henry's loyalty. It was a Chinese proverb that bad time builds good relationship, and that Chinese will use a crisis to test the true nature of guanxi. Henry remembered that foreign companies that had pulled out of China at the time of the Tiananmen crisis in 1989 had been unwelcome when they tried to come back later. Other companies that stayed in China had been rewarded later for their loyalty to China during a time of crisis.

Yet Peter hadn't sounded at all confident about his imminent return—all that talk about dragons bullied by little fish—and if he didn't come back within a couple of years it could be too late. Realistically, the point of guanxi was to invest your time and energy with those who could benefit you the most either now or sometime in the future. The giver always benefited equally or even more than the recipient especially when the recipient was the tiger and the giver was the fox. The world was like a pyramid of people struggling with each other. You didn't have a choice about whether you joined the struggle—that was just life. You could, however, choose where you struggled. You didn't want to fight your battle at the bottom of the pyramid in the midst of the crowd. It was easier to fight at the top. In China, conditions changed quickly and unpredictably. The government could pass a new economic manifesto and suddenly the basis of competition was completely different. The man who governed today could be in disgrace tomorrow and someone else would be in charge. It was important to remember the Taoist proverb of the staunchness of the oak and the yielding of the grass. The grass bends easily in the wind but the great oak stands unmoved. A strong wind can uproot the oak but no wind, however strong, can uproot the grass that bends flat before it. It was important to honor and maintain your values but it was also important to know which were the true standards that should govern your life and which were arbitrary standards that you upheld hoping that others would like you. Sometimes you had to have the courage to do what you must without regard for what others might think. If Henry stuck with Peter and he was not rehabilitated, then Peter might be pleased but Red Dragon would lose the COA and Henry would lose face with his colleagues who were counting on his abilities. It was another proverb that the successful man played leapfrog. People and relationships that had no further use were cast off. You always did your best to leap to the top to gain endorsement from the established authorities and to ally yourself with the powerful and the wise. You must always leap towards an association with the tiger.

Henry wondered if he could switch his guanxi building efforts to Mr. Holt. Holt was apparently the new tiger of HCC's logistics department and represented the German half of the joint venture. He could entertain Holt by taking him sightseeing, shopping and to meals but, in his experience, Germans were less likely than Chinese to trade friendship for business. Mr. Holt probably thought that business was business and would make his decisions about the COA based on the service and the cost, and not based on whether he was friends with Henry. He said,

> I find the whole prospect of building guanxi with Mr. Holt very confusing. I don't quite know what to do because my experience is building guanxi with Chinese. Do the same things work with Germans or other foreigners?

Or, Henry could start again. It had taken him a few months to identify Peter as the person to build guanxi with and his efforts had taken about a year. He still had two or three years left. If he could find a Chinese manager higher than Mr. Holt, perhaps that manager could influence Mr. Holt to support signing a COA with Red Dragon China. Certainly, this was the option Henry felt most confident about.

Standing in the window of his office looking down at Pudong and the Yantze River, Henry worried that just when he was ready to walk through the forest with his friend the tiger, he was being cast down to struggle again at the base of the pyramid. Pudong was the shining symbol of China's transformation of world commerce. Henry needed the COA with HCC as his shining symbol ensuring that Red Dragon China would continue to be a part of the Chinese economic miracle. What should he do now?

Casablanca Kids

Lisa Giguere and David Rose

In October 2005, Ricki Glinert assumed the new position of Artist & Repertoire and Marketing Manager for Casablanca Kids, a private Canadian-based children's music label. The owners of Casablanca Kids believed that children's music required more attention and gave Ricki the task of increasing artist signings, overseeing product development and increasing brand recognition and marketing of the product line to increase sales. As Ricki began gathering information to develop a plan for increasing sales and profitability in the next year, she realized that her new position was going to be very challenging.

The Company

Ed Glinert and Jennifer Mitchell founded Casablanca Kids in 2001, as a division of Casablanca Media Acquisitions Inc. ("Casablanca"). Casablanca Kids produced children's music, while Casablanca's other divisions were involved in the production and distribution of a variety of music genres as well as music publishing and television production services. Casablanca Kids' products were well-produced quality entertainment of various musical styles (i.e. blues, jazz, reggae, etc.), designed for children, without being patronizing. The founders strongly believed that their company had one of the most impressive children's music catalogues in all of North America. They had titles from well-established artists, most of whom had over 20 years of experience in the industry. Notable signed artists included Sharon, Lois and Bram, Fred Penner, Jack Grunsky, Al Simmons, Norman Foote and Bob King. Casablanca Kids' releases included original CDs by established artists, compilation CDs by lesser known artists, DVDs and interactive games. According to Jennifer Mitchell, the company's products were "competitively priced at a mid-range level of approximately $9.99 to $12.99 per CD, midway between the high end products and the discount products". As a testament to the quality of the product, Casablanca Kids had won numerous consumer choice awards including Parents Choice Awards, National Parenting Publications Awards, iParenting Awards and Juno Awards. However, Mitchell acknowledged that although these awards were meaningful to consumers, they had little impact on the retailers that Casablanca Kids relied on to distribute their products. (Exhibit 1 provides biographies for Ricki Glinert, Jennifer Mitchell and Ed Glinert.)

Typical of a company with less than $1 million in sales, Casablanca Kids faced some challenges as its net income continued to decrease from declining sales and a lower profit margin as Wal-Mart continued to force retail prices down and CD manufacturing costs remained the same. (Exhibit 2 provides a breakdown of variable costs for CDs.) In 2005, over 50% of total sales volume was attributed to budget compilations (or discount CDs). Although margins on mid-range CDs were much higher, the discount CDs had a much higher potential sales volume. Casablanca was considering whether to enter the dollar store market where margins would be even lower but volumes could be much higher, perhaps several hundred thousand units per sale.

Casablanca Kids had limited financial resources for any marketing initiatives. Compounding this challenge was the need to "front-end" the marketing of children's music products (i.e., upfront marketing costs that cannot be recouped until two years after the expenses are incurred). "Front-end" marketing costs totaled approximately 10% of Casablanca Kids' mid-range CD sales. Marketing expenses were a requirement in order to promote mid-range CDs, whereas discount CDs were sold on the basis of low price with little marketing support. Dollar store CDs would receive no marketing support and would not even carry the Casablanca Kids name.

Casablanca Kids had no current television presence to assist in promoting the product line, as none of the company's signed artists currently had a regular television program. Further, Casablanca Kids was very reliant on a single act as over 50% of total Canadian sales volume was attributed to Sharon, Lois and Bram.

The Children's Music Market

While the total world market for children's music was unknown, Ricki thought there had been little sales growth during the past few years. Recently, the preschool market (children under the age of six) had been declining due to a decrease in the number of families having children. However this market was expected to experience moderate growth within five years as the Echo generation (the children of the Baby Boom generation) started having children. Casablanca Kids estimated that Canada represented about 10% of the total world market for children's music, while the US market was estimated to be as much as 45% of the total world market.

More detailed information was available about the overall music industry, compared to the limited data about the children's music market. According to figures available to Casablanca, in 2005:

■ Tracking firm Nielsen SoundScan, which measured point-of-sale purchases across the United States, indicated that total album sales, including current and catalogue titles, fell 7.2 percent from 2004 to 618.9 million units, the lowest since 1996, when they were 616.6 million. After enjoying an "up" year in 2004, prompting predictions that the worst was over, sales flagged during 2005, hurt by competition from illegal downloads, rival forms of entertainment such as video games, and a lack of breakout musical acts.

■ Overall music sales, which included albums, singles, music videos, and digital tracks, jumped 22.7 percent to just over a billion units in 2005. The rise was fuelled by a 194 percent increase in digital downloads.

■ Sales of physical albums bought via the internet were up 11.3 percent.

■ Breaking down sales by genre, every type of music took a hit in 2005 with the exception of Latin, which saw a 12.6 percent increase.

Distribution

The primary channel of distribution for Casablanca Kids' products in Canada was through two large music distributors, EMI and Universal. These two distributors accounted for approximately 75% of the total sales volume for the company. EMI and Universal sold the product directly to mass merchants including Wal-Mart, Zellers, and Best Buy; major book chains including Indigo and Chapters; major record chains such as HMV; and non-traditional outlets such as major grocery and drug chains. In terms of an overall promotion mix strategy, EMI and Universal used a push strategy, directing all marketing activities (mainly personal selling and trade promotion) toward wholesalers and retailers to encourage them to stock the product and promote it to the end consumer.

Ricki recognized that sales in the children's music industry were dominated by mass merchant accounts including Wal-Mart, Zellers, and Best Buy. She thought that in 2005 Wal-Mart accounted for 50% to 60% of total retail sales of children's music in Canada. She described non-traditional outlets such as grocery and drug chains as "problematic since these stores are not used to selling music. There is often low compliance from staff to ensure that the product is properly merchandised." Compounding this issue was the fact that Casablanca Kids did not have dedicated staff to call on retailers and maintain merchandising displays.

EMI and Universal also sold the product to wholesalers who would stock the titles for smaller retail accounts including small chain stores and privately owned independent stores who would be likely to purchase less than 10 copies of a single title in the span of a year.

Direct sales accounted for the remaining 25% of total company sales volume. This included sales to small retailers who might, for example, purchase products from the Casablanca Kids website as well as direct sales to consumers who could purchase the product directly 'off-stage' during the artists' concerts and from the online store at the Casablanca Kids website (**www.casablancakids.com**). According to Ricki, "There are no plans to expand the direct sales channel as this would require a huge financial investment." Exhibit 3 provides an illustration of the various distribution channels.

Buying Behaviour of Retailers

In the children's music industry, product was 100% returnable for a full refund. This meant that retailers could return the product to Casablanca Kids for a full refund if the product did not sell. In addition, the two primary distributors, EMI and Universal, charged a refurbishing cost to Casablanca Kids for all returned product. Ricki felt that mass merchants such as Wal-Mart were most concerned with profit per square foot and would rather carry CDs from well known adult artists that would be guaranteed to move quickly.

> If the CDs are not sold within a couple of weeks, mass merchants and non-traditional retail outlets will return the product to Casablanca Kids for a full refund. They tend to buy low priced children's music products or brands advertised nationally on television. Mass merchant buyers are not particularly knowledgeable about children's music.

Ricki believed that children's music occupied the least amount of shelf space, relative to other categories of music, in all retail stores. Further, she recognized that with the maturation of the CD format, retailers were beginning to carry far less CD inventory in general.

Buying Behaviour of Consumers

The primary purchasers of children's music were parents who tended to purchase the same music that was purchased for them as a child, prompting Ricki to describe the industry as being "evergreen". In addition, grandparents, other relatives and friends also purchased children's music as gifts. However, children's music was a low priority purchase for the vast majority of buyers. According to Ricki:

> A fundamental problem is that the majority of parents don't believe that children need to be exposed to music. With the introduction of DVD players in automobiles, parents can now choose to let children watch a DVD in the car instead of listening to music.

Buyers of children's music could be divided into four main categories. The "keep them quiet" buyer group purchased children's music to keep children occupied and quiet, particularly during long car trips. These buyers were not well informed about the quality of children's music or the developmental benefits of exposing children to music at an early age. The second group of buyers, the "developmental buffs", believed that regular exposure to music from birth was fundamental to a child's brain development. This group purchased children's music because they firmly believed that exposing children to music at an early age made them smarter. These buyers were searching for a quality music product and were willing to pay a premium to ensure that children had the proper exposure to music. The third group, "music enthusiasts", were music lovers themselves and wanted to share their love of music with children. This group was very knowledgeable about a variety of music and was willing to pay more for a quality recording. A fourth group, "gift givers" included a wide range of behaviours, depending on a number of factors such as the occasion and the relationship of the giver to the child.

Most buyers who shopped at big box stores such as Wal-Mart and Zellers tended to be looking to purchase low-end product for $2.00 to $5.00 per CD. Although big box stores did stock some mid-range product, i.e., approximately $9.99 to $12.99 per CD, the focus was on offering a wide range of low-end product to meet the needs of the target customers. Conversely, buyers who shopped at specialty children's stores such as Mastermind were prepared to spend more money. As such, children's music sold in these specialty stores tended to be high-end product in the $16.00 to $19.99 per CD range.

Children's music was generally not purchased by the person who would listen to the music, i.e., the child, so the product had to be appealing to both the buyer (parents, relatives, friends) and the user (the child). Both parents and children chose children's music based on familiarity with the performing artist. According to Ricki:

> Most parents grew up listening to Sharon, Lois and Bram. That's what is driving our high sales for this act. Parents are choosing Sharon, Lois and Bram because they know that the music is great.

Ricki felt that the target demographic for Casablanca Kids' product was getting younger, as children were growing up at a younger age, a phenomenon often called "age compression".

> With artists like Sharon, Lois and Bram, we need to focus on younger children, as kids today are growing up faster at an earlier age. Our target demographic has become children under the age of five. The industry is in a cycle of animation, meaning that the majority of children's music performers are animated characters. Children are being exposed to and love animated characters. This presents a challenge as our signed artists are not animated, but are real people. However, this trend is slowly beginning to change in our favour with the movement toward live performances.

Promotions

In terms of marketing to retail accounts, Casablanca Kids provided catalogues and 'sell sheets' that contained information about a CD that would be released in the near future. The release information contained in both the sell sheets and catalogues served as marketing tools to convince the distributors, wholesalers and retailers to carry the product. In addition, Casablanca Kids advertised in trade magazines including Canadian Music Network, Canadian Entertainment Network and Billboard Magazine.

Marketing efforts by Casablanca Kids towards end consumers were more limited. Whenever possible, public relations was used as a tool to promote new releases in the various media including print, television, radio and the website. The main exception was the budget compilation CDs, where the primary factor driving the consumer purchase decision was price. However, it was generally very difficult to interest the media in the company's news. According to Ricki:

> The media is just not that interested in children's music. Ideally, we like to get positive product reviews in the media, but this is a challenge given the media's overall lack of interest in the industry.

Giveaways had proven to be a more successful form of promotion. For example, Casablanca Kids often provided prizes for draws held at "Movies for Mommies", movie viewings restricted to mothers who brought their babies with them. Some advertising was placed in parenting magazines and on children's television and radio shows, but only a very limited amount due to the relatively high cost.

Opportunities for Growth

In 2005, Casablanca Kids introduced Jazz Baby, a CD with traditional children's songs recorded by celebrities and famous musicians including Jim Belushi, Cybill Shepherd, Megan Mullally and Taj Mahal. Short-term promotional plans for Jazz Baby included the creation of t-shirts with the Jazz Baby logo and the possibility of a live concert on television, which would result in a DVD for sale.

Casablanca Kids was attempting to increase its music DVD product line. Given the maturation of the CD format, more retail shelf space was available for music DVDs than CDs. The company was also beginning to introduce interactive music games.

Casablanca Kids planned to aggressively enter the US market in 2006. In the longer term, the company planned to expand internationally into the UK market, given the cultural similarities between the Canadian and UK markets. However, each country had its own group of notable children's music artists and it was very difficult for a children's music artist to gain international exposure. Such exposure was only obtained through the television media. The Wiggles, an Australian act, had gained international recognition with children through their own television program, which aired in many countries. The Casablanca Kids' artists were not well known in the US, making it difficult for the company to effectively penetrate the market. Recently, the company had been trying to sign more US artists in an effort to overcome this lack of awareness.

Casablanca Kids had been exploring the potential of digital music stores as another distribution channel for the product. Use of this channel would require a relationship with a digital aggregator who would then distribute the Casablanca Kids recordings to the digital music stores. According to Ricki, the digital music market was growing significantly.

Another opportunity existed in the educational market, selling music to schools, but it was not a market that Ricki found attractive:

> The educational segment is difficult to penetrate and restricted by funding guidelines. In addition, it's very hard to reach the buyers, i.e., the teachers, and building relationships with these individual buyers would take a long period of time. If we were to go after this market, the best way for us to reach the buyers directly would be to have a strong presence at relevant industry trade shows. But this presents a challenge given our limited resources.

Competitors

Casablanca Kids' largest direct competitor was Disney, who produced the best known products in the industry. In 2005, Ricki estimated that Disney's share of the worldwide children's music market was approximately 30%. Other significant competitors included:

- branded television characters, such as the Wiggles and Sesame Street
- "tween" entertainers, such as Hilary Duff, who targeted children aged 9 to 12
- budget compilation CDs consisting of collections of songs by unknown artists, selling for $1 to $2
- video/early learning games, such as Baby Einstein (a Disney product).

In addition to direct competitors, indirect competition existed in the form of other children's entertainment products such as DVDs, toys, games, and books. The total market in Canada for children's entertainment products was estimated to be at least $2 billion. Most of the sales were through large retailers such as Wal-Mart and Zellers, with a much smaller amount through specialty retailers. Typically products were not carried by the large discount retailers and the specialty retailers at the same time, with specialty retailers tending to carry newer, higher-end products. Once products ended up at the large discount retailers, where they were often heavily discounted, it was difficult for specialty retailers to continue selling them.

The Decision

Ricki wondered how she could increase the brand recognition and therefore sales of Casablanca Kids' products. The company had an established relationship with both EMI and Universal, but was that the best method of distribution? Were there other channels that might provide more support? The mass merchant retailers currently accounted for the vast majority of the company's sales, but would that continue, given their limited interest in children's music? Which consumer groups represented Casablanca's most attractive target market? She wondered how she could increase sales when it seemed like the distribution channels were not interested in carrying the products and consumers were not aware they existed. Ed and Jennifer were anxious to hear what Ricki had planned for the business so she soon needed to make some important decisions.

Exhibit 1   Biographies

Ricki Glinert, Artist & Repertoire and Marketing Manager
Ricki has over 25 years of experience in television production and has most recently focused on kids tv because she can look them directly in the eye. Ricki was the creator and producer of Treehouse TV's "Crazy Quilt", as well as the creator and producer of "100% True" for Discovery Kids. She has also written numerous television series for kids and spent 5 years at TVO producing, directing and writing in the children's department. Her credits include "Join In", "Way Up There", "World of Nature" and "Mathica's Mathsop". She has also worked on children's shows for OWL Communications and CTV. At Casablanca Television she has served as Executive In Charge of Production on the 13 part space series "Rocket Science" and produced, directed and wrote the 2 hour special on the science of wrestling, "Slam Bam". Both of these series aired on The Discovery Channel.

Jennifer Mitchell, Vice-President
Jennifer has specialized in the areas of entertainment, media and corporate law for the past 10 years, working with Edmund L. Glinert in private practice and co-founding Casablanca Media Acquisitions Inc. She has been involved in the acquisition and sale of numerous entertainment related transactions as well as film and television tax shelters. Ms. Mitchell is the Senior Vice President of Casablanca Media Acquisitions Inc. and is involved in the buying, selling, administration, and exploitation of music publishing and recording catalogues and has been overseeing the day to day operations of all areas of Casablanca since its inception.

Ed Glinert, President
Ed has specialized in the areas of entertainment, media and communications law for the past 25 years. Prior to becoming a lawyer, he founded, owned and operated Frederick Lewis Artist Placement Bureau, one of Canada's largest theatrical agencies, from 1967 through 1971. From 1977 through 1982, he was also a co-owner of National Variety Promotions ("NVP"), one of Canada's largest adult contemporary concert promoters, which presented such acts as Liza Minnelli, Frank Sinatra, Don Rickles and Steve Lawrence as well as producing the stage play, Pirates of Penzance starring Barry Bostwick and Andy Gibb at the Royal Alexandra Theatre. In 1990, he co-founded The Children's Group, owner of the hit series "Classical Kids" which has been one of the most successful series of children's records in history. In 2000, he founded Casablanca Media Acquisitions Inc., along with Jennifer Mitchell.

Exhibit 2   Variable Costs Per CD*

	Dollar Store CD	Budget CD	Mid-Range CD
Retail Price	$1.00	$5.99	$9.99
Wholesale Price	$ 0.50	$2.99	$4.99
Distribution Costs 25%	$0.12	$ .75	$1.25
Manufacturing	$0.25	$1.00	$1.30
Mechanical Licenses	$0.05	$0.32	$0.50
Master Licenses	$0.05	$0.32	$0.50
Casablanca Income	$0.03–$0.04	$0.60	$1.44

*Figures represent estimates of average costs for music companies with less than $1 million in sales. Some figures may have been disguised.

Exhibit 3   Distribution Channels

Mediaspark

In September of 2001, Mathew Georghiou, the President and CEO of MediaSpark (**http://www.mediaspark.com**) in Sydney, Nova Scotia, finished a phone conversation with IBM Canada. IBM had just informed Georgiou that they were interested in exclusively carrying MediaSpark's new product, GoVenture Entrepreneur (**http://www.goventure.net**) in the Canadian market. Georghiou had been researching possible distribution channels for GoVenture in North America. The phone call with IBM completed Georghiou's research and he now needed to sift through the information and decide how he was going to get his product to market.

BACKGROUND

Georghiou completed a two year engineering diploma at Cape Breton University (then University College of Cape Breton), before transferring to Dalhousie University in Halifax, Nova Scotia, to complete his Electrical Engineering Degree. After Georghiou's second year at Dalhousie, IBM awarded him a sixteen month internship in Toronto, an offer which he took. In 1991, Georgiou received a national award for innovation during his internship which led IBM to guarantee him a position upon graduation.

Doug Lionais, Sherry Finney, and Melissa Cameron

After graduating in 1993, Georghiou immediately moved back to Toronto to work for IBM. While employed at IBM, Georghiou gained much experience in the engineering field which included programming and computer product manufacturing.

Georghiou had a vision to establish his own business and left IBM in 1994. He moved back to Sydney, Nova Scotia, and with personal savings and financing from Enterprise Cape Breton Corporation (ECBC), he established MediaSpark. The business began in the basement of his home and after only two years, he needed to expand and he relocated his offices downtown. MediaSpark focused on technology and design; the business offered a wide range of services such as multi-media production, Internet development, e-learning, technology consulting, and image and print design.

GOVENTURE ENTREPRENEUR

In 2000, MediaSpark launched GoVenture Entrepreneur, an educational software program which simulated establishing and running a small business (Exhibit 1, page C–34). This software created a practical replication of an entrepreneur's business start-up, daily management, and personal activities. Georghiou felt GoVenture Entrepreneur would be a perfect learning tool for any business education class because it provided students the opportunity to gain experience and knowledge without risk. Georghiou described GoVenture Entrepreneur as a "flight simulator for business."

In the GoVenture Entrepreneur simulation, participants establish and manage a small business start-up. The program simulates all aspects of entrepreneurial decision making, including business and personal outcomes. Performance evaluation tools included in the simulation allow the user and/or the instructor to set goals, adjust performance evaluation weightings and measure outcomes in terms of business success and personal work-life balance. MediaSpark designed the product to be as flexible as possible for teachers.

MediaSpark identified the broader market for GoVenture Entrepreneur as middle school to adult; however, the primary target was high school classes. Georghiou saw GoVenture Entrepreneur as enhancing the existing curriculum. MediaSpark positioned it for use in business, marketing, and entrepreneurship courses. Georghiou identified three general ways of using GoVenture Entrepreneurship in the classroom. First, educators could use GoVenture Entrepreneurship as an introduction to a course to demonstrate the purpose of learning the concepts in the course. Second, they could use it to end a course as a capstone module to apply the lessons of the course. Third, educators could use it throughout a course to complement ongoing lessons.

To serve the educational market, MediaSpark developed a number of support materials for GoVenture Entrepreneurship. For example, institutions that purchased software licenses received an "Experiencing Entrepreneurship" text. MediaSpark developed this book as an easy to use summary of the subject that educators could use either as a textbook or as a complement to existing textbooks. MediaSpark's educational bundle also included an instructor's manual, lesson plans focusing on different topics, and a test bank.

THE MARKET

Georghiou divided the educational publishing industry between the K–12 market and the university market. Georghiou's target market fell in the K–12 category. Georghiou felt the market in the United States was much larger than the Canadian market, with more growth in the educational software sector. There were 90 000 to 100 000 elementary and secondary schools in the United States while there were only 16 500 in Canada, and Canada's K–12 enrolment was 5.3 million students, approximately one-tenth the size of the United States. According to market studies that Georghiou had reviewed, U.S. schools spent $5.50 per student on software and the market for CD-ROMs in schools approximated US$300 million. Georghiou hoped to generate significant sales in both the Canadian and the U.S. market, but the focus was on the U.S. market because it was much larger than the Canadian market and it had greater access to funding.

MARKETING AND PRICING STRATEGY

Georghiou was concerned about how to sell and distribute the product. The education market was accustomed to purchasing texts rather than multimedia products. Whereas a catalogue description can describe a text fairly well, Georghiou felt that educators would need to experience GoVenture Entrepreneur before considering it for use in the classroom. Georghiou felt that it would be difficult to convince educators of the value of his product as either a text complement or as a text replacement without a hands-on trial. Georghiou commented, "To sell the product, people need to see it; they need to try it out for themselves." Thus, he was only interested in marketing channels which placed the product in educators' hands for a decision or at least provided an opportunity to demonstrate the product in action.

The price of GoVenture Entrepreneur varied depending on the user and country. Georghiou identified six user groups: individuals, educational K–12, educational post-secondary, home school, non-profit or government, and all others. He wanted his initial target market to be the educational K–12 and offered this segment a 50% price reduction for a limited time in an effort to break into the market. The regular price varied per package depending on the quantity purchased (Exhibit 2, page C–34). The cost of goods sold was generally 5% to 10% of the suggested retail price.

DISTRIBUTION CHANNELS

Georghiou identified two basic distribution alternatives for GoVenture Entrepreneur: direct or indirect. Indirect distribution channels would include catalogue companies, textbook publishers, or software publishers. If Georghiou was to sell directly, MediaSpark would have to handle the full advertising and distributing duties.

Educational product catalogue companies sold thousands of products to educational institutions through published or on-line catalogues. The larger publishers would send out educational catalogues to most schools in North America, though Georghiou questioned how many actually got to teachers he wished to reach. Catalogue companies would typically only list a product in exchange for an exclusive deal. Thus, Georghiou would not be able to sell GoVenture Entrepreneur in the same region through any other channel. Georghiou had researched the reseller discount for all possible distribution channels. The reseller discount was the percentage of the final price that the reselling company retained. For catalogue companies, Georghiou reported the reseller discount to be between 20% and 35%.

Georghiou's second indirect option, textbook publishers, supplied most schools with their core text books. Textbook publishers differed from catalogue companies as they employed a sales force as well as a published catalogue of products. Sales representatives would travel to schools and trade shows to present the product catalogue, and potential purchasers would have a better chance of seeing a demonstration of the product. Text publishers, however, would also require an exclusive deal to carry a product and would demand a reseller discount of 40%–60%.

Georghiou had identified two main text publishers: Glencoe McGraw-Hill and Southwestern. Georghiou knew that Glencoe was already carrying a competing product: Virtual Business (**http://www.knowledgematters.com**). Georghiou had heard that Southwestern had turned down his competitor's product, but thought it would likely want to pick up a competing product since Glencoe started carrying Virtual Business. Georghiou identified Southwestern as the leading business education provider to the K–12, higher education, and professional markets in the United States. It did not, however, distribute in Canada. Its main focus was text books; however, it had distributed some interactive software in keyboarding, marketing, management, and accounting. Glencoe also focused on text books with a small amount of software titles (like Virtual Business).

Because of the technological nature of his product, Georghiou also considered software distribution companies as a third indirect distribution channel. A software distributor could give Georghiou's product more profile when compared to being "lost in the thousands of traditional text products in a publisher's catalogue." Again, software distributors would require an exclusive deal to carry a product. Georghiou found that the software distribution market was highly fragmented. There were no companies that operated in both the Canadian and the U.S. markets. Furthermore, in the United States, there were very few national distributors; many were small companies who would carry other firms' products as well as their own. The reseller discount for software distributors was comparable to that of text publishers at 40% to 60%.

One option within the United States was to distribute through a non-profit company called MarkED, a consortium of 40 state education departments and other organizations. As an industry-run organization, MarkED would lend credibility to the products it supported. MarkED sold products through a catalogue it distributed to its constituent organizations. However, it did not have a sales force to complement the catalogue and Georghiou could not be sure that the catalogue would reach the right teachers.

In Canada, the software distribution choices were much different. The most prominent distributor was IBM which operated a software distribution division in Canada.[1] Established in 1880, IBM was the world's largest and most recognizable information technology company. IBM Canada had its own sales force which was already distributing to schools. Since 1995, IBM invested $75 million in its Reinventing Education program which it established to break down barriers to academic achievement. IBM estimated that this program would reach 100 000 teachers and 10 million students in 10 countries by the end of 2004. IBM provided research and technical expertise, as well as equipment and cash contributions, to improve teaching and learning. The educational software currently available to the K–12 market focused on reading, language arts, mathematics, and science. In addition to this, IBM supplied many schools with the interface and internet software for their computers, as well as interactive white boards.

Georghiou felt that IBM was a good candidate because it was technology based, had brand recognition, and was already distributing to schools.

---

[1] IBM also sold software in the United States but it was in the midst of changing its strategy and moving towards only carrying a very small number of products. Because it was undergoing some changes, MediaSpark saw no real opportunity to work with them.

IBM had proposed a two-year exclusive deal with MediaSpark to distribute to the K–12 educational market. Georghiou's only reservation was that he felt IBM may focus its attention on its hardware sales rather than software.

Finally, Georghiou could also consider an in-house direct distribution channel. MediaSpark currently employed only one marketing/sales person. Georghiou estimated that to effectively market GoVenture, he would have to hire 5 to 10 sales representatives and an additional 2 to 3 marketing people located in various areas throughout Canada and the United States. The majority of his sales would originate from tradeshows, events, and inside sales calls. Georghiou expected that MediaSpark would have to appear at over ten trade shows in the United States and at least two in Canada. MediaSpark's sales team would have to be responsible for inside sales calls, email campaigns, direct mail, CD demos, seminars, public speaking, and catalogue sales. Georghiou estimated that if MediaSpark did market and sell GoVenture independently, he would not be able to hire all the sales representatives he required and would have to survive with only one or two marketing/sales people. In such a situation, Georghiou himself would likely attend a number of tradeshows and make sales trips throughout the year. The advantage of selling in-house was that MediaSpark would make a much higher margin on each unit sold as there would be no reseller discount. However, tradeshows were expensive and the need to sell GoVenture Entrepreneur may distract MediaSpark from new product development.

THE DECISION

Georghiou struggled with the distribution decision. He first had to decide whether or not to go with a third party distributor and if he did, which one or ones to go with. Georghiou was most worried about the exclusivity required by distributors. In essence, if Georghiou went with a distributor, he was putting all his eggs in one basket; he had to have absolute confidence in the distributor he chose. If the distributor did not succeed in selling the product, Georghiou would have no other avenues to make a sale. Georghiou worried that his product would be one product among many in any distributor's product line and that they may put more focus on other products. The lack of technology knowledge of some of the potential distributors was another worry. As Georghiou explained, "Success depended on leveraging a distributor's brand awareness and market reach to sell more units than we can on our own."

Exhibit 1   **MediaSpark GoVenture Entrepreneur Website**

GoVenture Entrepreneur is a highly visual and realistic business simulation that recreates the day-to-day experiences involved in starting and running a small business.

Like a flight simulator for small business, Entrepreneur engages you in realistic situations and problems. Take your own test flights, at your own speed. Within the world of Entrepreneur, the decisions and the consequences are highly realistic. So virtual entrepreneurs rapidly gain the authentic wisdom that normally only comes from on-the-job experience.

The GoVenture Experience

- **Experience** what it is like to manage numerous business and personal tasks.

- **Make** necessary compromises to reach both business and personal success.

- **Learn** what you need to know to start a business in minutes, not months.

This simulation makes learning about being an entrepreneur fun. You can run the simulation for as long as you want. You can dive in using the Quick Start feature or take the time to go through the Personal and Business Profiles to select and start a business. You can conduct business, get advice, attend training seminars, and even close or sell your company. At any point, you may save your simulation and return to it later.

There is no penalty for failure, so if your first business doesn't succeed, try another. You can even control how fast the simulation time clock runs!

You can check your own personal financial status or your company's at any time. Review the business' financial statements and charts on recent operations. If you're doing well, you can pay yourself a bonus and buy one of those items on your wish list.

Watch out for random events—you could become injured and have to stay home for a while. Or if you forget your spouse's birthday your stress level may go up. If your stress level is too high, you may have to take some time off from the company. Can your employees run it without you?

The simulation immerses you in a life-like world of entrepreneurship and small business—a world where you still have to remember to pay your bills and get enough sleep.

It is an engaging experience, which makes learning fun, as you build an understanding of what it is like to be an entrepreneur and to meet the challenges of starting and running a small business.

The Entrepreneur CD-ROM simulation can be used in schools, in self-paced home or work study, in life-long learning programs, and in corporate training initiatives for employees or customers. Never before has it been so easy to experience the life of an entrepreneur.

Exhibit 2   **MediaSpark GoVenture Entrepreneur Pricing**

GOVENTURE ENTREPRENEUR PRODUCT PRICE

	1 SEAT*	5 SEAT*	30 Seat*	SITE**
GoVenture Entrepreneur Software License – Educational (USD)	$199	$349	$749	$1199
GoVenture Entrepreneur Software License - Educational (CAD)	$199	$499	NA	$1499

Software License Includes:

- License for a specified number of concurrent user(s). See Software License Descriptions below for important information.

- 1 CD-ROM for Windows (GoVenture Entrepreneur is also compatible with Macintosh). Program can be copied from CD to computer hard drives or network drive.

- User Guide.

- Performance Reports (built into the software).

- FREE Experiencing Book (text on Entrepreneurship).

- FREE Education Bundle (including instructor guide, lesson plans and test bank).

- FREE Value Option for 1 Year (includes additional customer service support).

* **SEAT License:** This license allows for many people to use the software at the same organization (or school) at one physical address location. The number of seats purchased determines how many computers may run the software concurrently (at the same time). For example, a 5-Seat License allows for the software to be run on up to 5 computers at the same time. In this example, the software may be installed on a network, or installed on more than 5 computers, but the software may not be run on more than 5 computers concurrently. Individual Seats cannot be shared amongst different organizations (or schools).

** **SITE License:** This license allows for use of the software on all your organization's (or school's) computers at one physical address location at any time. There are no limits on how many computers may run the software concurrently—as long as they are on the same site (one physical address location). A SITE License cannot be shared amongst different organizations.

Reference Notes

Chapter 1

1 *Financial Post Business*, Special Edition, 2006, 64.

2. See Robert A. Collinge and Ronald M. Ayers, *Economics by Design: Principles and Issues*, 2nd ed. (Upper Saddle River, NJ: Prentice Hall, 2000), 41–42; Michael J. Mandel, "The New Economy," *Business Week* (January 31, 2000): 73–77.

3. Karl E. Case and Ray C. Fair, *Principles of Economics*, 6th ed. (Upper Saddle River, NJ: Prentice Hall, 2003), 224–225.

4. Richard I. Kirkland, Jr., "The Death of Socialism," *Fortune* (January 4, 1988): 64–72.

5. See Karl E. Case and Ray C. Fair, *Principles of Economics*, 5th ed. (Upper Saddle River, NJ: Prentice Hall, 1999), 69–74; Robert A. Collinge and Ronald M. Ayers, *Economics by Design: Principles and Issues*, 2nd ed. (Upper Saddle River, NJ: Prentice Hall, 2000), 51–52.

6. Deborah Orr, "The Post Office with a Ticker," *Forbes* (November 29, 1999): 77–78; Matthew L. Wald, "Canada's Private Control Towers," *The New York Times*, October 23, 1999, C1. See also National Center for Policy Analysis, "Privatization," www.public-policy.org/~ncpa/pd/private/privat.html, March 8, 2000.

7. Andy Hoffman, "Labatt Convicted in Quebec Discount Beer Case," *The Globe and Mail*, November 24, 2005, B10

8. Barrie McKenna, "Hyundai Gorged on Federal Funds," *The Globe and Mail*, March 25, 1994, B3.

9. See Karl E. Case and Ray C. Fair, *Principles of Economics*, 5th ed. (Upper Saddle River, NJ: Prentice Hall, 1999), 70–90; Robert A. Collinge and Ronald M. Ayers, *Economics by Design: Principles and Issues*, 2nd ed. (Upper Saddle River, NJ: Prentice Hall, 2000), 74–77.

10. Joel Millman, "Metal is so Precious that Scrap Thieves Now Tap Beer Kegs," *The Wall Street Journal*, March 14, 2006, A1, A15.

11. Wendy Stueck, "Ginseng Growers at Root of Problem," *The Globe and Mail*, May 21, 2001, B1, B3.

12. See Paul Heyne, Peter J. Boettke, and David L. Prychitko, *The Economic Way of Thinking*, 10th ed. (Upper Saddle River, NJ: Prentice Hall, 2003), 190, 358–359.

13. See Gina M. Larson, "bebe Bridges Style Gap," www.office.com/global/0,2724,509-10386_1,FF.html, July 10, 2001; Natural Fibers Information Center, "Ranking of Top U.S. Public Apparel Companies," www.utexas.edu/depts/bbr/natfiber, June 2001; "bebe.com Finishes #1," *Fashion Windows.com*, www.fashionwindows.com/beauty/2002/bebe.asp, January 14, 2002.

14. Karl E. Case and Ray C. Fair, *Principles of Economics*, 6th ed., updated (Upper Saddle River, NJ: Prentice Hall, 2003), 300–309.

15. *Hoover's Handbook of World Business 2002* (Austin, TX: Hoover's Business Press, 2002), 74–75.

16. John Partridge and Lawrence Surtees, "Rogers Faces Assault from Telcos," *The Globe and Mail*, March 28, 1994, B1–B2.

17. "Royal Mail's Reign Comes to an End," *The Globe and Mail*, January 2, 2006, B7.

18. Madelaine Drohan, "Ottawa Targets Interprovincial Barriers," *The Globe and Mail*, May 14, 1991, B5.

Chapter 2

1. See Jay B. Barney and William G. Ouchi, eds., *Organizational Economics* (San Francisco: Jossey-Bass, 1986), for a detailed analysis of linkages between economics and organizations.

2. Karl E. Case and Ray C. Fair, *Principles of Economics*, 6th ed., updated (Upper Saddle River, NJ: Prentice Hall, 2003), 432–433.

3. Karl E. Case and Ray C. Fair, *Principles of Economics*, 6th ed., updated (Upper Saddle River, NJ: Prentice Hall, 2003), 15.

4. Karl E. Case and Ray C. Fair, *Principles of Economics*, 6th ed., updated (Upper Saddle River, NJ: Prentice Hall, 2003), 15.

5. *Bank of Canada Banking and Financial Statistics*, Table H1 (April 2006), S94.

6. Barry Marquardson, "GDP Fails as a Measurement," *The Globe and Mail*, July 16, 1998, B2.

7. Richard Bloom, "Report Analyzes Income Gap with U.S.," *The Globe and Mail*, October 6, 2003, B1, B4.

8. Olivier Blanchard, *Macroeconomics*, 3rd ed. (Upper Saddle River, NJ: Prentice Hall, 2003), 24–26.

9. Jay Heizer and Barry Render, *Operations Management*, 6th Ed. (Upper Saddle River, NJ, Prentice Hall, 2001), 15–16.

10. *Bank of Canada Banking and Financial Statistics*, Table J1 (April 2006), S108.

11. Greg Hitt and Murray Hiebert, "U.S. Trade Deficit Ballooned to a Record in 2005," *The Wall Street Journal*, February 11–12, 2006, A1, A10.

12. *Bank of Canada Banking and Financial Statistics*, Table G1 (May 2006), S83.

13. This section is based on Paul Heyne, Peter J. Boettke, and David L. Prychitko, *The Economic Way of Thinking*, 10th ed. (Upper Saddle River, NJ: Prentice Hall, 2003), 491–493.

14. See Warren J. Keegan, *Global Marketing Management*, 7th ed. (Upper Saddle River, NJ: Prentice Hall, 2002), 39–42.

15. Tavia Grant, "Lard in 1913, Plasma TV Now: CPI Tracks Changes," *The Globe and Mail*, April 21, 2005, B1, B15.

16. Bruce Little, "There's Been a Huge Shift in How Consumers Spend," *The Globe and Mail*, July 5, 2004, B4.

17. Paul Heyne, Peter J. Boettke, and David L. Prychitko, *The Economic Way of Thinking*, 10th ed. (Upper Saddle River, NJ: Prentice Hall, 2003), 403–409, 503–504.

18. Statistics Canada, *Industrial Research and Development, 2005 Intentions*: 10.

19. Statistics Canada, *Industrial Research and Development, 2005 Intentions*: 10.

20. Statistics Canada, *Industrial Research and Development, 2005 Intentions*: 17.

21. Statistics Canada, *Industrial Research and Development, 2005 Intentions*: 10.

22. Statistics Canada, *Industrial Research and Development, 2005 Intentions*: 10.

23. Thomas Wheelen and J. David Hunger, *Strategic Management and Business Policy* (Upper Saddle River, NJ: Pearson, 2004), 280.

24. L. G. Franko, "Global Corporate Competition: Who's Winning, Who's Losing, and the R&D Factor as One Reason Why," *Strategic Management Journal* (September–October, 1989): 449–474.

25. Roberta S. Russell and Bernard W. Taylor III, *Operations Management*, 4th ed. (Upper Saddle River, NJ: Prentice Hall, 2003), Chapter 12.

26. Terrence Belford, "The Little Guys Are Getting with Big Boys' Program," *The Globe and Mail*, June 2, 2005, B16.

27. Brian Laghi, "U.S. Backlash Seen Growing," *The Globe and Mail*, March 27, 2003, B1, B10.

28. Sinclair Stewart, "CIBC's Solid Profit Overshadowed by Woes," *The Globe and Mail*, February 27, 2004, B1, B6.

29. KPMG, "Eleventh Annual Survey of Canada's Most Respected Corporations, 2005," www.mostrespected.ca.

30. Michael Porter. *Competitive Strategy: Techniques for Analyzing Industries and Competitors* (New York: The Free Press, 1980).

31. Judy Strauss and Raymond Frost, *E-Marketing* (Upper Saddle River, NJ: Prentice Hall, 2001), 245–246.

32. Tessa Wegert, "Advertisers Get Creative in Bid to Infect the Internet," *The Globe and Mail*, October 27, 2005, B13.

33. Lee J. Krajewski and Larry P. Ritzman, *Operations Management: Strategy and Analysis*, 6th ed. (Upper Saddle River, NJ: Prentice Hall, 2002), 3–4.

34. Lee J. Krajewski and Larry P. Ritzman, *Operations Management: Strategy and Analysis*, 6th ed. (Upper Saddle River, NJ: Prentice Hall, 2002), Chapter 3.

35. Lawrence Surtees, "Takeover Concern Prompts BCE Poison Pill Plan," *The Globe and Mail*, February 25, 2000, B5.

36. Margot Gibb-Clark, "Share Plans Can Benefit More Than Employees," *The Globe and Mail*, February 14, 2000, B6.

37. "Nunavut Diamond Find Sends Shares Soaring," *The Winnipeg Free Press*, February 4, 2003, B10.

38. "Inco, LionOre Mining Form Strategic Alliance," *The Winnipeg Free Press*, March 14, 2003, B6.

Chapter 3

1. Constance L. Hays, "Aide Was Reportedly Ordered to Warn Stewart on Stock Sales," *The New York Times*, August 6, 2002, C1, C2.

2. Thomas Donaldson and Thomas W. Dunfee, "Toward a Unified Conception of Business Ethics: An Integrative Social Contracts Theory," *Academy of Management Review* 19, no. 2 (1994): 252–284.

3. "Drug Companies Face Assault on Prices," *The Wall Street Journal*, May 11, 2000, B1, B4.

4. John Saunders, "Bitter Air Carrier Dogfight Heads to Court," *The Globe and Mail*, July 8, 2004, B3.

5. Ann Zimmerman and Anita Raghavan, "Diamond Group Widens Probe of Bribe Charges, *The Wall Street Journal*, March 8, 2006, B1-B2.

6. This section follows the logic of Gerald F. Cavanaugh, *American Business Values with International Perspectives*, 4th ed. (Upper Saddle River, NJ: Prentice Hall, 1998), Chapter 3.

7. Patricia Sellers, "Crunch Time for Coke," *Fortune* (July 19, 1999): 72–74+.

8. Mark Schwartz, "Heat's on to Get an Effective Code," *The Globe and Mail*, November 27, 1997, B2.

9. Jeffrey S. Harrison and R. Edward Freeman, "Stakeholders, Social Responsibility, and Performance: Empirical Evidence and Theoretical Perspectives," *Academy of Management Journal* 42, no. 5, 479–485. See also David P. Baron, *Business and Its Environment*, 3rd ed. (Upper Saddle River, NJ: Prentice-Hall, 2000), Chapter 17.

10. James R. Healey, "Ford to Reveal Plans for Think Brand," *USA Today*, January 10, 2000, 1B; Gwen Kinkead, "In the Future, People Like Me Will Go to Jail," *Fortune* (May 24, 1999): 190–200.

11. David P. Baron, *Business and Its Environment*, 4th ed. (Upper Saddle River, NJ: Prentice Hall, 2003), Chapter 11.

12. Jeremy Main, "Here Comes the Big New Cleanup," *Fortune* (November 21, 1988): 102–118.

13. Patrick Brethour, "Canada's Big Emitters Brace for Investment Climate Change," *The Globe and Mail*, February 19, 2005, B4.

14. Bill Curry, "Ottawa Wants Kyoto Softened," *The Globe and Mail*, May 12, 2006, A1, A7.

15. Andrew C. Revkin, "Who Cares About a Few Degrees?" *New York Times*, December 12, 1997, F4.

16. Catherine Collins, "The Race for Zero," *Canadian Business* (March 1991): 52–56.

17. Allan Robinson and Allan Freeman, "Mining's Dam Problem," *The Globe and Mail*, May 16, 1998, B1–B2.

18. "Hot Spots," *Canadian Business* (March 17, 2003): 30–31.

19. Geoffrey Scotton, "Cleanups Can Hurt, Companies Warned," *The Financial Post*, June 25, 1991, 4.

20. Marc Huber, "A Double-Edged Endorsement," *Canadian Business* (January 1990): 69–71.

21. Egle Procuta, "One Man's Garbage is Another's Gold," *The Globe and Mail*, April 11, 2006, B7.

22. Richard B. Schmitt and Robert Langreth, "American Home Products Agrees to Pay Up to $3.75 Billion in Diet-Drug Lawsuits," *WSJ Interactive Edition*, www.productslaw.com/diet21.html, July 11, 2001. See also Nancy Shute, "Pills Don't Come with a Seal of Approval," *U.S. News Online*, www.usnews.com/usnews/issue/970929/29fen.htm, July 11, 2001.

23. John Saunders, "Polar Plastic Plot Flops," *The Globe and Mail*, June 10, 1994, B1.

24. John Wilke, "Cases, Fines, Soar in Fraud Probes of Drug Pricing," *The Wall Street Journal*, June 7, 2005, A1, A10.

25. Jonathan Cheng, "False Ads: Chinese Consumers Awaken to a Western Problem," *The Wall Street Journal*, July 8, 2005, B9.

26. Shawn McCarthy, "Crackdown on New York's Canal Street," *The Globe and Mail*, August 30, 2004, B1, B11.

27. Jeff Sanford, "Knock-off Nation," *Canadian Business* (November 8–21, 2004): 67–71.

28. Gordon Fairclough, "Tobacco Firms Trace Fakes to North Korea," *The Wall Street Journal*, January 27, 2006, B1–B2.

29. Tim Barker, "Word-of-Mouth Advertising Grows in Influence, Concern," *Orlando Sentinel*, March 17, 2006, A1, A19.

30. Michael McCarthy and Lorrie Grant, "Sears Drops Benetton After Controversial Death Row Ads," *USA Today*, February 18, 2000, 2B.

31. Shona McKay, "Willing and Able," *Report on Business Magazine* (October 1991): 58–63.

32. "Why Business Is Hiring the Mentally Abled," *Canadian Business* (May 1991): 19.

33. J. Southerst, "In Pursuit of Drugs," *Canadian Transportation* (November 1989): 58–65.

34. G. Bylinsky, "How Companies Spy on Employees," *Fortune* (November 4, 1991): 131–140.

35. Greg Farrell, "Enron Law Firm Called Accounting Practices 'Creative,'" *USA Today*, January 16, 2002, 1B.

36. Jerald Greenberg and Robert A. Baron, *Behavior in Organizations: Understanding and Managing the Human Side of Work*, 7th ed. (Upper Saddle River, NJ: Prentice Hall, 2000), 374–375.

37. Rick Lyman, "A Tobacco Whistle-Blower's Life Is Transformed," *The New York Times*, October 15, 1999, A24.

38. Cora Daniels, "'It's a Living Hell,'" *Fortune* (April 15, 2002): 367–368.

39. Andy Pasztor and Peter Landers, "Toshiba to Pay $2B Settlement on Laptops," *ZD Net News* www.zdnet.com/zdnn/stories/news/0,4586,2385037,00.html, July 12, 2001.

40. Greg Farrell, "Enron Law Firm Called Accounting Practices 'Creative,'" *USA Today*, January 16, 2002, 1B.

41. Daniel Stoffman, "Good Behavior and the Bottom Line," *Canadian Business* (May 1991): 28–32.

42. Tom Kierans, "Charity Begins at Work," *Report on Business Magazine* (June 1990): 23.

43. Theresa Ebden and Dawn Walton, "Walkerton Recipient of New-Style Corporate Giving," *The Globe and Mail*, June 3, 2000, B1, B6.

44. Theresa Ebden and Dawn Walton, "Walkerton Recipient of New-Style

Corporate Giving," *The Globe and Mail*, June 3, 2000, B1, B6.

45. "Private Sector Comes to Rescue in Asia," *The Globe and Mail*, December 30, 2004, B5.

46. Paul Waldie, "Firms Mull Response to Disaster," *The Globe and Mail*, December 31, 2004, B1–B2.

47. Sandra Waddock and Neil Smith, "Corporate Responsibility Audits: Doing Well by Doing Good," *Sloan Management Review* (Winter 2000): 75–85.

48. Janet McFarland, "Are You Making Yourself Accountable?" *The Globe and Mail*, April 20, 2006, B12.

49. Alison Arnot, "The Triple Bottom Line," *CGA Magazine* (January–February 2004): 27–32.

Chapter 4

1. Statistics Canada, *Business Dynamics in Canada*, Catalogue no. 61-534-XIE (Ottawa: Minister of Industry, 2006).

2. P. D. Reynolds, S. M. Camp, W. D. Bygrave, E. Autio, and M. Hay, *Global Entrepreneurship Monitor: 2001 Executive Report.* (Kansas City, MO: Kauffman Center for Entrepreneurial Leadership, 2001); P. D. Reynolds, M. Hay, W. D. Bygrave, S. M. Camp, and E. Autio, *Global Entrepreneurship Monitor: 2000 Executive Report* (Kansas City, MO: Kauffman Center for Entrepreneurial Leadership, 2000).

3. Industry Canada, *Key Small Business Statistics* (Ottawa: Public Works and Government Services Canada, 2006), 24.

4. Industry Canada, Key Small Business Statistics, (Ottawa: Public Works and Government Services Canada, 2006), 3.

5. Monica Diochon, Teresa Menzies and Yvon Gasse, "Exploring the Relationship Between Start-up Activities and New Venture Emergence: A Longitudinal Study of Canadian Nascent Entrepreneurs," *International Journal of Management and Enterprise Development* 2, no. 3/4 (2005): 408–426.

6. Nancy M. Carter, William B. Gartner and Paul D. Reynolds, "Firm Founding," in *Handbook of Entrepreneurial Dynamics: The Process of Business Creation*, ed. W. B. Gartner, K. G. Shaver, N. M. Carter, and P. D. Reynolds (Thousand Oaks, CA: Sage, 2004), 311–323.

7. William D. Bygrave and C. W. Hofer, "Theorizing About Entrepreneurship," *Entrepreneurship Theory and Practice* 16, no. 2 (Winter 1991): 14; Donald Sexton and Nancy Bowman-Upton, *Entrepreneurship: Creativity and Growth*, (New York, NY: MacMillan Publishing Company, 1991), 7.

8. John Cooper, "A Pint of Success," *CMA Management* (December 1999/January 2000): 44–46.

9. Angela Dale, "Self-Employment and Entrepreneurship: Notes on Two Problematic Concepts," in *Deciphering the Enterprise Culture*, ed. Roger Burrows, London: Routledge, 1991), 45, 48; Holt 1992, 11.

10. Donald Sexton and Nancy Bowman-Upton, *Entrepreneurship: Creativity and Growth* (New York, NY: MacMillan Publishing Company, 1991), 11; Kao, 1991, 21.

11. Allan A. Gibb, "The Enterprise Culture and Education: Understanding Enterprise Education and Its Links with Small Business, Entrepreneurship and Wider Educational Goals," *International Small Business Journal* 11, no. 3 (1993): 13–34; Donald Sexton and Nancy Bowman-Upton, *Entrepreneurship: Creativity and Growth*, (New York, NY: MacMillan Publishing Company, 1991).

12. Terrence Belford, "Intrapreneurs Combine Big-biz Clout with Entrepreneurial Style," CanWest News (March 23). Retrieved June 25, 2006, from CBCA Current Events database. (Document ID: 1009719591).

13. Statistics Canada, Business Register, National Income and Expenditure Accounts 2005; Estimates of Population by Age and Sex for Canada, the Provinces and the Territories, June 2005.

14. Industry Canada, *Key Small Business Statistics* (Ottawa: Public Works and Government Services Canada, 2006), 10

15. Industry Canada, *Key Small Business Statistics* (Ottawa: Public Works and Government Services Canada, 2006), 10.

16. Industry Canada, *Key Small Business Statistics* (Ottawa: Public Works and Government Services Canada, 2006), 23.

17. William B. Gartner, Kelly G. Shaver, Nancy M. Carter, and Paul D. Reynolds, *Handbook of Entrepreneurial Dynamics* (Thousand Oaks, CA: Sage Publications, Inc., 2004), ix.

18. Statistics Canada, *Business Dynamics in Canada 2003* (Ottawa: Minister of Industry, March 2006), Catalogue no. 61-534-XIE, 6.

19. Richard Bloom, "Building a Future on Sweet Dreams," *The Globe and Mail*, October 21, 2004, B9.

20. Angela Barnes, "Doing It for Themselves," *The Globe and Mail*, October 19, 2005, E1–E2.

21. Virginia Galt, "Female Entrepreneurs to be Honoured Tonight," *The Globe and Mail*, November 22, 2005, B9.

22. Christine Carrington, "Women Entrepreneurs," *Journal of Small Business and Entrepreneurship* 19, no. 2 (2006): 83–94.

23. Murray McNeill, "Patience Pays Off for Native Owner," *The Winnipeg Free Press*, November 6, 2002, B3.

24. Sarah Kennedy, "Self-Styled Pioneer Aims to Alter Face of Fashion," *The Globe and Mail*, July 1, 2002, B12.

25. Geoff Kirbyson, "Market-Research Firm Lands Major Contract," *The Winnipeg Free Press*, July 19, 2004, D7.

26. Donald F. Kuratko and Richard M. Hodgetts, *Entrepreneurship: Theory, Process, Practice*, 7th ed. (Mason, OH: Thomson South-Western, 2007), 118–125; John A. Hornday, "Research About Living Entrepreneurs," in *Encyclopedia of Entrepreneurship*, ed. Calvin Kent, Donald Sexton, and Karl Vesper (Englewood Cliffs, NJ: Prentice-Hall, 1982), 26–27; Jeffry A. Timmons and Stephen Spinelli, *New Venture Creation: Entrepreneurship for the 21st Century* (Boston, MA: McGraw-Hill Irwin, 2007), 9.

27. Jeffry A. Timmons and Stephen Spinelli, *New Venture Creation: Entrepreneurship for the 21st Century*, 7th Edition (Boston, MA:McGraw-Hill Irwin, 2007), 19.

28. J. D. Kyle, R. Blais, R. Blatt, and A. J. Szonyi, "The Culture of the Entrepreneur: Fact or Fiction," *Journal of Small Business and Entrepreneurship* (1991): 3–14.

29. R. H. Brockhaus and Pam S. Horwitz, "The Psychology of the Entrepreneur," in *The Art and Science of Entrepreneurship*, ed. D. L Sexton and Raymond W. Smilor (Cambridge, MA: Ballinger Pub. Co., 1986); William B. Gartner, "What Are We Talking About When We Talk About Entrepreneurship?" *Journal of Business Venturing* 5, no. 1 (1990): 15–29; Allan A. Gibb, "The Enterprise Culture and Education: Understanding Enterprise Education and Its Links with Small Business, Entrepreneurship and Wider Educational Goals," *International Small Business Journal* 11, no. 3 (1993): 13–34; J. C. Mitchell, "Case and Situation Analysis," *Sociological Review* 31, no. 2 (1983): 187–211.

30. Donald Sexton and Nancy Bowman-Upton, *Entrepreneurship: Creativity and Growth* (New York, NY: MacMillan Publishing Company, 1991); Karl H. Vesper, *New Venture Strategies* (Englewood Cliffs, NJ: Prentice Hall, 1990); W. D. Bygrave and C. W. Hofer, "Theorizing About Entrepreneurship," *Entrepreneurship Theory and Practice* 16, no. 2 (Winter 1991): 14.

31. Walter Good, *Building a Dream*, (Toronto: McGraw-Hill Ryerson, 1998), 40.

32. Wayne A. Long and W. Ed McMullan. *Developing New Ventures* (San Diego: Harcourt Brace Jovanovich, 1990), 374–375.

33. "Sally Fox: Innovation in the Field," www.vreseis.com/sally_fox_story.htm, June 27, 2006.

34. Michael E. Porter, "Know Your Place," *Inc.* 13, no. 9 (September 1992): 90–93.

35. Howard H. Stevenson, H. Irving Grousbeck, Michael J. Roberts, and Amarnath Bhide, *New Business Ventures and the Entrepreneur* (Boston: Irwin McGraw-Hill, 1999), 19.

36. Howard H. Stevenson, H. Irving Grousbeck, Michael J. Roberts, and Amarnath Bhide, *New Business Ventures and the Entrepreneur* (Boston: Irwin McGraw-Hill, 1999), 21.

37. Marc J. Dollinger, *Entrepreneurship: Strategies and Resources* (Upper Saddle River, NJ: Prentice Hall, 1999), 94–101.

38. Thomas W. Zimmerer and Norman M. Scarborough, *Essentials of Entrepreneurship and Small Business Management*, 4th ed. (Upper Saddle River, NJ: Pearson Prentice Hall), 359.

39. Michael E. Porter, "Know Your Place," *Inc.* 13, no. 9 (September 1992): 90–93.

40. Karl H. Vesper, *New Venture Mechanics* (Englewood Cliffs, NJ: Prentice Hall, 1993), 105.

41. Jeffry A. Timmons, *New Venture Creation* (Boston: Irwin McGraw-Hill, 1999), 277.

42. Lisa Stephens, "With Some Shape Shifting, This Company Has Legs," *The Globe and Mail*, October 5, 2005, B10.

43. Gordon Pitts, "An Empire Looks to the Future," *The Globe and Mail*, March 26, 2005, B4.

44. George Anders, Carol Hymowitz, Joann Lublin, and Don Clark, "All in the Family," *The Wall Street Journal*, August 1, 2005, B1, B4.

45. Ronald J. Ebert, Ricky W. Griffin, and Frederick A. Starke, *Business Essentials*, 4th Canadian ed. (Toronto: Pearson Education Canada, 2006), 63.

46. Mary Agnes Welch, "When Name Is Everything," *The Winnipeg Free Press*, May 12, 2002, B1–B2.

47. Quoted in Lowell B. Howard, *Business Law* (Woodbury, NY: Barron's Woodbury Press, 1965), 332.

48. Richard Bloom, "IPO's Surge on Mood Swing," *The Globe and Mail*, February 8, 2005, B3.

49. Richard Bloom, "Cara Shareholders Vote to Take Company Private," *The Globe and Mail*, February 25, 2005, B7; and Greg Keenan, "Magna Reverses Strategy, Plans to Take Parts Subsidiaries Private," *The Globe and Mail*, October 26, 2004, B1, B10.

50. Terry Pedwell, Income Trusts Face Tough Rules," *The Winnipeg Free Press*, November 1, 2006, B7.

51. "An Overview of Available Business Structures," www.umanitoba.ca/afs/ agric_economics/MRAC/structures.html #Cooperatives, July 2, 2006.

52. Monica Diochon, Teresa Menzies, and Yvon Gasse, "Nascent Entrepreneurs' Start-up Efforts: Outcomes and Individual Influences on Sustainability," *Journal of Small Business and Entrepreneurship* (2005), 53–74.

53. Kevin Marron, "Want to Succeed? Read This," *The Globe and Mail*, October 19, 2005, E1, E5. Several excellent articles on starting and operating a small business are found in Section E, "Report on Small Business" in *The Globe and Mail*, October 19, 2005.

54. See Norman M. Scarborough and Thomas W. Zimmerer, *Effective Small Business Management: An Entrepreneurial Approach*, 7th ed. (Upper Saddle River, NJ: Prentice Hall, 2003).

Chapter 5

1. Ricky W. Griffin and Michael W. Pustay, *International Business: A Managerial Perspective*, 2nd ed. (Reading, MA: Addison-Wesley, 1999), 431–433; John J. Wild, Kenneth L. Wild, and Jerry C.Y. Han, *International Business: An Integrated Approach* (Upper Saddle River, NJ: Prentice Hall, 2000), 456–458.

2. Ricky W. Griffin and Michael W. Pustay, *International Business: A Managerial Perspective*, 2nd ed. (Reading, MA: Addison-Wesley, 1999), 44–45. See also Warren J. Keegan, *Global Marketing Management*, 6th ed. (Upper Saddle River, NJ: Prentice Hall, 1999), 42–45.

3. Trade Partners UK, "Automotive Industries Market in Mexico," www.tradepartners.gov.uk/automotive/ mexico/profile/characteristics.shtml, July 10, 2001; NAFTA Works, "Mexico Auto Sector Sees $15 Billion Investment in 5 Years," www.naftaworks.org/papers/ 2000/automex.htm, July 10, 2001.

4. David Fairlamb and Gail Edmondson, "Work in Progress," *Business Week* (January 31, 2000): 80–81+.

5. David Fairlamb and Gail Edmondson, "Work in Progress," *Business Week* (January 31, 2000): 80–81+.

6. Edmund L. Andrews, "The Metamorphosis of Germany Inc.," *The New York Times*, March 12, 2000, section 3, 1, 12.

7. Mark Landler, "Mapping Out Silicon Valley East," *The New York Times*, April 5, 1999, C1, C10; Bruce Einhorn with Cathy Yang, "Portal Combat," *Business Week* (January 17, 2000): 96–97.

8. John Wild, Kenneth Wild, and Jerry Han, *International Business*, 2nd ed. (Upper Saddle River, NJ: Prentice Hall, 2003), 239.

9. Ricky W. Griffin and Michael W. Pustay, *International Business: A Managerial Perspective*, 2nd ed. (Reading, MA: Addison-Wesley, 1999), Chapter 3. Dominick Salvatore, *International Economics*, 6th ed. (Upper Saddle River, NJ: Prentice Hall, 1998), 27–33; Karl E. Case and Ray C. Fair, *Principles of Economics*, 5th ed. (Upper Saddle River, NJ: Prentice Hall, 1999), 813–817.

10. This section is based on Michael Porter, *The Competitive Advantage of Nations* (Boston: Harvard Business School Press, 1990), Chapters 3 and 4; Warren J. Keegan, *Global Marketing Management*, 6th ed. (Upper Saddle River, NJ: Prentice Hall, 1999), 312–321; John J. Wild, Kenneth L. Wild, and Jerry C.Y. Han, *International Business: An Integrated Approach* (Upper Saddle River, NJ: Prentice Hall, 2000), 175–178.

11. Heather Scoffield, "Canada's Slipping on the World Stage, WEF Study Shows," *The Globe and Mail*, September 27, 2006, B7.

12. Madelaine Drohan, "Dependency on U.S. Leaves Canada 'Vulnerable': WTO," *The Globe and Mail*, November 20, 1996.

13. Table J2, *Bank of Canada Banking and Financial Statistics*, April 2006, S110.

14. Karl E. Case and Ray C. Fair, *Principles of Economics*, 5th ed. (Upper Saddle River, NJ: Prentice Hall, 1999), 818–821.

15. Robyn Meredith, "Dollar Makes Canada a Land of the Spree," *The New York Times*, August 1, 1999, sec. 3, 1, 11.

16. "Exports, Eh?" *Canadian Business* (January 1997): 21.

17. "China Rising: Where We're At," *The Globe and Mail*, October 29, 2005, introduction to the "Report on Business" section.

18. Shirley Won, "Small Firms Beating a Path to the Middle Kingdom," *The Globe and Mail*, August 31, 2004, B7.

19. Ray August, *International Business Law: Text, Cases, and Readings*, 3rd ed. (Upper Saddle River, NJ: Prentice Hall, 2000), 192–197.

20. Paola Hjelt, "The Fortune Global 500," *Fortune* (July 22, 2003): 144–147.

21. Celeste Mackenzie, "Rumble in the Jungle," *Canadian Business* (February 28–March 13, 2005): 57–63.

22. Warren J. Keegan, *Global Marketing Management*, 6th ed. (Upper Saddle River, NJ: Prentice Hall, 1999), 290–292; Ricky W. Griffin and Michael W. Pustay, *International Business: A Managerial Perspective*, 2nd ed. (Reading, MA: Addison-Wesley, 1999), 427–431; John J. Wild, Kenneth L. Wild, and Jerry C.Y. Han, *International Business: An Integrated Approach* (Upper Saddle River, NJ: Prentice Hall, 2000), 454–456.

23. Ricky W. Griffin and Michael W. Pustay, *International Business: A Managerial Perspective*, 2nd ed. (Reading, MA: Addison-Wesley, 1999), 431–433; John J. Wild, Kenneth L. Wild, and Jerry C.Y. Han, *International Business: An Integrated Approach* (Upper Saddle River, NJ: Prentice Hall, 2000), 456–458.

24. Shirley Won, "Small Firms Beating a Path to the Middle Kingdom," *The Globe and Mail*, August 31, 2004, B7.

25. Shirley Won, "Small Firms Beating a Path to the Middle Kingdom," *The Globe and Mail*, August 31, 2004, B7.

26. John J. Wild, Kenneth L. Wild, and Jerry C.Y. Han, *International Business: An Integrated Approach* (Upper Saddle River, NJ: Prentice Hall, 2000), Chapter 7; Ricky W. Griffin and Michael W. Pustay, *International Business: A Managerial Perspective*, 2nd ed. (Reading, MA: Addison-Wesley, 1999), 436–439.

27. Eric Beauchesne, "Foreign Control of Economy Hits 30-Year High," *The Winnipeg Free Press*, November 19, 2005, B7.

28. Eric Beauchesne, "Foreign Control of Economy Hits 30-Year High," *The Winnipeg Free Press*, November 19, 2005, B7.

29. Shawn McCarthy, "Business Sounds Alarm on Vulnerability," *The Globe and Mail*, May 8, 2000, B1, B3.

30. Steven Chase, "Canada Slaps Duties on Chinese-made Barbecues," *The Globe and Mail*, August 28, 2004, B2.

31. Peter Kennedy, "Softwood Decision Gets Mixed Reviews," *The Globe and Mail*, December 8, 2005, B6.

32. Jennifer Ditchburn, "Canada, U.S. Pen Deal to End Lumber Dispute," *The Winnipeg Free Press*, July 2, 2006, A6.

33. Paul Veira, "Emerson Warns Lumber Leaders of 'Consequences'," *Financial Post*, August 1, 2006, FP1, FP5. Steve Merti, "Lumber Exporters Taste Sting of Softwood Deal," *The Winnipeg Free Press*, September 22, 2006, B5.

34. Scott Kilman and Roger Thurow, "In Fight Against Farm Subsidies, Even Farmers Are Joining Foes," *The Wall Street Journal*, March 14, 2006, A1, A16.

35. Roger Thurow and Geoff Winestock, "How an Addiction to Sugar Subsidies Hurts Development," *The Wall Street Journal*, September 16, 2002, A1, A10.

36. "WTO Strikes Down U.S. Cotton Subsidy Appeal," *The Globe and Mail*, March 4, 2005, B10.

37. Scott Kilman and Roger Thurow, "To Soothe Anger Over Subsidies, U.S. Cotton Tries Wooing Africa," *The Wall Street Journal*, August 5, 2005, A1, A6.

38. Simon Tuck, "Farmers to WTO: If It Ain't Broke...," *The Globe and Mail*, August 9, 2004, B1–B2.

39. Anthony DePalma, "Chiquita Sues Europeans, Citing Banana Quota Losses," *The New York Times*, January 26, 2001, C5; Brian Lavery, "Trade Feud on Bananas Not as Clear as It Looks," *The New York Times*, February 7, 2001, W1; David E. Sanger, "Miffed at Europe, U.S. Raises Tariffs for Luxury Goods," *The New York Times*, March 4, 1999, A1, A5.

40. Wendy Stueck, "Mining Firms Hit Again By Chavez Threat," *The Globe and Mail*, September 23, 2005, B4; Barrie McKenna, "A Nation of Big Riches, Bigger Risks," *The Globe and Mail*, September 24, 2005, B4.

41. Konrad Yakabuski, "Quebec Courts Margarine War," *The Globe and Mail*, October 14, 1997, B1, B4.

42. Bertrand Marotte, "Ontario Calls for Dispute Panel in Quebec Margarine Battle," *The Globe and Mail*, March 26, 2002, B10.

43. Neville Nankivell, "Spilled Milk Over Provincial Trade," *National Post*, April 24, 2000, C9.

44. Gerry Stobo, "Cross-Border Mobility," *CGA Magazine* (May–June 2005): 13–16.

45. "The 2005 Transparency International Corruption Perceptions Index," www.infoplease.com/ipa/A0781359.html.

46. Geoffrey York, "Blowout in Bangladesh," *The Globe and Mail*, April 1, 2006, B4–B5.

47. Barrie McKenna, "Aluminum Producers Whispering Dirty Word," *The Globe and Mail*, March 5, 1994, B1, B5.

48. Jalil Hamid, "Coffee Rally Reignited," *The Globe and Mail*, May 22, 1997, B9.

49. Oliver Bertin, "Coffee Cartel Moves Fast on Price," *Globe and Mail*, May 20, 2000, B3.

50. Steven Chase, "Canadian Bike Makers Fear Hit from Cheap Chinese Imports," *The Globe and Mail*, September 7, 2004, B4.

51. "New Global Trade Regulator Starts Operations Tomorrow," *The Winnipeg Free Press*, December 31, 1994, A5.

52. Helene Cooper and Bhushan Bahree, "World's Best Hope for Global Trade Topples Few Barriers," *The Wall Street Journal*, December 3, 1996, A1, A8.

53. Heather Scoffield and Greg Keenan, "Canada Told to Scrap Auto Pact," *The Globe and Mail*, October 14, 1999, A1, A2.

54. Barrie McKenna, "NAFTA Dealt Blow by WTO Ruling," *The Globe and Mail*, July 12, 2003, B1, B5.

55. Michelle MacAfee, "Trade Protest Turns Violent," *The Winnipeg Free Press*, July 29, 2003, A9.

56. "European Union Expands into 10 New Countries," *Reuters*, news release, April 30, 2004.

57. Bruce Little, "Free-Trade Pact Gets Mixed Reviews," *The Globe and Mail*, June 7, 2004, B3.

58. Andrew Purvis, "Super Exporter," *Time* (April 28, 1997): 36.

59. Peter Cook, "Free Trade Free-for-All Causes Confusion," *The Globe and Mail*, December 5, 1994, B7.

Chapter 6

1. *Hoover Handbook of American Business 2006* (Austin, TX: Hoover's Business Press, 2006).

2. Stephen P. Robbins and Mary Coulter, *Management*, 7th ed. (Upper Saddle River, NJ: Prentice Hall, 2002), 202–204; Thomas L. Wheelan and J. David Hunger, *Strategic Management and Business Policy*, 7th ed. (Upper Saddle River, NJ: Prentice Hall, 2000), 107.

3. Melanie Wells, "Red Baron," *Forbes* (July 3, 2000): 150–160; Andrew Ross Sorkin, "Taking Virgin's Brand into Internet Territory," *The New York Times*, February 9, 2000, C1, C17.

4. Brent Jang, "CanJet Plans Steady Growth, One Airplane at a Time," *Globe and Mail*, April 11, 2005, B1–B2.

5. Michael Porter, *Competitive Strategy: Techniques for Analyzing Industries and Competitors* (New York: The Free Press, 1980).

6. Bertrand Marotte, "Gildan Takes T-shirt Making to the Cutting-Edge of Casual Apparel," *The Globe and Mail*, July 3, 2004, B3.

7. "Cruise-Ship Delays Leave Guests High and Dry," *The Wall Street Journal*, October 24, 1997, B1, B10; *Hoover's Handbook of American Business 2000* (Austin, TX: Hoover's Business Press, 2000), 1512–1513.

8. Richard Bloom, "How Parmalat Juggled the Struggle," *The Globe and Mail*, May 23, 2005, B3.

9. Richard Bloom, "McMakeover on Fast-Food Strip," *The Globe and Mail*, April 23, 2005, B4.

10. Peter Burrows, "The Hottest Property in the Valley?" *Business Week* (August 30, 1999): 69–74.

11. Alex Taylor III, "How a Top Boss Manages His Day," *Fortune* (June 19, 1989): 95–100.

12. Gordon Pitts, "Taking a Stand: How One CEO Gained Respect," *The Globe and Mail*, January 31, 2006, B8.

13. Virginia Galt, "Lousy People Skills Are Biggest Hurdle for Leaders," *The Globe and Mail*, October 15, 2005, B11.

14. Frank Rose, "Vivendi's High Wireless Act," *Wired*, www.wired.com/wired/archive/8.12/vivendi.html, July 18, 2001;

Mike Trigg, "Vivendi Grabs Houghton Mifflin," *The Motley Fool*, www.fool.com/news/2001/v010601.htm, July 18, 2001.

15. "The 2005 Rankings," *The Globe and Mail*, May 9, 2006, B8.

16. Kamal Fatehi, *International Management: A Cross-Cultural and Functional Perspective* (Upper Saddle River, NJ: Prentice Hall, 1996), 5–8, 153–164.

17. Andrew Wahl, "Culture Shock," *Canadian Business* (October 10–23, 2005): 115–116.

18. Ric Dolphin, "Magna Force," *Canadian Business* (May 1988).

19. Isadore Sharp, "Quality for All Seasons," *Canadian Business Review* (Spring 1990): 21–23.

20. Bruce McDougall, "The Thinking Man's Assembly Line," *Canadian Business* (November 1991): 40–44.

21. Peter Verburg, "Prepare for Takeoff," *Canadian Business* (December 25, 2000): 95–99.

22. Doug Nairne, "Mounties Riding the Vision Thing," *The Winnipeg Free Press*, September 16, 1996, A5.

23. Sinclair Stewart and Andrew Willis, "Hunkin is De-Risking the Place," *The Globe and Mail*, December 11, 2004, B4.

24. Gordon Pitts, "It Boiled Down to a Culture Clash," *The Globe and Mail*, June 11, 2005, B5.

Chapter 7

1. Robert L. Simison, "Ford Rolls Out New Model of Corporate Culture," *The Wall Street Journal*, January 13, 1999, B1, B4.

2. Joann Muller, "Ford: Why It's Worse Than You Think," *Business Week* (June 25, 2001): 80–84.

3. John A. Wagner and John R. Hollenbeck, *Management of Organizational Behavior* (Englewood Cliffs, NJ: Prentice Hall, 1992), 563–565.

4. Jay Diamond and Gerald Pintel, *Retailing*, 6th ed. (Upper Saddle River, NJ: Prentice Hall, 1996), 83–84.

5. Industry Report: Restaurant Industry," *U.S. Business Reporter*, July 19, 2001; Michael Arndt, "There's Life in the Old Bird Yet," *Business Week* (May 14, 2001): 77–78.

6. Michael E. Raynor and Joseph L. Bower, "Lead from the Center," *Harvard Business Review* (May 2001): 93–102.

7. Bruce Horovitz, "Restoring the Golden-Arch Shine," *USA Today*, June 16, 1999, 3B

8. Joann Muller, "Thinking Out of the Cereal Box," *Business Week* (January 15, 2001): 54–55.

9. Dan Morse, "A Hardware Chain Struggles to Adjust to a New Blueprint,"

The Wall Street Journal, January 27, 2003, A1, A4; Chad Terhune and Dan Morse, "Tweaking Home Depot," *The Wall Street Journal*, June 25, 2002, B1, B5; Debbie Howell, "The Super Growth Leaders—The Home Depot: Diversification Builds Bridge to the Future," *DSN Retailing Today* 40, no. 23 (December 10, 2001): 17–18.

10. Lee Hawkins, "Reversing 80 Years of History, GM is Reining in Global Fiefs," *The Wall Street Journal*, October 6, 2004, A1, A14.

11. Donna Fenn, "Redesign Work," *Inc.* (June 1999): 75–83.

12. Gary Yukl, *Leadership in Organizations*, 5th ed. (Upper Saddle River, NJ: Prentice Hall, 2002), 35–36.

13. "Multi-Tasking: Cost-Reduction Strategy at Case Corp.," *Machinery Systems Inc.*, www.machinerysystems.com/RavingFan/CaseCorp.html, July 20, 2001.

14. Donna Fenn, "The Buyers," *Inc.* (June 1996): 46–48+.

15. Nelson Wyatt, "Bell Canada Plan Creates 3 Divisions," *The Winnipeg Free Press*, May 8, 2003, B7.

16. Robert Berner and Kevin Helliker, "Heinz's Worry: 4,000 Products, Only One Star," *The Wall Street Journal*, September 17, 1999, B1, B4.

17. J. Galbraith, "Matrix Organization Designs: How to Combine Functional and Project Forms," *Business Horizons* (1971): 29–40; H.F. Kolodny, "Evolution to a Matrix Organization," *Academy of Management Review* 4 (1979): 543–553.

18. Interview with Tom Ward, operations manager for Genstar Shipyards.

19. Lawton R. Burns, "Matrix Management in Hospitals: Testing Theories of Matrix Structure and Development," *Administrative Science Quarterly* 34 (1989): 48–50.

20. Diane Brady, "Martha Inc.," *Business Week* (January 17, 2000): 62–66.

21. Gail Edmondson, "Danone Hits Its Stride," *Business Week* (February 1, 1999): 52–53.

22. Thomas A. Stewart, "See Jack. See Jack Run," *Fortune* (September 27, 1999): 124–127+.

23. Jerald Greenberg and Robert A. Baron, *Behavior in Organizations: Understanding and Managing the Human Side of Work*, 7th ed. (Upper Saddle River, NJ: Prentice Hall, 2000), 308–309.

24. Tyler Hamilton, "Welcome to the World Wide Grapevine," *The Globe and Mail*, May 6, 2000, B1, B6.

Chapter 8

1. See Angelo S. DeNisi and Ricky W. Griffin, *Human Resource Management* (Boston: Houghton Mifflin, 2001) for a complete overview.

2. Elizabeth Church, "Store Owners Struggle with Staffing," *The Globe and Mail*, November 25, 1996, B6.

3. Elizabeth Church, "Nortel Recruits to a Different Beat," *The Globe and Mail*, August 23, 2000, M1.

4. Virginia Galt, "Extreme Blue Is the Taj Mahal of Internships," *The Globe and Mail*, July 17, 2004, B9.

5. Wallace Immen, "Prospective Hires Put to the Test," *The Globe and Mail*, January 26, 2005, C1, C2.

6. Wallace Immen, "Prospective Hires Put to the Test," *The Globe and Mail*, January 26, 2005, C1, C2.

7. Katie Rook, "Curveball Job Questions: How Not to Strike Out," *The Globe and Mail*, September 3, 2005, B9.

8. Malcolm MacKillop, "An Employer's Guide to Drug Testing," *The Globe and Mail*, April 9, 1998, B13.

9. Margot Gibb-Clark, "Ruling Narrows Options for Drug Testing," *The Globe and Mail*, July 28, 1998, B11.

10. Mark Blanchard, "Pilots Enter Superjumbo Virtual Reality," *The Globe and Mail*, January 20, 2005, B8.

11. Charles Davies, "Strategy Session 1990," *Canadian Business* (January 1990): 50.

12. Scott Feschuk, "Phi Beta Cuppa," *The Globe and Mail*, March 6, 1993, B1, B4.

13. Abby Ellin, "Training Programs Often Miss the Point on the Job," *The New York Times*, March 29, 2000, C12.

14. "The 2005 Rankings," *The Globe and Mail*, May 9, 2006, B8.

15. Elizabeth Church, "Nortel Workers Pick Tailor-Made Perks," *The Globe and Mail*, December 8, 2000, B11.

16. David Roberts, "A Long Way from Cambodia," *The Globe and Mail*, July 5, 1994, B18.

17. Ken Kilpatrick and Dawn Walton, "What a Joy to Work for Dofasco," *The Globe and Mail*, February 23, 2000, B1, B8.

18. Peter Verburg, "The Man of Steel's Fed Up," *Canadian Business* (June 26/July 10, 1998): 69.

19. Virginia Galt, "Medicare Cut Seen Raising Labour Costs," *The Globe and Mail*, February 12, 2002, B10.

20. Virginia Galt, "Companies, Unions, Expect Little Relief," *The Globe and Mail*, September 15, 2004, B4.

21. Elizabeth Church, "Pension Funding Shortfall Increases Dramatically," *The Globe and Mail*, November 8, 2005, B5.

22. Elizabeth Church, "Pension Fund Shortfall Soars in First Half," *The Globe and Mail*, November 23, 2005, B1, B7.

23. Elizabeth Church, "Cost of Retiree Benefit Liabilities 'Sleeping Giant,'" *The Globe and Mail*, August 23, 2004, B4.

24. Virginia Galt, "Gift of Time Pays off for Savvy Employers," *The Globe and Mail*, December 28, 2004, B3.

25. Virginia Galt, "Gift of Time Pays off for Savvy Employers," *The Globe and Mail*, December 28, 2004, B3.

26. Erin White, "Sabbaticals: The Pause That Refreshes," *The Wall Street Journal*, August 2, 2005, B1, B4.

27. Elizabeth Church, "Workplace Daycare Takes Baby Steps Toward Acceptance, But Some Not Sold," *The Globe and Mail*, July 2, 2001, B1, B3.

28. Bruce McDougall, "The Thinking Man's Assembly Line," *Canadian Business* (November 1991): 40.

29. John Partridge, "B of M Lauded for Promoting Women's Careers," *The Globe and Mail*, January 7, 1994, B3.

30. Vivian Smith, "Breaking Down the Barriers," *The Globe and Mail*, November 17, 1992, B24.

31. Bob Cox, "Women Gaining on Men's Wages," *The Globe and Mail*, January 18, 1994, B4.

32. Marie Drolet, "The Male-Female Wage Gap," *Perspectives on Labour and Income*, the Online Edition (December, 2001), www.statcan.ca/english/freepub/75-001-XIE/01201/hi-fs_200112_01_a.html

33. Richard Blackwell and Brent Jang, "Top Court Sides with Airline Attendants," *The Globe and Mail*, January 27, 2006, B1, B6.

34. Neco Cockburn, "Clerks to Get $150 Million in Back Pay," *The Winnipeg Free Press*, October 8, 2005, A3.

35. Bruce Little, "Male Earning Power Wanes," *The Globe and Mail*, September 18, 1997, B1, B4.

36. Keith McArthur, "Criticism of Women's Fitness for Top Jobs Causes International Stir," *The Globe and Mail*, October 21, 2005, A1, A14.

37. Ted Kennedy, "Beware of Health and Safety Law: It Could Bite You," *Canadian Business* (December 1990): 19.

38. Wallace Immen, "Post-65 Workers 'Productive and Engaged,'" *The Globe and Mail*, March 18, 2005, C1.

39. Omar El Akkad, "A Woman's Work May Never Be Done," *The Globe and Mail*, March 28, 2006, B1, B4.

40. Max Boisot, *Knowledge Assets* (Oxford: Oxford University Press, 1998).

41. Thomas Stewart, "In Search of Elusive Tech Workers," *Fortune* (February 16, 1998): 171–172.

42. Matt Richtel, "Need for Computer Experts Is Making Recruiters Frantic," *The New York Times*, December 18, 1999, C1.

43. Aaron Bernstein, "When Is a Temp Not a Temp?" *Business Week* (December 7, 1998): 90–92.

Chapter 9

1. David Lipsky and Clifford Donn, *Collective Bargaining in American Industry* (Lexington, MA: Lexington Books, 1981).

2. Susan Bourette, "Organized Labour Lures Growing Number of Youth," *The Globe and Mail*, July 4, 1997, B1, B4; Susan Bourette, "Women Make Strides in Union Movement," *The Globe and Mail*, August 29, 1997, B1–B2.

3. Statistics Canada, "Perspectives in Labour and Income," Autumn 2003, 15, 3, p. 50.

4. Statistics Canada, "Perspectives in Labour and Income," Autumn 2003, 15, 3, p. 51.

5. Virginia Galt, "Worn-Out Middle Managers May Get Protection," *The Globe and Mail*, January 3, 2005, B1, B8.

6. Greg Keenan, "CAW Targets Honda, Toyota," *The Globe and Mail*, June 15, 1999, B1, B8.

7. Sarah Binder, "McDonald's Store Closes, Union Wails," *The Globe and Mail*, February 14, 1998, B23.

8. Paul McKie, "Goldcorp Workers Accept Offer, Dismantle Union," *The Winnipeg Free Press*, April 22, 2000, A6.

9. Murray McNeill, "Hotel Workers Sever Relationship with Union," *The Winnipeg Free Press*, July 22, 2005, B14.

10. Paul Waldie, "How Health Costs Hurt the Big Three," *The Globe and Mail*, March 22, 2005, B1–B2; Virginia Galt, "Companies, Unions Expect Little Relief," *The Globe and Mail*, September 15, 2004, B4.

11. Catherine McLean, "Telus, TWU Settle Labour Conflict," *The Globe and Mail*, October 11, 2005, B1.

12. Jack Mintz, "The Perils of the Picket Line," *Canadian Business* (February 27–March 12, 2006): 15.

13. Andrew Nikiforuk, "Why Safeway Struck Out," *Canadian Business* (September 1997): 27.

14. Margot Gibb-Clark, "Wounds Left by Strike Require Healing," *The Globe and Mail*, September 30, 1991, B4.

15. Martin Cash, "Tractor Plant Workers Locked Out," *The Winnipeg Free Press*, March 28, 2001, B3; Paul McKie, "A Bitter End at Versatile," *The Winnipeg Free Press*, August 14, 2001, A1–A2.

16. Jeffrey Ball, Glenn Burkins, and Gregory White, "Why Labor Unions Have Grown Reluctant to Use the S-word," *The Wall Street Journal*, December 16, 1999, A1, A8.

17. Patrick Brethour, "Telus Gets Injunction Against Union," *The Globe and Mail*, July 25, 2005, B1, B4.

18. Peter Verburg, "The Man of Steel's Fed Up," *Canadian Business* (June 26–July 10, 1998): 68.

Chapter 10

1. Michael Stern, "Empowerment Empowers Employees," *The Globe and Mail*, December 9, 1991, B4.

2. For a detailed treatment of this entire subject area, see Gregory Moorhead and Ricky W. Griffin, *Organizational Behavior*, 6th ed. (Boston: Houghton Mifflin, 2001).

3. Virginia Galt, "Keeping Key Workers a Tougher Task," *The Globe and Mail*, October 25, 2005, B6.

4. Frederick W. Taylor, *Principles of Scientific Management* (New York: Harper and Brothers, 1911).

5. Douglas McGregor, *The Human Side of Enterprise* (New York: McGraw-Hill, 1960).

6. Abraham Maslow, "A Theory of Human Motivation," *Psychological Review* (July 1943): 370–396.

7. Frederick Herzberg, Bernard Mausner, and Barbara Bloch Snydeman, *The Motivation to Work* (New York: Wiley, 1959).

8. Victor Vroom, *Work and Motivation* (New York: Wiley, 1964); Craig Pinder, *Work Motivation* (Glenview, IL: Scott, Foresman, 1984).

9. Edwin Locke, "Toward a Theory of Task Performance and Incentives," *Organizational Behavior and Human Performance* 3 (1968): 157–189.

10. Andy Holloway, "How the Game Is Played," *Canadian Business* (April 2, 2001): 26–35.

11. Interviews with Sterling McLeod and Wayne Walker, senior vice-presidents of sales for Investors Group Financial Services.

12. Wilfred List, "On the Road to Profit," *The Globe and Mail*, July 10, 1991, B1, B3.

13. Virginia Galt, "Change Is a Good Thing When Everyone Is Involved," *The Globe and Mail*, June 25, 2005, B11.

14. Margot Gibb-Clark, "BC Telecom Managers Get an Overhaul," *The Globe and Mail*, July 23, 1994, B3;

15. Brent Jang, "High-Flying WestJet Morale Gets Put to the Test," *The Globe and Mail*, November 25, 2005, B3.

16. Gregory Moorhead and Ricky W. Griffin, *Organizational Behavior*, 6th ed. (Boston: Houghton Mifflin, 2001), Chapter 7.

17. Gregory Moorhead and Ricky W. Griffin, *Organizational Behavior*, 6th ed. (Boston: Houghton Mifflin, 2001), Chapter 7.

18. Gregory Moorhead and Ricky W. Griffin, *Organizational Behavior*, 6th ed.

(Boston: Houghton Mifflin, 2001), Chapter 7.

19. Virginia Galt, "Flex-Time Helps to Attract, Keep Best Workers," *The Winnipeg Free Press*, August 12, 2003, D7.

20. Robert White, "Changing Needs of Work and Family: A Union Response," *Canadian Business Review* (Autumn 1989): 31–33.

21. Margot Gibb-Clark, "Banks' Short Work Week Improves Service," *The Globe and Mail*, September 23, 1991, B4.

22. "Telecommuting Causing Work Condition Worries," *The Globe and Mail*, January 7, 2000, B8.

23. Margot Gibb-Clark, "What Shaped the Workplace in 1998," *The Globe and Mail*, December 29, 1998, B6.

24. Margot Gibb-Clark, "Satellite Office a Hit with Staff," *The Globe and Mail*, November 18, 1991, B4.

25. "Slaves of the New Economy," *Canadian Business* (April 1996): 86–92.

26. Dawn Walton, "Survey Focuses on Job Sharing," *The Globe and Mail*, June 10, 1997, B4.

27. Andy Holloway, "How the Game Is Played," *Canadian Business* (April 2, 2001): 26–35.

28. David Dorsey, "Andy Pearson Finds Love," *Fast Company* (August 2001): 78–86.

29. Gordon Pitts, "Taking a Stand: How One CEO Gained Respect," *The Globe and Mail*, January 31, 2006, B8.

30. Jason Kirby, "In the Vault," *Canadian Business* (March 1–14, 2004): 69.

31. Jason Kirby, "In the Vault," *Canadian Business* (March 1–14, 2004): 69.

32. Madelaine Drohan, "What Makes a Canadian Manager?" *The Globe and Mail*, February 25, 1997, B18.

33. Natalie Southworth, "Canadian Team Builders Turn U.S. Heads," *The Globe and Mail*, August 28, 2000, B8.

34. Zena Olijnyk, Mark Brown, Andy Holloway, Calvin Leung, Alex Mlynek, Erin Pooley, Jeff Sanford, Andrew Wahl, and Thomas Watson, "Canada's Global Leaders," *Canadian Business* (March 28–April 10, 2005): 37–43.

35. Gregory Moorhead and Ricky W. Griffin, *Organizational Behavior*, 6th ed. (Boston: Houghton Mifflin, 2001), Chapters 13 and 14.

36. Gregory Moorhead and Ricky W. Griffin, *Organizational Behavior*, 6th ed. (Boston: Houghton Mifflin, 2001), Chapters 13 and 14.

37. "A Better Workplace," *Time* (April 17, 2000): 87.

38. Stephanie Armour, "More Dads Tap into Family Benefits at Work," *USA Today*, June 16, 2000, 1B.

39. Employee-Friendly Workplaces Raises Issues for Unions," *The Globe and Mail*, December 27, 2000, B1, B4.

Chapter 11

1. Andrew Nikiforuk, "Pure Profit," *Canadian Business* (April 3, 2000): 70–76.

2. Eryn Brown, "America's Most Admired Companies," *Fortune* (March 1, 1999): 68, 70–73; www.walmartstores.com, April 24, 2000.

3. Judy Strauss and Raymond Frost, *Marketing on the Internet* (Upper Saddle River, NJ: Prentice Hall, 1999), 266–271.

4. Intel Corp., "Digital and Intel Complete Sale of Digital Semi-Conductor Manufacturing Operations," news release, May 18, 1998.

5. Mark Lander, "Slovakia No Longer a Laggard in Automaking," *nytimes.com*, April 13, 2004, www.nytimes.com/2004/04/13/business/worldbusiness.

6. Neal Boudette, "Chrysler Gains Edge by Giving New Flexibility to Its Factories," *The Wall Street Journal*, April 11, 2006, A1, A15.

7. Greg Keenan, "Ford's New Maxim: Flex Manufacturing," *The Globe and Mail*, May 10, 2006, B3.

8. Gordon Pitts, "Industrial Evolution," *The Globe and Mail*, May 29, 2006, B1, B4.

9. Don Marshall, "Time for Just in Time," *P&IM Review* (June 1991): 20–22. See also Gregg Stocker, "Quality Function Deployment: Listening to the Voice of the Customer," *APICS: The Performance Advantage* (September 1991): 44–48.

10. Lee J. Krajewski and Larry P. Ritzman, *Operations Management: Strategy and Analysis*, 6th ed. (Upper Saddle River, NJ: Prentice Hall, 2002), 153–154, 828–829; Robert S. Russell and Bernard W. Taylor III, *Operations Management*, 4th ed. (Upper Saddle River, NJ: Prentice Hall, 2003), 221–222, 593–595.

11. Robert S. Russell and Bernard W. Taylor III, *Operations Management*, 4th ed. (Upper Saddle River, NJ: Prentice Hall, 2003), 222–224.

12. Lee J. Krajewski and Larry P. Ritzman, *Operations Management: Strategy and Analysis*, 6th ed. (Upper Saddle River, NJ: Prentice Hall, 2002), 595.

13. Tom Murphy, "E Cyber Squeeze: The Pressure Is On," *Ward's Auto World* (December 2000): 44–47.

14. "The Disney Institute," www.disney.go.com/DisneyWorld/DisneyInstitute/ProfessionalPrograms/DisneyDifference/index.html, April 25, 2000.

15. Bruce Little, "Stock Answers," *The Globe and Mail*, June 6, 1995, B12.

16. Bruce McDougall, "The Thinking Man's Assembly Line," *Canadian Business* (November 1991): 40.

17. Alan Freeman, "Why Firms Avoid Taking Inventory," *The Globe and Mail*, December 12, 1994, B1, B4.

18. Clare Ansberry, "A New Hazard for Recovery: Last-Minute Pace of Orders," *The Wall Street Journal*, June 25, 2002, A1, A12.

Chapter 12

1. Gordon Pitts, "Message for Manufacturers: Go Big, Don't Stay at Home," *The Globe and Mail*, December 6, 2005, B1, B7.

2. United States Department of Labor, "International Comparisons of Manufacturing Productivity and Unit Labor Cost Trends, 2005," news release, September 26, 2006, www.bls.gov/news.release/prod4.nr0.htm.

3. Bart VanArk and Robert McGuckin, "International Comparisons of Labor Productivity and per Capita Income," *Monthly Labor Review* (Washington, DC: U.S. Department of Labor, July 1999), 33–41.

4. Harvey Enchin, "Canada Urged to Stop Living Off Fat of the Land," *The Globe and Mail*, October 25, 1991, B1, B6.

5. Jon Hilsenrath, "Behind Surging Productivity: The Service Sector Delivers," *The Wall Street Journal*, November 7, 2003, A1, A8.

6. John Sheridan, "More Steel Productivity Gains Ahead?" *Industry Week* (September 15, 1997): 86–96.

7. Peter Kennedy, "Canfor Goes High Teach to Cut Costs," *The Globe and Mail*, July 29, 2000, 3.

8. Lee J. Krajewski and Larry P. Ritzman, *Operations Management: Strategy and Analysis*, 5th ed. (Reading, MA: Addison-Wesley, 1999), 229–230.

9. Bruce McDougall, "The Thinking Man's Assembly Line," *Canadian Business* (November 1991): 40.

10. Thomas Foster Jr., *Managing Quality: An Integrative Approach* (Upper Saddle River, NJ: Prentice Hall, 2001), 22–23.

11. Joel Kurtzman, "Is Your Company Off Course? Now You Can Find Out Why," *Fortune* (February 17, 1997): 133.

12. Ted Wakefield, "No Pain, No Gain," *Canadian Business* (January 1993): 50–54.

13. Tootsie Roll Industries Inc. *Annual Report, 2003* (Chicago, 2004), 1.

14. Thomas Foster Jr., *Managing Quality: An Integrative Approach* (Upper Saddle River, NJ: Prentice Hall, 2001), 325–339.

15. Thomas Foster Jr., *Managing Quality: An Integrative Approach* (Upper Saddle River, NJ: Prentice Hall, 2001), 325–329.

16. James Evans and James Dean Jr., *Total Quality: Management, Organization, and Strategy*, 2nd ed. (Cincinnati, OH: South-Western, 2000), 230.

17. Margot Gibb-Clark, "Hospital Managers Gain Tool to Compare Notes," *The Globe and Mail*, September 9, 1996, B9

18. "Customer Service You Can Taste," *Canadian Business* (July 1991): 19–20.

19. Del Jones, "Baldrige Award Honors Record 7 Quality Winners, *USA Today*, November 26, 2003, 6B.

20. "ISO 9001 Registration Helps Improve Airport Security," *Quality Digest*, www.qualitydigest.com/currentmag/html/news.html, June 9, 2002; "A Call for Consistency in the Quality of Airline Security Screening Services," *American Society for Quality*, www.asq.org/news/interest/airportsecurity.html, December 18, 2002.

21. Roberta S. Russell and Bernard W. Taylor III, *Operations Management*, 4th ed. (Upper Saddle River, NJ: Prentice Hall, 2003), 658–662; and Thomas Foster Jr., *Managing Quality: An Integrative Approach* (Upper Saddle River, NJ: Prentice Hall, 2001), 85–86.

22. Roberta S. Russell and Bernard W. Taylor III, *Operations Management*, 4th ed. (Upper Saddle River, NJ: Prentice Hall, 2003), 137–140.

23. Sunil Chopra and Peter Meindl, *Supply Chain Management: Strategy, Planning, and Operation*, 6th ed. (Upper Saddle River, NJ: Prentice Hall, 2001), 3–6; Lee J. Krajewski and Larry P. Ritzman, *Operations Management: Strategy and Analysis*, 5th ed. (Reading, MA: Addison-Wesley, 1999), Chapter 11; Roberta S. Russell and Bernard W. Taylor III, *Operations Management*, 4th ed. (Upper Saddle River, NJ: Prentice Hall, 2003), Chapter 7; and Thomas Foster Jr., *Managing Quality: An Integrative Approach* (Upper Saddle River, NJ: Prentice Hall, 2001), Chapter 9.

24. Sunil Chopra and Peter Meindl, *Supply Chain Management: Strategy, Planning, and Operation*, 6th ed. (Upper Saddle River, NJ: Prentice Hall, 2001), Chapter 20.

25. Sunil Chopra and Peter Meindl, *Supply Chain Management: Strategy, Planning, and Operation*, 6th ed. (Upper Saddle River, NJ: Prentice Hall, 2001), 348–349.

26. Catherine Greenman, "An Old Craft Learns New Tricks," *The New York Times*, June 10, 1999, G1, G7.

27. Gillian Babicz, "Six Sigma Software Generates Improvements," *Quality* (April 2002): 28.

28. Terrence Belford, "Real Estate Heaven Is No Mistake," *The Globe and Mail*, March 22, 2005, B9.

29. Evaluate the Value of Training," *Quality* (April 2002): 48.

30. Leonard L. Berry, A. Parasuraman, and Valarie A. Zeithaml, "Improving Service Quality in America: Lessons Learned," *Academy of Management Executive* 8, no. 2 (1994): 32–45.

Chapter 13

1. Kenneth C. Laudon and Jane P. Laudon, *Management Information Systems: Managing the Digital Firm*, 7th ed. (Upper Saddle River, NJ: Prentice Hall, 2002), 7–11.

2. Kenneth C. Laudon and Jane P. Laudon, *Essentials of Management Information Systems*, 3rd ed. (Upper Saddle River, NJ: Prentice Hall, 1999), 267.

3. Kenneth C. Laudon and Jane P. Laudon, *Essentials of Management Information Systems*, 3rd ed. (Upper Saddle River, NJ: Prentice Hall, 1999), 273.

4. Mary J. Cronin, "Ford's Intranet Success," *Fortune* (March 30, 1998): 158.

5. Lee J. Krajewski and Larry P. Ritzman, *Operations Management: Strategy and Analysis*, 6th ed. (Upper Saddle River, NJ: Prentice Hall, 2002), 106.

6. Lee J. Krajewski and Larry P. Ritzman, *Operations Management: Strategy and Analysis*, 6th ed. (Upper Saddle River, NJ: Prentice Hall, 2002), 232–233.

7. Joshua Macht, "The Ultimate Head Trip," *Inc. Technology* 3 (1997): 77.

8. Gene Bylinsky, "Industry's Amazing Instant Prototypes," *Fortune* (January 12, 1998): 120(B-D).

9. Kenneth C. Laudon and Jane P. Laudon, *Essentials of Management Information Systems*, 3rd ed. (Upper Saddle River, NJ: Prentice Hall, 1999), 383–391.

10. Geoffrey Rowan, "Unique Software Thinks Like a Human," *The Globe and Mail*, December 31, 1996, B1, B4.

11. Kenneth C. Laudon and Jane P. Laudon, *Essentials of Management Information Systems*, 3rd ed. (Upper Saddle River, NJ: Prentice Hall, 1999), 383–388; E. Wainwright Martin et al., *Managing Information Technology: What Managers Need to Know*, 3rd ed. (Upper Saddle River, NJ: Prentice Hall, 1999), 225–227.

12. Emily Smith, "Turning an Expert's Skills into Computer Software," *Business Week* (October 7, 1985): 104–107.

13. Heather Green et al., "It's Time for Rules in Wonderland," *Business Week* (February 21, 2000): 82-88+; Ira Sager et al., "Cyber Crime," *Business Week* (February 21, 2000): 36-42; Ira Sager, Neil Gross, and John Carey, "Locking Out the Hackers," *Business Week* (February 28, 2000): 32–34.

14. Larry Long and Nancy Long, *Computers: Information Technology in Perspective*, 9th ed. (Upper Saddle River, NJ: Prentice Hall, 2002), 52–54.

15. Simon Avery, "Hunting Season for Computer Attackers," *The Globe and Mail*, July 6, 2005, B1, B4.

16. Ann Carrns, "Trial Highlights Vulnerability of Databases," *The Wall Street Journal*, August 3, 2005, B1, B3.

17. Mark Blancahrd, "A Day in the Life of Superhighway Cops," *The Globe and Mail*, October 7, 2004, B15.

18. Larry Long and Nancy Long, *Computers: Information Technology in Perspective*, 9th ed. (Upper Saddle River, NJ: Prentice Hall, 2002), 101–106.

19. Kenneth C. Laudon and Jane P. Laudon, *Management Information Systems: Managing the Digital Firm*, 7th ed. (Upper Saddle River, NJ: Prentice Hall, 2002), 237–244.

20. "Canada's Software Piracy Rate Decreases," *The Winnipeg Free Press*, May 24, 2006, B7.

21. Nathalie Raffray, "Portal Power," *Communications International* (August 2001), 30–35; and David Maloney, "The Newest Better Idea at Ford," *Modern Materials Handling* (June 2000), 34–39. Kenneth C. Laudon and Jane P. Laudon, *Management Information Systems: Managing the Digital Firm*, 7th ed. (Upper Saddle River, NJ: Prentice Hall, 2002), 239–244.

22. Nathalie Raffray, "Portal Power," *Communications International* (August 2001): 30–35; David Maloney, "The Newest Better Idea at Ford," *Modern Materials Handling* (June 2000): 34–39; Kenneth C. Laudon and Jane P. Laudon, *Management Information Systems: Managing the Digital Firm*, 7th ed. (Upper Saddle River, NJ: Prentice Hall, 2002), 239–244.

Chapter 14

1. Ronald Hilton, *Managerial Accounting*, 2nd ed. (New York: McGraw-Hill, 1994), 7.

2. Brian Christmas, "Buttoned Down and In Demand," *The Globe and Mail*, April 19, 2006, B13.

3. Brian Christmas, "Buttoned Down and in Demand," *The Globe and Mail*, April 19, 2006, B13.

4. Brian Christmas, "Buttoned Down and in Demand," *The Globe and Mail*, April 19, 2006, B13.

5. Elizabeth MacDonald, "Accounting Sleuths Ferret Hidden Assets," *The Wall Street Journal*, December 18, 1996, B1–B2.

6. Philip Mathias, "Non-Profits Fight Move to GAAP Accounting," *The Financial Post*, March 5, 1994, 15.

7. Charles T. Horngren, Walter T. Harrison Jr., and Linda Smith Bamber, *Accounting*, 5th ed. (Upper Saddle River, NJ: Prentice Hall, 2002), 11–12, 39–41.

8. Charles T. Horngren, Walter T. Harrison Jr., and Linda Smith Bamber, *Accounting*, 5th ed. (Upper Saddle River, NJ: Prentice Hall, 2002), 41–56.

9. Charles T. Horngren, Walter T. Harrison Jr., and Linda Smith Bamber, *Accounting*, 5th ed. (Upper Saddle River, NJ: Prentice Hall, 2002), 17–20.

10. Ronald Hilton, *Managerial Accounting*, 2nd ed. (New York: McGraw-Hill, 1994), 402–403.

11. Billie Cunningham, Loren Nikolai, and John Bazley, *Accounting: Information for Business Decisions* (Fort Worth, TX: Dryden, 2000), 133–134.

12. Charles T. Horngren, Walter T. Harrison Jr., and Linda Smith Bamber, *Accounting*, 4th ed. (Upper Saddle River, NJ: Prentice Hall, 1999), 562–563; Arthur J. Keown et al., *The Foundations of Finance: The Logic and Practice of Financial Management*, 2nd ed. (Upper Saddle River, NJ: Prentice Hall, 1998), 89–95.

13. Charles T. Horngren, Walter T. Harrison Jr., and Linda Smith Bamber, *Accounting*, 4th ed. (Upper Saddle River, NJ: Prentice Hall, 1999), 201–202.

14. Frederick D. S. Choi, Carol Ann Frost, and Gary K. Meek, *International Accounting*, 4th ed. (Upper Saddle River: Prentice Hall, 2002), 267–279.

Chapter 15

1. American Marketing Association, "Marketing Services Guide," www.ama.org/about/ama/markdef.asp, August 23, 2001.

2. Philip Kotler, *Marketing Management*, 11th ed. (Upper Saddle River, NJ: Prentice Hall, 2003), 76–78.

3. Warren J. Keegan and Mark C. Green, *Global Marketing*, 3rd ed. (Upper Saddle River, NJ: Prentice Hall, 2003), 8–15.

4. Philip Kotler and Peggy Cunningham, *Marketing Management* (Toronto: Prentice-Hall, 2004), 18.

5. Chris Isadore, "Sweet Spot: Luxury SUV's are Hot," *CNN/Money*, January 7, 2004, http://cnnmoney.com.

6. Aparita Bhandari, "Ethnic Marketing—It's More Than Skin Deep," *The Globe and Mail*, September 7, 2005, B3.

7. Lauren Goldstein, "Dressing Up an Old Brand," *Fortune* (November 9, 1998): 154–156.

8. Jane Perlez, "Joy of Debts: Eastern Europe on Credit Fling," *The New York Times*, May 30, 1998, A3.

9. Philip Kotler, *Marketing Management*, 11th ed. (Upper Saddle River, NJ: Prentice Hall, 2003), 292–294.

10. Marina Strauss, "The Secret to Gaining Success in Quebec," *The Globe and Mail*, September 27, 2005, B4.

11. John Morton, "How to Spot the Really Important Prospects," *Business Marketing* (January 1990): 62–67.

12. Barrie McKenna, "Coke Plans Major Revamp to Put Fizz Back in Its Shares," *The Globe and Mail*, November 12, 2004, B1, B6.

13. Paul Sutter, "How to Succeed in Bubble Gum Without Really Trying," *Canadian Business* (January 1992): 48–50.

14. Alvin C. Burns and Ronald F. Bush, *Marketing Research*, 3rd ed. (Upper Saddle River, NJ: Prentice Hall, 2000), 70–84.

15. Marina Strauss, "First You Have to Get Their Attention," *The Globe and Mail*, July 12, 1991, B1.

16. Emily Nelson, "P&G Checks Out Real Life," *The Wall Street Journal*, May 17, 2001, B1, B4.

17. Joseph Pereira, "Spying on the Sales Floor," *The Wall Street Journal*, December 21, 2004, B1, B4.

18. Alvin C. Burns and Ronald F. Bush, *Marketing Research*, 3rd ed. (Upper Saddle River, NJ: Prentice Hall, 2000), Chapter 9.

19. Marina Strauss, "Mining Customer Feedback, Firms Go Undercover and Online," *The Globe and Mail*, May 13, 2004, B1, B25.

20. Deborah Ball, Sarah Ellison, and Janet Adamy, "Probing Shoppers' Psyche," *The Wall Street Journal*, October 28, 2004, B1, B8.

21. Oliver Bertin, "John Deere Reaps the Fruits of Its Labors," *The Globe and Mail*, September 2, 1991, B1, B3.

22. Alvin C. Burns and Ronald F. Bush, *Marketing Research*, 3rd ed. (Upper Saddle River, NJ: Prentice Hall, 2000), 140–148.

23. Kenneth C. Laudon and Jane P. Laudon, *Management Information Systems: Managing the Digital Firm*, 7th ed. (Upper Saddle River, NJ: Prentice Hall, 2002), 221–222.

24. Kenneth C. Laudon and Jane P. Laudon, *Management Information Systems: Managing the Digital Firm*, 7th ed. (Upper Saddle River, NJ: Prentice Hall, 2002), 222–224.

25. Paul S. Foote and Malini Krishnamurthi, "Forecasting Using Data Warehousing Model: Wal-Mart's Experience," *The Journal of Business Forecasting Methods & Systems* (Fall 2001): 13–17.

26. Robyn Greenspan, "The Web as a Way of Life," www.cyberatlas.com, May 21, 2002.

Chapter 16

1. Dan Verton, "Oracle Scraps Unpopular Database Pricing Model: Oracle Faces Challenges in the Marketplace," *Computerworld* (June 18, 2001): 6, 8.

2. Philip Kotler, *Marketing Management*, 11th ed. (Upper Saddle River, NJ: Prentice Hall, 2003), Chapter 3; Roger J. Best, *Market-Based Management: Strategies for Growing Customer Value and Profitability*, 2nd ed. (Upper Saddle River, NJ: Prentice Hall, 2000), 87–100.

3. Simon Tuck, "Bombardier to Gamble on New Jet," *The Globe and Mail*, March 16, 2005, A1–A2; Bertrand Marotte, "Bombardier Shelves C Series," *The Globe and Mail*, February 1, 2006, B1, B6.

4. Richard Blackwell, "High-Definition TV a Bit Fuzzy, Poll Finds," *The Globe and Mail*, May 2, 2005, B4.

5. James C. Anderson and James A. Narus, *Business Market Management: Understanding, Creating, and Delivering Value* (Upper Saddle River, NJ: Prentice Hall, 1999), 203–206.

6. Philip Kotler, *Marketing Management*, 11th ed. (Upper Saddle River, NJ: Prentice Hall, 2003), 328–339.

7. Keith McArthur, "Big Mac, Coke, Marlboro and...China Mobile?" *The Globe and Mail*, April 4, 2006, B1, B9.

8. Keith McArthur, "How to Survive an Identity Crisis," *The Globe and Mail*, November 14, 2005, B1, B11.

9. Caroline Alphonso, "A Great Place to Do Business—Just No Beacon for Culture," *The Globe and Mail*, August 2, 2005, B1, B9.

10. John Gray, "What's in a Brand?" *Canadian Business* (December 26, 2005–January 15, 2006): 73–74.

11. Gordon Pitts, "New Irving Generation Broadens Horizons," *The Globe and Mail*, January 18, 2003, B1, B4.

12. Keith McArthur, "Tim Hortons Scores Winning Goal as a Brand," *The Globe and Mail*, June 6, 2005, B3.

13. Lori Mitchell, "Branding Equals Smart E-Business," *InfoWorld*, www.InfoWorld.com/articles/tc/xml/00/12/18/001218tcbranding.xml, December 15, 2000; Robyn Greenspan, "Brand Opening," *ECommerce-Guide*, http://ecommerce.internet.com/news/insights/ectips/article/0,,6311_557131,00.html, January 10, 2001; Kris Wadia, "Top 10 Myths of E-Branding," *Business-Minds*, www.business-minds.com/article.asp?item=68, May 17, 2001.

14. Eloise Coupey, *Marketing and the Internet* (Upper Saddle River, NJ: Prentice Hall, 2001), 174–179.

15. John Frook, "Cisco Scores with Its Latest Generation of Empowering Tools," *B to B* (August 20, 2001): 20.

16. Cyndee Miller, "Little Relief Seen for New Product Failure Rate," *Marketing News* (June 21, 1993): 1; Nancy J. Kim,

"Back to the Drawing Board," *The Bergen [New Jersey] Record*, December 4, 1994, B1, B4.

17. Brian Milner, "Canada's Franklin the Turtle Heads South," *The Globe and Mail*, February 14, 2000, B1, B10.

18. Marina Strauss, "Shoppers Sees Gold in Private Labels," *The Globe and Mail*, January 3, 2005, B1–B2.

19. Richard Bloom, "Taking on the World, One Jar at a Time," *The Globe and Mail*, July 4, 2005, B3.

20. Keith McArthur, "Why Molson Is Crying in Its Beer," *The Globe and Mail*, July 10, 2004, B4.

21. Marina Strauss, "Consumers Less Trusting of Brands," *The Globe and Mail*, February 13, 2003, B3.

22. David Square, "Mouse Pad Gets Oodles of Nibbles," *The Winnipeg Free Press*, July 26, 1997, B10.

23. Paul Waldie, "How RIM's Big Deal Was Done," *The Globe and Mail*, March 6, 2006, B1, B14.

24. Simon Avery, "RIM Faces New U.S. Fight Over Patents," *The Globe and Mail*, May 2, 2006, B3.

25. Deborah Ball, "The Perils of Packaging: Nestle Aims for Easier Openings," *The Wall Street Journal*, November 17, 2005, B1, B5.

26. Keith McArthur, "Oh? Canada? Ads Beg to Differ," *The Globe and Mail*, July 1, 2004, B1, B18.

27. William Pride and O.C. Ferrell, *Marketing*, 5th ed. (Boston: Houghton Mifflin, 1987).

28. Robert Berner, "The Rolls-Royce of Leather Jackets Is Hard to Come By," *The Wall Street Journal*, November 22, 1996, A1, A10.

29. Kenneth E. Clow and Donald Baack, *Integrated Advertising, Promotion, and Marketing Communications* (Upper Saddle River, NJ: Prentice Hall, 2002), Chapter 5.

30. John Heinzl, "Buckley Wants U.S. to Swallow Its Bad Taste," *The Globe and Mail*, November 11, 1999, B1, B12.

31. Marina Strauss, "Towel War Turns to Name-Naming," *The Globe and Mail*, December 5, 1995, B1, B10.

32. Andrew Wahl, "Red All Over," *Canadian Business* (February 13–26, 2006): 53–54.

33. Allan Kreda, "Advertisers Lured by Super Bowl's Glitz, Huge Ratings," *The Globe and Mail*, December 30, 2004, B3.

34. Marina Strauss, "This Billboard Wants to Pass You By," *The Globe and Mail*, February 27, 1992, B4.

35. Erin White, "Word of Mouth Makes Nike Slip-On Sneakers Take Off," *The Globe and Mail*, June 7, 2001, B1, B4.

36. P. Kotler, G. Armstrong, and P. Cunningham, *Principles of Marketing*, 6th Canadian ed., (Toronto: Pearson, 2005), 88.

37. Andrew Wahl, "Red All Over," *Canadian Business* (February 13–26, 2006): 53–54.

38. P. Kotler, G. Armstrong, and P. Cunningham, *Principles of Marketing*, 6th Canadian ed., (Toronto: Pearson, 2005), 89–91.

39. Simon Tuck, "Security Rated Top On-Line Fear," *The Globe and Mail*, July 5, 1999, B5.

40. James Hagerty and Dennis Berman, "New Battleground in Web Privacy War: Ads that Snoop," *The Wall Street Journal*, August 27, 2003, A1, A8.

41. Stuart Elliott, "Real or Virtual? You Call It," *The New York Times*, October 1, 1999, C1, C6.

42. William Wells, John Burnett, and Sandra Moriarty, *Advertising: Principles and Practice*, 5th ed. (Upper Saddle River, NJ: Prentice Hall, 2000), 77–83.

43. Ann Gibbon, "Ad Group Tries to Demystify Quebec," *The Globe and Mail*, November 25, 1993, B6.

44. "Regulators Wary of Ads Rapping Rivals," *The Globe and Mail*, May 23, 1991, B4.

45. Ira Teinowitz and Cara B. Dipasquale, "Direct Marketers Take Issue with Proposed FTC Rules," *Advertising Age* (January 28, 2002): 3, 29; Larry Neilson, "Look Out for Telemarketing Speed Bumps," *National Underwriter* (September 17, 2001): 12–14.

46. John Heinzl, "Beer Firms Rethink Giveaways," *The Globe and Mail*, March 3, 2003, B1, B5.

47. Joanna Slater, "Coke, Pepsi Fight Product-Contamination Charges in India," *The Wall Street Journal*, August 15, 2003, B1, B5.

48. Warren J. Keegan, *Global Marketing Management*, 7th ed. (Upper Saddle River, NJ: Prentice Hall, 2002), Chapter 14.

49. Norman M. Scarborough and Thomas W. Zimmerer, *Effective Small Business Management: An Entrepreneurial Approach*, 6th ed. (Upper Saddle River, NJ: Prentice Hall, 2000), Chapter 11.

Chapter 17

1. Constance L. Hays, "Coke Tests Weather-Linked Pricing," *The Globe and Mail*, October 29, 1999, B11.

2. Stefan Fatsis, "The Barry Bonds Tax: Teams Raise Prices for Good Games," *The Wall Street Journal*, December 3, 2002, D1, D8.

3. Stephen Kindel, "Tortoise Gains on Hare," *Financial World* (February 23, 1988): 18–20.

4. Ethan Smith, "Universal Slashes CD Prices in Bid to Revive Music Industry," *The Wall Street Journal*, September 4, 2003, B1, B8.

5. Chet Zelasko, "Acesulfame-K," *Better Life Institute*, www.blionline.com/HDB/Acesulfame-K.htm, May 17, 2001.

6. Stewart A. Washburn, "Establishing Strategy and Determining Cost in the Pricing Decision," *Business Marketing* (July 1985): 64–78.

7. Marina Strauss, "Why Everyday Low Prices Failed Zellers," *The Globe and Mail*, March 22, 2005, B8.

8. Judy Strauss and Raymond Frost, *E-Marketing*, 2nd ed. (Upper Saddle River, NJ: Prentice Hall, 2001), 166–167; Eloise Coupey, *Marketing and the Internet* (Upper Saddle River, NJ: Prentice Hall, 2001), 281–283.

9. Marina Strauss, "Taking 'e' Out of E-commerce: Meet the eBay Middleman," *The Globe and Mail*, October 6, 2004, B1, B19.

10. Ahmad Diba, "An Old-Line Agency Finds an Online Niche," *Fortune* (April 3, 2000): 258.

11. Dell Annual Report: *FY2001 Year in Review*, www.dell.com, April 22, 2002.; Qiao Song, "Legend Outlines Role in China's Wireless Future," *ebn* (March 25, 2002): 3; Faith Hung, "Legend Looks to Defend Its Turf—WTO Entry Will Force China's Top PC Maker to Fend Off Unrestricted Rivals," *ebn* (December 17, 2001): 44; Neel Chowdhury, "Dell Cracks China," *Fortune* (June 21, 1999): 120–124.

12. Keith McArthur, "Para Paints' Bold Stroke," *The Globe and Mail*, October 18, 1999, M1.

13. Dale M. Lewison, *Retailing*, 5th ed. (New York: Macmillan, 1994), 454; Louis Stern and Adel I. El-Ansary, *Marketing Channels*, 4th ed. (Englewood Cliffs, NJ: Prentice Hall, 1992), 129–130.

14. *Expedia.com*, www.expedia.com, July 8, 2002.

15. Ann Bednarz, "Acquisitions Tighten Supply-Chain Market," *Network World* (February 9, 2004): 21–22.

16. Direct Selling Association, May 4, 2004, www.dsa.org.

17. American Teleservices Association, May 4, 2004, www.ataconnect.org.

18. Marina Strauss, "E-tailing in Age of Refinement," *The Globe and Mail*, August 3, 2005, B6.

19. Zena Olijnyk, "Dot-Com Wonder Boys, *Canadian Business* (April 14, 2003): 30–36.

20. Tessa Wegert, "Catalogue Shopping Is So Yesterday," *The Globe and Mail*, November 24, 2005, B13.

21. "Did You Know?" *Catalog News.com*, www.catalog-news.com, April 8, 2002; Judy Strauss and Raymond Frost,

E-Marketing, (Upper Saddle River, NJ: Prentice Hall, 2001), 140.

22. Carolyn Brackett, "Setting Up Shop in Cyberspace," *Inc.com*, www.inc.com/conducting_commerce/advice/15237.html, May 20, 2002; David Radin, "'Electronic Mall Syndrome' Gives Way to Unified Buying," *eBusiness News*, http://ebusiness.dci.com/articles/1998/05/14radin.htm, May 20, 2002; Garrett Wasny, "Free Electronic Storefronts," www.howtoconquertheweb.com/gohome111.htm, July, 2000.

23. Peter Elkind, "Shhhhh! Amway's on the Web," *Fortune* (March 6, 2000): 76.

24. "LivePerson.com™," www.liveperson.com, April 19, 2000.

25. Gordon Jaremko, "River Highway in Canada's North Open for Business," *The Winnipeg Free Press*, July 25, 2006, B10.

26. Anne T. Coughlan et al., *Marketing Channels*, 6th ed. (Upper Saddle River, NJ: Prentice Hall, 2001), 458–462.

27. Bill Redekop, "The Crow Subsidy Is History," *The Winnipeg Free Press*, February 28, 1995, 1.

Chapter 18

1. Andrew Higgins, "Lacking Money to Pay, Russian Firms Survive on Deft Barter System," *The Wall Street Journal*, August 27, 1998, A1, A6.

2. *Bank of Canada Banking and Financial Statistics*, Table E1 (April 2006), S50.

3. John Partridge, "Phony $10, $20 Bills Rampant in '04," *The Globe and Mail*, March 15, 2005, B5.

4. Dean Beeby, "Canadians Worry About Counterfeit Cash: Survey," *The Winnipeg Free Press*, June 26, 2006, B8.

5. Omar El Akkad, "Canada's $5 Bill Offers New Security Features," *The Globe and Mail*, April 5, 2006, B5.

6. *Bank of Canada Banking and Financial Statistics*, Table E1 (April 2006), S50.

7. *Bank of Canada Banking and Financial Statistics*, Table C1 (May 2006), S16.

8. Nancy Carr, "More Canadians Turning to Alternative Banks," *The Winnipeg Free Press*, July 21, 2003, B7.

9. "Statistics for Smart Cards," *ePaynews.com*, June 14, 2004, www.epaynews.com/statistics/scardstats.html.

10. Karen Horcher, "Reconstruction Zone," *CGA Magazine* (June 1997): 19.

11. Andrew Willis, "American VC Firms Trouncing Canadians at Home," *The Globe and Mail*, June 13, 2005, B1, B3.

12. Andrew Willis, "CIBC Leads Underwriting Pack for Fourth Year," *The Globe and Mail*, January 26, 2005, B7.

13. Andrew Willis, "RBC Dominion King of the Debt Dealers," *The Globe and Mail*, January 26, 2005, B7.

14. Robert J. Carbaugh, *International Economics*, 5th ed. (Cincinnati: South-Western, 1995), Chapter 11.

Chapter 19

1. Joseph Nocera, "Do You Believe? How Yahoo! Became a Blue Chip," *Fortune* (June 7, 1999): 76–81.

2. Cory Johnson, "The Internet Blue Chip," *The Industry Standard*, www.thestandard.com/article/0,1902,4088,00html, August 7, 2001; and Chris Nerney "Yahoo!: Bargain or Big Trouble?" *The Internet Stock Report*, www.internetstockreport.com/column/print/0,,530021,00.html, August 7, 2001.

3. George G. Kaufman, *The U.S. Financial System: Money, Markets, and Institutions*, 6th ed. (Englewood Cliffs, NJ: Prentice Hall, 1995), 432.

4. Louise Lee and Lauren Young, "Is Schwab's Latest Come-On Enough?" *Business Week* (June 7, 2004): 44.

5. Borzou Daragahi, "E-Finance Forecast," *Money* (March 2001): 129–133; and Joseph Kahn, "Schwab Lands Feet First on Net," *The New York Times*, February 10, 1999, C1, C5.

6. Richard Blackwell, "TSE Sees Few Gains from Realignment," *The Globe and Mail*, May 23, 2000, 12.

7. Gordon J. Alexander, William F. Sharpe, and Jeffery V. Bailey, *Fundamentals of Investments*, 3rd ed. (Upper Saddle River, NJ: Prentice Hall, 2001), 36–39.

8. Gordon J. Alexander, William F. Sharpe, and Jeffery V. Bailey, *Fundamentals of Investments*, 3rd ed. (Upper Saddle River, NJ: Prentice Hall, 2001), 44–46.

9. *NASDAQ*, www.nasdaq.com/about/timeline.stm, June 25, 2000.

10. *NASD*, www.nasd.com, June 25, 2000.

11. Keith Damsell, "Ethical Investing Proving a Hard Sell in Canada," *The Globe and Mail*, August 12, 2004, B10.

12. Rob Carrick, "Tread Carefully in the World of Hedge Funds," *The Globe and Mail*, May 27, 2006, B8.

13. Paul Waldie and Sinclair Stewart, "Hedge Funds in the Crosshairs," *The Globe and Mail*, May 30, 2005, B4; Sinclair Stewart and Paul Waldie, "The New Breed of 800-Pound Gorilla," *The Globe and Mail*, May 31, 2005, B7.

14. Richard Blackwell, "TSE 300 Shift Will Shrink Index," *The Globe and Mail*, January 31, 2002, B17.

15. Rob Carrick, "Direct Plans Cut Brokers Out," *The Globe and Mail*, August 21, 1999, B8.

16. Gordon J. Alexander, William F. Sharpe, and Jeffery V. Bailey, *Fundamentals of Investments*, 3rd ed. (Upper Saddle River, NJ: Prentice Hall, 2001), 37–38.

17. U.S. Securities and Exchange Commission, "SEC Charges Former ImClone CEO Samuel Waksal with Illegal Insider Trading," June 12, 2002, www.sec.gov/news/press; Andrew Pollack, "ImClone's Ex-Chief in Talks with U.S. on Plea Agreement," *The New York Times on the Web*, July 13, 2002, www.nytimes.com/2002/07/13/business; "Martha Scrutiny Heats Up," *CNNMoney*, June 14, 2002, www.cnnfn.com.

Chapter 20

1. David F. Scott et al., *Basic Financial Management*, 8th ed. (Upper Saddle River, NJ: Prentice Hall, 1999), 626–627.

2. "Britain's Third Biggest Bank Sees 2001 Net Profit Fall as Bad-Debt Provisions Rise," *CNNMoney*, www.cnnfn.com, February 15, 2002; "SocGen, Abbey National Set Aside Money for Bad Loans, Profits Decline," *CNNMoney*, www.cnnfn.com, February 21, 2002; and James Cox, "Argentina Pins Hope on Debt-Swap Proposal," *World Business*, www.usatoday.com, November 11, 2002.

3. John Heinzl, "Good Strategy Gone Awry, Top Retailer's Tale of Woe," *The Globe and Mail*, March 7, 1992, B1, B4.

4. The State of Small Business, 1989 Annual Report on Small Business in Ontario (Toronto: Ministry of Industry, Trade and Technology, 1990).

5. J. W. Duncan, *D&B Reports* (September–October 1991): 8.

6. Norman M. Scarborough and Thomas W. Zimmerer, *Effective Small Business Management: An Entrepreneurial Approach*, 6th ed. (Upper Saddle River, NJ: Prentice Hall, 2000), esp. 298–300.

7. Susan Hodges, "One Big Step Toward a Loan," *Nation's Business* (August 1997): 34–36.

8. Richard S. Boulton, Barry D. Libert, and Steve M. Samek, "Managing Risk in an Uncertain World," *Upside* (June 2000): 268–278.

9. Thomas Fitch, *Dictionary of Banking Terms*, 2nd ed. (Hauppauge, NY: Barron's, 1993), 531.

10. Mark S. Dorfman, *Introduction to Risk Management and Insurance*, 6th ed. (Upper Saddle River, NJ: Prentice Hall, 2000), Chapter 1.

11. Denyse O'Leary, "The Scams That Drive Up Premiums," *The Globe and Mail*, May 2, 1995, B1; Denyse O'Leary, "Insurers United Against Fraud Face Serious Obstacles," *The Globe and Mail*, May 2, 1995, B1.

12. Sinclair Stewart, "Insurers Take a Category 5 Hit in the Pocketbook," *The Globe and Mail*, October 27, 2005, B1, B26.

13. Sinclair Stewart, "Sun Life's Insurance Policy: The Great Indian Middle Class," *The Globe and Mail*, October 1, 2005, B1, B6.

14. Yochi Dreazen, "As Iraq Terror Rises, Businessmen Find Niche in Life Insurance," *The Wall Street Journal*, August 19, 2005, A1, A16.

15. Mark S. Dorfman, *Introduction to Risk Management and Insurance*, 6th ed. (Upper Saddle River, NJ: Prentice Hall, 2000), 420–421.

Appendix B

[1]See Chris Arthur J. Keown, *Personal Finance*, 3rd ed. (Upper Saddle River, NJ: Pearson Prentice Hall, 2004), 600–609.

[2]Christopher Farrell, "No Need to Hit the Panic Button," *Business Week*, July 26, 2004, 76–80.

Source Notes

Chapter 1

Canadian Megaprojects Wendy Stueck, "Vindication of Voisey's Bay," *The Globe and Mail*, September 3, 2005, B4; Dave Ebner, "CNQ Bets $25 Billion on Oil Sands," *The Globe and Mail*, November 3, 2005, B1, B6; Patrick Brethour, "Alberta's Earth-Shaking Ambitions," *The Globe and Mail*, April 4, 2005, B4, B5; Wendy Stueck, "Voisey's Bay at Last Getting Off the Ground," *The Globe and Mail*, June 17, 2004, B1, B4; Wendy Stueck, "Nickel Prices Continue to Shine" *The Globe and Mail*, October 13, 2003; Wendy Stueck, "Inco Shares Fall on Voisey's Overrun," *The Globe and Mail*, March 21, 2003, B13; Allan Robinson, "Inco, Province Inch Toward Deal on Voisey's Bay," *The Globe and Mail*, October 12, 2001, B3; James Stevenson, "Inco Grilled Despite Impressive Rebound," *The Winnipeg Free Press*, April 20, 2000, B7; "Giant Newfoundland Nickel Project May Soon Proceed," *The Winnipeg Free Press*, November 23, 1999, B8; Allan Robinson, "Inco President Willing to Compromise on Voisey's Bay," *The Globe and Mail*, April 29, 1999, B1, B4; Allan Robinson, "Inco to Halt Voisey's Bay Work," *The Globe and Mail*, July 28, 1998, B1, B6; Allan Robinson, "Inco Chairman Defends Actions," *The Globe and Mail*, April 23, 1998, B3. **Business Accountability** Andres Oppenheimer, "Latin America Is Skeptical," *The Orlando Sentinel*, February 20, 2006, A19; Bradley Martin, "Hermit Kingdom Mixes Stalin, Profits," *The Globe and Mail*, December 29, 2005, B1, B8; James Kynge, "Private Firms' Growth in China Striking: Report," *National Post*, May 11, 2000, C14; Howard French, "On the Street, Cubans Fondly Embrace Capitalism," *The New York Times*, February 3, 1994, A4. **Table 1.1** *Financial Post Business*, Special Edition, 2006, 128; Material reprinted with the express permission of "National Post Company," a CanWest Partnership. **Entrepreneurship and New Ventures** "Murad Al-Katib Quickens the Pulse of the Saskatchewan Agricultural Industry," Business Development Bank of Canada website www.bdc.ca/en/about/mediaroom/news_releases/2005/2005101811.htm; Bruce Johnstone, "Al-Katib Named Young Entrepreneur of the Year," Saskatchewan News Network, *Regina Leader-Post*, Tuesday, October 15, 2005, A8, www.saskcan.com/news.html. Material reprinted with the express permission of Regina Leader Post Group Inc., a CanWest Partnership. **Concluding Case 1-1** Barrie McKenna, "Welcome to the Age of Scarcity," *The Globe and Mail*, May 22, 2005, B15; Harris Anwar, "Are Saudi Reserves Drying Up?," *The Globe and Mail*, May 21, 2005, B19; Peter Tertzakian, "Canada: Energy Superpower?" *The Globe and Mail*, May 28, 2005, B6; Michael Lynch, "Oil Discovery Forecasts Doomed," *The Globe and Mail*, May 28, 2005, B6; John Heinzl, "Now's a Good Time to Cut Back on that Coffee Drinking Habit," *The Globe and Mail*, February 25, 2005, B10; "Price of Oil Spurts to $42.90 a Barrel," *USA Today*, July 29, 2004, 1B; "Higher and Higher—Again: Gasoline Prices Set Record," *USA Today*, May 25, 2004, 1B; Brad Foss, "Drivers Pay Price for Imported Gas," Associated Press Wire Story, May 22, 2004; Allan Sloan, "Why $2 Gas Isn't the Real Energy Problem," *Newsweek*, May 24, 2004, 40; Gregory L. White, "How Ford's Big Batch of Rare Metal Led to $1 Billion Write-Off," *The Wall Street Journal*, February 6, 2002, A1, A6. **Concluding Case 1-2** Dan Lett, "Wine Stores Collect $8 Million," *The Winnipeg Free Press*, June 21, 2006, A3; Eric Reguly, "Ontario's Liquor Stores Look Good, but Where's the Profit?" *The Globe and Mail*, July 19, 2005, B2; Trevor Harrison, "Demon Rum and the Perils of Privatization," *The Winnipeg Free Press*, June 19, 2003, A13; John Cotter, "Privatized Liquor Stores a Flop, Study Suggests," *The Winnipeg Free Press*, June 6, 2003, A20; Bill Redekopp, "Private Wine Stores Cheesed with MLCC," *The Winnipeg Free Press*, July 8, 2000, A6; David Menzies, "Sour Grapes," *Canadian Business*, February 26, 1999, 28–35; Brian Hutchinson, "Cheers!," *Canadian Business*, November 1994, 23–28.

Chapter 2

Productivity and the Standard of Living Virginia Galt, "Productivity Buckling Under the Strain of Stress, CEO's Say," *The Globe and Mail*, June 9, 2005, B1, B15; John Partridge, "Several Causes Seen Possible for 'Unprecedented' Productivity Gap," *The Globe and Mail*, June 24, 2005, B6; "Canada Lags in Productivity, Investment: Study," *The Winnipeg Free Press*, October 19, 2005, B12; Gordon Pitts, "Ottawa's New, Improved Mantra: Productivity," *The Globe and Mail*, October 3, 2005, B1, B6; Simon Tuck, "Canada's Standard of Living Takes Downturn," *The Globe and Mail*, March 3, 2005, B1, B9; Jacquie McNish, "'Mediocre' Report Card Says Canada not Making the Grade," *The Globe and Mail*, October 4, 2004, B1, B10; Bruce Little, "Board Warns Productivity Must Rise," *The Globe and Mail*, October 5, 2004, B3; "Canada's Standard of Living," *National Post Business*, June 2003, 19–20; Pierre Fortin, "Differences in Annual Work Hours per Capita Between the United States and Canada," *International Productivity Monitor* (Spring 2003): 38–46; Frank Graves and Richard Jenkins, "Canadian Attitudes Towards Productivity: Balancing Standard of Living and Quality of Life," *The Review of Economic Performance and Social Progress* (2002): 243–258; Andrew Sharpe, "Why Are Americans More Productive Than Canadians?" *International Productivity Monitor* (Spring 2003): 19–37; Pierre Fortin, "Canadian Productivity: When Do We Catch Up?," *ISUMA* (Spring 2002). **Figure 2.3** 2005 data is from the *Bank of Canada Banking and Financial Statistics*, Table H8, May 2006, S-102-103 **Figure 2.4** *Bank of Canada Banking and Financial Statistics*, Table H5, May 2006, S-99. **Figure 2.5** Statistics Canada, Industrial Research and Development, 2005 *Intentions*, 13. **Entrepreneurship and New Ventures Want a MacBrioche with That MacEspresso?** Amy Tsao, "For McDonald's, the Fat's in the Fire," *Business Week*, October 15, 2003, 52–53; Julie Forster, Thinking Outside the Burger Box," *Business Week*, September 16, 2003, 66–67; Shirley Leung, "Armchairs, TVs and Espresso—Is It McDonald's?" *Wall Street Journal*—August 30, 2003, A1, A6. **Business Accountability** John Partridge, "Agency Predicts Further Outsourcing," *The Globe and Mail*, April 26, 2005, B5; Rebecca Buckman, "Outsourcing with a Twist," *The Wall Street Journal*, January 18, 2005, B1, B4; Norihiko Shirouzu, "Big Three's Outsourcing Plan: Makes Parts Suppliers Do It," *The Wall Street Journal*, June 10, 2004, A1, A6; Lee J. Krajewski and Larry Ritzman, *Operations Management: Strategy and Analysis*, 6th ed. (Upper Saddle River, NJ: Prentice Hall, 2002), 102–106; Virginia Galt, "Take Our Business, Take Our People: BMO," *The Globe and Mail*, May 19, 2003, B1, B4; Anne T. Coughlin et al., *Marketing Channels*, 6th ed. (Upper Saddle River, NJ: Prentice Hall, 2001), 168–172. **Concluding Case 2-1** Ronald Alsop, "Ranking Corporate Reputations," *The Wall Street Journal*, December 6, 2005, B1, B14; Gordon Pitts, "The RBC Dynasty Continues," *The Globe and Mail*, January 30, 2006, B1, B10. **Concluding Case 2-2** Gautam Naik, Vanessa Fuhrmans, Jonathan Karp, Joel Millman, Farnaz Fassihi, and Joanna Slater, "Global Baby Bust," *The Wall Street Journal*, January 24, 2003, B1, B4.

Chapter 3

The Price of Bad Behaviour James Bagnall, "Enron Verdict Sends CEO's Strong Message," *The Winnipeg Free*

Press, May 27, 2006, B10; Mark Maremont, "Tyco Ex-Officials Get Jail Terms, Big Fines," *The Wall Street Journal*, September 20, 2005, C1, C4; Simon Houpt and Shawn McCarthy, "Ebbers' Storied Career Ends with Record-Fraud Conviction," *The Globe and Mail*, March 16, 2005, B1, B7; Peter Brieger, "$2.4 Billion Gets CIBC Out of Class Action," *The Winnipeg Free Press*, August 3, 2005, B7; Paul Waldie and Richard Blackwell, "Several Charges Against Drabinsky Dropped," *The Globe and Mail*, September 23, 2005, B5; Karen Howlett, "Livent's Auditors Charged with Misconduct," *The Globe and Mail*, April 6, 2004, B1, B4; Barbara Shecter, "Black's $80 Million Fraud Charges," *The Winnipeg Free Press*, November 18, 2005, A1, A4; Shawn McCarthy, "The Case Against Black," *The Globe and Mail*, November 18, 2005, B1, B6; Jacquie McNish, "How the OSC Tipped the Scales on Rankin," *The Globe and Mail*, November 2, 2005, p. B13; Shirley Won, "Rankin Gets Six Months in Jail," *The Globe and Mail*, October 28, 2005, B1, B16; Elena Cherney, "Radler Pleas May Trigger Showdown," *The Globe and Mail*, September 19, 2005, p. B4; Sinclair Stewart, "RBC Pays Enron to Resolve Lawsuit," *The Globe and Mail*, July 29, 2005, B1–B2; Paul Waldie, "Black's Right-Hand Man Pleads Guilty to Fraud," *The Globe and Mail*, September 21, 2005, A1, A7; Jacquie McNish and Shirley Won, "OSC Wins Trading Case Against Andrew Rankin," *The Globe and Mail*, July 16, 2005, B1, B3; Gillian Livingston, "Scandal Hits Canada," *The Globe and Mail*, October 23, 2002, B3; David Wessel, "Why the Bad Guys of the Boardroom Emerged en Masse," *The Wall Street Journal*, June 20, 2002, A1, A6; Barrie McKenna, "Andersen Hit with Charges," *The Globe and Mail*, March 15, 2002, B1, B4. **Figure 3.1** Based on Gerald S. Cavanaugh, *American Business Values: With International Perspectives*, 4th ed. (Upper Saddle River, NJ: Prentice Hall, 1998), 71, 84. **Business Accountability** Andrew Willis, "CIBC Puts Ethics on the Line," *The Globe and Mail*, January 8, 2005, B2; Sinclair Stewart, "CIBC Sues 6 Former Employees, Alleges They Took Confidential Data, Recruited Colleagues to Upstart Genuity," *The Globe and Mail*, January 6, 2005, B1, B4; Andrew Willis, "CIBC Sues 6 Former Employees, Lawsuit Makes Both Parties Look Bad—But the Bank Gets the Worst of the Deal," *The Globe and Mail*, January 6, 2005, B1, B13. **Figure 3.2** Courtesy of Mountain Equipment Co-op, *www.mec.ca*. **Figure 3.3** David P. Baron, *Business and Its Environment*, 4th ed. (Upper Saddle River, NJ: Prentice Hall, 2003), 768. **Entrepreneurship and New Ventures** Abridged with permission from Ralph Shaw, "Peak Performance: Mountain Equipment Co-op has a better way of climbing," *Alernatives Journal*, Jan/Feb 2005, Vol. 31, Issue 1, p. 19–20. Annual subscriptions $35.00 <www.alternativesjournal.ca>.;

Figure 3.5 Based on Andrew C. Revkin, "Who Cares About a Few Degrees?" *The New York Times*, December 12, 1997, F1. **Concluding Case 3-1** Bill McAllister, "Alaska Still Out Front on Environmental Monitoring," *The Juneau Empire*, May 29, 2004; Marilyn Adams, "Former Carnival Exec Says He Was Fired for Helping Federal Inquiry," *USA Today*, November 8–10, 2003; Marilyn Adams, "Cruise-Ship Dumping Poisons Seas, Frustrates U.S. Enforcers," *USA Today*, November 8–10, 2003; Michael Connor, "Norwegian Cruise Line Pleads Guilty in Pollution Case," Reuters, December 7, 2002; "What Is a Dead Zone?" *Oceana Interactive* (June 10, 2004), www.oceana.org. **Concluding Case 3-2** Stephen Power and Matthew Karnitschnig, "VW's Woes Mount Amid Claims of Sex Junkets for Union Chiefs," *The Wall Street Journal*, November 17, 2005, A1, A8, A9; Gabriella Mitchener, "VW Agrees to Big Settlement with GM," *The Wall Street Journal*, January 10, 1997, A3; "Lopez Indicted for Taking from GM," *The Globe and Mail*, May 23, 2000, B9.

Chapter 4

Stepping Up Robeez Footwear Ltd. website: www.robeez.com/en-us/about/sandra.htm?PriceCat=1&Lang=EN-US; Rebecca Gardiner, "It Pays to Be Nice," *Profit* 24, no. 6 (December 2005): 23. Reprinted with permission of Robeez Footwear Ltd. and Profit Magazine. **Figure 4.1** Statistics Canada, Business Register, June 2005. **Figure 4.2a and Figure 4.2b** Statistics Canada, Business Register, June 2005. **Figure 4.3a and Figure 4.3b** Statistics Canada, Survey of Employment, Payrolls and Hours (SEPH), March 2005, and calculations by Industry Canada. **Entrepreneurship and New Ventures** © Rick Spence, "The Fastest Five," *Profit* 24, no. 3 (June 2005): 49. Retrieved May 14, 2006, from ABI/INFORM Global database. (Document ID: 856224751). Reprinted with permission; BDC website, www.bdc.ca/en/about/mediaroom/news_releases/2005/2005101808.htm, accessed June 12, 2006. **Table 4.3** *Financial Post Business*, Special Edition, 2006, 64; Material reprinted with the express permission of "National Post Company," a CanWest Partnership. *Financial Post Business*, Special Edition, 2006, p. 64. **Business Accountability** "Report on Business Corporate Governance Rankings," *The Globe and Mail*, October 17, 2005, B5; Louis Lavelle, "The Best and Worst Boards," *Business Week*, April 7, 2004; Stefani Eads, "Why Amazon's Board Is Part of the Problem," *Business Week*, April 7, 2004; "Mixing It Up," *Corporate Board Member*, November/December, 2003; Jacquie McNish, "Onex Chief Ripped for Appointing Wife," *The Globe and Mail*, May 9, 2003, B1, B7; Jennifer Reingold, "Dot.Com Boards are Flouting the Rules," *Business Week*, December 20, 2003; Janet McFarland, "How ROB Created the Rating System,"

The Globe and Mail, October 7, 2002, B6. **Concluding Case 4-1** Paul Judge, "From Country Boys to Big Cheese," *Fast Company* (December 2001): 38–40; Sue Robinson, "Saving Our Farms," BurlingtonFreePress.com, November 27, 2001. **Concluding Case 4-2** Marlene Cartash, "My Best Sale: Asked to Recall the Defining Moment of their Selling Careers, 10 Celebrated Entrepreneurs Cited Gutsy Moves that Still Fill Them with Pride," *Profit* 13, no. 4 (1995): 34–41; Bruce Erskine, "Gibson got in on ground floor," *The Halifax Herald Limited*, Wednesday, April 26, 2006, www.thechronicleherald.ca/external/bbi/index11.html, July 3, 2006. Used with permission.

Chapter 5

Canadian Exporters: Opportunities and Problems Gordon Pitts, "Manulife's Army of Agents on the March for Middle Class," *The Globe and Mail*, October 23, 2004, B4; Rick Cash, "Dealing with the Dragon," *The Globe and Mail*, October 23, 2004, B3; Stephanie Nolen, "McCain Learns Tough Cultural Lesson on South Africa," *The Globe and Mail*, October 21, 2004, B1, B19; Bertrand Marotte, "Coutu Takes on Fortress Retail, U.S.A.," *The Globe and Mail*, September 4, 2004, B5; Gordon Pitts, "Learn This Mantra: Customer Is King in China," *The Globe and Mail*, July 12, 2004, B1, B5; Gordon Pitts, "McCain Boss Picks up Pace of Global French Fry Assault," *The Globe and Mail*, June 14, 2004, B1, B12; John Heinzl, "China Feasts on Canada's Resources," *The Globe and Mail*, May 22, 2004, B6; Oliver Bertin, "Firms Face Major Hurdles en Route to U.S. Markets," *The Globe and Mail*, April 29, 2004, B16; Shirley Won, "Small Furniture Firm Pegged for Success," *The Globe and Mail*, April 10, 2004, B5; "Exports, Eh?" *Canadian Business* (January 1997): 21; Peggy Berkowitz, "You Say Potato, They Say McCain," *Canadian Business* (December 1991): 44–48. **Figure 5.3** *Bank of Canada Banking and Financial Statistics*, Table J1, May 2006, S108. **Table 5.1** *Bank of Canada Banking and Financial Statistics*, Table J3, May 2006, S111. **Entrepreneurship and New Ventures** Ron Lieber, "Give Us This Day Our Global Bread," *Fast Company* (March 2001): 164–167. **Table 5.3** *Financial Post Business*, Special Edition, 2006, 121; Material reprinted with the express permission of "National Post Company," a CanWest Partnership. *Financial Post Business*, Special Edition, 2006, 121. **Business Accountability** Clay Chandler, "Japan's Horror Show," *Fortune* (November 10, 2003): 114–118; "Quick Studies," *Business Week* (November 18, 2003): 48–49. **Concluding Case 5-1** Wal-Mart, "International Operations," "Wal-Mart International Operations," "Wal-Mart Stores Inc. at a Glance," *2002 Annual Report* (November 27, 2002), www.walmartstores.com; Amy Tsao, "Will Wal-Mart Take Over the

World?" *Business Week* (November 27, 2002): 76–79; Geri Smith, "War of the Superstores," *Business Week* (September 23, 2002): 60; "The 2002 Global 500," *Fortune* (July 8, 2002). **Concluding Case 5-2** Martin Cash, "China Wins Apparel War?" *The Winnipeg Free Press*, July 30, 2005, B8, B11; Gordon Pitts, "Peerless on a Mission: Stop China Now," *The Globe and Mail*, January 14, 2005, B8; Bertrand Marotte, "Gildan Takes T-shirt Making to the Cutting-Edge of Casual Apparel," *The Globe and Mail*, July 3, 2004, B3; Gordon Pitts, "Who Will Be the Next Huntingdon?" *The Globe and Mail*, January 8, 2005, B7.

Chapter 6

Looking for Redemption? Shawn McCarthy, "Bronfman Is Eager to Gain Redemption for His Music Gambit," *The Globe and Mail*, January 4, 2005, B4; Allen Swift, "Bronfman Jr. Wants His Toy Again," *The Winnipeg Free Press*, May 26, 2003, B7; Shawn McCarthy, "Bronfman Jumps Back into Music with Winning Bid," *The Globe and Mail*, November 25, 2003; Brian Milner, "Broken Spirits," *Report on Business Magazine* (September 2002): 26–38; Allan Swift, "Polygram Bid Heats Up," *The Winnipeg Free Press*, November 5, 1998, B12; Brian Milner, "Seagram's Top Gun Shoots for the Stars," *The Globe and Mail*, June 6, 1998, B1, B6; Brian Milner, "Seagram Snares Polygram," *The Globe and Mail*, May 22, 1998, B1, B4; Brian Milner, "The Selling of Edgar Bronfman Jr.," *The Globe and Mail*, February 15, 1999, B15. **Figure 6.1** Based on Stephen P. Robbins and Mary Coulter, *Management*, 7th ed. (Upper Saddle River, NJ: Prentice Hall, 2002), 199. **Entrepreneurship and New Ventures** © Rick Spence. Used with permission; Reprinted with permission of Pet Health Inc. **Figure 6.2** Based on Thomas L. Wheelen and J. David Hunger, *Strategic Management and Business Policy*, 7th ed. (Upper Saddle River, NJ: Prentice Hall, 2000), 13. **Business Accountability** Henry Mintzberg, *The Nature of Managerial Work* (New York: Harper and Row, 1973); Harvey Schachter, "Monday Morning Manager," *The Globe and Mail*, November 8, 2005, B2. **Concluding Case 6-1** "Coach's Driver Picks Up the Pace," *Business Week* (March 29, 2004): 98–100; Julia Boorstin, "How Coach Got Hot," *Fortune* (October 28, 2003): 131–134; Marilyn Much, "Consumer Research Is His Bag," *Investor's Business Daily*, December 16, 2003; "S&P Stock Picks and Pans: Accumulate Coach," *Business Week* (October 22, 2003). **Concluding Case 6-2** Andrew Willis, Jacquie McNish, and Grant Robertson, "How the Deal Was Done: Embarking on Project Odyssey's Stormy Water," *The Globe and Mail*, December 3, 2005, B4; Gordon Pitts, "Bell Adopts a New Party Line," *The Globe and Mail*, May 14, 2005, B4; Simon Avery, "Sabia Lays Out a New BCE: Lower Costs, More Wireless,"

The Globe and Mail, December 16, 2004, B1, B7; Dave Ebner, "BCE Cutting Costs, Staff, Focusing on Bell Canada," *The Globe and Mail*, December 19, 2002, B1, B4; Jacquie McNish and Paul Waldie, "BCE Reacquiring 20% Stake in Bell Canada," *The Globe and Mail*, June 29, 2002, B1, B4; Karen Howlett and John Saunders, "Teleglobe to Abandon Huge Internet Investment," *The Globe and Mail*, May 16, 2002, B1, B11; Ian Austen, "On the Hook," *Canadian Business* (May 13, 2002): 35–39; Bertrand Marotte, "Sabia: BCE Committed to Emergis," *The Globe and Mail*, May 8, 2002, B5; Eric Reguly, "Decision Time for BCE Boss Is Now," *The Globe and Mail*, March 22, 2002, B1–B2; Gordon Pitts, "Monty Ends 28 Years with a Clean Break," *The Globe and Mail*, April 25, 2002, B3.

Chapter 7

Frantic Films Is Getting More Organized Interviews with Jamie Brown, CEO of Frantic Films, as well as documents provided by Frantic Films. **Business Accountability** Joann Lublin, "Place vs. Product: It's Tough to Choose a Management Model," *The Wall Street Journal*, June 27, 2001, A1, A4; Richard Blackwell, "New CIBC Boss Promises Shakeup," *The Globe and Mail*, April 2, 1999, B1, B4; Rekha Bach, "Heinz's Johnson to Divest Operations, Scrap Management of Firm by Region," *The Wall Street Journal*, December, 1997, B10-B12; Jana Parker-Pope and Joann Lublin, "P&G Will Make Jager CEO Ahead of Schedule," *The Wall Street Journal*, September, 1998, B1, B8. **Entrepreneurship and New Ventures** *Profit* magazine, "The 18th Annual *Profit* 100 Ranking of Canada's Fastest Growing Companies," http://canadianbusiness.com, Tuesday, June 13, 2006; Business Development Bank of Canada *www.bdc.ca*. **Concluding Case 7-1** Sara Lee "Our Brands," www.saralee.com, July 3, 2002; Deborah Cohen, "Sara Lee Opens Alternative to Victoria's Secret," *The Wall Street Journal*, January 3, 2003, B4; Julie Forster, "Sara Lee: Changing the Recipe—Again," *Business Week* (September 10, 2001): 87–89; "Sara Lee: Looking Shapely," *Business Week* (October 21, 2002): 52.

Chapter 8

Celebrating Workforce Diversity Virginia Galt, "P&G Leverages Its Cultural Diversity," *The Globe and Mail*, April 7, 2005, B1, B18; Jill Mahoney, "Visible Majority by 2017," *The Globe and Mail*, March 23, 2005, A1, A7; Kamal Dib, "Diversity Works," *Canadian Business* (March 29, 2004): 53–54; Valerie Marchant, "The New Face of Work, *Canadian Business* (March 29, 2004): 38; Ann Zimmerman, "Defending Wal-Mart," *The Wall Street Journal*, October 4, 2004, B1, B10; Virginia Galt,

"Western Union Remakes 'Canadian' Image," *The Globe and Mail*, November 23, 2004, B1, B24. **Entrepreneurship and New Ventures. The Guru of Fun Takes a Meeting with the V.P. of Buzz** Eric Wahlgren, "Online Extra: Goodbye, 'Guru of Fun,'" *Business Week*, February 6, 2003, 74–77; Lee Clifford, "You Get Paid to Do What?" *Fortune*, January 20, 2003, 106–108. **Table 8.1** *Financial Post Business*, Special Edition, 2006, 122. Material reprinted with the express permission of "National Post Company," a CanWest Partnership. **Business Accountability** Celene Adams, "Interview Style Probes Past to Predict Future," *The Globe and Mail*, April 29, 2002, B16. **Concluding Case 8-1** "While Hiring at Most Firms Chills, Wal-Mart's Heats Up," *USA Today*, August 26, 2003, 3B; "Personnel File," *Fast Company* (January 2003): 118–122; *Hoover's Handbook of American Business 2004* (Austin: Hoover's Business Press, 2005), 554–555.

Chapter 9

What Happened to Hockey Night in Canada? Tim Wharnsby, "NHL: Zero Hour Looms," *The Globe and Mail*, February 10, 2005, A1, A15; Ingrid Peritz, "A Hockey Family Loses Faith," *The Globe and Mail*, February 10, 2005, A1, A15; Pierre LeBrun, "Union's OK of Cap Was Key," *The Winnipeg Free Press*, July 14, 2005, C3; David Shoalts, "NHL Sides Agree on Salary Cap," *The Globe and Mail*, June 9, 2005, A1, A9. **Figure 9.1.** Statistics Canada, "Perspectives in Labour and Income," Autumn 2003, 15, 3, p. 50. **Entrepreneurship and New Ventures.** "Arcelor: a strong commitment to value creation." Canada NewsWire, February 27, 2006, 1; www.imfmetal.org/main/index.cfm?n=47&l=2&c=12371; http://biz.yahoo.com/iw/060216/0110163.html; www.goiam.org/content.cfm?cID=5563. **Business Accountability** Peter Rakobowchuk, "Early Closing of Unionized Wal-Mart Called Cowardly," *The Winnipeg Free Press*, April 30, 2005, C15; Marina Strauss, "Wal-Mart Faces Another Unionized Store in Quebec," *The Globe and Mail*, January 20, 2005, B4; Barrie McKenna, "Unions Starting to Make Inroads at Wal-Mart," *The Globe and Mail*, August 23, 2004, B1, B12; Aldo Santin, "Wal-Mart vs. Union Battle Now Shifts to Manitoba," *The Winnipeg Free Press*, August 5, 2004, B3; Patrick Brethour, "Wal-Mart Hails Saskatchewan Court Ruling in Union Drives," *The Globe and Mail*, July 28, 2004, B1, B20; Virginia Galt, "Wal-Mart Must Give Union Access," *The Globe and Mail*, May 13, 2003, B5; "Union Is Trying to Organize Staff at Wal-Mart," *The Winnipeg Free Press*, May 13, 2003, A7; Zena Olijnyk, "CAW Walks Away from Wal-Mart," *National Post*, April 20, 2000, C5; Susan Bourettte, "Wal-Mart Staff Want Out of Union," *The Globe and Mail*, April 23, 1999, B9; John Heinzl and Marina Strauss, "Wal-Mart's Cheer Fades," *The Globe and Mail*, February 15, 1997, B1, B4; Margot Gibb-Clark, "Why Wal-Mart Lost the Case," *The Globe and Mail*, February 14, 1997, B10. **Table 9.2.** Source: Human Resources and Social Development Canada, Union Membership in Canada—January 1, 2006. Reprinted with the permission of Her Majesty the Queen in Right of Canada 2006. www.hrsdc.gc.ca/en/lp/wid/union_membership.shtml. **Figure 9.3** Labour Canada, *Labour Organization in Canada, 1991*, xxv. Used by permission of the Minister of Supply and Services Canada. **Concluding Case 9-1** Brent Jang, "Air Canada Labour Relations Tested," *The Globe and Mail*, January 21, 2005, B4; Keith McArthur, "Cuts Take Harsh Toll on Air Canada Employees," *The Globe and Mail*, May 2, 2004, B1, B16; "Unions, Airline Give Nod to Deal," *The Winnipeg Free Press*, May 25, 2003, A6; Cassandra Szklarski, "Air Canada Reaches Tentative Deal with Machinists," *The Winnipeg Free Press*, May 28, 2003, B6, B10; "1,000 AirCan Mechanics Told to Take Summer Off," *Winnipeg Free Press*, May 16, 2003, B7; David Paddon, "Airline Charting New Territory," *The Winnipeg Free Press*, April 2, 2003, B4, B5; Keith McArthur, "Air Canada to Fight Hostile Motions," *The Globe and Mail*, April 21, 2003, B1, B8; Allan Swift, "Air Canada Unions OK Cuts," *The Winnipeg Free Press*, April 1, 2003, B1, B8; David Paddon, "Air Canada to Shed More Jobs," *The Winnipeg Free Press*, April 23, 2003, B9. **Concluding Case 9-2** Barrie McKenna, "As Big 3 Skid, UAW Braces for Inevitable World of Pain," *The Globe and Mail*, October 21, 2005, B10; Robert Matthews and Kris Maher, "Labor's PR Problem," *The Wall Street Journal*, August 15, 2005, B1, B4; Kris Maher, "Unions' New Foe: Consultants," *The Wall Street Journal*, August 15, 2005, B1, B4; Greg Keenan, "CAW Crisis? No Way, Hargrove Says," *The Globe and Mail*, December 28, 2004, B1, B5; Bruce Little, "EU's Expansion Bound to Put the Screws to Cushy Labour Rules," *The Globe and Mail*, August 4, 2004, B2; Greg Keenan, "CAW Renews Drive to Unionize Toyota," *The Globe and Mail*, July 13, 2004, B1, B4; Virginia Galt, "Their Backs Against the Wall, Unions Are Opting for Compromise," *The Globe and Mail*, July 5, 2004, B1, B9; Greg Keenan, "GM and CAW Forge an Improved Relationship," *The Globe and Mail*, October 23, 1999, B1, B14.

Chapter 10

Keeping Employees Satisfied and Motivated Wallace Immen, "The Continuing Divide Over Stress Leave," *The Globe and Mail*, June 10, 2005, C1; Jeff Buckstein, "In Praise of Praise in the Workplace," *The Globe and Mail*, June 15, 2005, C1, C5; Virginia Galt, "This Just In: Half Your Employees Ready to Jump Ship," *The Globe and Mail*, January 26, 2005, B1, B9; David Sirota, Louis Mischkind, and Michael Meltzer, "Nothing Beats an Enthusiastic Employee," *The Globe and Mail*, July 29, 2005, C1; Virginia Galt, "Business's Next Challenge: Tackling Mental Health in the Workplace," *The Globe and Mail*, April 12, 2005, B1, B20; Virginia Galt, "Canadian Take Dour View on Jobs, Bosses, Angels," *The Globe and Mail*, October 18, 2004, B1, B7; Virginia Galt, "Worker Stress Costing Economy Billions, Panel Warns," *The Globe and Mail*, July 21, 2000, B9. **Entrepreneurship and New Ventures** © Andy Holloway, "The Dream Team," *Profit* magazine (June 2006) www.canadianbusiness.com/rankings/profit100/index.jsp?pageID=article&type=top10&year=2006&content=top10&page=9&print=. **Figure 10-2** Ricky Griffin and Ronald Ebert, *Business*, 2nd ed. (Englewood Cliffs, NJ: Prentice Hall, 1996). **Business Accountability** Virginia Galt, "Ideas: Employees' Best-Kept Secrets," *The Globe and Mail*, June 18, 2005, B11; Frederick A. Starke, Bruno Dyck, and Michael Mauws, "Coping with the Sudden Loss of an Indispensable Worker," *Journal of Applied Behavioural Science* 39, no. 2 (2003): 208–229; Timothy Aeppel, "On Factory Floors, Top Workers Hide Secrets to Success," *The Wall Street Journal*, July 1, 2002, A1, A10; Timothy Aeppel, "Not All Workers Find Idea of Empowerment as Neat as It Sounds," *The Wall Street Journal*, September 8, 1997, A1, 13. **Concluding Case 10-1** A. G. Lafley, "Letter to Shareholders," Procter & Gamble, *2002 Annual Report*; "A Healthy Gamble," *Time* (September 16, 2002): 46–48; Katrina Booker, "The Un-CEO," *Fortune* (September 16, 2002): 88–96; Robert Berner, "Procter & Gamble's Renovator-in-Chief," *Business Week* (December 11, 2002): 98–100; Robert Berner, "The Best and Worst Managers: A. G. Lafley, Procter & Gamble," *Business Week* (January 13, 2003): 67. **Concluding Case 10-2** Virginia Galt, "Statscan Studies Workplace Stress," *The Globe and Mail*, June 26, 2003, B3; Anne Howland, "There's No Place Like Work," *CGA Magazine* (July–August, 2000): 21–25; David Leonhardt, "Did Pay Incentives Cut Both Ways?" *The New York Times*, April 7, 2002, BU1-3; Dean Foust and Michelle Conlin, "A Smarter Squeeze?" *Business Week* (December 31, 2001): 42–44; Rick Perera, "Siemens Offers Workers 'Time-Outs' to Save Cash," *The Industry Standard*, August 31, 2001; Tischelle George, "Bye-Bye Employee Perks," *Information Week* (October 15, 2001).

Chapter 11

Toyota: The New Number 1? Barrie McKenna, "Made in America, Toyota-Style," *The Globe and Mail*, June 10, 2006, B4; Jathon Sapsford, Norihiko Shirouzu, and Joseph White, "Toyota Maps Plan to Displace GM as Top Car Maker," *The Wall Street Journal*, November 19–20, 2005, A1, A4; Greg Keenan, "Global Domination, the Toyota Way," *The Globe and Mail*, June 18, 2005, B4; Greg Keenan, "Japan's Big Three Still Lead Race," *The Globe and Mail*, June 19, 2003, B6; Alex Taylor, "How Toyota Defies Gravity," *Fortune* (December 8, 1997): 100–108. **Entrepreneurship and New Ventures** Business Development Bank of Canada, "Scott MacDonald Brings the Sound of Silence to Alberta and Beyond," news release, October 18, 2005, www.bdc.ca/en/about/mediaroom/news_releases/2005/2005101812.htm. **Business Accountability** Greg Keenan, "Ford's New Maxim: Flex Manufacturing," *The Globe and Mail*, May 10, 2006, B3; Timothy Aeppel, "Workers Not Included," *The Wall Street Journal*, November 19, 2002, B1, B11; Martin Stinson, "Assembly Line Robots Taking Workers' Jobs: UN Report," *The Globe and Mail*, February 8, 2000, B6; Wally Dennison, "Robotics Paint System Makes Splash at CN," *The Winnipeg Free Press*, October 6, 1988, 30. **Concluding Case 11-1** Pasadena Convention and Visitors Bureau, "Pasadena Tournament of Roses Parade and Rose Bowl Game: A Grand Tradition," news release, March 29, 2004, www.pasadenacal.com; Burbank Tournament of Roses Association, "2004 Float Entry Fact Sheet," March 29, 2004, www.burbankrosefloat.com; Cindy Chang, "Finally, a Chance to Relax," *Pasadena Star-News*, January 1, 2004, www. pasadenastarnews.com, March 29, 2004; Bill Hetherman, "Overnighters in Partying Mood," *Pasadena Star-News*, January 1, 2004, www.pasadenastarnews.com, March 29, 2004; Naush Boghossian, "Float Volunteers Feel the Moosic of Rose Parade," *Los Angeles Daily News*, December 26, 2003, www.dailynews.com, January 6, 2004; personal observations of the author as a volunteer assembling the float on December 28, 2003. **Concluding Case 11-2** Simon Tuck, "Ottawa Taking Brakes Off Auto Lures," *The Globe and Mail*, November 23, 2005, B1, B4; Gordon Pitts, "GM Economic Aftershocks Set to Hit Southern Ontario," *The Globe and Mail*, November 22, 2005, B1, B11; Greg Keenan, "GM Scraps New Car Platform Intended for Oshawa Plant," *The Globe and Mail*, March 22, 2005, B1–B2; Greg Keenan, "Ford Plans SUV's for Oakville," *The Globe and Mail*, June 18, 2003, B1, B18; Oliver Bertin, "Appliance Makers in Canada: A Dying Breed," *The Globe and Mail*, March 31, 2003, B5; Greg Keenan, "Auto Sector's Best-Paid Jobs Vanishing," *The Globe and Mail*, March 29, 2003, B1, B2; Thomas Watson, "Car Trouble," *Canadian Business* (March 17, 2003): 69–71; Steve Erwin, "Auto Workers 'Angry and Frustrated,'" *The Winnipeg Free Press*, May 23, 2003, B5; Bertrand Marotte, "Quebec GM Plant

Closing the End of an Era," *The Globe and Mail*, August 24, 2002, B1, B5; Todd Zaun, Gregory White, Norihiko Shirouzu, and Scott Miller, "Auto Makers Get Even More Mileage from Third World," *The Wall Street Journal*, July 31, 2002, A1, A8; Greg Keenan, "Auto Plants Gone with the Wind," *The Globe and Mail*, June 24, 2002, B1, B4.

Chapter 12

Meeting the Productivity Challenge Gordon Pitts, "Ottawa's New, Improved Mantra: Productivity," *The Globe and Mail*, October 3, 2005, B1, B6; Greg Keenan, "GM Oshawa Cranks Out Productivity Award," *The Globe and Mail*, June 3, 2005, B1, B8; Grant Robertson, "In the Boardroom at the General Motors Oshawa Plant Is a Baseball Bat. Two Words are Carved on It: Beat Toyota," *The Globe and Mail*, September 15, 2005, B16; Gordon Pitts, "Manufacturers' Choice—Compete or Die," *The Globe and Mail*, October 5, 2005, B7; "Canada's Standard of Living," *National Post Business*, June 2003, 19–20; Jeffrey Bernstein, Richard Harris, and Andrew Sharpe, "The Widening Canada–US Manufacturing Productivity Gap," *International Productivity Monitor* (Fall 2002): 3–22; Pierre Fortin, "Differences in Annual Work Hours per Capita Between the United States and Canada," *International Productivity Monitor* (Spring 2003): 38–46; Frank Graves and Richard Jenkins, "Canadian Attitudes Towards Productivity: Balancing Standard of Living and Quality of Life," *The Review of Economic Performance and Social Progress* (2002): 243–258; Andrew Sharpe, "Why Are Americans More Productive Than Canadians?," *International Productivity Monitor* (Spring 2003): 19–37; Jason Myers, "Back to Basics: Canada's Productivity Challenge," *Canadian Manufacturers and Exporters* (April 2003): 14–18; Pierre Fortin, "Canadian Productivity: When Do We Catch Up?," *ISUMA* (Spring 2002). **Figure 12.1** Bart Van Ark and Robert McGuckin, "International Comparisons of Labor Productivity and Per Capita Income," *Monthly Labor Review* (July 1999): 33–41. **Business Accountability** Calvin Leung, "Diamonds in the Rough," *Canadian Business* (February 28–March 13, 2005): 65–67; Joel Baglole, "Political Correctness by the Carat," *The Wall Street Journal*, April 17, 2003, B1, B3; Matthew Hart, "The Ice Storm," *Canadian Business* (November 2002): 52–62. **Figure 12.2** Adapted from D. Daryl Wickoff, "New Tools for Achieving Service Quality." *The Cornell Hotel and Restaurant Administrative Quarterly* (November 1984): 89. Cornell HRA Quarterly. Used by permission. All rights reserved. **Figure 12.5** Adapted from Richard B. Chase, Nicholas J. Aquilano, and F. Robert Jacobs, *Production and Operations Management*, 8th ed. (Boston: Irwin McGraw-Hill, 1998), 771. **Entrepreneurship and New Ventures** © Camilla Cornell, "The Dream

Team," *Profit* magazine (June 2006), www.canadianbusiness.com/rankings /profit100/index.jsp?pageID=article&type= top10&year=2006&content=top10&page= 11&print=, June 13, 2006. **Concluding Case 12-1** Chris Isidore, "Mercedes Loses Top Resale Spot," *CNNMoney* (November 10, 2003), http://cnnmoney. printthis.clickability.com; Alex Taylor III, "Mercedes Hits a Pothole," *Fortune* (October 27, 2003): 140–146; Neal E. Boudette, "DaimlerChrysler Drops Truck Plant," *Wall Street Journal*, September 24, 2003, A11; Scott Miller and Karen Lundegaard, "An Engineering Icon Slips—Quality Ratings for Mercedes Drop in Several Surveys," *Wall Street Journal*, February 4, 2002, B1. **Concluding Case 12-2** Marina Strauss, "Loblaw's Supply Chain Reaction," *The Globe and Mail*, February 25, 2006, B4; "Canadian Retailer Loblaw's Earnings Hit Due to Delays and Challenges in Supply Chain Network Redesign Project," www.scdigest.com/assets, November 17, 2005; Blaise Robinson, "Bay Street Week Ahead—Food Fight in Canada Grocery Aisle," www.globeinvestor.com/servlet/ ArticleNews/story/ROC, January 6, 2006; "Analysts Dismiss Loblaw's Woes," www.canada.com/national/nationalpost/ financialpost/investing/story.html, April 28, 2006.

Chapter 13

The Information Revolution Simon Avery, "Radio Frequency Identification the New Bar Code," *The Globe and Mail*, June 30, 2004, B10; Derrick Penner, "High-Tech Devices an Important Part of Canfor's Future," *The Globe and Mail*, December 30, 2005, B10; Marina Strauss and Simon Avery, "New System Gets a Boost in Bar Code Battle," *The Globe and Mail*, April 6, 2005, B4; Kevin Lubin, "The Last Retailer in Canada?" *Canadian Business* (March 18, 2002): 31–40; Casey Mahood, "Wal-Mart Claims Another Victim," *The Globe and Mail*, February 7, 1998, B1, B5; Mark Stevenson, "The Store to End All Stores," *Canadian Business* (May 1994): 20–29. **Table 13.1** *Financial Post Business* (Special Edition, 2006): 142. Material reprinted with the express permission of "National Post Company," a CanWest Partnership. **Figure 13.3** Adapted from Kenneth C. Laudon and Jane P. Laudon, *Essentials of Management Information Systems: Managing the Digital Firm*, 5th ed. (Upper Saddle River, NJ: Prentice Hall, 2003), 16. **Entrepreneurship and New Ventures**. "They All Want a Piece of Bill Gross," *Fortune*, November 11, 2002, 139–144; Patty Enrado, "Here Comes the Lynch Mob," *Upside*, June 2002, 15; Seth Lubove, "The Final Act," *Forbes*, March 4, 2002, 44; Christopher Palmeri and Linda Himelstein, "The Bloom Is Off Idealab," *Business Week*, December 31, 2001, 10; Joseph Nocera, "Bill Gross Blew through $800 Million in 8 Months (and He's Got Nothing to Show for It). Why Is He Still Smiling?" *Fortune*,

March 5, 2001, 81–83. **Figure 13.5** Kenneth C. Laudon and Jane Laudon, *Essentials of Management Information Systems*, 3rd ed. (Upper Saddle River, NJ: Prentice Hall, 1999), 39. **Figure 13.7** Adapted from Kenneth C. Laudon and Jane P. Laudon, *Essentials of Management Information Systems: Managing the Digital Firm*, 5th ed. (Upper Saddle River, NJ: Prentice Hall, 2003), 44. **Business Accountability** Daniel Roth, "Catch Us if You Can," *Fortune* (February 9, 2004): 64–74. **Concluding Case 13-1** Erick Schonfeld, "The Wizard of POS," *Business 2.0* (April 2004): 101–110; Michael Gros, *CRN* (August 25, 2003): 93; "No Tools Required for This Work Station," *Computing Canada* (November 14, 2003): 29; Gary Hilson, "Hardware Fit for a King," *Computing Canada* (February 14, 2003): 19; Larry Greenemeier, "Retailers Buy into Real-time Business," *Information Week* (January 20, 2003): 22. **Concluding Case 13-2** Paul Samyn and Leah Janzen, "Bulk-Sale Ban Hailed by Online Drug Industry," *The Winnipeg Free Press*, June 30, 2005, B15; Mia Rabson, "Feds Would Kill City Jobs to Safeguard Drug Supply," *The Winnipeg Free Press*, December 16, 2004, A1, A4; Dan Lett, "Drug Pipeline Goes Underground," *The Winnipeg Free Press*, July 18, 2004, B1; Marton Dunai, "Duty-Free Site's Cigarette Sales Draw Scrutiny," *The Wall Street Journal*, August 5, 2004, B1, B7; Leonard Zehr, "Net Pharmacies Cheer New U.S. Import Bill," *The Globe and Mail*, July 26, 2003, B1, B4; Leah Janzen, "Internet Pharmacy's Drug Search Denounced," *The Winnipeg Free Press*, July 5, 2003, A3; David Kuxhaus, "An Internet Pharmacy Primer," *The Winnipeg Free Press*, June 22, 2003, A1, A8; Carol Sanders, "Net Druggists Pen Deal," *The Winnipeg Free Press*, June 3, 2003, B1; David Kuxhaus, "U.S. Drug Agency Deals Blow to Net Pharmacy Operation," *The Winnipeg Free Press*, March 27, 2003, A3; Paul Samyn, "Competition Bureau Backs Drug Giant," *The Winnipeg Free Press*, March 22, 2003, B3.

Chapter 14

Do We Need to Audit the Auditors? Jeff Buckstein, "SOX Provision Holds Management's Feet to the Fire," *The Globe and Mail*, April 19, 2006, B13; Claire Gagne, "The Sarbanes-Oxley Act Restores Shine to Auditors' Reputation—and Fills Their Coffers," *Canadian Business* (September 27–October 10, 2004): 47–49; Karen Howlett, "Livent's Auditors Charged with Misconduct," *The Globe and Mail*, April 6, 2004, B1, B4; Karen Howlett, "Accounting Hearing Is Told Misconduct Charges Against Auditors Are 'Rubbish,'" *The Globe and Mail*, April 14, 2004, B3; Shawn McCarthy, "Investors Expect Too Much: Deloitte CEO," *The Globe and Mail*, October 17, 2005, B10; Elizabeth Church, "Accounting Overhaul Coming," *The Globe and Mail*, December 23, 2002,

B1, B6; Richard Blackwell, "Auditing Firms Get Tighter Rules," *The Globe and Mail*, July 18, 2002, B1, B6; John Partridge and Karen Howlett, "CIBC Restricts Its Auditors," *The Globe and Mail*, March 1, 2002, B1, B4; Lily Nguyen, "Accountants Primed for Change," *The Globe and Mail*, February 4, 2002, B9; Richard Blackwell, "Accountants to Issue New Rules," *The Globe and Mail*, March 28, 2002, B1, B7; John Gray, "Hide and Seek," *Canadian Business* (April 1, 2002): 28–32; Steve Liesman, Jonathan Weil, and Michael Schroeder, "Accounting Debacles Spark Calls for Change: Here's the Rundown," *The Wall Street Journal*, February 6, 2002, A1, A8; Edward Clifford, "Big Accounting Firms Face Insurance Crunch," *The Globe and Mail*, November 13, 1993, B3; Patricia Lush, "Gap Widens Between Views on Auditor's Role in Canada," *The Globe and Mail*, February 14, 1986, B3; Chris Robinson, "Auditor's Role Raises Tough Questions," *The Financial Post*, June 22, 1985. **Table 14.1** *Financial Post Business* (Special Edition, 2006): 160; Material reprinted with the express permission of "National Post Company," a CanWest Partnership. **Business Accountability** Luis Millan, "Death Knell of the Nest Egg?," *CGA Magazine* (May–June, 2006): 13–19; "Addressing the Pension Dilemma in Canada" and "The State of Defined Benefit Pension Plans in Canada," www.cga-online.org/canada/ar; Elizabeth Church, "Pension Fund Shortfall Soars in First Half," *The Globe and Mail*, November 23, 2005, B1, B7; Elizabeth Church, "Cost of Retiree Benefit Liabilities 'Sleeping Giant,'" *The Globe and Mail*, August 23, 2004, B4; Elizabeth Church, "Accounting Overhaul Coming," *The Globe and Mail*, December 23, 2002, B1, B6. **Entrepreneurship and New Ventures** "Brew Tour Update Form," *The Real Beer Page* (February 14, 2003), www.realbeer.com; "Black Oak Nut Brown Ale," *Beer Advocate.com* (February 14, 2003), www.beeradvocate.com; Stephen Beaumont, "Lament for a Brewpub—February 2003," *Stephen Beaumont's World of Beer* (February 14, 2003), www.worldofbeer.com; "Brewery Profile," *The Bar Towel* (February 14, 2003), www.bartowel.com/breweries/blackoak.phtml; John Cooper, "A Pint of Success," *CMA Management* (December 1999–January 2000): 44–46. **Concluding Case 14-1** Beth Ellyn Rosenthal, "Deloitte Study Discovers 75 Percent of Global Financial Institutions Plan to Outsource Offshore," *BPO Outsourcing Journal* (June 2003), www.bpo-outsourcing-journal.com; Lawrence M. Gill, "Questions Loom as Accountants Outsource Work Abroad," January 26, 2004, *Chicago Lawyer* (Chicago: Law Bulletin Publishing Company); "How to Evaluate an Outsourcing Provider and Watch the Bottom Line," *The CPA Journal* (June 2002): 19; Liz Loxton, "Offshoring—Offshore Accounting," *Accountancy* (February 2004): 48; Todd Furniss and Michel Janssen, "Offshore Outsourcing Part 1: The Brand of India," *OutsourcingAsia.com* (April 2003) www.outsourcing-asia.com; Todd Furniss, "China: The Next Big Wave in Offshore Outsourcing," *OutsourcingAsia.com* (June 2003) www.outsourcing-asia.com; "Outsourcing the Finance Function—Out with the Count," *Accountancy* (September 1, 2001): 32. **Concluding Case 14-2** Elizabeth Church, "Pension Funding Shortfall Increases Dramatically," *The Globe and Mail*, November 8, 2005, B5; Elizabeth Church, "Pension Fund Shortfall Soars in First Half," *The Globe and Mail*, November 23, 2005, B1, B7; Elizabeth Church, "Cost of Retiree Benefit Liabilities 'Sleeping Giant,'" *The Globe and Mail*, August 23, 2004, B4; Paul Waldie and Karen Howlett, "Reports Reveal Tight Grip of Ebbers on WorldCom," *The Globe and Mail*, June 11, 2003, B1, B7; Barrie McKenna, Karen Howlett, and Paul Waldie, "Probes Cite Ebbers in 'Fraud,'" *The Globe and Mail*, June 10, 2003, B1, B16; Elizabeth Church, "Accounting Overhaul Coming," *The Globe and Mail*, December 23, 2002, B1, B6; Richard Blackwell, "OSC Targets Tech Accounting," *The Globe and Mail*, September 26, 2000, B1, B6.

Chapter 15

Marketers Pay Attention to the Older Folks David Pringle, "In Mobile Phones, Older Users Say, More Is Less," *The Wall Street Journal*, August 15, 2005, A1, A9; John Partridge, "Leisureworld Purchase Revs Up Retirement Debate," *The Globe and Mail*, March 24, 2005, B15; Kelly Greene, "Marketing Surprise: Older Consumers Buy Stuff, Too," *The Wall Street Journal*, April 6, 2004, A1, A12; Andre Mayer, "Star's New Paper Woos Tween Readers," *The Globe and Mail*, March 12, 2003, B7; Gautam Naik, Leslie Chang, and Joanna Slater, "Leveraging the Age Gap," *The Wall Street Journal*, February 27, 2003, B1, B4; Cris Prystay and Sarah Ellison, "Time for Marketers to Grow Up?," *The Wall Street Journal*, February 27, 2003, B1, B4; Sebastian Moffett, "For Ailing Japan, Longevity Begins to Take Its Toll," *The Wall Street Journal*, February 11, 2003, A1, A12; John Heinzl, "Crayon Maker Draws in an Older Kid," *The Globe and Mail*, March 5, 1998; Shawna Steinberg, "Have Allowance, Will Transform Economy," *Canadian Business* (March 13, 1998): 59–71; Lisa Bannon, "Little Big Spenders," *The Wall Street Journal*, October 13, 1998, A1, A6; Sheryl Ubelacker, "Magazines Target Over-50 Crowd," *The Winnipeg Free Press*, April 9, 2000, B3; Allen St. John, "Baseball's Billion Dollar Question: Who's On Deck?" *American Demographics* (October, 1998): 60–62, 65–69. **Business Accountability** Keith McArthur, "A Year Later: No Medium for the Message," *The Globe and Mail*, November 1, 2004, B3; Cheryl Healton and Kathleen Nelson, "Reversal of Misfortune: Viewing Tobacco as a Social Justice Issue," *American Journal of Public Health*, February 2004, 186 *t.*; *Federal Trade Commission Cigarette Report for 2001* (June 15, 2003), www.ftc.gov/os/2003/06/cigreport.pdf. **Figure 15.5** Adapted from Naresh K. Malhotra, *Marketing Research: An Applied Orientation*, 3rd ed. (Upper Saddle River, NJ: Prentice Hall, 1999), 10. **Entrepreneurship and New Ventures** © Susanne Ruder, "When in Rome..." *Profit* (March 2006), www.canadianbusiness.com/entrepreneur/sales_marketing/article.jsp?content=20060210_125140_5560, June 12, 2006. Used with permission. **Concluding Case 15-1** Kevin Maney, "Dell to Dive into Consumer Electronics Market," *USA Today*, September 25, 2003, 1B–2B; David Teather, "Michael Dell Quits as Chief of His Own Company," *The Guardian*, March 5, 2004. **Concluding Case 15-2** Brooks Barnes, "New TV Ratings Will Produce Ad-Price Fight," *The Wall Street Journal*, December 22, 2005, B1, B3; Brooks Barnes, "Where're the Ratings, Dude?" *The Wall Street Journal*, March 7, 2005, B1, B6; Keith McArthur, "New TV Ratings Devices Know What You're Watching," *The Globe and Mail*, November 29, 2004, B1, B12; Keith McArthur, "Advertisers Wary of Plan to Fuse TV Ratings Systems," *The Globe and Mail*, July 13, 2004, B1, B20; Brooks Barnes, "For Nielsen, Fixing Old Ratings System Causes New Static," *The Wall Street Journal*, September 16, 2004, A1, A8; Elizabeth Jensen, "Networks Blast Nielsen, Blame Faulty Ratings for Drop in Viewership," *The Wall Street Journal*, November 22, 1996, A1, A8.

Chapter 16

The Fuel Cell: Still a Long, Rough Road Ahead Peter Kennedy, "Ballard's Celebrated Drive Hits a Bumpy Road," *The Globe and Mail*, July 17, 2004, B6; Peter Kennedy, "GM Aims to Finish First in Fuel Cell Race," *The Globe and Mail*, June 10, 2003, B5; Chris Nuttall-Smith, "Waiting for the Revolution," *Report on Business* (February, 2003): 44–54; Jeffrey Ball, "Hydrogen Fuel May Be Clean, But Getting It Here Looks Messy," *The Wall Street Journal*, March 7, 2003; Rebecca Blumenstein, "Auto Industry Reaches Surprising Consensus: It Needs New Engines," *The Wall Street Journal*, January 5, 1998, A1, A10. **Entrepreneurship and New Ventures** Cris Prystay, "Bio-Boost," *Far Eastern Economic Review* (February 6, 2003): 38; Charles Bickers, "Medicine Man Returns," *Far Eastern Economic Review* (August 23, 2001): 30–33. **Table 16.1** Keith McArthur, "Big Mac, Coke, Marlboro and...China Mobile?" *The Globe and Mail*, April 4, 2006, B1, B9. Reprinted with permission from The *Globe and Mail*. **Table 16.2** *Financial Post Business*, (Special Edition, 2006): 146; Material reprinted with the express permission of "National Post Company," a CanWest Partnership. **Business**

Accountability Joe Mandese, "The Age of Accountability," *TelevisionWeek* (February 16, 2004): 28; Joe Mandese, "Shifting Ad Accountability to Media," *TelevisionWeek* (October 6, 2003): 15; Erin White, "Media & Marketing— Advertising: Making Sure the Work Fits the Bill," *The Wall Street Journal*, February 3, 2004, B8. **Concluding Case 16-1** Keith McArthur and Grant Robetson, "CRTC Ponders Impact of Product Placement," *The Globe and Mail*, November 21, 2005, B1, B10; Grant Robertson and Richard Blackwell, "Eased Satellite Radio Rules Could 'Shock' System," *The Globe and Mail*, September 23, 2005, B7; Tessa Wegert, "On-Line Marketing Concept Gives Consumers a Say," *The Globe and Mail*, October 13, 2005, B13; Aaron Patrick, "Commercials by Cellphone," *The Wall Street Journal*, August 22, 2005, B1, B3; Frazier Moore, "You Can't Fast-Forward Past These Commercials," *The Winnipeg Free Press*, July 25, 2005, D3; Simon Tuck, "CRTC Turns Radio on Its Head with Landmark Satellite Ruling," *The Globe and Mail*, June 17, 2005, B1, B6; Eric Reguly, "Blame the Act, Not the Regulator," *The Globe and Mail*, June 16, 2005, B2; Joe Flint and Brian Steinberg, "Procter & Gamble Tweaks Its Traditional TV Ad Strategy," *The Wall Street Journal*, June 13, 2005, B6; Peter Grant, "Interactive Ads Start to Click on Cable and Satellite TV," *The Wall Street Journal*, May 26, 2005, B1, B6; Keith McArthur, "Branded Content Generates Buzz," *The Globe and Mail*, April 6, 2005, B4; Keith McArthur, "A Year Later: No Medium for the Message," *The Globe and Mail*, November 1, 2004, B3. **Concluding Case 16-2** Alexander Wolff, "Rockin' the Retros," *Sports Illustrated* (December 22, 2003): 46–54; Sean Gregory, "How Old Jerseys Got Hot," *Time* (online edition), April 7, 2003, www.time.com/time/insidebiz/article/0,9171,1101030407.

Chapter 17

The Importance of Price "Avery Wine's Brandman," *Venture*, March 27, 2005; Andy Hoffman, "Cheap Suds Give Lakeport Rivals Brand Hangover," *The Globe and Mail*, March 14, 2006, B6; Derek DeCloet, "Trouble Brewing in Beer Industry, " *The Globe and Mail*, May 7, 2005, B4; Jon Swartz, "Some eBay Sellers Are Going, Going, Gone," *USA Today*, February 2, 2005, 3B; Keith McArthur, "In Hamilton, They Like Beer Cold...and Cheap," *The Globe and Mail*, July 10, 2004, B4; Keith McArthur, "Why Molson Is Crying in Its Beer," *The Globe and Mail*, July 10, 2004, B4; Greg Keenan, "Toyota Kills No-Haggle Sales Price Strategy, " *The Globe and Mail*, June 17, 2004, B1, B25; Ann Zimmerman, "Behind the Dollar-Store Boom: A Nation of Bargain Hunters," *The Wall Street Journal*, December 13, 2004, A1, A10; Gordon Fairclough, "Four Biggest Cigarette Makers Can't Raise Prices as They Did," *The Wall Street Journal*,

October 25, 2002, A1, A8; Timothy Aeppel, "After Cost Cutting, Companies Turn Toward Price Increases," *The Wall Street Journal*, September 18, 2002, A1, A12. **Business Accountability** David Wessel and Susan Carey, "Airlines Captive to Costs and Competition," *The Wall Street Journal*, September 19, 2005, B8; Evan Perez and Nicole Harris, "Despite Early Signs of Victory, Discount Airlines Get Squeezed," *The Wall Street Journal*, January 17, 2005, A1, A6; Melanie Trottman, "Equalizing Air Fares," *The Wall Street Journal*, August 17, 2004, B1, B4; Julia Boorstin, "JetBlue's IPO Takes Off," *Fortune* (April 29, 2002): 96–100; Melanie Wells, "Lord of the Skies," *Forbes* (October 14, 2002): 130–138; Paul C. Judge, "How Will Your Company Adapt?" *Fast Company* (February 2003): 105–110. **Table 17.1** *Financial Post Business* (Special Edition, 2006): 144; Material reprinted with the express permission of "National Post Company," a CanWest Partnership. **Entrepreneurship and New Ventures** Chris McDougall, "Closing the Deal," *Inc.* (March 2004): 70–84. **Concluding Case 17-1** Keith McArthur, "Why Molson Is Crying in Its Beer," *The Globe and Mail*, July 10, 2004, B4; Kevin Kelleher, "66,207,896 Bottles of Beer on the Wall," *Business 2.0* (January–February 2004): 47–49; Tim Davis, "Surfin' the Net, Bud Style," *Beverage World* (August 1995): 28; "This Budnet's for You," *Progressive Grocer*, (May 1996): 16; *2003 Annual Report* (St. Louis: Anheuser-Busch Companies Inc., 2004). **Concluding Case 17-2** Shawn McCarthy, "U.S. Court Shuts Door on Internet File-Sharing," *The Globe and Mail*, June 28, 2005, B3; "File Sharing Firm Will Shut Down," *The Winnipeg Free Press*, November 8, 2005, A11; Nick Wingfield, "Online Music's Latest Tune," *The Wall Street Journal*, August 27, 2004, B1, B2; Nick Wingfield, "New File-Swapping Software Limits Sharers to a Select Few," *The Wall Street Journal*, October 4, 2004, B1, B4; Sarah McBride, "Stop the Music!" *The Wall Street Journal*, August 23, 2004, B1; Vauhini Vara, "On Campus, iTunes Finds an Illicit Groove, *The Wall Street Journal*, August 23, 2004, B1–B2; Nick Wingfield and Sarah McBride, "Green Light for Grokster," *The Wall Street Journal*, August 20, 2004, B1, B3; Nick Wingfield, "The Day the Music Died," *The Wall Street Journal*, May 2, 2003, B8; "The End of File-Shares as We Know Them," *The Winnipeg Free Press*, July 4, 2003, A8; Ted Birdis, "Music Industry Escalates Net Fight," *The Winnipeg Free Press*, June 26, 2003, A12; Matthew Ingram, "Digital Music Industry Gets New Spin on Napster Judge's Decision," *The Globe and Mail*, February 26, 2002; Nick Wingfield, "Napster Boy, Interrupted," *The Wall Street Journal*, October 1, 2002, B1, B3; Anna Matthews and Charles Goldsmith, "Music Industry Faces New Threats on Web," *The Wall Street Journal*, February 21, 2003, B1, B4.

Chapter 18

Who Could Have Imagined This? Tim Campbell, "Hockey Plays Dollar Game," *The Winnipeg Free Press*, June 30, 2006, D8; Murray McNeill and Larry Kusch, "Manitoba's Manufacturing Sector Suffers While Buck Rises," *The Winnipeg Free Press*, May 2, 2006, B1, B6; Eric Beauchesne, "Loonie Predicted to Hit Par Next Fall," *The Winnipeg Free Press*, May 2, 2006, B1, B6; "20 Ways the Rising Loonie Is Changing Canada's Landscape," *The Globe and Mail*, July 5, 2003, B1, B4; John Saunders, "Exporters Facing Some Loonie Math," *The Globe and Mail*, May 7, 2003, B1, B4. **Table 18.1** *Financial Post Business* (Special Edition, 2006): 156; Material reprinted with the express permission of "National Post Company," a CanWest Partnership. **Entrepreneurship and New Ventures** Canada NewsWire, "Announcing CHEQ-IT Ltd. System Sales," October 13, 2005, p. 1; CHEQ-IT Ltd. home page; Reprinted with permission of Cheq-It Ltd. **Business Accountability** Nocolas Parent, Phoebe Munro, and Ron Parker, "An Evaluation of Fixed Announcement Dates," *Bank of Canada Review* (Autumn 2003): 3. **Table 18.2** *Financial Post Business* (Special Edition 2006): 156; Material reprinted with the express permission of "National Post Company," a CanWest Partnership. **Table 18.3** http://economist.com, June 9, 2005. **Concluding Case 18-1** "Newfoundland Aquaculture Industry Association Receives Funding for Cod Aquaculture Initiative,", January 30, 2006; Lindsay Royston, "Cod Walloped," *Canadian Business* (November 21–December 4, 2005): 110–114; "Newfoundland Projects Work Toward Cod Commercialization," April 2005; "Newfoundland Cod Comeback," January 16, 2004; CBC series "Land & Sea," May 21, 2006. **Concluding Case 18-2** "Business: Tested by the Mighty Euro," *The Economist* (March 20, 2004): 78; G. Thomas Sims, "Tale of Two Recoveries: EU and Tokyo Diverge," *The Wall Street Journal*, April 2, 2004, A7; Justin Lahart, "Is the Euro Too Strong?" *CNNMoney*, January 8, 2004, http://cnnmoney. com; Jamie McGeever, "Dollar May Gain More Against Euro on ECB Outlook," *The Wall Street Journal*, March 29, 2004, C5.

Chapter 19

The Urge to Manipulate the Stock Market "Scandalist," CBC *Venture* series, November 6, 2005; Richard Blackwell, "OSC Scores Trading Conviction," *The Globe and Mail*, July 22, 2000, B1–B2; "CEO Jailed for Insider Trading," *The Winnipeg Free Press*, September 19, 2000, B8; Karen Howlett, "Below The Decks of Treasure Ship Deals," *The Globe and Mail*, July 19, 2003, B1, B4; Karen Howlett, Sinclair Stewart, and Paul Waldie, "Brokers Caught Up in Police Probe," *The Globe and Mail*, June 20, 2003, B1, B20; Richard Blackwell, "Firm, Ex-CEO Pay Millions in Penalties," *The Globe and*

Mail, December 20, 2001, B1, B6; Andrew Willis, "Paterson's Words Give Ugly Spin to Debacle," *The Globe and Mail*, December 20, 2001, B1, B6; David Paddon and Hollie Shaw, "Top Heads Roll at Royal After Scandal," *The Winnipeg Free Press*, July 21, 2000, B7, B12; Karen Howlett, Janet McFarland, and Dawn Walton, "Stock Rigging Appears Widespread," *The Globe and Mail*, July 1, 2000, B1, B4; Keith McArthur, "Business Seeps Away from Royal Pensions," *The Globe and Mail*, July 1, 2000, B1, B5; Richard Blackwell and Jacquie McNish, "OSC Prepared to Deal with RT," *The Globe and Mail*, July 1, 2000, B5; Jacquie McNish, "How the High Closing High Fliers Got Caught," *The Globe and Mail*, July 3, 2000, B1, B3. **Figure 19.1** "Yahoo Inc (YHOO)/Wal-Mart Stores Inc (WMT)," *Quicken.com*, www.quicken.com/investments/charts/, July 13, 2002. **Table 19.1** *Financial Post Business* (Special Edition, 2006): 98; Material reprinted with the express permission of "National Post Company," a CanWest Partnership. **Table 19.2** *National Post* (June 2000): 168. **Table 19.3** *Financial Post Business* (Special Edition, 2006): 158; Material reprinted with the express permission of "National Post Company," a CanWest Partnership. **Entrepreneurship and New Ventures** Camilla Cornell, "The Dream Team," *Profit* (June 2006), www.canadianbusiness.com June 13, 2006. **Business Accountability** "Our True Identity Revealed: AIMR Changes Name to CFA Institute," CFA Institute (April 19, 2004), www.cfainstitute.org. **Concluding Case 19-1** Karen Howlett and John Saunders, "Fund Firms Admit Role in Market Timing Trades," *The Globe and Mail*, December 17, 2004, B1, B4; Janet McFarland and Rob Carrick, "The Fee Crunch: Not All Investors Get Value for Money," *The Globe and Mail*, June 24, 2004, B6; Christine Dugas, "Putnam Ousts CEO in Midst of Fund Probe," *USA Today*, November 3, 2003, www.usatoday.com/money; "Senators Blast SEC over Mutual Fund Trading Scandal," *USA Today*, November 3, 2003, www.usatoday.com/money; John Waggoner, Christine Dugas, and Thomas A. Fogarty, "Scandal Outrage Keeps Growing," *USA Today*, November 3, 2003, www.usatoday.com/money; "NYC Pensions Pull Assets from Putnam," *CNNMoney*, November 4, 2003, www.cnnmoney.com; "Chairman of Strong Mutual Resigns," *USA Today*, November 3, 2003, www.usatoday.com/money. **Concluding Case 19-2** Janet McFarland, "Companies Reform Stock Option Plans," *The Globe and Mail*, February 24, 2003, B1, B5; Matt Murray, "Options Frenzy: What Went Wrong?," *The Wall Street Journal*, December 17, 2002, B1, B3; David Wessel, "Why the Bad Guys of the Boardroom Emerged En Masse," *The Wall Street Journal*, June 20, 2002, A1, A6.

Chapter 20

The Increasing Importance of Risk Management Oliver Bertin, "Sector Hit Hard by Sharp Increases in Premiums," *The Globe and Mail*, April 27, 2004, B14; Oliver Bertin, "Firms Face Major Hurdles En Route to U.S. Markets," *The Globe and Mail*, April 29, 2004, B16; Harris Anwar, "Chief Risk Officer: A Valuable addition to the C-Suite," *The Globe and Mail*, June 20, 2005, B13; "Singer 'Incited' Crowd," *The Winnipeg Free Press*, August 15, 2005, D2; Leslie Scism," If Disaster Strikes This 'Titanic,' Chubb Could Lose Millions," *The Wall Street Journal*, April 9, 1997, A1, A4; Leslie Scism, "Maybe Julie Andrews Could Offer Insurers a Spoonful of Sugar," *The Wall Street Journal*, April 4, 1997, A1, A4; Patrick Reilly, "Insurers Are Downbeat on Rap Concert Tours," *The Wall Street Journal*, March 26, 1997, B1, B12. **Entrepreneurship and New Ventures** Tom Stein, "Every Step You Take, LPs Will Be Watching You," *Venture Capital Journal*, January 1, 2003, 1; Yasmine Chinwala, "US Survey Shows Gender Gap," *eFinancial News*, February 25, 2002, www.marcusventures.com/financialnews.html; Alison Maitland, "An Idea from the Ladies Room," *FT.com/Financial Times*, February 2, 2003, www.marcusventures.com/FT.html. **Business Accountability** Michael S. Hopkins, "Because He Learns, and Teaches," *Inc.* (April 2004): 119–120. **Table 20.2** *Financial Post Business* (Special Edition, 2006): 158; Material reprinted with the express permission of "National Post Company," a CanWest Partnership. **Concluding Case 20-1** Ian Mount, " Be Fast, Be Frugal, Be Right," *Inc.* (January 2004): 64–70; Winston Chai, "Linksys Finds Its Voice," *CNET News.com*, April 21, 2004, http://news.com.com; Drew Robb, "Linksys Router Named Top Wireless Product," *Datamation*, March 25, 2004, www.wi-fiplanet.com; Mark Boslet, "Cisco Pushes into New Market: the "Digital Living Room," *The Wall Street Journal*, January 21, 2004, 1. **Concluding Case 20-2** Shirley Won, "What's in a Name? Plenty, if It's Brascan," *The Globe and Mail*, September 16, 2005, B3; Shirley Won, "Brascan's Plan Pleases Analysts, but Some Preach Wait-and-See," *The Globe and Mail*, March 18, 2005, B12; Andrew Willis, "Brascan Remakes Itself, This Time with Trees," *The Globe and Mail*, February 19, 2005, B7; Andrew Willis, "How Flatt Is Reforging Brascan," *The Globe and Mail*, September 25, 2004, B6; John Partridge, "Brascan Looks to Power Plants for Added Juice in Bottom Line," *The Globe and Mail*, August 6, 2004, B9; Andrew Willis, "Investors Betting on Brascan Dismantling," *The Globe and Mail*, July 19, 2004, B1, B10.

NAME AND ORGANIZATION INDEX

"AS IS" LICENSE AGREEMENT AND LIMITED WARRANTY